MW01518257

ADULT EDUCATION IN CANADA

Historical Essays

Gordon Selman

University of
British Columbia

Thompson Educational Publishing, Inc.

Toronto

Canadian Cataloguing in Publication Data

Selman, Gordon R., 1927-
    Adult education in Canada: historical essays

ISBN 1-55077-074-8

1.   Adult education - Canada - History.
I.   Title.

LC5305.G67 1995   374'.971   C95-932047-4

Book design: *Danielle Baum*
Cover design: *Mike McAuliffe*

Printed and bound in Canada.

1234 98 97 96 95

TABLE OF CONTENTS

Introduction

*B*esides the obvious one—the focus on adult education in Canada—the essays which make up this volume have one major connecting link; it is one of intention. When I entered the world of practice in adult education in 1954 (like so many of us, not realizing at first the real nature of the field) and in due course started to take stock of the enterprise I had fallen in with, I began to see that, although we had a proud tradition in this field in Canada, very little of our story had as yet been told. I had been trained as an historian and I think had a strong sense of wishing to find the roots of the work in which I increasingly felt a personal stake. Such feelings became even more intense when, in 1974, I left university continuing education activities and became a professor in the academic professional training program in adult education. I soon was able to specialize in the "foundations" and historical aspects of the field and the more knowledgable I gradually became about the development of adult education in this country and its relationship with our society as a whole, the more I regretted—and felt limited by—the paucity of Canadian historical materials we had to work with.

Some useful research had already been done, of course, and I felt grateful, as their work became known to me, to people like Ned Corbett, M.M. Coady, Roby Kidd, Alec Laidlaw, Donald Cameron, Isabel Wilson, Ron Faris, David Armstrong, Bert Wales and others who had contibuted by documenting some features of the field. I was also aware of the fact, however, that in other countries with which we were closely associated in the field, notably the United States and Great Britain, much more had been accomplished by way of historical study, including comprehensive national accounts of the development of the movement.

The "intention" to which I refer above as the connecting link among the papers here assembled was a gradually developing ambition to make whatever small contribution I could to our understanding of the historical development of the field of adult education in Canada, with some special emphasis as well on my native province of British Columbia. I did some work of this kind back in my years as an Extension worker, but my opportunities (and commitment) to do so were greatly expanded when I became a professor and such work became part of my job, and was expected of me.

The character of my historical writing has I believe changed somewhat over the years. Much of my early work was "documentary" in a sense, in that I was exploring topics and materials which had never been examined before from the point of view of adult education. A strong element of some of my early work therefore was to get "on the record" hitherto unknown facts about the field. This related mainly, but not only, to my work on British Columbia. As I moved on, there was a stronger element of interpretation in my work, partly because I was gaining in knowledge and confidence concerning the handling of such material, partly because my sense of commitment to certain philosophical and other points of view was becoming more clear to me, and thirdly, because in at least some instances I was in part reacting to or commenting on other people's work in the same areas.

I have in recent years given some thought to why it was that I pursued certain topics and not others in my research. It is clear that for one thing, some research tasks were simply more "doable" than others. The research I did into adult education in the early decades of its development in B.C. was based in the main on newspapers and government documents which were available at my university or in the provincial archives. My study of the history of the Canadian Association for Adult Education came to mind because of my long involvement with that organization and was made possible by the co-operation and generosity of the Director of the Association at the time, Ian Morrison. In other cases the research I undertook arose from a keen personal interest and involvement in the organizations and topics which I studied. This would be true of my histories of two of our provincial adult education associations, and several pieces on university extension/ continuing education work. Some of the individual, "set pieces" to which I turned my hand were either just that, spur of the moment decisions (such as my article on the year 1972 as a key year for the field), or ones which, although relatively isolated topics at the time, were in my mind parts of larger projects which I hoped subsequently to complete. Examples of the latter are my history of adult education in B.C. in the Great Depression (which I hoped would contribute to an overall provincial history of the field); my study of the 1950s as a "pivotal decade" in the history of adult education in Canada; and research into six short-lived provincial associations of adult educators in the 1930s and 1940s. (The full scale comprehensive history of adult education in Canada to which such research was to contribute was never achieved, however.) A few pieces which were of a more philosophical bent arose from my studies of the foundations of the field and my efforts to understand the evolution of the enterprise. I was all too conscious of my lack of background for philosophical discussions, but I have been encouraged by the extent to which some of these pieces appear to have been useful to students and practitioners.

Back in my Extension years (1954-74) almost all my research work had to do with adult education in British Columbia. My thesis for my degree was about the development of university extension work at my home institution, The University of British Columbia. I wrote a number of articles based on that research, both before and after the thesis was completed. As well, the Canadian Association for Adult Education published a shortened version of the thesis. The other major research work I carried out in those years was a study of the development of adult education in the colonies and subsequently the Province of British Columbia in the years prior to 1914. The main document which resulted from this work has never been published (and was not intended to be), but I subsequently wrote for publication a series of articles and monographs which were based on parts of the study. I have continued to draw on that work over the years.

After I became a faculty member, the dynamics of the enterprise changed somewhat. For one thing, I had more time to give to such work. Concerning my research and writing, I had certain major goals in mind, such as comprehensive histories of adult education in B.C. and in Canada, and a major study of the history and contributions of certain associations of adult educators—each of which was a multi-year project—but there were at the same time sometimes conflicting pressures (largely self-imposed) to have things published each year—to show that I was "producing." One owed it to one's colleagues, as a contribution to the overall scholarly productivity of our academic group, and also I wished to be seen personally as producing useful work which met scholarly standards. Having been appointed with tenure from the very beginning of my time as a faculty member, I did not feel strong external pressure to publish extensively, but one's sense of self-esteem and wish to contribute to one's chosen field was motivation to keep at it. Because those strong external pressures were not there, I felt I could to a large extent follow my own interests and not worry too much about whether my work was of the kind that would be published in the most highly regarded juried journals. There is satisfaction in having work published in journals which are juried by one's peers, but there are also certain "homogenizing" pressures in such systems which are not pleasant to deal with and which work against certain forms of creativity. Seeking that form of publication also imposes limitations of length which did not suit many of the topics I wished to study. I tried to keep these factors in balance. During this period of almost twenty years as a faculty member, I had significant parts of my writing published in academic journals, but a great deal of it elsewhere.

The publishing possibilities for much of my work have been quite limited. The picture is changing now, but for most of my professional career, the outlets for my writing were few. Some of my colleagues published a great deal of their work in American and international journals. This was possible for them because their subject matter—such things as instruction, program planning, learning and motivation, administration and research methodology—were not country-specific and were of use and interest to practitioners and scholars in other countries. In my case, a great deal of my work had to do with the field in Canada, and even in the Province of British Columbia. The number of journals in our field in Canada was extremely limited, although it improved in the Eighties, and commercial publishers were understandably very cautious about investing in material for which there would be a limited audience, even in Canadian market terms. I did what I could through those outlets, but what really made the difference for me was the publishing program of the Centre for Continuing Education of The University of British Columbia, which was managed by Jindra Kulich, a segment of which specialized in the main in B.C. and Canadian topics. This monograph series provided an outlet for a number of my more substantial research projects and thereby made that work available to a circle of interested colleagues in the field.

In the last few years before I was due to retire from the university, I began to feel that it was time to move to a different stage in my research and publications. There were at least two lines of thinking which were at work. One arose from the fact that I was aware that there were very few of us who were concentrating on the history of adult education in this country and that I had a "responsibility" to try to turn my hand to some larger tasks which would be useful to students and scholars, and to interested practitioners. The other feeling was that I had done quite a lot of work on aspects of the history of the field and that it was time to try to pull some of it together—to see whether the various things I had done could be made to add up to some larger whole. With these things in mind, I turned my hand to three main tasks.

The first was, if feasible, to produce a history of adult education in British Columbia. There weren't (and still aren't) any other provincial histories of the field in Canada and so I felt it was a challenge to produce one. I started out with a full length book in mind, but came to feel as the work progressed that there were too many gaps in our knowledge of the subject for the completion of a work on that scale. I therefore decided that a substantial monograph would be more appropriate and was pleased that my colleague, Jindra Kulich, agreed to publish it in his Occasional Papers in Continuing Education series. The history, entitled *The Invisible Giant*, was published in 1988 and appears in its entirety in Part 4 of this volume.

The second major goal was a textbook on the social foundations of adult education in Canada. We had for years in Canada been forced (as far as textbooks were concerned) to rely largely on American and British materials as a basis for our courses. Our teaching colleagues who had come from the United States did not appear to be overly concerned about this matter, but many Canadian-born professors felt the lack of texts and other books which drew on the rich heritage of our Canadian experience in the field. Here we were, teaching about the historical foundations of adult education in a country which had produced remarkable projects of world-wide reputation, such as the Antigonish Movement, National Farm Radio Forum and Citizens' Forum, Frontier College, the National Film Board and the Canadian Broadcasting Corporation, and utilizing textbooks published in other countries which made no mention of these accomplishments. I was determined to do something about this and set out to write such a book. As I got into the planning, and saw it in the context of other responsibilities, it became clear that it would be preferable to share the task with someone else. Paul Dampier, a former student and valued colleague, agreed to become a partner in the project and together we produced a volume which was published in 1991 by Keith Thompson, under the title *The Foundations of Adult Education in Canada*.

I had for some years been working on a history of what I saw to be the central tradition of significant achievements in Canadian adult education, projects related to the general field of citizenship education. Much of my published work (including the three extended monographs about the Canadian Association for Adult Education which are included in the present volume) touched on that subject, as had much of my teaching. As a result of assistance once again from my colleague Jindra Kulich, I was able to secure funding for my further research and a publishing arrangement for a book of that kind, and was able to complete it in 1991. It appeared under the title, *Citizenship and the Adult Education Movement in Canada* and is a history not of the whole adult education movment in Canada, but of many of its best known projects.

*   *   *

I hope that at least some of the essays in this volume convey the sense of excitement which lay behind their creation. In much of the historical research which is reported on here, I was buoyed up in doing the work because I was finding my way in territory which had never been explored before. A great deal of my research has been based on primary sources. My masters thesis got me started on this, based as it was on personal interviews, the decades-old files of the President's Office of the university, the Faculty of Agriculture files which were gathering dust in a storage room, and the back files of the Extension Department, which were stacked in the basement of a campus building, the lower six inches of which had at one time been flooded during a firefighting operation. In carrying out that first major piece of research, I discovered what a pleasurable experience it was (for me, at any rate) to go where no person had gone before in search of historical evidence.

My second major experience with that kind of work was required when I decided to write a history of adult education work in British Columbia from the earliest days of European settlement up to 1914. This was largely virgin territory, though two earlier authors, Henry Johnson and Bert Wales, had touched on the subject in studies which were devoted largely to other topics and in other time frames. For all practical purposes, no one had done any research on the subject. It was clear that I was going to have to rely largely on the newspapers as a source of information, with some minor help from biographies and government reports. The main newspapers had been indexed, after a fashion, but by people who had no knowledge of adult education, and who were working on a period in which there was little if any awareness of what adult education was. The indexes were of next to no use for my purposes, therefore. As a result, I simply had to go through reel after reel of microfilmed newspaper files looking for stories and information which I would term adult education activity, but which were not referred to as such by the writers of the day, and were not indexed as such. A few examples of such items are as follows: a newspaper account of the annual meeting of a local mechanics' institute; an advertisement for the opening of a new business school; a news snippet about a touring cleric having spoken to a local church institute; an account of the opening of a short course for dairymen conducted by the Dominion Department of Agriculture; mention of a box of books having been received by the Barkerville Literary Institute's library; or an account of a debate in the provincial legislature about granting public support for local libraries. Such research was very taxing work, but what kept me at it was the sense that I was going where no one else had gone before and that the product of my efforts, if I could do something useful with it, would be a historical record or account which simply had not existed before and which could serve others in their subsequent efforts. The result of this work was a manuscript which was bound and placed in a few local libraries, but which suffered from the defect that it was really an account which strung together my many factual items, rather than being a history in the full sense of the term. Nevertheless, the material assembled there has been a valuable source for me in some of my subsequent work, most notably my general history of adult education in the province. I would go home at night after a few hours of plowing through the old newspapers, sore of eye and weary of limb, but with an underlying sense of excitement that I had been exploring in uncharted territory.

A third example of work which engendered the same kind of interest for me were the historical monographs covering some 35 years of the development of the Canadian Association for Adult Education (which are contained in this volume). In this case, much the same kind of basic research was required (though this is more true of the last two in the series than the first). It involved reading files, minute books, correspondence, the publications of the association, briefs to public commissions, the association news contained in the journal which the association published over the years, and interviews with key persons in the story. The added dimension in the case of this study was that as the story proceeded to the late Fifties and into the Sixties, I became an actor in what I was researching. This brought fresh interest, but also hazards for the historian. A great deal of the pleasure I derived from doing this work was, however, once again based on the fact that I had gathered information from primary sources of a depth which had not been available to the field before.

All three of the examples described in the preceding paragraphs involved an enormous amount of detailed work, based in the main on primary sources. I had the satisfaction that I was producing studies which, even though my own interpretation of the story might not be accepted by everyone, placed in the public domain a lot of material which simply had not been available to the field before my work had been done. Further, I was able in the later years to build on that earlier work with more interpretive studies, with a sure sense of what lay behind the data with which I was working.

* * *

The essays included in this volume are extremely diverse. They represent a selection from my writings over the last twenty-five years. Most, but not all, are included because they seem to have been among the pieces which have been of greatest interest to the field. They were originally published in various places and appear here, as noted in each case, with the permission of those other publishers. In a few cases the selections have been edited in order to convert them to the APA reference style being used in this volume.

Part 1 of the volume consists of pieces which in one way or another deal with the nature of adult education and its relationship with the society of which it is a part. This has been a growing element in my writing over the years, as I have tried increasingly to see broader meaning in my work, and have had an opportunity to teach about the foundations of the field.

Part 2 contains several articles in which I have tried to examine the evolution of the field in Canada. Only one of these attempts to discuss the whole sweep of development over the years, but others examine particular periods in the light of their significance for the bigger picture.

Part 3 contains several long pieces on the history of the Canadian Association for Adult Education. The detailed histories cover the decades from the founding of the organization in 1935 until the departure of its third Director in 1971. These monographs are included in the volume not only because they represent a major part of my historical research, but also because, in the period covered by these three studies, the CAAE was a major force in the development of adult education in this country and a major contributor to Canada's outstanding international reputation in the field.

Part 4 involves a shift in focus from the national scene to the Province of British Columbia. This section contains a monograph devoted to the general history of adult education in the province and a substantial article which describes the two periods in which the Provincial government provided very active leadership in the field.

Part 5 deals with the history of adult education in B.C. prior to 1914. This work takes us back to the colonial period, when what is now British Columbia consisted of two British colonies, Vancouver Island and British Columbia. The two were united in 1866 and this entity then joined the Canadian Confederation in 1871. The section contains one article which surveys the whole period (in the case of the City of Vancouver) and others on more specialized topics.

Part 6 contains the result of some of the considerable work I have done at various times on the development of adult education in British Columbia during the Great Depression of the 1930s. I do not remember exactly what got me started on the detailed study of that period, but as I got into it I found it to be of absorbing interest. I discovered that this was the period when adult education programs and services were more central to the aims and efforts of the provincial government than at any other time in our history, and that enormously creative work was carried out, much of it based on a most enlightened sense of partnership between government and the voluntary sector.

* * *

I live beside the sea—on Bowen Island, near Vancouver—and for that as well as other reasons I have long been attracted to the writings of Joseph Conrad, who wrote a great deal about the sea. One of the many things in his stories which I have found meaningful are his comments about the responsibilities of professionalism—in his case, that of ship's officers. I have found this helpful in my own professional life as well as in some of my writing, a good part of which deals with professionalism and its impact on the field of adult education. Conrad also wrote memorably about the sea itself, in its many moods. In one of his novels, *An Outcast of the Islands*, he puts in the mind of one of his characters a comment about the sea which I have always thought might apply equally well to the task of being an historian. He writes of Willems' "disappointment with the sea that looked so charming from afar, but proved so hard and exacting on closer acquaintance". Like most tasks that are "hard and exacting," however, there is fun as well as pain in the doing of them, an all-too-frequent awareness that things might have been done better, and some satisfaction when the job is done.

G.S.
Smuggler's Cove
Bowen Island, B.C.
January, 1995

To Jindra Kulich

Friend

And invaluable contributor to
our knowledge of adult education
in Canada

Part 1

The Meaning of Adult Education

*T*here is an old saying in the history business: "Antiquarians want to know; historians want to understand." All historical writing involves reaching to some extent for some understanding of the people and events being described. Such interpretations need to be carefully handled. At times they can get in the way of a satisfactory appraisal of the facts. In other cases, historians can be accused of not reaching sufficiently for an explanation of events. This section is made up of several papers which put considerable emphasis on interpretation.

In late 1983 I was approached by those in the International Council for Adult Education who were organizing an international seminar to be held in Shanghai the following spring (held in co-operation with the Chinese authorities and other organizations). There were to be two papers on each of the major themes to be dealt with at the meeting, one presented by an expert from China and the other by an appropriate person from among the invited guests from other countries. There was much said at the meeting by our hosts about their wish to "catch up" with research developments in the field, ones from which the Chinese scholars and leaders had been cut off during the Cultural Revolution. I was very pleased to be invited to be one of the thirty or so guests from outside China, but sobered by the task I was asked to perform. I was asked to prepare one of the opening statements for the symposium, one which was to be on the subject of the history of adult education in the world, and to be done in no more than ten pages! Clearly an impossible task, but I was consoled by the fact that everyone present at the meeting would recognize that this was the case and would hopefully accept the shortcomings of my efforts as the inevitable consequence of the difficulties I faced.

It was clear that it would not serve a useful purpose to tell the story of adult education in any one country, though it did occur to me to present contrasting "cases" from several nations. In the end, however, I opted for the identification of a number of themes which I saw to be present in the field of adult education in all societies, even though the programmatic and institutional responses to the themes had differed greatly from nation to nation, depending on such factors as political philosophies, stage of political and social development and cultural traditions. The result is "Adult Education: An Awakening Force," which is the first essay in this section.

The second paper, "The Adult Educator: Change Agent or Program Technician?" began life as a talk I gave to students and faculty in the Adult Education program area at The University of British Columbia. It was part of a series of such events being given my our faculty and guests from the community. My paper prompted a lively discussion among those present and was one of my hesitant forays into philosophical matters. It was not until a couple of years later that it occurred to me that it might be worth publishing and I submitted it to the *Canadian Journal of University Continuing Education*, which was at that time still our only juried journal in the field in Canada. I have been heartened over the years since that time to hear that the article is being used in professional training programs across Canada. I do not think it is at all sophisticated as a piece of philosophical writing, but it seems to have "worked" as one which bridges the gap between practice and philosophical considerations. It also to some extent grounds philosophical considerations in the Canadian context.

One of my most consistent interests over the years has been to study the impact on the behaviour of the field of the trend towards professionalization, which has been with us since at least the 1950s. There are two essays in this section which focus on this matter particularly. The first was one I wrote jointly with my friend and colleague, Jindra Kulich, which appeared in a longer version (in German) in a German publication and subsequently in English in the British journal, *Studies in Adult Education*, in the fall of 1980. It was entitled "Between Social Movement and Profession: A Historical Perspective on Canadian Adult Education." The other, more detailed article on this subject is entitled "The Fifties: Pivotal Decade in Canadian Adult Education." It was suggested by the thinking which had gone into the other article and by the work I had done a few years earlier on the role of Dr. Roby Kidd while he had been Director of the Canadian Association for Adult Education during the Fifties. When the Canadian Association for the Study of Adult Education began the publication of its new juried research journal and issued a call for papers for the first issue, I suggested to the editor that I write such an article, warning him that it might be a reasonably long one. He accepted the idea and I was pleased to have it appear in May of 1987 as the lead article in the first issue of *The Canadian Journal for the Study of Adult Education*.

Linked with my ideas about the impact on the field of increasing professionalism and with my research into adult education in the Depression of the 1930s, I watched with fascination how adult educators were responding to the serious economic slump which hit the Canadian economy in the early Eighties. The product of this thinking was a paper I presented at the Annual Research Conference of the Canadian Association for the Study of Adult Education in the spring of 1982, entitled "Adult Education in Two Depressions." One of the suggestions made in the paper was that partly because of its increased professionalization between the two events, adult education was less able to respond to social and individual need in the Eighties than it had been in the Thirties. The paper attracted some notice at the time, one of the speakers at a plenary session of the conference mentioning it as one of the most important on the program. I also received a number of requests in ensuing months for copies of the paper—not a common occurrence. Although this paper concentrates on British Columbia, the case made is a more general one and it has been decided to place it in this section, which is considering the general nature of the field.

1.1

Adult Education:
An Awaking Force

udyard Kipling pointed out that "there are nine and sixty ways of constructing tribal lays, and every single one of them is right." The same sort of situation is faced by anyone attempting a general historical overview of the development of adult education. The number of choices open to the author is exceeded only by the number of possible pitfalls. One is reminded of the response of a Canadian Prime Minister, admittedly a man noted for his caution in such matters, who responded to an awkward inquiry by saying, "To that question I must answer yes and no, and qualify both—but don't quote me." Similar caution is perhaps appropriate in the face of the formidable subject entrusted to me on this occasion.

The nature of adult education is such that to describe its state at any given time, in any one country, is a daunting enough task. To describe it adequately over the span of its historical development, and in the many nations, is well nigh impossible. One of the most striking characteristics of adult education as a field is its diversity and the fact that it is so widely dispersed throughout society, much of it in the private sector and virtually invisible to the casual observer. It is far from a tidy enterprise, which is at once a problem and a source of strength. Indeed it might be argued that a tidy mind is a distinct disability in dealing with the subject.

The story of adult education over the past two centuries is intimately linked with the struggle of humanity for freedom and dignity, for progress and development—for the good life. It has gained significance, even majesty, not so much as a particular or specialised aspect of human activity, not for itself, but because of the goals it has served and continues to serve. Learning, and its handmaiden education, are vital dimensions of the continuing struggle of mankind towards what Moses Coady of the Antigonish Movement in Canada termed "the good and abundant life."

Adults have throughout the history of mankind been helped by their society to learn the things it was thought important and appropriate for them to know. The task before us, however, is to examine particularly the modern adult education movment as it has existed in the last two centuries or so, during which time new and specialised forms of provision have been made to assist adults to learn what they, and their society, thought it was important for them to know.

Research and reflection on the history of adult education in various parts of the world indicate a number of themes or perspectives which are relevant to the story everywhere.

The Individual and the Society

One of the most important dichotomies in the field, and to some extent a point of creative tension, has been represented by the concepts of education for individual development and education for citizenship. The concepts are of course, inseparable. Only individuals can learn. But the use to which they put their knowledge, skills or attitudes may be either largely personal in emphasis or directed towards community life. Much of the earliest British adult education activity described by Kelly (1970), such as study groups on science and efforts to teach people to read the scriptures, were clearly undertaken for the purpose of individual growth and development. In the case of the Danish Folk School, the struggle for national ethnic revival in several central European countries in the nineteenth century, or the Canadian National Farm Radio Forum—and the number of possible examples is large—the purpose had clearly to do with the individual as citizen.

Liberal and Instrumental Learning

There has throughout the history of adult education been emphasis upon that education which develops the power of the person as ends in themselves (here termed liberal education) and education which is undertaken to strengthen the person's capacity to carry out other tasks (instrumental). The line between the two is a mysterious one. It was said of the Danish Folk School, for instance, that without ever mentioning the word butter, they trained generations of farmers to make the best butter in Europe. And the Workers' Educational Association of Britain, through a liberal education curriculum, helped to produce a corps of leaders for organizational and public life. The same can be said of the Swedish Study Circle movement. In all of our countries, we have examples of the instrumental approach, such as the agricultural extension movement in the United States, the public health education effort in the People's Republic of China, the Yugoslav Worker's Universities and other Third World programs designed to produce the skills required for the process of development.

The Movement and the Profession

In perhaps most, if not all countries, adult education in its many forms began as a people's movement and frequently was seen as an instrument for improving society. Many of those providing leadership for adult education saw it as a way of improving the quality of life, promoting citizen participation, social justice and equality. The names of Mao, Mansbridge, Grundtvig, Freire and Nyerere come to mind, as do many others. In recent decades we have in many countries promoted the professionalization of adult education. Specialised training has been provided in order to create a corps of leaders, researchers, administrators and other specialists for the field. Particularly notable efforts have been made, for instance, in the socialists countries and the United States. In many societies, there has developed a type of professional approach which tends to be committed more to the standards and problems of practice (and often to institutional and self-interest) than to the more traditional goals of the adult education movement. The result is sometimes a tension in the field, a competition of aims and priorities.

Private and Public Sponsorship

The differing political and social arrangements in our countries have produced strikingly different organizational approaches. For many nations, however, this has been historically— and is—an important perspective on adult education. In my own country and many others I am familiar with, adult education, in the early decades of its development, was sponsored predominantly by the private, voluntary, non-governmental sector. With the emergence of what has been termed "the strong remedial state," the public authority has accepted this as well as other instruments of intervention and to an increasing degree adult education has been provided by the public sector. In many more revolutionary situations this shift has come about dramatically. Many of us have actively sought an enlarged role for the public authority, believing that some needs can be met adequately only by government action. At the same time, many believe that there is a power, a dynamic, in the private and voluntary sector which can facilitate learning and outreach in ways and to an extent not possible for the public authority. The channelling of public funds through non-governmental organizations for the support of adult education is a prominent feature in the Scandinavian countries, an approach which seeks to combine the advantages of public and voluntary contributions. But in all countries there has been concern for strengthening the public role in the interests of broadening provision, setting standards and promoting equity in the system.

Response and Initiative

Generally adult education has developed as a response to individual and societal needs. It would be strange if this were not the case. Many examples spring to mind, such as the mechanics' institutes of nineteenth century Britain, the part-time post-secondary program in the U.S.S.R., vocational education as a response to the needs for development in the Third World, the large-scale literacy campaigns in many countries, and the paid educational leave policies in several European countries. Indeed it is possible to write the history of adult education in my own country, and I suspect in others, in terms of the major advances which came as a response to the crises and dramatic changes in our lives as a people. What has followed upon many of the revolutions of the present century provides notable examples, including, of course, that of China. It has long been debated by educational philosophers and historians whether educational provision can or should bring about intentional social change. Opinion is divided and the record is at best unclear. Current voices in the field (Botkin 1979) are calling upon adult education to be more pro-active rather than reactive in its outlook, and for a shift from what is sometimes termed "maintenance/shock" learning to "innovative" learning. It has long been a tradition in adult education that the promotion and facilitation of social change is one of adult education's major tasks. In many countries, the efforts of adult education leaders to promote and advance towards a system of lifelong learning may be among the most important initiatves ever taken by the field.

These perspectives—in some cases, contrasting tendencies—account for many of the forces and points of view which have shaped adult education through its modern history to the present day. The second part of this paper will be devoted to certain developments which have been of particular importance in the most recent decades, especially the last twenty-five years, during which time the nature of the international community has changed so profoundly.

Education and Development

Significant evolution in thinking has taken place over the past few decades with respect to the concept of development and the role of education in the development process. There has been increasing realization that development must be seen in many dimensions as well as the economic. Much literature has focused on "the educational core of development" and latterly on the crucial role to be played by nonformal as well as formal education, if development programs are to live up to their potential. There is widespread discussion of the shortcomings of much development effort over the past generation and concern about cynicism in some quarters. Many aspects of the role of adult education in development are dealt with in the "Design for Action" developed by the 1976 conference of the International Council for Adult Education held in Dar es Salaam (Hall & Kidd 1978: 284-85):

- the *educative dimension* of all strategies for economic, social, cultural and political development;
- *participation* of the people in decisions;
- policies responsive to *basic human needs*;
- implementation of the *UNESCO Recommendation* on the Development of Adult Education;
- regional and national *organizations* to develop adult education capacity;
- action to *assist countries* least developed in adult education;
- *training* for adult education through regional centres;
- accent on particularly *deprived groups* in society—women, illiterates, peasants, migrants;
- *research* that emphasizes participatory methods of investigation and evaluation;
- *integrated* rural development;
- *workers' education* for those in the rural sector;
- promotion of and respect for *indigenous cultures*;
- adult education *content* concerned with development issues of food, health, environment.

Recognition of the essential role of adult education in the development process has surely been the most important single fact in the history of the field in our generation. President Nyerere has put it well:

First, we must educate adults. Our children will not have an impact on our economic development for five, ten or even twenty years. The attitudes of adults, on the other hand, have an impact now. (Institute of Adult Education 1973:4)

Of particular significance in the relationship between adult education and development has been the field of literacy education. The functional literacy projects sponsored by UNESCO from 1967 to 1973 for its Experimental World Literacy Program, the recommendations of the first World Conference of Ministers of Education on the Eradication of Illiteracy in Tehran in 1965 (which proposed and created the mechanisms for the EWLP) the Persepolis Declaration of the 1975 International Symposium for Literacy, and the large-scale literacy campaigns in many countries are some of the significant features and achievements of an enterprise devoted to the world's most compelling educational task. That, in spite of much successful effort, the absolute number of illiterate persons in the world is increasing is recognized by all educational authorities as an urgent call to further effort. That there will be, according to optimistic predictions, at least 900 million adult illiterates by the year 2000 (Lowe 1982:65) is a fact which will continue to place literacy education at the head of the international community's educational agenda.

The Impact of Technology

One of the most obvious features of the development of the field in recent decades has been the influence of increasingly rapid technological change on both the educational needs of our people and the methodologies of the field. The situation varies widely from one country and region to another. To take only one example, but perhaps it is one of the most dramtic: the impact of technology on what used to be called correspondence instruction and now is usually termed distance education. A method which was highly developed in many countries in the inter-war period of the 1920s and 1930s but began to languish in many regions after the Second Word War, has been augmented and transformed as a result of the application of recent technological developments. A methodology which was seen by many as out of date and very restricted in its use has now returned to centre stage of adult education.

Meeting the Needs of Special Groups

It was a remarkable feature of the Tokyo Conference in 1972 that there was such a broad base of agreement among the nations represented—no matter what their stage of development or political orientation—that increased priority must be attached to meeting the educational needs of certain groups which our systems of adult educastion had not served adequately. Foremost among these were the most educationally disadvantaged in our populations. Great emphasis was placed on what was termed the democratization of the field, and since that time great efforts in many countries have been devoted to serving such disadvantaged groups more effectively. The education of women was also identified by virtually every participating nation as a priority and important progress has been made in some areas. The list of special needs is long, and one can but mention several others: the urban and rural poor, migrant workers, ethnic minorities and handicapped persons. Judging by international surveys and reports, many countries have made concerted efforts in these and other areas of special need.

Provision in Public Policy

One of the most striking changes in the period between the second (1960) and third (1972) UNESCO World Conferences on Adult Education was the development of public policy in this area. That trend has continued apace. Just as adult education as a field of practice is decentralized in our societies, so public policy with respect to it has appeared in various sectors, such as labour, welfare, economic planning and development, agriculture, health and of course education. Education and training have come to be seen increasingly as indispensible means of intervention to cope with a complex of problems such as chronic high levels of unemployment, including youth unemployment, the need to upgrade or alter the skills of the workforce and the increasing burden of welfare costs. As a result, adult education has been transformed from what in many cases was a marginal state of genteel poverty and obscurity to a major role in public policy and practice. Adult educators accustomed to seeing their area neglected even in plans for the broad field of education have now seen it come to the fore in national social and economic policy. For many, the process began or was accelerated with *Learning to Be*, the report of the UNESCO International Commission on the Development of Education, in 1972. The rest of the decade has brought many important policy recommendations and actions, including international consensus on the Recommendation on the Development of Adult Education, adopted by the UNESCO General Conference in 1976.

Lifelong Education and the Learning Society

Although the concept and reality of lifelong learning are in some respects as old as recorded history (and we are aware of The 1919 Report in Britain and the Declaration of the Montreal Conference in 1960) the active promotion of the concept as a basis for policy development perhaps dates from the UNESCO Faure Report (*Learning to Be*) and subsequent elaborations by UNESCO, the Organization for Economic Cooperation and Development (OECD) and other intergovernmental organizations. Adult education does not "own" the idea of lifelong learning—far from it—but adult educators have played a major role in the development of the idea and represent what must be a major element in its implementation. Many adult educators are particularly accepting of one of the central ideas inherent in lifelong learning, the focus on learning as distinct from education. There is a realization and reliance on the fact that, seen in a lifelong and lifewide perspective, the growth and development of the individual is influenced by all the elements of society, not just those formally designated as educational. Indeed some proponents of lifelong education see the diversity of sources of assistance for learning, including self-directed learning of all kinds, as important protection for the individual against some of the forces seeking to influence him or her (Gelpi 1979). The intellectual and philosophical thrust behind the concept of lifelong education and the related ideas of *l'education permanente* and recurrent education has had profound impoact both on our field and on broader circles of national policy, and will continue to do so.

A World Community of Ideas

One of the most beneficial and profound changes in the field of adult education in recent decades has been the creation of an international community of ideas. If it was ever the case that the flow of influence, advice and assistance was overwhelmingly a one way flow—from the more to the less developed nations—this has now ceased to be the case. The experience and ideas of the Third World are having profound impact on the First and Second. Concern for development and the struggle to improve our approaches to adult education are things which we share. The international conferences on the field and on specialized aspects of it are of great importance. They are but the tip of the iceberg of international sharing and mutual benefit. Montreal, Tokyo, Tehran, Dar Es Salaam and Paris remind us of important efforts to share experience and launch new lines of development. An increasing number of instruments have been developed to promote communication at the international level. To the traditional avenues available to the scholarly world have been added the work of UNESCO (of central importance to our field) and that of other intergovernmental organizations, the regional adult education bodies, and since its formation in 1973, the International Council for Adult Education. Through these and many other international instruments, we have created the means to support and learn from each other.

The history of adult education to the present day is wonderfully complex. It is interwoven with the story of the struggle of the human family to achieve its individual and social goals. The record of the past reveals impressive and inspiring achievement. As the poet John Milton reminded the leaders of his day, "peace hath her victories no less renowned than war." The past has contained its problems, frustrations and disappointments. It is both the lessons of the past and a vision of a possible future which arm us for our further efforts.

References

The following includes the sources referred to in the text and a few other works which were the most useful among the many consulted.

Anderson, L. and Windham, D.M. (Ed.) (1982), *Education and Development*, Lexington: Lexington Books.

Botkin, J., Elmandjra, M. and Malitza, M. (1979), *No Limits to Learning*, Oxford: Pergamon.

Coombs, P.H. (1968), *The World Educational Crisis: A Systems Analysis*, New York: Oxford Universtiy. Press.

Gelpi, E. (1979), *A Future for Lifelong Education*, Manchester: Manchester Universtiy, Manchester Monographs, vol. 1 and 2.

Hall, B. and Kidd, J.R. (Ed.) (1978), *Adult Learning: A Design for Action*, Oxford: Pergamon.

Institute for Adult Education (Tanzania) (1973), *Adult Education Handbook*, Dar es Salaam: Tanzania Publishing.

Kelly, T. (1970), *A History of Adult Education in Great Britian*, Liverpool: Liverpool Universtiy. (Second edition).

Kidd, J.R. (1974), *Whilst Time is Burning*, Ottawa: International Development Research Council.

Lowe, J. (1982), *The Education of Adults: A World Perspective*, Paris: Unesco/Toronto, OISE Press, (Second edition).

Simmons, J. (Ed.) (1980), *The Education Dilemma*, New York: Pergamon.

Titmus, C. (1981), *Strategies for Adult Education*, Chicago: Follett.

UNESCO (1972), Learning to Be: *Report of the Unesco International Commission on the Development of Education*, Paris: UNESCO.

World Bank (1980), *Education Sector Working Paper*, Washington: World Bank.

Originally published in Duke, C. (Ed.) (1987), *Adult Education: International Perspectives from China*, London: Croom Helm, pp. 3-12. Reprinted with permission.

1.2

The Adult Educator: Change Agent or Program Technician?

*W*hat would the average adult educator today think the origin might be of the following statements: "Social controls and planning are a necessary expression of (a) sense of social responsibility" and "It is probable that the area of public ownership and control should be extended in enterprises most essential to human welfare."

Are these statements from a political party's platform—perhaps the founding conference of the CCF? As some will know, that is not the case. They are quotations from a declaration approved—and approved unanimously—by a national conference of adult educators in Canada in 1943 (Kidd 1963:108-9). And what about the following: "The main task (of adult education) is the imaginative training for citizenship." How long has it been, or have we ever heard the functions of adult education put in such exclusively social terms? This statement was approved as a declaration by another Canadian national adult education conference, in 1946 (Kidd 1963: 109).

Writing in the mid-60s, an American, Webster Cotton (1964), in one of the most interesting essays we have in our field, summons up the great traditions of adult education— its sense of movement—and laments that too many adult educators see themselves as what he terms "program technicians." He saw two traditions in adult education: the "social reformist tradition," those who see adult education as the key to improving society, and the "professional tradition," those who see adult education largely in terms of meeting individual needs. He lamented the kind of professionalism he saw developing and a narrowing of vision in the field. One does not need to agree with all that Cotton says, but it seems clear that he raises important issues.

These two traditions continue to co-exist in adult education today. It may be helpful to examine them from several perspectives as a means of asking, as we regularly should, what adult education is for. Robert Blakely usually puts it well. He has said:

> We can—and usually do—refrain from asking philosophical questions, but we cannot avoid acting according to philosophical assumptions. (Blakely 1957: 93)

Adult educators are affected every day in their approach to their tasks, in every professional decision they make and in their relationships with all the people with whom they deal, by their view of what we as adult educators are essentially in business to do.

Historians, such as Cotton, who have watched the development of adult education as a social enterprise in our society generally conclude that the field has in recent decades gone from being a movement to being a profession. Or, to put it another way, adult education is becoming professionalized. The argument goes that at one time adult education was a movement. By this is meant that it was a field the purpose of which, essentially, was to improve society. This was sometimes stated in terms of making democracy work more effectively, or bringing about a more equitable sharing of society's resources. Although the leadership of the movement may not have had what today we would see as expert professional skills in the practice of adult education, one thing they did have was a very strong sense of the goals of the movement. They wanted a better world, a better society, through adult education. This was the social reformist tradition of which Cotton speaks. E.A. Corbett (1941), the founding Director of the Canadian Association for Adult Education, told his organization in his Director's Report for 1941 that they must: "...re-affirm our belief that a democratic way of life is the good way of life. . . .That's our job, to show people what a living, shining thing democracy can be."

Moses Coady, the leader of the Antigonish Movement of St. Francis Xavier University, told his radio audience in 1945 that, "We need continuous adult learning to achieve the high objective of social progress," and his biographer has said that to Coady, "the adult educator worth his salt was an aggressive agent of change and adult education a mass movement of reform" (Laidlaw 1971: 83, 57). And in the same tradition, the American scholar and adult education leader, Eduard Lindeman (1961) put it this way:

> Adult education will become an agency of progress if its short-time goal of self-improvement can be made compatible with a long-time, experimental but resolute policy of changing the social order. (p.105)

Corbett spoke of having set off on the road to Damascus (for him, the road to the Protestant ministry) and falling among adult educators. What he and many others fell among was a movement—a secular movement—aimed at creating a better world here on earth. It is no coincidence that many of the early leaders of adult education came from the churches, a strong church background, or the Y.M.C.A.

Generally speaking, that sense of movement has faded into the background in adult education. The field is becoming professionalized and institutionalized. There is much less emphasis or consensus in the field about the social goals of adult education, or indeed whether it does or should have any such goals. There is a tendency to think increasingly of the delivery of (hopefully) expert services to individuals. There is increased concern about theory and research as a basis for practice and about the organizational aspects of the field. The adult educator's perspective is closer now to how a dentist or any other professional approaches the task at hand. If there is a cavity, the dentist will fix it. If the adult student wants to learn how to repair an outboard motor, we can teach that. We have gone from a sense of movement, with broad social goals, to a sense of meeting individual needs.

If this dichotomy in the field is looked at historically, it is possible to see some periods which brought one tendency or the other to the fore. In the very early years of the modern adult education enterprise, the middle decades of the Eighteenth Century, much that went on was of a very individualized approach. Thomas Kelly (1970), in his history of adult education in Great Britain, tells us of early literacy work, coffee houses, circulating libraries and "science for the citizen." From the 1790s to the mid-1800s, however, society was profoundly affected by the ideas of the American and French Revolutions, and there was an upsurge of adult education as an arm of political reform, through such movements as the corresponding societies, Owenite socialism, and most prominently, the Chartist movement (Kelly 1970; Silver 1975). Coming to the present century, from the 1920s to the 1940s, in response to two World Wars and the Depression, much of adult education was inspired once again by social goals. What had gone wrong with society? Is it possible to build a better world? It was a time of study groups, the co-operative movement and major emphasis on citizenship education, of the origins of the Antigonish Movement, National Farm Radio Forum and Citizens' Forum (Kidd 1950; Selman 1982). After 1945, many people had had more than enough of group activities during the war period, and we entered a much more individualistic age, the age of do-it-yourself. This was a period, too, of the emergence of professionalism in adult education (Cotton 1968; Selman 1982). The 1960s brought a new concern about social issues, human rights and participatory democracy. In adult education, there was an upsurge of peer group learning efforts, increased attention to the needs of disadvantaged groups and increased reliance on community development approaches. Not all, but much of that faded in the 1970s. Today, in response to widespread economic and social distress, there is some increased emphasis on social concerns, but against the background of a much more professionalized and institutionalized field. And so it is possible to see in the historical record adult education changing as the needs and conditions of the society as a whole were changing.

The third perspective on the topic which might be explored is the light that it sheds on the emerging concept of recurrent education. Recurrent education is a scheme whereby society is so arranged that people can switch back and forth throughout their working lives between the world of work and the world of education. Paid educational leave is a crucial component of such a system. The conceivers of this scheme, the Scandinavians, saw its impact largely in social terms. It promised to alleviate the increasing problem of high school dropout and the creation of a large group of alienated and undereducated young adults, it aimed at improving the quality of life in the workplace and also it was hoped that by such a scheme the gap could be narrowed between the younger generation and the older workers. Its potential for updating and upgrading the qualifications of the workforce was of course also seen to be important. But the idea has been picked up by national planners and economists in the industrialized world, it would appear, mainly on the strength of its economic potential and the promise of upgrading the skills of individual members of the workforce. The two major studies of the concept in Canada to this point, significantly, have emphasized its potential for skill development and economic productivity (*Education and Working Canadians,* 1979; *Learning a Living in Canada,* 1983). Thus recurrent education, an approach to adult education which was conceived largely out of a sense of its social impact, its potential for social change, may be adopted for quite other reasons—to make the status quo function more efficiently.

What one thinks of the basic issue, adult education as a force for social transformation or as a profession which concentrates on the delivery of expert services, depends very largely on one's personal philosophy or view of society. There is a view, perhaps the dominant one, which might be described as the liberal position, which sees change as gradual and tends to see it individualistically. This view recognizes problems and inequities in society; it wishes to create opportunities for everyone to better his or her lot (in the present context, by means of adult education); it seeks to put in place a wide range of services and programs in which there are opportunities to learn, to get ahead and contribute to society; and it tends to be comfortable with the professionalization of the field if this will result in good programs and in services being delivered as widely and as expertly as possible.

The other main point of view in the field—perhaps it might be termed the social transformation view—sees the world of adult education quite differently. It sees the adult education enterprise as it now exists as serving mainly the middle class. It describes our present arrangements as the "free market view" of education, in which the provider of education is the entrepreneur and the public are the consumers. It is critical of what is termed the "technical function" view of education, aimed at providing people to play a part in the existing social and economic order and at adapting men and women to the system. It accuses society of what is termed "the individualization of failure"; we continue the rhetoric of individualism and individual responsibility and opportunity, when in fact the problems are based in a social pathology, in collective problems within the social and political arrangements (Thompson 1980). And in the words of an eloquent exponent of this view, Paulo Freire, it believes that there is no neutral education. Either education is a force for change or it reinforces the status quo, and any thought adult educators might have that they are simply delivering a technically competent service which expresses no social view is a delusion.

There are those who are deeply concerned about what they see to be a tendency to "politicize" adult education. Some educators simply do not agree with the social philosophy of the "transformation" view. But many are fearful for adult education, believing that education is for personal development and making it the servant of anything else is dangerous, for society and for adult education. In the words of R.W.K. Paterson (1984: 20), "the limits of objectivity are the limits of education." Whatever the adult educator's view of all this, it is clear that one's personal philosophy has a profound impact on the role that one sees for adult education.

Does being a professional adult educator carry with it a view of what kind of society we should have? There are two aspects of this question. Does being a professional adult educator imply that we should have a view about society, and seek to implement it? Or is it implied that being a professional adult educator should lead one to a commonly accepted particular view of society? There is general criticism in Western society of the older professions as tending to be ultra-conservative and more inclined to turf-guarding and seeking their own interests than seeking to promote the general interest. The Canadian Association for Adult Education (and its French language counterpart) published recently a statement on the field which they entitled *From the Adult's Point of View* (1982). The title made a significant point; it stated clearly that what was intended was to speak on behalf of the interests of the learner, not for the interests of the professional adult educator or the adult education institutions. This consistent effort by C.A.A.E. to be the voice of the adult education movement rather than the voice of the adult education "establishment" is a part of their tradition and is in sharp contrast to many other organizations of adult educators. Perhaps it is also one reason why such a small percentage of adult educators choose to join the organization.

As a profession—if that is what adult education is on its way to becoming—or as individuals who are trying to approach their work in a responsible manner—do we have a view of what kind of society we should have? Do we have a view of the range of opportunities for learning, for growth and development, which all Canadians should have? And if we do, what do we feel we should be doing about it? Is that part of our professional responsibilities?

In attempting to raise these questions, it is by no means my intention to suggest what the answers should be. It is to suggest that the questions themselves are important and that each practitioner would do well to consider them. Whether one seeks to promote a particular view, or wishes to rest content with a field which Malcolm Knowles has described as a "patternless mosaic of pluralistic aims," we would do well from time to time to return to the wisdom of Robert Blakely which was referred to at the outset:

> We can—and usually do—refrain from asking philosophical questions, but we cannot avoid acting according to philosophical assumptions. (Blakely 1957: 93)

References

Blakely, R.J. (1957), "The Path and the Goal," *Adult Education*, VII (2), 93-98.

CAAE/ICEA (1982), *From the Adult's Point of View*, Toronto: CAAE/ICEA.

Corbett, E.A. (1941), *Director's Annual Report to CAAE*.

——. (1957), *We Have With Us Tonight*, Toronto: Ryerson.

Cotton, W.E. (1964), "The Challenge Confronting American Adult Education," *Adult Education*, XIV (2), 80-88.

——. (1968), *On Behalf of Adult Education*, Boston: CSLEA.

Education and Working Canadians (1979), Report of the Commission of Inquiry on Educational Leave and Productivity, Ottawa: Labour, Canada.

Kelly, T. (1970), *A history of Adult Education in Great Britain*, Liverpool: University of Liverpool.

Kidd, J.R. (Ed.) (1950), *Adult Education in Canada*, Toronto: CAAE.

——. (1963), *Learning and Society*, Toronto: CAAE.

Laidlaw, A.F. (Ed.) (1971), *The Man from Margaree*, Toronto: McLelland and Stewart.

Learning a Living in Canada (1983), Report, Skill Development Leave Task Force Vol. I and II, Ottawa: Employment and Immigration Canada.

Lindeman, E. (1961), *The Meaning of Adult Education*, Montreal: Harvest House.

Paterson, R.W.K. (1984), Objectivity as an Educational Imperative, *International Journal for Lifelong Learning*, 1 (1), 17-29.

Selman, G.R. (1981), *The Canadian Association for Adult Education in the Corbett Years: A Re-evaluation*. Occasional Papers in Continuing Education, U.B.C. Centre for Continuing Education, No. 20.

——. (1982), *Roby Kidd and the Canadian Association for Adult Education 1951-1961*, Occasional Papers in Continuing Education, U.B.C. Centre for Continuing Education, No 22.

Silver, H. (1975), *English Education and the Radicals*, London: Routledge and Kegan Paul.

Thompson, J.L. (Ed.) (1980), *Adult Education for a Change*, London: Hutchinson.

Originally published in *Canadian Journal of University Continuing Education*, 11 (2), 1985: 77-86. Reprinted with permission.

1.3

Between Social Movement and Profession: A Historical Perspective on Canadian Adult Education

(Co-authored with Jindra Kulich)

*T*he intention of this article is to examine briefly the development of adult education in Canada (largely in English-speaking Canada), with emphasis on the shifting balance between adult education as a social movement and as a professional field.

The term "adult education" will be used in the broad sense typical of North America. It is meant to include all purposeful efforts by adults, or on behalf of adults, to promote learning—in all areas of human concern. The "social movement" aspect of the field refers to all conscious efforts to improve the nature of the society by means of adult education and its wider application in the community. This approach usually has involved considerable numbers of volunteers and has stressed citizen involvement in leadership. By the "professionalization" of the field is meant those elements which have placed emphasis on providing adult education with a sound theoretical base, have emphasized research and the application of scientific standards to methods, materials and the organization of the field and have promoted the need for professional training and staffing. This point of view has advanced with the increase in the number of full-time people working in the field, many with a serious commitment to improving the effectiveness of their efforts. These two thrusts are not, of course, mutually exclusive.

One of the most difficult problems facing the authors of this study is that the history of adult education in Canada is not, as yet, well documented. There is no comprehensive history of the field such as Kelly (1970) has provided for Great Britain, Knowles (1977) for the United States or Hall (1970) for New Zealand. This article is to some extent exploring new ground in the examination of the field in Canada, utilizing insights from a recent paper by Kidd (1979) and also from Cotton's (1968) treatment of similar forces in the United States.

One reason why more progress has not been made on the national history of the field in Canada, and at the same time one of the basic features of adult education in this country, is the fact that under the Canadian constitution education is assigned as a responsibility of the Provinces. The development of the field has not been one story, therefore, but at least twelve (the ten Provinces, the Northern Territories, plus certain national efforts under both private and public auspices).

For the purposes of this exploratory study, the development of edult education in Canada has been divided into four periods. The first of these includes the years up to 1935, the second from then until 1959, the third covers the Sixties and the fourth the Seventies. These are of course arbitrary time periods, but they have been chosen in the light of some features of Canadian development, including the balance of thinking about the field as social movement and as an arena of professional activity.

Prior to 1935

Before 1935 the Canadian population was small and—as settlement and immigration advanced—spread over an enormous territory. The economy was based largely on agriculture and resource industries, with some manufacturing emerging, especially during the First World War and the buoyant 1920s.

Adult education was mainly in voluntary and private hands. It was organized largely through means which had been developed in other countries—the churches, mechanics' institutes, the Y.M. and Y.W.C.A., folk schools, labour unions, co-operatives, and Chautauqua. Three significant Canadian innovations of the period were: Frontier College, which recruited university students to work in isolated camps and to teach the other men in their spare time; the Women's Institute movement, which subsequently became world wide; and the "Antigonish Movement," the extension work in co-operative education carried on by St. Francis Xavier University (Fitzpatrick 1923; Powell 1958; Coady 1939).

Public authorities began to play a larger role with every passing decade. Departments of agriculture, public health and some others took up the task. Some provinces launched correspondence instruction. Some public universities began extension work, a few on the older lecture course model and especially in the West, some adopting the newer, more broadly based North American approach. Some local school boards entered the field and a few provincial governments provided funds to support this work. The Federal government provided some matching funds in support of agricultural and other vocational training. During the Depression, which hit Canada particularly hard, some governments enlarged the scope of their activities from what had been mainly remedial, vocational and academic, to include as well other activities which were designed to improve the morale of the people.

This was a period of predominantly non-governmental, much of it voluntary, activity in adult education. The training of workers, of which there was little, was still largely in the hands of voluntary organizations such as the churches and the Y.M.C.A. Writing in the field was almost nil and the few efforts to form associations devoted specifically to adult education were short-lived. In 1934, however, steps were taken which resulted in the following year in the formation of a national body for the field.

1935 to 1959

This period began in the Depression years and carried Canada through the trials of the Second World War, from which it emerged with fresh confidence and a greatly expanded economy. The Fifties, until near the close of the decade, was a buoyant time in almost every sphere of Canadian life. Adult education was no exception. The social movement dimension in adult education reached its high point in the Forties and early Fifties, with elements of professionalism developing rapidly by the end of the period.

The Canadian Association for Adult Education (CAAE), founded in 1935, was originally intended to be a clearing house for the field and to serve largely professional ends, but with the coming of the War, and as a result of the leadership of E.A. Corbett, the Association moved into direct programming, largely in the field of citizenship education (Armstrong 1968; Faris 1975). The two main programs were National Farm Radio Forum and Citizens' Forum, both combining broadcasting (in co-operation with the Canadian Broadcasting Corporation), print material and local listening/discussion groups, and both being national in scope. Public statements issued by the Association in the 1940s were in the social reform tradition and earned the organization the reputation in some quarters of being on the left of centre politically. A third major CAAE project in this period was the Joint Planning Commission, a network of national organizations active in adult education, aimed at co-ordination and increasing the impact of their work, again with some emphasis on matters of citizenship, social and cultural development. By the 1950s, under the leadership of Roby Kidd, the CAAE was also stimulating professional development: training, research and publication, and the shaping of public policy.

Other program trends included the considerable expansion of university extension, the steady growth of vocational education for adults and of activity in the arts and crafts, human relations training, and the development of hundreds of community centres offering education and recreation. School board programs expanded in a few areas. Several voluntary organizations greatly expanded their educational efforts: the Parent-Teacher Federation, organized labour, the United National Association, the Canadian Council on Education for Citizenship (later the Canadian Citizenship Council), the Y.M. and Y.W.C.A., the Women's Institutes and the Men's and Women's Canadian Clubs, to name just a few.

Provincial governments began to pay more attention to the field. Many departments of government carried out in-service development work for own their staff and in some cases for the public as well. By the end of the period, seven of the ten provincial governments had units within their departments of education which were designated as being responsible for the field of adult education.

Professional organizations for the field emerged strongly in the Fifties. University extension workers formed an association early in the decade. The CAAE began holding regional conferences and by the end of the decade all four Western Provinces had formed provincial organizations and those in other regions were holding periodic conferences.

Training opportunities expanded. The CAAE conducted several studies and convened meetings about training needs. Some regional bodies sponsored non-credit training courses. Universities began by offering single credit courses in the field, the first at the undergraduate level being given at Sir George Williams as early as 1934 and the first graduate course by the Ontario College of Education in 1951. By 1957, seven universities had offered courses in the field, and in that year The University of British Columbia launched the first graduate degree program in adult education.

Research and publication were still operating at a minimal level. The Dominion Bureau of Statistics carried out national surveys in 1951 and 1958. The CAAE was the chief source of publications, including a journal, books and pamphlets. Institutional studies, biographies and a collection of historical articles (Kidd 1950; "Learning for Living" series (1952-54); Cameron 1956; Corbett 1957). These few were the exceptions.

By the end of the Fifties, the public agencies had become more dominant in the field and there were increased numbers of people who were identifying themselves and their work with adult education. The social movement element in the field, focussed largely on the CAAE, was still present, but seemed to have passed its peak by approximately 1955. Just at the end of this period, when a more professionalized field seemed to be on the horizon, the Declaration of the Second World Conference on Adult Education, held in Montreal, sounded once again a strong call for the social relevance of this work.

The 1960s

This decade was marked by increasing social and economic difficulties, growth of Canadian (and of Quebec) nationalism, and the maturing of Canada as a nation. During the same period society in Canada experienced simultaneously a trend in the search for individual development and fulfilment approaching at times extreme individualism and hedonism among a considerable segment of the population, and a trend of social consciouness and service to the community manifested in organizations such as the Company of Young Canadians (an organization created by the Federal government through which young adults could serve in social and community development projects).

These developments had their influences on Canadian adult education. The most pervasive of these were the measures involved in the "war on poverty" which in adult education found their manifestation in a significant expansion of Federal government funding of technical and vocational education through the Technical and Vocational Training and Assistance Act of 1960. This was replaced in 1967 by the Occupational Training Act which constituted a major Federal incursion into the sphere of education and training, with the retraining of unemployed and underemployed adults as the main thrust. The Quebec question and the Federal government's response generated only limited public affairs programming, but brought about an explosion in second language programs (English and French).

During the 1960s, through Federal government initiatives such as ARDA (Federal Agricultural Rehabilitation and Development Act 1961), Challenge for Change (National Film Board work in community development) and NewStart (Federal initiative in adult basic education), Canadian citizens were assisted to take an active part in the economic, social and educational regeneration of their regions. Social animators and adult educators were an important part of this activity.

An explosive growth of adult education at the local public school board level in the mid-1960s and at the community and regional college level in the late 1960s brought with it an unprecedented growth in the number of full time and part time organizers and program planners. With the increase in the number of personnel (practically all of whom entered the field of adult education from another profession or vocation) came an increased concern for professional preparation and skills.

As was mentioned earlier, the first Masters program in adult education was established in 1957. The first adult education program offered by a French Canadian university was established at the University of Montreal in 1968. During the ten years from 1960 to 1970, the number of Canadian universities offering Masters programs in adult education increased from one to seven (two of these, The University of British Columbia and the

Ontario Institute for Studies in Education, by 1970 also offered a Doctoral program), while a number of additional universities offered individual credit courses.

The Canadian Association for Adult Education played a leadership role in the professionalization of adult education in Canada during the 1960s, while at the same time acting as an advocate for the interests of the adult learner in Canadian society. In 1966 the CAAE organized a national conference on professional training of adult educators. In December of the same year the formation of a committee of professors was discussed; some links were established and informal meetings held, but no formal structure emerged. One important result of the 1966 conference was the first Canadian survey of training opportunities in adult education (Tough 1968). A second was published in 1970 (Draper &Yadao 1970).

The professionalization of adult education, which started to gather momentum in the 1960s, expanded rapidly in the 1970s.

The 1970s

During the 1970s many of the trends established in the previous decade continued, but the initiative passed from the Federal to the Provincial governments. This was consistent with the gradual shift in the political arena from Federal to Provincial power in many social and economic areas.

A number of Provincial reports and commissions in the field of post-secondary and adult education had impact on the field in this period. Among these were the 1972 Wright Report in Ontario, the 1972 Worth Report in Alberta, a report on community colleges in Saskatchewan in 1974, and the Winegard Report, Goard Report and Faris Report of 1976 and 1977 in British Columbia.

At the Federal level, one major intiative in the late 1970s was the Commission of Inquiry on Educational Leave and Productivity established in 1978 by the Minister of Labour. The Commission held hearings throughout Canada and delivered its very comprehensive report in 1979.

Two major thrusts occurred during the 1970s on the social movement level. One of these initiatives was assisted by the CAAE, while the other one occurred spontaneously in many parts of the country. The first centred on the education of women. Although some local projects predated this, the CAAE organized in 1973 the first national workshop in this area, resulting in the creation of an informal group, the Canadian Committee on Learning Opportunities for Women. With financial support from the Federal government the CCLOW held its first national conference in 1977, which led to the establishment of a national organization in 1979.

The second area of rapid development is Adult Basic Education. Federal occupational training initiatives had revealed the extent of the need in this area but neither Ottawa nor the Provinces responded adequately to the task. In spite of weak encouragement from the Provincial governments, and in the face of many obstacles, an increasing number of committed adult educators became involved in ABE in the 1970s and late in the decade they banded together to form organizations at both the national and provincial levels. The national focal point in this activity is the Movement for Canadian Literacy.

While in the 1960s the CAAE actively supported all the major trends in Canadian adult education (vocational training and upgrading; community development and citizen participation in economic, social and educational regeneration; the individualistic human potential movement; and the professionalization of the field), the early 1970s saw a definite shift by the CAAE towards support of the social movement aspects of the field. Unfortunately the result of this change in direction was that for most of the early 1970s the CAAE became separated from the main stream of development, with a committed and well meaning board but little effective activity.

Meanwhile, major thrusts in vocational education continued, while a number of citizen participation and community development programs were phased out. The four major new developments in the early and mid-Seventies were the nation-wide expansion of community colleges, the growth in the number of part time students in colleges and universities, the rapid growth of continuing education in the professions and the establishment of women's programs.

With the expansion of publicly sponsored adult education through local school boards, colleges and universities, independent provincial associations of adult educators came into being in a number of Provinces (British Columbia, Alberta, Saskatchewan, Manitoba, Ontario, Nova Scotia and Newfoundland). These associations took divergent positions on the professionalization versus social movement issue.

Into the 1980s

Looking back we can see the broad trends in Canadian adult education to be: the organizational stage of the early period; the height of the social movement phase of the CAAE in the 1940s and 1950s; the Federal government initiatives and the development of the human potential movement of the 1960s; and the provincial initiatives, diversification of adult education and rapid growth on all levels of the 1970s. Ever since the 1930s there has been creative tension between the professionalization and social movement trends. While at times one or the other seemed to predominate, at no time did Canadian adult education fall completely under the spell of one or the other. In our opinion, as with the yin and the yang, commitment to both these forces are necessary for the vitality and effectiveness of this field of social practice. Adult education in Canada will play a significant role in the life of our citizens and of the society to the degree it is able to unite both forces in its further development.

References

Armstrong, D.P. (1968), *Corbett's House: The Origins of the CAAE and its Development During the Directorship of E.A. Corbett 1936-1951*, Unpublished M.A. Thesis, University of Toronto.

Cameron, D. (1956), *Campus in the Clouds*, Toronto: McLelland and Stewart.

Coady, M.M. (1939), *Masters of Their Own Destiny*, New York: Harper and Bros.

Corbett, E.A. (1957), *We Have With Us Tonight*, Toronto: Ryerson.

Cotton, W.E. (1968), *On Behalf of Adult Education*, Boston: Centre for the Study of Liberal Education for Adults.

Draper, J. and Yadao, "Adult Education as a Field of Study in Canada," *Continuous Learning*, March-April, 1970, pp. 65-82.

Faris, R. (1975), *The Passionate Educators*, Toronto: Peter Martin.

Fitzpatrick, A (1923), *University in Overalls*, Toronto: Frontier College Press.

Hall, D.O.W. (1970), *New Zealand Adult Education*, London: Michael Joseph.

Kelly, T. (1970), *A History of Adult Education in Great Britain*, Liverpool: University of Liverpool Press.

Kidd, J.R. (1950), *Adult Education in Canada*, Toronto: Canadian Association for Adult Education.

Knowles, M.S. (1977), *A History of the Adult Education Movement in the United States*, Huntington N.Y.: Robert E. Krieger.

"Learning for Living," series of 11 pamphlets on outstanding projects in Canadian adult education published from 1952 to 1954 by the Canadian Association for Adult Education.

Powell, V. (1958), *Forty Years and Growing: Ontario Women's Institutes*, Toronto: Ontario Women's Institutes.

Tough, A. (1968), "Adult Education as a Field of Study in Canada," *Continuous Learning*, January-February 1968, pp. 4-14.

Originally published in *Studies in Adult Education*, 12 (2), 1980: 109-116. Reprinted with permission.

1.4

The Fifties: Pivotal Decade in Canadian Adult Education

*O*f the recent decades in our history, two stand out as having a pronounced character or flavor of their own, the 1930s and the 1960s. The 1940s are synonymous with World War II. The Fifties and the Seventies are generally seen as quieter interludes during which our crises were less extreme and most people could get on with their lives in pursuit of personal interests. Donald Creighton, in his history of the period, referred to the Fifties as a "sober and conventional period" (1976: 245) and, in his history of social policy, Tom Kent has termed it "our conservative decade" (cited in Guest 1985:142). Research carried out in recent years is indicating that as far as the field of adult education is concerned, at least, the 1950s were far from a quiet period. It was a time during which the character of adult education in Canada was transformed dramatically, a new spirit of professionalism began to emerge, and generally the foundations were laid for many developments which have become more pronounced in the subsequent decades.

This article examines the nature of the changes which took place in the Fifties. The scene is set by a brief examination of the nature and reputation of adult education in Canada at the beginning of the decade, with particular reference to The Canadian Association for Adult Education and to Dr. Roby Kidd, who became its Director in 1951. Kidd was to be the leading personality in many of the developments during the decade. The signs of emerging professionalism in adult education are then examined under four headings: a sense of vocation or profession, the development of training opportunities, institutional development, and the literature of the field. In each case, these topics are examined from a national perspective and then, as appropriate, from a regional point of view.

The article is an attempt to take a closer look than we have before at the Fifties and to identify some of the major developments and forces in connection with adult education which were at work, both nationally and regionally. The author having for some years carried out historical research on adult education in British Columbia, that region will be used mainly to illustrate some of the more important changes at the more local level. The evidence indicates that for adult education in Canada, the 1950s may justifiably be judged a "pivotal" decade.

In what sense may it be seen to be pivotal? It would appear that the institutional base of the field, especially in the public educational systems of Canada, was significantly strengthened across the country. The number of persons who came to identify themselves and their careers with the field of adult education was greatly enhanced during the decade. Generally the period was one of an expanding sense of professionalism on the part of growing number of workers in the field, involving increased concern about the systematic and appropriate use of methodology and the development of appropriate adult curricula. This in turn led to a demand for training opportunities in adult education. Leaders in the field came to an increasing realization of the significance of Canadian achievements in adult education. This decade also saw the creation of a number of organizations of adult educators at the national and provincial levels.

It is interesting to note that, according to several authorities in the field in the United States, the corresponding period of development in that country was perhaps fifteen or twenty years earlier. Based on a study of the literature of the field, Webster Cotton (1968) concluded that there was a strong trend towards the professionalization of adult education "in the middle and late 1930s" (p. 7). Cotton contrasted what he termed the social reformist tradition of adult education, one which existed in the early years of the movement and supported adult education as a means of improving society, with what he termed the professional position, which placed greater emphasis on serving individual needs, building a sense of common cause among practitioners based on expertise and, as he put it, transforming the adult education enterprise "from one primarily oriented toward social reform to that of a more purely educational undertaking" (p. 9). Cotton identified the emergence of the professional point of view with the creation of the American Association for Adult Education in 1926, the launching of its journal three years later, Columbia University's introduction of a doctoral degree in the field in 1935 and the publication of the first textbook for the field in 1936 (Bryson 1936). Other American scholars who have studied this trend in their country, most notably Malcolm Knowles (1977) and Cyril Houle (1956, 1960), are in general agreement on the timing of these developments.

Although it is possible in this way to identify some elements of emerging professionalism in adult education in the United States as early as the 1920s and 1930s, a profession in the full or classical sense of the term has never been realized. The late A.A. Liveright examined this question at some length in the landmark American study, *Adult Education: Outlines of an Emerging Field of University Study*, which was published in 1964, and he concluded that adult education could not then be classified as a profession in the full sense of the word. It is certainly not being suggested here that, in the decade being studied, anything approaching professional status in the full sense was even aimed for, much less achieved in Canada. Rather, attention is focused here on signs of an emerging sense of a profession-like approach, or professionalism on the part of practitioners, efforts made to promote such a tendency and the growing institutionalization of the field.

The Role of J. R. Kidd

Many of the noteworthy developments towards the professionalization of adult education during the 1950s can be connected with the efforts of Dr. J. Roby Kidd, whose tenure as Director of the Canadian Association for Adult Education (CAAE) coincides with the period. Kidd worked for eleven years with the Y.M.C.A in Montreal and Ottawa early in his career and earned his Masters degree at McGill University. After the war, he went to

New York to study for his doctorate in the field of adult education at Columbia University, graduating in 1947 and thus becoming the first Canadian to receive a doctorate in this field. (Kidd enjoyed making the point that his claim to this distinction hung on a technicality, in that Florence O'Neill of Newfoundland had earned her doctorate at the same institution three years earlier, but that until 1949 Newfoundland was not a part of Canada!) Kidd returned to Canada upon graduation to become Associate Director of the CAAE. When E.A. Corbett retired in 1951, Kidd became Director, a post he held until the spring of 1961.

Kidd's effectiveness with respect to the building of the adult education enterprise in Canada during this period and the encouragement of a more professional view of the field can be explained on several grounds. First of all, the fact that he had earned a doctorate in adult education, and from the most prestigious university in the field at that time, opened certain doors for Kidd. He could deal with educational officials, government leaders and academic institutions and be seen by them as having outstanding formal qualifications in his field of operations, qualifications beyond what any but a handful of Canadians possessed. Secondly, his position with CAAE provided him with unique opportunities. In a country where education was a provincial responsibility, there were few organizations concerned with education at the time which had a national membership and mandate. The fact that the CAAE was a small organization and represented a field of activity which was little recognized at the time was a handicap from certain points of view. But this meant that Kidd and the organization were a threat to no one, and could move relatively freely in the politically sensitive national and interprovincial educational scene, promoting the development of educational activities. A further advantage of his position with the CAAE was that Kidd had at his disposal the national information networks which had been built up by the organization, in terms of both personal contacts and publications. Of course, all of this would have been of little avail if Kidd himself had not been committed to the promotion of the institutionalization of, and a more professional approach to, the field. His belief in the importance of these matters, demonstrated in so many ways, was basic to his efforts. As the decade of his tenure as Director of the CAAE progressed, Kidd gained increasing stature in the field, most notably through his published works and also his growing reputation at the international level (Cochrane 1986; Selman 1982). The final attribute which contributed to Kidd's effectiveness as a promoter of adult education at this time was his capacity to build relationships and attract the respect and affection of others with whom he worked and had contact. He was effective in inspiring in others—fellow workers in adult education and others outside the field—a sense of the significance of adult learning and the importance of promoting and supporting it effectively in Canadian society. This he pursued in three main ways: the promotion of a more expert or professional work force in adult education; the documentation of Canada's accomplishments in that field; and the strengthening of the institutional base of operations for the field. There were, of course, many other persons who contributed to the developments at this time, and a number will be mentioned in this article, but Kidd was undoubtedly the most important figure.

The Field at the Beginning of the Fifties

At the beginning of the Fifties, adult education in Canada had already achieved a considerable reputation among those who were knowledgable about the field, largely on the basis of several outstanding projects. These would include, certainly, two programs sponsored by the CAAE and the Canadian Broadcasting Corporation (CBC): the National Farm Radio Forum and the Citizens' Forum, which made imaginative combined use of broadcasting, print and local discussion groups. The extension program in education about co-operatives, sponsored by St. Francis Xavier University in Nova Scotia under the leadership of the Rev. Moses Coady, was widely known internationally. The work of Frontier College in bringing basic education to men in isolated centres on the frontier, that of the Banff School of Fine Arts in providing education in the arts, and the activities of the Joint Planning Commission as a clearinghouse for organizations involved in the social and cultural development of the country, were also well known in some circles. There was, of course, much adult education being conducted in other settings, in voluntary organizations, co-operatives, university and agricultural extension, and a few local school boards, but this work was on the whole not noteworthy on an international scale.

The CAAE was also widely known as an organization by this time, at least in adult education circles. Its reputation rested on two main things. First, under the leadership of Ned Corbett, its founding Director, the organization had established several projects of importance. National Farm Radio Forum and Citizens' Forum have already been mentioned and the methodologies developed for those programs were being adapted for use in many other countries (Sim 1954; Faris 1975). In 1947, Corbett found funding and launched the Joint Planning Commission, a vehicle for consultation and co-operation among over a hundred national organizations and departments of government (Clark 1954). North America was strewn with the corpses of defunct clearinghouse bodies of this kind, but Canada's Joint Planning Commission seemed to work and visitors came from several other countries to study its structure and methods.

These and other significant projects had established the reputation of the CAAE as an innovative and capable programming agency. While these projects were important in themselves, it was the nature of their overall purpose and content which constituted the basis for the second characteristic of the CAAE which had attracted wide attention. The CAAE was founded in 1935, largely by persons from the universities and government, to serve as a clearinghouse for the field, generally to be the servant of practitioners and institutions. Before long, however, as a result of the leadership of Corbett and other early leaders, and also of the conditions brought on by the Second World War and the period of reconstruction thinking in the late and post-war period, the Association was transformed from a clearinghouse body to a direct programming agency, largely in the field of education about public affairs (Faris 1975; Selman 1981).

In the somewhat radicalized period of reconstruction thinking in the latter war years, the CAAE conference of 1943 approved a "Manifesto" which gained it a reputation in some quarters of being a leftist, anti-free enterprise group. The legacy of this incident and the almost inevitable controversy which flared up from time to time over its handling of public issues in the Farm Forum and Citizens' Forum series plunged the organization into disputes in the late Forties and early Fifties, just as Kidd took over as Director (Faris 1975). In the October 1951 issue of *Food For Thought*, the CAAE's journal, in an unsigned portion of the editorial column, but no doubt written by Kidd himself, a statement was printed which explained that the CAAE's advocacy role was restricted to speaking about "adult education in Canada" and that the Association would "take no partisan position on controversial questions" (The CAAE and Social Action, 1951:9). It was with considerable feeling, no doubt, that in his first report as Director of the Association, in the spring of 1952, he told his colleagues that during the year the Association had been subjected to criticism from all parts of the compass, and while much of it was undeserved and misguided, there was need for caution:

> An organization like ours has bounds and limitations which we must recognize. It is not, and by its nature cannot be, the radical agency of social action which some of you might prefer. Nor can it be a research agency only—simply observing and reporting facts. Our work cannot be done in splendid isolation; we must stay close to where groups are living and working. The CAAE is concerned about the welfare of, but cannot be the mouthpiece of, the farmer, the union member, the housewife, the businessman. (p. 5)

For all this, however, it would be a mistake to interpret Kidd's remarks as signalling a rejection of the citizenship education thrust of the organization. He was cautioning against an extreme social action position, but it is clear from his actions as Director of the Association in the ensuing decade that he was firmly committed to the citizenship education mission of the CAAE. With respect to the field as a whole, what he promoted was a more professionalized field of practice, with the strongest possible institutional base, but one which at the same time retained a lively sense of the social as well as the individual needs to be served, and benefits to be delivered.

A Sense of Vocation

The emerging sense of professionalism or profession-like commitment on the part of practitioners in adult education was pronounced in the 1950s, although it perhaps came into greater prominence in the following decade. The concept of the adult education leader as a professional person did not of course originate in the 1950s. In the report of the survey of the field which was undertaken at the time of the formation of the CAAE in the mid-Thirties (Sandiford 1935), there was an obvious assumption that the leadership of adult education in Canada would be an increasingly professionalized group, and that the field would become more tightly co-ordinated at the provincial level. At the first Western Regional conference on adult education, held in Saskatoon in March of 1938, the need for trained leaders in the field was stressed (Rayner 1938). When, for instance, the Public Library Commission of British Columbia conducted a comprehensive survey of the field in B.C. in 1941, the recommendations in its report called for a co-ordinated system of adult education, led by "specialists in adult education, not child educationists" (B.C. Public Library Commission 1942:7). During the 1940s at least three Canadians earned doctoral degrees in adult education in the United States—Roby Kidd and Florence O'Neill, who have already been mentioned, and John Friesen of Manitoba (Houle & Buskey 1966). In 1947, successive issues of *Food For Thought* carried articles on the history of adult education written by Corbett (1947, 1947b) and, later in the year, a long description was carried of the report of the Manitoba Royal Commission on Adult Education (Tweedie 1947). The first of a series of biographical sketches of adult education leaders in Canada appeared in the CAAE Journal in late 1947, a further sign of an emerging self-conscious adult education movement (Corbett 1947c). In the same issue, an article appeared describing the Adult Education Division of the Department of Education in Saskatchewan, written by its Director (Smith 1947), and early in the following year an article appeared which examined the "democratic safeguards" which needed to be adopted if governments were to get into the business of financing adult education (Needler 1948). At the annual meeting of the CAAE in June, 1948, consideration was given (as far as can be determined, for the first time in Canada) to policy concerning the development of training programs for adult educators. Recommendations called for the development of university degree programs (In Our Opinion, 1948). In the same year the first article carried by the Association's journal on the training of adult educators appeared, making reference to the "elements of a profession" as they relate to adult education (Hallenbeck 1948). Attention had been given earlier to "leadership training" for a variety of community workers. These few examples serve to illustrate that prior to 1950, recognition of professional concerns and of the need for professionally qualified adult educators was present in the field. What occurred in the Fifties was a very considerable further development along these lines.

As has been suggested, the most important person in the promotion of a sense of professionalism or of the need for well trained leadership in the field was undoubtedly Roby Kidd (Selman 1983, 1986). His work took him back and forth across the country and provided many opportunities to talk to both adult educators themselves and also employers, such as senior officials in educational institutions and large voluntary organizations, and key officials in departments of government. The fact that in some respects he was the epitome of the professional adult educator, with a doctoral degree from the most highly regarded graduate program in the field on the continent, who frequently was teaching degree credit courses in the field at Canadian universities, and who was the head of the only national organization in Canada devoted to adult education, helped to open many doors for him. His very great capacity to convince and influence others and his skills, however cloaked with personal modesty, to present his case in compelling, winning ways, contributed to his undoubted success in getting support for his point of view.

Kidd seemed to lose no opportunity to emphasize the responsibility of adult educators to address and make use of the increasing knowledge that was becoming available about how adults could be assisted in their learning. As well, he persistently stressed to the employers of adult educators the importance of selecting first-class people and providing them with opportunities to study about the field. A study of the major addresses, reports and publications produced by Kidd and his organization during the 1950s reveals what a consistent theme this was (Selman 1982, 1983). For example, in his Director's Report to the CAAE in 1956, which was devoted in large part to professionalism in the field, Kidd spoke strongly about the need for good personnel and training:

> I have only one serious apprehension about the future. More and more the conception of continuous learning is being accepted. But will we have the staff who are numerous and talented enough? Every year several important positions are open which require men and women of considerable capacity and long experience. So we quickly look around for a suitable person as if we did not fully understand that such people aren't just found, they must be "grown", and the growing period starts many years before.

In the latter 1950s, more space was devoted than before in the Association's journal to professional concerns such as training, information services and research. In his consultations with educational authorities across Canada, Kidd repeatedly stressed the need to employ able people to take charge of adult education. For instance, in his major report to the Toronto Board of Education, written late in the decade, he included strong recommendations on the need for training in adult education for teachers and counsellors of adults and for administrators and planners of adult education programs (Kidd 1961).

Other people were providing leadership in this same direction within their spheres of influence. In British Columbia, Dr. John Friesen, Director of the Extension Department of the University, and one of few Canadians holding a doctoral degree in the field, urged and enabled his staff members to advance their study of adult education. He was joined in this in mid-decade at the University by Alan Thomas, who had completed all but his dissertation at Columbia University at that stage and who was by the end of the decade writing articles in *Food For Thought* on professional matters (Thomas 1959, 1959b). Dr. Bert Wales, who earned his doctorate in the field from Oregon State University in 1958, and who became Director of Adult Education for the Vancouver School Board the following year, was leading by example towards a more professionalized approach to adult education, particularly among the rapidly increasing number of school board adult educators. Encouragement in this direction was also provided by L.J. Wallace, who became provincial director of adult education in B.C. early in the decade and who, by various means, encouraged the adult educators employed by the school boards to take a broader, more professional view of their responsibilities (Report of the Provincial Conference 1955). British Columbia was one of the regions in Canada showing leadership with respect to the development of adult education in this period. It was perhaps not typical of the country as a whole. At least four other Canadians earned doctoral degrees in the field during the 1950s (Houle & Buskey 1966), and it is clear from other developments, described later, that some similar things were happening elsewhere.

Training Opportunities

Opportunities in Canada for acquiring training in the field of adult education expanded very greatly during the 1950s. There had been some work of this general kind going on for many years in certain quarters. The literature of the Forties contains many accounts of "leadership training" activities in fields such as group work, recreation, and especially late in the decade, human relations training. The Y.M. and Y.W.C.A., and other voluntary organizations, the folk school, co-operative and labour movements were active in this work. Roby Kidd recalled that he had been a student in a credit course in adult education at Sir George Williams College in 1934-35, which may have been the first such course in Canada (Selman 1982).

When Kidd returned from his doctoral studies in 1947 and joined the staff of the CAAE, the promotion of training opportunities for adult educators was one of his priorities. He suggested the formation of a CAAE "Committee on Personnel in Adult Education", whose initial report in 1948 has already been mentioned. It indicated that, of the 86 full-time adult educators in Canada who responded, only two had any training in the field, even a single course, and recommended that the CAAE take a lead in the promotion of both formal and non-formal training programs (Kidd 1950). The endorsement of this report provided Kidd with a mandate for his continuing efforts to these ends during the Fifties. He pursued this goal in various ways: by encouraging the organization of training programs by various organizations, including the CAAE, and playing a leading role as instructor in this work; by fostering regional meetings of adult educators at which in-service development training could take place; by assisting with the formation of regional and provincial associations of adult educators; by encouraging senior administrators in employing institutions to seek training for their adult education staff; by raising funds from foundations which could be used to assist individuals to engage in professional training; and by assisting interested universities in the development of credit courses and programs.

Non-credit, in-service development activities for adult educators were an important new feature of the period and Kidd played a leading role. A few examples will indicate the types of programs which were organized. The first training course for adult educators in the western region, a two week program on "Extension Methods and Techniques", was held at Banff in 1949, co-sponsored by the CAAE and the University of Alberta. Kidd took part in the planning and the instruction. He frequently taught courses for adult educators in the labour movement. In 1951, he secured a foundation grant to support a two-year series of training programs designed for workers in the outports of Newfoundland. The first regional training course for the Atlantic region was organized by the CAAE in 1958.

In 1950, at Kidd's suggestion, the CAAE made a decision to hold national conferences every second year and to sponsor regional conferences in the Western and Atlantic regions in the intervening years. The chief reason for this suggestion was that the regional meetings would be more accessible to practitioners than were national ones and could serve as a vehicle for in-service professional development. The Atlantic region was the first to pick up on the idea; the "first Atlantic Region Conference" was held at Amherst, Nova Scotia, in June of 1951 (Maritime Conference 1951:32). Further such meetings followed every second year throughout the decade, the programs focusing mainly on the social and economic development of the region. In the West, the meetings did not begin until 1953, the first being held in Banff, but were held regularly thereafter. Although the conferences in the West, like those in the Maritimes, devoted some attention to social development, there was much more focus in the West on the formation of provincial organizations of adult educators, their functions and their relationship with the national organization. It is clear from the reports of these meetings, East and West, that the decision to facilitate the holding of regional meetings under CAAE sponsorship was an important factor in stimulating in-service development activities in both regions (Selman 1982). In the case of the Western region, there was also a great impact on the development of provincial organizations.

There had been a few local and regional associations of adult educators in Canada prior to the Fifties—one in Winnipeg in the mid-Thirties, in Ontario and the Eastern Townships of Quebec in the early Forties and in Alberta beginning in 1943 (Selman 1982)—but by the late Forties, no such organizations were functioning. Arising out of suggestions discussed at Banff in 1953, and worked out by leaders in the field in British Columbia, steps were taken in that province to create a provincially based organization. An organizational dinner which was addressed by Roby Kidd in September of 1954 led to the first of what were to be a continuing series of semi-annual conferences on adult education which continued on a regular basis until 1961 (Selman 1969). The B.C. organization was a council of agencies rather than a personal membership body, but the B.C. Adult Education Council sponsored a significant series of in-service development activities within the framework of the semi-annual conferences. In 1956, all four Western provinces held provincial conferences of adult educators and in all but B.C. (where an organization already existed), plans were discussed for the possible creation of provincial bodies (Selman 1957). As it turned out, plans developed more quickly in Saskatchewan than in the other two provinces and under the terms of a revision in the CAAE constitution passed in 1958, the B.C. and Saskatchewan organizations subsequently became "affiliated" with the CAAE and had representation on that organization's National Council. The meetings in the Atlantic region did not lead to the promotion of provincial bodies as they had in the West and that development did not come until the following decade.

Apart from the CAAE, there were other organizational developments in the field at the national level. The French language national body, the Institute Canadien d'Education des Adultes, which had developed out of a standing committee of the CAAE, was reorganized in 1952 and became a more vigorous and effective instrument for that language group. Those who worked in the field of university extension, after a considerable period of consultation with an already existing organization of colleagues responsible for summer session activities, joined with them in 1954 in forming the Canadian Association of Directors of Extension and Summer Sessions (Kidd 1956). Educators interested mainly in the rural and agricultural aspects of adult education had formed an Extension Group under the Canadian Society of Technical Agriculturalists in 1940, but this organization met only sporadically during the following decade and disappeared by 1953. In 1959, a decision was made to revive such a body, and the Canadian Society of Rural Extension came into existence the following year (Adema 1984).

Similarly, the decade was one of significant beginnings at the provincial level. In British Columbia, as described above, the first organization of adult educators (more accurately, of adult education organizations) was formed in the year 1954, with leadership coming from three institutions: the University Extension Department, the Vancouver School Board and the provincial Department of Education. The Vancouver School Board, which had, since early in the century, been the leading board in the province in adult education, gave strong support to the field and by the 1950s employed a considerable number of program administrators who had come to identify themselves in career terms with adult education. In 1955, the dynamic director of adult education in the Department of Education, L.J. Wallace, organized an ambitious five-day conference of night school directors in the province in which 22 night school directors and 16 resource persons took part and which, in retrospect, may be seen to have marked the beginning of a major expansion of school board sponsored adult education. The result was that in the ensuing decade such work in B.C. became the leading example of this aspect of adult education in all of Canada (Wales 1958). Dominion Bureau of Statistics figures showed school board adult education enrolments in 1959-60 to be leading the country and proportionately approximately twice as large as the national average (Dominion Bureau of Statistics, 1962). Further regional conferences of night school directors were held within the province in 1959 and 1960 and in his annual report in the latter year, the provincial director made the point that the traditional term "night school" was giving way to "adult education" as a better reflection of the broad community service for adult learners which the school boards were aiming to provide.

By the end of the decade, there were large numbers of educators in British Columbia who identified themselves and their careers with the field of adult education. At the thirteenth semi-annual conference of the B.C. Adult Education Council, held in the spring of 1961, there was a concerted effort to plan for the decade ahead and one among several task forces was asked to consider what kind of organization for adult educators would serve the field appropriately in the future. In reporting to the conference, this group stated emphatically that the existing Council, which was an inter-agency clearinghouse, was no longer adequate because there had been such a large increase in the number of adult educators who wished a personal commitment to the field and desired an organization to which they could belong on a professional basis and through which they could receive assistance in their professional continuing education (Selman 1969, 1980).

A further dimension of working towards adequate training opportunities for adult educators involved efforts directed at employers of adult educators, most notably educational institutions, school boards and provincial departments of education. At the CAAE conference in 1950, a working group gave attention to "Provincial Divisions of Adult Education" (meaning units within departments of education). In 1957, 1959 and 1961, conferences on the role of governments and school boards in the field were organized in co-operation with the Canadian Education Association. Beginning in the late Fifties, the CAAE had standing committees both on governments in adult education and on school boards in the field. Reference should also be made to Kidd's pamphlet, *Adult Education and the School* (1950b), and his major study of adult education in the Metropolitan Toronto area carried out in 1961 on behalf of the Board of Education of that city (Kidd 1961). The committee organizing the Second Canadian Conference on Education, held in 1962, commissioned Kidd to write a background study on adult education, which was one of several on specialized topics, and by means of this substantial pamphlet, he made the most of the opportunity to address the educational establishment of Canada with respect to the system's responsibilities in adult education (Kidd 1961b).

Kidd was also active in raising funds from foundations for the purpose of financing training activities. Reference has already been made to the funds he raised for training work in Newfoundland beginning in 1951. In 1953, a party of leading adult educators from English and French Canada was enabled, with the help of funds secured from Carnegie, to visit outstanding people and projects in Europe. In 1955, school board adult educators from Nova Scotia and New Brunswick were assisted with a study tour to American and Canadian centres. For several years in the late fifties, some $15,000 a year which he secured from the Fund for Adult Education in the United States was used to make study tours or degree study possible for individual adult educators.

This was also the period during which academic degree programs in adult education were inaugurated in Canada. With his doctoral degree, Kidd was clearly qualified to be appointed to teach university courses. In the late Forties and during the Fifties he taught the first credit course in adult education at several Canadian universities and, in 1951, he taught the first graduate course to be offered, at the Ontario College of Education. A course he taught at the University of British Columbia in the summer of 1956 was utilized by several leaders at that institution as the first step in developing and securing official approval for a masters degree program in the field, which when introduced in 1957 became the first degree credit program in adult education in Canada. By this time there were at least twelve universities in the United States which were offering advanced degree programs in the field (Houle 1960). The University of Guelph became the second institution to offer such a program when it admitted its first masters candidates in this field in 1960 to a Master of Science degree with a specialization in agriculture and rural matters (Personal Communication, M.W. Waldron, September 10, 1986). It is apparent from the foregoing that during the Fifties considerable strides were taken in both providing various kinds of training opportunities and attempting to convince both adult educators and their employers that such training was desirable.

Institutional Development

The matter of institutional development has already been touched upon in several ways. The efforts made during the decade to convince the public educational authorities were in large measure directed to this end. Kidd made use of the available opportunities, at meetings and in the course ot his constant travel back and forth across Canada to promote the field and the need for adequate institutional provision for this work. CAAE standing committees on school board and government adult education work have already been mentioned, as have several conferences held during the decade with representatives of those sectors of the field. The consultation carried out for the Board of Education in Toronto (Kidd 1961) and the opportunity to write one of the study pamphlets for the Second Canadian Conference on Education in 1962 (Kidd 1961b) were high-profile opportunities to address the educational establishment in Canada. Another opportunity presented itself in 1953, when the National Conference of Canadian Universities commissioned Kidd to write a study concerning adult education in the university. The outcome was a volume entitled *Adult Education in the Canadian University*, which was published in 1956. Although it is impossible fully to determine the influence of such reports, several universities in Canada subsequently created extension departments.

There were grounds for encouragement particularly with respect to provision for adult education within the structure of the provincial departments of education. Kidd attached particular importance to this matter and approached it not only by means described above, but also through personal representations whenever possible. He also gave whatever prominence he could, through the Association's journal and by other means, to accounts of successful examples of work by the provincial departments. The stormy events surrounding Watson Thomson and his work as Director of the Adult Education Division in Saskatchewan in 1944-45 (Welton 1983) were largely ignored but, when the government of Nova Scotia created a Division of Adult Education a year later, Kidd gave great prominence to that development, carrying frequent news items in *Food For Thought* and printing a full account of the work of the Division as one of several pamphlets he arranged to have published in the early Fifties (Henson 1954). Advances in this area were most satisfactory in this period. In 1945, only one provincial department of education in Canada—Saskatchewan—had an adult education unit (as distinct from just an official with responsibility in this area). When Kidd wrote his pamphlet entitled *Continuing Education* in 1961, he could report that all ten provinclal departments had such a unit (Kidd 1961b). It was this kind of development which prompted J.D. Wilson and his colleagues in their general history of education in Canada to identify the Fifties as a period during which adult education "lost much of its amateur status" (Wilson, Stamp & Audet 1970:412).

The Literature of the Field

The literature of adult education in Canada was another area in which there was significant advance during this decade. It is generally understood that a field of practice, in order to advance towards professional status, must have a body of knowledge on which to base its growth and development. While adult education in Canada could not be said to have reached the stage of theory building or other advanced forms of research and scholarshlp at this time, what was attempted was to document the nature and history of the field in Canada and to assist adult educators who were ready to do so, to take an increasingly serious interest in the methods and problems of practice.

There was very little literature about the field in Canada published before the Fifties. There were the accumulated files of the two CAAE journals, *Adult Learning* (1936-39) and *Food For Thought* (1940-), Fitzpatrick's plea for and account of the early years of Frontier College (1920), the survey of adult education activities in Canada edited by Sandiford (1935) as part of the process of founding the CAAE, and Rev. Moses Coady's account of the philosophy and methods of the Antigonish Movement, *Masters of Their Own Destiny* (1939). Aside from a few other articles, institutional and government reports, and a very few pamphlets, these seem to be the only published works on adult education in Canada prior to 1950 (Kidd 1950). Due to the efforts of Roby Kidd as both author and publisher and those of a growing, but still small circle of practitioners in Canada, this picture changed substantially during the fifties.

Walter Stewart, in his study of the content of the CAAE journals over the years (1983), perceived a distinct shift of emphasis in *Food For Thought* in 1950 compared to five years earlier:

> The clearly intended audience of the 1950 issues was those who were engaged in educating adults and not those who were being educated as had been true in the 1940s. (p. 36)

He commented further that at this time the journal became "a magazine about adult education rather than an instrument of adult education" (p. 54). He noted that an interest in the history of the field was being reflected In the journal and that, by 1960, the journal was including articles on philosophical issues, on methods and techniques and on evaluation. He comments that by that time, the journal "had made some moves towards becoming a professional journal" (p. 39).

Kidd's own writing about the field during the Fifties was prolific, extremely varied, and may be seen to fall into five main categories. The first, that of descriptive studies of the field in Canada, is represented by two books of collections of articles about Canadian adult education, *Adult Education in Canada* (1950) and *Learning and Society* (1963) and two pamphlets, "People Learning from Each Other" (1953), the summary pamphlet in the "Learning for Living" series which appeared from 1952 to 1954, and "Continuing Education" (1961b), written to represent the field at the 1962 National Conference on Education. On several occasions during the decade, Kidd produced substantial publications as a result of consultations which he or the CAAE undertook. These several reports have already been mentioned, one on the field as it related to the school (1950b), one on the place of adult education in the university (1956), and the major report to the Toronto Board of Education (1961). There were several publications on methodological aspects, two on film and film utilization (1953, 1959) and a guide for discussion leaders, a pamphlet published in 1956 (1956b). As Kidd became progressively more involved in the international dimensions of adult education, he began to write about that sphere of interest, this taking the form of articles in the main during the Fifties. Kidd's most notable publication during the period in some respects was his textbook for the field, *How Adults Learn*, published in 1959. The first text for the field is generally considered to be Lyman Bryson's *Adult Education*, which appeared in 1936. Two others were published during the Fifties in the United States (Sheets, Jane & Spence 1953; Kempfer 1955), but Kidd's was the first to be produced in Canada and was a significant departure from all its predecessors in at least one major respect, the relative prominence given to learning theory. The book was well received in the field in North America, but especially so in other countries and it has since been translated into at least five other languages (Cochrane 1986) and has been used as a text in at least forty countries (Selman 1982).

Over and above Kidd's own writing, the field benefitted from his efforts in encouraging and publishing a great deal of material through the CAAE. Soon after his publication of *Adult Education in Canada* in 1950, he secured a grant from the Fund for Adult Education to make it possible to continue the program of documenting Canadian achievements in the field. The result was a series of eleven substantial pamphlets entitled "Learning For Living", which appeared between 1952 and 1954. A few other representative examples of CAAE publications during the decade were: a survey of labour education in Canada (Smith 1951), a bibliography of Canadian writings in adult education (Thomson & Ironside 1956), and *Residential Adult Education: A Canadian View* (Loosley 1960). There were as well several other notable volumes about the field which were published commercially at this time. They included Donald Cameron's history of the Banff School of Fine Arts (Cameron 1956), E.A. Corbett's reminiscences, *We Have With Us Tonight* (1957), and at the end of the decade A.F. Laidlaw's history of the Antigonish Movement (1961).

Other organizations at the national level were publishing material at this time: the Canadian Labour Congress, the Canadian Library Association, the Canadian Film Institute and the Canadian Citizenship Council. As well, an increasing amount of material about adult education was being published at the local and provincial level. The bibliography published by the CAAE in 1956 (Thomson & Ironside 1956) selected a number of items related to adult education from Saskatchewan Community and Community Courier (Ontario) and listed a number of other newsletters and bulletins published at the provincial level. The Extension Department of the University of British Columbia began in 1954 the publication of a series of monographs under the title, "Occasional Papers on Adult Education" and they appeared at the rate of one a year for the balance of the decade.

At the beginning of the 1950s there was very little Canadian literature in the field of adult education, whereas by the end of the decade, practitioners and students had a considerable and growing body of writings from Canadian sources on which to call, covering not only aspects of practice but also Canadian perspectives, policies and achievements in the field.

Summary and Comment

While it is certainly not suggested, by way of summary of this account, that by 1960 adult education had become a professionalized field, or that Canada had reached an advanced stage in the institutionalization of this activity, it does seem justifiable to conclude that the field had moved very substantially in those directions during the previous decade. Whether this matter is approached in terms of the number of persons who identified themselves and their careers with adult education, the opportunities available for professional training and in-service development, the expansion of the institutional base and provision for adult education, or the growing body of knowledge and literature available about the field in Canada, it is clear that the 1950s were a period of rapid advance towards a more professionalized field. In the terminology of the economists, the period might be seen as the "take-off" stage in which lines of development were established, ones which would set the general directions for the ensuing period.

At the beginning of the Fifties, professionalism was simply not a significant issue in the field as a whole in Canada. But ten years later, during the period of preparation for the National Conference on Adult Education to be held in the fall of 1961, Alan Thomas, writing in *Food For Thought* under the pen name of Parameter, was expressing concern that adult education in Canada, in the face of rapidly advancing professionalism and institutionalization, was in danger of losing its quality of being a movement (Thomas 1961). In his closing address to the National Conference, Boris Ford, a visitor from Britain, commented on the obvious emphasis in the keynote address on "The Social Implications and Responsibilities of Adult Education" and the concern which had been expressed that with advancing professionalism in the field, education for adults would come to be seen too predominantly in terms of meeting individual needs to the neglect of social needs (National Conference on Adult Education 1961:60). Such concerns were far removed from the situation a decade earlier.

References

Adema, B. (1984), *The History of the Canadian Society of Extension*, Unpublished M. Sc. Thesis, University of Guelph.

British Columbia Public Library Commission (1942), *A Preliminary Study of Adult Education in British Columbia: 1941*, Victoria: B.C.P.L.C.

Bryson, L. (1936), *Adult Education*, New York: American Book Co.

Cameron, D. (1956), *Campus in the Clouds*, Toronto: McClelland & Stewart.

"[The] CAAE and Social Action" (1951), *Food For Thought*, 12 (1): 8-9.

Clark, C. (1954), The Joint Planning Commission, Toronto: CAAE.

Coady, M.M. (1939), *Masters of Their Own Destiny*, New York: Harpers.

Cochrane, N. et al (1986), *J.R. Kidd: An International Legacy of Learning*, Vancouver: University of B.C. Centre for Continuing Education.

Corbett, E.A. (1947), "A Short History of Adult Education," *Food For Thought*, 7 (5): 14-17.

——. (1947b), "A Short History of Adult Education: Part II," *Food For Thought*, 7 (6): 29-33,43.

——. (1947c), "Dr. James Tompkins: Priest and Prophet," *Food For Thought*, 8 (3): 10-13.

——. (1957), *We Have With Us Tonight*, Toronto: Ryerson.

Cotton, W.E. (1968), *On Behalf of Adult Education*, Boston: Centre for the Study of Liberal Education for Adults.

Creighton, D. (1976), *The Forked Road: Canada 1939-1957*, Toronto: McClelland & Stewart.

Dominion Bureau of Statistics (1962), *Survey of Adult Education 1959-60*, Ottawa: D.B.S.

Faris, R. (1975), *The Passionate Educators*, Toronto: Peter Martin.

Fitzpatrick, A. (1920), *University in Overalls*, Toronto: Hunter-Rose.

Guest, D. (1985), *The Emergence of Social Security in Canada*, Vancouver: University of B.C. Press.

Hallenbeck, W.C. (1948), Training Adult Educators, *Food For Thought*, 9 (1): 13-15, 25.

Henson, G. (1954), *Adult Education in Nova Scotia*, Toronto: CAAE.

Houle, C.O. (1960), "The Education of Adult Education Leaders," in Knowles, 1960.

Houle, C.O. and Buskey, J.H. (1966), "The Doctorate in Adult Education," *Adult Education*, 16 (3); 131-68.

"In Our Opinion" (1948), *Food For Thought*, 9 (1): 1-2.

Kempfer, H. (1955), *Adult Education*, New York: McGraw-Hill.

Kidd, J.R. (Ed.) (1950), *Adult Education in Canada*, Toronto: CAAE.

———. (1950b), *Adult Education and the School*, Toronto: CAAE.

———. (1952), A Kind of Partnership: Director's Report, *Food For Thought*, 13 (1): 4-7.

———. (1953), *People Learning from Each Other*, Toronto: CAAE.

———. (1953b), *Pictures with a Purpose*, Toronto: CAAE.

———. (1956), *Adult Education in the Canadian University*, Toronto: CAAE.

———. (1956b), *Putting Words to Work*, Toronto: CAAE.

———. (1969), *How Adults Learn*, New York: Association Press.

———. (1961), *18 To 80: Continuing Education in Metropolitan Toronto*, Toronto: Toronto Board of Education.

———. (1961b), *Continuing Education*, Ottawa: Canadian Conference on Education.

———. (1963), *Learning and Society*, Toronto: CAAE.

Kidd, J.R. and Storr, C.B. (1951) *Film Utilization*, Toronto: CAAE.

Knowles, M.S. (Ed.) (1960), *Handbook of Adult Education in the United States*, Chicago: Adult Education Association of the U.S.A.

———. (1977), *The Adult Education Movement in the United States*, Huntington: Robt. E. Krieger.

Laidlaw, A.F. (1961), *The Campus and the Community*, Montreal: Harvest House.

Loosley, E. (1960), *Residential Adult Education: A Canadian View*, Toronto: CAAE.

Maritime Conference (1951), *Food For Thought*, 12 (1): 32-33.

National Conference on Adult Education (1961), Toronto & Montreal: CAAE & ICEA.

Needler, M.C. (1948), "Government Assistance in Adult Education," *Food For Thought*, 8 (5): 21-25.

Rayner, J.G. (1938), "Four Western Provinces Discuss Adult Education," *Adult Learning*, 2 (6): 18-21.

Sandiford, P. (Ed.) (1935), *Adult Education in Canada: A Survey*, Toronto: University of Toronto.

Selman, G. (1957), "Western Variations on the Theme," *Food For Thought*, 18 (1): 5-9.

———. (1969), *Toward Co-operation: The Development of a Provincial Voice for Adult Education in British Columbia 1953-1962*, Vancouver: University of B.C. Centre for Continuing Education.

———. (1980), *The British Columbia Division of the CAAE 1961-1971*, Vancouver: Pacific Association for Continuing Education.

——. (1981), *The CAAE in the Corbett Years: A Re-evaluation*, Vancouver: University of B.C. Centre for Continuing Education.

——. (1982), *Roby Kidd and the CAAE 1951-1961*, Vancouver: University of B.C. Centre for Continuing Education.

——. (1983), "Roby Kidd and the Continuing Education of Adult Educators," *Canadian Journal of University Continuing Education*, 9 (2): 10-16.

——. (1986), "Roby Kidd and the Professionalization of Adult Education," in Cochrane et al, 1986.

Sheats, P.H., Jane, C.D. and Spence, R.B. (1953), *Adult Education: The Community Approach*, New York: Dryden Press.

Sim, R.A. (1954), *Canada's Farm Radio Forum*, Paris: UNESCO.

Smith, D. (1947), "Adult Education in Saskatchewan," *Food For Thought*, 8 (3): 24-27.

Smith, D. (1951), *A Survey Report on Labour Education in Canada*, Toronto: CAAE.

Stewart, W. (1983), *A Comparison of a Historical Model of the American Literature in Suport of Adult Education with the literature in the Journals of the CAAE*, Unpublished Major Paper, University of B.C.

Thomas, A.M. (1959), "Who Are the Professionals?, *Food For Thought*, 19 (8): 362-69.

——. (1959b), "The Making of a Professional," *Food For Thought*, 20 (1): 4-11, 45.

——. (1961), "Something to Think About," *Food For Thought*, 21 (4): 180-82.

Thomson, M. and Ironside, D. (1956), *A Bibliography of Canadian Writings in Adult Education*, Toronto: CAAE.

Tweedie, A.S.R. (1947), "Adult Education," *Food For Thought*, 8 (1): 42-45.

Wales, B.E. (1958), *The Development of Adult Education in British Columbia*, Unpublished Ed. D. Thesis, Oregon State University.

Wilson, I. (1980), *Citizens' Forum: Canada's National Platform*, Toronto: Ontario Institute for Studies in Education.

Wilson, J.D., Stamp, R. and Audet, L. (Ed.) (1970), *Canadian Education: A History*, Scarborough: Prentice-Hall.

Originally published in *The Canadian Journal for the Study of Adult Education*, 1 (1): 5-24. Reprinted with permission.

1.5

Adult Education in
Two Depressions

*I*t is notoriously perilous to try to compare any social phenomenon in two periods of time, but the fascination of the exercise persists. The fact that Canada, in common with other countries, is experiencing a sharp economic depression at the present time (1982) suggests to the historian a comparison with that worst of all depressions, that of the 1930s. This is particularly so for the historian of adult education; in spite of the great stress and difficulties of the 1930s (or was it because of them?), that decade was a most creative one in our field. It witnessed the founding of the Canadian Association for Adult Education (CAAE), the Banff School, the Canadian Broadcasting Corporation and the National Film Board, the early testing time for the Antigonish Movement, many experiments with leadership training, group and community development, a flowering of drama groups, and of course widespread study group activity connected with political movements and with the social gospel wing of several church denominations (Selman & Kulich 1980). It was clearly a time when adult educators responded vigorously to the widespread social distress. The author has carried out detailed research on adult education in British Columbia during the Great Depression and this reveals an equally creative response at the provincial level as well (Selman 1976). In this article a comparison is made between the response of adult educators to the conditions of the 1930s in British Columbia to that of the current period.

At the outset it must be said that there are certain important differences between the Thirties and the present period. The first is that the depression of the Thirties lasted for almost an entire decade, from the late Twenties until the outbreak of the war, whereas the comparable period of sharpest distress at the present time has extended so far for only some three or four years. Secondly, because of the welfare legislation of the late war and post-war period, the distress experienced by those affected by the current depression is on the whole not as desperate or extreme as was the case in the Thirties. People in large numbers are out of work, displaced and discouraged today, but generally they are not starving, without housing and going without adequate clothing. In the broader society, while there is widespread discontent with the present conditions, and considerable hardship, there is not the same depth of despair and there is perhaps less feeling of things being totally out of control.

While there are some important differences between the Thirties and the early Eighties, there are also some striking prarallels. The economic downturn in recent years in Canada has been of such proportions that 1982 has been characterised as the worst year in economic terms since 1933 (*Globe and Mail*, Mar. 1, 1983). The number of unemployed in Canada in March of 1983 was the highest in the history of the nation and the rate of unemployment at that time reached a total of 16.3 per cent, only three per cent lower than in the depth of the Depression (*Globe and Mail*, Apr. 12, 1983). As in the Thirties, unemployment in parts of B.C. has been particularly severe (B.C. Ministry of Labour 1982), much higher than the national average, partly because of the vulnerability of B.C.'s primary industries to the decline in exports. In January of 1983, the unemployment rate in the Southern Interior of B.C. was 26.3 per cent and some other major regions were also much above the national average. Individual communities have unemployment rates close to 80 per cent (*Tough Times News*, Mar. 1983). Soup kitchens and lineups to receive free bags of groceries have become a familiar part of the scene in B.C. towns again.

* * *

What has been the response of the public and private sectors of adult education and related social services to these conditions, and how does it compare to that of the 1930s? In terms of the Federal role, the situations are very different. In the Thirties, the most obvious features of Ottawa's measures were relief payments, the relief camps for single men and beginning in 1937, the provision of funds for vocational education for the unemployed. In the current period, the Federal role is much more varied and comprehensive, including a share of unemployment and welfare support programs, training activities under C.E.I.C. and a range of special project funding schemes such as the Local Employment Assistance Program. In what follows, the focus will be largely on provincial and local activities.

The Provincial government in British Columbia took bold initiatives in the field of adult education in the Thirties. The Liberal Patullo government, which came to office late in 1933, was elected on a "New Deal" type of platform and moved with energy on a number of fronts. With leadership from George Weir, a professional educator who became Minister of Education, ably assisted by John Kyle, the Director of Night Schools, the Department of Education responded to the human needs of the day in several ways: offering educational programs in some of the Federal relief camps in the Province, both on-site instruction and correspondence courses; free vocational and general interest classes offered directly by the Department in unused schools in the larger population centres; free mining classes offered in several centres in the Province; co-sponsorship with a voluntary organization, the Council of Women (which had started the program) of the Self-Help project, a social and educational program designed for women from families on relief; a large provincial recreation program which conducted training as well as purely recreational activities; and a large-scale program of play-reading groups throughout the Province (Selman 1976). The report of this work for the year 1934-35 described it as for the benefit of unemployed persons, with the aim of "the preservation of their skill, self-respect, and morale" (B.C. Public Schools Report 1934-35, p. 68), a statement of goals which is at the same time a reflection of the desperate conditions of the day and a quite remarkable declaration by an agency of the government. These activities were guided by an advisory committee of knowledgable citizens and officials and were in addition to the regular adult education activities of the Department, such as the support of school board night classes and an excellent corresondence course program.

The record of the Provincial authority in the current period is more limited and less clear in its directions. The present Social Credit government has been in power since 1975 and is a conservative administration. In the field of adult education, there has been at an intermediate level imaginative leadership and concern for the quality and direction of the services provided by the public institutions in the system. In terms of the response to the conditions of the current depression, there is clearly not the degree of commitment on the part of the Minister and senior officials to emergency measures that the Liberal government in the Thirties displayed. However, Dr. Ron Faris, Executive Director for Continuing Education, who has given effective leadership to the Ministry's role in the field since 1976, has taken advantage of the few opportunities which have been open to him. In May of 1982, the Deputy-Minister of Education, Jim Carter, suggested in his remarks to a conference on adult education that a limited amount of adult education funds might be re-allocated to those school boards and colleges which wished to respond to the effects of high unemployment in their areas. Later the same month Faris called a meeting of all interested agencies, indicating that the Lake Cowichan School District (southern Vancouver Island) was to administer the funds for the project and Dorothy Clode, the district's Director of Adult Education, would be the convenor (Memo, Faris to Colleges and School Districts May 28, 1982). Out of this initiative and a first meeting held on June 21, came the Adult Education Consortium on Economic Dislocation (AECED). The AECED has since met several times, assisted by an experienced community educator, Michael Clague, who was hired by the project, and has undertaken or financed a number of projects: the publication of a newsletter, *Tough Times News* (first issued Dec. 1982), which carries information about economic trends and news about relevant activities undetaken by institutions and organizations in B.C.; the publication of a resource kit containing ideas for services and programs; a survey of community economic self-help projects; a study of the role of continuing education in high unemployment areas, and a conference in one school district on innovative economic enterprises. The columns of *Tough Times News* indicate that several colleges and school boards in the province are sponsoring courses designed to assist people to manage in times of financial difficulty through barter of services, self-help and co-operation, and the prudent use of credit and other financial resources.

The private sector has responded to the times, as always. Much of the effort has concentrated on welfare activities, but some has included an educational component. Three of the most prominent volunteer projects back in the Thirties had been the Council of Women's Self-Help program, already mentioned; a series of vocational courses organized by the A.O.T.S. (a men's United Church organization); and a number of correspondence courses in vocational subjects provided free of charge to men in the relief camps by a group of teachers at the Vancouver Technical School (Selman 1976). In the current crisis, some projects among the many which have been organized are: some thirty Unemployment Action Centres sponsored by the B.C. Federation of Labour, which provide welfare services, mutual support, information about services available, and workshops about local issues; the United Way Employment Centres (13 in the Lower Mainland area) which provide counselling, referral and workshops for job-seekers; and the co-operation of community groups and educational institutions in the sponsorship of meetings and surveys and the establishment of action groups. These are but a few of many community services which have been created in response to the conditions of the day.

* * *

A comparison of the responses of adult educators in the Thirties and in the present crisis does not provide conclusive results, but justifies some observations and raises some significant questions for further consideration. By the mid-Thirties, the Depression had done its worst for several years and British Columbians elected a government which from the outset was committed to relief measures. The Minister of Education was familiar with adult education before he took office and used it as one of the instruments of ameliorative services for the unemployed. The present government in British Columbia appears to have no such vision of the importance, or even the utility of adult education to meet the situation. Thanks to the leadership of a few officials in the Ministry, a few tens of thousands of dollars are being used for special projects, but these are minor exceptions to the general picture.

A few colleges and school boards in the province, it should be said, are making a substantial commitment of leadership and time (and a more modest one of funds) to exploring ways in which adult education can serve the needs of citizens who are in distress. They are the honorable exceptions; most colleges and school districts have made only token efforts. A number of community agencies—service clubs, welfare agencies, labour organizations, churches, etc.—are making substantial efforts, mostly in the welfare areas, sometimes with an educational component.

What of the adult educators and the adult education organizations in the province? Here is a clear demonstration, if evidence were needed, that adult education as a whole has ceased to be a social movement, has ceased to have a corporate concern for all dimensions of human need to which learning is an appropriate response, and in large measure has become the servant of institutional interests. There are a modest number of individual adult educators, most of them working at the local level and in what might be described as community education settings, who have rallied to the current crisis. In organizational terms, they are most evident in the Association for Community Education (B.C.) and the Adult Basic Education Association (B.C.) and the programs of these associations have reflected those concerns. The other adult education organizations appear to be largely inward looking and none has taken any significant initiatives in terms of services or advocacy by way of response to the economic crisis facing so many adult learners.

It may be argued, perhaps with some justification, that "our" depression has been relatively short and that it is unfair to compare the response to the one of the Thirties, which went on for a decade. It is open to all interested adult educators to make their own judgments as to the nature of the field's response. The comparison with the Thirties must also, however, be seen in the context of the vastly greater number of adult educators today and the far greater resources adult educators currently have at their disposal. The writer is reminded of the question asked by a respected adult educator a few years ago when she was evaluating the field's response to the women's movement (Thom 1977, p. 8), "Can it be that continuing education...has lost its ability to respond?" Perhaps, almost as serious, the main body of adult education in our country has narrowed the range of human learning needs to which it feels called upon to respond.

References

British Columbia Ministry of Labour, "Special Report—B.C. Labour Force Statistics," July 1982.

British Columbia Public Schools Report 1934-35 and selected other years, B.C. Department of Education.

CE Newsletter, Continuing Education Division, B.C. Ministry of Education.

Selman, G. (1976), *Adult Education in British Columbia During the Depression*, Vancouver: University of B.C. Centre for Continuing Education.

Selman, G and Kulich, J. (1980), "Between Social Movement and Profession: A Historical Perspective on Canadian Adult Education," *Studies in Adult Education*, 12 (2): 109-16.

Thom, P. (1977), "Tokenism," *Learning*, 1 (3): 8-10.

Tough Times News, 1 1-3 (Dec. 1982 - Mar. 1983), published by Pacific Association for Continuing Education for the Consortium on Economic Dislocation.

Published originally in *Proceedings,* Canadian Association for the Study of Adult Education, Toronto, 1982. Reprinted with permission.

Part 2

Some Historical Dimensions of Adult Education in Canada

*O*ne of my long-term goals was to write a general history of adult education in Canada. It is perhaps more appropriate to call it a hope rather than a goal, because it never reached the stage of seeming to be realizable. Without any provincial or regional histories on which to rely and lacking a capacity to function in French, there remained too many gaps in the material available to allow anything like a national history to be within reach. I did a lot of writing over the years from a national point of view (at least in English Canadian terms), including the three major monographs on the Canadian Association for Adult Education, the historical sections in the Selman and Dampier *Foundations* book, the historical volume, *Citizenship and the Adult Education Movement in Canada*, and a number of individual articles, a selection of which appear in this section.

Apart from brief attempts by Kidd and Thomas (which are referred to in the first essay in this section), my paper entitled "Stages in the Development of Adult Education in Canada" was the first attempt to provide a comprehensive view of the development of adult education in Canada from the beginning of European settlement until the present day. It was published in 1984 and I was pleased to hear subsequently from several adult education faculty members across the country that they were using it in their classes. It seems now to have been a very tentative beginning, but it is an indication of the under-development of this branch of scholarship in the field that it was picked up and used by others. It was all we had.

As the Canadian Association for Adult Education was approaching its 50th anniversary in 1985, I was already well launched in my series of detailed monographs on its history and took a great interest in the activities which were organized by way of observance of the event. I was a member of a Vancouver-based committee which wrote early drafts of the "Declaration" which was issued by the Association at the time and I also wrote one of the papers which were used as a basis of discussion at regional conferences across the country. These papers and some others were then assembled in a volume entitled *Choosing Our Future: Adult Education and Public Policy in Canada*, which was edited by Frank Cassidy and Ron Faris and appeared in 1987. My paper, "Adult Education and Citizenship," is reprinted here and in some respects anticipated my *Citizenship* book, which appeared in 1991.

Quite a different kind of an approach was adopted for an article which appeared in 1989 under the title, "1972—Year of Affirmation for Adult Education." For reasons which I do not recall, it struck me at some point that the year of the appearance of the landmark UNESCO volume, *Learning to Be*, which was important to us all because it had the effect of putting adult and lifelong education "on the map" of the international world of educational planning, was also of special meaning in the Canadian context. We had become accustomed in Canada to having Royal Commissions or provincial committees studying education but practically ignoring the field of adult education. In the year 1972, however, two high profile provincial studies—the Worth Commission in Alberta and the Wright Commission in Ontario—were published, both of them, like the UNESCO document, giving unaccustomed prominence to adult education and lifelong learning. It seemed reasonable, therefore, to focus attention on that special year as a way of bringing several threads of development together.

I have included two articles in this section which have to do with adult educators' professional associations, a subject to which I have given quite a lot of attention. The first is brief, having been a paper presented to the Adult Education Research Conference in 1992. It has to do with six adult education associations which existed in Canada for varying lengths of time from the late 1920s to the 1940s, but all of which were gone from the scene by 1950. The second article is more substantial and examines the proliferation of organizations of adult educators in more recent decades. It was published in 1988. It examines the nature of the organizations, suggests a typology, comments on their activities from several points of view, and asks some questions about the future.

Stages in the Development of Canadian Adult Education

*W*e do not have a comprehensive account of the development of adult education in Canada. There is not even such a description for any province or region. The varied nature of the field is reflected in the three volumes which come as close as anything to providing a general picture of adult education in this country, two edited by J.R. Kidd, *Adult Education in Canada* (1950) and *Learning and Society* (1963) and the third edited by Kidd and G.R. Selman, *Coming of Age* (1978). Each of these is comprised of articles dealing with various aspects of adult education occurring over the last several decades and taken together they represent something of the panorama of programs, institutions and people which have constituted Canadian adult education.

Adult education in Canada has gained a considerable reputation internationally for imagination and excellence. National Farm Radio Forum and Citizens' Forum, the extension work of St. Francis Xavier University, Frontier College, the Joint Planning Commission, the Banff School and the Women's Institute movement are some of the well-known Canadian projects which have gained recognition abroad and in some cases have been borrowed and adapted for use elsewhere. It is all the more surprising, therefore, that we have not managed as yet to produce a general history of Canadian adult education.

Canada has created many programs and institutions, such as those mentioned above, which are original and unique responses to our experience as a people in this northern half of the North American continent. We have also borrowed institutional forms from other sources, mostly from Britain (mechanics' institutes, the Y.M.C.A., the Workers' Educational Association and newer forms of distance education) and the United States (correspondence education, types of agricultural extension, school board and college programs and the newer form of university extension).

There have been compelling reasons prompting Canadians to learn. We have been an immigrant society and we have had to adjust to new conditions. We have jointly undertaken the enterprise of nation building, with all its challenges at both the personal and community level. In addition to these ongoing factors, we have experienced a series of major shocks and crises which have required a response on a massive scale, based largely on our capacity to learn. These have included such events as the two World Wars and the Depression, the technological revolution of recent decades and the periodic stresses and strains within Canadian confederation.

In recent years, three efforts have been made by Canadian scholars to sum up the history of adult education in Canada within certain time frames. The earliest of these was in a paper by J.R. Kidd (1979). He took as his starting point the creation of Canada and extended that first period to the outbreak of World War I. Subsequent periods extended to 1945, and thence to the present time. In those periods, he saw progressive stages of development, down to the present "Coming of Age." In a second recent interpretation, Selman and Kulich (1980) have set their focus on more recent decades, focussing on the field's growing professionalism. Their milestone years were 1935, 1960 and 1979. In the most recent such analysis, Alan Thomas (1981) he deals with what he terms the "modern period". Thomas organizes his study into three periods: the 1930s to 1955, the late Fifties to mid-Sixties and the years since 1966, during which he sees an increased recognition of non-formal education and a readiness to focus less on adult education and more on adult learning.

In what follows, an effort is made to establish periods of development which go back to the earliest days of European settlement in Canada and which, it is suggested, provide a satisfactory framework within which to seek coherence and some measure of consistency in the development of the field. Such time frames are, of course, artificial creations, but they are sometimes helpful in identifying significant trends and notable milestones in the advancement of the field of activity.

Before 1867

This was largely a period of scattered, informal beginnings under private and voluntary auspices. It was a time of book clubs, literary and scientific societies, music, handicraft and art associations. It has been pointed out that the well-known "l'ordre de bon temps" group formed at Port Royal in 1605, in which members took turns in entertaining and edifying fellow group members, may be seen as the earliest peer learning group in what later became Canada.

An important development of this period was the creation of large numbers of mechanics' institutes in several of the colonies, the earliest appearing in Nova Scotia, Quebec and Ontario in the early 1830s (approximately a decade after their origins in Britain). The first Y.M.C.A.s appeared in Montreal, Toronto and elsewhere in the 1850s and night classes under their sponsorship were organized beginning about the time of Confederation. Libraries, under public and private auspices, had their beginnings at this time. Several of what were to become long-lived cultural associations such as L'institut Canadien of Montreal (1844) and the Royal Canadian Institute of Toronto (1849) were formed in this period.

Aside from public libraries, little is known about the origins of public support for adult education in this period. In 1851, the Government of Upper Canada began to subsidize the classes offered by the mechanics' institutes, and the Toronto School Board offered night school classes for a few years beginning in 1855.

1867 - 1914

In this period, adult education was still predominantly under private auspices, but some important steps were taken by government and other public authorities and institutions which laid the groundwork for the expansion of the public sector.

As the population increased and settlement pushed West and North, there was a continuation of the phenomenon of study groups, institutes and associations devoted to educational and cultural matters. Mechanics' institutes, Y.M.C.A.s and after 1868, Y.W.C.A.s were formed in increasing numbers. In 1895 there were 311 mechanics' institutes in Ontario alone. Representative of the wide range of other voluntary organizations which were active in the field are the National Council of Women (founded in 1893) and the forerunner of the home and school movement founded in Beddeck, Nova Scotia, two years later.

Agricultural extension, under private and public auspices, came into its own in this period. The Grange (the first in 1872), Farmers' Institutes (the first in 1894) and other agricultural societies flourished. The C.P.R. and the Federal government operated experimental farms beginning in the mid-Eighties. After the turn of the century, the Federal and some Provincial departments of agriculture became engaged on a large scale in educational activities by means of information services, demonstration schools and through the appointment of district agriculturalists. Co-operative education was under way early in the new century. In 1913, the Federal parliament passed the Agricultural Instruction Act, which made Federal funds available for use by the provinces for agricultural extension work, an important step in itself, but also significant in that it pioneered the means subsequently to be used by Ottawa to fund other types of vocational education as well. Other departments of government, for instance Marine and Fisheries and the Geological Survey, began to offer educational services in this period.

Public educational institutions began in greater numbers to get into the field. The Toronto School Board re-instituted its night classes in 1880 on a permanent basis. Night classes in technical subjects were greatly expanded at the turn of the century. Queen's University became the first university in Canada to begin extension work on a permanent basis, in 1889, and the University of Toronto and McGill soon followed suit. After the turn of the century, with the creation of provincial universities in Saskatchewan and Alberta, these two adopted the more broadly based approach to university extension which had been pioneered at the University of Wisconsin.

Three other important organizations had their origins in this period. The first Women's Institute was founded in Stoney Creek, Ontario, in 1897. An organization devoted to the education of rural women and to improving the quality of rural life, the Women's Institute movement subsequently spread quickly and became worldwide. The Canadian Reading Camp Association began its activity in 1899 and has continued its work in frontier camps and communities ever since, changing its name in 1919 to Frontier College. The origins of co-operative education in Canada are obscure, but the founding of the Caisse Populaire in 1900 should be noted in that connection.

1915 - 1939

A traumatic period in the life of the country, these twenty-five years also witnessed the beginning of a conscious adult education movement in Canada and the creation of a number of noteworthy projects. The best known program during World War I was Khaki College, which made available a wide range of educational services to Canadian armed forces personnel in Britain and Europe. In the Second World War, such services were organized by the Canadian Legion Educational Services, which was formed in 1939 and served both overseas and Canadian-based armed forces personnel.

A number of important adult education institutions were created in Canada during this period. University extension was begun at many universities, the best-known project being the co-operative education program of St. Francis Xavier University in Nova Scotia, often referred to as the Antigonish Movement. Begun in 1928, the work addressed itself to the impoverished fishermen, farmers and industrial workers of northern Nova Scotia and proved so successful, under the leadership of Rev. Moses Coady, that it gained international fame and has over the decades been studied and adapted for use in many countries in the Third World. The Workers' Educational Association was established in several centres in Canada in 1918 and although it had a short history in most places, has continued its activity ever since in Ontario. Sir George Williams University, long an evening college and an important source of part-time degree study, was founded in Montreal in 1926. The Banff Centre, originally the Banff School of Fine Arts, was founded under University of Alberta auspices in 1933 and began its remarkable success story in the depth of the Depression. The first of the famous institutes on public affairs was held at Lake Couchiching in 1932. And in the late Thirties, two of our most important national institutions were created, the Canadian Broadcasting Corporation and the National Film Board.

In 1935, following an organizational meeting the previous year and the carrying out of the first national survey of adult education in Canada (Sandiford 1935), the Canadian Association for Adult Education (CAAE) was established. Founded largely by university and government people, the CAAE was originally intended to be a clearing house and information centre for adult education in Canada, but under the dynamic leadership of E.A. Corbett, it was soon, partly because of the crisis presented by the World War, transformed into a direct programming agency, largely in the field of citizenship education.

Certain government services developed extensively during this period. In 1919, with the passage of the Technical Training Assistance Act, the Federal government provided funds for use by the Provinces in vocational training, a device which was used to circumvent the constitutional barrier to Ottawa's direct involvement in education. This device was used consistently up until the 1960s, making it possible to channel Federal funds into "training" programs. Further important legislation in 1937 made possible much significant educational provision for unemployed adults in the later years of the Depression, including vocational training in many fields and the well known "Youth Training Schools." At the Provincial level, the pace of development varied from one Province to another. Taking British Columbia as an example, where the Minister of Education and his government (elected in late 1933) were very much of the interventionist, New Deal tradition, many progressive steps were taken in order, in the words of the day, to "improve the morale of the people." The measures adopted included free evening classes in vocational subjects for the unemployed, the imaginative extension of correspondence education, life skills and social education (in partnership with voluntary associations) for women from families on relief, a progressive Apprenticeship Act, implementation of regional library services, an innovative recreation and leadership training project ("Pro-Rec"), and the organization of hundreds of drama and play reading groups.

The crisis of the Depression and the deep concern about the future of Canadian society produced many efforts during the Thirties to study and rethink the basic elements of man's relationship to his fellow man, and the nature and role of government. A great deal of this effort was directly related to politics and produced several political movements, most notably the Co-operative Commonwealth Federation Party in 1932. But much of such study group activity was carried out under other sponsorship, for instance the groups under United Church auspices which prepared and issued a major proposal, "Christianity and the Social Order" and other policy statements. The Social Gospel movement was very lively in these desperate days, as were many forms of radical political advocacy.

1940 - 1959

This was a vibrant time in the life of Canada, in war and peace, and also in the field of adult education. Many of the best-known accomplishments in Canadian adult education were created or gained prominence during these years and there was considerable expansion of provision by public authorities for this work.

The wartime period mobilized Canadians to unaccustomed tasks on an unprecedented scale. Whether in the armed forces, war industries or the vast network of civilian and voluntary support services, Canadian men and women responded, and learned, as never before. Canada emerged from the War with an expanded economy and a new sense of identity as a nation. The educational efforts of the Wartime Information Board and many other organizations during the War years contributed to these changes.

The CAAE, under the leadership of Corbett and his successor, J.R. Kidd, made remarkable contributions in these two decades. Foremost among these were the two projects in the field of citizenship education undertaken in co-operation with the Canadian Broadcasting Corporation, National Farm Radio Forum and Citizens' Forum. Listening groups were organized at the local level across Canada and each week were provided with background information and stimulation by means of a pamphlet (produced by the CAAE) and a broadcast (produced by the C.B.C.) on the week's topic. The local groups, having read the pamphlet and heard the broadcast, then discussed the subject, afterwards reporting their opinions on certain questions listed in the pamphlet. By such feedback, the opinions of the groups were obtained, as were suggestions for future topics. These programs attracted a great deal of international attention and were adopted for use in many other countries. The CAAE also organized the Joint Planning Commission in this period, a remarkably successful and flexible instrument for consultation and joint planning at the national level, for public and private agencies, in the fields of adult education, cultural and social development. The CAAE also provided significant leadership in two other areas of adult education which emerged in these years, human relations training and study-discussion groups in the liberal arts.

The post-war period was one of continuing large-scale immigration to Canada and both government, through the newly-formed Citizenship Branch, and the voluntary sector, with the effective leadership of the Canadian Citizenship Council, provided services to many "New Canadians."

Cold War tensions and Canada's active role as a leading middle power on the world scene at this time encouraged the activities of several important organizations concerned with education about international affairs, including the United Nations Association, the Canadian Institute on Public Affairs and the Canadian Institute on International Affairs. Canadian adult educators, most notably J.R. Kidd, also began to play an important role at UNESCO and elsewhere in the international dimensions of the adult education movement.

Local and Provincial governments in parts of Canada became involved more activley in the field. The community centre movement swept the country, creating new means of making educational and recreational services accessible at the neighbourhood level. School board adult education programs began to expand rapidly in some areas, most notably in B.C. Whereas in 1945, only one province in Canada had a formally constituted adult education section within its Department of Education, by 1957 seven provinces had taken that step. In Saskatchewan, the landmark Royal Commission on Agriculture and Rural Life demonstrated how the research and public hearings of such a body could be used as an educational instrument among the citizens. In Manitoba, the provincial government launched an important community development project among the Métis people. The Federal government also greatly expanded its educational work with the native people, Indian and Inuit.

The National Film Board gained world recognition in this period for the excellence of its productions. In order to carry out its mission of interpreting Canada to Canadians, it devised an outstandingly successful domestic distribution system. Through its field staff, and in co-operation with other agencies in each Province, it created a far-flung series of local film councils and film distribution circuits, through which its excellent documentaries and other non-commercial productions were seen by a remarkable number of Canadians on a regular basis.

This was a period, especially in the 1950s, in which a sense of professionalism was emerging in adult education. Organizations of adult educators began to appear in some Provinces and the CAAE inaugurated a series of regional conferences in both the West and the Maritimes. Several universities offered individual credit courses on the subject of adult education for the first time in the Fifties (many of them taught by J.R. Kidd) and in 1957, The University of British Columbia introduced the first full-degree (Masters) program in Canada in this field.

1960 - 1982

The most recent period has seen enormous strides made in the field of adult education and this account can at best mention only some highlights. In very broad terms, the 1960s may be seen as a period of important Federal initiatives and the subsequent years as ones of more active provincial leadership, perhaps reflecting the state of Canadian confederation in general. Canada's stature in the field of adult education was demonstrated in 1960, when UNESCO's Second World Conference on Adult Education was held in Montreal and J.R. Kidd was elected as its President. The conference is generally seen to have articulated for the field that adult education had passed the stage of being seen largely as a remedial activity, something one engaged in to make up for something that was missed earlier, and instead should be seen as part of a normal pattern of lifelong learning in which all persons would expect to take part as a customary dimension of adult life.

The Federal government has made enormous contributions to adult education in these years. The character of technical and vocational education in Canada has been transformed as a result of three major pieces of Federal legislation: the Technical and Vocational Training Assistance Act (1960), which made unprecedented amounts of money available for vocational training facilities and programs and made possible the creation of many of our colleges, vocational schools and technical institutes; the Occupational Training

Act (1967), which continued this development and also brought the Federal authorities into a more direct role in purchasing training and selecting and supporting students; and the National Training Act (1982), which appears to be placing greater emphasis on training on-site in industry and on high skill vocations. Related to the vast expansion of vocational education has been the Federal role in the development of adult basic education and English as a second language instruction. In both these areas, Federal efforts have accelerated educational provision (the role of the NewStart Corporations in six provinces was an important dimension of ABE) and has resulted in pressure on the provinces to increase their efforts as well. Another important area of Federal contributions flowed from the War on Poverty approach which originated in the mid-Sixties and which spawned a great range of community development, local initiative and social development agencies and policies. The bilingualism drive in Canada, within the civil service and outside it, has spurred much educational activity. Finally, in this necessarily selective review of Federal initiatives, mention should be made of the large Federal grants to the labour movement in recent years to help strengthen its educational activities.

Developments at the provincial level are perhaps even more diverse and impressive and only some examples can be mentioned. That important new policy approaches were under consideration was signified by the reports of the Parent, Wright and Worth Commissions in Quebec, Ontario and Alberta. Policies to match these progressive recommendations were not always forthcoming, but in the last decade significant steps have been taken in such areas as the creation of community colleges, the expansion of school board adult education programs and fresh approaches to distance education offerings. Examples of more specific measures include the community college policy in Saskatchewan, policies on further education and community schools in Alberta, and the use of community development and ABE in Quebec and elsewhere.

Distance education and educational broadcasting have made great advances in recent years. Many long-established institutions have greatly expanded their distance education offerings (the University of Waterloo being a leading example) and new, special purpose institutions such as Athabasca University in Alberta and the Open Learning Institute in B.C. have been created. Educational broadcasting has made great progress, especially in Quebec, Ontario, Saskatchewan and B.C.

Community colleges have been mentioned in passing. The vast expansion of the college systems (and similar institutions such as post-secondary institutes) has enormously increased the opportunities for adult education in some parts of the country. Colleges from the outset have been designed with the educational needs of adults and part-time students in mind and they have altered the face of educational provision for adults in Canada.

Several program areas of adult education have greatly expanded in recent years. The professions have seen clearly the urgency of continuing professional education for their members and have mounted substantial programs. Major businesses have in some cases developed very large training enterprises within their organizations. The women's movement, which has emerged in the last twenty years, has placed great emphasis on appropriate counselling and educational provision for women, in their various roles and circumstances. Access to university degree study on a part-time basis has increased greatly, with institutions such as York University and the University of Toronto creating new colleges to serve the needs of part-time students. Community development programs proliferated impressively in the Sixties and early Seventies, with the National Film Board, Indian Affairs, the ARDA program, the Centre for Community Studies (Saskatchewan), several institutions in Quebec and Memorial University of Newfoundland being among the leading agencies in this work. Related to community development has been the growth of a broadly based community education movement.

With the increased acceptance of adult or lifelong education as a normal expectation for increasing numbers of Canadians has come an increasing professionalization of the field. Professional training programs, largely at the graduate level, are available in most Provinces. Many organizations of adult educators have been formed, provincially and nationally, some relating to the field as a whole (such as the CAAE) and some being concerned with particular areas of practice (ABE, English as a second language, university extension, training in industry, etc.). A national organization concerned with research about the field, the Canadian Association for the Study of Adult Education, was founded in 1981.

The most recent attempt to estimate the participation rate of Canadian adults in adult education activities was completed in 1980 by Brundage and Clark (1980) and indicated that approximately 23 per cent of adults were participating each year. Clearly adult education has become an accepted part of life for a great, and growing, section of our population.

At the time of writing [1983], the depressed economy and resulting austerity budgets are causing havoc in adult education. Programs are being cut back and cancelled, many adult educators are losing jobs, or having them reduced in scope. Programs which are least able to pay their way out of fees are particularly vulnerable and many of the people who are most in need of adult education opportunities are facing long waiting lists or the elimination of services entirely. The situation is not entirely black, of course, and adult educators, who as a breed are all too accustomed to functioning on slender resources, are accomplishing much. It is hoped that as times improve, opportunities for adults in Canada to continue their growth and development through learning will be provided on an ever-increasing scale, and with a degree of imagination and vigour which is consistent with our historical tradition.

References

Brundage, D. and Clark, R. (1980), "Canada," in Peterson, R. et al (1980), *Adult Learning Opportunities in Nine Industrialized Countries,* Princeton: Educational Testing Service.

Kidd, J.R. (Ed.) (1950), *Adult Education in Canada,* Toronto: Canadian Association for Adult Education.

——. (Ed.) (1963), *Learning and Society,* Toronto: Canadian Association for Adult Education.

——. (1979), *Some Preliminary Notes Concerning the Heritage of Canadian Adult Education,* Vancouver: University of B.C. Centre for Continuing Education.

Kidd, J.R. and Selman, G. (Ed.) (1978), *Coming of Age,* Toronto: Canadian Association for Adult Education.

Sandiford, P. (Ed.) (1935), *Adult Education in Canada: A Survey,* Toronto: University of Toronto (typescript multilith).

Selman, G. and Kulich, J. (1980), "Between Social Movement and Profession: A Historical Perspective on Canadian Adult Education," *Studies in Adult Education,* 12 (2): 109-16.

Thomas, A.M. (1981), "Education: Reform and Renewal in the 80s," in Wilson, J.D. (Ed.) (1981), *Canadian Education in the 1980's,* Calgary: Detselig.

Originally published in *Canadian Journal of University Continuing Education,* 10 (1), 1984: 7-16. Reprinted with the permission of the *CJUCE.*

Adult Education and Citizenship

*I*t is particularly appropriate that among the papers being commissioned in connection with the fiftieth anniversary of the Canadian Association for Adult Education there is one on the connection between adult education and citizenship. Because if adult education in Canada, and the CAAE itself, have any claim to fame—and they most certainly do—it is largely because of their contributions in just this field. Adult education in Canada is known around the world for programs such as National Farm Radio Forum and Citizens' Forum, the Antigonish Movement (of St. Francis Xavier University), Frontier College, and the Women's Institutes, all of which had as their focus the quality of life in a democratic society and the relationship between the individual and the community. And many of the important names in the history of adult education in our country—Fitzpatrick and Bradwin, Tompkins and Coady, Hoodless, and Corbett and Kidd, to name only a few—are seen to be great Canadians largely for their contributions in these same areas.

But the intellectual climate in which the field of adult education operates has changed dramatically in the last few decades. Adult education itself and the leadership of the field have changed. The relationship between adult education as a social enterprise and the development of the society in which it operates is being re-examined. The traditional liberal democratic assumptions which inspired and informed the thinking of many of our leaders in adult education are being challenged. No part of the field of adult education is more forcefully required to rethink its position and its underlying assumptions than what we generally describe in terms of "education for citizenship."

The effort to define with any precision what is properly included in the field of adult education for citizenship plunges us at once into the essentials of the current debate. We have traditionally seen such education as efforts to help people learn those things which relate most directly to their role in the functioning of the community, be it the local, regional, national or international community. Education for citizenship has concentrated on several elements which were felt to be relevant to the action of a citizen in a democratic society: the development of intellectual capacity and understanding to support independent thought (liberal education); knowledge about the ways in which the political system operates, how decisions are made and change achievable; skills of participation, leadership and organization which are involved in operating effectively within the system; and the promotion of knowledge about particular issues on which the community must make decisions. In approaching these tasks we have recognized the differences in approach required in working with recent immigrants on the one hand, and established Canadians on the other.

Perhaps the best-known statement about adult education in Canada consists of the words of the declaration approved by the conference of the CAAE in 1946:

> The adult education movement is based on the belief that quite ordinary men and women have within themselves and their communities the spiritual and intellectual resources adequate to the solution of their problems.

And in summarizing the functions of adult education, the statement declared, "In short, the task is the imaginative training for citizenship." This declaration, formulated by the adult education leaders at the time, and approved unanimously by a conference at which many national organizations were represented, was very much a response to the circumstances of the day, but also may be said to represent many of the best-known elements in adult education in Canada for the last half century.

Canada is an immigrant society. We have throughout our history been dependent for our sense of identity and our social and economic development on the capacity of our citizens to learn. The times of crisis we have faced—world wars, depressions, inter-regional tensions—have made more urgent the need for learning at certain periods, but throughout our history the national-building tasks we have faced have required a constant process of growth, development, and adjustment on the part of Canadians. It is not surprising, therefore, that our adult education movement has devoted a great deal of its energy and imagination to citizenship education. Indeed it is possible to argue that the central tradition of adult education in Canada lies in this area. I undertook a survey some years ago of what some leaders in adult education in Canada felt have been our most important contributions to the field. Of the top ten projects or programs in that poll, the first five, and eight of the top ten, are in the field of citizenship education. All these and others are mentioned in the following summary of some of our best-known accomplishments in citizenship education.

Citizenship Education and the Immigrant

Some of the earliest adult education activities of which we have a record, most conducted under private auspices (churches, ethnic groups, organized labour and so on), were aimed at assisting immigrants to learn about and adjust to Canadian society and to conditions of life in Canada (Kidd 1950; 1963; Kidd & Selman 1978). Frontier College (which began as the Reading Camps Association) conducted its work, beginning at the turn of the century, in mining, lumbering, construction, and other isolated camps and communities. Most of the people it served—and the same is true of the "railway camps" of the Y.M.C.A., which began about the same time—were men, many of whom needed language instruction and basic education. Beginning in the 1920s, especially in the Prairies, increased efforts were made by school authorities and the Canadian National Railway, among others, to assist immigrants to learn the dominant language of the area and to adjust to Canadian ways, at the same time retaining a pride in their native culture.

In 1940, a group of leading educators (concerned mostly with the schools, initially) created the Canadian Coucil of Education for Citizenship, later the Canadian Citizenship Council. It did important work over the years, after the War concentrating heavily on services for immigrants. When the Federal government created the Citizenship Branch in the late Forties, the two organizations worked closely together on many projects. The Federal government has, of course, played an important role over the decades since, partially funding language instruction and citizenship education (via the provinces) and also supporting in a variety of ways the activities of local organizations which work on behalf of immigrants.

In recent years activities in the field of English as a second language and adult basic education have expanded rapidly, much of it provided locally but financed by government. There is growing attention being paid in both fields to cultural dimensions and to citizenship education.

Citizenship Education for the General Population

Soon after its creation in 1935, the CAAE, under the leadership of E.A. Corbett, took the lead in creating two outstanding citizenship education projects, National Farm Radio Forum (1939) and Citizens' Forum (1943). Both were co-sponsored with the Canadian Broadcasting Corporation and, in the case of the former, the Federation of Agriculture. Involving a unique combination of print, broadcasts, discussion groups and feedback to the sponsoring organizations, these projects earned an international reputation and the became a model for similar work in many other countries.

A second type of citizenship education for the general population took the form of "leadership training", a widespread activity beginning in the late Forties and continuing for at least twenty years thereafter. Related to the "boom" in group development and human relations training, this activity was sponsored by a myriad of voluntary organizations and educational institutions and was aimed at fostering the skills required in functioning as leaders and members in organizational and community life. Related to such activity was the operation of folk schools, youth training schools, community life institutes, and other forms of leadership training and residential education.

Also in the area of general citizenship education are the activities of two public corporations: the National Film Board and the Canadian Broadcasting Corporation. Both organizations have outstanding records over the years since their creation in the Thirties in informing Canadians about public affairs, providing a basis for an emerging sense of national identity, and bridging the geographic, social, and cultural gaps among our people. In the case of the Film Board, particular reference should be made to the film councils and film circuits, which were developed in the Forties and were the key to the distribution system in subsequent years.

Canada has also had a series of very successful organizations which have been devoted to the study of public affairs and international relations, and in some cases to social action with respect to such matters. Several of the most active of these were started in the Thirties, including the Canadian Institute on International Affairs, the League of Nations Society (and subsequently the United Nations Society), and the Canadian Institute on Public Affairs, which conducts the annual Couchiching Conference in co-operation with the C.B.C.

It is difficult to define the citizenship education role of voluntary organizations in general, but it seems clear that many Canadians have learned skills of participation, were drawn into thinking and learning about public affairs, and were given a means of exercising an influence over policy development by means of their participation in such organizations.

Examples of such groups, although there are many, would include the Women's Institutes, the Council of Women, the Y.M. and Y.W.C.A.

National and Community Development

While it is not possible to make a clear distinction between the previous category and this one, there has been such a strong and continuing tradition of community development in Canada, much of it closely related to the adult education movement, that it deserves recognition in its own right.

Perhaps the best known adult education project in Canada, at home and abroad, is the Antigonish Movement, led by St. Francis Xavier University. By means of this work, fishermen, farmers and industrial workers in northern Nova Scotia were encouraged to examine their conditions and communities and to undertake action (much of it with an economic emphasis and involving co-operative enterprises) aimed at improving their lot. This work was so successful, and so relevant to the situation in the developing world, that it has been the object of study for decades on the part of workers from many other countries by means of visits and study in Canada and through the export of training programs.

A very different but also well-known project is the Joint Planning Commission. It provided a meeting ground, at the national level, for public and private organizations concerned with a broad spectrum of educational functions and made a vital contribution for some twenty years (beginning in 1947) to the social and cultural development of Canada. Not a "membership" organization and not a social action group in its own name, the J.P.C. provided a meeting ground for government agencies, educational, cultural, business, labour, church and other voluntary groups which came together to share word of each other's plans, learn about and research significant issues, and provide a basis for advocacy activities as the separate organizations saw fit.

Community development projects of a more traditional kind have had a long history in Canada, going back at least to the early experiment at The Pas which was conducted by the CAAE in the late Thirties. Community development work among the Métis of Manitoba, which began in the late Fifties, seemed to mark the growth of a new interest in such work, and the landmark Saskatchewan Royal Commission on Agricuture and Rural Life and its successor organizations, the Centre for Community Studies, exemplified new standards of excellence in terms of appropriate research and social action being productively combined. It is clear that the Quiet Revolution in Quebec during the Sixties and thereafter involved several forms of community development and related activity.

The "War on Poverty" undertaken by the Fedral government beginning in the Sixties spawned a variety of different approaches to community development, including the development aspects of ARDA, work among Native people, projects undertaken by the Company of Young Canadians, and under O.F.Y. and L.I.P. grants, to name a few. Frontier College expanded its work and moved into community development projects as well. A Canadian initiative which has attracted a great deal of attention both here and in other countries in the last decade has been the Challenge for Change project of the Film Board, one major thrust of which used film, and subsequently videotape, in the community development process. Early successful experiments in Newfoundland were followed by projects in other regions of Canada, and the methodology has since been adapted for use in other countries.

Communications between French and English Canada

Adult Education in Canada—like the nation itself—has not been very effective in efforts to create mutual awareness and understanding between English and French speaking Canadians. The best known exception to this was the series of residential summer programs involving young adults from the two communities, Camp Laquemac. Begun as "Camp Macdonald" in 1941, and co-sponsored by Laval and McGill Universities, this project pioneered many leadership training and community development approaches and made possible contact among emerging leaders in both language communities.

Philosophical and Professional Perspectives on Education and Citizenship

There are two major factors which over the past few decades have had a profound impact on how we see the relationship between adult education and citizenship. One is the changes which have taken place in the nature of adult education as an occupation. The other is the increasingly insistent philosophical debate which centres on the relationship between adult education and social change.

Writing in the mid-Sixties, Webster Cotton (1964) summed up the great tradition of adult education—as he saw it, the field's sense of being a movement—and lamented that too many adult educators had abandoned that view and saw themselves as what he termed "program technicians." He saw two tendencies in adult education: the "social reformist tradition," those who see adult education as the key to improving society; and the "professional tradition," those who see adult education largely in terms of meeting individual needs. He lamented the *kind* of professionalism he saw developing and a narrowing of vision in the field. One does not need to agree with all that Cotton says but it seems clear that he raises important issues.

Those who have watched adult education as a social enterprise in our society generally conclude that the field has in recent decades gone from being a movement to being a profession, or is becoming professionalized. The argument goes that, at one time, adult education was a movement. By that is meant that it was a field, the purpose of which, essentially, was to improve society. This was sometimes stated in terms of making democracy work more effectively, or to bring about a more equitable sharing of society's resources. The leadership of adult education had a very strong sense of the goals of the movement. They wanted a better world, a better society, through adult education. This was the social reformist tradition of which Cotton wrote. And so we have E.A. Corbett, the founding Director of the CAAE, telling his organization in 1941 to:

> Re-affirm our belief that a democratic way of life is the good way of life.... That's our job, to show people what a living, shining thing Democracy can be. (CAAE Director's Report 1941)

Moses Coady, the leader of the Antigonish Movement, told his radio audience in 1945 that, "We need continuous adult learning to achieve the high objective of social progress," and his biographer said that to Coady, "the adult educator worth his salt was an aggressive agent of change and adult education a mass movement of reform" (Laidlaw 1971: 57, 83). In the same tradition, the American scholar and adult education leader, Eduard Lindeman, put it this way:

> Adult education will become an agency of progress if its short-time goal of self-improvement can be made compatible with a long-time experimental but resolute policy of changing the social order. (Lindeman 1926:105)

Corbett spoke of having set off on the road to Damascus (for him, the road to the protestant ministry) and falling among adult educators. What he, and many others, fell among was a movement—a secular movement—aimed at creating a better world here on earth. It is no co-incidence that many leaders of adult education in the early years came from the churches and the Y.M.C.A.

The sense of movement has faded into the background in adult education. The field is becoming professionalized and institutionalized. There is much less emphasis or consensus in the field about the social goals of adult education, or indeed whether it does, or should, have any such goals. There is a tendency to think increasingly of the delivery of expert services to individuals. We have gone from a sense of movement with broad social goals, to a sense of meeting individual needs.

The other factor which is having a profound impact on adult education's view of education for citizenship is the philosophical debate which has been evident in Canadian adult education for decades—certainly throughout the life of the CAAE—and which has taken on additional dimensions in recent years.

The adult education movement, as it existed in this country and others some decades ago, was clearly based on the assumption that adult education was an instrument for social change. This position was commonly based on a humanistic optimism as well as on belief in the "saving power" of liberal education. If people could only be given a real opportunity to learn the things they needed to know, including the skills of operating successfully in democratic society, there would be increased democratic participation, decisions would be made on the basis of a better level of information and quality of thought, and adult education would thereby have been the means of achieving the good and abundant life for both individuals and society. There were incipient conflicts between the liberal democratic and social democratic views within the adult education movement, so clearly identified in the case of Canada in Ron Faris's excellent book, *The Passionate Educators* (1975), but for a time, there was a willingness to submerge these differences, in the interest of promoting adult education. So we had the classic liberal education view co-existing in relative comfort with social reformers such as Moses Coady and Eduard Lindeman.

With the onset of a more strident conflict of political views beginning in the late 1940s with the Cold War and McCarthyism, such an alliance could not hold. Faris sees adult education losing its sense of movement at this time. It is clear that certain of the more radical elements which had been influential in the CAAE up to that point either left or retreated to a more moderate position. It was in this period too that we see the emergence of adult education as a profession (Wilson et al 1970; Selman 1982). Organizations of adult educators began to appear at the provincial level and professional training programs for personnel in the field began at several universities in the late Fifties. The enormous expansion of the public education systems in the late Fifties and Sixties and the vast increase in technical and vocational education combined to expand greatly the number of people who identified themselves with the field of adult education. While the CAAE itself in many respects continued to be a voice for the movement elements in adult education (CAAE 1966; Selman 1983), it was evident in the 1960s that even within the counsels of

Shift from movement to professionalism 1940-1960

that organization, it was becoming increasingly difficult to reconcile the aims of the emerging professional cadre, as expressed through the provincial associations of adult educators, and the traditional movement elements which were represented in the national organization. By the end of the Sixties, these divergent views brought about open conflict and separation of the provincial bodies from the national organization.

At the end of the Sixties, and increasingly noticeably in the subsequent years, new voices entered the debate. While professionalism continued to develop in the rapidly expanding work force of adult education, other forces in the field, which had received fresh impetus from developments in the tumultuous Sixties, were further encouraged and inspired by the ideas of two figures who both produced major books in 1970, Ivan Illich and Paulo Freire (Illich 1970; Freire 1970). Both saw established, professionalized state education as essentially conservative and negative forces, from the point of view of social change and human development, and both called for new approaches to education and a fresh alliance between education and the forces of social change. The relationship between education and citizenship was thereby placed back in the spotlight, and became the centre of debate.

Freire's ideas have been taken up vigorously in the field of adult education. The reasons are clear. Many of his ideas had been worked out most fully in the context of literacy or basic education and became known just at the time when basic education was being greatly expanded in many countries. In addition, Freire's philosophical position became known at a time when an increasing number of voices were being raised in alarm over the possible effects of increased professionalization in the field of adult education. Those who wished to strengthen, or had a stake in strengthening the role of adult education in the promotion of social change, took up his ideas and made them the basis of fresh initiatives. The work of Jim Lotz (1977) in Canada, Ira Shor (1980) in the United States, and Tom Lovett (1983) and Jane Thompson (1980) in Great Britain are examples of this movement, although some have since gone beyond Freire in their thinking, drawing on the ideas of Gramsci and others.

The liberal view of adult education, as expressed by Alan Thomas (1983) and others, sees change as gradualist and tends to see it individualistically. This view recognizes problems and inequities in society. It aspires to creating opportunities for everyone to better his or her lot (in the present context, by means of adult education); it seeks to put in place a wide range of services and programs through which there are opportunities to learn, get ahead and contribute to society; and it tends to be comfortable with the professionalization of the field if this will result in good programs and in services being delivered as expertly as possible and being made widely accessible.

The other main point of view in the field—the social transformation view—sees the world of adult education quite differently. It sees the adult education enterprise as it now exists as serving mainly the middle class. It describes our present arrangements as the "free market view" of education in which the provider of education is the entrepreneur and the public are the consumers. It is critical of what is termed the "technical function" view of education, aimed at providing people to play a part in the existing social and economic order and at adapting men and women to the system. It accuses society of what is termed "the individualization of failure." We continue the rhetoric of individualism and individual responsibility and opportunity, when in fact the problems are based in a social pathology, in collective problems within the social and political arrangements

(Thompson 1980). And in the words of Paulo Freire, it believes that there is no neutral education. Either education is a force for change or it reinforces the status quo. Some of this school, following Gramsci, would go beyond Freire's position and call for a disciplined, politically directed adult education aimed at the mobilization of the "subordinate social classes" and at equipping them to take control of and manage society (Lovett 1983).

These views of education as an instrument or means of bringing about social change have been countered vigorously in the last decade particularly by a number of writers, including K.H. Lawson and R.W.K. Paterson, generally described as professing an "analytical" philosophical point of view. Starting from a careful analysis of concepts and terminology rather than from philosophical systems, these writers have expressed grave concerns about what happens to education when it is "allowed" to become the handmaiden of what they see to be extrinsic political and social objectives. In the first major statement of this position to become widely known in the field, Lawson identified the pitfalls of justifying education by reference to the "goods" it leads to, such as economic growth or political change, and defends it instead of the basis of its capacity to enhance the powers of the human being (Lawson 1975). Some of the same issues are taken up at length by Paterson in his *Values, Education and the Adult* (1984) and he sums up his argument dramatically in a recent article when he states that "the limits of objectivity are the limits of education (p. 20).

At the present time, then, there is vigorous debate in adult education circles—or perhaps it should be termed disagreement of views, because the debate is not very often joined—over the relationship between education and citizenship, or education and the social order. The social transformation view holds that education cannot and should not be separated from the struggle for social change. Those espousing the liberal education or analytical point of view are more inclined to see education in terms of its impact on developing the powers of the individual. Furthermore, they are fearful for the welfare and efficacy of education should it become a weapon in the arsenal of those seeking social change.

Adult Education in the Process of Social Change

In the foregoing section, the focus has been on examining different views of the role of adult education, as seen largely from the perspective of the field itself. Another important question to ask, which raises many of the same issues but sees them from another vantage point, is what adult education has to offer individuals and groups in our society who are seeking to play an active role in determining the nature of their society and are looking for assistance.

In their study of the relationship between university extension and public affairs questions, Houle and Nelson (1956) pointed out some years ago that, with respect to any area of public concern, there were at least four identifiable groups: the specialists in that area who had a professional concern with respect to it; the actively concerned citizen who played an active part in citizen action with respect to the issue; the "attentive" citizen who could be rallied to action when an issue came to the forefront in community affairs; and the "inattentive" citizen who was not likely to play an active part regardless of the circumstances. The authors' view was that a different sort of approach was required on the part of adult educators and programming agencies for each of these four constituencies.

This approach to the matter of public affairs or citizenship education tends to be individualistic in its approach. It is necessary as well to see the matter from an organizational or community perspective. The community development and community education approach to involving people in determining the character of the society in which they live is at least as important. But community development, for instance, poses difficult problems for some adult educators. Can one draw the line between education about community affairs and involvement in social action? Some adult educators see it as going beyond their role as educators if they step over that line. One of the most helpful analyses of this issue is the one provided by Tom Lovett in his book *Adult Education, Community Development and the Working Class* (1975). This provides a clear delineation of the role of adult education in the community development process and an instructive case history showing how this was worked out in the case of a project in Liverpool, England, in the early Seventies.

While it is important for those in adult education to think clearly about their role as educators in community and social development, this may not be the most important question to resolve. Another perspective on the matter is produced by reversing the situation. Where there are groups of citizens who are asking questions about the nature of their society and who are exploring alternative solutions or directions, or where there are groups who have a clear sense of direction of change which should be pursued, what is the response of adult education and adult educators to their needs?

One solution is indicated by the well-known statement by the Chartist leader, Ernest Jones, who insisted that "the people's education was safe only in the people's hands" (Jones 1975:41). In keeping with this belief, interest groups and popular movements rely as much as possible on their own efforts to organize the educational resources they require, and the distinction between propaganda or proselytizing on the one hand, and that of education on the other, simply do not arise, or not in the same form. The educator operating in these settings is a facilitator of the goals of the sponsoring organization; he or she assists the leadership in acquiring the information, skills and membership support needed to further those goals. Although in most instances such interest group efforts are supported only by the group of organization itself, in some cases the public authority assists with the task. The present grants by the Federal government to the educational activities of organized labour in Canada are an example of the latter, as is the assistance which public bodies make available to interest groups which are preparing submissions on environmental and other issues. In other countries, in Scandinavia for instance, a great deal of public money which goes into adult education is channelled into work sponsored by private or voluntary organizations.

Conclusion

We are only beginning in Canada to examine the relationship between adult education and the goals of our society. Indeed the OECD team which reviewed the whole of education in Canada was struck in the mid-Seventies by the gap between our thinking about education and our social and political goals (OECD 1976). If they had given more attention to adult education in this country, their views of at least that part of education might have been somewhat different. In the work of authors such as Draper (1971), Faris (1975), Lotz (1977), Baum (1980) and Roberts (1982), we are beginning to look more closely at these matters.

For those who have a particular interest in the relationship and contribution of adult education to citizenship matters, the present time of budget restraint and conservative government policies raises particular concern. Many see a tendency in public policy to downgrade support for education related to social matters and an undue concentration on vocational pursuits and technology. There is particular concern about the reduction of support for efforts aimed at enabling disadvantaged Canadians to play a fuller part in Canadian society. There is a tendency to centralize control over our educational institutions and thereby render them less able to respond to community needs. Some fear, with Leslie Armour, that "egocentrism is on the march, and that social bonds are creaking" (Armour 1981:31).

No nation has had a richer, more varied experience than has Canada with respect to the application of adult education to the tasks and problems of citizenship. But a respected tradition is not enough. As conditions change, the means of living in and controlling the society must also change. Helping Canadians—all Canadians—to live a life and mold their world remains a major challenge for adult education and adult educators. To ignore this aspect of adult education's task in our society would run the danger of justifying the kind of charge which the leading Chartist newspaper hurled in its day, when it referred to educationists as "the pretended friends, but the real enemies of the people" (Cited in Jones 1975:41).

References

Armour, L. (1981), *The Idea of Canada*, Ottawa, Steel Rail.

Baum, G. (1980), *Catholics and Canadian Socialism*, Toronto: James Lorimer.

CAAE (Canadian Association for Adult Education), *1941 Director's Report*, Toronto: CAAE.

——. (1966), *A White Paper on the Education of Adults in Canada*, Toronto: CAAE.

Cotton, W. (1964), "The Challenge Confronting American Adult Education," *Adult Education*, 14 (2): 80-88.

Draper, J. (1971), *Citizen Participation: Canada*, Toronto: New Press.

Faris, R. (1975), *The Passionate Educators*, Toronto: Peter Martin.

Freire, P. (1970), *Pedagogy of the Oppressed*, New York: Herder & Herder.

Houle, C. and Nelson, C. (1956), *The University, the Citizen and World Affairs*, Washington: American Council on Education.

Illich, I. (1970), *Deschooling Society*, New York: Harper & Row.

Jones, D. (1975), *Chartism and the Chartists*, London: Allen Lane.

Kidd, J.R. (Ed.) (1950), *Adult Education in Canada*, Toronto: CAAE.

——. (1963), *Learning and Society*, Toronto, CAAE.

Kidd, J.R. and Selman, G. (Ed.) (1978), *Coming of Age*, Toronto: CAAE.

Laidlaw, A. (Ed.) (1971), *The Man from Margaree*, Toronto: McClelland & Stewart.

Lawson, K.H. (1975), *Philosophical Concepts and Values in Adult Education*, Nottingham: University of Nottingham.

Lindeman, E. (1961 (1926)), *The Meaning of Adult Education*, Montreal: Harvest House.

Lotz, J. (1977), *Understanding Canada*, Toronto: NC Press.

Lovett, T. (1975), *Adult Education, Community Development and the Working Class*, London: Ward Lock.

Lovett, T. et al. (1983), *Adult Education and Community Action*, London: Croom Helm.

OECD (Organization for Economic Co-operation and Development) (1976), *Reviews of National Policies for Education: Canada*, Paris: OECD.

Paterson, R.W.K. (1984), "Objectivity as an Educational Imperative," *International Journal of Lifelong Education*, 3 (1): 15-28.

Roberts, H. (1982), *Culture and Adult Education*, Edmonton: University of Alberta.

Selman, G. (1982), *Roby Kidd and the CAAE 1951-1961*, Vancouver: University of B.C. Centre for Continuing Education.

Selman, G. (1983), "CAAE 1935-1982," *Learning*, 3 (4): 14-19.

——. (1985), *Alan Thomas and the CAAE 1961-1970*, Vancouver: University of B.C. Centre for Continuing Education.

Shor, I. (1980), *Critical Teaching and Everyday Life*, Boston: South End Press.

Thomas, A. (1983), *Learning in Society*, Ottawa: Canadian Commission for UNESCO.

Thompson, J. (Ed.) (1980), *Adult Education for a Change*, London: Hutchison.

Wilson, J.W. et al. (Ed.) (1970), *Canadian Education: A History*, Scarborough: Prentice-Hall.

Originally published in Cassidy, F. and Faris, R. (1987), *Choosing Our Future,* Toronto: Ontario Institute for Studies in Education. Reprinted with permission.

2.3

1972: Year of Affirmation
for Adult Education

We therefore offer as our central concern, not education, in its formal and institutional sense, but learning. (Thomas 1961:16)

*T*he year 1972 was one of startling developments for those in Canada who were involved in the field of adult education and who were concerned about the place of that activity in public policy. For some decades, supporters of adult education in Canada had been advancing their case through various forms of advocacy, all too frequently with little if any effect (Selman 1988). A long sequence of royal commissions and other public inquiries about education had received representations about adult education and their reports either had ignored the field completely or had paid only lip service to it. An extreme example was the Royal Commission on Education in British Columbia which when it reported in 1960 devoted less than half a page to adult education in a 460 page report (Report 1960). Although that commission made several hundred recommendations on some 158 different subjects, none was made on the education of adults. There had been a few other more satisfactory public documents, but adult educators who were active in advocacy activity had become inured to having their point of view largely ignored, at least by those public inquiries which were concerned with an overview of the whole field of education.

The events of the year 1972, seen against this background, were truly startling and tremendously encouraging for adult educators in Canada. In that year the reports of not one, but two high profile provincial inquiries—in Ontario and Alberta—were published, giving great prominence to adult education and the concept of lifelong learning (*A Choice of Futures* 1972; *The Learning Society* 1972). At the international level, the United Nations Educational, Scientific and Cultural Organization (UNESCO) published the report of its International Commission on the Development of Education, a report which espoused the concept of lifelong education and singled out adult education as one area which should be accorded priority treatment (UNESCO 1972). These and other significant events during the same year resulted in adult education gaining an unaccustomed prominence of place in public discussion about educational policy, and more broadly, in national development strategy. The phrase "triumphal affirmation" which Alan Thomas used with reference to the Ontario Report (Thomas 1973) conveys something of the reaction of informed adult educators at the time.

While it is reasonable to single out a particular year—in this case 1972—as one in which a number of significant events took place, such an eventful year was not, of course, an isolated period. The closer one looks at the developments during that year, the more one becomes conscious of the background which led up to these occurrences. It is justifiable to state, however, that the events of 1972 broke with dramatic impact on many adult educators in Canada, many of whom were not aware of the previous events which were stirring in educational circles.

The three major reports identified above—two originating in Canada and the third at UNESCO—adopted the concept of lifelong learning (although this was restricted in the case of the Ontario report as the terms of reference of that report focussed on post-secondary education). All three reports put particular stress on the fact that the educational influences in society should not be viewed as confined to what traditionally have been termed educational institutions, but were much more broadly pervasive in various economic, social, and cultural aspects of society. In other words, education should be considered as not only lifelong but lifewide. The concept of the "learning society" was not only central to all three reports but was adopted as the title of the Ontario document.

The three commissions were operating in very different circumstances. The UNESCO document, *Learning To Be*, addressed the international community and of necessity had to express its analysis and recommendations in very general terms, leaving their application to the various member states. The international panel of seven experts, chaired by Edgar Faure of France, was doing its work in an atmosphere of urgency. The alliance which had been forged in the early years of de-colonization between economic planners and educators, and the "educational euphoria" of the Sixties, had given way in the minds of many to what P.H. Cooms termed in his landmark study published in 1968 "the world educational crisis" (Coombs 1968). It was being discovered that huge expenditures on education in both the developing and the more industrialized countries, based on what Coombs called "the linear expansion of existing or inherited systems," simply was not working. The costs were rising beyond what many nations could afford to put into education and it was becoming increasingly clear that the strategy, however expensive, was not achieving the desired results (Psacharopoulos & Woodhall 1985).

The recommendations of the UNESCO panel, as expressed in *Learning To Be*, were provided as general guidelines and based on three main themes: the widening gulf between the developed and the developing countries; the need to find a wider concept of education, one which was both lifelong and lifewide; and the need to break through some of the traditional pedagogical notions and to develop "democratic systems and methods more appropriate to the education of the mass of the people" (Scott 1973:93). This "learning society" as described by the report was to result in the individual playing a more active part in his/her education. "Responsibility will replace obligation," it stated (UNESCO 1972:163). An emphasis on adult learning infused the whole document as did the potential role of non-formal as well as formal education.

In an analysis of several reports which appeared in the early Seventies, Alan Thomas developed a continuum upon which he placed the various documents in terms of the breadth of the reports' concerns (Thomas 1973b). The UNESCO report was placed at one end of the scale, concerned as it was with the whole world and with the entire life span. Next to the UNESCO report he placed *A Choice of Futures*, the report of the commission chaired by Dr. Walter Worth in Alberta. This latter report, too, took as its major focus the concept of lifelong learning, but in keeping with its mandate, explored the application to a single jurisdiction, the Province of Alberta. The Worth Commission, in developing the application of lifelong learning in Alberta, did so from a philosophically liberal point of view, with an emphasis on pragmatism, individualism, rewards based on individual achievement, an optimistic view of society's capacity for reform, and a belief in a progress through technological advance (Moore 1973).

The achievement of maximum opportunity for lifelong learning on the part of Albertans was seen to require strong development in two previously neglected areas, early childhood education and adult education (referred to by Worth as "further education"). It was recommended that both these areas be given equal status with the K-12 and higher education sectors. Opportunities for adult education and support for adult learning were to come from various agencies in society, both educational and "non-educational" (e.g. employers) and from a new agency which was to be created called the "Alberta Academy." The latter agency was to facilitate adult learning by various and flexible means, with an emphasis upon the use of the media and non-formal approaches (*A Choice of Futures* 1972).

The Worth Commission clearly was influenced by the concept of recurrent education (described later) as well as by the concept of lifelong education. An examination of the report indicates the espousal of a humanistic, lifelong learning concept and a belief that these goals could be reached largely by the enlightened utilization of the institutions already in place. Priority was placed on the democratization of education but there was little indication of how this goal was to be realized.

The Ontario report, *The Learning Society*, frequently referred to as the Wright Report after the Chairman of the Commission, was a more limited document in the sense that its focus was upon the post-secondary sector. Nevertheless, there was frequent reference to "lifetime learning" and to what was termed "continuing education." Post-secondary education was described as "not an activity confined within the walls of the familiar institutions of teaching and learning" and education was to be seen as "a continuous, lifelong process" (*The Learning Society* 1972:vii).

Post-secondary education in Ontario was to have four major sectors, each with its governing council: the universities; the colleges; the creative and performing arts; and the Open Education Sector. The latter sector was to foster a range of flexible and non-formal learning activities provided by many agencies, including a new institution, the "Open Academy of Ontario." The report referred to continuing education as "a transforming concept whose time has come" (p. 22) and the ideal of "The Learning Society" infused all sections of the report. As with the Alberta report, a great deal of stress was placed on access to post-secondary and continuing education on the part of any citizen who wished to make use of them. Major provision was recommended for information and counselling services.

How the world had changed in one year! Adult educators, accustomed to having their field and their concerns practically ignored by such public documents, now found their proposals and aspirations in the limelight and the subject of widespread public discussion. As is usually the case with such public documents, the presentation of the reports carried with them no assurance that corresponding action would follow. The nature of these reports and the prominence given to many matters of interest to adult educators also resulted in the dramatic widening of the forum within which these ideas were discussed. Adult educators, used to talking mainly to each other, now were faced with the challenge of moving out of their comfortable professional circles and taking part in a wider forum. The basic point, however, is that such concepts as adult education, lifelong learning and the learning society had "arrived" and were on the public agenda. It is easy almost two decades later to forget that the changed context within which we function today was brought about to a significant extent by the impact of these reports.

A Historical Background to the Three Reports

Although some of the concepts which informed these three reports (and others of the period) burst with considerable impact upon the world of education, they were not entirely new. As Denis Kallen has reminded us, "Every major idea can with some goodwill and much artisanship be traced back to antiquity" (Kallen 1979:46). Leaving aside consideration of such long-range ancestry, we should note that in the decade or so leading up to the early Seventies, many of the key ideas embraced by the three reports were under active discussion and development.

In the case of recurrent education, which was such a prominent feature of both the language and the structure of the Worth Commission report, the idea had emerged in Sweden in the late 1960s. It was brought to increased prominence when Olaf Palme of that country presented the idea to the Conference of European Ministers of Education in 1969. The idea was subsequently taken up by the Organization for Economic Co-operation and Development (OECD) which published a report on it as early as 1971 (Kallen 1979).

Recurrent education was basically a strategy or administrative device which allowed alternating periods of work and study for adults throughout their working lives. The scheme appeared to hold promise by assisting governments to cope with current challenges common to many of the industrialized countries: high levels of unemployment (especially among youth); soaring costs of formal education; and the need to upgrade the skills of the workforce. Recurrent education was accepted in varying degrees by many OECD members in a remarkably short period of time (Titmus 1981).

The concepts of lifelong education and lifelong learning undoubtedly have as long a lineage as that suggested by Kallen. In this century, the idea found eloquent expression in the language of the well-known *1919 Report* in the United Kingdom, was coin of the realm in adult education circles in subsequent decades, and found a prominent place in the final declaration of the UNESCO (Second) World Conference on Adult Education which was held in Montreal in the summer of 1960 (UNESCO 1960). As documented by Parkyn (1973) and Alenen (1982) in their studies, lifelong education was the subject of particularly active development in UNESCO committees from 1965 onwards, with Paul Lengrand of the secretariat being undoubted the key figure.

Lengrand produced a working document for UNESCO's International Committee for the Advancement of Adult Education in 1965 and at that time urged that UNESCO endorse the concept of lifelong education. The first version of his book, *An Introduction to Lifelong Education*, was published by UNESCO in 1970 and contained many of the basic ideas subsequently adopted by the Faure panel and reflected in *Learning To Be*. A remarkable document, Lengrand's small book reflects both the analytical detachment of social science and a passionate commitment to human values. *Learning To Be* also reflected the critique of educational systems which emerged from student unrest in the late Sixties and from the work of contemporary authors such as Freire (1970), Illich (1970) and Coombs (1968).

These developments at the international level were well known in certain circles in Canada and certainly among those engaged in the Worth and Wright studies. Additional voices at work within Canada most certainly had an impact. Dr. Roby Kidd emerged from the Montreal World Conference of 1960 as a prominent world figure in educational circles. During the Sixties he published several volumes in which he developed the idea of lifelong learning (Kidd 1961; 1961b; 1966). Dr. Alan Thomas was the Director of the Canadian Association for Adult Education for most of the Sixties and in a series of statements and briefs to the Worth and Wright Commissions developed the implications of the concept of lifelong learning (Thomas 1966). Of particular importance with respect to the work of Kidd and Thomas was the fact that they had been stressing for at least a decade before the reports of 1972 the point which all three reports endorsed and indeed made central to their recommendations: that what is most essential is learning, rather than education, and that learning takes place throughout society, not just in the traditional educational institutions.

The Tokyo Conference of 1972

Another event of the year 1972 which was less surprising to adult educators but which added to the overall impact of the year's events was the UNESCO (Third) World Conference on Adult Education held in Tokyo in the summer of that year. By far the largest of the three World Conferences which had been held since the War, the Tokyo meeting was distinguished from its predecessors by the fact that many countries sent as delegates not adult educators, but senior officials of government and of ministries of education. Adult education was no longer the concern of only adult educators; it had now become the concern of educational and national planners as well, and was considered an important component of national development strategies (UNESCO 1972b). Kidd has described the Tokyo meeting as more professional than its predecessor (1974), an indication that the adult education field was strengthening its position in formal educational structures.

The dominant theme of the conference was the need for the increasing democratization of adult education, both in the sense that the field should serve a broader spectrum of society, and that adult learners should have an effective voice in the choice of educational goals, methods and content. Lifelong learning was widely accepted and referred to as a master planning concept at the conference (Hall and Stock 1985).

Other Developments in Canada

There were other developments taking place at this time which added cumulatively to Canadian adult educators' sense that fresh winds were blowing. The publication in the United States in 1970 of Malcolm Knowles' *The Modern Practice of Adult Education*, with its exposition of the concept of andragogy, provided many Canadian practitioners with a stronger sense of the uniqueness and significance of their field. The suggestion that increased attention should be paid to learning, as distinct from education, encouraged in the previous decade by the work of Kidd and Thomas, was further enhanced by the publication in 1971 of Allen Tough's major study of adults' self-directed learning efforts (Tough 1971). A sense of both the accumulation of significant experience in Canadian adult education and of emerging expertise and professionalism was re-enforced by substantial volumes about community development (Draper 1971) and adult basic education (Brooke 1972) which also were published at this time.

Following the Tokyo Conference, the Canadian Commission for UNESCO established a task force, the purpose of which was to communicate to adult educators across Canada some of the insights which had emerged from the conference. While the working group was engaged in this task, *Learning To Be* was published (four months after the Tokyo Conference). It was decided to incorporate that publication into the Canadian task force's work. The Commission published a summary of the UNESCO report for use in Canada (Canadian Commission for UNESCO 1973). It also contracted with the two national adult education organizations, the Canadian Association for Adult Education and the Institut canadien d'education des adultes, to organize conferences in several cities across Canada (held in 1973) through which the ideas contained in the UNESCO report could be publicized.

Another important event of the year 1972 in Canada was the publication of a report on community colleges in the Province of Saskatchewan (Province of Saskatchewan 1972). At the heart of the report and its recommendations was that the focus should be on the individual learner in his/her community and that community resources should be mobilized in support of learning needs. It was very much a lifelong learning model with an emphasis placed upon information and counselling services and on the use of non-formal as well as formal educational approaches. As such it was to a high degree consistent with the main elements of the Worth, Wright and UNESCO reports.

Canada as Part of a World Community of Ideas

It is significant that adult educators in Canada not only drew inspiration from the prominence given to adult education in the several development discussed, but it is also clear that at the same time Canada was taking its place in an international community of ideas about adult education. The Worth Commission in Alberta had drawn considerably upon the OECD thinking about recurrent education, and its report makes repeated reference to the concept of lifelong learning. The Ontario report drew its title and a great deal of its language and thinking from the literature of lifelong education which was emerging in Europe. In *Learning To Be*, the UNESCO panel quoted at some length from the discussion paper issued by the Worth Commission which was focussed on the nature of lifelong learning. Reference is also made in the Faure report to the Quebec TEVEC project, the multi-media adult basic education project, and to Tough's research on self-directed learning (UNESCO 1972: 184-5, 121-2, 210).

Following the Tokyo Conference, UNESCO commissioned John Lowe of England, who had prepared much of the documentation for Tokyo, to write a book which examined "the state of the art" internationally (Lowe 1975). In his book, Lowe made reference to a number of features of adult education in Canada, singling out for particular praise the report of the Wright Commission in Ontario.

Canada's relationship with the international community of ideas concerning lifelong learning was further enhanced at this time by the central role played by Roby Kidd in the discussions leading to the formation of the International Council for Adult Education (ICAE). Kidd was the leading figure in consultations about the ICAE before and during the Tokyo Conference. Based in Toronto, the ICAE was established in 1973 with Kidd serving as its first Secretary-General.

In his examination of the Worth Commission report, Barry Moore makes an observation which adds a dimension to the significance of these events of 1972 (Moore 1973). He pointed out that, as of approximately 1970, the "second generation" of educational planning began. He attributed the development of this new approach to the OECD, UNESCO and other planners at the international level such as P.H. Coombs. Rather than seeing educational systems as separate entities, and instead of concentrating almost exclusively on formal education, the newer approach called for educational planning to be both "comprehensive" (including both non-formal and informal aspects of the field) and "integrated" (that is, developed as an integral part of broader social and economic planning processes). In 1985 Coombs referred to the former as the comprehensive "learning network" of the society in question (Coombs 1985:57). He also pointed to what he saw as a prolific increase in human learning needs in the 1980s, an increase brought about by development, in the sense that the term is used in international planning circles.

This kind of educational planning of necessity brings non-formal, adult and lifelong education into a central role in planning strategy. The authors of the Worth, Wright and UNESCO reports realized the importance of these matters and framed documents which accorded a new and unaccustomed prominence and priority to adult education as part of a larger strategy. Adult educators found themselves catapulted from the margin into the mainstream of educational thought and debate.

Conclusions

The publication of *Learning To Be* by UNESCO and of the Worth and Wright reports in Canada did not by any means bring about an immediate or spectacular series of revisions in public policy. Nor can it be claimed that the other events of 1972 which are described here had any such major effect. However, these developments, taken together, may now be seen to have been important in at least two ways. First, they encouraged and spurred on to renewed effort many adult educators who had been attempting to promote the advancement of educational opportunities for adults in our society. It was indeed an important time of affirmation for many of us. Second, the concepts foreshadowed the future development of education. With every passing year since that time, we have seen increasing currency and significance accorded to the ideas which were central in the reports discussed here.

Within Canada there has been in the last two decades an increasing acceptance of continuing and lifelong education as bases for educational planning. A number of major new institutions and educational services have been established in order to make educational opportunities for adults more accessible and effective. Examples include several Provincial educational television networks, the creation of distance education institutions such as Athabasca University (Alberta) and the Open Learning Agency (British Columbia), and the expansion of opportunities for part-time degree study. At the international level, organizations such as UNESCO, OECD and the World Bank have broadened their roles in education, and more partularly within the field of adult education. For instance, one can note the OECD's promotion of the concept of recurrent education and the World

Bank's decision in the 1970s to broaden its loan policy so as to include education or human resource development projects. Development planning increasingly has been influenced by ideas such as "the learning society," lifelong learning and the importance of non-formal and informal educational influences, all of them concepts and strategies which were given fresh impetus by the events of 1972.

References

Alenen, A. (1982), "Lifelong Education—Permanent Education—Recurrent Education," *Adult Education in Finland*, 19 (2): pp. 3-41.

Brooke, M. (Ed.) (1972), *Adult Basic Education*, Toronto: New Press.

Canadian Commission for UNESCO (1973), *Summary of the Faure Report*, Ottawa: Canadian Commission for UNESCO.

(A) Choice of Futures (1972), *Report of the Commission on Educational Planning*, Edmonton: Queen's Printer, Province of Alberta.

Coombs, P.H. (1968), *A World Educational Crisis: A Systems Analysis*, Oxford: Oxford University Press.

——. *The World Crisis in Education: The View from the Eighties*, New York: Oxford University Press.

Draper, J. (Ed.) (1971), *Citizen Participation: Canada*, Toronto: New Press.

Freire, P. (1970), *Pedagogy of the Oppressed*, New York: Herder & Herder.

Hall, B. and Stock, A. (1985), "Trends in Adult Education Since 1972," *Prospects*, 15 (1): 13-26.

Illich, I. (1970), *Deschooling Society*, New York: Herder & Herder.

Kallen, D. (1979), "Recurrent Education and Lifelong Learning: Definitions and Distinctions," in Schuller, T. and Megarry, J. (Ed.) (1979), *Recurrent Education and Lifelong Learning*, London: Kegan Paul.

Kidd, J.R. (1961), *Continuing Education*, Ottawa: Canadian Conference on Education.

——. (1961b), *18 To 80: Continuing Education in Metropolitan Toronto*, Toronto: Toronto Board of Education.

——. (1966), *The Implications of Continuous Learning*, Toronto: W.J. Gage.

——. (1974), *A Tale of Three Cities*, Syracuse: University of Syracuse.

Knowles, M.S. (1970), *The Modern Practice of Adult Education*, New York: Association Press.

(The) Learning Society: Report of the Commission on Post-Secondary Education in Ontario (1972), Toronto: Ontario Ministry of Public Services.

Lengrand, P. (1970), *An Introduction to Lifelong Education*, Paris: UNESCO.

Lowe, J. (1975), *The Education of Adults: A World Perspective*, Paris: UNESCO.

Moore, B.D. (1973), *Two Approaches to Educational Planning: Freire and Worth*, Unpublished Ph.D. Thesis, Edmonton: University of Alberta.

Parkyn, G.W. (1973), *Towards a Conceptual Model of Lifelong Education*, Paris: UNESCO.

Province of Saskatchewan (1972), *Report of the Minister's Committee on Community Colleges*, Regina: Department of Continuing Education.

Psacharopoulus, G. and Woodhall, M. (1985), *Education for Development*, Oxford: Oxford University Press.

Report of the Royal Commission on Education (B.C.) (1960), Victoria: Province of British Columbia.

Scott, P. (1973), "Education at the Hour of Choosing," *Prospects*, 3 (1): 90-99.

Selman, G. (1988), "Advocacy for Adult Education in British Columbia," in Kulich, J, (Ed.) (1988), *Advocacy for Adult Education in British Columbia*, Vancouver: Pacific Association for Continuing Education, pp. 115-166.

Thomas, A.M. (1966), *A White Paper on the Education of Adults in Canada*, Toronto: Canadian Association for Adult Education.

———. (1973), "The Learning Society," *Canadian University and College*, Toronto: Association of Canadian Community Colleges.

———. (1973b), *A Summary and Critique of Various Reports on Post-Secondary Education in Canada 1969-1973*, Toronto: Canadian Association for Adult Education.

Titmus, C. (1981), *Strategies for Adult Education*, Chicago: Follett.

Tough, A. (1971), *The Adult's Learning Projects*, Toronto: O.I.S.E. Press.

UNESCO (1960), *World Conference on Adult Education: Final Report*, Paris: UNESCO.

———. (1972), *Learning To Be*, Paris: UNESCO.

———. (1972b), *Third International Conference on Adult Education on Adult Education: Final Report*, Paris: UNESCO.

United Kingdom, Ministry of Reconstruction (1919), *The 1919 Report*, Reprinted 1980, Nottingham: Department of Adult Education, University of Nottingham.

Originally published in *The Canadian Journal for the Study of Adult Education*, 3 (1), 1989: 33-45. Reprinted with permission.

2.4

Early Adult Education Associations in Canada: Short-Lived Organizations in the 1930s and 1940s

 esearch in the field has made clear that, in the main, the establishment of provincial associations of adult educators in Canada came about in the 1950s and the 1960s (Selman 1988; Selman & Dampier 1991). Accounts of that earlier research, however, noted that there had been several earlier short-lived bodies, established in the Thirties and Forties, all of which had disappeared by 1950. It is the purpose of this paper to examine those earlier organizations—to the extent this is possible—and to indicate something of their origins, nature and activities.

Investigation reveals that there were six such organizations, in Alberta, Manitoba, Ontario, the Eastern Townships of Quebec, Prince Edward Island and Newfoundland (in this period not yet part of Canada). It is clear that the six associations referred to were varied in character and functions. We know very little about most of these organizations. Perhaps the chief intention of the author is to bring these groups to the attention of interested scholars in the hope that further research will be carried out at the local and provincial levels.

The Associations

Newfoundland

The earliest to be formed, the Newfoundland Association, was founded in late 1929, the apparent product of an invitation to Albert Mansbridge of the Workers Educational Association (U.K.) and the World Association for Adult Education (WAAE) to make a speaking tour of the territory (Newfoundland and Adult Education 1930; Newfoundland: The Inception of a Movement 1930; Burke 1939). The Association was closely linked with the WAAE, whose annual reports described it as a regional body within the WAAE structure. The government of Newfoundland funded programs through the Association and in some respects absorbed it within the government services in 1936, but WAAE reports as late as 1943 indicated its continued existence. In the latter year, the Association "operated 31 centres and maintained work in lumber camps" as well as in St. John's (Personal communication of D. Balsom to author; WAAE Annual Report 1943:4). The work was restricted by shortages of funds and personnel both before and during the war years, but existed until at least the mid-war period (Newfoundland 1937; Farwell 1943).

Prince Edward Island

An association was formed in P.E.I. in 1936 under the name of the Adult Education League. An article which appeared the following year indicated that the chief activity was to furnish material for study groups (to be operated through the public library system) the content of which seems to have been closely related to the work of the Antigonish Movement (Adult Education in P.E.I. 1937). Subsequent accounts appearing in 1939 confirmed these impressions, one in November stating that the League currently had 300 study groups functioning and was working closely with a large number of credit unions and co-operatives (Croteau 1937; Corbett 1939). An article about Farm Forum which appeared in 1941 stated that the League was the organizer of Farm Forum in P.E.I. (Morrison 1941).

Eastern Townships of Quebec

With financial assistance from the Carnegie Corporation, McGill University employed a community worker in the person of R. Alex Sim in 1938 to conduct a program aimed at strengthening the sense of community of the English-speaking areas of the Eastern Townships. Known as the "Community Council for Adult Education" or the "Eastern Townships Adult Education Council," this body was based initially at Lennoxville, then Sherbrooke and, beginning in 1942, at Macdonald College (of McGill). The work may be seen as falling within the community development tradition. It involved a considerable social dimension as well as instructional programs. An account of the work published in 1943 states that "over 10,000" adults were using the service and that the activities included: 125 Farm Forum groups (with 2,000 members), 13 community schools, leadership training schools, Film Board circuits, a monthly journal and a travelling library service (Adult Education in Quebec 1939; Corbett 1941; Eastern Townships 1943; personal communication of R.A. Sim to author). The latest known reference to this activity appeared in 1948, when it was referred to as the Committee for School Programs of the Protestant School Boards of the area (Adult Night Schools 1948).

Ontario

Remarkably little is known at this point about the Ontario Association for Adult Education. It was established at least as early as 1936, because there is a notice in the CAAE journal in 1939 that Mrs. H.P. Plumptre was resigning as President after serving a three-year term (Ontario Association for Adult Education 1939). It is known as well that, during 1937, the Association ran a "literary competition," inviting contestants to write essays on the subject, "Adult Education in My Community" (Literary Competition 1937). At the time of writing, nothing else is known about the activities of the Ontario body. It is possible that, unlike the other associations mentioned previously, it was not in the main a programming organization, but rather a meeting place for those engaged or interested in the field.

Manitoba

The Manitoba Association was established in 1934 (England 1980; Selman 1991) and appears to have been a "clearing house and co-ordinating body," so termed by E.A. Corbett in 1937 (Corbett 1937:14). Leading figures included Dr. David Stewart, the founding President (a medical doctor), Robert England and Andrew Moore, among others. The

Manitoba body seems to have been a product of the "idealistic" approach to adult education, the leadership coming from persons in various walks of life who believed in the benefits, both individual and social, of such activity. The Association continued in existence until at least 1941 (Progress in Western Canada 1941), though the report of the Manitoba Royal Commission on Adult Education in 1946 indicates that the Association gave up at least some of its functions in 1939 when the University of Manitoba secured Carnegie funds for related activities (Manitoba 1946).

Alberta

We have more information about the Alberta Adult Education Association than about any of the others. Because the organization was initiated by government figures, a number of key documents have been preserved in archives; the organization was able to employ professional staff, who wrote about the work (for example, Bercusson 1944); and two scholars have in recent years devoted attention to the Association (Clark 1985; Blevins 1990). The Department of Education of Alberta called a meeting of interested parties in 1943, out of which eventually came the Alberta Association (a somewhat parallel Adult Education "Council" was operative for a brief period as well, but was soon dropped). Both the Premier and the Minister of Education took part in the initial meetings, using such phrases as the need to promote "a well-organized system of adult education" and the wish to promote democratic values (cited in Blevins 1990:2). There was some suspicion on the part of the University Extension people that the government was attempting to undermine its leadership in this field (Clark 1985). The government made funds available to employ central staff, led by Leonard Bercusson, and to assist communities with the development of adult education services, in the main through programming grants to the school boards. It also promoted the establishment of "Community Councils on Adult Education," which functioned in Lethbridge, Calgary, Lacombe, Edmonton, Wetaskiwin and Medicine Hat. Bercusson stressed that the objective was not to duplicate services, but to "encourage and co-ordinate activities which were already under way" (Bercusson 1944:15; See also Stearn 1944). The Association did carry out some programming of its own, however, including radio-based discussion groups. The local councils also ran evening class programs. Over time funding fell increasingly behind what was required to maintain the work which had been put in motion. This came to a crisis point in 1948, when the government withdrew its support and the Association was disbanded.

National Perspectives

E.A. Corbett, the Director of the Canadian Association for Adult Education, was of course aware of these events in the regions. In 1939, he presented a paper in the United States in which he described the state of the field in Canada. The paper, or a version of it which was subsequently published in the CAAE journal, contained a section entitled "Regional Committees," in which the following appeared:

> In several of the provinces, Provincial Committees on Adult Education have been formed to serve as clearing houses of local interests, giving common direction to activities within the provinces and providing points of easy contact with the parent body. (Corbett 1939b:13)

He went on to say that he saw the provincial bodies as a useful means for the distribution of literature, the organization of study clubs, the development of educational broadcasting, the holding of conferences and the training of leaders.

There are several significant points which arise from Corbett's comments. One is that although he stresses the clearing house and co-ordinating functions of these bodies, the other accounts we have seem to put more stress on their direct programming role, except perhaps in the case of the Manitoba (and perhaps the Ontario) groups. A second point has to do with the emphasis he places on the use of broadcasting and the organization of study groups. We know of Corbett's abiding interest and creative leadership in this area (Corbett 1957; Armstrong 1968), and in this case the other sources we have stress the role played by the provincial bodies in this area. The third item raises different kinds of issues. In his paper, Corbett mentioned that some members of the National Council had doubts about the wisdom of encouraging these provincial associations, feeling that their presence might have the effect of halting the growth of "national unity in education" (Corbett 1939b:13). But Corbett puts himself on record as being in favor of the regional developments. Similar concerns arose in the 1960s when further provincial organizations emerged (Selman 1985).

Another national perspective is provided in an article by Eugene Bussiere, then with the Extension Department of Laval University. He wrote a piece for the CAAE journal, *Food For Thought*, in 1947 which sheds some light on somewhat parallel developments in French language adult education circles. His article was mainly about La société canadienne d'enseignement postscolaire. Bussiere carefully pointed out that the organization which he was describing, though mainly Quebec based, was "national in scope" and in that sense was "parallel to the CAAE" (Bussiere 1947:28). He also referred to the provincial level of activity. He stated that in 1939, quite separate from the national French language organization, "the Province of Quebec was organizing its own provincial Association for Adult Education" and that "the French-speaking Canadians of the West had also organized...their own organizations in Manitoba, Saskatchewan and Alberta". He also stated that currently [1947], "Ontario and the Maritimes" were working on establishing "similar associations" (Bussiere 1947:29).

Comment and Analysis

From the perspective of the present day, we might expect that provincial adult education "associations," such as those being described here, would be "professional" bodies, established to facilitate communication among workers in the field. The limited research done so far reveals, however, that with the exception of the Manitoba Association (and perhaps Ontario) these bodies were rather coalitions of agencies—public and private/ voluntary—devoted to programming for the general public. The Manitoba Association seems to have been of a different character from the others, a product of what has been termed the "idealistic" point of view towards the field (Selman 1991). The key figures in Manitoba were not adult educators; they were leading figures from various walks of life who believed in the potential of adult education and were willing to associate their names with the movement.

Why did such groups form? There were no doubt different circumstances from one province or region to another, but one of the impulses may have been the co-operative ethos of the Depression and Reconstruction periods. These were lean times in Canada, as elsewhere, and there was a tendency to utilize co-operative approaches to tasks which may have been beyond the resources of individual groups. The Depression years were also ones which saw government enter into various kinds of partnerships with voluntary bodies in the field of human services (see Selman 1976), and the role of government as funder and co-sponsor in several of the provincial associations is consistent with such practices.

Why did they typically last for such a short time? Three reasons may be suggested. The first has to do with the extensive changes in Canadian society resulting from the outbreak of the war in 1939 and the end of the Depression. Governments adopted new priorities and may in some cases have lost their commitment to their role within the associations. The second reason is a related one. In some cases, the provincial groups were rather fragile creatures, with the leadership coming from very few persons. Changes brought about by wartime conditions could very easily remove one or more persons on whose enthusiasm and talent the associations depended. The third reason may be that as the war "stirred up" Canadian society, the adult education programs of many agencies took a spurt ahead. At least some of the organizations which had been involved in the associations, and conducting their programs through them, may have felt less need for such co-operative arrangements.

What connections can be seen between these relatively short-lived associations of the Thirties and Forties and the more professional bodies which appeared in the subsequent two decades, especially the Sixties? The author began this research on the assumption that these earlier organizations were pretty much the same as the later ones, but fleeting because the field was just beginning to take shape and the number of persons feeling a commitment to such bodies were therefore few. On closer examination, however, the earlier groups turned out in the main to be programming bodies, based on co-operation among several organizations, sometimes including government. We must conclude, therefore, that these earlier associations have little connection with or relationship to the more professionally oriented ones which emerged later.

References

(Note: *AL* = Adult Learning; *FFT* = Food For Thought.)

"Adult Education in P.E.I." (1937), *AL* 2 (1): 18-19.

"Adult Education in Quebec" (1939), *AL* 3 (4): 22.

"Adult Night Schools" (1948), *FFT* 8 (8): 27.

Armstrong, D. (1968), *Corbett's House; The Origins of the CAAE*, Unpublished M.A. Thesis, University of Toronto.

Bercusson, L. (1944), "First Steps in Alberta," *FFT* 4 (9): 14-16.

Blevins, J. (1990), *The Alberta Adult Education Association*, Unpublished Paper Dept. of Adult, Career and Technology Education, University of Alberta.

Burke, V.P. (1939), "Adult Education in Newfoundland," *AL* 3 (4): 10-15.

Bussiere, E. (1947), "La société canadienne d'enseignement postscolaire," *FFT* 8 (2): 28-30.

Clark, R. (1985), *History of the Department of Extension of the University of Alberta 1912-1956*, Unpublished Doctoral thesis, Ontario Institute for Studies in Education.

Corbett, E.A. (1937), "Note and Comment," *AL* 1 (4): 13-16.

——. (1939), "Progress in the Maritimes," *AL* 4 (2): 17-20.

——. (1939b), "The Canadians March," *AL* 4 (1): 5-12.

——. (1941), "Eastern Townships," *FFT* 2 (3): 18-19.

——. (1957), *We Have With Us Tonight*, Toronto: Ryerson.

Croteau, J.T. (1939), "Developments in Adult Education in P.E.I.," *AL* 3 (3): 18-19.

Eastern Townships Rural Adult Education Service (1943), *FFT* 3 (5): 19-20.

England, R. (1980), *Living, Learning, Remembering*, Vancouver: University of B.C. Centre for Continuing Education.

Farwell, E.M. (1943), "Adult Education in Newfoundland," *Bulletin (World Association for Adult Education)*, XXXIII (Second Series): 1-2.

"Literary Competition" (1937), *AL* 1 (4): 16.

Manitoba (1946), *Report, Manitoba Royal Commission on Adult Education*, Winnipeg: Queen's Printer.

Morrison, N.M. (1941), "Farmers Air Their Problems," *FFT* 16: 1-19.

"Newfoundland" (1937), *AL* 1 (3): 18.

"Newfoundland and Adult Education" (1930), *Bulletin* (WAAE) XLIII: 19-20.

"Newfoundland: The Inception of a Movement" (1930), *Bulletin* (WAAE) XLIV: 1-9.

"Ontario Association for Adult Education" (1939), *FFT* 3 (6): 22.

"Progress in Western Canada" (1941), *FFT* 16: 21-22.

Selman, G. (1976), *Adult Education in B.C. During the Depression*, Vancouver: University of B.C. Centre for Continuing Education.

——. (1985), *Alan Thomas and the CAAE 1961-1970*, Vancouver: University of B.C. Centre for Continuing Education.

——. (1988), "Specialization or Balkanization: Organizations of Adult Educators," *Can. Journal of University Continuing Education*, 14 (1): 24-44.

——. (1991), "Yesterday Speaks to Today," *Proceedings*, Canadian Association for the Study of Adult Education, 221-226.

Selman, G. and Dampier, P. (1991), *The Foundations of Adult Education in Canada*, Toronto: Thompson Educational Publishing.

Stearn, C. (1944), "These Community Councils!," *FFT* 4 (6): 14-16.

Trends in Adult Education (1949), *FFT* 9 (5): 16-20.

World Association for Adult Education, Annual Report (1943), *Bulletin* XXXV:1-12.

Personal communications: D. Balsom, J.K. Friesen, E. Harris, R.A. Sim, A.M. Thomas, S. Wigmore.

Originally published in *Proceedings,* Canadian Association for the Study of Adult Education, 1992, 279-284. Reprinted with permission.

2.5

Specialization or Balkanization: Oganizations of Adult Educators

*I*n the last 50 years, and especially the last 30, we have witnessed the emergence in Canada of quite a large number of organizations of adult educators, at both the provincial and national levels. These organizations were established in order to serve a variety of goals, the most common being to provide a means of communication among people working in the field, to render services to the members of assistance to them in their work, and in the case of at least some of the organizations, to create a vehicle for joint advocacy. While a major goal of the organizations has been to promote communication among those working in adult education, the proliferation in the number of groups in recent years, as useful as this has been in some respects, has perhaps now begun to work against this happening. Specialization is verging on balkanization, and perhaps it is time to examine this phenomenon.

This paper will trace the history of these developments in Canada, noting the emergence of a number of the groups of adult educators. A typology of the organizations will be presented and some significant differences among them will be identified. The functions of the several types of organizations will be examined, with some reference to philosophical currents in the field of practice. Some strengths and problems arising from the present organizational pattern will be examined and some suggestions made concerning ways our organizational arrangements can be made to serve the interests of the field more satisfactorily.

Historical Perspective

The development of national and regional adult education associations in Canada does not lend itself to tidy summary, but some general observations can perhaps be made. Aside from a few short-lived exceptions at the regional level, the first three decades of development, from 1935 to the early sixties, tended to be ones for the formation of national organizations. The sixties were a period during which provincially based organizations of a general or "umbrella" coverage of the field came into being. The most recent two decades have brought the development of a variety of more specialized organizations at the provincial level, and in the last 10 years, at the national level as well.

The Canadian Association for Adult Education (CAAE) was the first national organization of adult educators formed in Canada. A planning meeting was held in 1934, certain preparatory work carried out in the ensuing year (including a survey of adult education activities in Canada (Sandiford 1935), and the CAAE was officially formed in 1935. It followed its American counterpart, the American Association for Adult Education, by some nine years, a point that is worth noting mainly because some of the same dynamics were at work in the two countries, including some stimulation and financial assistance from the Carnegie Corporation of New York (Armstrong 1968; Faris 1975).

Short-lived more local associations came and went in these early years: in Winnipeg (which actually predated the CAAE) (England 1980), Ontario (Ontario Association 1940); the Eastern Townships of Quebec (Eastern Townships 1941), and in Alberta (Bercusson 1944; Clark 1985), but the CAAE was alone in the field again by 1950, as far as English-speaking Canada was concerned.

In French Canada the field had at first been represented by a French-language sub-committee of the CAAE, an arrangement that continued for some nine years. In 1946, however, a new, autonomous French-language organization was created, La société d'enseignement postsecondaire. In 1956, this organization was reconstituted as the Institut canadien d'education des adultes (ICEA) (Morin 1950; Quebec 1981; Roberts 1982). The CAAE and the ICEA remain today as the two general or "umbrella" organizations in the field, one for the English and the other for the French-speaking communities in Canada, and both have for some 20 years received financial support on a regular basis from the federal government.

More specialized organizations came along in the subsequent decades. Some of those interested in the rural and agricultural dimensions of the field formed an Extension Group in 1940 under the Canadian Society of Technical Agriculturalists. This body met sporadically through the forties, but had disappeared by the early fifties. A fresh start was made in 1960 with the formation of the Canadian Society of Rural Extension. This body continues to the present day, the word "Rural" having been dropped from the name in 1970 (Adema 1984; H. Baker, personal communication, January 13, 1987). Some of those involved in university extension work joined in 1954 with colleagues who were in charge of administering summer schools in forming the Canadian Association of Directors of Extension and Summer Schools (CADESS). This organization is still in existence, having changed its name in 1974 to the Canadian Association for University Continuing Education (CAUCE), (CAUCE Handbook 1987). In 1965, those working in French language and bilingual universities created a parallel organization, L'ACDEULF, L'association canadienne d'education des adultes dans les universités de langue française (Bourgeault et al. 1982). And finally, as far as this period was concerned, following the passage of federal manpower training legislation in 1960, which had the effect of enormously expanding the number of persons engaged in vocational training programs, the federal government supported the formation of a national organization of those engaged in this work, the Canadian Vocational Association (CVA) (Selman 1980).

The sixties were an active period in the formation of associations of adult educators at the provincial level. The main reason for this development was active promotion by the national body, the CAAE. There had been provincial organizations of adult educators in B.C. and Saskatchewan in the fifties. The B.C. group, which had been in existence since 1954 (Selman 1969), put forward a proposal in 1961 that the CAAE revise its constitution in such a way as to allow for the formation of provincial associations of adult educators, not as separate organizations but as integral parts or "divisions" of the national body. This change having been brought about, six provinces formed such divisions during the decade: B.C. (1962), Nova Scotia (1963), Ontario (1966), Manitoba (1966), Saskatchewan (which became affiliated in 1963 and a division in 1967), and Newfoundland (1967) (Selman

1985). By the late sixties, it became apparent that a change in the structure of the CAAE was imminent, and for this and other reasons adult educators in Alberta, when they formed an association in 1967, decided not to become part of the national body (Tewnion & Robin 1978; Roberts 1982). After the CAAE did change its structure in 1971, the provincial divisions were all reconstituted as autonomous organizations, affiliated with the CAAE and with representation on its Board of Directors. An additional development at the provincial level in the sixties was the formation in 1965 of the broadly based Rural Learning Association of Ontario. While not representing the full spectrum of adult education in the province, its coverage was quite extensive in that it was formed as a result of the amalgamation of the Ontario Farm Radio Forum, the Folk School Council and the Rural Leadership Forum (Fleming 1972).

The latter years of the sixties were the starting point in the development of a number of more specialized associations at the provincial level. For reasons of clarity (and because the author is not informed sufficiently about the details of developments in all provinces), this will be illustrated in the case of one province only, British Columbia. In 1964, a group of those involved in adult vocational training in the province (who had a short time earlier formed an autonomous provincial organization) reconstituted it as a provincial chapter of the new national group, the Canadian Vocational Association. This provincial chapter remained in existence until it was amalgamated with the Pacific Association for Continuing Education in 1972 (Buttedahl 1986: Selman 1982). In 1965, a group of directors of adult education employed by the school boards of the province formed the B.C. Association of Continuing Education Administrators. As the community college system developed, beginning in 1965, many of the adult education programmers in the colleges joined this organization as well. In 1967, those teaching English as a second language (approximately half of whom were in adult education), formed B.C. TEAL, Teachers of English as an Additional Language. In 1974, a number of those involved in training activities in business and industry and in government departments formed the Training and Development Society of B.C. (Some of these people had been active previously in the B.C. chapter of the American Society of Training Directors.) The next provincial organization to be formed was the Association for Community Education, which was established in 1976 and is made up largely of those working in neighborhood houses, community schools, community centers and others working at the community level, including those with a community development emphasis. In 1977, initial steps were taken that resulted two years later in the formation of the Private Career Training Association of B.C., a body that involves people from private postsecondary career training institutions in the province. In 1979, a group of those involved in Adult Basic Education in the province, with stimulation from both the Movement for Canadian Literacy and the provincial Ministry of Education, formed the ABE Association of B.C. The last of these provincial organizations to be established was the Adult Special Education Association (now the ASE Network), formed in the early 1980s and concerned with educational services for handicapped persons (see Kulich 1986 for all these provincial bodies). At the provincial level, the Canadian Congress for Learning Opportunities for Women is still in a stage of development, with "networks" existing in Victoria and Vancouver. All of these provincial bodies, including the Pacific Association for Continuing Education mentioned earlier, are still active in the field at the present time, making at least nine organizations of adult educators in the province, quite apart from the national bodies in which some educators are active.

The last decade has brought the formation of several new national organizations. Although it was not established as an autonomous organization until 1979, the Canadian Congress for Learning Opportunities for Women traces its beginnings back to committee status under the CAAE beginning in 1973 (CCLOW 1986). In 1977, a number of persons interested in literacy work formed the Movement for Canadian Literacy, successor organization to World Literacy of Canada, which was formed in the early fifties (Thomas 1983). Two years later, the first conference was held of TESL Canada, the national organization for teachers of English as a second language (personal communication of N. Collins to author). The Canadian Association for the Study of Adult Education (CASAE/ACEEA) held an organizational conference in 1980 and a formal founding conference the next year. It is devoted to stimulating and making known research about adult education in Canada (Bourgeault 1982). Laubach Canada Inc. was also formally established in 1981, though literacy work utilizing its methods and materials dated back to 1970 in Canada (L. Batdorf & Audrey Thomas, personal communication, February 25, 1987). Community educators from several provinces established the Canadian Association for Community Education in 1984. And perhaps most recent among these national organizations, the Canadian Association for Distance Education functioned for a year under the auspices of the university extension body, CAUCE, and became an autonomous organization in 1985.

This list of organizations is not complete. At the national level there are undoubtedly gaps. At the provincial level, for reasons referred to above, British Columbia is used in this article as a case example.

A Typology of Organizations

The organizations referred to above have been classified into a typology in an effort to examine them from the point of view of their basis of organization. There have been many attempts to do this for the field with respect to the agencies providing programs, most notably the work of Schroeder (1970, 1980), but little attention has been given to the organizations of adult educators. William Griffith (1980) has done some useful work in examining a particular type of organization, co-ordinating bodies in the field. The author has made an earlier attempt to classify organizations of adult educators (Selman 1983) and the present treatment is a further development and expansion of that analysis.

Basically, this represents an attempt to identify a number of categories into which the organizations of adult educators will fit appropriately. At the same time, an effort has been made to keep the number of categories relatively small, at the risk of making some compromises. The common observation that adult education is a diverse, unsystematic enterprise, a "patternless mosaic," as one writer has put it, is amply borne out.

The categories that have been utilized here are as follows:

1. **General or umbrella organizations:** These are ones that attempt to represent or relate to the whole field of adult education.

2. **Institutional:** These are organizations that are based on the organizational or institutional setting within which the members carry out their work.

3. **Content and Clientele:** This category includes the organizations that are based on the subject matter or content of the programs being delivered, and in some cases on the nature of the clientele being served .

4. **Methodology:** These are organizations that have been formed on the basis of the methods or techniques employed by or of concern to the members.

A Typology of Organizations of Adult Educators

	General or Umbrella Organizations	Institutional	Content and Clientele	Methodology
National	Canadian Association for Adult Education Institute Canadien d'education des adultes	Canadian Association for University Continuing Education	Canadian Soc. of Extension Movement for Canadian Literacy	Canadian Association for Distance Education
	Canadian Association for the Study of Adult Education		Canadian Congress for Learning Opportunities for Women	Canadian Association for Community Education
			Canadian Vocational Association TESL Canada Laubach Canada Inc.	
Provincial	Pacific Association for Continuing Education	B.C. Association of Continuing Education	Teachers of English as Additional Language	Association for Community Education (B.C.)
(B.C. examples)		Private Career Training Soc. of B.C.	Training and Development Soc. of B.C.	
			Adult Special Education Network	
			Adult Special Education Network	
			Network of Canadian Congress for Learning Opportunities for Women	

This classification scheme has its strengths, but also its difficulties. Two examples of problems will illustrate this. In the case of the Canadian Congress for Learning Opportunities for Women, although the primary basis of organization is service to a particular clientele—women—the range of content is very wide. The same applies to the Canadian Society of Extension. The case of the Association for Community Education presents other problems. It is not easy to see where it fits, but it has been decided that its members' concerns are focused predominantly on the relationship among the learner, the institutions/organizations providing services, and the broader community. This is essentially a matter of relationships and therefore may be seen in terms of approach or methodology, broadly conceived. Such problems of "sorting" or classification are signs of a less than ideal typology, and perhaps further refinement is necessary.

Philosophical and Methodological Issues

Behind the typology used above lie a number of issues on the basis of which the various organizations listed here may be seen to vary, in some cases to represent contrasting views. Three of these will be identified and discussed briefly.

Movement "vs." Profession

There is considerable comment in the literature of the field on the phenomena of professionalization and institutionalization in adult education and the effects of these on the long-standing tradition of adult education as a social movement, and ally of other movements (Selman and Kulich 1980; Selman 1985a). One can see considerable variation among the Canadian organizations of adult educators with respect to these issues. Generally, members of the organizations in the institutional category and some in the "content" category are reasonably comfortable with the tendencies towards a more professionalized field, whereas many others, such as the ABE Association and the Association for Community Education, and at the national level, the Canadian Association for Adult Education, among others, are uncomfortable with many of the dimensions of professionalization and are actively concerned with the social impact of their educational endeavors.

Educators and Learners as Members

Perhaps another dimension of the issues identified above is the degree to which learners and community representatives, as well as educators, are active participants in these organizations. This is more likely to be the case with those groups that are closely associated with other social movements, as with the Canadian Congress for Learning Opportunities for Women, or with the organizations which have retained a sense of social mission themselves, such as the ABE and Community Education groups. Quite the opposite is true of the Canadian Association for University Continuing Education, the B.C. Association of Continuing Education Administrators, and the Canadian Association for the Study of Adult Education.

Philosophical Stance

Some of the organizations, almost "by definition," or on the basis of their customary mode of operations, are identified with a social change position, or at least with an active critique of our present social arrangements. This tends to be true of the Congress for Learning Opportunities for Women, the ABE and Community Education Associations, and the CAAE.

The fact that there are clear differences of view on issues such as the three mentioned above clearly has impact on the level of communication that exists between groups of adult educators. Indeed it no doubt affects even the willingness to seek dialogue or common ground. Historically it may even be the case that the very formation of some of our organizations has taken place because the interests or point of view some persons represent were not being adequately addressed in the other organizations.

Common Elements

What are the functions of all these different organizations? Reference has been made to at least 30 bodies, and there are more, some at the national level and many in other provinces and territories. On the basis of examining the statements of purpose of quite a number of these bodies, several common elements can be identified.

1. **Communication among the members.** The purposes for which such communication is promoted are variously stated, but this seems to be a common aim.

2. **Promotion of effective practice.** In various ways, most if not all organizations seek to assist their members to be more effective practitioners, by means of the contacts, activities and services provided.

3. **Advocacy.** All the associations examined see advocacy as part of their task. The range of causes to be promoted, however, appears to vary widely. In some cases, the advocacy is intended to be on behalf of the members' institutions or programs, and to increase the status of their work. In others, there is advocacy for the rights or welfare of the clients being served, or of whole sections of society — the "empowerment of women," for instance (CCLOW 1986: 7).

4. **Critical examination, research and demonstration.** Some of the organizations seek to improve the state and knowledge about their fields in ways that go beyond what we normally think of as in-service professional development. This takes the form of research, the critical examination of programs, practices, policies and/or institutions, inter-institutional co-operation, and demonstration projects.

There are other functions performed by some of these associations, but the foregoing outline covers the ones shared by substantial numbers of them.

Discussion

What is one to make of this proliferation of organizations of adult educators? The phenomenon can fairly be seen as a sign of a growing, rapidly developing field, with growth bringing specialization. The rate of social and technical change, which we are fond of writing and talking about from the point of view of its motivating impact on our students/members, is also having its effect on us professionally. For instance, the continuing influx of immigrants and refugees has heightened the need for English or French as a second language. The increased complexity of many occupational roles, and the efforts of governments to cope, has brought greater emphasis on basic education and technical and vocational training. Changing aspirations on the part of women have created a need for educational support services. The changing technology of communication has brought new opportunities for the delivery of educational assistance.

The four categories of organizations used in the typology above suggest grounds for establishing separate organizations. General or umbrella organizations are not likely going to be able to provide sustained, highly relevant services in a wide range of specializations. Organizations that are identified with the affairs of educational institutions and the "professionals" who work in them are not likely to be much interested in the welfare of particular social movements. Organizations that are giving major emphasis to their role in relation to social movements will likely not be concerned about broadly-based research projects or about problems of professional status. And so as the field of practice has grown and become more complex, there has been a natural tendency for practitioners to form associations that would meet their particular needs.

One of the drawbacks to the proliferation of organizations is the fact that it almost inevitably leads to barriers to communication across the field as a whole. Specialization can lead to balkanization, and in large measure has. In theory, the field could gain the best of both worlds if all adult educators belonged to the specialized organization(s) that best served their particular area of practice and also to an umbrella organization that was concerned with the broader concerns of the field. But there are several problems with this suggestion. First, not everyone has the time, interest or energy to play a part in several organizations. And further, although certain organizations may legitimately be categorized as umbrella organizations, they may not be perceived in those terms by all adult educators, or be acceptable to them all. The CAAE, for instance, which is the general organization for English-speaking Canada, has chosen to involve itself heavily with several social movements at the present time. It has at the same time decided not to respond to many other concerns of adult education practitioners. For any one of a number of reasons, therefore, adult educators, even those who might have been ready to join an umbrella organization, may decide not to join the CAAE, given its present policies. Educators who might be inclined to look to an umbrella organization at the provincial level might face similar problems, finding these bodies either too preoccupied with professional concerns or too strongly linked with social causes for their taste.

There clearly are important advantages that are resulting from the present proliferation of adult educators' associations. The several functions of such bodies—communication, support services, joint advocacy, and research and demonstration—can in many cases be carried out more effectively, as far as the practitioner is concerned, if it is in as specific an area as possible. Those in adult basic education or distance education, to take two examples, wish on the whole to go to meetings, or receive journals, or lobby governments, etc., with focus on their own immediate interests rather than those covering the whole spectrum of adult education. The existence of such specialized organizations is also frequently seen as helpful in raising the visibility and status of the particular area of practice. Most adult educators see such specialization as resulting in a more beneficial use of their time, energy and funds. There seems no reason to question their judgment. Indeed it seems entirely likely that the proliferation of specialized agencies will continue.

At the same time, there seem to be some real and potential disadvantages resulting from this phenomenon. They flow from the barriers to communication that result from the balkanization of the field, and also from the difficulties that are thereby created in mounting advocacy efforts that speak on behalf of the field as a whole and on behalf of all adult learners' interests. It is not only a question of who will speak for the general interests of the adult learners, but also who sees it to be within their mandate to do so. If government receives representations from various parties or organizations about particular policy issues and "the experts disagree" in their recommendations, then the case may be badly damaged. But perhaps more seriously, if major issues are not spoken of at all because they do not seem to fall mainly within any specialized area, then the field may be guilty of letting the welfare of adult learners suffer by default.

In the present context, special reference might appropriately be made to the matter of scholarly journals. There has for some years been a serious dearth of opportunities within Canada to publish scholarly articles about adult education. The CAUCE Journal has been the only outlet for such work over a broad range of topics, although others, such as the TESL Canada Journal, have been available for particular sectors. The picture is now changing rapidly, however. Both the Canadian Association for Distance Education (first issue in Fall '86) and the Canadian Association for the Study of Adult Education (first issue in May '87) have entered the field, publishing juried, scholarly journals. The Ontario Association for Continuing Education has begun to publish a popular journal, which will take its place alongside the CAAE's sporadic publication, *Learning*, and some other provincial publications. There is room for consultation on the part of these associations with regard to the scope and focus of their publications.

It would not appear to be realistic to expect a very large percentage of adult educators to play an active role both specialized and umbrella organizations. Specialization is in general the path of future development. What we need to be doing is to seek sensible ways for such specialized groups to act in concert when the situation calls for such action.

Two examples of inter-organizational co-operation, one national and one provincial, will be referred to briefly. In recent months (*i.e. in late 1987 and early 1988*), the CAAE has begun to develop a cooperative relationship with other organizations and social movements in seven areas of concern: cultural development, ecology, literacy, local economic development, peace, women's access to education, and learning and work. What is envisaged is a period of active co-operation focused on the educational components in each of these areas of social, cultural and economic development. It is seen as a "from now until further notice" arrangement and is based on a strong sense of common cause that exists at the present time among the leaders of the several organizations. But it is seen to be an ad hoc arrangement.

The provincial example is provided by the efforts of the Pacific Association for Continuing Education (PACE) to give stimulation to collaboration among the nine organizations of adult educators in B.C. In this case, the intention is more than an ad hoc arrangement, but it is a "limited" one in that the focus is primarily on advocacy activities. This initiative has been pursued since the early Eighties, but has not included an attempt to establish a joint organization. Currently referred to as a "Council of Presidents," the group gets together at the call of the chair, who by mutual consent is the President of PACE. The present agenda focuses on the need to strike up effective communication with the new provincial government. Participation in the group is voluntary and implies no commitment in advance to take part in joint action. It is a forum for discussion and a potential vehicle for joint action. In the view of this writer, the two examples just described are useful and appropriate models for further development.

As has been documented above, the last two decades have seen an almost explosive proliferation of organizations of adult educators. There is in the author's view little if any readiness on the part of these organizations to think in terms of an ongoing commitment to a federated or coordinating agency, either provincially or nationally. But what is more likely is a willingness to engage with others in a joint approach to particular tasks, be it programming or advocacy, where there is a clear advantage to be gained from joint action and where there is freedom for the parties to engage in the joint activity for as long as, and to the extent that is desired by each participating group.

A recipe for chaos? Perhaps. But we are old hands at living with chaos. There are jobs we can do together in the best interests of the adult learners we are serving. Our capacity to do this is thrown into question by the compartmentalization of the field into the many separate organizations. We need to devise ways and to develop the skills of working productively together, so that on those occasions where such joint action would be in the interest of the field as a whole, and of the welfare of adult learners in Canada, there will be a basis on which to act.

The proliferation of specialized sub-groups within the workforce of adult education, which is a product of both the diversity of settings in which our work is based and also the increased specialization of our functions, seems to this writer to be inevitable, and in many respects desirable. However, to the extent that one holds the view that adult education is a single field of activity—however multifaceted—that has a shared concern for our society's provision for the needs of adult learners, specialization brings with it danger or disadvantages as well. If the proliferation of organizations results in the balkanization of the field, with attendant barriers to communication and a narrowing of concerns, then we are in danger of placing professional and institutional interests ahead of the interests of the adults we are attempting to serve. For many adult educators, such a tendency is anathema. By means of reconsidering the nature of our umbrella organizations or by seeking creative and effective inter-organizational means for our specialized groups to act in concert on matters of common concern, we have a chance of gaining the best of both worlds. It will not be easy—far from it. But let it not be said that we didn't try.

Founding Dates of Canadian Organizations Mentioned in this Article

1935   Canadian Association for Adult Education

1940   Extension Group, Canadian Society of Technical Agriculturalists

1946   Société d'enseignement post-secondaire (see 1956)

1954   Canadian Association of Directors of Extension and Summer Schools (see 1974)

1954   B.C. Adult Education Council (see 1962)

1956   Société . . . (1946) becomes Institut canadien d'education des adultes

1960   Canadian Society of Rural Extension (drops "Rural" in 1970)

1962   BCAEC (1954) becomes B.C. Division of CAAE

1963   Canadian Vocational Association

1963   Nova Scotia Division of CAAE

1963   Saskatchewan Association for Continuing Education (see 1967)

1964   B.C. Chapter, Canadian Vocational Association

1965   L'Association canadienne d'education des adultes dans les universités de langue française

1965   Rural Learning Association of Ontario

1966	Ontario Association for Continuing Education (Ontario Division of CAAE)
1966	Manitoba Division of CAAE
1966	B.C. Association of Continuing Education Administrators
1967	Sask. Assoc. (see 1963) becomes Sask. Division of CAAE
1967	Newfoundland Division of CAAE
1967	Alberta Association for Continuing Education
1967	B.C. Teachers of English as an Additional Language
1972	B.C. Div. of CAAE (1962) becomes Pacific Association for Continuing Education
1973	B.C. Training and Development Society
1974	CADESS (see 1954) becomes Canadian Association for University Continuing Education
1976	B.C. Association for Community Education
1977	Movement for Canadian Literacy
1979	Canadian Congress for Learning Opportunities for Women
1979	B.C. Association for Adult Basic Education
1979	TESL Canada
1980	B.C. Adult Special Education Association (now "Network")
1981	Canadian Association for the Study of Adult Education
1981	Laubach Canada Inc.
1984	Canadian Association for Community Education
1985	Canadian Association for Distance Education

References

Adema, B. (1984), *The History of the Canadian Society of Extension*, Unpublished M.Sc. major paper, University of Guelph.

Armstrong, D. P. (1968), *Corbett's House: The Origins of the Canadian Association for Adult Education and its Development During the Directorship of E.A. Corbett 1936 - 1951*, Unpublished M.A. Thesis, University of Toronto.

Bercusson, L. (1944), "First Steps in Alberta," *Food for Thought*, 4(9): 14-16.

Bourgeault, G. et al (1982), *Les practiques d'education permanente au Quebec et les universités: Emergences et convergences*, Montreal: University of Montreal.

Buttedahl, K. (1986), "Pacific Association for Continuing Education." In J. Kulich (Ed.). *Adult Educators and their Associations in British Columbia* (pp. 239-252), Vancouver: PACE, (Pace Papers 2).

CAUCE (1987), (Canadian Association for University Continuing Education) *Handbook/Manual*, Toronto: CAUCE.

CCLOW (1986), (Canadian Congress for Learning Opportunities for Women.) *Policy and Procedures Manual*, Toronto: CCLOW.

Clark, R. (1 985), *A History of the Department of Extension at the University of Alberta 1912-1956*, Unpublished Ph.D. Thesis, University of Toronto.

"Eastern Townships Adult Education Council (1941)," *Food for Thought*, 2(3): 18-19.

England, R. (1980), *Learning, Living, Remembering*, Vancouver: University of B.C. Centre for Continuing Education.

Faris, R. (1975), *The Passionate Educators*, Toronto: Peter Martin.

Fleming, W. G. (1972), *Educational Contributions of Associations. (Ontario's Educative Society, Vol. VII)*, Toronto: University of Toronto.

Griffith, W. S. (1980), "Coordination of Personnel, Programs and Services." In J. M. Peters and Associates (Eds.). *Building an Effective Adult Education Enterprise* pp. 78-114, San Francisco: Jossey-Bass.

Kulich, J. (Ed.) (1986), *Adult Educators and their Associations in British Columbia*, Vancouver: PACE, (PACE Papers 2).

Morin, R. (1950), Adult Education for French-speaking Canadians in Quebec. In J. R. Kidd, (Ed.). (1950), *Adult Education in Canada*, Toronto: CAAE, 65-72.

"Ontario Association for Adult Education." (1940), *Food for Thought*, 1(5): 19.

Quebec Commission d'etude sur la formation des adultes. (1981), *Adult Education in Quebec: Possible Solutions*, Quebec: Government of Quebec.

Roberts, H. (1982), *Culture and Adult Education*, Edmonton: University of Alberta.

Sandiford, P. (Ed). (1935), *Adult Education in Canada: A Survey*, Toronto: University of Toronto.

Schroeder, W. L. (1970), "Adult Education Defined and Described." In R.M. Smith, G. F. Aker & J. R. Kidd (Eds.), *Handbook of Adult Education* (pp. 25-43), New York: MacMillan Co.

———. (1980), Typology of Adult Learning Systems." In J. M. Peters and Associates. (Eds.), *Building an Effective Adult Education Enterprise* pp. 41-77, San Francisco: Jossey-Bass.

Selman, G. (1969), "Toward Cooperation: The Development of a Provincial Voice for Adult Education in British Columbia, 1953 to 1962." *Occasional Papers in C.E., Extension Department*, Vancouver: University of British Columbia, No. 3.

———. (1973), "An Organization for the Study and Development of Adult Education," *Dialogue*, 1(2): 51-54.

———. (1980), "The British Columbia Division of the CAAE 1961-1971," Vancouver: *PACE Occasional Paper* No. 7.

———. (1983), "Organizations of Adult Educators—Canada and British Columbia." In University of British Columbia, Education 412, Introduction to Adult Education: 67-74, Vancouver: University of British Columbia (Guided Independent Study course).

———. (1985), "Alan Thomas and the Canadian Association for Adult Education 1961-1970." Vancouver, *Occasional Papers in C. E.,* Center for Continuing Education, University of British Columbia, No. 24.

———. 1985a), "The Adult Educator: Change Agent or Program Technician?" *Canadian Journal of University Continuing Education*, 11(2): 77-86.

Selman, G. and Kulich, J. (1980), "Between Social Movement and Profession— a Historical Perspective on Canadian Adult Education," *Studies in Adult Education*, 11(2): 109-16.

Tewnion, J. and Robin, K. (1978), "Origins of the Alberta Association for Continuing Education," *Journal of the Alberta Association for Continuing Education*, 6 (1): 6-10.

Thomas, Audrey. (1976), *Adult Basic Education and Literacy Activities in Canada 1975-76*, Toronto: World Literacy of Canada.

Thomas, Audrey. (1983), "Adult Literacy in Canada: A Challenge," Ottawa: Canadian Commission for UNESCO, *Occasional Paper 42.*

Personal Communication from:

Batdorf, Luke (February 25, 1987)

Baker, Dr. Harold (January 13, 1987)

Blaney, Dr. John P. (March 2, 1987)

Campbell, Audrey (November 26, 1986)

Collins, Nick (February 20, 1987)

Thomas, Audrey (December 17, 1986)

Waldron, Dr. Mark (December 9, 1986)

Originally published in *Canadian Journal of University Continuing Education*, 14 (1): 1988), pp. 24-44. Reprinted with permission.

Part 3

The Canadian Association for Adult Education

*A*s I gained increasing awareness of the history of adult education in this country, I became ever more aware of the importance of the leadership to the field as a whole provided by the Canadian Association for Adult Education and its Directors. This was especially true in the period from 1935, when the CAAE was established, up until approximately 1970. After that time, the field had become so large and complex, and the goals of the CAAE so focussed in particular aspects of it, the organization's influence, though still substantial, became more circumscribed.

The CAAE also loomed large in my own professional development and in my sense of the unique contributions which Canada had made to the field. Based on my early experience in organizations of adult educators at the provincial level, I subsequently became involved in representing British Columbia at the national level, and for many years thereafter served as a board member and officer of the national association. At the same time, as I learned more about the history of our field in Canada, I became aware that the CAAE itself, and its first three Directors—E.A. (Ned) Corbett, J. Roby Kidd and Alan M. Thomas—were important factors in the development of adult education in this country, as well as leaders of significant adult education projects, several of which gained international influence and recognition.

I knew all three of the men in question. I met Ned Corbett only a few times, but in those fleeting contacts, gained some insight into his personality and leadership skill. Roby Kidd and Alan Thomas became my close personal friends, based on many joint enterprises and happy times we shared, and in the case of Alan Thomas, based as well on the fact that we worked together in the Extension Department at U.B.C. for five years in the late Fifties.

All of the foregoing contributed, I'm sure, to my decision to write substantial accounts of the history of the CAAE under the leadership of these three men. But the main underlying reason was my growing realization over the years of the importance of the role the organization had played in the development of the field throughout Canada, and beyond. The "triggering" event which got me going in the first instance was, I think, the publication of Ron Faris's volume, *The Passionate Educators*, in 1975. I admired the book and welcomed such a substantial contribution to our knowledge of the history of the field.

But, at the same time, I was not sure that Faris's interpretation of the story was satisfactory. It was his view, as I understood it, that when at the end of World War II, the CAAE abandoned its somewhat radicalized view of adult education, as symbolized by its "1943 Manifesto," it thereby gave up its significant leadership of the adult education movement in Canada and, with it, a claim to leadership in what had been its main field of operation, education for citizenship. I questioned this judgment. In my view, the CAAE, in order to find a satisfactory basis for co-operation with a wide variety of voluntary organizations and government agencies in the post-war period, had abandoned a more radical stance for one which could be accepted by its many working partners. The CAAE had gone from taking a particular position on social and political policy questions to espousing the cause of citizenship education—what the 1946 Declaration called "the imaginative training for citizenship." Such a declaration seemed to me to represent a continued commitment to what I understood by citizenship education. Ron Faris saw it otherwise. By the late Seventies, I had become a faculty member and had the time to engage in detailed research on this matter. It mattered deeply to me both because I had by that time given a great deal of time and energy to the affairs of the CAAE and had served as its President, but also because the differing interpretations referred to above were clearly based on different philosophical orientations, raising issues which I was still in the process of clarifying for myself.

The events just described got me going on what turned out to be a very substantial series of research projects. They also raised the question of where monographs of that length (much longer than any journal would accept as articles) could be published. Once again, I turned to the publications program of the Centre for Continuing Education at The University of British Columbia and its editor, Jindra Kulich. Recognizing that such monographs would not find a large audience, but continuing in his commitment to publish significant contributions to our understanding of adult education in Canada, Jindra Kulich agreed, as each of this series of three studies was being completed, to publish them in his Occasional Papers series. They re-appear here in their entirety, thus becoming available to a wider (and to some extent a new) audience.

As I have stated, the Corbett study was suggested to me by my disagreement with an aspect of Faris's interpretation of the story. I also had the advantage, when carrying out that project, that both Faris's book (a reworking of his doctoral dissertation) and David Armstrong's thesis on Corbett's years as Director of the CAAE, were already completed. As I moved on from there, however, into the Kidd years (the Fifties) and the Thomas years (the Sixties), no such earlier studies had been conducted. In these cases, I was not in the position of relying on and reacting to the work of others, but rather I had to do all the original research myself and arrive at my own interpretations. This turned out to be a most stimulating and rewarding task and I consider these three publications, taken together, as among the most significant contributions I have been able to make to our knowledge of the field in Canada.

3.1

The Canadian Association for Adult Education in the Corbett Years: A Re-evaluation

*T*he Canadian Association for Adult Education has since its creation been a key element in the adult education movement in Canada. Founded in the Depression years, it has played a leadership role ever since. Unlike many counterpart organizations in other countries, many of which engage mainly in clearing house activities and the provision of support services to practitioners, the Canadian body became actively engaged in direct programming for adult learners. Its activities in this connection, most notably National Farm Radio Forum and Citizens' Forum, attracted world-wide attention and were adapted for use in many countries.

This monograph is not a history of these projects, but rather an attempt to trace the philosophical or ideological development of the CAAE during the years of E.A. "Ned" Corbett's leadership of the organization, from its founding in 1935 to his retirement in 1951. These were troubling and exciting years in the history of Canada, years of economic depression, of World War II and the emergence of a more vigorous Canadian nation, and years of vibrant post-war development. Three major studies already exist of Corbett and the Corbett years. Ned Corbett himself wrote an episodic autobiography, *We Have With Us Tonight*. David Armstrong (1968) wrote his M.A. thesis on the CAAE during the Corbett years, and Ron Faris subsequently published the most significant interpretive study we have on adult education during the period, *The Passionate Educators* (1975).

Why another treatment of this period? For one thing, because of its importance as a time when adult education and the CAAE were providing vigorous leadership in their sphere of influence in matters of central concern to the larger Canadian society. Secondly, some significant further sources of information, not available to earlier writers, have since appeared. And finally—and most important of all—any serious student of such matters, myself included, has the feeling that scholars before him, as enlightened and well informed as they may have been, did not get it "quite right."

The Early Years and the Commitment to Citizenship Education

The Canadian Association for Adult Education (CAAE) was formally established in 1935, but events leading up to its formation went back almost a decade prior to that. Frederick P. Keppel, President of the Carnegie Corporation of New York, and his assistant, Morse A. Cartright, had been instrumental in launching the American Association for Adult Education in 1926 and encouraging the creation of a Canadian national adult education organization. This was discussed by the two of them at least as early as the same year (Armstrong 1968:12). C.M. MacInnes, a Canadian who was teaching in Great Britain and who represented Canada on the Council of the World Association for Adult Education, edited a book for the Association entitled *Adult Education in the Dominions*, which appeared in 1929. MacInnes wrote the section dealing with Canada and in it he stated that there soon would be need for a national organization for the field in Canada (MacInnes 1929:40). An historian of the early years of the CAAE, David Armstrong, states that MacInnes was prompted to take this stand by Morse Cartright (Armstrong 1968.24). Three years later, Cartright was expressing some impatience with the "dilatory tactics of the Canadians" with respect to the matter. By means of a grant to the American Association, the Carnegie Corporation made it possible for eight Canadians (two in 1932 and six the following year) to visit Scandinavia to study the folk school movement. They were to make a report to the Corporation and make recommendations as to what they thought could be done to foster the adult education movement in Canada. In the meantime, Keppel and Cartright had taken the matter up directly with three Canadian leaders, W.J. Dunlop, Drummond Wren and W.L. Grant, while they were attending the meeting of the American body in Buffalo in May of 1932.

Dunlop, who was Director of University Extension at the University of Toronto, took the lead by calling a meeting of Canadians in late May, 1934, stating in advance that the objective was "to establish a national clearing house for adult education." At the suggestion of Cartright, Dunlop proposed a three-stage process leading towards the formal establishment of the new organization. The initial conference was to establish an organizing committee which would conduct a survey of adult education activities in Canada and investigate the feasibility of a national organization for the field. This would then be followed by a further conference to hear the committee's report and make a decision about an organization.

Throughout this whole process, which culminated in mid-June of 1935, when a conference at Macdonald College decided to create the CAAE, it is clear that the emphasis in the minds of those taking part was on a clearing house type of organization, one that would strengthen professional concerns in the field. Keppel and Cartright clearly had such an organization in mind (Armstrong 1968:17). The call for the 1934 conference referred to creating a "clearing house." The report on the national survey, which was edited by Peter Sandiford of the University of Toronto, argued for the co-ordination of adult education and a stronger role on the part of the provincial governments (Sandiford 1935: Chapt XX p.3ff.).

And when the CAAE was established, its stated goals were as follows:

1. To serve as a clearing house and to maintain a working library.
2. To develop interest by means of publications, radio, conferences.
3. To suggest methods and improve the work in adult education.
4. To provide for study and research.
5. To undertake experiments and demonstrations.
6. To advise grant-giving bodies, educational trusts, and private donors regarding

the status of any organization which makes application for a grant (I. Wilson in Kidd 1950:42).

There is a clear preponderance of professional concerns in this statement.

In the first issue of *Adult Learning*, the journal which was launched by the CAAE in late 1936, both the "Foreword" by Sir Robert Falconer, the Honorary President, and an editorial by Dunlop, the first President, in referring to the functions of the organization, make no mention of the social goals of the adult education movement, referring only to the need for more effective communications in the field (*Adult Learning*, Nov., 1936:2-4). Looking back in 1943 from the vantage point of seven years experience in the organization (and at a time when a strikingly different approach was being taken) E.A. Corbett observed that the original intention of the founders of the organization was that it be "a clearing house in all matters relating to adult education" (Director's Report 1943:3). He wrote a year later that the CAAE had subsequently "moved out of the Ivory Tower" (Corbett 1944a:1). In 1935, the goals of the organization focussed on adult education itself, not on society as a whole.

By 1935, when the CAAE was formed, there was already a great deal of adult education going on in all parts of the country. The Sandiford survey of 1935 had confirmed that fact, if proof was needed, although the survey provided only a partial picture of what was actually happening. The organization was formed in the depression years, a period during which many national voluntary organizations came into being (Ostry 1978:47), and one might have expected greater evidence of the social reform tradition in adult education in the founding documents of the new organization—especially in view of its subsequent history. Perhaps the explanation lies partly in the fact that the majority of the key figures in the new organization represented the interests of the universities and government services and that they tended to have in common a desire to improve the efficiency of practice, not a commitment to a common social goal. Also, there having previously been no satisfactory means of communication within the field across the country, it is not surprising that purposes related to communication should at least initially be given priority. The Carnegie Corporation officers clearly had some influence in the process too, the statement of the new Association's functions, which was approved by the executive in October, 1935, having been originally drafted by Morse Cartright, who was also present at the meeting (Armstrong 1968:46-49). The American Association, which had also been supported by Carnegie from its founding in the previous decade, had a similar set of goals.

If there was a clear priority at the outset for the CAAE over and above the specific matters covered in the statement of goals, it was to help improve the adult education opportunities in rural areas. The Sandiford survey had taken note of this need and Corbett, whose professional experience in Alberta had given him considerable experience in rural work, was receptive to that idea. The CAAE consistently emphasized rural educational needs for at least fifteen years after its founding (Faris 1975:26, 28).

The first and long-time Director of the CAAE, E.A. "Ned" Corbett, was one of the great charismatic leaders of adult education in Canada. He dominated the CAAE, and to some extent, the adult education movement as well. It is perhaps characteristic of small organizations that the paid director, especially when he or she has a strong personality and point of view, dominates the affairs of the organization. Certainly this was true of Corbett, and his successors Roby Kidd and Alan Thomas.

Corbett had strong views about society and the role which adult education should play in moulding it. He had graduated from a Presbyterian Theological College but subsequently decided that the ministry was not for him. He did possess, however, as Faris has put it, a "burning social conscience, fired by the social gospel theology which characterized divinity schools of the day" (Faris 1975:23-4). He had been wounded in a gas attack during the First World War, had a horror of war and a fervent belief in the merits of the democratic system, including the fullest possible participation by an informed citizenry in the working of society. As Armstrong and Faris have pointed out in their studies, Corbett was also a Canadian nationalist and was concerned about the task of building a single nation in spite of the geographical facts of Canada. As he put it in the fall of 1937, "In Canada we are so far apart geographically that frequent interchange of ideas and opinions will always be difficult" (Corbett 1937:2). In his study of the Wartime Information Board, W.R. Young refers to Corbett as "a leader of [the] intellectual mafia" who were "promoters of a Canadian national consciousness" (Young 1978:23-4). Such views help to explain Corbett's commitment to citizenship education as a priority and his readiness to work closely with the Canadian Broadcasting Corporation and the National Film Board, both instruments designed to bridge the gaps in Canadian society and to promote a feeling of national identity.

Corbett took over the leadership of an organization whose goals were stated largely in terms of dispassionate and professional interests, and transformed it into one which was heavily engaged in the promotion of particular social values. The founders of the CAAE had seen its role as that of a clearing house and information center for agencies and individuals in the field. Corbett led the organization into an active program role of its own.

During the prewar period, Corbett gave a great deal of his time to building up the new organizatian—making contacts with key persons in government, consolidating relationships with adult education leaders across the country and building up a remarkably effective network of contacts and communication with key figures in the national life of the country. The organization's emphasis on rural education was manifested by two projects which began in this period—a community development experiment at The Pas, Manitoba and the Community Life Training Institute in Barrie, Ontario, a leadership development program. These projects may be seen as the CAAE's first ventures into direct programming, but could be "justified" in terms of CAAE's stated goals as demonstration or experimental efforts designed to try out certain methodologies.

The first clear signal of the readiness of the CAAE to move into a sustained direct programming role appeared in the fall of 1937. At a meeting of the executive in mid-September, Corbett was authorized (no doubt at his own suggestion) to begin publishing pamphlets for use by study groups and to enter into discussions with the Canadian Broadcasting Corporation about possible joint programming. The CAAE made an arrangement with Ryerson Press for the publication of a series of pamphlets and in early 1938, with a series of radio talks about adult education, launched its long period of close co-operation with the C.B.C. (Armstrong 1968:102-7). By mid-1939, the organization was well launched on the promotion of study groups (in co-operation with local adult education organizations) and radio listening groups. In the summer of 1939, it employed Neil Morrison to serve as liaison officer with the C.B.C., organize listening groups and arrange training for group leaders. The posture of the organization was revealed clearly by a telegram which its executive sent to the Prime Minister the day following Canada's declaration of war on Germany in early September:

> The Canadian Association for Adult Education, comprising all university extension departments, having a total of forty-seven affiliated organizations and offering courses and radio listening groups throughout the Dominion, lays at the disposal of the federal government its services and facilities for information and education in citizenship and public affairs. (Armstrong 1968:117)

What these developments reveal was that the CAAE had for its own purposes, subsequently reinforced by urgent wartime needs, moved to a position where it had added to the original clearing house function of the organization, the direct promotion of citizenship education by means of publications, study groups and broadcasting. Such citizenship education had a long history in the field of adult education, going back to at least the late 1700s. The whole ideological atmosphere in the country at the beginning of the war leant emphasis to the necessity of strengthening the democratic nature of society, in the face of the challenge from the totalitarian, fascist states abroad and anti-democratic forces within.

Corbett later described in this way the situation he faced as Director of the CAAE:

> To create from a document of aims and purposes a national institution dedicated to the idea that continued learning throughout life was not only possible, but necessary if democratic institutions were to survive. (Corbett 1957:113)

And as he put it in a report to the Carnegie Corporation in March of 1941:

> In a country at war, the educational needs and wants of its citizens must not be overlooked or forgotten. This is supremely important if democracy is to be strong and vital in opposing the totalitarian states. (Armstrong 1968:116)

Armstrong, in his study of Corbett's leadership role in the CAAE, describes his aim during the war years as "to involve the whole adult education movement in the gigantic task of educating for democratic citizenship and effective post-war reconstruction" (Armstrong 1968:130).

In the period between the founding of the CAAE in 1935 and the early months of the war, it is clear that the CAAE changed its goals by adding to the original clearing house and information center idea a direct programming role in the field of citizenship education. There is a crucial distinction, however, between fostering adult education about questions of concern to the citizen—public affairs topics and social goals—and taking a position on those questions. Up until 1940, or early 1941, the CAAE had done only the former. It was at this point that Corbett's leadership set the CAAE on a course which in the ensuing two years resulted in the Association taking a position on national policy questions.

It is useful to pause here to remind ourselves of the intellectual climate in which this step was taken. Canada, in common with other nations, had had to endure the terrible shock of the Depression, with its widespread misery and profound questioning of the workings of contemporary society. The Thirties had witnessed the widespread acceptance of socialist ideas, and in some circles, Marxist ones, the formation of the C.C.F. Party and the propagation, within heretofore conservative circles such as the leading Protestant denominations, of discussion of radical ideas about the future direction of Canadian economic and social arrangements. With the outbreak of the war, the government itself was plunged into the propaganda business. Through the Bureau of Public Information (later replaced by the Wartime Information Board), it sought to define the issues for which the war was being fought and to establish a concept of Canadian nationalism which would rally all Canadians behind the war effort. Publicity and educational techniques were employed to mobilize Canadians for wartime activity (Young 1978:1-4). It was amidst this sort of atmosphere—the yeasty, somewhat radicalized legacy of the Depression years, with an "overlay" of the widespread use of propaganda by official government sources, that the CAAE was sorting out its role.

As Corbett subsequently observed, "The coming of the war gave CAAE its first opportunity to depart from its prescribed course as a clearing house and to participate in a national program of action" (Corbett 1946:99). Looking at these events from outside the adult education movement, W.R. Young has commented that the adult educators viewed the war as "a great opportunity for citizenship education." The educators hoped that their activities could provide the framework within which citizens could be encouraged "to read, to listen, to think and to decide" (Young 1978:27-30).

One can see the evolution of CAAE policy in this two year period, 1941 to 1943, as falling into two stages. The first of these represented a decision to join in with or enhance the efforts being made by the government to marshall support for the cause of democracy, as a means of strengthening the war effort. (Of course this was consistent with the deep convictions of most Canadians anyway and was a longstanding goal of many persons and organizations in the adult education movement.) The message to the Prime Minister at the outbreak of war had offered the CAAE'S services "for information and education in citizenship and public affairs." In his report to the annual meeting of CAAE in 1941, Corbett went further. He called upon the Association to:

> [R]e-affirm our belief that a democratic way of life is the good way of life....
> That's our job, to show people what a living, shining thing Democracy can be.
> [The CAAE must] throw off its attitude of academic detachment and make it quite
> clear that it intends to use whatever methods of propaganda are sound and legitimate
> in helping people to think clearly about the kind of world we have the right to look
> for when this war is over.

With the exception of the use of the word propaganda in the foregoing, adult educators of the day would on the whole accept this view.

This then represents the first stage of the transformation of the CAAE from a clearing house to a programming agency. While some individuals within the CAAE may have questioned the wisdom of the organization moving into direct programming, few if any would have questioned the move on grounds of principle. Especially in view of the absence of other national educational agencies (the constitution of the country assigning education to the provinces) it seemed appropriate for the CAAE to engage in "national" educational activities such as co-operation with the C.B.C. on Farm Radio Forum and with the National Film Board on its film circuits and the publication of materials for use by study groups across the country. Many adult educators in Canada, then and since, have seen this as an appropriate role for the CAAE and it has continued in diverse ways over the years to engage in and encourage citizenship or public affairs education.

But beginning in 1942-43, the CAAE moved one step further. In addition to raising public affairs questions for consideration, the CAAE resolved to take a stand on some broad matters of national policy. Here the organization, in the view of many, crossed over the line between education and propaganda, between raising questions and answering them. This second stage surfaced in 1941 and culminated in the declaration which was endorsed by the CAAE conference of 1943. In the process, the CAAE allied itself with the "social reform tradition" which had been present in the adult education movement since its earliest years. This stand by the CAAE was a source of some controversy within the organization, caused considerable suspicion of and trouble for the Association, but did not, on the whole, make a profound or abiding impact on the CAAE's work. What stayed with the organization was a commitment to citizenship education. The avowal of certain political or social policy positions by the Association, very much a product of the period of "reconstruction" planning during the war, did not have a strong lasting effect on the future activities of the organization.

Colors to the Mast: The 1943 Manifesto—and After

One of the first hints of the move towards a distinct social or political position on the part of the CAAE came in the same report of the Director to the annual meeting of 1941 which has already been quoted from above. In addition to arguing that the CAAE should be active in education about public affairs, Corbett went further; he said that adult education is:

> [M]ore than a method or system.... It is a social philosophy. The CAAE can at least affirm our faith that a working democracy need not countenance poverty and starvation.... We can insist that changes in the social [and] economic [systems] do not come from wishful thinking or resolutions passed at conventions but as the result of careful study and long-term planning. This does not mean that we should become propagandists...but it does mean that we take our stand with the men and women who believe in progress.

Corbett carried the CAAE with him along these lines in the months that followed. Reform was "in the air" in Canadian society at that time and a small band of thirty or forty people, a few of them quite radical in their views, provided leadership and carried their ideas through to acceptance by the significant conferences in 1942 and the following year. In looking back on this period from the vantage point of 1947, Corbett saw it as of particular significance:

> In 1942-43, we began to realize that the time had come to broaden our base of operations; to restate our objectives, and to outline as clearly and comprehensively as possible the working philosophy of the movement. (Director's Report 1947 quoted in Armstrong 1968:134)

In May of 1942, in speaking to the National Farm Radio Forum conference in Winnipeg, Corbett indicated that sobering decisions faced Canadians in their reconstruction policies and he raised the spectre of "returning to free enterprise with cycles, poverty, and special privilege...or a type of regimentation that may destroy the very thing we are fighting for" (Faris 1975:31). In November of that year, the Council of CAAE formally endorsed the view that the organization needed to give the most earnest attention to its responsibilities in stimulating and giving guidance to a process of public enlightenment and awakening regarding the issues of the war and objectives in the post-war world (Nov. 16, 1942, quoted in Faris1975:31).

A Special Program Committee was established to work out a statement of principles to be endorsed by the Association. The committee consisted of Corbett, Watson Thomson (University of Manitoba), R.E.G. Davis (Y.M.C.A. and Canadian Youth Commission) and W.H. Brittain (Macdonald College). The committee involved several other persons in its work and during the Christmas break in 1942, convened a small but representative meeting at Macdonald College to complete a statement of the philosophy of the movement, in the light of wartime conditions and planning for reconstruction. The report of that meeting, containing a statement of principles, was then submitted for consideration at the Annual Meeting held in May, 1943 in London, Ontario.

There was clearly a heightened "sense of occasion" at the London conference, which was the first general conference for the members which had been held for two years. The President of the Association, Dr. Sydney Smith, President of the University of Manitoba, opened the meeting with a stirring call to action. After reminding those assembled of the original purposes of the Association and indicating how each had been performed successfully, he said:

> But I assert that the record is not good enough for today, and certainly not for tomorrow. I plead with you to examine carefully, in this Annual Meeting, the *raison d'etre* of the Association.

He posed three alternatives: continuing as a clearing house, becoming a government agency, or the one that he endorsed:

> Working voluntarily with governmental and other agencies, the CAAE, by leadership, and even direction, should suggest, promote or initiate, for itself and its member organizations, policies and projects that will enable their respective constituencies to foster national unity and strength of purpose, and that will transcend social, political and economic conflicts.

He lauded the virtue of democratic values and stressed the importance of education in preparing citizens for carrying out their civic duty. He stressed the need for change so that those fighting in the war would not have to return to the likes of "the dizzy Twenties and the dismal Thirties."

He stressed that the CAAE was not being called upon to "espouse any particular 'ism:"

> The Association should direct people to examine basic human problems affecting their own welfare...and relate these problems to certain invaluable and inviolable standards, values and absolutes or imperatives.... We are dealing with the very stuff of individual and national strength and purpose.

Dr. Smith stopped short of suggesting a particular path for the Association, but he did clearly support a change of role, commended the special committee's statement of principles to the attention of the meeting, and called for fashioning "a new dynamic for adult education" (Smith 1943:5-8). Corbett's Director's Report to the conference went further. After drawing attention to recent developments in the program of the Association and the urgency of wartime conditions, he described the process and decisions which had led up to the conference. He made reference to recent social legislation introduced by the government and then moved to the heart of the matter, as far as the future of the Association was concerned:

> Can we depend on private enterprise to provide full employment or will a considerable measure of government planning and regulation be required? Many of our members may feel that it is not the business of an association such as ours to propagate any particular point of view on such questions, but rather to present all the facts in a completely detached and objective fashion. If, however, we believe that the only hope for world peace in the future lies in some kind of international order based on co-operation, and the concept of selective security, we surely have the right to say so. Such a planned international economy however, implies and depends upon controls which operate effectively in the domestic field as well as in the international field. The Canadian Association for Adult Education has, it seems to me, a definite obligation to make clear its conviction that any return to a laissez-faire social and economic philosophy means a return to those social and economic disorders that must inevitably lead again to war.

And he asked:

> What can we do to assist in the crystallization of public opinion in support of necessary social and economic reforms in the national and international fields? (Director's Report 1943:2-3)

Corbett was clearly throwing his weight behind a social reform position on the part of the Association.

Neil Morrison introduced the report of the planning committee to the conference, stressing the section dealing with "fundamental principles," and a committee was struck to produce overnight a simplified version of that section for possible approval by the conference. A draft "Manifesto" was ready by the next day, and after discussion, and some amendment, was moved by Sydney Smith and seconded by Donald Cameron (of the University of Alberta) and unanimously adopted.

The Manifesto is a brief statement containing a general introduction and a statement of seven principles. It refers to the need for "a new Canadian and world society" and invites interested individuals and groups to join in the "urgent educational task" of working towards that end. It declares that "academic aloofness and neutrality are not enough" and declares itself in support of certain principles:

1. Mutual responsibility for each other's welfare among individuals and nations.

2. Social controls and planning are necessary. It "is probable that the area of public ownership and control should be extended...."

3. Human beings are ends, not means. Need to prevent regimentation.

4. Status of the individual should rest on efficient service to the cormmunity, "not social privilege, financial power or property rights."

5. Meeting consumption needs "should be the main incentive of economic life."

6. "Social goals take precedence over individual and sectional purposes of profit or advantage."

7. Neither "the old individualism" nor "the newer mass collectivism" but a principle of "voluntary co-operation which balances rights with responsibilities" should be the basis of the social order.

And the Manifesto concludes:

> The CAAE will seek the co-operation of all individuals and organizations who endorse these principles in formulating and executing a whole-hearted campaign of public education directed towards the winning of a people's war and a people's peace. (Kidd 1963:108-9)

It is an indication of the times that this statement—even the title, "Manifesto"— could have been approved unanimously by the conference, which was attended by 230 persons. This was a time in Canadian society when reform was in the air. In the words of a Wartime Information Board report to Cabinet in November of this same year, "Public opinion favored great changes—almost anything to prevent the return to poverty and insecurity." There was "an undercurrent of public nervousness" (Bothwell and Kilbourn 1979:180-81) and a concern about post-war conditions "something akin to dread" (Granatstein 1975:251). Charles Ritchie, then a junior staff member of the Canadian High Commission in London, recorded at this time (late 1943), "The war will make people impatient and ready for change. The post-war period is our great opportunity" (Ritchie 1974:149). So this was clearly a time in the life of the country when the Manifesto, which at other times might seem clearly socialistic and therefore both unacceptable to some attending the conference and unwise in terms of the Association's public relations, could be unanimously accepted by the meeting. In fact, some of those who attended, especially those representing some university extension departments and representatives of provincial departments of education, voiced objections privately but "sat in sullen silence as [the Manifesto] was unanimously adopted" (Faris 1975:138 quoting interview with Alex Sim).

The London conference in May, 1943, in order to begin to implement this program of citizenship education, resolved to launch a major program, somewhat parallel to the existing National Farm Radio Forum but dealing with more general citizenship and reconstruction problems. In order to plan this project (which became Citizens' Forum), a further conference, on "Education for Reconstruction," was called for September, at Macdonald College.

The September conference was concerned mainly with the organization of Citizens' Forum. It embodied the practical application of the "reconstruction educational program" which had been called for by the Special Program Committee in its report and endorsed by the annual meeting in London. It was from the beginning envisaged as a project which would involve the use of radio and local discussion groups. The Wartime Information Board played a prominent part in the organization of the planning conference, no less than ten of their staff taking part in the final planning meeting in July. There was an enthusiastic response from many of the organizations approached about the project and the originally intended 100 participants grew to 165, representing 120 organizations (Avison 1943:18). The practical measures undertaken by the meeting to launch Citizens' Forum need not detain us. What is of relevance here are the further indications of the general mood and directions of the Association's thinking. The report of the conference printed in *Food For Thought*, (by this time, the name of the Association's journal) (Anon 1943:ff) dealt only with the report of the three commissions (on curriculum, methods and organization) and contained little of an ideological nature. The following issue carried the text of the concluding conference address by Gregory Vlastos, a socialist (Young 1978:81) then in the R.C.A.F. and subsequently on the staff of the Wartime Information

Board. He called for a sense of commitment to democratic ideas and "the sense of community releasing the hidden greatness of the common man" (Vlastos 1943:8). It appears that at the Macdonald College conference the CAAE, having to work out co-operative arrangements with many other organizations, did not stress ideological matters, but got on with the practical implementation of Citizens' Forum, which was launched later in the same fall, with remarkable success.

It is clear that the year 1943, with the endorsement of the Manifesto, marks the high point in the social reform position of the CAAE. Watson Thomson, one of the members of the planning committee and a leading activist for the ideas in the Manifesto, was asked to write an article on the conference for the Association's journal. He stated that the adult education business in Canada had "jelled" and the CAAE had acquired a momentum from within. But the great event of the London Conference was a decision which, in effect, implies a radical transformation and extension of the structure and functions of the CAAE.

Thomson pointed out, somewhat scornfully, that the frequent stance of adult educators with respect to social issues was "a pale neutrality and restraint." He referred to it as offering people "stones when they are crying for bread. So as not to be accused of belonging to any camp, they have refused to come down to earth at all." Concerning the principles in the Manifesto, Thomson stated:

> In short, the Manifesto is a necessary declaration without which the CAAE could hardly dare go to the citizens of Canada, regardless of race, class or creed. It testifies that, in this crisis, we offer men and women not only information, but something of vision and faith. It testifies that, as for us, social change—radical social and economic change—is not something to be feared.

> Such a stand is obligatory upon men and women to whom adult education is not just a job and a technique but a passionate preparation for a new society....At London, we did something we all wanted to do, some more consciously than others. We took a stand. We gave ourselves a moral and ideological basis from which to act. (Thomson 1943:9-11)

In the spring of 1944, the CAAE chose to reprint an address which John Grierson, Director of the National Film Board and, until a few months previous, of the Wartime Information Board, had given in England five years earlier. Much of it had to do with the place of communications media in citizenship education, but one can see its appeal to the CAAE in the Manifesto period: "On the other hand, if education is to be an active instrument of the democratic idea, it must first be socialized. By that I mean that it must at every turn take hold of its role as a social instrument" (Grierson 1944:5).

Over the summer of 1944, Corbett went on a speaking tour of Canadian armed forces bases in England and Scotland, at the request of the Wartime Information Board. He talked with the men and women mainly about problems of rehabilitation and reconstruction. He found them very anxious about the kind of world which would face them on their return and Corbett drew the lesson that civilians at home had the "heavy responsibility" of creating a kind of community in which the veterans would be able to play an active and meaningful part (Corbett 1944:4-8).

The CAAE annual meeting for 1944 was held in Ottawa in September of that year. Corbett's Director's Report to the meeting is a significant statement of how he saw the current position and priorities of the Association. Some parts of the report perhaps reflect some uneasiness in the Association over the stand that was taken in the Manifesto:

> During the past four years the policy of this Association has undergone a complete change. In the first four years of our existence, we followed closely the terms of reference laid down in our Dominion Charter. The Association was a clearing house: a center of adult education interest, and of experimental promotion. But with the development of the National Farm Radio Forum, we automatically entered the program field. Our name became associated with the active propagation of certain points of view. While we might protest our complete educational objectivity, the fact is that through our close relationship with the Canadian Federation of Agriculture, and our sponsorship of a program dealing with practical problems of rural living, we moved out of our Ivory Tower and began to take a look at the world we lived in. We had allied ourselves with people of progressive temper, we began to be accused of having ideas about human affairs, which is always dangerous in Canada.

Corbett reviewed the events which led up to the approval of the Manifesto. He maintained that the Manifesto did not depart:

> [I]n any way from the original purposes of the Association, but simply clothes the dry bones of an official statement with a working philosophy and gives it direction. It states only the basic assumptions regarding human welfare that we believe can be made by all thinking people. It testifies that in the crisis through which the world is passing, the CAAE proposes to offer men and women something more than information: it suggests national leadership in social vision and faith: it testifies that social and economic change are not something to be feared, nor something to be promoted in the interest of any special group. It is to be demanded and fought for in the interest of the whole society. That adult education is not just a technique or a special field of education, but a means, perhaps the only means by which men and women can be prepared for a new social order, a means of establishing the moral and ideological basis from which action can take shape.

Corbett described the Macdonald College conference, calling it "the most significant in the history of the Association" in that it brought the CAAE into close working relationships, both at the conference and subsequently in the launching of Citizens' Forum, with "literally hundreds of societies":

> We are no longer alone. We are no longer a voice crying in the wilderness. Our emphasis upon the value of adult education as a medium of social change is supported by thousands of people now who formerly had no interest in or knowledge of the possibilities of adult education. There is therefore now no way out for this Association. It must either proceed ideologically along the lines laid down in its Manifesto and practically in the areas developed by National Farm Radio Forum, Citizens' Forum and by other media, or it must retreat ignominiously from the field. (Director's Report 1944 and Corbett 1944 a:1-2)

There is some impression here of cheering on the flagging troops and it is clear that there was some unease in the Association about its ideological directions (Faris 1975:137ff). There had been some adverse response in the press about the matter (Thomson 1943:10). In his study of the period, Ron Faris makes this comment:

> Considering the concepts and even the terminology used in the Manifesto and in Corbett's defence of social action, it is not surprising that conservative observers subsequently accused the Association and its Director of "left-wing" leanings. To a conservative, this social democratic rhetoric, set in a period of rapid growth of the C.C.F. movement, may have been conclusive proof that the CAAE was a partisan propaganda weapon. (Faris 1975: 34)

Faris describes in detail efforts made by members of the Liberal cabinet in the fall of 1944 to influence the balance of speakers who were to appear on the early Citizens' Forum broadcasts, on the grounds that they were loaded in favor of the C.C.F. and the socialist point of view (Faris 1975:104-07). Corbett's active role in civil liberties issues during this same period added to his—and the Association's—reputation in some quarters for leftist tendencies.

At this distance in time, it can be seen that the Manifesto of 1943 and the Director's reports of that year and the following were the most extreme stands taken by the Association with respect to its ideological position. Thereafter, strong statements were occasionally made in individual articles, but the tendency was to fall back from the more extreme position to one in which the goal was not so much change of a particular kind and direction, but rather the animation of discussion and study about social issues.

An example of the continuation of insistence upon social reform may be found in an article by Watson Thomson which was carried in *Food For Thought* in early 1945. (By this time, Thomson had become Director of adult education in the Saskatchewan Department of Education—under the new C.C.F. government there.) He said that the legacy of the war demanded an adult education with a "new Philosophy." The new adult education must be "social through and through" and must be "activist;" "glad to associate with the Common Man and serve him in his historic struggle towards a more abundant life."

He raised the matter of the acceptability of a "neutral" stance on the part of the educator, in the context of a study of fascism, for instance:

> Such neutrality is impossible.... Education cannot detach itself in that way from the historic process. Teachers and professors and adult educationists have to make up their minds, like everybody else, whether they are on the side of the people and on the side of social change or on the side of the enemies of the Common Man and on the side of the status quo. To play the neutral role means, like the political policy of appeasement, to play into the hands of the enemies of progress. (Thomson 1945:5-6)

This sort of article, which was "answered" in a subsequent issue (Gordon 1945), was the exception (as was Thomson himself) and on the whole, CAAE avoided thereafter strident statements of the sort contained in the 1943 Manifesto. It had by then, however, become the target of attack and suspicion in conservative circles. Young, in his study, quotes W.H. Brittain of Macdonald College as stating late in 1943 (after the Manifesto of that year) that "even various wings of the adult education movement had come to view each other suspiciously." Young also states that in this period, the Wartime Information Board, the C.B.C. and the CAAE were seen by many businessmen as attempting to "downgrade the free enterprise system" (Young 1978:99). Mention of such attacks was noted in an editorial in *Food For Thought* in the fall of 1950 (Anon 1950:1-2).

For the balance of Corbett's years as Director of the Association, CAAE came under periodic attack for what were termed leftist views. These attacks mainly focussed on the choice of speakers and program materials in the Farm Radio and Citizens' Forum programs and many of them are reviewed in Faris's book (Faris 1975). The most "spectacular" of these incidents involved the President of the Association, James Muir, then President of the Royal Bank of Canada, who, in 1951 and 1952, had a series of battles with the staff and some committees over the "bias" which he and some business associates believed the CAAE had allowed at times to creep into both broadcasts and pamphlets of the two Forum programs (Faris 1975:141-50).

The 1946 Declaration—and After

The next comprehensive test of the ideological climate of the Association came at the annual meeting of 1946. In the intervening period, the energies of the Association appear to have been focussed on managing Farm and Citizens' Forum, publishing *Food For Thought*, and beginning in 1945, on closer co-ordination with other organizations. Articles in the journal gave a great deal of attention to the various forms of citizen education and involvement—leadership training, rural adult education, community centers and councils, outstanding institutions in the field such as St. Francis Xavier in Nova Scotia, the film circuits and of course the two broadcast Forum projects. Editorially, the journal pursued most of these same subjects, education for citizenship in its various forms being the most frequent theme. Early in this two year period (1944 to 1946), much attention was given to the interests of the returning veterans. In the fall of 1944, for instance, in an editorial entitled, "When the Boys Come Home," the emphasis was placed on building a society in which there would be jobs for the veterans and in which they would have a meaningful place as participating citizens (Morrison 1944:1-2). In the spring of 1945, an article by Corbett on adult education and the schools stressed the significance of the study group as a setting in which people not only learn from each other, but practice the methods and skills of democratic living in so doing (Corbett 1945). A long editorial in April of 1945 dealt with the issue of education and propaganda, taking a moderate stand.

The important conference in Winnipeg in the spring of 1945 will be dealt with in greater detail below, but it is appropriate to note here that because it was concerned with co-operation and co-ordination in the field of citizenship education, involving other agencies, including public bodies, the emphasis was on method and general philosophy, not on particular political ends. For instance, on the opening night of the conference, John Grierson stated that:

> The basic problem of education lies not so much in the acquisition of literacy or knowledge or skills, as in the pattern of civic appreciation, civic faith and civic duty which goes with them. I suggest, in fact, that the crisis in education today lies in the realm of the imaginative training for citizenship and not anywhere else. (Grierson 1945:5-6)

At the opening of a new program year in September of 1945, the editorial in *Food For Thought* was a call to action "for those interested in adult education, public information and responsible citizenship," who were entreated not to let down now that the war was won, but "to find out how to steer the political machine instead of letting ourselves be crushed beneath its wheels" (Morrison 1945:1). In a thoughtful article in the same issue,

Alex Sim surveyed the task of citizenship education lying ahead and questioned whether peacetime challenges such as unemployment and poverty could be seen "as dreadful an emergency" as "Dunkirk, Pearl Harbor and the siege of Leningrad" (Sim 1945:24). In a brief to the Ontario Royal Commission on Education in 1945, the CAAE pointed out that it was not involved in vocational or degree credit adult education. "Its [CAAE's] basic creed is that well-informed citizens are vital in a democracy and that a well-developed program of adult education is essential to good citizenship" (8-page brief in Association files). In November of 1945, the editorial lamented the demise of the Wartime Information Board, stressing its importance in public affairs education (its successor was to be concerned only with information services abroad). This same position was taken in an article by Martin Estall in the same issue (Estall 1945).

Reference has been made to the annual conference of the Association held in Winnipeg in May of 1945. Corbett was convinced that the CAAE should play a role as a co-ordinator of a network of national agencies—public and otherwise—which were broadly concerned with citizenship education. The CAAE was successful at the Winnipeg meeting in bringing together representatives of many of these agencies, some of them (the Wartime Information Board and the C.B.C.) having been involved in the planning as well. At the end of the meeting, the CAAE was asked to take the lead in establishing a national committee to facilitate co-operative programming. This committee, chaired by Corbett, convened a further national conference in the following year which was on the subject of joint planning by voluntary and government agencies in adult education.

The resulting Kingston Conference of May, 1946, was instrumental in creating the Joint Planning Commission, described below. The conference also produced a declaration (drafted largely by Harry Avison of Macdonald College) on the role of adult education:

> The adult education movement is based on the belief that quite ordinary men and women have within themselves and their communities the spiritual and intellectual resources adequate to the solution of their own problems. Through lack of knowledge and lack of leadership these resources are often not mobilized or not directed in constructive ways.
>
> The primary tasks of adult education, therefore, are to awaken people to the possibilities and dangers of modern life, to help them with knowledge and leadership, and to provide channels of communication between different cultural, occupational and social groups so that the solution of human problems may be sought against the broadest background and in the interest of all. In short, the task is the imaginative training for citizenship. Adult education should deal with the actual and living concerns of actual and living people.
>
> Adult education is a natural continuation and fulfillment of schooling. The lessons of mature citizenship can really only be learned by mature people. While provision must always be made for the training of the underprivileged and the neglected and for the occupation of leisure time, adult education must be seen as a normal activity of a developing and healthy society. (Kidd 1950:24-5)

This eloquent statement of the "mission" of adult education in the field of citizenship education indicates that the CAAE saw itself still committed firmly to education for citizenship and to the rights and capacities of the individual citizen, but it stopped considerably short of the language of the 1943 Manifesto.

There was presumably no need this time for university and government representatives to abstain from supporting the declaration. Indeed the nature of the meeting was such that it was essential that the declaration be acceptable to the representatives of a variety of public and private agencies. Although it could be argued that this latter fact greatly influenced what ideas went into the declaration, it should also be said that from this point on, the CAAE seemed to take as policy and purpose the mission outlined in 1946, rather than to return to the language of the 1943 statement. The commitment now was to "the imaginative training for citizenship," not to some of the more explicit political goals of the Manifesto, such as the expansion of public ownership and "social controls."

For the ensuing five years, until the end of his time as Director of the Association in 1951, Corbett continued to be a dynamic leader, although it is probably fair to say that by this latter period he had fought most of his battles and the Association was concerned largely with operating along already established lines. Ron Faris, in his study, suggests that during this period, the "social movement activists" realized that they had lost the struggle for control of the Association and left (Faris 1975). It would be fairer to say, however, that the activists who saw the CAAE as a means of advancing certain social and political ends had left, but that there remained others who still thought of adult education as a movement, one which had potential to transform society in significant ways, ways and directions to be left for decision by the learners, the citizens.

Aside from the comparatively strident notes in his annual reports in 1943 and 1944, Corbett tended to couch his philosophical statements about the field in fairly moderate terms. In his Director's Report in 1946, he said, "It seems to me that the CAAE has an opportunity and a duty now to emphasize the need for a more dynamic concept of citizenship in this new and dangerous world we live in."

In 1947 the CAAE published a small pamphlet by Corbett entitled *A Short History of Adult Education*, the text of which had shortly before appeared in *Food For Thought*. He pointed out there that earlier experience with adult education in the United Kingdom, where much adult education was a response to social problems, made it clear "that the social problem is partly an educational problem. It always has been, and it always will be" (Corbett 1947:4). Later in the publication he describes what he terms his "working philosophy" of adult education as being based on the conviction that the desire for knowledge is a normal human appetite, and that the capacity to acquire knowledge continues throughout life:

> I also know from long experience that through study, discussion and planning together people can change their social and economic environment and in so doing change themselves. (Corbett 1947:12)

He set forth six principles of adult education which he and M.M. Coady of St. Francis Xavier University had worked out together:

a. That the individual, his rights, his moral and spiritual significance, is of supreme importance in a democracy.

b. That social progress can only come about through improvement in the quality of human beings, and that improvement can only come through education.

c. That adult education must suit its efforts to the intimate interests of the individual or the group, and in most instances these interests are economic.

d. That adult education functions most effectively through group study and group action.

e.   That the ultimate objective of all education, particularly adult education, is the development of the individual's capacity to live a fuller and more abundant life.

f.   That education, like religion, can only be truly vital in the measure of its freedom from external authority. (Corbett 1947:12)

Both these six principles and the preceding "working philosophy" apparently still had appeal for Corbett ten years later because he used them, unchanged, in his autobiography, *We Have With Us Tonight*, published in 1957 (Corbett 1957:220-1).

Corbett shed further light on his views on the occasion of a dinner in honor of his retirement in 1951. He said that to be an adult educator one must like people, be flexible and tough, and have a philosophy of life, He pointed out that a lot of ministers and ex-ministers had gone into adult education:

> The reason is, I think, because in adult education they have found an activity in which they can express in their own peculiar way whatever passion for justice and righteousness may possess them. The working philosophy of these men can be summed up in a few words. They have believed that people can be creative and that they can live in fellowship. (Anon 1951)

This statement reveals some of the fervor and social gospel thinking of the man. He led the CAAE into adopting a broad citizenship education task, and in 1943, into a social activist posture. Armstrong, in his study of the man and his influence, adds:

> Corbett's values too—his belief in voluntarism, his nationalism. and the importance which he attached to free discussion, rural adult education, civil liberties and citizenship training—are indelibly etched in the historical record of the Association during this period. (Armstrong 1968:205)

Programs and Services

With the decision taken in 1937 to enter into citizenship education, initially by means of the publication of pamphlets for study groups and through broadcasts, in co-operation with the C.B.C., the foundation was laid for much future work. In this connection, especially after the beginning of the war, the CAAE became an active partner in various ventures with several private and public organizations which had an interest in promoting study and discussion of public affairs questions facing Canadians. These organizations included the Canadian Legion Educational Services (which the CAAE had helped to organize), the Canadian Institute of International Affairs, the Canadian Federation of Agriculture, the Canadian Council on Education for Citizenship, the Wartime Information Board (especially after Grierson became its Manager in early 1943), the C.B.C. and the National Film Board. Corbett was almost legendary in his ability to create and maintain productive working relationships with many of the leaders of these—and other—organizations. In his book, Faris has studied the nature of these alliances, on ideological and other lines (Faris 1975).

The relationship among these organizations—different combinations for different programs—was complex and it is often difficult from the records to determine where one organization's efforts leave off and those of another begin. Pamphlets produced by one organization would be used by another in its programs. Those produced by two organizations co-operatively would he used by both of them—and others—in their study group activities. The same was true for many study outlines, films and broadcasts.

Basic to an understanding of the efforts of those several organizations in the late Thirties and the succeeding fifteen years is the fact that very heavy reliance was placed on the small study group as a technique. The churches, the Y.M. and Y.W.C.A., university extension departments, rural voluntary organizations, political parties and many other groups had begun, during the Thirties, to rely heavily on this means of promoting study and discussion. (It had been a prominent technique from the very early period of the adult education movement in the late 18th century.) The well-known and successful "Antigonish Movement" of St. Francis Xavier University in Nova Scotia, which relied heavily on the study group, gave increased prominence to this approach through its outstanding leaders, J.J. Thompkins and M.M. Coady. They built their whole program around the study group and eloquently promoted its use, a position Corbett and many other adult education leaders of the day endorsed. Corbett's "basic principles of adult education," listed above, indicate the priority which he attached to that setting and method of adult education.

As the CAAE moved into the field of citizenship education, in the company of the other organizations, heavy reliance was placed on the study group and as, a result, on the production of materials which would provide such groups with information and guidance for their work. Two of the major projects of the Association, Farm Radio Forum and Citizens' Forum, relied heavily on pamphlets produced especially for that work. In addition, CAAE produced, and otherwise made available for use, a great many pamphlets on other subjects.

A major instrument utilized by the Association for the assistance of study groups was its regular journal, called *Adult Learning* from 1936 to 1939 and *Food For Thought* thereafter. *Adult Learning* had been a general adult education journal, with articles about what was going on in the field, but the changeover in 1940 was made with the deliberate intention of producing instead a publication which could serve as the basis of individual or group study. Each issue was almost wholly taken up with an article on some public affairs topic, sometimes one related to adult education ("What About the C.B.C.?," "Farmers Air Their Problems," etc.). With the first issue of volume II, in the fall of 1941, it went to a smaller format and to a larger number of shorter articles, although the announced intention was to continue carrying one longer article in each issue on "some outstanding Canadian problem." The intention was to carry "editorial comment [and] discussion helps, information concerning material suitable for adult education groups" (Anon 1941b:4). In the fall of 1944 (Vol.V, No. 1) the magazine was converted to a yet smaller size, with a picture on the cover and became generally more attractive in appearance. Among the goals listed at the time of this change was that of providing "practical guidance for those who are giving leadership in Citizens' Forum, Farm Radio Forum, and other types of discussion groups or educational clubs" (Morrison 1944a). Significantly, the lead editorial in this first issue was the one by Corbett commenting on the 1943 Manifesto and announcing that the CAAE had moved "out of our Ivory Tower" (Corbett 1944a:1). Throughout the decade, *Food For Thought* gave particular emphasis to public affairs questions and to matters of direct relevance to the interests of those in study groups, such as Forum project news, discussion and group techniques, leadership education, and reviews, notices and descriptions of materials for use in study activities—pamphlets, films, books and radio broadcasts. Towards the end of the Forties one can see a noticeable increase in the number of articles on international affairs.

The Association's journal represented only a portion of its publishing activities during this period, however. Many pamphlets, individually and in series, were produced, most of them related to some major program. The first publishing activity, apart from the Association's journal, was a series of pamphlets undertaken jointly with the Canadian Institute for International Affairs. They began to appear in late 1939 under the series title of "Behind the Headlines" and by the fall of the next year, there were nine on the list. They were on public affairs topics, including international affairs, civics and economics, and were written by leading writers of the day such as B.K. Sandwell, H.G. Skillings and J.W. Holmes. In his Director's Report for 1943, Corbett stated that 3,500 copies a month of the "Behind the Headlines" series were being used.

Early in 1940, the CAAE held an invitational conference on rural adult education out of which came plans for a series of 16 bulletins on "Canadian Farm Problems." They were edited by W.H. Brittain and became extremely popular. They were subsequently used as study guides for listening groups in a C.B.C. series broadcast in the Eastern Townships and the Maritime provinces, the precursor of Farm Radio Forum. The CAAE also assisted the Canadian Teachers' Federation and the Canadian Council on Education for Citizenship with the production of a series of twelve pamphlets on public affairs topics, for use in the schools. In its early stages of development, the Canadian Legion Educational Services were largely a result of CAAE leadership and this involved a substantial publications program as well. In his Director's Report for 1943, referred to above, Corbett stated that the C.L.E.S. took 500 copies of the "Behind the Headlines" pamphlet series each month and that a similar arrangement was being worked out for "educational officers of the armed forces."

The most sustained publication effort on the part of the CAAE consisted of the pamphlets and study guides produced in connection with Farm Radio Forum (beginning in 1939) and Citizens' Forum (1943). Generally, there was a new pamphlet produced each week for both programs throughout the length of each season. These usually presented factual information about the week's topic, a list of other related readings, and suggested questions for study and discussion. Each member of each listening group had to receive a copy of this publication, and on time to accompany the broadcast on the same subject.

The CAAE also utilized in its work many pamphlets produced by other organizations. Many of these were reviewed or listed in *Food For Thought* and many could be purchased from the CAAE offices. Perhaps the most outstanding example of this activity was the "Canadian Affairs" pamphlet series, which in May of 1943 was taken over by the Wartime Information Board from the Department of National Defence. They were used by the W.I.B. for their general educational work and also supplied regularly to those who were involved in "Servicemen's Forum," a project they ran for members of the armed forces. The CAAE was in close working relations with the W.I.B. and made use of the "Canadian Affairs" Pamphlet series on a large scale, as did other organizations.

Corbett frequently used the total circulation of pamphlets from the CAAE offices as a way of conveying an impression of the scale of the Association's activities. For instance, in his report to the annual meeting in 1944, just after the second major forum project, Citizens' Forum, was launched, he reported that four years earlier, the circulation of the journal, the "Behind the Headlines" series and miscellaneous other publications had totalled approroximately 5,000 items per month. In the year 1943-44, however, Farm Radio Forum alone distributed 20,000 copies per week (560,000 for the seven month program year) and "Of Things to Come" (the early name for Citizens' Forum), 15,000 copies per week (450,000 for the program year). In an article published in March of 1945, Corbett states that the combined monthly mailing for the two Forum projects was 26,000 copies of study bulletins (Corbett 1945:8).

Over and above this publications program, and the close working relationships with the other organizations which have been mentioned, the chief program initiatives undertaken by the CAAE under Corbett's direction were the two experimental rural projects—the citizenship training center at The Pas, Manitoba and the Community Life Training Institute at Barrie (Simcoe County), Ontario.

Joint Planning Commission

The Joint Planning Commission functioned for fifteen years and was one of the most notable and successful features of adult education at the national level in Canada. It may be seen primarily as an aspect of adult education, or more broadly as an instrument of "the social growth of Canada" (McLeish 1978:103) but in both contexts it fits within the ample philosophy of Corbett, and is seen as one of his most creative contributions to the field (Armstrong 1968:150).

Efforts to co-ordinate the activities of bodies interested in adult education within particular jurisdictions have been many and varied, usually unsuccessful. The Joint Planning Commission—usually called the "J.P.C."—was the product of the efforts of many people and organizations, but the idea was developed initially, in its distinctive Canadian form, by Corbett from his base at the CAAE, and John Robbins, the Head of the Education Section of the Dominion Bureau of Statistics and the part-time, unpaid secretary of the Canadian Council on Education for Citizenship.

As far as the CAAE was concerned, co-ordination of adult education at the national level was consistent with its terms of reference from the beginning. During the war there developed an effective network of communication and co-operation among key people in several agencies interested in education about public affairs. In his Director's Report to the annual meeting in 1944, Corbett suggested a somewhat more formal effort to consult regularly with other organizations, recommending that the CAAE provide "a medium through which all the varied adult education activity in Canada can be integrated and co-ordinated to serve an agreed purpose" (Director's Report 1944). In an article written in 1946, Corbett said:

> At the annual meeting in 1944 it became apparent that some practical steps must be taken to bring about a more systematic method of co-operation at the national, provincial and community levels. (Corbett 1946:101)

The leaders of several agencies which had worked together closely during the war were determined to foster the continuation of that co-operation in peacetime (Corbett 1957:213). Early in 1945, the CAAE Executive decided to call a conference "of those organizations which had already worked out a pattern of integration in their work" (Corbett 1946:101). This included Farm Radio Forum, Citizens' Forum, C.B.C., W.I.B., the National Film Board, the Canadian Council on Education for Citizenship and the Canadian Legion Educational Services. The chief parties in planning this conference were the CAAE, the National Film Board, the C.B.C. and the Wartime Information Board. Invitations were sent to the organizations mentioned above and some others. The meeting was held in late

May, 1945, and was attended by 125 delegates. The conference authorized the CAAE to take the lead in establishing a national planning committee which would in future be responsible for working out national programs co-operatively and more effectively integrating work at the provincial and community levels (Director's report to the CAAE National Council Nov. 21, 1945, quoted in Faris 1975:41).

The committee formed as a result of this initiative was chaired by Corbett and the secretary was John Robbins. Corbett remembered particularly the contributions as well of Harry Avison, John Grierson, Geoffrey Andrew (of the W.I.B.), Neil Morrison and George Grant (who was briefly on the staff of the CAAE) to the development of the project at this early stage. A national conference on the idea of joint planning and co-ordination among voluntary and public bodies was organized for Kingston in May, 1946. The outcome of this conference, in the form of the general declaration on adult education, has already been described.

With respect to the co-ordinating committee, its functions were considered and extended. They were stated as:

a.   To facilitate the exchange of information on program and activities between the different agencies in the field.

b.   To avoid overlapping and duplication of effort, particularly in the production of program materials.

c.   To work out more effective ways of using available materials and agencies.

d.   To consider areas of adult education not being covered and to reach groups not now being reached.

e.   To make suggestions about program needs (Clarke 1954:8-9).

The committee at this time established its basic pattern. Meetings of agency representatives were held approximately three times a year, in Toronto, Ottawa or Montreal. At these, there was an exchange of information about programs, program materials and other matters of mutual interest, and usually there was a major address and/or half-day session on some topic of the day. The CAAE provided the staff work for the meetings. A unique and important feature of the arrangement was that there was no formal "membership" or membership fees or constitution of the committee. Organizations were simply invited each time to take part and because the committee continued to be useful to them, they kept coming. It was recognized that to introduce the notion of formal membership requirements, when the participants were of such a varied nature— representatives of government departments, other public agencies, voluntary associations, business and labor—would have raised needless complications. And so the group simply went on, from meeting to meeting and year to year, on the basis of the mutual benefits being received.

A significant step was taken early in 1947 when Corbett was successful in securing a two-year grant from the Carnegie Corporation, which made possible the appointment of a part-time paid Secretary for the Committee. (Dr. J. Roby Kidd was subsequently employed, to fill this role and also to serve as Associate Director of the CAAE itself.) In that same year too, the name of the "Co-ordinating Conrmittee" was changed to the "Joint Planning Commission."

The Joint Planning Commission was a success story for the almost twenty years of its existence. It was so regarded by the vast majority of those who played a part in it and by many visitors from abroad who studied its work as a possible model for their own countries. It did a great deal more than just exchange information. Its work was organized by an administrative committee which was representative of the broader "membership." The staff work was provided by the CAAE under the leadership of Roby Kidd, until he became Director of the Association in 1951, and thereafter by Mrs. Clare Clarke. The "permanent chairman" of J.P.C. meetings was Walter Herbert, Director of the Canada Foundatlon, who did it on a volunteer basis. Meetings were held three times a year, usually hosted by one of the participating organizations or by some business enterprise. At the fall meeting, emphasis was placed on the exchange of information about program, resource development and other matters for the coming program year. (An editorial in *Food For Thought* in the spring of 1949 stated, "It has more than justified its existence in preventing duplication of effort in the preparation of program materials and in providing for the better use of those materials available" (Anon 1949a:2)) The other two meetings in the year normally put greater stress on some selected topic(s) for the day, with some attention being given in the spring as well to the following year's activities. The members did not just sit and listen to speakers, however. The J.P.C. had a series of active committees, some of which were designated as standing committees, which carried out regular tasks such as adjudicating for film and broadcasting awards. Also, there were ad hoc committees which were formed from time to time to conduct a study or prepare a report for the J.P.C. Some of these reports carried recommendations for action; some were more information or "state-of-the-art" reports.

Although the J.P.C.'s work resulted in action being taken, the Commission was not an action body in a political sense:

> One agreement is basic—no decisions are taken that will commit an organization to any prescribed course of action by reason of its participation in the J.P.C. This is fundamental to the continued existence of the Commission. In no other way would it be possible to keep such diverse groups together. (Clarke 1954:22)

But action did take place as a result of the J.P.C.'s activities:

> When the members agree upon the need for a study of a certain problem, the work is assigned to a special committee. When the report is completed it is reviewed and discussed by the members. The usual step is for it to be circulated—not as a report by the Commission but as a report prepared for the Commission. The J.P.C. takes no further responsibility itself. But if action is called for the lead is taken by the organization most concerned, in concert with all other groups who wish to and are able to take part.

The topics studied by the Commission over the years were many and varied. A small sample list includes the following:

Inter-cultural relations
Civil liberties
Labor and management in relation to the community
Professional personnel in adult education
Experimentation and research in adult education
Need for a National Commission for UNESCO

Broadcasting policy in relation to television
Censorship
Canadian distribution of U.N. publications
Distribution of program materials
Labor education
Education in correctional institutions
Retraining and employment

The J.P.C. is somewhat elusive in terms of efforts to define its accomplishments and operations. At the time she wrote her history and description of the project in 1954, Clare Clarke stated that there were then 120 organizations which took part in the J.P.C.'s meetings. She pointed out that many organizations sent the same representatives to each meeting and that over the years considerable friendship and confidence was built up within the group. As Corbett later summed up the accomplishment of the J.P.C., "it has made a friendly family of the organizations and the people who are at work in the field of adult education" (Corbett 1957:214). This made possible a quality of consultation and mutual reliance which was quite remarkable. The galaxy of agencies taking part in the J.P.C. was varied in nature and subject matter interest. The people attending, and the organizational resources behind them, were such that J.P.C. could call upon expert opinion and information sources of a great range and depth. As Clare Clarke pointed out in her study, the tasks undertaken by the J.P.C. of co-ordination and development were not unique, and neither were the principles which guided its actions. But the combination of the particular circumstances in Canada at that time and the skill of the leadership and staff work which went into the enterprise were such that it achieved a remarkable success story.

The CAAE had a delicate relationship to the J.P.C. The latter was a "standing committee" of the CAAE and the CAAE appointed the chairman annually. The cost of operating and staffing the J.P.C. was provided in the CAAE's budget, but the J.P.C. had a character of its own. "It is at once both a dependent of the CAAE, but as a new kind of informal association it leads a life apart from its parent body" (Clarke 1954:15). Although the CAAE was the parent body, during the meetings and deliberations of the J.P.C., the CAAE "does not take its place as the senior partner, but simply as one of the participating groups that both gives and receives help from its deliberations" (Clarke 1954:16).

In his history and description of the extension work of St. Francis Xavier University, Alexander Laidlaw included a preliminary chapter describing the field of adult education. He states that in the year 1954-55, "over 100" organizations took part in the J.P.C. and he categorized them as follows: (Laidlaw 1961:15)

Business and professional groups	15
Labor organizations	4
Churches	5
Government departments and agencies	18
Provincial departments of education	6
University extension	17
Voluntary organizations	49
Total	114

In the fall of 1955, the tenth anniversary meeting of the J.P.C. was held. On that occasion, "nearly 100" people were in attendance, including three "charter members,"

Corbett, Avison and Neil Morrison. The day consisted of historical addresses, a demonstration of film strips, the screening of two N.F.B. films, and a presentation by a panel of three outstanding figures from the press, Clifford Sifton, T.E. Nichols and W.B. Burgoyne (Anon 1956:184-5). One of the last J.P.C. sessions was held in late 1963, at which several of the senior members of the Royal Commission on Bilingualism and Biculturalism addressed the delegates. It was significant that the J.P.C. could attract such senior people to speak to its meetings.

The J.P.C. was disbanded by the CAAE in the early 1960s. The new Director of the Association, Dr. Alan Thomas, felt that it had served its purpose, was not attracting as many participants as it once had, and was in decline. Any judgment about the validity of this conclusion is made difficult by the fact that in the last few years of its existence, J.P.C. altered its modus operandi. Instead of holding three meetings a year, with a group of participants who tended to attend regularly, the pattern was established of holding less frequent meetings, each on a special topic. This procedure was seen as not working very satisfactorily and in the end, the J.P.C. was terminated by the CAAE. There is some opinion that what destroyed the effectiveness of the J.P.C. was the decision to depart from the established way of operating, which had supported and sustained the network of informal communication and action.

The J.P.C. was created at the instigation of a group of organizations whose mutual interests were in the field of adult education, broadly defined. The emphasis of its activities over the years was mainly in the areas of adult education, social and cultural development and as such, was embraced by the citizenship emphasis which was stressed by the CAAE beginning in the late 1930s. A demonstration of the ways in which the J.P.C. carried out its task is provided by this account by Ron Faris of its role with respect to the Massey Commission:

> When the Royal Commission on National Development in the Arts, Letters and Sciences was appointed on April 8, 1949, to examine and make recommendations on such topics as the principles of Canadian Radio and Television policy, government-voluntary association relationships, and Canadian relations with UNESCO, the CAAE and many of its J.P.C. partners sprang into action. The Secretary of the Planning Commission, Mrs. W.H. Clark [sic] subsequently recalled the role of the J.P.C. vis a vis the Royal Commission by describing the J.P.C. office as a kind of temporary information center on the work of the Royal Commission in that it answered innumerable inquiries, searched out relevant material and consulted with the organizations, many of whom needed encouragement as much as information. The report on Radio and Television Broadcasting "was completed in time to serve as a guide to member organizations preparing briefs for the Royal Commission." (Faris 1975:120; internal quote from Clarke 1954)

This provides a glimpse of a further "informal" dimension of the way in which J.P.C. "network" was of use to member groups, and was used to encourage efforts in support of political action. It was a further dimension of the adult education movement of the day, acting in what it saw to be the best interests of its society.

Advocacy Activity

The lobbying activities carried out by the CAAE during the Corbett years represent another manifestation of its citizenship activities. They involved adult educators speaking together on matters which they saw to be relevant to the interests of adult learners and adult education.

These activities have been well documented by Faris (Faris 1969; Faris 1975) and Armstrong (Armstrong 1968) in their studies of the period. The main briefs submitted during this period were:

1937 - to Rowell Sirois Commission
1944 - to Parliamentary Committee on Radio Broadcasting
1945 - to Ontario Royal Commission on Education
1945 - to Government of Canada
1946 - to Parliamentary Committee on Radio
1948 - to the Prime Minister
1949 - to the Massey Commission

The brief to the Rowell Sirois Commission advocated an expanded federal role in the field of education, offered the services of the CAAE in an advisory capacity and sought federal funds to support the CAAE. The briefs to the Government of Canada in 1945 and 1948 sought financial aid, on the earlier occasion for the Canadian Council on Education for Citizenship with which the CAAE worked closely, and in 1948, for the CAAE itself. The brief to the Ontario Royal Commission in 1945 put heavy stress on CAAE's role in citizenship education and sought a grant in support of the Association's work.

Two submissions on broadcasting policy, in 1944 and 1946, represented the continuation of Corbett's—and other CAAE members'—commitment to a broadcasting policy which gave priority to the public interest and the information and education function of broadcasting, over the private interest and private profit interests. In 1944, the CAAE joined with the Canadian Federation of Agriculture, its partner in Farm Radio Forum, in presenting a brief to the Special Parliamentary Committee on Radio Broadcasting. It spoke generally in support of the C.B.C., its performance and its role as both broadcaster and governor of the broadcasting system in the country, and referred particularly to the C.B.C.'s role in education for citizenship. In 1946, the CAAE appeared again before the parliamentary committee, this time appearing on its own. It had used its Farm Radio and Citizens' Forum mailing network to urge other groups to make representations as well, (Faris 1975:117) a step which led to some criticism in the committee hearings and in the parliamentary debates. Again, the CAAE in its brief strongly supported the principle of public ownership and control of broadcasting and praised the C.B.C. for its efforts in citizenship education. It urged the committee to support the C.B.C. in both its regulative and operating functions (Estall 1946).

The most ambitious submission made by the Association to any such body was that presented to the Massey Commission on National Development in the Arts, Letters and Sciences, in July of 1949. The Association's journal, *Food For Thought*, frequently carried editorials and information notes about the Commission while it was at work. It had welcomed the creation of the Commission (Anon 1949) and stressed the relationship of its areas of concern to adult education. Reference has been made already to the use of the J.P.C. network to encourage responses from other organizations as well. The CAAE's submission consisted of 35 closely typed pages and covered a lot of ground. Among other matters touched upon, it sought financial support from the Federal Government for the Association; supported once again the performance of the C.B.C. and defended the existing arrangements under which the C.B.C. both ran its own operations and controlled the whole system—recommending a similar arrangement for television, which was on the horizon; strongly supported the National Film Board and described further work in the film field which it should be funded to undertake; and supported the creation of a National Commission for UNESCO (a cause CAAE had been promoting through *Food For Thought* and the J.P.C. for some time) (Clarke 1949). Borrowing from the language of its 1946 declaration, the submission stated that, "the CAAE believes the task of adult education is the imaginative training for citizenship." It also said that "the destiny of adult education (and of Canadian democracy itself) is intimately connected with the way in which we manage our media of communication" (CAAE 1949:2). The two statements combined represent a form of summary of Corbett's work and views.

The Report of the Massey Commission, which appeared in 1951, gave some grounds for satisfaction in the CAAE. It was a landmark document in terms of cultural policy in Canada (Ostry 1978:64) and it placed the CAAE and its major adult education projects (making several references to them) in the context of the nation-building process. In this sense it supported the philosophical position of Corbett and others with respect to the basic mission of adult education. The two Forum projects were praised by the Commission as "rewarding and distinctive Canadian programs" which "are of great value in making better citizens of us, in that they awaken our critical faculties" (Report 1951:37). The activity of the J.P.C. was also commended for its role in promoting co-operation among voluntary associations and between voluntary and government agencies (Report 1951:74-5).

Summing up the Corbett Years

Ned Corbett led the CAAE from what the founders had foreseen, a clearing house body, to one which placed its chief emphasis on education for citizenship, through direct programming. Corbett was in the liberal democratic tradition and his view of education as it related to social action and change was to place the issues, with relevant information, before the people, leaving them free to choose the most appropriate course of action. The initial steps in moving the CAAE into citizenship education were taken before the war, but with the onset of World War II, this tendency was accelerated, and in association with other agencies in the same field, the C.B.C. the National Film Board, the Wartime Information Board, the Canadian Council on Education for Citizenship and the Canadian Federation of Agriculture, the CAAE moved more vigorously and effectively into education for social change. In the midst of the war, at a time typified by a considerable body of radical thinking about reconstruction planning, the CAAE produced, in the 1943 Manifesto, a fairly radical statement of its goals and beliefs, the day having been carried by a relatively small number of the more doctrinaire figures in the counsels of the Association. And for at least twenty years thereafter, the CAAE was in some quarters seen as being a left-leaning organization. But by the end of the 1940s, the more radical leaders in the CAAE had given up on the organization and it continued in the hands of leadership which was committed to the idea of education for citizenship, but not as a means of producing a particular social policy. Corbett was a liberal democrat, but in the interests of producing a dynamic organization, he gave reign at times to some of the more radical figures interested in the organization (Armstrong 1968).

Further perspective on Corbett's leadership and the course of action pursued by the CAAE is provided from two other sources. The first is an article by S.A. Wunder which appeared in the *New York Times* in 1941 and was reprinted in *Food For Thought* in December of that year. The author described the striking contrast between the American national adult education body, which he saw to have retrenched in the wartime period, and the CAAE, which had taken on additional wartime responsibilities and whose program and activities were expanding rapidly (Wunder 1941:15-16). In his memoirs, published in 1980, Robert England, who was working in Western Canada during the early years of the CAAE, saw at the time a related contrast between the two organizations. He had seen something of the work of the American organization:

> Its work was on a high plane and somewhat remote on occasion. Our new Canadian Association for Adult Education, while it emulated the older sister organization, had in Ned Corbett as its director a "grass roots" practitioner of the art of adult education. (England 1980:68)

In his view, Corbett kept the CAAE in close touch with the rest of the field of practice— more a part of the field rather than just a service organization for the field.

The central themes which are clearly identifiable in Corbett's leadership of the CAAE are citizenship education, rural adult education and Canadian nationalism. The Forum projects, the J.P.C., the publications program and the other joint activities with the several other closely related organizations are clear evidence of his concern for all three areas. The period of his directorship of the CAAE, from the mid-thirties through the war and into the post-war world, were exciting years for Canadians. The struggles of the depression, the remarkable achievements of Canadian industry and armed forces during the war, and Canada's emergence as a leading middle power in international affairs in the years after the war were the basis for a new sense of Canadian identity and pride. Few, if any, Canadian leaders, outside of government, played a more central and significant role during this turbulent period in helping Canadians come to a new sense of what it meant to be a Canadian than did Ned Corbett. He molded the CAAE into an effective and flexible instrument to that end.

References

Allen, R. (1975), *The Social Passion*, Toronto: University of Toronto.

Andrew, G.C. (1967), "What's Past is Prologue," *Continuous Learning*, (Hereafter, *CL*, 6 (1): 5-15.

Anon. (1940), "Conference on Education for Citizenship," *Food For Thought*, (Hereafter *FFT*), 10: 12-13.

———. (1940a), "Workers' Education," *FFT*, 5: 18-19.

———. (1941), "Learning and—What Next?," *FFT*, 12: 3-12.

———. (1941a), "Community Life Training Institute," *FFT*, 11: 15-16.

———. (1941b), "The New Editorial Policy," *FFT*, 2 (1): 3-4.

———. (1943), "Education for Reconstruction," *FFT*, 4 (2): 11-13,22.

———. (1947), "Trade unions and Democracy." *FFT*, 7 (5): 4-9.

———. (1949), "Brief Summer," *FFT*, 10 (2): 2-3.

———. (1949a), "Joint Planning," *FFT*, 9 (7): 2-3.

———. (1950), "National Conference on Adult Education," *FFT*, 11 (1): 1-8.

———. (1951), "The CAAE and Social Action," *FFT*, 12 (1): 8-9.

———. (1951), "Massey Commission," *FFT*, 12 (8): 1-2.

———. (1956), "Joint Planning Commission," *FFT*, 16 (7): 327-30.

Armstrong, D.P. (1968), *Corbett's House: The Origins of the Canadian Association for Adult Education and its Development during the Directorship of E.A.* Corbett 1936-51, Unpublished M.A. Thesis, University of Toronto.

Avison, H. (1943), "New Directions in Adult Education," *FFT*, 4 (2): 10-18.

———. (1945), "Wanted: A Layman's Movement," *FFT*, 5 (6): 32-3, 45.

———. (1947), "New Developments in the CAAE." *FFT*, 7 (4): 17-18, 34.

Bothwell, R. and Kilbourn, W. (1979), *C.D. Howe: A Biography*, Toronto: McClelland & Stewart.

Bovey, W. (1950), "Canadian Legion Educational Services," in J.R. Kidd (1950), 216-20.

Brittain, W.H. (1943?) "The Role of the CAAE," Typescript, CAAE files.

Canada Department of Manpower and Immigration (1974), *Canadian Open Adult Learning Systems*, Prince Albert.

CAAE (1950?), "Questions and Answers about Adult Education in Canada," Toronto: CAAE.

Canadian Citizenship Council (1948), *From Immigrant to Citizen*, Ottawa: C.C.C.

Chapman, E. (1947), "Learning Community Living," *FFT*, 7 (6): 9-12.

———. (1950), "The Women's Institutes," in Kidd 1950, 210-15.

Clarke, C. (1949), "What Kind of Commission?," *FFT*, 10 (3): 27-31.

———. (1954), *The Joint Planning Commission*, Toronto: CAAE.

Coady, M.M. (1939), "Adult Education in Action," *Adult Learning* (hereafter *AL*) 3 (5): 2-6.

———. (1939), *Masters of Their Own Destiny*, New York: Harper and Bros.

———. (1950) "Mobilizing for Enlightenment," in Kidd 1950, 198-203.

Corbett, E.A. (1937), "Foreword," *AL*, 2 (1): 1-2.

———. (1939), "The Canadians March," *AL*, 4 (1): 5-12.

———. (1942), "Agriculture Looks to the Future," *FFT*, 3 (4): 7-11.

———. (1944), "The Soldiers are Saying," *FFT*, 5 (1): 4-8.

———. (1944a), "Post-Invasion, Pre-Peace," *FFT*, 5 (1).

———. (1945), "Adult Education and the Schools," *FFT*, 5 (6): 4-10.

———. (1946), "The Canadian Association for Adult Education." *Canadian Education*, 1 (2): 98-102.

———. (1947), *A Short History of Adult Education*, Toronto: CAAE.

———. (1950), "What Can We Do?," *FFT*, 11 (2): 1-4.

———. (1953), "Farm Forum Twelve Years After," *FFT*, 13 (6): 15-18.

———. (1957), *We Have With Us Tonight*, Toronto: Ryerson Press.

———. (1959), "Dr. M.M. Coady: A Tribute," *FFT*, 20 (1): 34-36.

———. (1961), "Harry Avison," *FFT*, 21 (7): 292-97.

Dilworth, I. (1951), "The Image of Canada," *FFT*, 12 (1): 9-10.

Dunlop, W.J. (1936), "Editorial," *AL*, 1 (1): 3-4.

———. (1936), "Adult Education in Canada," *Bulletin*, The World Association for Adult Education, 11 (5): 1-11.

England, R. (1980), *Living, Learning, Remembering*, Vancouver: University of B.C. Centre for Continuing Education.

Estall, M. (1945), "After the W.I.B.—What?," *FFT*, 6 (3): 9-12.

———. (1946), "We Speak our Piece on Radio," *FFT*, 7 (1): 20-23.

Faris, R. (1975), *The Passionate Educators*, Toronto: Peter Martin.

Feir, D.L. (1940), *A Survey of Adult Education in Canada*, Unpublished M.A. Thesis, University of Alberta.

Ferguson, G. (1967), "E.A. Corbett: Adult Education in Canada," *CL*, 6 (1): 21-24.

Fletcher. B.A. (1939), "Growing Points in Adult Education," *AL*, 3 (4): 2-7.

Friesen, J., and Parsey, J. (1951), *Manitoba Folk Schools: The First Ten Years 1940-1950*, Winnipeg: King's Printer.

"G.G." (George Grant?) (1944), "Citizen's Forum," *FFT*, 4 (8): 15.

Gaynor, M.F. (1948), "Education for New Canadian, *FFT*, 8 (4): 12-15, 28

Gelley, T.F. (1949), "Khaki University," *FFT*, 9 (7): 29-34.

Granatstein, J.L. (1975), *Canada's War: The Politics of the MacKenzie King Government 1939-1945*, Toronto: Oxford University Press.

Grant, G. (1943), "Citizens' Forum—So Far," *FFT*, 4 (3): 20.

Gray, C.W. (1973), *Movies for the People*, Montreal: N.F.B.

Grierson, J. (1944), "Searchlight on Democracy," *FFT*, 4 (7): 4-9.

——. (1945), "Education in a Technological Age," *FFT*, 5 (9): 4-8.

Haas, A. (1941), "A Folk School in Ontario," *FFT*, 2 (1): 15-17.

Hannam, H.H. (1936), "The Cape Breton Experiment: A Bird's Eye View," *AL*, 1 (2): 4-11.

Harman, L. (1939), "An Experiment with a Folk School," *AL*, 3 (5): 11-13.

——. (1943), "A Citizens' Forum on Canada in the Post-War World," *FFT*, 4 (2): 14-15, 23.

——. (1944), "Adult Education and the Farm Movement," *FFT*, 4 (6).

Kelly, T. (1970), *A History of Adult Education in Great Britain*, Liverpool: Liverpool University Press.

Kidd, J.R. (1948), "The Canadian Citizenship Council," *FFT*, 8 (4): 16-20.

——. (1950), *Adult Education in Canada*, Toronto: CAAE.

——. (1950b), "Present Developments and Trends," in Kidd 1950, 11-22.

——. (1952), "A Kind of Partnership," *FFT*, 13 (1): 4-7.

——. (1963), *Learning and Society*, Toronto: CAAE.

Knowles, M. (1977), *A History of the Adult Education Movement in the United States*, Huntington: Robt. E. Krieger.

Laidlaw, A. (1961), *The Campus and the Community*, Montreal: Harvest House.

——. (1971), *The Man from Margaree*, Toronto: McClelland Stewart.

Lotz, J. (1973), "The Antigonish Movement," *Studies in Adult Education*, 5 (2): 97-112.

——. (1977), *Understanding Canada*, Toronto: NC Press.

MacInnes, C.M. (1950), "Canadian Adult Education in 1925," in Kidd 1950, 4-21.

——. (1929), *Adult Education in the British Dominions*, London: World Association for Adult Education.

McLeish, J.A.B. (1978), *A Canadian for All Seasons*, Toronto: Lester and Orpen.

Morrison. J.H. (1943), "Editorial," *FFT*, 4 (2): 3.

——. (1945), "The Winnipeg Conference," *FFT*, 5 (9): 1-3.

Ostry, B. (1978), *The Cultural Connection*, Toronto: McClelland and Stewart.

Peers, F.W. (1969), *The Politics of Canadian Broadcasting*, Toronto: University of Toronto.

Ritchie, C. (1974), *The Siren Years*, Toronto: MacMillan of Canada.

Sandiford, P. (Ed.) (1935), *Adult Education in Canada: A Survey*, Toronto: University of Toronto.

——. (1937), "Editorial," *AL*, 1 (4): 2-3.

Sim, A. (1944), "School for Community Leaders," *FFT*, 5 (2): 19-23.

——. (1945), "Patriotism is Enough If...," *FFT*, 6 (1): 20-24.

Smith, S. (1943), "The President's Address," *FFT*, 3 (10): 5-8.

Thomson, W. (1943), "The London Conference," *FFT*, 3 (10): 9-11.

——. (1945), "Adult Education—New Model," *FFT*, 5 (4): 4-8.

Vlastos, G. (1943), "Education for Morale," *FFT*, 4 (3): 4-8.

Wilson, I. (1980), *Citizens' Forum: Canada's National Platform*, Toronto: Ontario Institute for Studies in Education.

Wunder, S.A. (1941), "Adult Education Gains in Canada," *FFT*, 2 (4): 15-16.

Young, W.R. (1978), *Making the Truth Graffic: The Canadian Government's Home Front Information Structure and Programs During World War II*, Unpublished Ph.D. Dissertation, U.B.C.

Originally published in *Occasional Papers in Continuing Education,* University of British Columbia Centre for Continuing Education, No. 20, 1981. Reprinted with permission.

3.2

Roby Kidd and the Canadian Association for Adult Education 1951 - 1961

*I*t is a sad fact that when I started the work on this monograph, Roby Kidd was alive—and I talked and corresponded with him about it on several occasions—but during the course of its preparation, he died, on March 21, 1982. It is likely too soon to attempt an assessment of his life and contributions to the field, but the present study deals with his work while Director of the Canadian Association for Adult Education some twenty to thirty years ago and there has been time to gain some perspective on that period. The task took on new significance and poignancy following his death.

I am grateful to a number of people for their assistance and co-operation with this project. In addition to Roby Kidd himself, I have received help from his wife, Margaret; his long-time colleague and successor at the CAAE, Alan Thomas, who supplied information on several points; Ian Morrison and his colleagues at the CAAE, who made records and minute books available; and my colleague, Jindra Kulich, whose encouragement and editorial advice have been invaluable, as always.

Sources of information for this study have been of four main types: information from individuals, including Kidd himself; the minutes, records and reports of the CAAE for the period; the journal published by the Association; and the writings of Kidd himself. In addition, a number of general works in the field have been called upon.

References which could be handled in the usual way are included in the text and listed at the end. References to the minutes of the Annual Meetings (AM), the National Council (NC), the Executive Committee (Exec.) and the Director's Reports (DR) are listed with these abbreviations and the appropriate dates. The Association's journal, *Food For Thought*, is referred to as *FFT*.

This monograph is dedicated to Margaret Kidd.

The Times

The period during which Roby Kidd was a senior staff member (1947-51) and then Director (1951-61) of the Canadian Association for Adult Education was an eventful one in the life of Canada. These were times of growth and dramatic change in social, cultural, economic and political terms.

The post-war years were a buoyant period of economic growth for Canada, with government playing a leading role (Bothwell and Kilbourn 1979). The mid-Fifties, especially 1954 to 1957, were boom years. The population was growing rapidly, a result of both high birth rates and a high rate of immigration. The Canadian economy was becoming more closely integrated with those of other countries, especially the United States (Creighton 1976:186). In 1957, the long period of rapid economic growth came to an end and a recession set in which lasted into the Sixties. Unemployment rose to between six and seven per cent of the work force, unprecedented levels in the post-war period (Bothwell et al 1981:222).

The year 1957 was a time of change politically as well as economically. In that year the long period of Liberal domination in national politics under the King and St. Laurent governments came to an end with the victory of the Conservatives, under John Diefenbaker. Faced with economic problems and other crises at home and abroad, and actively pursuing the goals of the new leader, the Conservative government was "actively interventionist" in its approach to national development (Bothwell et al 1981:264) and introduced a number of measures which had direct effects on adult education and the role of the CAAE. Concern about American domination of Canadian life in many of its dimensions came to the fore in this period as well and tensions between the two countries were if anything heightened by the actions of the Diefenbaker government.

Two factors contributed to an increased concern at this time about vocational and technical training. All the Western countries were taken aback when in October of 1957 the U.S.S.R. successfully launched the first global satellite. This had considerable impact in economic and educational circles and heightened concern about the effectiveness of education systems generally and more particularly the technical capacity of the work force. The sharp recession and attendant high unemployment which struck in the late 1950s focussed attention on the need for training and retraining of the work force, especially those who were unemployed. In 1960, the Diefenbaker government produced the Technical and Vocational Training Assistance Act, which provided funds on an unprecedented scale for vocational and technical training institutions and programs in the provinces. One authority has stated that a total of 538 capital projects were approved under the Act in the first three years of operations alone, 265 of which were totally new institutions (Bothwell et al 1981:259).

This was a lively period in Canadian cultural development. Canada emerged from the Second World War with a new sense of national pride and self-awareness. The Canadian Broadcasting Corporation and the National Film Board developed rapidly and gained in stature in these years, both achieving international recognition for their outstanding achievements. Many Canadians took interest and pride in such events as the founding of the Stratford Shakespearean Festival in 1953. The Report of the Massey Commission in 1951, rightly termed "a watershed in Canadian cultural policy" (Ostry 1978:63), sounded alarm bells about the extent of American domination of Canadian culture and led to the eventual creation of the Canada Council and the National Commission for UNESCO in 1957. The arrival of television in 1952 introduced a powerful new dimension for entertainment and education and had a major impact on adult education.

Of particular relevance to education also was the fact that this was the period in which the political initiative began to shift from the federal to the provincial governments. Although the more spectacular dimensions of this development may not have taken place until later, during the days of the Pearson government, certainly in the area of social policy the provinces had taken over the initiative by the mid-Fifties. St. Laurent and his colleagues saw the need for a new accommodation with the provinces and the election of the Liberals in Quebec in 1960 was an important stage in the development of new movements in terms of provincial rights and regional interests.

The late Forties and Fifties were dramatic times from the point of view of Canada's international role. This period was the high point of Canada's position as a leading middle power on the world scene. Both the St. Laurent and Diefenbaker governments were active in support of the United Nations and its international police actions and also in foreign aid and technical assistance to developing nations. The Suez crisis of 1956 was a matter of sharp controversy at home and abroad, and Lester Pearson won international recognition for his leadership in that connection. This was also a period of sharp Cold War tensions and Canada played an active part in NATO, in the Korean War and other crises.

These years have perhaps accurately been characterized as a "sober and conventional" period compared to the Sixties (Creighton 1976:245), but it was also a time for the most part of vibrant growth, and for many it was an exciting time to be a Canadian. With the pipeline debate crisis of 1956 and the victory of the Conservatives in 1957, Canada moved from a period of relative calm on the political front to a "new era of doubtful, contentious politics" (Bothwell et al 1981:191).

Priorities and Assessment

When Roby Kidd took over the leadership of the Canadian Association for Adult Education (CAAE) in 1951, the organization already had established an enviable reputation as an outstanding national organization in the field. The story of the contributions of E.A. Corbett, the charismatic founding Director whom Kidd succeeded, and of the Association, through such internationally recognized programs as National Farm Radio Forum, Citizens' Forum and the Joint Planning Commission, are well known and have been described at length elsewhere (Corbett 1957; Armstrong 1968; Faris 1975; Selman 1981).

The Association had been established in 1935, largely by leaders from the universities and government, and the intention of the founders was that it be a national clearing house and information centre for the field, a servant of the institutions and increasing number of practitioners across Canada. However, as a result of the leadership of Ned Corbett and the conditions created by the outbreak of the Second World War and the reconstruction period which followed, the CAAE was transformed from what had originally been intended to a direct programming agency. Instead of a service agency to the emerging adult education establishment, the CAAE became an active provider of citizenship education. For a brief period in the early-to-mid 1940s, in the yeasty early days of reconstruction thinking, the Association took a stand itself on particular social and political issues. Although this action gained the Association some criticism, the somewhat radical manifesto of 1943 was soon replaced with a more moderate declaration of principles in 1946. From this point on the Association was committed to "the imaginative training for citizenship" (the words of the 1946 Declaration), but took no positions itself on the issues of the day, other than submissions to government bodies on matters clearly related to the interests of adult education and the adult learner.

Corbett himself was a remarkable leader of the Association. He had long experience in adult education before taking over the CAAE, had originally trained for the ministry, was strongly in the "social gospel" tradition, and a liberal in political philosophy. He was an attractive and vigorous person, with an outstanding capacity for forming friendships and working relationships with an astonishing range of people, including many leading figures in business, government and other educational and social agencies. He was a gifted creator of projects and skilled at developing productive relationships with others, and nowhere were these talents demonstrated more successfully than in the creation of the two Forum projects, the Joint Planning Commission and other citizenship education activities carried out by the CAAE during his years as Director. With the retirement of Corbett in 1951, the Associate Director of the Association, Dr. Roby Kidd, who had been on the staff for four years, was appointed to take his place. Roby Kidd grew up in Western Canada during the depression years and had worked for the Y.M.C.A. in Montreal and Ottawa before studying for a doctorate in adult education at Columbia University. His masters thesis at McGill University had been a biographical study of Dr. H.M. Tory, the institution builder in higher education in Canada (and promoter of adult education), and his doctoral dissertation was about education for citizenship and the Canadian Council on Education for Citizenship (CCEC), to which he expected to return in a paid capacity on the completion of his doctoral studies. The organization ceased to exist while Kidd was away, however, and Kidd was recruited instead, in 1947, to the staff of the CAAE, his chief task to direct the affairs of the newly-created Joint Planning Commission. Hiring Kidd had been suggested to Corbett by an officer of the Carnegie Corporation, from which Corbett had sought a grant in support of the establishment of the J.P.C. (For the first year of his employment with the CAAE, Kidd spent half his time in Ottawa, finishing up some projects for the by-then-defunct CCEC.)

Kidd was 32 years old when he returned to Canada to join the staff of the CAAE and 36 when he became Director. He was a quiet and friendly person with a quick and ready sense of humor. Like Corbett, he had a great capacity for forming friendships. He respected as a colleague anyone who was working in the field of adult education, in however humble a capacity, and people with whom he came into contact were attracted—and heartened— by that sense of comradeship which he displayed. He was a lively companion and enjoyed the company of others, especially on a one-to-one basis, or in small groups. He was not a particularly eloquent or dramatic speaker, but he always prepared carefully and people appreciated the professional skill and integrity, imagination, humanity and humor always evident in his presentations. The warmth of the man came through most effectively in smaller groups and personal conversation.

Kidd was a prodigious worker. How he accomplished all that he did was a mystery to his colleagues. He never took a holiday, in the normal sense of the term, but there was much change of activity in his professional life, and that may have helped. He was a sports fan, played and coached various games in his youth, and would take some time out from work occasionally to watch or listen to a game.

Kidd was a friendly and generous-spirited person who liked most other people, and most of them liked him. And he worked effectively with many persons for whom he had no particular affection. He did not have a very high toleration level, however, for people he judged to be mean-spirited or who in any way seemed to deny the potential of others for growth and development. Kidd had a strong sense of the mission of adult education and of the potential significance of the CAAE and other associations for whose welfare he was in any way responsible. There were a very few people in adult education whom he judged to be unduly negative, untrusting or destructive, for whom he developed negative feelings, which were often reciprocated. These were a very few exceptions to the general situation. The overwhelming number of people who knew Kidd admired his capacity, enjoyed his company and worked easily with him.

Kidd was a different style of leader than Corbett had been, although he had many of the same sympathies. He was no less a Canadian nationalist, but increasingly as the years went by, he supported and became involved in international contacts and projects. Like Corbett, he strongly supported the development of the arts in Canada. And like Corbett too, he had a capacity for relating to a wide range of people and winning their loyalty and affection. The most striking difference, perhaps, between his leadership and Corbett's arose from the fact that he had received advanced professional training in adult education, being the first Canadian to earn a doctorate in that field. This tempered his approach to the field as a whole and also made it possible for him to contribute—which he did more than any other person—to the advancement in Canada of adult education as a field of study and professional training.

Kidd was a pacifist at the outbreak of the Second World War, when he was 24 years old, and at first did not wish to participate in any way. As the war went on and the issues became clearer to him, he tried to arrange participation in a non-combat role, but he could not find an opportunity which seemed to him more important than the work he was doing for boys and young men in the Y.M.C.A. Kidd was involved in human rights activities all his adult life, but during his years at the CAAE, although actively engaged in this work, he kept it quite separate from his role in the Association.

Kidd had many of the same social and political convictions that Corbett, Coady and other leaders of the field had demonstrated. But for two main reasons, he manifested them differently. He saw, for one thing, the needs of an emerging professional group of adult educators and realized that the goals of that group would have to be less overtly political than the CAAE's had been in the previous period. Secondly, there was by the 1950s a wave of conservatism in North American society which made an overt left-of-centre image a distinct liability in seeking support and attaining one's other goals. Kidd was a practical leader of organizations and projects and he was sensitive to the winds which were blowing. He was not afraid of controversy, but he chose his ground carefully.

The change in the political climate had been abundantly clear to Kidd before he assumed the directorship of the organization. In the context of his J.P.C. duties, he had had to deal with strident conflict of views over broadcasting policy and other issues. More telling were the series of conflicts which surrounded Farm and Citizens' Forum in the closing years of Corbett's directorship (see Faris 1975), some of them spearheaded by James Muir, the President of the CAAE itself. Kidd spoke to these matters directly in his first Director's Report to the Association in 1952:

> This year we have been subjected to criticism in pretty equal doses from all parts of the compass and all parts of Canada. We have been castigated on many counts, from the ads we have accepted in *Food For Thought* up to policy decisions of the Executive Committee. (Kidd 1952b:5)

Kidd pointed out that anyone dealing with "bread and butter questions affecting the daily lives of Canadian people" could not expect to be immune from criticism "because of good intentions." He went on to point out, perhaps especially to the more activist members:

> But an organization like ours has bounds and limitations which we must recognize. It is not and by its nature cannot be the radical agency of social action which some of you might prefer. Nor can it be a research agency only—simply observing and reporting facts. Our work cannot be done in splendid isolation; we must stay close to where groups are living and working. The CAAE is concerned about the welfare of, but cannot be the mouthpiece of, the farmer, the union member, the housewife, the business man. (Kidd 1952b:5)

In the same way that Kidd cautioned the organization against seeking to pursue a partisan course of action, he was inclined at a personal level to speak in eclectic and inclusive terms about educational philosophies, rather than make strong personal statements in the Corbett style. He was fond of quoting Gandhi's statement:

> I do not want my house to be walled in on all sides and my windows to be stuffed. I want the cultures of all lands to be blown about my house as freely as possible. But I refuse to be blown off my feet by any.

For Kidd, this applied to educational philosophies as well. When in 1950, he published the first comprehensive book about adult education in Canada, his section on "A Working Philosophy for Canadian Adult Education" drew on the 1943 and 1946 CAAE statements and the words of both social activists and the more traditional liberal education point of view, active citizenship being the common element (Kidd 1950:24-39).

Although Kidd seemed, in a paper prepared in 1975, to accept the Faris thesis (Faris 1975) that in the post-war period adult education became less concerned than previously with social change (Kidd 1975:260), this would not be a fair conclusion to draw with respect to Kidd himself. This may be one reason why he was drawn to the international dimensions of the field, the Third World generally seeing adult education as a means of social change. The English statesman, George Canning, said in a speech in 1826 (following his use of the Monroe Doctrine in the European power politics game), "I called the New World into existence, to redress the balance of the old." In a way, Kidd did the same thing, helping to draw in the ethos of adult education in the developing countries, where it was closely associated with social and political goals, to offset the tendencies towards disinterested professionalism which he saw emerging in Canada and North America. Kidd also pointed out in his 1950 book that foreign visitors to Canada had a strong sense of adult education in this country being a movement, with a "sense of shared purposes" (Kidd 1950:13). It is significant that Kidd perceived this, and clear from his language that he took some pride in it. In the period of Kidd's directorship, the early stages of professionalization and institutionalization of the field of adult education in Canada were developing, and at an accelerating pace. No one contributed more to that trend than Kidd himself. But at the same time, no one gave more effective leadership in the direction of avoiding the negative aspects of professionalization.

In some respects, the Kidd years at the CAAE can be seen as a transitional period. It was one in which the social movement tradition in Canadian adult education was being tempered by an emerging professional ethic. Adult education—at least as it was reflected in the CAAE—was to some extent losing the sense of identity which it had derived from taking a stand on some social issues and was still in the process of reformulating its objectives in response to the outlook of a more professionalized field.

Citizenship education, in the broad sense in which the term is being used here, continued to be a central feature of the CAAE's work during the Kidd years. In his first annual report as Director, Kidd spoke of the network of partnerships with other organizations on which the CAAE relied:

> This concept of the CAAE as a partnership, in fact and in the making, working with many organizations and interests towards the goal of responsible citizenship, is an essential key to an understanding of this report. (Kidd 1952b:4)

The standing of the CAAE in this field was revealed when in 1953 the Citizenship Branch of the federal government held a national seminar on citizenship matters. Attendance was by invitation and at least 12 of the 88 attending, including Corbett, Kidd and Clark of the CAAE staff, were prominent figures in the CAAE. Most of these persons also gave papers at the meeting. The recommendations of the seminar recognized the efforts of the CAAE in citizenship education and urged the Citizenship Branch to work with and support the meritorious CAAE projects (Citizenship Branch 1953).

In early 1954, the Association's journal published an article by Rev. Moses Coady, according it warm editorial support. It included a strong statement in support of the citizenship education function of adult education:

> Education is the key that unlocks life to man in organized society. Adult education is the mobilization of all people, including those who are today poor and illiterate, for continuous learning. It is based on the conviction that people should not be allowed to float down the river of events—that positive, purposeful effort should be put into the business of guiding them up the rushing streams of progress. They should come under their own power, of course. It is the work of educational institutions to organize them to do this. (Coady 1954:4)

In his report to the twenty-first anniversary annual conference of CAAE in 1956, Kidd returned to the theme of citizenship education, saying that adult education is "a basis, perhaps *the* basis, for responsible citizenship." He stressed that the Association "must always be found...in the thick of life's urgencies and its passions" (in *FFT* 17:1:13).

In 1960, towards the end of Kidd's term as Director, a bilingual pamphlet on *Adult Education in Canada* was published jointly with CAAE's French language counterpart, the ICEA. Under the heading of "Aims and Objectives," the purposes of adult education were stated in a form which gave primary emphasis to citizenship, very much in the same vein, and using some of the same words as the 1946 CAAE declaration (CAAE/ICEA 1960:4-6).

Kidd's leadership of the CAAE consistently gave emphasis to the citizenship education function and tradition of the organization. He was supported in this effort by Gordon Hawkins, who served as Assistant Director of the Association from 1955 to 1959. Hawkins had come from England to the Extension Department of The University of Alberta, and thence to the CAAE. He was in the tradition of English adult education which placed particular emphasis on the importance of liberal education and the social and political relevance of adult education. He was an eloquent speaker and talented writer and organizer and gave strong leadership to the liberal and citizenship education activities of the Association, as well as to its general administration and organizational development.

Shortly before joining the staff, Hawkins commented in an article in *Food For Thought* on what he saw to be the leading characteristics of adult education in Canada and the CAAE's role, compared to the situation in Britain:

> [In Canada] the concern is more with what one might call the "community" aspects of adult education. Partly this is a consequence of geography and time. With newly formed and changing communities, with immigrant groups, with the awful challenge of distance, methods and aims are bound to be different. But there is also a newer, consciously evolved philosophy of adult education. It stems from a deep concern with the processes of democracy—with how the individual and the group and the community work, as much as with what they set out to achieve. Hence the emphasis in their scheme of things on group work, community organization, discussion methods and techniques, leadership courses and so on, and, as a background to all that, on the use of the mass media to spread a common basis of information for their discussion and their social actions. The Canadian Association for Adult Education [is] the prime mover and clearing house in this work....(Hawkins 1954:2)

Throughout the Kidd years, the Association continued its leadership of its major citizenship education projects, Farm and Citizens' Forum and the Joint Planning Commission, carried out many other programs in the citizenship education field, often in association with the Canadian Citizenship Council and/or the Citizenship Branch of the federal government, and promoted informed citizenship through the Commission for Continuous Learning and the National Commission on the Indian Canadian. Education for citizenship, in the broad sense of the term, remained, as it had under Corbett, the core of the CAAE's work.

Another of Kidd's priorities was the improvement of practice in adult education. With his considerable experience as a practitioner and his advanced training from the most highly regarded graduate school in his field, Kidd had both the knowledge and the credibility which enabled him to provide effective leadership. His efforts towards the improvement of practice took two main forms—the advancement of research and professional training, and experimentation with new forms of organization, methods and materials.

Kidd's contributions to the development of professional training for adult educators are described in some detail below. The need for professional competence in the field, for something a great deal beyond idealism concerning the potential role of adult education in Canadian society, was a theme which Kidd almost invariably addressed himself to in any review he made of the general state of the field. He once described his concern about the state of professional strength and competence in the field as his only "serious apprehension about the future" of adult education (CAAE DR 1956). He spent a great deal of his time teaching training courses for adult educators, both degree credit and non-formal activities, counselled many in the field concerning their further training and career development, and especially in the latter years of his directorship, helped to increase the capacity of the Association and its library as an information centre and clearing house for research activities.

The Association carried out many projects in these years which aimed at improving practice by experimenting with and demonstrating new forms of organization, new media and new kinds of learning materials. The American foundation, the Fund for Adult Education (F.A.E.), financed some of these activities, including the study-discussion group experimental work conducted by Alan Thomas in the mid-Fifties and the substantial program conducted by the Commission for Continuous Learning and its successor, Living Library, in the later years of Kidd's tenure. The Citizenship Branch of the federal government made possible several projects of this kind also, some devoted to general citizenship matters and some to the needs of recent immigrants. In association with its allied organization, the Joint Planning Commission, the CAAE did a great deal of work facilitating the exchange of program materials among organizations and also promoting the educational use of television, which arrived on the scene in Canada early in the decade. Workshops about the use of television were held in all parts of Canada, with the co-sponsorship of local or provincial organizations.

Kidd also attached priority to helping adult education serve more effectively a number of special groups in the population. His efforts related both to the affairs of the CAAE itself and to the field as a whole. He worked actively with the labor movement, giving a great deal of time to teaching at union-sponsored courses. He was anxious that the CAAE not become the preserve of professional educators and it was due to his influence that two business leaders became President of the organization during his time as Director. He worked hard to strengthen ties with allied fields such as communications and the arts, using the Association's annual Henry Marshall Tory Award and working relationships cultivated through the J.P.C., as well as other means of continuing contact. In these ways, as well as that of establishing standing committees of the Association on such areas as business and industry, labor, the mass media, and governments and school boards, he sought to relate the CAAE's activities to important interest groups.

Beyond the affairs of the CAAE itself, Kidd was one of the earliest voices in the field calling for more effective service by the adult education enterprise to certain neglected groups. Such ideas became a prominent feature of the scene in the next decade and beyond, but one is struck, when reviewing Kidd's work in the Fifties, and that of the Association as a whole, with the leadership role which was played in this important area. Although the Diefenbaker government began to look into these matters in the late Fifties, the War on Poverty and other consciousness-raising activities of the mid-Sixties were still several years ahead. But throughout the Fifties, Kidd, and some others in the Association, were expressing concerns, developing specialized programs and drawing public attention to the special needs of older persons, women, single parents, immigrants, prison inmates and native people.

One of the most striking features of Kidd's leadership was his involvement in international dimensions of the field. His clear commitment to international contacts and assistance appeared early in the decade in the form of assistance in the Caribbean, the CAAE campaign for the creation of a UNESCO Commission in Canada and Kidd's increasingly frequent contacts with UNESCO and other international bodies. His eight-month technical assistance mission in the West Indies in 1957-58 gave Kidd further experience in the problems of developing nations and increased the confidence with which he carried out his international role. His scholarship became increasingly well known abroad. This, plus his increasing ties with UNESCO, his chairmanship of the Adult Education Committee of the World Confederation of Organizations of the Teaching Profession, and most of all, his spectacularly successful leadership of the World Conference on Adult Education in Montreal in 1960, established Kidd by the end of the decade as perhaps the best known adult educator in the world.

But Kidd's priority task in these years was developing the CAAE into an ever-more useful servant of and participant in the adult education movement. His growing prominence, at home and abroad, brought credit to the Association, as did his scholarship and publications. His unusual ability to raise funds for worthwhile projects helped to increase the effectiveness of the Association and expand its work and staff. He attracted a number of especially talented persons to the staff of the Association and to leadership positions in its policy and executive bodies.

Kidd had his critics within the Association, as all directors did. As in the case of almost all organizations which cannot support themselves out of fees from their membership, there is an inherent contradiction in their affairs. On the one hand, the membership expects to direct the activities of the association and establish its priorities. On the other hand, so long as the director is left to raise much of the money, especially for the main projects, he must go where he finds the money to be, often along the lines of his own priorities and enthusiasm. In such a situation, there is a danger of the membership, and even the policy-making bodies, coming to feel that they are not in effective control. Kidd was not a by-the-book administrator and was not always able to keep his National Council fully informed. Most colleagues understood that the director must be given his head and freedom to follow up on opportunities which appeared. And most of those involved in the Association's affairs were fond of Kidd, respected and admired his accomplishments, and both understood his situation and were willing to "overlook" occasional lapses in communication. But there were a few who could not accept Kidd's style, or were not willing to do so, and who became alienated from him and the Association.

By and large, however, Kidd's leadership of the Association and his many personal accomplishments as scholar, teacher, organizer and international leader, increased the CAAE's effectiveness and worked to the benefit of both the Association and the movement as a whole. He was a man of many parts, with a prodigious capacity for work and an unusual ability to relate to and attract the admiration of others. His contributions to adult education and to the CAAE were impressive, but complex, and not readily summarized. He contributed substantially to the professionalization of the field but retained the sense of movement and was effective in attracting many from other fields of interest into the circle of the CAAE. He cared deeply about and contributed significantly to the social and cultural development of his country but also brought the CAAE and many Canadian adult educators into participation in international developments. He valued highly the strengths of the established CAAE projects, the Forums and the J.P.C., but also pioneered important new program initiatives. He believed that a strong CAAE had important contributions to make but also encouraged regional and provincial organizations. He was a leader of adult education at a world level but he found time to spend hours in his office with a new recruit to the field, welcoming him to the family of adult educators and challenging him with its hopes and potential.

In a monograph in which he described the three World Conferences on adult education (Kidd 1974), Kidd used a quotation from *All's Well that Ends Well*, in referring to the field:

> Our doubts are traitors
> And make us lose the good we oft might win
> By fearing to attempt.

Part of Kidd's success as leader of and advocate for adult education was his deep belief in its importance and his confidence in fighting for its interests. A man who worked closely with Kidd in these years, Walter Herbert (who was the longtime chairman of the J.P.C.), has said that during Kidd's time studying at Columbia, he rubbed shoulders with American leaders and the officers of some of the large foundations and that he learned "to think big about adult education" (Herbert 1959:14). Kidd constantly tried to persuade his Canadian colleagues of the richness of Canada's accomplishments in adult education and of the field's rightful claim for more substantial recognition and support. In the introduction to one of Kidd's pamphlets, published early in the Fifties, the writer stated that it was "recommended reading for pessimists" (Kidd 1953c:4) because of the life, promise and challenge reflected in it. The same may be said of Kidd himself. He thought big about adult education and he invited others to do so as well.

The CAAE 1951-1961—Organization

Administration and Staff

The CAAE went through a period of very considerable growth and development during Kidd's years as Director. He was anxious that it not become tied in only with the educational institutions of the country, as much as he valued those associations, and he made considerable efforts to engage people from many parts of society in the work—business and industry, organized labor, government services, other professions, and voluntary organizations—as well as from the field of education. During the decade of Kidd's directorship, of the five presidents of the Association, two were businessmen (J. Muir and W.R. Carroll), two were university presidents (R.C. Wallace and N.A.M. MacKenzie) and one an adult education administrator (and by this time a Senator), Donald Cameron. Of the chairmen of standing committees in 1958-59, for instance, committees concerned with aspects of practice were all chaired by professional educators and of the remaining twelve, five were chaired by persons other than educators. Soon after Kidd took over as Director, with the assistance of the President, an experienced businessman, a more adequate pension and fringe benefit package was arranged for the staff (CAAE NC Nov. 24, 1951; Exec. Jan. 10, 1952). The Association's offices, at 143 Bloor St. West, Toronto, had become increasingly overcrowded and were moved to more spacious quarters at 113 St. George Street.

Finances were a constant concern, as always, for the Association. The Finance Committee, chaired for most of the period by H.H. Edmison, did steady service in securing and maintaining donations from corporations, provincial governments and individuals. The budget of the Association more than tripled in the Kidd years and there was a deficit—a modest one—in only one year, 1957-58, when he was away in the Caribbean. Membership campaigns were carried out from time to time, and membership was maintained at a fairly satisfactory level, but memberships did not help the net financial picture. On the program side, Kidd was very successful in raising funds for projects. During this period it was two American foundations—Carnegie and the Fund for Adult Education—and departments of the federal government, most notably the Citizenship Branch, from which he raised the largest amounts. Kidd gained the reputation, beginning in this period, of being a wizard at raising money. He always maintained that it was simple enough. Perhaps one key to his success was the fact that he and the CAAE earned the reputation of achieving a great deal on slender resources. Kidd told close colleagues that he had been told by an American foundation executive that the CAAE could do more with a dollar than any other organization he knew of. Most grants, however, were used up mostly in paying out-of-pocket costs, with only modest amounts, if any, to cover any administrative overhead. What made the system work as well as it did was the fact that in some of the major grants, Kidd built staff time (mainly his own) into the projects to be carried out. He frequently "sold" his time several times over for such projects, which was fine so long as he could deliver. This he did, by virtue of prodigious effort and productivity (and to a lesser extent, that of some of the other professional staff). A review of his major writing accomplishments alone during this decade is very impressive. When it is remembered he also ran the organization, taught a great deal, and travelled widely in Canada and abroad—the record is truly to be wondered at.

The size of the staff of the Association grew considerably during the period, and included some remarkably able people. Corbett did some consulting work, on a retainer fee, for a short time after his retirement. Throughout, there was the National Secretary of Citizens' Forum, Isabel Wilson, and the editor of *Food For Thought*. Six different persons served in the latter capacity during the decade. Clare Clark took over staffing the Joint Planning Commission when Kidd became Director and retained it until she became president of the Commission on the Indian Canadian in 1957. Alan Thomas was on staff as a program officer from 1953 to 1955, largely to carry out demonstration work under a grant from the F.A.E.

In the middle of the decade, expanded revenue (much of it from project grants) made possible an increase in the staff. The most notable addition of the period was the hiring of Gordon Hawkins as Associate Director in September, 1955, a post he held until April, 1959. Hawkins was a fine organizer, a gifted speaker and writer (he was an outstanding "permanent" chairman of Citizens' Forum broadcasts for a time) and complemented Kidd and his abilities very well.

Hawkins filled in ably for Kidd when the latter was on leave in the West Indies for most of the 1957-58 year. Another most valuable addition in 1955 was Diana Ironside, who served as librarian and information officer until 1957, when she expanded her work to include the J.P.C. (for a brief period) and some other projects. Other able staff joined the Association for briefer periods—Peter Martin and Catherine McLean to staff the Commission for Continuous Learning and Living Library, respectively; Muriel Jacobson, who took over the J.P.C. and staffed other projects; and John Melling, who was on staff briefly as Director of the Commission on the Indian Canadian, until it became an autonomous body in 1960. In late 1960, Arthur Pigott joined the staff as assistant to the Director and when Kidd left in April of 1961, Pigott served briefly as Director, until replaced by Alan Thomas in the fall of 1962.

Regional Developments and Structure

The organizational structure of the CAAE remained basically the same during the Kidd years, but some modifications were made to accommodate regional and provincial interests, and by the early Sixties, major changes were on the way. In this respect, perhaps the affairs of the CAAE anticipated developments in the larger society, with the emergence of regional and provincial claims, which became so prominent in the Sixties.

The constitution of the CAAE, as is customary with voluntary associations, vested ultimate control over its activities in the membership, as expressed by ballot and at the annual meetings. Between annual meetings, policy matters were directed by a National Council (NC). At first, it was simply left to the good judgment of the nominating committee and the membership to see that there was satisfactory representation from across the country on the NC, but soon after Kidd became Director, he urged that more deliberate provision be made in this regard and at the annual meeting in 1951, the size of the NC was increased and a formula written into the constitution whereby the NC would be made up of 24 persons from the Central Provinces, 16 from the Atlantic region and 16 from the West (CAAE AM April 27, 1951). Between meetings of the NC (which normally met three times a year) the affairs of the Association were managed by a small Executive Committee, the Director and staff.

One of the most important developments during Kidd's time, and an aspect of the work to which he gave vigorous leadership, was the emergence of regional and provincial organizations of adult educators. There had been a few relatively short-lived organizations of this kind in the earlier years—one in Winnipeg in the mid-Thirties (Selman 1963:230), in Ontario and the Eastern Townships of Quebec in the early Forties (*FFT* 1:5,19 and *FFT* 2:3, 18-19) and in Alberta beginning in 1943 (Bercuson 1944), but by the late Forties no such organizations were functioning. Because of the growth of the field across the country, and the increased numbers of institutions, programs and personnel involved, it was decided in late 1950 to begin the policy of holding national conferences of CAAE on alternate (even numbered) years and to promote the holding of regional meetings in the years in between (CAAE Exec. Nov. 4, 1950). The aim was, by means of such regional meetings, to provide in-service development opportunities for adult educators in the regions and to promote the general development of adult education in those areas as well. There was no intention at the outset of promoting the development of provincial or regional organizations, just to provide periodic opportunities for meetings at the regional level.

As it turned out, organizational developments were quite different in the two regions, East and West. (There was one Ontario region conference during the period, but apparently the national meetings and conferences of the CAAE generally met the needs of the region.) In the Atlantic provinces, regional conferences were held every second year throughout the decade, but no provincial organizations resulted. In the West, provincial adult education bodies were formed, and there was discussion about a Western regional organization as well, but as in the Atlantic region, all that happened on the regional level was the formation of planning committees for the biennial conferences.

The first regional conference under CAAE auspices was held at Amherst, Nova Scotia, in June of 1951. (There is record of a "Maritimes Conference on Adult Education" in Saint John in March, 1939, but it was apparently not sponsored by the CAAE (*FFT* 16:7, 300).) Referred to as "the first Atlantic Region Conference" (Anon 1951:32), the meeting in 1951 dealt largely with the co-ordination of efforts among the agencies represented. Two years later, in June of 1953, a four-day regional meeting was held at Antigonish, attended by more than 200 delegates. A booklet describing the work of many agencies in the region had been prepared since the previous conference and was distributed at this second meeting. The program dealt with a variety of professional concerns and with the general development of the region. There was reference in the report to the "incoming executive" of the conference, and certain tasks were referred to it for action, but there was no indication of the range of its activities (Timmons 1953). The third conference, held in Charlottetown in 1955, focussed mainly on the economic development of the region (Anon 1955). In contrast to the somewhat parallel series of meetings which took place in the West at this time, there was little if any attention given in the Atlantic region to the CAAE as an organization, or to the relationship of the region or the provinces to the national organization. Indeed, in reporting to the national Executive in December of 1956, Gordon Hawkins indicated that whereas the West was pressing for structural changes in the CAAE, the Atlantic region was not (CAAE Exec. Dec. 6, 1956), and early the following year, he reported in the same terms to the National Council (CAAE NC Jan. 5, 1957).

The fourth regional meeting was held in Sackville in June of 1957 and was devoted to community development and its impact on the region (Jones 1957). Although there was no evidence of it in the subsequent account of the conference printed in *Food For Thought*, some thinking was apparently going on in the region about organizational structure. At a founding conference of an Alberta organization of adult educators held in May of 1957, Hawkins stated that whereas the West was moving in the direction of provincial organizations, the Atlantic region was likely to have a regional body (Minutes in O.I.S.E. files). There was a fifth regional conference held at Bathurst in June of 1959, but organizational matters were apparently not discussed (Kidd 1959:45).

Although the regional conference scheme was established in 1950 and the Atlantic region held its first conference the following year, the Western provinces did not get going until 1953. Kidd had indicated to the Executive of the CAAE the previous year that some people in the West were thinking of a "Western Council on Adult Education" (CAAE Exec. April 16, 1952). Two months before the first Western conference, Kidd informed the NC that there was interest in the West (B.C. was mentioned particularly) in the formation of provincial bodies which would be linked to the national organization (CAAE NC Mar. 7, 1953), and at a further meeting held just days before the first Western conference, he indicated that committees had been established to study "organization in the provinces" (CAAE NC May 19, 1953).

The first Western Regional Conference was held in Banff in May, 1953. Resolutions from the meeting dealt with professional training and other matters and endorsed the idea of further such meetings (Anon 1953). One recommendation called for study of "co-ordination of educational policies and programs in the provinces and in local communities" (Selman 1969:3-4). Not recorded in the report but significant in the light of future developments was the fact that at the Banff meeting, the suggestion was discussed among some B.C. delegates that a provincial adult education organization be formed in that province (Selman 1969:3). These plans materialized in the fall of 1954, when following an organizational meeting in September (which was addressed by Kidd), the first semi-annual meeting of adult educators in British Columbia was held in December (Selman 1955; Selman 1969). (These semi-annual conferences continued on a regular basis until the early Sixties, organized on an ad hoc basis until 1957, when the B.C. Adult Education Council was established as the organizing body.) A similar meeting was held in Manitoba in 1954 as well (CAAE NC Jan. 22, 1955). The Western regional conference in 1955 was held in Saskatoon in May and the program dealt mainly with aspects of social and community development. A strong resolution was passed in support of arranging professional training experiences for adult educators (Anon 1955a). In an article which appeared in the CAAE journal late in the year, Selman indicated that there was some support in B.C. for the idea of a "provincial counterpart" of the CAAE, and ultimately, "a provincial division of the CAAE" (Selman 1955:124). Such a development was still some six years away.

The following year, 1956, was a year for the national conference. The NC, at its meetings in January and June, discussed the regional developments. Kidd had prepared for the January meeting a "Memorandum on Regional Participation in the Management of CAAE", which outlined a number of possibilities for more effective liaison with the regions, including opening regional offices, appointing a travelling staff member who would spend time in each region, appointing more regional representatives to the NC, and regional J.P.C.s or divisions of CAAE. These suggestions were discussed at the two meetings (CAAE NC Jan. 28 and June 10, 1956) and at the national conference. The report on the latter which appeared in *Food For Thought* indicated that some of these alternatives had been discussed and stated that "it was evident that strong regional organization was just in the beginning stages" (Hawkins 1956:8). In the fall of the year, the regular semi-annual conference in B.C. decided that something more in the way of organizational structure was required for their purposes and established a committee to make recommendations in that connection, instructing it as well to look into the relationship between any such organization and the CAAE. Hawkins reported to the national Executive in December (having met with the Western region conference planning committee shortly before) that those in the West wanted some change in relationships with the regions (CAAE Exec. Dec. 6, 1956). A committee was appointed to look into the various dimensions of the issue.

The year 1957 was one of considerable regional and provincial activity. In January, the NC indicated its clear willingness to be responsive to regional wishes, deciding to consider "the basis for regional and other types of representation on the National Council, with a view to making any changes that may be necessary" (CAAE NC Jan. 5, 1957). In February, Gordon Campbell, Director of Adult Education for the Government of Saskatchewan, who had earlier sent to Kidd, Hawkins and several other people in the Western provinces some suggestions about the possible form a Western regional organization might take, circulated to these same people the responses he had received from them all (Corresp. dated Feb. 18, 1957 to author, et al). The responses were mixed, many calling for further discussion of the matter at the upcoming regional conference, and several saying that provincial organization should be given preference over regional dimensions. In early May, all four Western provinces held adult education conferences, B.C.'s and Manitoba's being the latest in their regular series and the other two being the first such provincial meetings, certainly in recent years (Selman 1957).

These meetings were then followed by the third Western regional conference, which dealt mainly with organizational matters. It was here that a model for provincial organizations was developed, which delegates from the several provinces were invited to take back to their own provinces for possible application. In terms of the relationship between the provincial bodies and the CAAE, the meeting examined two alternatives. One involved the provincial bodies being affiliated with the national organization and, the other that the CAAE members in each province elect the NC members representing their area. What would be involved in affiliation was spelled out in some detail by the meeting. In structural terms, the two essential elements were that the provincial organization be responsible for the nomination of those from their region running for membership on the NC, and that the provincial body itself be entitled to name its own representative on the NC (CAAE 1957). These suggestions formed the basis for the subsequent constitutional amendments put into effect by the CAAE.

Careful and detailed consideration was also given at this meeting to the possible form of a Western regional organization, and the matter was referred to the next meeting. Shortly after the regional meeting, Hawkins reported its conclusions to the national Executive, which approved the suggestions in principle and appointed a committee to draw up corresponding changes in the constitution (CAAE Exec. June 8, 1957). These were duly approved at the annual meeting in May of 1958 (CAAE AM May 23, 1958) and as a result, formal recognition was provided in the CAAE structure for the role of provincial or regional affiliated organizations. (A representative of a provincial body attended a NC meeting for the first time in February, 1959.) This arrangement remained the basis of the relationship with the provinces until 1959. At the Western regional conference in that year, most of the time of the meeting was devoted to organizational matters. Thinking in the region had progressed further by this time and concern was now expressed that there was no CAAE presence in the provinces. It was pointed out that although provincial organizations, which were of a consultative, informal nature, performed certain local functions adequately, they were not able to carry out advocacy activity on behalf of the field or to raise funds or solicit memberships on behalf of the CAAE. After consideration of this problem, the conference approved a recommendation whereby the persons in each province who were members of the NC of the CAAE would be constituted as a provincial executive of the national organization and carry out functions at that level on behalf of the national body (CAAE 1959:14). This recommendation was accepted by the CAAE and a few months later, Kidd indicated to the Executive that the Saskatchewan group had already met (CAAE Exec. Sept. 8, 1959).

Although no further change in the relationship between the CAAE and the provincial or regional organizations was made in the years while Kidd was Director, change was very much in the air by the time he left. At the annual meeting in 1958, both Selman and Thomas from B.C. raised the prospect of creating chapters or divisions of the CAAE at the provincial level (CAAE AM May 23, 1958). Ever alert to thinking in the regions, Kidd suggested to the national Executive that it appoint a committee to keep the whole matter under review, and this was done (CAAE Exec. Sept. 8, 1959). The next major initiative came in the spring of 1961 from the B.C. organization. At its thirteenth semi-annual conference, which was at the same time a preparatory meeting for the national bilingual conference to be held in Ottawa in the fall, the B.C. group adopted the report of a committee which had been chaired by Alan Thomas and which proposed the abandonment of the B.C. Adult Education Council in favor of the creation of a provincial division of the CAAE. The latter would be an integral part of the CAAE, not an affiliated body. In the end, the CAAE accepted this proposal for provincial divisions. The process thus begun was not completed until long after Kidd had left the Association, preliminary discussions taking place in the fall of 1961 at the national conference and the necessary constitutional amendments being given final approval by the CAAE annual meeting on June 2, 1962 (Selman 1969; Selman 1980).

Of particular interest in connection with all these developments was the role played by Kidd and his colleagues at the national office. Kidd had stated:

I think the record will show that the national office and staff and Executive were always in favor of and encouraging local organization but did not set out conditions under which it should happen, leaving that to local planners and negotiation. (Letter to author Aug. 26, 1969)

Kidd and his associate for part of the period, Gordon Hawkins, were back and forth across the country a great deal attending almost all regional meetings and many provincial ones. They were in a position to report developments first hand to the national body and the record indicates that they consistently supported the necessary adjustments in CAAE procedures or constitutional arrangements so as to facilitate the changes desired in the regions.

The CAAE 1951-1961—Program

Farm and Citizens' Forum

National Farm Radio Forum and Citizens' Forum were creations of the pre-Kidd period and were already well known internationally by the time Kidd became Director of the Association. In his introduction to Adult Education in Canada, published in 1950, E.A. Corbett stated that at the World Conference in Denmark the year before, "every English-speaking delegate" was familiar with "the new techniques in radio education developed through National Farm Radio Forum" (Kidd 1950:xi).

In terms of the affairs and apportionment of resources of the Association, the two Forum projects lost something of their dominance during the decade. Kidd believed in their importance, an aspect of his strong sense of the centrality of citizenship education as a function of the field, but it was only natural that as new programs and new goals for the Association appeared, they should claim attention. This trend is made quite obvious, for instance, from a review of Food For Thought over the decade. In the early years of the Fifties, every issue had pages devoted to news about the Forum programs. By the end of tlhe decade, it was the exception when something about them appeared. Both programs were by the end of the decade in a period of decline, and their years were numbered.

National Farm Radio Forum was the older of the two programs and the best known. After his retirement from the directorship, Corbett was still active on behalf of the Association and one assignment he took was representing it on the Board of Farm Forum. Farm Forum was a special favorite of Corbett's and this was a congenial arrangement. Because of the involvement of the Canadian Federation of Agriculture in the management of Farm Forum, there was an independent governing board; it was not an integral part of the CAAE in the same way that Citizens' Forum was. It was perhaps at least partly for this reason that in the latter years of the decade, news of Citizens' Forum appeared more frequently in the Association's publications than that of Farm Forum. The period of the Fifties was for the most part one of continued relatively high level of activity for Farm Forum, but there was a gradual decline in the number of listening groups. The highest level of activity preceded Kidd's years as Director; in 1948-49 there were 1,600 listening groups, with approximately 30,000 members (Ohliger 1967:42). In the early Fifties, the number of forums hovered between 900 and 1,000 (Anon 1952; Wilson et al 1954). By 1957-58, the figure was down to 772 and the following year to 600 (CAAE DR's). In 1958, considerable efforts were made to reverse the trend, but although initial results were encouraging, the decline set in again (Ohliger 1967).

Farm Forum engaged in a broader range of activities than did Citizens' Forum. Its publication, *Farm Forum Guide*, had many features in addition to background information about the week's program topic, including such things as news of activities undertaken by groups in their local cormnunities. Indeed, there are those who argue that the decline and eventual termination (1965) of the national program were not an indication of failure but rather a sign that many of the groups had become preoccupied with local development tasks and had gone on to other things.

One significant event of the decade was the commissioning by UNESCO in 1951 of a study about Farm Forum, the purpose of which was to make the project widely known in the international community, for possible application in the developing countries. UNESCO put $16,000 into the project and other funds were raised elsewhere (CAAE Exec. Nov. 23, 1951). The volume was prepared by Alex Sim, the pioneer of the project in Canada, and was published in 1954 under the title *Canada's Farm Radio Forum*. Farm Forum, along with the extension work of St. Francis Xavier University (the Antigonish Movement) were perhaps the best known Canadian adult education projects in the international movement.

Citizens' Forum continued to operate throughout the decade as well, but on a declining scale, as far as the number of organized listening groups was concerned. Having reached a high of 1,215 groups in its first year and 800 the next (1944), the number declined until it stood at 400 for several years in the late Forties and early Fifties. Decline set in again during the Fifties (Wilson 1980: 28). In 1953, there were 315 groups functioning and the following year the number dropped off to 200. Television had begun on a national scale in 1952 and the system got up to full production the following year. It was felt that if Citizens' Forum was to continue to attract an audience (which went far beyond the organized listening groups), it would have to go on television as well. This move was not wholeheartedly supported by everyone involved. The radio version became just the audio of the televised broadcast, and the length was reduced to 30 minutes (from the traditional 45) in order to conform to the requirements of the television schedule. The broadcast in its first year was moved out of prime time, to the 10:00 to 10:30 time slot, too late for its use in the usual way as a discussion starter for listening groups, and then moved to Sunday afternoons. Provincial input on the broadcasts, which had been used to promote the formation of groups and maintain a network of communication among them, was eliminated with the reduction to a half hour broadcast (Wilson and Stinson 1957; Anon 1958c).

By the end of the 1958-59 season, there were only between 40 and 60 discussion groups functioning and it was decided to do away with the provincial offices for the program, which were located in university extension departments and some other centres across the country (and run on a part-time basis as part of the host organization's program, at no charge to the CAAE). The television version was clearly reaching a larger audience than radio had, and the volume of mail from listeners about the programs had increased greatly, but the broadcasts now mentioned only the national office and the number of listening groups did not justify maintaining the provincial offices.

In 1963-64, after many trials and experiments with format, and increasing signs of lack of interest in the arrangement with the CAAE on the part of the C.B.C., Citizens' Forum lost even its longstanding title, which was changed to "The Sixties," and the radio version was converted to an open line show, the precursor of "Cross Canada Checkup."

The program had thereby been changed out of all recognition and for all practical purposes ceased to exist.

Such a short treatment leaves out of account a great range of experimental and special activities during the period—broadcasts from community meetings, variations in program format, dramatic presentations, etc. Of importance too were the pamphlets which were produced on the topic of every program, year after year, under the general editorship of Isabel Wilson. These pamphlets were often the first study materials created on what, over the years, became an amazingly wide range of public issues facing Canadians, and not only were they important to the functioning of the program at the time, but as time goes by they become an increasingly interesting reflection of concerns of Canadians throughout the life of the project.

In the early years of Citizens' Forum, there were several controversial incidents, involving a cast of characters ranging on different occasions from Liberal cabinet members, to right wing elements, to representatives of business interests—including on one memorable occasion in 1951 the President of the CAAE itself (the President of the Royal Bank of Canada). These disputes have been described elsewhere at some length (Faris 1975:104-08, 134-50). It is sufficient to note that dispute centred around the balance of spokespersons who were selected to represent various points of view on the broadcasts, and occasionally on the way in which issues were dealt with in the pamphlets. Considering the fact that the very essence of Citizens' Forum was to deal with controversy, it is not surprising that there were occasional "incidents" and it is a credit to the skill of all those involved that there were in fact so few.

Joint Planning Commission

It is likely fair to say that the Joint Planning Commission had a special place in the heart of Roby Kidd. When he joined the staff of the CAAE in 1947, his chief assignment was to act as the founding executive secretary of the project and he saw it through its formative years, relinquishing the task when he became Director of the Association in 1951. The origins of the J.P.C. have been described elsewhere (Clark 1954; Selman 1981:26-33). It was an imaginative approach to voluntary co-ordination and consultation at the national level among agencies—public and private—concerned with adult education, social and cultural development. The biographer of John Robbins, a co-founder of the Commission along with Ned Corbett, has called it an instrument of "the social growth of Canada" (McLeish 1978:103).

The J.P.C. was active throughout Kidd's years at the CAAE. There was a regular pattern of three meetings a year, usually in Toronto, Ottawa and Montreal, through which programming and publication plans were exchanged and significant issues studied and debated. Meetings were attended by representatives of more than a hundred government departments, crown corporations, voluntary, church, business, labor, health and welfare, cultural and of course educational organizations. A report on J.P.C. "membership" given to the National Council in 1955 contained the following breakdown of the participating groups:

Business and Professional Groups	15
Labor Unions	4
Churches	5
Government Departments and Agencies	18
Provincial Departments of Education	6
University Extension	17
Voluntary Organizations	49
Total	114

It was further stated that of those organizations, 75 were making some contribution to the CAAE in the form of donations or grants (CAAE NC Jan. 26, 1955).

The J.P.C. was not a "membership" organization in the normal sense; this would have been awkward for some of the organizations, especially the public agencies. Organizations simply took part on a regular basis if participation was useful to them. The J.P.C. was staffed by the CAAE, which was at the same time the organizer and one among equals as a participant. The J.P.C. was not a social action body. It was understood that no organization, by virtue of its participation in the J.P.C., would be committed to social action measures. However, many organizations, singly or in co-operation with others, did take action on issues, at least partly on the basis of insights and information gained through the J.P.C.

Topics discussed at the regular meetings ranged far and wide. They included such as the following: retraining and employment, human resources and Canada's expanding economy, television policy, French Canada, policy with respect to Native people, the role of the press, channels and bottlenecks in organizations, UNESCO's educational activities, labor education, problems affecting Canadian families, the work of national cultural institutions, and issues as broad as "significant trends in Canadian national life."

Apart from the regular meetings of the Commission and the discussion of topics such as the above, special activities of other kinds were carried out as the need arose. Task forces were created from time to time to carry out studies on subjects of interest to a number of the members. Matters studied in this way included the marketing of U.N. publications in Canada, film services, censorship, the distribution of program materials, radio and television broadcasting and labor education. Reports on these studies were made to the J.P.C. when completed, often providing the basis for a full session of the Commission. Another type of special activity was carried out in the early days of television broadcasting in Canada. In the summer of 1953, the J.P.C. organized a six-day workshop on the educational use of television, bringing together people from educational institutions, voluntary organizations, churches, labor, broadcasters and government agencies. A briefer version of this program was made available to all member agencies, and a modified version was offered in several Canadian cities, in co-sponsorship with local agencies (Clark 1954:21; Wilson 1980:89). In addition, the J.P.C. organized for several years awards in the fields of film making and broadcasting, to recognize outstanding achievement by Canadians in those fields.

When the original grant from the Carnegie Corporation, which had made the organization of the J.P.C. possible, ran out in 1949, Carnegie was appealed to again and a further $22,500 was made available, not for general administration this time, but for special projects and experiments which grew out of the work of the Commission.

The J.P.C. did not long survive the change of leadership in the Association after Kidd left, being disbanded two years later. By any standard, the J.P.C. was a highly successful venture. It succeeded where many such organizations had failed. The J.P.C. was the subject of study by many visitors from elsewhere in North America and abroad (Clark 1954) and is generally considered to be one of Ned Corbett's major contributions to the field and one of the CAAE's and Canada's significant achievements in adult education. Corbett and others created it. Kidd was a key figure in making it work successfully.

Study-Discussion Programs and the Fund for Adult Education

Funds for program activities, as for everything else at the CAAE, were always in short supply. The main body of the CAAE's activities did not involve direct service to adult learners. As Kidd put it on one occasion, "we are a national organization working with and through others" (CAAE DR 1956). The two Forum projects were in some respects exceptions to this, as were a number of demonstration projects which were undertaken from time to time. During the Kidd years, much of this demonstration work was made possible by grants from an American foundation, the Fund for Adult Education, which was a subsidiary of the Ford Foundation.

Throughout Kidd's years as Director, he was able to secure funds, for various purposes, from the F.A.E. In the summer of 1951, Kidd engaged in successful negotiations with the F.A.E. and he placed before the Executive in September an outline of various projects which would be carried out under a series of grants from that organization, the "Learning for Living" pamphlet series being the outstanding item. The Executive approved the proposals (CAAE Exec. Sept. 10, 1951). More detailed information is available from the minutes of the National Council meeting later in the fall, where it is reported that the CAAE had been asked to "try out groups in Canada to evaluate the effectiveness of a film-discussion series on democratic ideas" and that funds had been secured to publish seven pamphlets (CAAE NC Nov. 24, 1951). In the December issue of *Food For Thought*, a preliminary list of topics and authors was provided, only some of which turned out to be accurate in the end (Anon 1951). A further grant of $5,000 was secured from the F.A.E. in 1953 to finance the remainder of the series (CAAE Exec. Jan. 14, 1953) and these are discussed elsewhere.

In the late 1940s, stemming from experimental work in the United States, there was a strong upsurge of interest in the small group as a setting for adult learning. Although much of that early work concentrated particularly on the functioning of the group itself— "group dynamics" or "group development" as it was often referred to—it led to a heightened interest in the small group as a setting for various types of education. The Fund for Adult Education took an interest in this matter and in the late Forties began to finance the development of study materials which were suitable for such groups, through such organizations as the Great Books Foundation and the American Foundation for Political Education. In Canada, small group study activity was already a familiar part of the scene. The two CAAE-C.B.C. Forum projects relied on discussion in small groups and the well known Antigonish Movement sponsored by St. Francis Xavier University had also depended on small group study. In 1947, Corbett of the CAAE and Coady of St. Francis Xavier published a jointly prepared series of six "principles of adult education," one of which was "that adult education functions most effectively through group study and group action" (Corbett 1947:12). Because of the considerable experience and reputation of the CAAE in the management of programs involving small group activity, it was presumably not difficult to convince the officers of the F.A.E. that the CAAE was a suitable partner for some of its programs involving that method.

However, it appears that the prospect of getting funds for testing the discussion series, which had been mentioned in the fall of 1951, did not materialize at that time. Late in 1953, Kidd reported to the Executive that a grant of $12,000 had been secured from the F.A.E. to finance an experiental discussion project and that Alan Thomas had been employed to carry out the work (CAAE Exec. Nov. 3, 1953). In the subsequent year and a half, Thomas organized and supervised demonstration groups which followed one of three different programs which had been underwritten by the F.A.E. The courses were generally known as study-discussion programs, the participants being required to read materials in advance of the session and then to come together and discuss them, under the leadership of a person who usually was not expert in the subject matter, but had been given some training in the leadership of such group discussion. The experimental work was carried out in several centres in Ontario and in Montreal. The three courses involved were: World Affairs are Your Affairs (based on a series of nine films), Ways of Mankind (involving recordings and readings) and World Politics (based on readings alone). There was liaison with the Great Books program, which had been launched in Canada two years before and involved similar methodology, but had its own separate organizational arrangements involving the public libraries. The groups which participated in the project were organized by Thomas through agencies such as the Y.M.C.A., community centres, unions and educational institutions. Thomas acted as a discussion leader for many of the groups, assisted by others. The film series was used with several local groups, but in addition, was broadcast over television station CFPL in London, Ontario, with discussion groups appearing on the broadcast, as well as participating at home. Thomas reported on the project to meetings of the National Council during 1954 and early 1955 and in May of that year he left to do further graduate study at Columbia University (CAAE NC Jan. 16, May 26, 1954; Jan. 26, May 3, 1955). The groups which took part in the demonstration were involved in evaluation of the courses at their conclusion (Hawkins 1956:28; Thomas 1957).

In the meantime, Kidd had advised the National Council in January of 1955 that further grants from the F.A.E. were a possibility (CAAE NC Jan. 26, 1955). In early June he announced that a grant of $35,000, to be received over three years, had been secured for the purpose of promoting further work in the field of study-discussion courses in the liberal arts for adults and also for what was termed "stabilizing the foundations" of the CAAE (CAAE NC June 7, 1955). Six months later, Kidd told the Council that a new unit had been formed within the CAAE, the Commission for Continuous Learning, which would organize the work under the grant, and that Peter Martin had been employed to direct the project (CAAE NC Dec. 6, 1956). Thus began a project which continued until the summer of 1961 (changing its name to Living Library and limiting its functions somewhat in 1960) and involved the CAAE in a long-term demonstration project, the development of Canadian courses and the general promotion of study-discussion courses in the liberal arts.

Under this project, the CAAE prepared, or commissioned, several study-discussion courses based on Canadian materials. Among these were: On Canada's Agenda, which utilized kinescopes of Citizens' Forum broadcasts; Canada in Folk Music; West Indies

Today; Canadian Plays and Playwrights, Shakespeare Seminar, including seeing plays at Stratford; Canada-U.S. Relations; Understanding French Canada; and a series on NATO. In addition, the project continued to use programs such as Ways of Mankind and World Politics, which had been developed elsewhere.

The CAAE project also acted as a sort of clearing house for several other organizations in Canada which were running study-discussion courses in the liberal arts, including the Thomas More Institute of Montreal, the North Toronto Y.M.C.A., Saskatchewan House in Regina and the Extension Department of U.B.C. Courses developed by the CAAE or elsewhere in Canada were made available to all these Canadian centres by means of this network and representatives of these several centres met from time to time.

Detailed information on the extent of the work carried on under this project is not available, but in December of 1958, towards the end of the work under the three-year grant, Martin reported to the Executive that some 35 to 40 groups had been helped to form and that he expected the total to reach 60 by the spring (CAAE Exec. Dec. 5, 1958). The three-year grant from the F.A.E. ran out in 1959, and by the fall of that year Martin had left the project and the work was reduced to an information service about the courses available (CAAE NC Nov. 12, 1959). Early in 1960, however, a long-time friend of Kidd and the CAAE, Kurt Swinton, arranged for his company, Encyclopedia Britannica, to provide $5,000 to strengthen the work. Catherine McLean joined the staff on a part-time basis to head up what was now named Living Library. In the May-June issue of *Food For Thought*, the chairman of the CAAE committee responsible for Living Library published an article describing the study-discussion method and the work of the project. The goals were listed as promoting study-discussion, facilitating the training of leaders and building up an inventory of courses. He stated that there were "some twenty" packaged courses available in Canada and estimated that there were "perhaps 150 groups now active, including 65 Great Books groups" (Baker 1960:370). The article indicated that there were plans to hold a weekend seminar "in chief centres across the country" in September of 1960 to promote interest in the project. Other sources indicate that the project also received support from the Citizenship Branch, Ottawa, during 1960, for the creation of program materials about citizenship, and from the UNESCO Commission for materials related to the UNESCO project on "East-West Cultural Values" (CAAE NC June 4, 1960; Jan. 20, 1961).

This project came to an end in the fall of 1961, as soon as Kidd had left the CAAE. Having run out of grant funds for the work, the chairman of the committee came to the Executive asking that $7,000 be made available out of the Association's budget so that a part-time staff person could be employed to continue the work. He was turned down on the grounds that the project involved direct service to the learner, which was said not to be the role of the organization, beyond the terms of a demonstration (CAAE Exec. Sept. 22, 1961).

There was one further major project of the CAAE which was supported by the F.A.E. For at least four years, 1957 to 1960, the foundation made $15,000 available annually which was used to support the in-service development of adult education workers. The grants were usually referred to as travel grants or funds for travel study projects and were used mainly to make it possible for selected persons to visit adult education projects in other centres. In some cases, the initiative was taken by the individuals, who applied for grants. In others, it was decided to gather information about a particular topic (for instance, the use of the mass media in programming about public affairs) and people were approached across Canada, each to undertake a part of the task (Anon 1957c; CAAE NC June 4, 1960).

Other Programs

In addition to the major projects described above, the CAAE carried out many other program activities during these years. The most substantial of these were the work of the National Commission on the Indian Canadian, which was created under CAAE auspices in 1957 and carried on its work until 1960, when it became an autonomous organization.

In the late 1950s, Canadians began to take a heightened interest in the problems of Native people, Indian and Eskimo. In their history of education in Canada, Wilson and associates date the upswing of government attention to educational needs in the North from 1955 (Wilson et al 1970:459-60), and Bothwell et al, in their general history of the period, point out that the new Diefenbaker government, elected in 1957, spoke of its "Northern vision" and gave increased attention to Indian and Eskimo education (Bothwell et al 1981:201). The voluntary sector responded in this same period and the CAAE, with the leadership of Clare Clark and Rev. Andre Raynaud O.M.I. (the latter a priest with long experience in education with Native people), established a unit to give special and continuing attention to the area. After two years of study and an organizational conference held in Kingston in June of 1956, the National Commission on the Indian Canadian was constituted, officially a standing committee. Activities included clearing house and information services, the publication of a newsletter, research activities, periodic meetings and conferences and various forms of advocacy activity. In the first year, for instance, a major conference was held in Calgary (May, 1957) and representatives of the Commission showed the flag while attending several other conferences. The Chairman of the Commission was Clare Clark, who had for some years been the executive secretary of the J.P.C., and a full-time Director, John Melling, was appointed in August of 1958. In the second year of operation, the Commission expanded its interests to include the Eskimo people as well and in January of 1959, with the co-operation of the Department of Northern Affairs and National Resources, a major Conference on the Canadian Eskimo was held.

It had been intended from the beginning that the Commission's status under the umbrella of the CAAE would be only an interim stage, prior to the group launching out on its own. During the program year 1958-59, a committee worked actively on this plan. In May of 1959, the National Council of the CAAE passed an enabling motion to prepare the way for transition to independent status (CAAE NC May 7, 1959) and as of January, 1960, the group began its separate existence as the Indian-Eskimo Association of Canada.

Roby Kidd had a particular interest in labor education. In late 1956, a major conference on Trade Union Education was held under CAAE auspices. Kidd always made a point of involving, and keeping in close touch with, representatives of the labor movement and frequently spoke or taught at labor-sponsored meetings. At the time of the World Conference in Montreal in 1960, labor educators were actively involved in the main conference and several of the satellite ones. Similarly, Kidd made an effort to keep in active liaison with the business sector. Two outstanding businessmen each served two years as President of the Association during the decade. In 1956, a series of President's Awards were made to several businesses for outstanding records in "the effective education of the public" (CAAE DR 1956) and, in 1958, a standing committee on business and adult education (jointly sponsored with the Canadian Chamber of Commerce) was created (CAAE Exec. Dec. 5, 1958). In 1959 a study of education in corporations was carried out.

Over and above the major citizenship education projects such as the Forums and the J.P.C., the Association engaged in other work in that field. A close relationship was maintained with the Citizenship Branch of the federal government and several persons who had been active with the CAAE held responsible positions in the Branch. Many grants were obtained from that source over the years, beginning in 1953, for financing meetings, the production of program materials and state of the art reports. In his report for the year 1955-56, Kidd stated that several of the Association's projects during the year had been made possible by the Branch (CAAE DR 1956). The close working relationship was acknowledged on other occasions as well. In the year 1958-59, for instance, grants from the Branch financed a major conference and study of residential adult education in Canada (Loosley 1960), a series of eight research papers on voluntary action for use in that sector, a series of study-discussion readings on constitution and government, an annotated list of Canadian fiction which bore on citizenship matters, and a collection of tapes and kinescopes on aspects of citizenship. The Citizenship Branch provided more grants for projects than any other outside agency during the Kidd years.

There was quite a highly developed system of standing committees in the Association, especially in the latter years of the decade. In 1958-59, there were eleven such committees in the management category and six in charge of activities. These committees, especially the latter category, frequently organized or initiated programs. For instance, the committees on Rural Extension, School Boards, Governments, and Residential Education all had major meetings in the 1958-59 program year.

The CAAE shared responsibility with the J.P.C. for the annual broadcasting and film making awards. The CAAE administered travel awards for adult educators, not only the ones supported by the F.A.E., which have been mentioned, but also others funded by Carnegie. The Association participated in, and sometimes chaired, the committees for Library Week and Education Week. An organization devoted to arranging educational travel experiences, Tourinco, was given assistance and office space.

The CAAE and the Canadian Citizenship Council were the first organizations in Canada to begin mobilizing other groups in connection with the celebration of Canada's centenary. In 1959 and again the following year, the two organizations jointly organized conferences on the subject, which were attended by representatives from both the voluntary and the public sectors. The 1950s were a time of great and growing interest in what was often at that time called "group dynamics," the study and development of process in small group activity. Much of the applied aspects of this field was referred to as "leadership training" at this time. The CAAE did not itself play a leading role in training work in this field, but it supported it in other ways. The journal of the Association, during the Corbett years, and especially in the first part of the Kidd years, carried a great deal of material designed to be of interest to group leaders—articles on group techniques and notices of books and pamphlets designed for group study. Publicity for the training courses at the National Training Laboratory at Bethel, Maine (the mecca of the movement) was frequently carried in the journal.

As the twentieth anniversary of the founding of the CAAE approached, thought was given to a suitable celebration of the event. In the end, it was decided to concentrate the efforts in the following year as a twenty-first birthday celebration (CAAE NC May 3, 1955). A committee chaired by J.A. Gibson proposed a general program of events for the year. The most spectacular was a cross-country tour made by J.B. Priestley, the English writer and broadcaster, who spoke to five public meetings in Toronto, Ottawa, Winnipeg, Edmonton and Vancouver, joined in each location by two outstanding people from the region. A total of 4,000 people attended the meetings and many more saw television interviews and read press accounts in each centre (CAAE Exec. May 11, 1956). Several special issues of *Food For Thought* were produced during the year—one a retrospective issue which reprinted excerpts from the files of the journal; one an assessment of the state of adult education in Canada; and one an extended account of the special anniversary annual meeting. With the assistance of the Canadian Library Association and the J.P.C., a display of CAAE publications travelled to all parts of Canada. Several significant publications were issued during the year, some of which will be dealt with elsewhere. Of particular interest at this point was the publication—in co-operation with the national associations in Britain and the United States—of excerpts from the well-known 1919 Report of the British Ministry of Reconstruction, under the title Design for Democracy (Hawkins 1956).

The foregoing paragraphs are intended not as a comprehensive account of CAAE program activities, but rather as mention of some leading examples, and a suggestion of their range. To all of these program activities must be added those which arose from other sectors of the work—national and regional conferences and training activities—which are described below.

The CAAE and the Development of the Field 1951-1961

Professional Training and Research

One of the most remarkable developments in the field of adult education during the period of Kidd's directorship, and one to which he gave effective leadership personally, was the creation of increased opportunities for professional training for workers in the field. Kidd himself was the first Canadian to have earned a doctorate in adult education and thus had the academic qualifications which made it possible to appoint him to teach university courses. He clearly made it a matter of high personal priority not only to spend his own time in this work but also to use the services of the CAAE in a number of ways to encourage and facilitate the growth of training opportunities for adult education workers.

Kidd lost no opportunity to emphasize the importance of training and staff development for the field. Not only did he teach courses himself, but also spoke frequently of the importance of training, sought funds to enable selected persons to get training, gave prominence of place in many CAAE conferences to consideration of training needs, and used the pages of *Food For Thought* for emphasizing the importance of training and publicizing the opportunities available. Through his own writings, he contributed in various ways to the literature of the field, in terms of theory, methodology and general description. The Kidd years may properly be seen as ones during which professionalism emerged in Canadian adult education and Kidd undoubtedly made by far the most significant single contribution to that development.

D.D. Campbell, in his recent study, has pointed out that Canadian efforts in the field of training of adult educators have lagged behind the United States (Campbell 1977: 125-6). Until the late Fifties, any Canadian wishing training in the field, even at the masters level, had to go to the United States, and even after 1957, it was for a few years only at The University of British Columbia that a masters degree could be obtained. But the matter of training opportunities involves much more than just university credit courses, and such developments moved forward on a broad front during the Fifties.

Some of the well known projects of the Corbett years such as the Community Life Training Institute in Barrie and Camp Laquemac, which was sponsored by Laval (for a time) and McGill Universities, provided significant training opportunities in group work and community development. One of the most remarkable early training programs in the field was a three-month course for Newfoundland adult educators held at Memorial College, St. John's (as it then was) in 1945, under the sponsorship of the Department of Education and directed by Per Stensland of Columbia University (who later moved to Canada) (Stensland 1946; Carter 1949). The first degree credit course on adult education in Canada, as far as can be determined, was one given at Sir George Williams College in the year 1934-35, in which Kidd was a student. The next, apparently, was taught by Kidd himself at the University of New Brunswick summer session for teachers in 1947, and the first graduate course was given at the Ontario College of Education in 1951, also taught by Kidd (Kidd 1970:117). This tended to be Kidd's practice during the decade, to teach such courses in the summer, when they could be compressed into a relatively short period of time, thus removing him from the home base in Toronto for as short a time as possible.

A short time after Kidd joined the staff of the CAAE, and presumably as a result of his influence, the organization set up a Committee on Personnel in Adult Education, which functioned for several years. The committee carried out a study in 1948 which indicated that out of 86 full-time adult educators surveyed, only two reported having had any training, even a single course, specifically in adult education. In a preliminary report issued in 1948, the committee called for "a full graduate program to be given in one or more universities" (Kidd 1950:19). In the fall of 1951, Kidd reported to the National Council that the previous summer he had taught a credit course at the Ontario College of Education and he described it as part of the overall development plan which the committee had devised (CAAE NC Nov. 24, 1951). In a paper presented at the National Seminar on Citizenship in 1953, Kidd summarized the report of the CAAE committee, indicating that the chief emphasis was on university credit courses, directed at several specialized types of adult education practice (Kidd 1953b:122).

In the meantime, other training projects were developing. The first short course in Extension Methods and Techniques offered in the West was held at Banff in the fall of 1949 and attended by 80 adult educators. It lasted ten days and was co-sponsored by the CAAE and the Extension Department of the University of Alberta (Anon 1949). In April of 1950, *Food For Thought* ran a page headed "Summer Courses in Adult Education", a feature which was frequently repeated in one form or another in subsequent years. On this first occasion, courses and conferences (all non-credit) to be held in six provinces (and two in Britain) were listed (*FFT* 10:7, 17). And in the summer of 1950, a credit course for teachers was given in Nova Scotia.

In 1953, in a pamphlet published by the Association, Kidd described some of the significant training activities going on in the field:

However, the number of training opportunities for full-time workers in adult education is still small. One unique program has been described in the booklet entitled "Camp Laquemac".... In Saskatchewan the Committee on Group Development (whose headquarters are in the Department of Education) conducts an annual training institute dealing with the principles of group development as well as providing a consultation service on conferences, workshops and institutes. For more than a decade now St. Francis Xavier has been providing courses and supervised fieldwork, not only for Canadians, but for many students from abroad. In Ontario the Community Programs Branch arranges an institute at a summer camp for representatives of ethnic societies and other community leaders where they jointly work out skills for the integration of immigrants The Ontario College of Education gives a course in principles and methods. All of these constitute a good start, but only a start. (Kidd 1953:26-7)

Kidd continued his efforts over the years to teach university credit courses and thus promote an interest in the field at universities across Canada. He taught the first such credit course at four universities. The effort which seemed to lead most directly on to further developments was the first course taught at The University of British Columbia in the summer of 1956. This event was then utilized by John Friesen, Alan Thomas and others at U.B.C. as part of a process leading up to the approval for a masters degree program in adult education. This was instituted in 1957 and became the first degree program in the field in Canada. By that time, seven universities in Canada were giving credit courses in adult education.

In 1951, the CAAE secured a two-year grant of $14,000 from Carnegie which made possible a two-year project in Newfoundland for programming in the outports. Under that project, a three-week intensive training course for rural workers was held in St. John's in January of 1952. In 1955, school board adult educators from Nova Scotia and New Brunswick were assisted with a study tour of adult education programs in several American and Canadian cities. With the aid of funds secured from the Fund for Adult Education and from the Carnegie Corporation, selected Canadian adult educators were awarded grants to enable them to travel and observe adult education projects in other centres—in North America and abroad. The first training course offered for the Atlantic region as a whole was held in March of 1958, under CAAE sponsorship (Anon 1958b). In addition to these training activities, Kidd utilized other opportunities to promote the cause of professional training. The regional conferences—East and West—were encouraged and assisted to direct attention to training needs (all the Western meetings, from 1953 to 1959, gave particular attention to this area). In his report to the annual meeting of the Association in 1956, which was devoted in large part to professionalism in the field, Kidd spoke strongly about the need for good personnel and training:

I have only one serious apprehension about the future. More and more the conception of continuous learning is being accepted. But will we have the staff who are numerous and talented enough? Every year several important positions are open which require men and women of considerable capacity and long experience. So we quickly look around for a suitable person as if we did not fully understand that such people aren't just found, they must be "grown," and the growing period starts many years before. (CAAE DR 1956)

In the latter 1950s and early Sixties, the pages of *Food For Thought* carried a great deal of material of interest to professionals in the field. More space all the time was given to professional concerns such as training, information services and research. In the spring and fall of 1959, two consecutive issues of the journal were subtitlted, "Adult Education as a Profession in Canada" (*FFT* 19:8; 20:1). The editorial introduction to the two issues, after reviewing the state of adult education in the country, spoke in somewhat negative terms:

> There continues to be more talk about than action on professionalism in adult education....The consensus of the moment is that there is no adult education profession in Canada. Uncertainty enters at the point; "Do we want a profession or don't we?" Willy-nilly, however, some things are happening to us as if we were a profession, notably the CAAE fellowships for study in adult education...and the surprising bibliography of current research in adult education. (*FFT* 19:8, 359-60)

The two issues contained two articles on professionalism in the field by Thomas, two on aspects of research, and other articles tangentially related to the theme. The first of the Thomas articles reports the results of a very inconclusive survey of adult educators in Canada concerning their experience, background, training and training needs (Thomas 1959). The second examines some of the issues involved in the professional training of adult educators, and in its introductory paragraph indicates something of the thinking about the matter at the time:

> There is a point reached by every movement when it must organize systematically or simply go into decline. The early leaders have died or retired, and new sharp-eyed careerists have begun to come to power; the old brotherhood derived from clear if unattainable goals, fiercely shared by all, has evaporated to be replaced by argument, a concern for technical proficiency, and devotion to method; and the more securely founded institutional outlines have begun to reassert themselves to divide even more sharply what was once a common endeavor. At this stage, to accept the responsibility of becoming professional, seems almost an act of treachery to the old order, designed to hasten its decline. (Thomas 1959b:4)

Thomas concludes by calling for combining the qualities of profession and movement, stating that "neither one seems able to exist satisfactorily without the other" (Thomas 1959b:11).

Another aspect of emerging professionalism, and of the CAAE'S leadership in this area was the work of the CAAE's library and information services. With the assistance of Diana Ironside after she joined the staff in 1955, the organization began to strengthen its library and information services and took increasing responsibility as cataloguer of research work in the field. In 1953, Kidd proposed to the National Council that the CAAE establish a national information service. This suggestion was approved, but his subsequent efforts to raise funds in support of such work were not immediately successful (CAAE NC Mar. 7, May 13, 1953). With the arrival of Ironside two years later, progress in this area became possible. The news, book review and resources columns of *Food For Thought* soon began to reflect increasingly the bibliographic skills and research such professional help made accessible. In 1956, the CAAE published a *Bibliography of Canadian Writings in Adult Education*, the first publication of its kind in Canada, which was compiled by Ironside, making use of some earlier work by Murray Thomson as well (Thomson and Ironside, 1956). It contained over 500 entries. Ironside updated that publication in 1959 in an article contained in the two issues of *Food For Thought* devoted to professional matters (Ironside, 1959). Kidd's attempts to secure grant funds in support of the information services of the Association were successful in 1960, when $7,500 was obtained from the

Atkinson Charitable Foundation for the purpose of strengthening the library and information work (CAAE NC Jan. 20, 1961).

Some of the momentum of Kidd's efforts in promoting aspects of professionalism in the field carried over into two important conferences which were held after he had left the Association—the national conference on adult education held in Ottawa in the fall of 1961, and the Second Canadian Conference on Education held in Montreal in March, 1962. (Kidd wrote the study on adult education published in the series of preparatory papers for this meeting.) In both of these meetings, professional concerns received considerable attention (CAAE/ICEA 1961; Price 1962).

The several dimensions of movement towards professionalism in adult education during the Kidd years, to which he gave such effective leadership, accelerated during the time of his successor, Alan Thomas, who if anything strengthened further the commitment of the CAAE to support of professional interests.

Provincial Governments and School Boards

In the Fifties, provincial government involvement in the field of adult education increased greatly, and many school boards entered the field for the first time. This was an aspect of the field to which Kidd and the CAAE gave active leadership. An indication of the growth of interest on the part of governments during this period is provided by the fact that whereas in 1945 only one province had a division of adult education within its department of education, by 1957, seven provinces had created such units (C.E.A. 1961:4) and by 1961, every province had taken that step (Kidd 1961:21). In their general history of education in Canada, J.D. Wilson and associates refer to this period as one in which adult education "lost much of its amateur status" and they link that development to the assumption of responsibility in adult education by the provincial ministries (Wilson et al 1970:412). The CAAE promoted the growth of government and school board sponsored adult education work by various means: discussions at CAAE conferences concerning the role and responsibility of governments in this field; the creation of committees of the CAAE on provincial governments and school boards in the field; the sponsorship of meetings and conferences about the matter; and the cultivation, by means of visits and correspondence, of relationships with department of education officials across the country.

It seems odd, given present attitudes on the matter, that as late as 1950, when the role of governments in adult education was discussed at the national conference of CAAE, it was apparently a matter of considerable controversy. In the general summary of the meeting carried in *Food For Thought*, the author indicated that it was the issue which had "produced the most heat and light" at the recent conference and considerable space was given in the editorial columns a few weeks later to discussing the merits of the issue.

One delegate at the conference was quoted as asking, "Why in the world are the departments of education meddling in adult education?" The writers of the editorial (Kidd and Isabel Wilson) acknowledged the grounds for concern: "Because the very fibre and heart of the adult education movement is voluntarism, it is little wonder that there should be a deep-seated suspicion of the intrusion of officialdom" (Anon 1950:3).

The editorial went on, however, to point out that the time had passed when there was much point in discussing whether provincial governments should play a role in the field—an increasing number of them already were. The critical question was rather:

> What are the conditions under which leadership in adult education from a
> government department can result in refreshing local enterprise, stimulating local
> groups, increasing the responsibility of individuals. (Anon 1950:3-4)

It was in this spirit that Kidd and his colleagues did what they could to promote the
participation of provincial departments of education in this work.

The report of the work group on "Provincial Divisions of Adult Education" on which
the editorial was commenting took note of the concerns of some participants. It was
reported that the group had endorsed the principle of participation of public authorities in
providing adult education services, but had also endorsed a second principle:

> In a free society, adult education is self-education on the part of responsible citizens,
> and methods of government support must take full account of the freedom of choice,
> effort, and initiative on the part of individuals and groups. (Anon 1950b:37)

As far as is known, this was the last occasion on which the very participation of
government in the support and provision of adult education was seriously questioned in
adult education circles, and as such was a milestone in the development of the field. As
has been indicated above, it was clear where Kidd's sympathies lay. Kidd understood that
it was important, in working with the departments of education and with school boards, to
co-operate with the Canadian Education Association and to build up their interest as well.
In the fall of 1955, he took part in the C.E.A. conference, stressing in his remarks the
emerging concept of lifelong learning (Anon 1956).

Arising out of informal discussions at the annual meeting of the CAAE in 1956, a
conference was organized on the role of provincial governments in the field of adult
education, which was held prior to the C.E.A. convention the following year. Eight
provinces, the CAAE and Dominion Bureau of Statistics were represented. The conclusions
reached dealt with the principle of public support and leadership in adult education,
indicating the functions which departments of education should perform, largely in support
of programs conducted by other agencies such as "voluntary associations, municipal
governments and local school authorities" (C.E.A. 1961:5).

In 1958, the CAAE established a committee on governments in adult education (CAAE
NC May 20, 1958). At a session held within the framework of the CAAE annual meeting
later in the year, a statement of purpose for the committee was drawn up and the intention
enunciated of conferring annually, on alternate years with the CAAE and the C.E.A.
(Anon 1958). Later in the year, this committee appears to have been augmented in its role
when another committee on school boards in adult education was created (CAAE Exec.
Dec. 5, 1958). The next major event in this sector was a one-day conference on the role
of school boards held in Toronto in November, 1959. It was organized by the CAAE, at
the invitation of Ontario officials, with participants drawn from Vancouver, Regina and
Halifax, as well as Ontario centres. The emphasis was placed on the need for boards to
appoint staff whose primary task was the organization of adult education programs and
the need for in-service training of teachers of adults (Anon 1960).

The year 1961 was one of major steps in this field. The program of the national
bilingual conference held in Ottawa in late October did not deal with institutional roles
directly. Among the recommendations arising from the meeting, however, were a number
which had to do with the role of government and school boards. Among these were ones
emphasizing the responsibility of boards to conduct adult education programs, the need

for competent, trained persons as directors of this work, and the need, at the provincial level, for adequate supporting legislation. A conference on Government and Adult Education, sponsored by the CAAE committee, was held directly following the national meeting. The conference considered such matters as the role of government, the type of leadership it could appropriately provide, and the range of programs (in terms of content and format) which should be provided (Campbell 1961). As described elsewhere, Kidd produced two major statements about adult education in 1961. One of these was a general description of the field and issues related to it, a background pamphlet prepared for the Canadian Conference on Education to be held the following year. In a section on provincial governments and school boards, Kidd described the growing participation of these bodies in the field in the post-war period and the functions they perform. He described also a transition in point of view which he saw taking place as school boards moved on from the old notion of "night schools," classes in "a narrow range of vocational and academic subjects," to a new concept, "continuing education for adults." He estimated that "about half a million" adults were currently enrolled in school board sponsored programs (Kidd 1961:21-3). Elsewhere in the paper, Kidd indicated that school boards could expand their work in the field, but cautioned that if the boards were going to be active in adult education, they must give evidence of their recognition that adults are very different from children and that their work with adults must take those important differences into account (Kidd 1961:94-5).

The major study of adult education in Metropolitan Toronto which was carried out in 1961 by Kidd and associates is discussed elsewhere but has particular relevance for this section. Kidd produced in this report, with particular reference to the role of school boards, a remarkably insightful and useful document which developed the concept of the educative society and at the same time outlined the practical steps the boards of the region could take to improve their service to their communities (Kidd 1961b).

Publications

The CAAE was by far the most important publisher of materials about adult education during this period. A few books were published elsewhere—Corbett's reminiscences (1957), Cameron's history of the Banff School (1956) and Laidlaw's book about the Antigonish Movement (1961)—but these were the exceptions. The CAAE was the dominant publisher in the field, in the form of their journal, *Food For Thought*, pamphlets and other occasional pieces, and full-length books.

Food For Thought was the regularly published journal of the Association throughout the period. It was issued six times a year and, during Kidd's time as Director, there were six different editors. The standard of article and of editorial work on the journal was outstanding. It served at least two main purposes. On the one hand it was very much a house organ—many editorials and news items dealt with the affairs of the Association; major portions of the Director's annual reports were carried and CAAE conferences, national and regional, were extensively reported; the availability of CAAE publications was announced; and on occasions such as the twenty-first anniversary of the founding of the Association, special issues were devoted to its history and development. On the other hand, the journal both reflected and served the field of practice. Articles on practice-related matters—teaching, publicity, discussion techniques, residential education, evaluation, etc.—were carried frequently. Articles on related aspects of sociology, psychology and social work were published. Emerging concerns of the field—aging, education in the labor and business sectors, working with immigrants and Native people, broadcasting policy, international dimensions of the field, and training opportunities— were frequently the subject of articles. Special issues devoted entirely or mainly to aspects of a single subject were published occasionally on such subjects as "Newcomers to Canada" (1953), "The Family in Canada" (1954), "Retrospective Issue" (1956), "French Canada" (1958) and "Education in the North" (1960). At the beginning of the decade there was considerable material in *FFT* designed for use by study and discussion groups, but this emphasis seemed to have disappeared by 1953 or so. Space was given throughout the period to pamphlet, book and film reviews, with television getting more attention as the decade progressed.

Circulation figures for *FFT* remained at much the same level during the decade, averaging between 2,000 and 2,500 an issue, with larger quantities for some special issues for which there were bulk orders (CAAE NC Nov. 24, 1951; Jan. 26, 195S; AR 1958-59).

Reference has already been made in the section on Citizens' Forum to the value and high calibre of the pamphlets which were produced each week for that program. They represented a very considerable publishing project in themselves.

A large number of pamphlets and monographs were published by the Association, some in series, some individual, some ad hoc ventures and some arising out of projects. At the beginning and near the end of Kidd's tenure, pamphlets about adult education and the Association were published—"Questions and Answers about Adult Education" in 1950 and a joint venture with the French language association in 1960, "Adult Education in Canada." Examples of individual pamphlets on aspects of the field include: Kidd's *Adult Education and the School*, published in 1950 and reprinted in 1952 (1950b); a study of the distribution of program materials (Parsons 1952); a report on adult education as carried out in health institutions and some prisons (Ross 1952); a *Bibliography of Canadian Writings in Adult Education*, which appeared in 1956 (Thomson and Ironside 1956); Kidd's *Putting Words to Work*, a guide for discussion leaders (1956); and Elizabeth Loosley's *Residential Adult Education: A Canadian View* (1960). Many other pamphlets and monographs were published (see annual reports), but these will serve as examples.

Some pamphlet series deserve mention. Ever since the late war years, the CAAE had co-operated with the Canadian Institute on International Affairs in producing the "Behind the Headlines" series of pamphlets on public affairs topics and had been a financial participant in the venture. It was mainly a C.I.I.A. project, however, and the CAAE was losing some money on it each year. Kidd proposed in the spring of 1952 that the CAAE remove itself from the arrangement and, after some negotiations back and forth, this was finalized the following year (CAAE Exec. Mar. 7, April 16, 1952; Nov. 3, 1953). Another series of a sort were the discussion courses and related leaders' manuals which were produced in the Commission for Continuous Learning project (See DR 1958-9, etc.). The project which is in some respects of the greatest long-term interest is a series of eleven pamphlets published from 1952 to 1954 under the series title, "Learning For Living." This was financed by the Fund For Adult Education, an initial grant coming in 1951 and further funds two years later (CAAE Exec. Sept. 10, 1951; Jan. 14, 1953). The series documented the development of adult education in Canada in many of its dimensions, dealing with outstanding institutions, pioneers in the field, the recent Massey Commission report, and including a final pamphlet by Kidd which contained a general assessment of the field in Canada at the time. Together the series made a valuable contribution to the literature of the field in Canada. At least some of the pamphlets were expanded versions of the work by the same authors which had appeared in Kidd's *Adult Education in Canada* (1950).

There were several book-length studies published by the CAAE in this period. Those by Kidd are discussed below, and they include the two books of readings about adult education in Canada published in 1950 and 1963: the study on *Adult Education in The Canadian University* (1956); and *Adult Education in the Caribbean*, an extended report on Kidd's study in that region in 1957-58 (1959b). The other book from this period was *Design for Democracy*, selections from the *1919 Report* of the British Ministry of Reconstruction. This book was prepared largely by Hawkins of the CAAE and was published as a co-operative venture among the three national adult education organizations in Canada, Britain and the United States (Hawkins 1956).

Advocacy

The CAAE had been active in an advocacy role on behalf of adult education throughout its history. Education being predominantly a provincial concern constitutionally, one of the important functions of a national organization was to speak out on issues at the national level which potentially had an impact on adult learning and access to educational opportunities. During the Corbett years, initiatives on the part of the CAAE had dealt with such matters as federal-provincial relations, economic, communications and cultural policy (Selman 1981:33-35).

The major activity during the Kidd years consisted of follow-up on the Massey Commission on the briefs in 1956 to both the Commission on Canada's Economic Prospects and the Commission on Broadcasting, and on a brief in 1961 to the Senate Committee on Manpower and Employment. In addition, representations were made from time to time to the Prime Minister's Office or through other cabinet ministers in continued efforts to obtain federal financial support for the Association, but these latter efforts did not bear fruit in this period (See CAAE NC May 26, 1954).

Kidd played a major role in the preparation and presentation of the Association's brief to the Massey Commission—the Royal Commission on National Development in the Arts, Letters and Sciences. The brief was a comprehensive one, the most ambitious ever prepared by the CAAE to that point, and it ranged over a large number of topics (See Selman 1981:33-35). The report of the Commission was a landmark document in terms of cultural policy in Canada (Ostry 1978:64) and gave grounds for satisfaction in the CAAE, whose views were generally supported and whose activities were mentioned and praised several times in the report (Canada 1951:37, 74-5). The report recommended federal support for higher education, the creation of the Canada Council and a UNESCO Commission and the strengthening of Canadian culture in many of its dimensions (Ostry 1978:56ff; Bothwell et al 1981:166-7; Creighton 1976:181ff; Shea 1952). The CAAE did not wish to let the matter rest there, however, and by every means at its disposal, the Association continued to press the government to implement the recommendations. The emphasis was placed on the creation of the Canada Council, and perhaps even more strongly on the creation of a National Commission for UNESCO, a measure for which

Kidd and the Association had been arguing for some time. As Kidd remembered it, the CAAE was "the first and for a while the only advocate of UNESCO in Canada" (Letter, Kidd to author Feb. 11, 1982). On many occasions in the following six years (until the government acted in the matter) the columns of *Food For Thought*, editorials, articles and news features, were used to pursue the matter. Other avenues were utilized as well—the J.P.C. became "a kind of information centre" on the subject (Clark 1954:25), the National Council sent messages directly to the Prime Minister (CAAE NC Jan. 26, 1955), and several CAAE conferences in the period passed resolutions on the matter. When the government announced late in 1956 that it was moving on the matter, the news was greeted enthusiastically in *Food For Thought* (Anon 1957; Anon 1957b), and it was hailed that the first chairman of the UNESCO Commission was the current President of the CAAE, N.A.M. MacKenzie.

The brief to the Gordon Commission on Canada's Economic Prospects was a short one, only three pages, and made no specific recommendations. In the area of broadcasting policy, however, the CAAE had twice before, in 1944 and again two years later, submitted substantial briefs, and it attached great importance to this area of public policy. Both Corbett and Kidd were stout defenders of the interests of public broadcasting. The submission to the Fowler Commission in 1956 ran to 15 pages and dealt with a wide range of issues. The most publicized issue at the time was whether the C.B.C. should continue to be both a participant in the broadcasting system and the controlling body for the system. The CAAE argued that it should, but this position was not supported by the Commission's report and the regulatory power was soon vested in a new agency, the Board of Broadcast Governors (Bothwell et al 1981:211-12). Shortly before Kidd left the CAAE, in early 1961, a brief was presented by the Association to the Senate Committee on Manpower and Employment. The brief, which was a lengthy one, was prepared largely by Arthur Pigott, the Associate Director. Excerpts were published in *Food For Thought* later in the year (CAAE Exec. Feb. 28, 1961; Anon 1961).

There was a wide measure of agreement in the Association on most matters on which views were put forward. From time to time, however, controversy appeared in this connection. At the annual meeting of 1951, a decision was made not to accept an invitation to take part in a delegation to the Prime Minister to urge the passage of a Bill of Rights. The decision was apparently a source of considerable consternation to some members, and the matter was discussed in the editorial column of *FFT* in the fall. The editorial stated, "The idea that the CAAE as an organization shall take no partisan position on controversial questions has been very well established" (Anon 1951c:19). Members were invited to submit their views on the question, which no doubt was of vital interest to Kidd himself because, in a private capacity, he was an active worker on human rights questions.

The issue arose again in early 1953. The Executive requested that the National Council discuss and clarify the role of the Association in social action activities. It was agreed at the end of a lengthy discussion that the CAAE had a responsibility to present views to appropriate bodies on matters directly related to adult education. It should not take action on matters outside of the field of adult education but might well encourage other groups to do so (CAAE NC Mar. 7, 1953). One further aspect of this question arose in connection with the submission to the Fowler Commission on broadcasting policy in 1956. When the delegation, headed by Kidd, appeared before the Commission, the chairman read into the record letters from two financial contributors to the CAAE who stated that they, as members of the Association, had not been consulted about the content of the submission (and were in fact associated with other submissions which took contrary views) and wished to disassociate themselves from the CAAE brief (Transcript in CAAE Archives).

Roby Kidd and International Commitments

Kidd came in later years to be a world traveller on a large scale and perhaps the best known adult educator in the world. In the record of the 1950s can be seen the beginning of his active involvement in adult education at the international level. Kidd has told associates that he was predisposed to taking an interest in international activities by the accounts he heard as a boy in the Baptist church from missionaries who had served abroad. He was further encouraged along these lines by his contacts with the increasing number of foreign adult educators who came as visitors to Canada and to the CAAE in the late Forties, after he had joined the staff of the organization. He believed strongly in the importance of international contacts and the exchange of people and ideas. He later commented that the CAAE was the first national adult education organization to take on major roles and activities in international development and he referred to the Association as being "a constant reminder that adult education was a universal idea" (Letter, Kidd to author Feb. 11, 1982).

A review of the files of the Association's journal indicates that throughout Kidd's years as Director, there was a large volume of international material printed. This seemed to increase noticeably in 1952 and to remain at a high level thereafter. From time to time, certain issues of the magazine would be dominated by articles about other countries and/ or international developments. The news columns of the magazine constantly included items of international news about the field and the reviews of publications included much material from abroad. In almost every issue, mention was made of visitors from other countries who had visited the offices of the organization. And in almost every one of Kidd's annual reports he made note of the fact that such visits took a significant amount of time and effort. Canadian adult education was becoming increasingly well known abroad and, as Kidd himself became an internationally known figure, both he and the Canadian adult education enterprise attracted visitors from afar.

Ned Corbett had given considerable attention to international aspects of the field and had attended the first UNESCO World Conference, which was held in Denmark in 1949. In his very first Director's Report, Kidd took his title and his opening remarks from the words of a recent Austrian visitor (Kidd 1952b:4). He also devoted some paragraphs to what he headed "international responsibilities," describing some of the events of the previous year and speaking directly to the possibility that some might feel that he and the staff were spending too much time on such matters. "And you might be right," he commented, but the reader does not get the impression Kidd intended to concern himself too much over such reservations (Kidd 1952b:6). The very next issue of the journal contained an article by him, "Thoughts on Returning to Canada," which followed a two-month trip to Europe (his first major trip abroad) during which he had visited Great Britain and several countries in Scandinavia and Western Europe and addressed a UNESCO conference on Workers' Education. His article was largely devoted to the difficulties put in the way of more effective contacts abroad by the failure of the Canadian government to create a national commission for UNESCO (Kidd 1952).

The links with UNESCO and involvement in its activities strengthened steadily in future years and came to be a continuing feature of Kidd's professional life. He was made a member of UNESCO's Advisory Committee on International Understanding and Co-operation in 1952 but could not attend a meeting of the group until the fall of 1954 (CAAE Exec. Aug. 27, 1953; Sept. 8, 1954; NC Jan. 26, 1955). In the fall of 1955, a whole issue of *Food For Thought* was devoted to the cause of international understanding, several of the articles having been arranged with the co-operation of the UNESCO Secretariat (*FFT* 16:2). Kidd had received two separate invitations in 1952 and the following year to carry out missions in the West Indies, but he arranged for others, Charles Topshee and Ned Corbett, to go instead. These activities launched the CAAE on its international development work. A further opportunity for Kidd himself arose later in the decade, however, and this time he went. He spent eight months, beginning in late September, 1957, in the West Indies Federation, at the invitation of the University College of the West Indies, carrying out a Carnegie-financed study of their extramural activities and making recommendations about its future development. Kidd told of his experiences in the Caribbean when he made his annual report to the CAAE the following spring and often referred to his time in the West Indies as his apprenticeship in the work of international development.

He took on an additional international responsibility in the summer of 1959, when he was asked to be the first chairman of the Committee on Adult Education constituted by the World Confederation of Organizations of the Teaching Profession. He presided at conferences organized by that group in Washington D.C. in 1959 and New Delhi in 1961 (CAAE Exec. Sept. 8, 1959). In 1958, Kidd organized a non-governmental foreign assistance venture in Canada called the Overseas Book Centre. It subsequently came to have operations in most major cities of Canada and shipped books to educational institutions in the Third World, soon exceeding a million books shipped each year to more than fifty developing countries.

The biggest event of the decade in adult education was the Second UNESCO World Conference on Adult Education, which was held in Montreal in the summer of 1960 and of which Roby Kidd was elected president. The goals of the meeting, the timing and the site were recommended to UNESCO by a consultative committee in 1957. Kidd took part in two planning meetings held in Paris in the months leading up to the event and had some warning that he would be nominated for the presidency of the meeting. By the time the conference was held, the world was plunged into a particularly tense period of the Cold War (following the U-2 incident) and it was widely predicted that the conference would break up before completing its work (Kidd 1974:13-14). That it did not was a tribute to the professional commitment of the delegates from the 54 countries which took part and to the ability, acumen and hard work of Kidd and a handful of others who managed to seek and find common ground when divisive issues arose. There was concern that a Soviet-sponsored resolution on disarmament would split the conference, but this was circumvented, after much negotiation, and a Canadian resolution on the same subject was introduced, around which all nations were willing to rally.

The conference worked in three commissions on matters of professional concern and subsequently approved a series of resolutions dealing with matters arising. The leading expert on the World Conferences and their impact on the field has summarized the outcome of the Montreal meeting as follows:

This was the first international assembly which, in its Final Report, set lifelong education as a goal for the future policies of governments: "Nothing less will suffice than that people everywhere should come to accept adult education as normal, and that governments should treat it as a necessary, part of the educational provision of every country." (Lowe 1975:10)

The internal quotation above was an excerpt from a special resolution passed by the conference and known as the Montreal Declaration. Seven satellite conferences on specialized topics were held in the general region of Montreal before or after the main conference.

The Montreal Conference was successful in a professional sense, in that it placed the challenge of lifelong education before the world community. It was a success in a political sense in surviving—and triumphing over—the acute dangers inherent in the Cold War tensions of the time (Anon 1960; Cameron 1960). Roby Kidd, who had already gained a considerable reputation in international adult education circles for his capacity and judgment, came away from the Montreal meeting as perhaps the most visible and respected leader in the field, on the world scene. He was to continue to make outstanding contributions to the field internationally for the rest of his life, his stature growing all the while.

Following Montreal, Kidd was named Chairman of UNESCO's Committee for the Development of Adult Education for a two-year period, and he was re-elected in 1963 and 1965. Another aspect of his recognition in the field was the fact that an address of his on the need for sharing and mutual assistance in the world community, entitled "The Creative Crusade," was awarded an international prize by the Fund for Adult Education in 1960 (Kidd 1961c).

The Writings of Roby Kidd 1951-1963

One of the most remarkable things about Kidd, during his years with the CAAE, was his capacity to produce such a quantity of useful writing for the field. It was difficult for anyone, perhaps other than members of his immediate family, to imagine when he did it, much less how he did it. In days—and years—full of administrative detail, meetings, fund raising, conferences, extensive travel (both inside Canada and increasingly as the decade progressed, outside as well) and all the other demands made on an organizational executive serving a far-flung field, he somehow managed as well to be the most prolific and useful writer in the field, certainly in Canada, perhaps anywhere. In the period 1950 to 1963, he wrote or compiled eight books, seven substantial pamphlets and an unknown number of articles, reports, briefs and other papers.

His writing, on the whole, is not outstanding for its powers of expression, although there were flashes of eloquence. The circumstances of some of the writing were such that he thought it useful to rely heavily on the writings of others, and the frequent inclusion of quotations from the work of others detracted from the power of the author's prose. Some of the writing is memorable, however, and he frequently expressed powerful ideas with brevity and modesty, tucked in amidst other material. What was outstanding about much of his writing was his powers of organization and the way in which he integrated new concepts and theory into his views of the field.

His writing was important from several other points of view. In Canadian terms, his two books of readings about the field, published in 1950 and 1963, and some of his pamphlets, helped give many practitioners a sense of the significance of their vocation and pride in their country's achievements. His textbook for the field, published in 1959, was the first (and only) one written in Canada and was widely used in other countries. His study of adult education in the City of Toronto (1961) was the only thorough examination of adult education at the municipal level ever carried out in Canada. His long pamphlet prepared for the 1962 Canadian Conference on Education was a significant effort to bring the nature and needs of adult education to the attention of officials and scholars in the rest of the field of education. In terms of the needs of the adult education practitioner, several of his works were of practical significance. His textbook made much knowledge and experience accessible. His pamphlets on discussion leadership and film utilization were full of useful information and suggestions.

Some of his work was addressed to policy makers and was written with a view to shaping their actions. This is true of *Adult Education and the School*; the study of the place of adult education in the universities; the report and recommendations on university extramural work in the West Indies; the book on adult education in the city of Toronto; and less directly, perhaps, the book on financing adult education and the pamphlet prepared for the Canadian Conference on Education.

All of his publications, because they were highly regarded, brought credit during this period to the CAAE as well as to Kidd himself. And in the case of many of the publications, they had a more direct, practical value to the CAAE as well. In many instances, the CAAE published these studies under grants from other organizations. Kidd consistently "sold" his time several times over on such projects, paying the price personally by having to produce the works which had been contracted—at the cost of unreasonable demands on his time and energy. His capacity to produce all this work, much of it of extremely high quality, was amazing to all his friends and colleagues and benefitted the coffers of the CAAE as well as the field as a whole.

Kidd's earliest major work was the collection of articles entitled *Adult Education in Canada*, which was published by the CAAE in 1950. Similar in intent and format was *Learning and Society*, which he produced in 1963, and the two will be considered together. Publication of the first was assisted financially by the Carnegie Corporation and the second by the Fund for Adult Education. There wasn't (and still isn't) a published history of adult education in Canada. This need was met in part by means of these two volumes, which contained a great deal of historical material as well as reflecting the state of the field in the period leading up to the time of publication. The books were organized along similar lines. The readings were grouped under broad themes such as "Aims, Origins and Development," "Organization" and "Some Selected Programs," with Kidd providing some introductory comments in each section and, as required, notes introducing individual items. The articles were selected on at least two grounds—to cover the material, describe the project, or reflect the point of view desired, and also, as much as possible, to have the key figures in the field in Canada represented among the authors.

In the first volume Kidd included a chapter he wrote especially for the volume entitled "Present Developments and Trends," which was the first review from a professional point of view of the field in Canada, under such headings as philosophy, functions, organization, methods, research and training. There was a clear effort to promote a professional approach to the field. *Learning and Society* clearly reflected the increased professionalization of the field which had taken place since the earlier volume was compiled. The second volume was a longer book and gave a great deal more attention to such areas as methodology, program planning, instruction, research and training. Many of the same authors appeared in the second volume, but as well, the emerging academic leaders of the field were represented. The second volume also reflected the growing concern in the field for providing more effective service to the educationally disadvantaged. Something of the excitement of the late Fifties and early Sixties—the new glimpse of the possibilities inherent in lifelong learning, increasing international contacts and sense of common purpose, and the increased focus on learning and its functions, as distinct from education— were reflected in the 1963 book. Taken together, these two volumes represent a tremendously valuable resource for students of adult education in Canada, containing much useful material about the field historically and reflecting the state of its development at the time these works were published.

Representing in some sense a sort of extension of the 1950 volume, the CAAE published in the years 1952 to 1954 a series of eleven pamphlets under the series title, "Learning for Living." The series was underwritten by the F.A.E., was planned by Kidd, and two of the pamphlets were written by him. One was called *Pictures with a Purpose* (1953) and dealt with various aspects of the distribution of non-theatrical films in Canada. The sections on film utilization drew on Kidd's earlier work in that field (Kidd and Storr 1951) but the bulk of the text concerned the history and current state of film distribution in Canada, most notably the work of the National Film Board. The other pamphlet by Kidd was *People Learning from Each Other* (1953). It was a summary of the series and a critique of the field as a whole, identifying some gaps and concerns which were to be prominent on the agenda of adult education in the ensuing years.

As is indicated elsewhere in this paper, one of the major developments in the field during the Fifties, to which Kidd gave a great deal of attention, was the increasing role of the provincial governments and the school boards in adult education. In terms of publications, he promoted this by means of a pamphlet called *Adult Education and the School* (1950), which was a very simple introduction to both adult education and the role of the school, and by means of a comprehensive study of adult education in the city of Toronto published in 1961, *18 to 80: Continuing Education in Metropolitan Toronto*. The latter was a book-length research report and series of recommendations which was carried out under contract with the Toronto Board of Education, at the suggestion of the newly formed Metropolitan Toronto Adult Education Council. It contained the findings of research into adult education services in Toronto, who the students were and why they came, and examined a range of professional concerns in such areas as goals, priority needs, programming, counselling, research, finance and training needs. In his quite remarkable introductory section to the report, "The Educative Society," and throughout his discussion of the issues, Kidd brought to bear what he had learned from his extensive practical experience, his considerable scholarship and international contacts. It is a wise, humane and discerning document which deserves to be better known.

In 1953, while R.C. Wallace, former principal of Queen's University, was President of the CAAE, an arrangement was made whereby the CAAE would carry out a study of adult education in the Canadian universities with the help of an advisory group representing the National Conference of Canadian Universities. The result was the publication of *Adult Education in the Canadian University* (1956), a book-length study of the subject. The report was based on widespread consultation with university people across the country, and because Kidd felt that the study was most likely to have an impact in the university community if it relied heavily on the views of university people, the text is heavily laden with quotations. There is much marshalling of arguments pro and con on issues and a minimum of stating the case for particular conclusions. In a brief final section, a few uncontroversial principles are stated but, perhaps wisely, the major conclusions and recommendations—which were very cautious at that—were presented in an accompanying document which was sponsored by the university members of the advisory group. The study was a useful document which contained much information and is of considerable historical interest but was not at the time judged to be very persuasive. It is hard to see how any such document could have been, the circumstances and traditions of the universities varying so greatly.

Kidd wrote a somewhat related study two years later, the result of an eight-month consultation with the University College of the West Indies, in which he examined in detail the institution, its relationship to its community (at that time, all the British possessions in the Caribbean—the islands, British Guiana and British Honduras) and its considerable program of extramural work, making a comprehensive set of recommendations and generally sharpening issues for consideration by the institution. The document, *Adult Education in the Caribbean* (1959), contains 293 pages of typescript and is characteristic of Kidd. It devoted considerable attention to the culture and conditions of the area, attaching great importance to the distinctive characteristics already inherent in the situation and suggesting that the institution value, strengthen and build upon its established adult education activities rather than adopting other, more traditional university extension patterns. The study is an interesting document in itself but also represents an important aspect of Kidd's development in his knowledge of the needs of Third World countries. Roby Kidd, the teacher and profession-builder, was represented once again in the late Fifties by two publications. The first was a slim pamphlet entitled *Putting Words to Work* (1956), which was a practical guide for discussion leaders. The other, *How Adults Learn* (1959), was one of the first textbooks in the field and represents one of Kidd's most important contributions. The title of the book is somewhat misleading in that it could be mistaken for one which deals only with the learning process rather than what it is, a text which covers such other areas as institutions, program planning, teaching and methods. It has been used as a text in more than forty countries and has been translated into five other major languages. But the title *is* appropriate in one important respect in that this text placed much greater emphasis than any before it on the adult learner and adult learning, as distinct from methodology and other institutional concerns. In this respect the book anticipated developments which are only now strongly coming to the fore in the field. In his discussion of such topics as learning theory, motivation and goals of the field, Kidd identifies himself more explicitly with what is usually termed the humanistic school of thought than is found anywhere else in his writing.

Brief reference should be made to *Adult Education in a Free Society*, a book of speeches by Robert Blakely, which Kidd edited and which was published in 1958. Blakely was a vice president of the F.A.E., an eloquent man who was sometimes referred to as the poet of the adult education movement, and he and Kidd had become close friends. The extent of Kidd's role in the preparation of this volume, aside from a delightful brief introduction, appears to be minimal. Shortly after he left the CAAE, and in order to fulfill the terms of an agreement made with the F.A.E., Kidd produced an extended essay which was published in book form, entitled *Financing Continuing Education* (1962). Rather general and somewhat discursive in nature, the book cannot be judged to be one of Kidd's better efforts, but it should be pointed out that it did develop some ideas which have come into prominence in recent years, the varying approaches which may be taken to the funding of adult education, depending on the function in society which each type of activity performs.

Kidd's other three major publications towards the end of the period under review all reflect the influence of his experience with the World Conference in Montreal in 1960 and the emergence of the concept of lifelong learning. Two of these have been described already, *18 to 80* and *Learning and Society*. The first, in its remarkable introduction and elsewhere, brings to bear the implications of lifelong learning on provision at the local level. The second emphasizes the international responsibilities of the movement in Canada and begins to explore some new dimensions of the role of adult education in society. The third publication was a long pamphlet (over 100 pages) entitled *Continuing Education* (1961) which Kidd wrote as one of a series of studies commissioned by the Canadian Conference on Education prior to their national conference in 1962. Designed to inform and appeal to persons from all aspects of education in Canada, it described the character and dimensions of adult education in this country, briefly ranged over a series of professional concerns (a sort of textbook in miniature) and concluded by identifying eleven "special issues," selected with an eye to appealing to and challenging educational decision makers in Canadian society. Throughout, the study is informed by ideas about the field which were highlighted by the Montreal Conference and develops some of the implications for Canadian life of the concept of lifelong learning.

Conclusion

Roby Kidd had obviously enjoyed great success in his years as Director of the CAAE, and his career had advanced tremendously. Why did he inform the officers of the Association early in 1960 that he would be leaving as of May 1 the following year? The answer would be reasonably clear if he had left to take a position at the international level or had decided to devote his energies full time to academic work and had accepted a university post. But instead, he moved to Ottawa and became Secretary-Treasurer of the Social Science Research Council and the Humanities Research Council. Such a move is understandable in the context of his many contacts in Ottawa and in the light of his continuing concern for the social and cultural development of Canada. But Kidd was not aware of the possibility of this position when he announced his resignation, and the responsibilities he assumed there were not in the direct line of his career development in adult education.

He left the CAAE because he felt it was time to leave and before he had any firm plans as to where he was going next. Perhaps some day, from Kidd's memoirs, we will learn more about his reasons for leaving, but it seems clear that he left because he felt it was in the best interests of the organization that he do so. He had demonstrated some concern over the degree to which he, as Director, had come to dominate the affairs of the organization. It is likely that he judged it time for the benefit of both the CAAE and himself to leave the Association.

Kidd and the Executive of the Association made efforts in the period prior to his departure to find a satisfactory successor. That task turned out to be a difficult one. Arthur Pigott, a person with varied experience in management and welfare circles and a specialist in education in relation to employment, was appointed Associate Director in 1960, succeeding Gordon Hawkins, and it was decided to appoint Pigott as Director when Kidd departed in May of 1961. Dr. Alan Thomas, who had worked for the Association in the mid-Fifties and had for five years been at The University of British Columbia, joined the staff of the CAAE in September, 1961, and within a year was appointed Director. Thomas was to remain with the Association throughout the Sixties and became the third of its long-term and outstanding Directors.

It is difficult, and perhaps unnecessary, to separate the man, J. Roby Kidd, from the Association, the CAAE. As a consequence of Kidd's leadership and the skilled work of Kidd and the able staff he attracted to the Association, the CAAE gained greatly in stature and accomplishment during the Kidd years. Kidd's time with the Association coincided with a period of enormous productivity on his part, the rapid development of his powers and range of experience, and his emergence on the world scene as one of the key figures in the field at the international level. Kidd's accomplishments internationally reinforced his capacity to provide leadership at home in Canada.

When Kidd inherited the leadership of the CAAE, that organization had already accomplished great things and was highly regarded in the field, mainly for its programs. By 1961, when he left this post as Director of the Association, the CAAE enjoyed an even higher reputation—in both programming and other areas of professional concern—both at home and abroad. That this was so was at least in part recognition of Roby Kidd as a person, his qualities and accomplishments.

Kidd did not often hand out advice or make ringing statements of principle in his writing. One of the few exceptions consists of his list of "ten commandments for educators," which he inserted in the second edition of his book, *How Adults Learn*. The statement says a great deal about the man, his values, texture and personal style. Such was the guiding spirit of the CAAE during his eventful years as its Director (1973:306-7).

1. Thou shalt never try to make another human being exactly like thyself; one is enough.

2. Thou shalt never judge a person's need, or refuse your consideration, solely because of the trouble he causes.

3. Thou shalt not blame heredity nor the environment in general; people can surmount their environments.

4. Thou shalt never give a person up as hopeless or cast him out.

5. Thou shalt try to help everyone become, on the one hand, sensitive and compassionate, and also tough-minded.

6. Thou shalt not steal from any person his rightful responsibilities for determining his own conduct and the consequences thereof.

7. Thou shalt honor anyone engaged in the pursuit of learning and serve well and extend the discipline of knowledge and skill about learning which is our common heritage.

8. Thou shalt have no universal remedies or expect miracles.

9.   Thou shalt cherish a sense of humor which may save you from   becoming shocked, depressed, or complacent.

10.   Thou shalt remember the sacredness and dignity of thy calling, and, at the same time, "thou shalt not take thyself too damned seriously."

References

(In the references which follow, the CAAE journal, *Food For Thought*, will be abbreviated as *FFT.*)

Andrew, G.C. (1954), "The Canada Council: A National Necessity," *FFT*, 15 (3): 12-17.

Anon (1949), "Extension Short Course," *FFT*, 10 (3): 39.

——. (1950), "In Our Opinion," *FFT*, 11 (1): 1-4.

——. (1950b), "Commissions and Workgroups," *FFT*, 11 (1): 37-40.

——. (1950c), "Canadians and the World," *FFT*, 11 (2): 4.

——. (1951), "Maritime Conference," *FFT*, 12 (1): 32-33.

——. (1951b), "The Massey Report," *FFT*, 12 (11): 1-8.

——. (1951c), "The CAAE and Social Action," *FFT*, 12 (1): 8-9.

——. (1951a), "CAAE Notes." *FFT*, 12 (3): 28.

——. (1952), "Farm Forum News," *FFT*, 12 (8): 37.

——. (1953), "Banff." *FFT*, 14, (1): 39-40.

——. (1954), "Canada and Unesco," *FFT*, 14 (8): 41-2.

——. (1955), "Atlantic Regional Conference," *FFT*, 16 (1): 3-5.

——. (1955a), "Western Regional Conference," *FFT*, 16 (1): 5-8.

——. (1956), "The School and Adult Education," *FFT*, 16 (4): 191.

——. (1956b), "Great Books Live On," *FFT*, 16 (4): 189-90.

——. (1957), "Jubilation," *FFT*, 17 (4): 167.

——. (1957b), "National Commission for UNESCO," *FFT*, 18 (1): 44-5.

——. (1957c), "Good News for Adult Education," *FFT*, 18 (11): 46-7.

——. (1958), "Conference Highlights," *FFT*, 19 (1): 30-39.

——. (1958b), "Professional Training," *FFT*, 18 (8): 405.

——. (1958c), "Citizens' Forum Conference," *FFT*, 19 (1): 35-37.

——. (1960), "Public Schools and Adult Education," *FFT*, 20 (4): 190-91.

——. (1960b), "Second World Conference on Adult Education," *FFT*, 21 (1): 21-30.

——. (1961), "Manpower and Unemployment," *FFT*, 21 (8): 265-76.

Armstrong, D.P. (1968), *Corbett's House: The Origins of the Canadian Association for Adult Education and Its Development during the Directorship of E.A. Corbett 1936-1951*, Unpublished M.A. Thesis, University of Toronto.

Baker, F.D. (1960), "Hard Sell and the Professor," *FFT*, 20 (8): 368-70.

Bercusson, L. (1944), "First Steps in Alberta," *FFT*, 4 (9): 14-16.

Bothwell, R., Drummond, I., English, J. (1981), *Canada Since 1945*, Toronto: University of Toronto Press.

Cameron, D. (1953), *The Banff School of Fine Arts*, Toronto: CAAE.

———. (1956), *Campus in the Clouds*, Toronto: McClelland and Stewart.

———. (1960), "A Diagnosis." *FFT*, 21 (3): 100-07.

Campbell, D.D. (1977), *Adult Education as a Field of Study and Practice*, Vancouver: University of B.C. Centre for Continuing Education.

Campbell, G. (1961), "Conference on Government and Adult Education," *FFT*, 21, Supp.B, 94-96.

Canada (1951), *Report*, Royal Commission on National Development in the Arts, Letters and Sciences 1949-1951, Ottawa: King's Printer.

CAAE (1950), *Questions and Answers about Adult Education in Canada*, Toronto: CAAE.

———. (1957), *Report of Western Regional Conference of CAAE*, Toronto: CAAE.

———. (1958), *Notebook on Citizenship Education*, Toronto: CAAE.

———. (1959), *Report of Proceedlngs, Western Regional Conference: CAAE* Toronto: CAAE.

CAAE/ICEA (1960), *Adult Education in Canada/L'education des adultes au Canada*, Toronto/Montreal: CAAE/ICEA.

———. (1961), *National Conference on Adult Education*, Toronto/Montreal: CAAE/ICEA.

Canadian Education Association (1961), *Report of the Conference on Government and Adult Education*, Toronto: C.E.A.

Carter, C.W. (1949), "Adult Education in Newfoundland," *FFT*, 9 (7): 10-14.

Citizenship Branch, Dept. of Citizenship and Immigration (1953), *Report of National Seminar on Citizenship*, Ottawa: Citizenship Branch.

Clark, C. (1949), "What Kind of Commission?", *FFT*, 10 (3): 27-31.

———. (1954), *Joint Planning Commission*, Toronto: CAAE

Coady, M.M. (1954), "The Secret of Leadership in Adult Education," *FFT*, 14 (4): 4-7.

Corbett, E.A. (1947), *A Short History of Adult Education*, Toronto: CAAE

———. (1952), *University Extension in Canada*, Toronto: CAAE.

———. (1957), *We Have With Us Tonight*, Toronto: Ryerson.

Creighton, D. (1976), *The Forked Road*, Toronto: McClelland and Stewart Faris, R. (1975), *The Passionate Educators*, Toronto: Peter Martin.

Hawkins, G. (1954), "As Others See Us," *FFT*, 14 (8): 2-8.

——. (1956), "Coming of Age in the CAAE: A Drama in Five Acts," *FFT*, 17 (1): 3-49.

——. (Ed.) (1956b), *Design for Democracy*, London: Max Parrish.

Henson, G. (1954), *Adult Education in Nova Scotia*, Toronto: CAAE.

Herbert, W.B. (1959), "Profile: J.R. Kidd," *FFT*, 20 (1): 12-17.

Ironside, D.J. (1959), "Canadian Investigations and Research in Adult Education." *FFT*,19 (8): 374-85.

Jones, T. (1957), "Economic Preoccupations in the East," *FFT*, 18 (1): 10-13.

Kidd, J.R. (Ed.) (1950), *Adult Education in Canada,*. Toronto: CAAE.

——. (1950b), *Adult Education and the School*, Toronto: CAAE.

——. (1952), "Thoughts on Returning to Canada," *FFT*, 13 (2): 30-31.

——. (1952b), "A Kind of Partnership," *FFT*, 13 (1): 4-7.

——. (1953), *People Learning from Each Other*, Toronto: CAAE.

——. (1953b), "Training for Democratic Leadership," in *Citizenship Branch* 1953, 105-24.

——. (1953c), *Pictures With a Purpose*, Toronto: CAAE

——. (1955), "Education for International Understanding." *FFT*, 15 (6): 13-19.

——. (1956), *Putting Words to Work*, Toronto: CAAE

——. (1956b), *Adult Education in the Canadian University*, Toronto: CAAE

——. (Ed.) (1958), *Adult Education in a Free Society*, Toronto: Guardian Bird.

——. (1959), "113 and All That," *FFT*, 20 (1): 44-45.

——. (1959b), *Adult Education in the Caribbean*, Toronto: CAAE.

——. (1959c), *How Adults Learn*, New York: Association Press.

——. (1961), *Continuing Education*, Ottawa: Canadian Conference on Education.

——. (1961b), *18 to 80: Continuing Education in Metropolitan Toronto*, Toronto, Toronto Board of Education.

——. (1961c), "The Creative Crusade." *FFT*, 21, Supp. A, 37-46.

——. (1962), *Financing Continuing Education*, New York: Scarecrow Press.

——. (Ed.) (1963), *Learning and Society*, Toronto: CAAE.

——. (1970), "The Imaginative Training for Citizenship," *Continuous Learning*, 9 (3): 111-25.

——. (1974), *A Tale of Two Cities*, Syracuse: University of Syracuse.

——. and Storr, C.B., (1951), *Film Utilization*, Toronto: CAAE.

Laidlaw, A.F. (1961), *The Campus and the Community*, Montreal: Harvest House.

Loosley, E. (1960), *Residential Adult Education: A Canadian View*, Toronto: CAAE.

Lowe, J. (1975), *The Education of Adults: A World Perspective*, Paris: UNESCO.

McLeish, J.A.B. (1978), *A Canadian For All Seasons*, Toronto: Lester and Orpen.

Martin, P. (1958), "Learning in Packages," *FFT*, 17 (7): 337-40.

Morin, R. and Potter, H.H. (1953), Camp Laquemac, Toronto: CAAE.

Morrison, J.H. (1953), *So-Ed in Canada*, Toronto: CAAE.

Ostry, B. (1378), *The Cultural Connection*, Toronto: McClelland and Stewart

Parsons, H. (1952), *Where and Why? A Study of the Distribution of Program Materials*, Toronto: CAAE.

Price, F.W. (1962), *The Second Canadian Conference on Education*, Toronto: University of Toronto.

Ross, M.G. (1952), Education in Canadian Institutions, Toronto: CAAE Rouillard, H. (Ed.) (1952), *Pioneers in Adult Education in Canada*, Toronto: CAAE.

Selman, G.R. (1955), "Mind Meets Mind in British Columbia," *FFT*, 16 (3): 121-25.

——. (1957), "Western Variations on the Theme," *FFT*, 18 (1): 5-9.

——. (1963), *A History of the Extension and Adult Education Services of The University of British Columhia 191S to 1955*, Unpublished M.A. Thesis, University of B.C.

——. (1969), *Toward Co-operation: The Development of a Provincial Voice for Adult Education in British Columbia, 1953 to 1962*, Vancouver: University of B.C. Centre for Continuing Education.

——. (1980), *The British Columbia Division of the CAAE*, Occasional Paper No. 7, Pacific Association for Continuing Education.

——. (1981), *The Canadian Association for Adult Education in the Corbett Years: A Re-Evaluation*, Vancouver: University of B.C. Centre for Continuing Education.

Shea, A.A. (1952), *Culture in Canada*, Toronto: CAAE.

Sim, R.A. (1950), "The Mondsee Seminar," *FFT*, 11 (2): 5-10.

——. (1954), *Canada's Farm Radio Forum*, Paris: UNESCO.

Stensland, P. (1946), "New Plans in Newfoundland," *FFT*, 6 (9): 4-9, 47.

Thomas, A.M. (1957), "London—and After," *FFT*, 17 (5): 230-33.

——. (1959), "Who Are the Professionals?," *FFT*, 19 (8): 362-69.

——. (1959b), "The Making of a Professional," *FFT*, 20 (1): 4-11, 45.

Thomson, M. and Ironside, D. (Compilers) (1956), *A Bibliography of Canadian Writings in Adult Education*, Toronto: CAAE.

Timmons, H.P. (1953), "Atlantic Regional Conference of the CAAE," *FFT*, 14 (2): 29-33.

Wilson, I. (1980), *Citizens' Forum: Canada's National Platform*, Toronto: Ontario Institute for Studies in Education.

——. and Stinson, A. (1957), "Has TV Helped Citizens' Forum?," *FFT*, 17 (5): 217-25.

——. et al (1954), *Education in Public Affairs by Radio*, Toronto: CAAE

Wilson, J.D.. Stamp. R.M., Audet, L. (Ed.) (1970), *Canadian Education: A History*, Scarborough: Prentice-Hall.

Originally published in *Occasional Papers in Continuing Education*, University of British Columbia, Centre for Continuing Education, No. 22, 1982. Reprinted with permission.

3.3

Alan Thomas and the Canadian Association for Adult Education 1961 - 1970

*T*he Canadian Association for Adult Education was established in 1935 and the story of its early years, under the direction of E.A. Corbett and Roby Kidd, has been told in some detail elsewhere (Faris 1975; Selman 1981, 1982). Founded in the midst of the Depression, although the original intention was that it be a clearing house and an agency-serving organization, the CAAE soon became something quite different. Under Corbett's leadership, and in response to the demands of wartime conditions and subsequently, the somewhat radicalized period of reconstruction planning, the organization, in Corbett's words, "moved out of [its] Ivory Tower" (CAAE DR 1944) and began to play a direct programming and leadership role in adult education. It pioneered in the use of radio and local discussion groups for public affairs education through National Farm Radio Forum and Citizens' Forum. It conducted experimental projects in the field of leadership training and community devopment. It established and led a network of national organizations active in adult education, social and cultural devopment, through the instrumentality of the Joint Planning Commission.

The Association, as a result of Corbett's vigorous leadership, went beyond providing citizenship education. For a time it espoused certain political and social policies itself. In what was called a "Manifesto," which was approved by its 1943 conference, the Association declared itself in favor of the expansion of public ownership and control and spoke strongly of the need for social goals to take precedence over "individual and sectional purposes of profit or advantage" (Kidd 1963: 108-9). The statement of such ideas earned the CAAE the reputation in some circles of being leftist. Corbett simply commented that the Association "had allied [itself] with people of progressive temper" (CAAE DR 1944) .

Although the position taken by the Association at this time seems less extreme when it is put against the background of the reconstruction period, it soon became clear that such a stance would not be a satisfactory basis for co-operation with a cross section of organizations in the postwar period. At a conference in 1946, the Association approved a new declaration, one which emphasized citizenship education and social animation. It sought to raise questions of public concern for examination, rather than suggest what the answers should be (Kidd 1963: 110-11).

After this point, the activists who sought to use the CAAE as a means of promoting leftist political and social goals tended to leave the Association. Others remained who thought of the CAAE as a movement and who wished it to contribute, in the words of the 1946 declaration, to "the imaginative training for citizenship"(Kidd 1963: 109).

Corbett retired from the directorship of the organization in 1951 and was replaced by Dr. Roby Kidd, who had been Associate Director for four years. Kidd was as committed to the citizenship education role of the Association as Corbett had been, but he added other dimensions as well. Kidd had been the first Canadian to gain a doctoral degree in the field of adult education and some of his chief contributions relate generally to the professionalization of the field.

Kidd saw that if the CAAE was to be able to provide leadership for the field over a broad front, it could not be partisan on the public issues of the day. He declared in his first annual report that the Association was not and could not be "the radical agency of social action" which some might prefer (CAAE DR 1952). Its advocacy must be on behalf of adult education. Kidd gave strong support, however, to the citizenship education projects, Farm and Citizens' Forum, the Joint Planning Commission and several other citizenship-related programs. He also spearheaded a vigorous series of advocacy activities involving submissions on behalf of the interests of adult learners to a variety of royal commissions and other public bodies.

Perhaps the most significant new dimension of Kidd's leadership was that of promoting the professionalization of the field. He emphasized the need for training in all his dealings with adult educators and their employers. He was extremely active in organizing and teaching training activities for practitioners. He taught university credit courses in the field at a number of Canadian universities, several of these being the first course on the subject given by those institutions. He raised funds from several sources to support Canadian adult educators in their career development. Kidd also was active in promoting the institutional development of the field, most notably in persuading provincial departments of education, school boards and universities to support and develop their adult education programs. He experimented with methodology in the field, pioneering the use in Canada of study-discussion programs in the liberal arts and public affairs. He also wrote and had published a great deal of material which was useful to practitioners. This included manuals of practice, descriptive material about the nature of adult education in Canada and a widely used textbook for the field. Kidd also encouraged, by various means, the formation of provincial associations of adult educators, arranging for them to have affiliation with the CAAE.

The other important dimension of Kidd's leadership was involvement in the international aspects of the field. Increasingly, as the decade of his directorship progressed, he—and through him, the CAAE—played an active part in international developments. He spent most of a year in the West Indies (1957-58) as consultant to the University College (as it then was), a time he subsequently referred to as his apprenticeship in the work of international development (Selman 1982). He became actively involved in the work of UNESCO, serving as chairman of its advisory committee on the field, and in 1960 acted as President of UNESCO's Second World Conference on Adult Education, which was held in Montreal. His skilled and diplomatic leadership saved the conference from foundering on cold war tensions, which it was widely predicted would ruin the meeting, and Kidd emerged from that event as perhaps the best-known adult educator in the world.

When Arthur Pigott (on a brief interim basis) and shortly thereafter, Alan Thomas, took over the directorship of the CAAE, they were stepping into large shoes. Corbett had been a charismatic, creative leader, whose major program innovations, the two Forum projects and the Joint Planning Commission, gained international reputations for excellence. Kidd pioneered other programs, skilfully promoted the professionalization and institutionalization of adult education and became a major world figure in the field by the time he left the Association. Anyone who was in the position of following these two leaders and who was anxious to make a significant conttibution in his own right must have seen the task as a large one.

The Sixties

"The Sixties," perhaps to a degree only exceeded by "The Thirties," is a decade the very name of which conjures up the flavour of the times. The Sixties in Canada were a time of accelerated change, of chaos, of participatory democracy, of co-operative federalism, populist movements, the counterculture, the War on Poverty, the Quiet Revolution and what has been termed the "youthquake" (Edmonds 1979: 25ff.). The traditional ways of the liberal democratic system were repeatedly challenged. As novelist Hugh MacLennan put it late in the decade, "We find ourselves cursed by the young for all the things we were proud of" (Quoted in Bothwell et al. 1981: 334).

It was a decade of economic prosperity, in overall terms, with considerable progress as well in social legislation (Brebner 1970). Such conditions might suggest times in which there was political stability and a pursuit of private interests, but though such may have been the ways of a silent majority, many Canadians, often spurred on by a New Left which was dominated by the young, contributed to the Sixties becoming a decade of intense political involvement (Granatstein 1983). Bothwell and colleagues (1981) have pointed out that both the New Left and society generally were dominated by the young and that this gave the decade its predominant image, that of a boisterous uprising of the young that threatened and sometimes tumbled over the fundamental institutions of our society (p.334).

Certainly the times brought unaccustomed political instability to Canada. The decade began with John Diefenbaker as Prime Minister. He was replaced by the Liberals under Lester Pearson in 1963, who was succeeded as leader of the party and Prime Minister by Pierre Trudeau in 1968. When Trudeau won a majority in the House of Commons later in the same year, it was the first majority government Canada had elected since ten years before. It was a time of great political unrest and strong citizen movements outside the traditional party and decision-making structures. Mass demonstrations, direct political confrontations and "media events" came to be a common style of operation. As Bothwell and his colleagues put it, "form was as important as content" (1981: 256).

But the content was strong stuff too. The increasing realization of the extent of poverty and its attendant evils in Canada engendered responses of many kinds, from both government and populist movements. The women's movement gathered momentum during the decade. Concern was felt by many about the increasing domination of sectors of the Canadian economy by American capital and head office control. While Canadians were largely bystanders with respect to the Vietnam war, which gave rise to so much protest in the United States, it had its effects here as well, and Canadians were also concerned with related issues of disarmament and regional defence agreements. Environmental concerns emerged strongly during the decade. as did matters of human rights.

In addition to these large issues, many of which were common to all countries or at least the industrialized ones, Canada had its own unique problems, most prominently perhaps, the social, cultural and political adjustments made necessary by the Quiet Revolution in Quebec and the changing expectations and demands of French Canadians within Canadian society. Government responded in various ways to Quebec's aspirations, in matters of language policy as well as a "co-operative federalism" which led Ottawa to accord Quebec a special status within Confederation. For this and other reasons, the other provinces made new demands for resources and consultation and there was a significant movement in the direction of the decentralization of power in Confederation to the provinces (Armour 1981; Bothwell et al. 1981).

There was a strong belief in Canada in the beneficial effects of education. When to this was added the shock the Western countries received when the U.S.S.R. was the first to launch a global satellite in 1957, fresh impetus was given to the need to expand and improve Canadian educational systems and practices. In the field of vocational and technical education, this led to two major pieces of federal legislation, the Technical and Vocational Training Assistance Act of 1960 and the Adult Occupational Training Act of 1967, the former making possible a massive expansion of facilities and programs and the second moving the federal government into a new and more direct role in the provision of training and the selection of students.

There were dramatic changes in the general educational systems as well, perhaps more than in any other comparable period in our history (Stevenson 1973). Most striking are the statistics of post-secondary education enrollments during the Sixties, as the postwar baby boom children came of age and public policy supported the expansion of educational facilities. There were 15 major provincial commissions on education between 1960 and 1973 (Wilson 1977). There was in this period great faith in the efficacy of education in supporting personal, social and economic development (Myers 1973; Stevenson 1973) and the public systems expanded enormously, most notably the universities and community colleges. There were 12 new universities founded between 1959 and 1966 (Kettle 1980) and full-time enrollments in universities increased from 106,000 in 1960 to 330,000 in 1970 (Granatstein 1983). The percentage of the GNP which was devoted to education rose from 4.3 in 1961 to 7.6 in 1969, and education's share of the expenditures of all levels of government in Canada rose from 14 percent in 1961 to 22 in 1971-72 (Pike 1981).

Even more dramatic were the developments concerning the community colleges, a movement with which the CAAE was closely connected. In 1958 there was only one college in the country, but by 1970, with major developments in Alberta, British Columbia, Ontario and Quebec, the number had increased to 130 colleges and related institutions (Dennison 1981; Martin and Macdonell 1978). The adult education movement had a particular interest in the community college because of its clear commitment to serving the needs of adult students and to responding to a wide variety of learning needs as expressed in the community. That such a phenomenal development of institution building could take place during this period was made possible by widespread belief in the benefits of education and the co-operation of both senior levels of government.

Education, according to the constitution, was a provincial responsibility, but it was one of several fields in which the provincial and federal levels of government had developed a shared leadership. Some of the reasons for the federal participation in this field are suggested by H.A. Stevenson (1981: 270):

> Since 1960, however, the federal government has developed a massive involvement in education because many national policies such as manpower training, multi-culturalism, bilingualism, research priorities, equalizing regional inequities, culture and the economy, involve education and the best interests of all Canadians regardless of where they live.

In terms which perhaps relate to the CAAE's efforts in the period to create a unitary national organization, Stevenson has referred elsewhere to "the truly national dimensions of most educational problems" and to the fact that in the early 1960s Canadians felt "a national dimension" to educational concerns (1973: 57, 59). During the Sixties, the federal government's share of the cost of post-secondary education rose from 23 percent in 1960 to 46 percent by 1969 (Martin and Macdonell 1978).

Of particular relevance to this study are the major measures taken during the decade in the field of vocational and technical training. Canada shared with other Western nations concern over relatively high unemployment rates and about the level and quality of training in the work force. The Act passed by the Diefenbaker government in 1960 provided for Ottawa to contribute 75 percent of the capital costs and 50 percent of the operating costs of a wide range of vocational and technical training facilities and programs. Some impression of the scale of operations under this Act is provided by the fact that by early 1967, the federal and provincial governments had agreed on projects valued at $1,476,000,000, provided 662 new institutions and 439,952 new places for students (Stamp 1970). Although much useful work was accomplished, there remained the problem of resentment, in some provincial quarters, over the fact that this federal legislation had the effect of forcing the hand of the provinces in a field which it was generally assumed was a provincial responsibility. At a federal-provincial conference in 1966, Prime Minister Pearson announced that his government intended to change the rules of the game. He stated that "manpower training was not 'education' in the constitutional sense" and that the federal government was going to move into a direct role in determining training need, selecting students for training, purchasing training for them, and providing training allowances, as required (Doerr 1981:48). These arrangements were provided for in the Act passed the following year.

There was also during the Sixties an increasing realization of the extent of illiteracy and under-education in the Canadian population. The facts revealed by the 1961 census (Adamson 1966) were reinforced as the decade progressed by the discovery of how many people who qualified for vocational training under the federal legislation did not have a basic education that was adequate to enable them to take advantage of such training. Federal financing of adult basic education increased rapidly under the 1960 legislation and with the change of federal policy in 1966-67 and the "War on Poverty" thrust of the government, commitment to this work increased and programs for the educationally disadvantaged, through the NewStart Corporations (Sloan 1972) and by other means, were expanded greatly (Brooke 1972).

Another significant development during the 1960s was the emergence of community development as a means of bringing about social change and the improvement of the quality of individual and community life. Relying on techniques developed by the United

Nations and others in the Third World, community development was suited to the desire for social improvement and democratic participation so typical of the 1960s and from its Canadian beginnings in Manitoba in 1960 (Legasse 1971; Lotz 1977) it was widely used elsewhere in the country, frequently financed by federal funds under the Agricultural Reconstruction and Development Act, or other measures (Draper 1971).

As a result of the foregoing developments, the field of adult education and the number of persons working as adult educators expanded enormously during the 1960s. The expansion of the formal systems led to greatly increased provision by school boards, colleges and universities in this field. Major developments such as those described above in the fields of vocational training, adult basic education and community development added to the field, as did a wide range of voluntary organizations and movements. University training programs for adult educators, the first of which had been inaugurated at the University of British Columbia in 1957, were established in the following decade at several other institutions across the country. Research activities increased rapidly (Draper 1978b).

The Canadian Association for Adult Education was seeking to provide support and leadership to a rapidly growing and diversifying field of educational activity. Education has been termed "the golden haired child of the Fifties and Sixties" (Myers 1973:60) and adult education shared in that rapid expansion. A field which according to educational historians had "lost much of its amateur status" by the late Fifties (Wilson et al. 1970:412), experienced further major expansion in the Sixties and became an important instrument in government strategy with respect to the goals of public policy. In such a time of emerging, unaccustomed prominence, it was advantageous for the movement to have at the head of the CAAE a person of such intellectual range and large ambition, not for himself, but for the role of adult education and adult learning in the life of the country.

Alan Thomas: Ends and Means

When Alan Thomas joined the staff of the CAAE in the fall of 1961, he felt he was "going home" (Thomas, personal communication, Mar. 10, 1982). He had worked for the Association in the mid-Fifties as director of an experimental project in study-discussion programs (Selman 1982), after working two earlier years as educational representative for a book publishing company. He had left the CAAE in 1955 to pursue a doctorate in adult education at Columbia University and then for five years worked at The University of British Columbia, giving part time to teaching in the Faculty of Education and part to directing a program in communications in the Department of University Extension. During his U.B.C. years, he kept in close touch with the CAAE and its Director, Roby Kidd. and contributed a number of articles to the Association's journal, *Food For Thought*. In September of 1961, he rejoined the staff of the CAAE as Associate Executive Director to Arthur Pigott, who had been Director since Roby Kidd's departure at the end of April. It was the general expectation, when Thomas joined the staff, that he would before long move into the directorship, Pigott not being a professional adult educator and having been seen as a caretaker appointment. In the summer of 1962, it was decided for financial and other reasons to discontinue the existing arrangement, Arthur Pigott resigned and Thomas became Director as of September 1. He continued in that post until the end of February 1970.

Thomas was 33 years old when he rejoined the staff of the Association. He was bright, quick-thinking and an able speaker, appealing to most people, but seen by some as brash and "too intellectual." He soon corrected that impression, on closer acquaintance, and inspired friendship with large numbers of people across the country and loyalty on the part of many.

It seems difficult to imagine anyone assuming responsibility for the CAAE with larger ambitions than Thomas held. From his position as Director of this small and impoverished organization, Thomas set out to move the CAAE to the forefront of national policy development and as he later put it, "to attach learning to all matters of public policy" (personal communication, Mar. 10, 1982). He sought to convince both policy makers in the country as a whole, especially at the federal level, and adult educators too, of the potential of adult learning as a force in human affairs (personal communication, Aug. 10, 1983). In his view adult educators were "riding a tiger," the tiger being the potential of adult learning, and he set out to use the CAAE as an instrument to bring that message to Canadians.

Commensurate with the scale of his ambitions, Thomas approached his mission with great flair and energy. He was seemingly tireless in his willingness to travel back and forth across the country to speak to a wide variety of audiences, to spend time in Ottawa, seeking to influence decision-makers there, and to write about his ideas. He redesigned and generally spruced up the Association's journal, hoping to reach a wider national audience; he styled the Association's library and information resources as the "National Research Library in Adult Education;" he renamed the offices of the Association as "Corbett House" and was successful in getting the federal Secretary of State to take part in the opening ceremonies; he instituted a series of annual reviews of adult education developments in Canada; he conceived of the publication of a policy statement about adult learning in Canada and arranged for its release by means of press conferences in all sections of the country; he saw the imminent emergence of the community college in Canada and sought to place the CAAE at the forefront of planning in that connection. Thomas thought in big terms about the potential of adult learning and about the leadership role of the CAAE and he pursued those goals with remarkable imagination and energy, reshaping the Association as an instrument to these ends.

Although the CAAE had from its creation, in the persons of E.A. Corbett and Roby Kidd, strong and extremely able leadership, at no time had the views and ideas of the Director been more dominant in the activities of the Association than during the Thomas years. It was not that Thomas set out to dominate the organization as an end in itself; rather he had ideas and convictions which he strongly wished to pursue—on behalf of adult education and the Association—and the CAAE was a means to those ends. Thomas' ideas were well known to the governing bodies of the Association before he was appointed; he had written and spoken widely about them and had made them abundantly clear in his year as Associate Director. The Association clearly knew what style and content would characterize Thomas' leadership—and liked what it saw.

The Learning Society

The most distinctive and important idea which Alan Thomas contributed to the field in this period was that the basic concept must be adult learning, as distinct from adult education. Learning is what has effects in the minds and lives of people; education consists of the deliberate efforts to promote or facilitate learning. Learning takes place everywhere in life, not just in educational programs and institutions, and it is learning that counts.

This emphasis on learning, and the implications of widening the field's concerns to include all the aspects of society which have an effect on learning, was the key to Thomas' professional activities (Thomas 1970b; 1980; 1981; 1983). He developed these ideas into coherent form in 1961, presented them to others by means of three major statements in that year, and amplified and applied them further throughout his directorship of the Association.

Some of his ideas—the emphasis on learning rather than education, the concern for the educative influences of forces in the society over and above the avowedly educational ones (the power of the media, the workplace, citizenship and other responsibilities) and the emphasis on the role of learning over the whole life span—were expounded by Thomas approximately a decade before they came into prominence in the field. Experts in adult education (Houle 1984; Kallen 1979) generally date the emergence of these ideas in the early seventies, with the publication of Lengrand's (1970) essay on lifelong education and the report of UNESCO's International Commission on the Development of Education (Faure 1972), and other developments. While the idea of "the learning society," as he entitled his major address in 1961, hardly originated with him in many of its dimensions— ideas of this kind can generally not be traced to any one person—Thomas' ideas burst upon the adult education scene in Canada as fresh and original. Thomas himself does not know with any clarity what led him to these ideas. He had been impressed by John Dewey's thought and had developed aspects of it in his masters thesis. He had been impressed during his short employment in the book trade with the differences between what people learned and were interested in, and the school curriculum. And he considers that the influences of Marshall McLuhan, under whom he studied as an undergraduate, and Roby Kidd, with whom he had worked in the mid-Fifties at the CAAE, had been important to his development (personal communication, Dec. 9, 1983).

There are four major statements written by Thomas in this period which outline his ideas. The first three were written in the spring and summer of 1961. They were a keynote address given on May 11 to the conference of the B.C. Adult Education Council (he was still living in B.C. at the time) under the title, "The Learning Society" (Thomas 1961g); an article published in the "Parameter" column of the CAAE's journal in the May-June issue of 1961 (Thomas 1961f), and his address, also under the title of "The Learning Society," to the bilingual national conference on adult education held in Ottawa in late October of that year (CAAE/ICEA 1961). The fourth statement was the *White Paper on the Education of Adults in Canada*, which was published by the Association in 1966. In addition to these four general statements, one may find his ideas applied to more specific contexts throughout his editorials and articles in the CAAE's journal during his tenure, other speeches and papers, and in the submissions made by the Association to royal commissions and other public bodies.

The National Conference on Adult Education, which was held in Ottawa beginning on October 30, 1961, was an unprecedented event. It was co-sponsored by the two national adult education organizations, the CAAE and the Institut canadien d'education des adultes (ICEA), functioned bilingually, and was the only one of its kind ever held in Canada. Leading personalities from the English- and French-speaking communities were invited to give the keynote addresses and it is evidence of the recognition of Alan Thomas' intellectual stature in the field that he was invited to give the English address. His major themes had already been stated in his speech in British Columbia and in several articles which had appeared in *Food For Thought* (1961b, 1961c, 1961d, 1961e, 1961f). In his address, Thomas paid tribute to the strong tradition of adult education in Canada, but stated that the nation was at present facing a "crisis of role, of character and of identity" of major proportions. It had need to call on that tradition of adult learning (CAAE/ICEA 1961:16):

> It is our belief that we can revitalize this tradition and make this capacity for learning the foundation of Canadian society. We therefore offer as our central concern, not education, in its formal and institutional sense, but learning. Whatever the explicit and various goals of the multitude of agencies which we here are associated with or represent, we have one conrmon concern, the ability of human beings to learn continuously, and the conditions under which learning best takes place. These conditions are the foundation of *the learning society*. It is the stimulation and encouragement of this unique human capacity throughout the whole of an individual life which is the core of our concern; and which can be the core of the entire country.

Thomas made the point repeatedly during the decade that learning far exceeds the limits of education, and at various times he made great claims for the potential and power of learning:

- The only human, dignified way to respond to change is by learning (1961a:264).
- Democracy depends on learning (1961e:316).
- Learning, the true currency of post-industrial society (1961d:264).
- Learning must be the true cornerstone of national policy (1962e:191).
- Learning together always breeds effective relationships among men (1964c:53).
- ....A whole new moral code, of which learning and competence are the cornerstones (1965:3).
- Learning is of course the only alternative to revolution (1961g:3).
- ...For surely most adult educators are aware that the morality lies in the learning, in the activity itself, and not in the effect of the subject matter (1966b:51).
- In every act of learning there is both an act of surrender and a great release of energy (1970:4).

Thomas suggested a view of Canadian history as seen from the point of view of learning. He pointed out that the Canadian people, like all people, have responded to the crises in their national life, in part by learning. The two World Wars, the Depression and other events have brought a response on a massive scale in the form of learning (Thomas 1961). By this means, the nation has risen to the challenges. He summed up this view (1970b:232) that, "Canada has been dominated from the outset by two overwhelming demands on human adaptation, learning—pioneering and immigration."And to these two factors he subsequently added a third, industrialization (1970b:234).

Learning must become "the cornerstone of national policy," he stated (1962e:191). "We have only begun to see the potential of free people learning all their lives long" (CAAE AR 1965-66:9). A strong element in Thomas' thinking was the importance of citizenship education and the role of learning in a democratic society. His interpretation of the tumultuous 1960s, written at the end of the decade, again stresses the centrality of learning (1970:2):

> What we have seen individually and collectively has been and remains a renaissance, we have seen learning bursting free from the institutions of the society and confronting them one after another, in particular, confronting the institutions of education.

In the fourth of Thomas' major statements, the White Paper issued by the Association in 1966, an effort was made to work out these ideas about learning as they related to public policy. Some aspects of this will be dealt with in the section on policy below, but it should be stated here that there was a clear commitment to what might be termed both a life-wide and a lifelong view of learning; that learning must be part of living throughout the life span and also that institutions of all kinds, not just those designated as educational, must play a role in promoting learning (CAAE 1966b). Thomas referred to this White Paper as the Association's "intellectual reference point" and he added, "We have only begun to see the potential of free people learning their lives long" (CAAE AR 1965-66:4, 9).

Something of the sweep of Thomas' ideas concerning the field of adult education may be seen in the peroration of his address to the 1961 conference (CAAE/ICEA 1961:20):

> We have offered this image of the learning society in Canada for two reasons. First, because we believe our country has some unique opportunities which we are not at present realizing. Second, because we think the same fact is true of the adult educators in Canada. We are convinced that not only Canada but adult educators face awesome alternatives. We, as eductors, can continue to run other people's errands, to jump when some other major institution or power wills and rush to do its bidding; we can remain, hat-in-hand, grateful for every small amount of support society chooses to give us—and we can leave this new energy, released by the greater demands of learning, undirected and unfulfilled. Or we can speak reasonably but with force and conviction to our citizens of the vision that the learning society affords, of the possibilities we have all seen arising from the determined nourishing of this capacity, and begin to realize the particular heritage that as a western, industrial, immigrant, pioneering society is ours alone to realize. We have said before that only the adult educators can do it if they choose. We commend this exhilarating prospect to this conference, to each and every one of our colleagues.

It seems clear that many of Thomas' colleagues were greatly attracted to his ideas, his vision of the centrality of learning and its power for both individuals and society. This was confirmed, at least as far as the affairs of the Association were concerned, by the fact that his ideas come through clearly in the advocacy activities of the Association, including most notably, the White Paper of 1966. But there were critics as well. A few voices were raised from more traditional quarters, which were uneasy with Thomas' view of the dominance of learning in human development. This seemed to be criticism based on a matter of degree. More basic was the criticism which came from the left. Thomas could appropriately be termed a liberal in social and political philosophy. His tendency was to see the world in terms of the individual and to seek changes in public, professional and institutional policies which would best serve the needs of individuals. Those from the left felt that Thomas' ideas did not go far enough and did not speak adequately to basic structural problems in society. Thomas once referred to the CAAE as being "respectably radical" (*Continuous Learning* [hereafter, *CL*] 5, 1, 1966:32), but there were few, if any, real radicals active in the CAAE in this period. Thomas' ideas dominated the work of the Association during his tenure as Director and what criticism there was on ideological grounds—and there was little of it—came largely from elsewhere.

A National Policy

In his "Learning Society" speech to the 1961 national conference, Thomas stated many of the principles which were to guide his efforts during the decade. One of the most notable of these was a call for what he often termed a "national policy" for adult education and adult learning. He stated in 1961 that (CAAE/ICEA 1961:14)

> Adult education has in a few years been transformed from an idealistic, determined, intermittent, fringe enterprise to a central, practical, everyday—if little understood—concern of many individuals and organizations.

A component of society as important as this should not be obstructed in its development by the constitutional arrangements which assigned responsibility for "the education of children" to the provinces. The need was for national policies and "a national governmental structure designed not to impede continuous learning but to support it" (CAAE/ICEA 1961:16). He returned to this theme repeatedly during the decade, the reference usually being to a national policy rather than to federal government structures. As the federal leadership in technical and vocational education developed, under the terms of the Technical and Vocational Training Assistance Act of 1960, Thomas hailed the federal role. In 1962, he urged the federal government, through the pages of *Continuous Learning*, not to give in to provincial complaints but to continue its leadership role (1962b). The following year he declared in an editorial that continuing education had "become inextricably a matter of national policy" (1963d:101).

While it may seem contradictory that Thomas was on the one hand very sensitive to the feelings of Quebec and worked energetically to build closer relations between the CAAE and the ICEA, and at the same time pressed for a national policy concerning adult education, a passage from an address given in 1963 gives some indication of his thinking (1963f:182):

> Adult education has become a matter of national policy....There is hardly a department of the Federal Government which is not engaged in education of some kind....The elaborate terminology used to conceal this fact, brought about by constitutional jitters, surely fools no one, particularly Quebec. I am convinced that Quebec in particular, partly because of the educational revolution now sweeping that province, would welcome a properly conceived, nationally planned and provincially administered system of continuing education.

In editorials in successive issues of *Continuous Learning* the following year (Thomas 1964e; 1964f). Thomas returned to the theme, taking his lead from the "War on Poverty" policies then declared by the Johnson government in the United States. He called for clear, forthright leadership in Canada and declared that a commitment to a learning society would be a commendable national policy for Canada. He went on to portray new federal programs emerging in Indian Affairs and the Agricultural Reconstruction and Development Agency as suitable components in such a policy.

The most substantial effort made by the CAAE in the decade to outline the features of a national policy was the *White Paper on the Education of Adults in Canada*, which was released in the spring of 1966 (CAAE 1966b). It called for "an articulated system of continuing education" for Canada, "a comprehensive national development" and "a logical national plan," one which was developed co-operatively between Ottawa and the provinces. The paper suggests a series of guiding principles for such a system, examines the roles to be played by educational institutions, governments, the voluntary and business sectors, and makes suggestions about matters of administration, research, professional development and finance. There is a final appeal for the development of a national policy along the lines suggested. Unprecedented efforts were made to publicize this White Paper and it was the most ambitious single effort by the Association, and Thomas himself, who wrote the statement, to convince the governmental and educational establishments about a national policy.

Later in the same year, there were grounds for encouragement. At the federal-provincial conference in the fall, the Pearson government announced that it was expanding its role in vocational training under its powers in the constitution related to promoting economic development (Bothwell et al. 1981:313-14) and these measures were implemented in the Adult Occupational Training Act of 1967. When the new bill was introduced, Thomas commented editorially as to the significance of the federal government taking "direct control of a great range of adult education, labelled occupational training" and welcomed this federal initiative, "because we believe that it is education, and because a national initiative in education is important to all of us" (Thomas 1967c:53). In an attempt some 15 years later to identify the various stages in the development of adult education in Canada, Thomas saw the 1967 Act as the watershed event, marking the realization on the part of the federal government that it had to take on more active leadership in this field (Thomas 1981b).

Other Advocacy

A great deal of thought and energy during the decade went into the CAAE's efforts to represent the interests of adult education and the adult learner in dealing with matters of federal policy. The Association had consistently over the years played an active role of this kind (Selman 1981, 1982) and if anything, this activity was even more prominent during the Sixties. Thomas had not only the traditional views of the adult education movement to speak for, but also his particular vision of the place of learning and the characteristics of a learning society.

The details, in terms of bodies to which representations were made, are dealt with in a later section. What may be pointed out here, hovever, is that the efforts of the Association took four main forms. The first was the continuing effort, which had been made sporadically over the years, to persuade the federal government to provide a direct supporting grant to the Association. Thomas and his predecessor, Roby Kidd, had been successful in getting many project grants from departments of the federal government, but it was not until 1966, after a meeting of Thomas and small group of the officers with Prime Minister

Pearson, that a federal grant for the general or administrative functions of the Association was achieved, initially for a five-year period. This effort was made in close consultation with the sister organization, the ICEA, and both received annual grants beginning at this time.

The second aspect of advocacy was the traditional role of making submissions to public bodies on behalf of adult education, as circumstances made that appropriate. The list of such briefs is provided elsewhere in this study and in the turbulent and in some respects chaotic years of the Sixties, there were many such opportunities. With the demise during the decade of Farm and Citizens' Forum and of the Joint Planning Commission, and because of Thomas' views and interest, the Association's advocacy efforts were focussed more predominantly than ever before on matters related to public policy as it affected the adult learner (Thomas 1980). There were significant opportunities to put the case before such bodies as the Royal Commission on Bilingualism and Biculturalism, the Senate Committee on Manpower and Unemployment, the Parliamentary Committee on Broadcasting, and the federal Task Force on Government Information, to name only a few.

A third category of advocacy, one to which Thomas gave a great deal of time in certain periods, is that of advising or persuading such public bodies to conduct their activities in such a way that there were maximum opportunities for the general public to both participate in the hearings and also learn from the process. The efforts in this connection constituted a new type of activity for the Association and the practical results during the period gave grounds for satisfaction.

The fourth type of advocacy was made possible by the fact that during the decade a large number of significant national conferences were held on aspects of Canadian life. These included conferences on education, resources, children, the family and at least ten more subjects. Leaders of the Association played an active part in many of these, most notably Thomas himself, who had earned a reputation as an outstanding conference planner, speaker and conference summarizer. By this means, adult education and adult learning were brought to the attention of many other active groups in Canada.

The Thomas years were extremely active ones in these areas, particularly 1965 to 1967, when a number of the foregoing efforts came to a head. In his annual report for 1966-67, Thomas even stated that the preoccupation with policy matters during the year had curtailed the other program activities of the organization. In words he used some years later in addressing the Association, Thomas displayed at this time "a determination to inject learning into the political process itself" (Thomas 1980:9).

Citizenship Education and National Unity

Since its earliest years, the CAAE had played an outstanding role in citizenship education activities. The Forum projects had brought credit to the Association at home and abroad. Thomas was no less committed to citizenship education than his predecessors, but the forms which it took were different. Citizen participation in activities related to the great issues of the day—the environment, human rights, the women's movement, disarmament, etc.—were the hallmark of the decade. Thomas stressed the learning component of citizenship, the emerging commmunity development movement and a major project on volunteerism in Canadian society, all of which are described below.

Of particular importance during the Thomas years were the activities involving the reports of certain public bodies. Especially after the termination of Citizens' Forum when the expert editorial skills of Isabel Wilson became available for other duties, the CAAE began to publish summaries of major royal commission reports, such as the Commission on Health Services and the Commission on Bilingualism and Biculturalism, and in a variety of ways to interest Canadians in giving close attention and study to these documents.

The report of the latter commission was on a subject of particular interest to Thomas. As explained elsewhere, he had close ties with the province of Quebec and deep affection for the French language and culture. He invested a great deal of effort in building satisfactory relationships between the CAAE and the ICEA. And as the strains on Canadian confederation developed during the decade, Thomas felt deeply involved personally in the outcome and took a great deal of interest in the procedures and the content of the "Bi and Bi Commission." He devoted much space in *Continuous Learning* to the issues involved. He persuaded the officers of the commission to take a second look at their intended procedures for the involvement of the public and personally carried out a contract the Association secured for the evaluation of the first four public hearings. Something of the depth of Thomas' feelings on the subject was revealed by a moving comment on the task of the commission published soon after it was appointed and which appeared in the journal under the nom de plume, "Saxon Roland." He dispatched with scorn the English Canadian tendency to pose the question, "What do the French Canadians want?". He stated the issue more broadly, and commented (Thomas 1963h:211):

> It will not be settled without deep and profound changes in the way we behave, in the way we imagine Canada, and in the way we perceive ourselves. It is a question of what we want, and it is time we began to pursue this investigation, for this is fundamentally what the French want to hear.

The Profession

The 1950s have been described as a period in which adult education emerged professionally in Canada (Selman 1982; Wilson et al. 1970). That process was of course still under way during the following decade. Thomas had himself earned a doctoral degree in the field (he completed his dissertation and received his degree in 1964), had played a leading role in the establishment of the first degree program in the field in Canada (at the University of British Columbia, in 1957) and was a very stimulating and admired teacher. A review of his copious writings while Director of the CAAE leaves one with the impression that he was speaking at least as much, perhaps more, to his fellow adult educators as he was to the rest of society. Like his predecessor, Roby Kidd, he strove to convince those working in adult education to take their vocation seriously in the sense of attempting to master the increasing knowledge available about the field of practice. To this, Thomas added the particular vision he had of the learning society and the role which those working in the field could play in helping to bring it about.

Thomas used all the means at his disposal to persuade adult educators of the significance of their calling. Conferences, standing committees of the Association, specialized newsletters for sections of the field, the pages of *Continuous Learning*—all these were employed as a means of communicating to the field. At the same time, he frequently reminded all who would listen of the historical roots of adult education as a social movement and the significance of learning as a means of improving the society.

Thomas taught a great deal during his time as Director and promoted the training of adult educators in many ways. In his first attempt to write an "annual review" of adult education developments in the country, published in the fall of 1964, he reviewed many aspects of the field and when he came to the training of adult educators, he termed it "the most troubled area of all" (1964i:204). He published articles about the development of professional training in Canada and as editor of the Association's journal carried annual directories of training opportunities for several years. A major conference sponsored by the Association was devoted to the subject in 1966 (CAAE 1966). He also demonstrated his interest in the field by preparing in 1963 on behalf of the Association a submission to the Kellogg Foundation for a $242,000, five-year project, which would have provided a "national program for training and development" (CAAE Exec. June 27, 1963). He established and supported a standing committee on research and training, which functioned throughout the period, and a standing committee of professors of adult education, which was formed in 1967 but which met infrequently.

Thomas made a concerted effort during the decade to bring to the attention of adult educators new and emerging challenges to the field. In his second annual review of the field, he wrote of "a series of intellectual comets that have flashed across the sky" and he referred to leisure, poverty, automation, women, community colleges, bilingualism and biculturalism, youth and aging, all of which were areas in which adult education had a role to play (1965e:193). To this list he added others on occasion—employment, health and communications, to name three. About all these areas, he published articles, articulated comments on public policy and generally attempted to bring the issues and their educational implications to the attention of practitioners.

There was a dimension of this which proved troublesome on occasion. Thomas' view of learning and of those who are concerned with learning was very inclusive. On occasion, when he made proposals to his board and executive concerning projects which involved co-operation with groups outside the traditional adult education circles, he was challenged and had to tread warily. It will be seen below that this matter arose in connection with the guidance and counselling group, the human relations trainers and some elements of the community college project. In an editorial he wrote in the spring of 1963, he somewhat pointedly asked, "Are we to remain only among our old and important associates, or actively seek new ones?" (1963d:101). He was clearly still having to sell his concept of the learning society and the role of the Association in promoting it.

Thomas took seriously the role of the Association in providing professional service to the field in the form of information and research facilities. The efforts to build up the library of the Association as a research centre for the field in Canada and the publication of a variety of newsletters to meet the needs of specialized groups of practitioners were ambitious, given the resources of the organization. He saw these professional activities as crucial. "It is our ability here that either will ensure us a commanding place in adult education or condemn us to watch the steady erosion of any imaginative unity in adult education" (CAAE Bd. Jan. 21-23, 1966).

The Association and its Program

Thomas saw—and used—the CAAE as a strategic place from which to influence both the field of adult education and the wider community. It was a small organization, with slender resources, one which threatened no one. It had links all across the country with its provincial divisions and could also "free-wheel" at the national level, where there was no constituted authority in the field of education and where it was possible to exercise influence both personally and in the name of the Association, during a decade in which many new ideas were being sought and experimented with by government.

Thomas cared deeply about the CAAE and had hoped to return to it ever since he had worked there with Roby Kidd and others in the mid-Fifties. He had large ambitions, not only for adult education and adult learning, but also for the CAAE itself. He hoped that by making the CAAE an instrument through which the concept of the learning society could be developed and promoted, the Association could, as he said in an editorial in 1963, "re-establish itself as a valuable, even indispensable factor in Canada" (1963d:100). In his first attempt at an annual review of the field, in 1964, he described the goals of the CAAE, "the unity of the field; the competence of the agents of adult education; and the application of the imagination of the country to the possibilities of continuous learning" (1964i:204). That the third of these goals received so much emphasis during the years of his directorship meant that the organization did not become what its counterpart organization in the United States became, one devoted largely to serving the needs of a professional membership (McClusky 1982), but one which retained many of the characteristics of a movement. The announcement of the crucial 1968 CAAE conference stated, "The CAAE is an Association that is a movement" (*CL*7 [4], 1968:145). In his report to that same conference, the Director asked those attending a series of pointed questions, two of which were (CAAE AM June 6-8,1968):

- Has the movement quality really vanished and is it romantic to hope to maintain it? Are we prepared to make sacrifices for the support of the Association...?

- Is membership basically a purchase of professional services, or a symbol of the wish to participate in the affairs of an organized movement whose first responsibility is to the community and to learning?

Elsewhere in the same year, Thomas called for the reinforcement of "the quality of movement" in the Association (CAAE AR 1967-68:61).

Something of the nature and seriousness of Thomas' aims for the Association is revealed by this excerpt from his speech to the CAAE conference in Vancouver in 1966 (CAAE 1966:61):

> This is the essence of the Association.... It is the attempt to make learning, the potential we all hold all our lives, effective in an organized way, at the most crucial frontiers and crevices of individual and social lives. To make it valuable, not as preparation for some undetermined future event, but as a replacement for hate, violence and destruction of other views, other ways, other hopes. The relationship of learning and loving has been clearly part of the life of the Association. It has been the attempt to create in a small way the true learning society which we hope to bring about in Canada.

In order to work effectively on behalf of this vision of the CAAE and its goals, Thomas felt he needed to reorganize the Association. He needed a smaller, more professional governing body than the old National Council, and with the constitutional changes of 1963, this was accomplished. He also sought a truly national organization in which provincial interests played a part, but were part of a unitary whole rather than of a loose federation. This was achieved in the form of the divisional structure, which included provincial representation on the smaller, more professional Board of Directors.

Basic to the functioning of the Association and always an elusive target, was achieving a sound and secure financial basis for its work. Of no small importance in the decision to create the divisional structure was the hope that this would result in more effective and continuous fund raising across the country. This proved not to be the case. Of great help, however, was the success in 1966, after many years of trying, in getting the federal government to provide an annual supporting grant.

With respect to the program sponsored by the Association, Thomas continued the strong emphasis placed by his predecessors on the field of citizenship education. Although the Forum projects were terminated, several other projects took their place. The CAAE's services to practitioners were considerably expanded. The Association gave prominence to a series of new issues and clienteles. The most substantial single program project during the period was the Commission on the Community College, which, with the assistance of the largest single grant ever received by the Association, attempted to assist in the development of the community college movement in Canada and to emphasize particularly the role of the colleges in serving the interests of the adult learner.

In his annual report in 1966, Thomas looked back on his work with the Association, in terms of what he saw to have been accomplished (CAAE AR 1965-66:9):

> I came to CAAE to accomplish three things; to build a strong Board and more widely conceived organization; to establish a reasonable financial basis; and to formulate a new statement of our concerns for the quality and quantity of adult learning. To some degree, some of those things are accomplished, not permanently...but enough to see a glimner of what they mean.

While this was by no means the end of Thomas' time with the Association, it was clearly a point by which much useful work had been accomplished: the new constitutional arrangements were in place and the division structure filling out; the federal government had been persuaded to provide annual sustaining grants for the Association; and the most ambitious advocacy activity ever undertaken by the organization, the White Paper, had been successfully launched. This appears to have been the high point of the decade for the CAAE.

The Organization

Divisional Structure and Organizational Change

The Thomas years involved an attempt to create a national organization which retained its unitary character but which at the same time encouraged and incorporated provincial bodies, to be called divisions. Indeed, Thomas himself was the chief architect of this new organizational structure, while still in British Columbia, and joined the staff of the CAAE at the time when the Association was evaluating the proposed new structure. He helped to convince the Executive and National Council that the plan would work and, having done so, had the task of managing the new system. By the time he decided to leave the CAAE in 1969 (to take effect early in 1970), it was clear that the divisional structure was not working to the satisfaction of many in the organization and that some basic change would take place.

The origins of the proposal which emanated from British Columbia in 1961 have been described in detail elsewhere (Selman 1969, 1980). Adult educators in B.C. had been meeting regularly, twice a year, since 1954. For the thirteenth semi-annual conference, to be held in May of 1961 (which was seen as well to be part of the preparation for the national conference in Ottawa to be held in the fall), working papers were prepared on several topics. Among them was one prepared by a committee chaired by Alan Thomas, entitled, "Study and Recommendations Regarding the Structure, Financing and Role of the CAAE with Special Reference to British Columbia." For several years prior to this point the national organization, the CAAE, was separate and distinct from the few provincial bodies which existed, but beginning in 1958 provincial groups which chose to do so could affiliate with the CAAE and name a representative to its National Council (Selman 1982). The committee chaired by Thomas proposed a basic change in this relationship. The national body would be asked to amend its structure so as to provide for provincial divisions, not as in the past, separate but affiliated bodies, but as integral parts of the CAAE. There would be a common membership between the two bodies, the provincial organization would raise funds and memberships for the two levels at the same time, and the provincial body would have suitable representation on the governing bodies of the CAAE. At the provincial level, at least in the case of B.C., the organization would be transformed from a council of agencies to a body in which there would be both personal and organizational memberships. These proposals were adopted by the B.C. conference.

There were both provincial and national purposes to be served by these arrangements. In B.C., the 1950s were a time of great growth in adult education programs and in the number of persons who were coming to identify themselves with the field of adult education. The structure of the former B.C. organization did not provide for personal memberships or a direct personal link to the field through the organization. It had become increasingly clear that some change was required (Selman 1969, 1980). At the same time, adult educators in the province who were active in the CAAE, who valued its work and sought to promote its welfare, felt that the new proposals would strengthen the national body while at the same time fully meeting the need for a new type of provincial organization. It was clear that provincially-based interests in adult education (institutions, programs and associations of adult educators) were gaining strength rapidly and that the CAAE, in Thomas' words, "had to support them or it would disappear" (personal communication, Mar. 10, 1982). There were also strong stirrings at this time in the rapidly-developing vocational education area (which was receiving massive injections of federal funds under the 1960 legislation) and some felt that it was important just then to strengthen the CAAE, which was devoted to a more comprehensive view of adult education. So, for reasons both provincial and national, the B.C. conference in May 1961 unanimously endorsed the recommendations and these were communicated to the national organization, on whose action their implementation depended.

The CAAE had had its constitution under review for some time (CAAE Exec. May 27, 1960; Sept. 22, 1961). The process was given fresh impetus, however, by the report of the B.C. recommendations. At this point, Thomas joined the staff of the CAAE (Sept. 1, 1961). Thus the chief architect of the B.C. proposals had become the Associate Director of the national body and took a lead in urging the adoption of the plan. Following informal discussions held at the time of the national conference, B.C. was authorized to proceed with the organization of a division, while the constitution committee of the CAAE prepared the necessary constitutional amendments (CAAE NC Oct. 26-Nov. 1, 1961). In March of 1962, the National Council approved an interim measure designed to accommodate the B.C. group and the annual meeting in June formally adopted a constitutional change which recognized the B.C. Division and, in effect, inserted the constitution of the B.C. body into the national by-laws (CAAE NC May 4; AM June 2, 1962). And at the annual meeting a year later, there was a total reorganization of the governing structure of the organization with provision made for the representation of any division which subsequently joined.

It is clear from the reports of the Constitution Committee that, by March of 1962, the committee had been assigned the task not only of providing for the creation of divisions. but also "to study the entire constitution" (CAAE NC Mar. 4, 1962). By June, it seems to have been decided that the National Council, which had grown to be a body of 56 members, should be replaced by a smaller Board of Directors (CAAE NC June 1, 1962) and by the end of the year, that the Board would contain some "at large" members (three from each region) and one from each provincial division or other provincial "affiliate," to a total of 28 members (CAAE Exec. Dec. 12, 1962). These and other amendments were formally approved at the annual meeting in June of 1963, the Executive being empowered to make minor changes in the light of the discussions at the meeting, the new constitution and by-laws to come into effect in 1964.

There was significance in this reorganization which went beyond the reduction in the size of the National Council/Board. Thomas has reflected that if the organization was to be vigorous and expertly informed in its advocacy role, he as Director had to have a reasonably compact and well-informed Board he could work with. It had to be the governing body, not just a committee, on whose authority action could be taken and, given the increasing professionalization of the field and the shifting focus of the advocacy activity, it was important that the Board be expert in its knowledge of the field (personal comunication, Aug. 10, 1983). Not only was the Board reduced in size (exactly in half), but it also became a more professional group.

The divisional structure of the Association filled out as the decade progressed. British Columbia was the first, its position being authorized in 1962 and its first budget being approved early in 1963 (CAAE Exec. Jan. 15, 1963). By January of 1963, two other provincial bodies, in Nova Scotia and Saskatchewan, were affiliated with the CAAE. The Nova Scotia Council for Adult Education had been organized in November 1962, was an affiliate of the CAAE for almost two years and became the Nova Scotia Division in the fall of 1964. The Saskatchewan organization remained an autonomous but affiliated group until the spring of 1967, when it became a division.

Three other provinces formed divisions in the balance of the decade. Adult educators in Manitoba had met sporadically since the late Fifties, had further meetings in 1962, but did not in fact form a division until late 1966. By a complicated process, the CAAE and adult educators in Ontario began working towards an organization in the spring of 1964. Further meetings, negotiations with other organizations and a grant-in-aid of $5,000 secured by the CAAE from the Atkinson Charitable Foundation, led to the creation of an Ontario Division in April 1966, the new organization being both a division of the CAAE and the

Continuing Education section of the Ontario Education Association. In December of 1967, Newfoundland, which had been represented on the National Executive for more than a year, formed a division of the Association, the last to be so formed. When adult educators in Alberta formed a provincial body in 1967, discussions at that time, and at the annual meeting the following year, produced a decision to remain independent rather than link up with the CAAE (Roberts 1982; Tewnion & Robin 1978).

The divisional structure lasted about a decade, roughly the period of Thomas' leadership of the organization. The aim was to create a strong national organization for the English-speaking adult education movement in Canada which could rely on and draw strength from the provincial divisions, while at the same time leaving the provincial bodies free to act according to the needs of their own situations. To this extent, the divisional structure worked. Problems arose in other areas.

The provincial divisions were all represented on the Board of the national body. The fiscal relationship was complex. It had been proposed originally that any funds that were raised provincially for the CAAE would be divided proportionally between the provincial and the national levels. In the restructuring which took place in 1963, however, it was decided instead (perhaps in an effort to strengthen the national ties) that all memberships and funds which were raised would go to the national body and the latter would annually negotiate a budget with each division, the funds to be paid back out to the division. (The CAAE had its own national Finance Committee and was raising funds on its own, in consultation with the divisions.) This fiscal relationship was the subject of a constitutional amendment in June of 1967, the effect of which was to define more precisely the obligation of the divisions to forward to Toronto all funds they received and which were properly those of the national body (CAAE Bd. June 22-23, 1967).

The financial resources of the divisions fell into three categories. All membership fees and donations for general purposes were in due course to be forwarded to the national office. The budget of the division was negotiated annually with Toronto and this amount was paid in quarterly instalments. The funds from the national office were intended primarily to cover the office and administrative expenses of the division and the expenses of provincial representatives in attending national meetings. A second account was usually maintained which was used to finance programs put on by the division locally or provincially, and balances in this account were the property of the division. Thirdly, the national organization occasionally undertook projects which were funded from elsewhere and which involved the divisions in their execution. In these cases, the divisions were sometimes paid an administrative overhead fee, which became the division's property.

This rather complex set of arrangements provided a great deal of difficulty between the divisions and the national organization. The divisions were not always careful enough in their record keeping and were sometimes slow in sending forward funds which belonged to the national office. The national was sometimes short of funds and could not always make their payments on time. Staff time was short at both levels and problems arose. Divisions, which were counted upon to carry out fund raising in their province for the national organization, frequently did not carry out this responsibility. Sometimes the national was desperate for funds and it was known that some divisions had considerable funds in their accounts, to the frustration and annoyance of those trying to raise funds nationally. The system was perhaps too complex for such a small organization.

There was also a great deal of detailed work to be maintained with respect to memberships. Members in any province where there was a division automatically became a member of both the division and the national and much information had to flow back and forth, records maintained, memberships billed and accounted for annually, and other details. Mailings from Toronto (the journal, newsletters, communications to members, etc.) depended upon Toronto having up-to-date membership records, which was not always the case. It was mainly in terms of problems in these two areas—finance and membership records—that Alan Thomas was to comment later, "It was a horror to manage, and eventually collapsed of its own weight" (personal communication, Mar. 10, 1982). In such a modest sized organization, there was simply not the staff time, provincially or nationally, to maintain the volume of administrative detail necessary for such complex arrangements. Such matters were but irritants, however. There were more basic problems, which in the end led to the dissolution of the divisional structure. First, organizations such as the CAAE are notoriously difficult to manage. The membership and governing bodies are theoretically responsible for goal setting and the approval of major activities. But, on the other hand, if fund raising for projects is left largely to the Director, as was the case, the Director must go where the money is to be found and will tend to explore most actively in areas for which he personally has most enthusiasm. This represents enough difficulty when the Board and Executive are representing national interests or a national perspective. But when, as in the case of the CAAE in the Sixties, a substantial number of the Board members were named by and representing provincial bodies, there was all the more likelihood that these persons could come to feel that the national body was not serving their interests.

A second major difficulty arose from the fact that as the field of adult education expanded rapidly in the Sixties, many people entered the field with little knowledge or understanding of the traditions of the CAAE and the leadership it had provided in the social movement dimensions of adult education. The provincial divisions were made up largely of people who looked to the divisions, and the national organization, for support services in their role as practitioners. There was inadequate understanding, much less approval, of the social activist role of the CAAE. As has been noted elsewhere, some elements in the provincial organizations came to speak with scorn of the "social crusaders" who in their view were dominating the leadership of the CAAE (Selman 1980:37).

Perhaps most basic of all was what was happening in Canadian society as a whole during the Sixties. It was a time of social unrest, of confrontational methods of seeking social change, of promotion of special interests and of single issue social and political movements. These populist elements appeared in the affairs of the CAAE, as in many such organizations in the period, and led, in the end, to pronounced changes in the CAAE's goals and style of operation. These new forces produced what could understandably be seen by some as social crusading tendencies. They also produced leaders in the CAAE who had little interest in or patience with the administrative details involved in maintaining the complicated relationships with the divisions and preferred instead a simpler, more directly "grass roots" or participatory style of operation. This eventually led to the abandonment by the national body of the divisional structure in 1970.

For the reasons indicated above, there were bound to be difficulties in the management of the organizational structure which was adopted in the early Sixties. Some of these related to the day-to-day administration, some to feelings in the divisions that the CAAE was not responding to the needs and interests of their members, and as the decade progressed, some related to differences of view as to how the CAAE should respond to the urgent social and political issues we associate with the late Sixties in Canada.

It is not surprising, therefore, that complaints and controversy appeared. At the Board meeting held in late January 1967, for instance, a demand was expressed by some members of the Board for a re-examination of the goals of the organization. Complaints were heard that a national membership drive was being conducted without adequate liaison with the divisions, and that the membership records were not being kept adequately. There was even a complaint that in the annual report the Executive Committee was listed before the Board members. Thomas, in his mid-year Director's Report to the same meeting, pointed out that the provincial bodies were not living up to their responsibilities in the national finance campaign (CAAE Bd. Jan. 28-29, 1967). At the June Board meeting, complaints were heard from Saskatchewan that the Association's newsletter and journal were too esoteric and not relevant to the members' interests (CAAE Bd. June 22-23, 1967). In the following year there were complaints about lack of provincial representation on CAAE standing committees (CAAE Bd. June 5-6, 1968). These are some examples of difficulties which appeared. In his comments to the annual meeting in June 1968, the President of the Association spoke wryly of the national body receiving "clear—and at times vigorous—advice from the divisions" (President's Report, CAAE AM June 6-8, 1968). None of this was particularly surprising, given the circumstances of the organization and the nature of the times. But at this distance in time, it can be seen that the discontents that began to be expressed in 1967 and which were brought to a head at the annual meeting and conference the following year, represented the seeds of destruction of the divisional structure of the Association.

It was decided to hold a conference in connection with the annual meeting in June 1968, and to make the CAAE itself the object of study at this meeting. This in itself was perhaps an acknowledgement that all was not well. The President's report to the annual meeting referred to the "winds of change" which were being felt in the organization (President's Report, CAAE AM June 6-8, 1968) and the proceedings of the meeting bore out the prior indications that change was wanted. There was clearly a feeling on the part of some participants that the CAAE, as represented by the Board of Directors, had got out of touch with the divisions and the members across the country. Thomas' editorial in *Continuous Learning* following the conference quoted one spokesman: "The CAAE is in a crisis, is at the crossroads. The Board had better deliver this next year or else" (1968b:147). A storm developed around the budget, containing a large deficit, which the Board submitted for approval. This sharpened up the debate about the general role of the organization and the relationship between the national and provincial levels. It was at times an abrasive conference and feelings ran high. Although the meeting identified problems, it did not chart a new course. It was decided to appoint a study committee to examine the issues and make recommendations.

A Committee on the Philosophy, Structure and Operation of the CAAE, chaired by Donald Snowden, the President of the Newfoundland Division and one of the most vocal critics of the Association, was organized in the summer and fall of 1968 (CAAE Exec. Aug. 12; Bd. Sept. 20, 1968) and worked through the following year. Its report was circulated to the divisions in the early spring of 1969, discussed at the Board meeting in June and considered at length at the annual meeting in Winnipeg in October. Discussions at the latter were organized around four areas—purposes, finance, programs and structure—and those attending had available the reactions to the Committee's report from all the divisions, the Board of Directors and the staff. The reports of the annual meeting (*CL* 8, [5 and 6], 1969) indicate that like its predecessor, it was vigorous and contentious, but that it failed to resolve the outstanding issues, referring them to the Board for "urgent consideration." There was some suggestion at the meeting of abandoning the divisional structure, but it was not pursued. Donald Snowden resigned from his offices in the Association in protest over the inconclusive outcome (CAAE Bd. Jan. 30, 1970).

It is not important for present purposes to examine the details of the Snowden Report in that they did not, as it turned out, have a determining effect on the directions of the organization. On the whole, the report stressed the need for greater involvement of the divisions in the decision-making of the national body and also the need for the Board of Directors to control more effectively the activities conducted by the staff, under the guidance of the Executive. In other words, the report reflected the continuing tension between the broad social purposes some favored for the national body, as exemplified in Thomas' leadership, and the membership-serving purposes, as stressed by the provincial divisions. The report put considerable emphasis on goals involving the delivery of services to practitioners. It was at this point, a few weeks after the 1969 annual meeting, that Thomas announced his resignation from the CAAE, to take effect at the end of February 1970 (CAAE Exec. Dec. 16, 1969).

Only a brief summary of subsequent changes in the structure of the CAAE need be provided. Those responsible for the finances of the national body became increasingly resentful of the inadequate efforts made by the divisions to raise funds for the CAAE. The Board meeting, held in late January 1970, was decisive. It was the scene of a vigorous discussion about the goals of the Association and the role of the divisions. A motion to terminate the divisional structure was lost by one vote and a notice of motion was tabled (for the next annual meeting) that the divisional structure be abandoned. Some alternative models were discussed. It was decided to appoint a committee under the chairmanship of Michael Clague, who had been a member of the Board and Executive for some time, to examine the goals of the organization and consider alternate forms of organizational structure (CAAE Bd. Jan. 30-Feb. 1, 1970).

Thus began a process which resulted in several organizational models being prepared as alternatives for consideration. While this was happening, two divisions, Newfoundland and Manitoba, indicated their impending withdrawal (CAAE Bd. May 23, 1970). At the annual meeting in the spring, by which time Thomas had left, six models were considered and what was termed the "developmental" or social action model was overwhelmingly adopted. This involved the termination of the divisional structure as such, but envisaged a continuing association or affiliation with these groups, which it was assumed would now become autonomous provincial bodies. The Board and Executive were authorized to prepare a new constitution for the CAAE, to be considered at a special meeting of the membership in the fall (CAAE AM May 22-23, 1970). This meeting was held in early December 1970, in Toronto. Clague had taken the lead in preparing the proposals which were presented. The new model was confirmed, a new constitution and by-laws discussed and adopted (to take effect in May 1971) and a "Transition Committee" named, which was to work with the Executive, establish procedures for the reconstituted organization and manage the phasing out of financial and other connections with the divisions (CAAE

AM Dec. 4-5, 1970). This was accomplished by the end of April 1971. By the time of the next annual meeting in June, the new model was in place and the new Director, Gordon Hodge, was on staff.

Administration

Reference has already been made to the complex forces which were present in the CAAE and the difficulties facing any director of an association such as the CAAE. Thomas had had only a modest amount of experience in matters of administration. However, he was clear as to what had to be done, organized himself and the support staff to carry out the tasks, and threw himself, in his highly personal style, into the effort. There was too much to be done. Discussion of getting him an administrative assistant was not pursued because of lack of funds. Such an appointment probably would have been beneficial, because with Thomas travelling a great deal, and his responsibilities for writing and speaking. which were also onerous, there was not always sufficient time for administrative details. The divisions tended to feel that they were not receiving sufficient service and attention. No one could have fully met the demands upon the Director, given the situation. Thomas was in constant demand to do the things he did best—teaching, speaking, program planning, consulting and writing—and it was sometimes difficult to find time for the "maintenance" functions. And the complicated nature of the divisional structure, described above, called for a great deal of attention to administrative details.

The governing structure of the Association was modified in 1963, as is described above. The large and broadly representative National Council, which had been in existence since the founding of the organization, was replaced with a smaller Board of Directors. Thomas attached considerable importance to the change, in relation to the advocacy activity of the Association. His predecessor, Roby Kidd, had been challenged, on occasion, by members of the Association who became aware that the CAAE was taking a certain public position on an issue, but did not feel that they had had an opportunity to give input to the policy paper. Thomas wished to avoid that problem by basing the Association's stance on the approval of the senior policy body. This was difficult to achieve in relation to the National Council, which was such a large body and could meet only infrequently. So he promoted the idea of a smaller group, which could meet more often (personal communication, Aug. 10, 1983). This was achieved in the constitutional revisions of 1963, with the creation of the Board of Directors to replace the National Council. He worked especially closely with the Executive Committee, an even smaller group, which met as needed, usually monthly. A review of the minutes of the Executive and Board in the following period indicates that the Board was more dominant, vis-à-vis the Executive, than the old Council had been. There was greater tendency on the part of the Executive to refer matters to the Board than had been the case before.

In early 1966, Thomas sought the consent of the Executive to employ a consulting firm to study the office management practices being used and to make recommendations (CAAE Exec. Mar 3, 1966). The recommendations were discussed at subsequent meetings (CAAE Exec. May 27, Dec. 14, 1966) and in his mid-year report to the Board in January 1967, Thomas commented that "most of the recommendations" had been implemented, the major exception being the hiring of an administrative assistant to the Director (CAAE Bd. Jan. 28-29, 1967). A consultant was also employed early in 1969, at the suggestion of the Board, to provide advice concerning the program planning processes being used. A new process was used in planning activities for the year 1969-70. It involved an attempt to estimate in some detail the time commitment involved in each activity and its relationship to the overall time resources available. In the plans for 1969-70, the time commitments of the office were shown as (CAAE Exec. Feb. 20, 1969):

Program	16%
Public policy	7%
Professional services	28%
Administration	28%
Organizational policy	21%

That this study was requested by the Board should perhaps be seen against the background of adverse criticism of the national office which was becoming more vocal in this period, especially from the divisions.

In addition to the Board and Executive, the Association maintained a series of standing committees. Some of these related to the ongoing services of the Association, such as the journal or the library and information services, some to specific projects, such as Citizens' Forum, and some to areas of concern or practice, such as residential adult education or voluntary action. In the year 1968-69, for instance, the list of standing committees was as follows (CAAE AM June 6-8, 1968):

- Public Affairs
- Finance
- Communications
- Research and Professional Development
- Poverty

- Library and Publishing
- School Boards
- Labour
- Residential Adult Education
- Voluntary Action

It should be mentioned as well that for a brief period, 1963 to 1965, there was a Program Committee, which was concerned with special program projects, ones which did not fall into the areas of the other committees and were a response to significant public affairs issues. Thomas was uncomfortable with this arrangement, generally preferring program decisions to be dealt with directly by the Board and Executive (personal communication, Mar. 14, 1978).

Thomas' sense of style and of history were nowhere revealed more fully than in his creation of "Corbett House," the name given to the new headquarters of the Association as a memorial to the founding director, who passed away in 1964. The offices at 113 St. George Street, Toronto, became increasingly crowded as the size of the staff grew during the Sixties. There was talk from time to time of moving the headquarters to Ottawa (CAAE Exec. Nov. 9, 1965; Bd. Jan. 21, 1966), but this was apparently not pursued seriously until the end of the decade (CAAE Exec. Feb. 13, April 8, 1970). As early as January 1965, consideration was given to naming the headquarters building "Corbett House" (CAAE Exec. Jan. 21, 1965), but this step was not taken until the Association moved its offices in the summer of 1966 to a linked pair of houses at 21-23 Sultan Street, still in the University of Toronto area. The new quarters were officially opened and dedicated on January 27, 1967. The issue of *Continuous Learning* in which the account of the opening appeared (*CL* 6, [1], 1967) was the first of many to carry a sketch of the new quarters on the cover. And Thomas' editorials *consistently thereafter* carried the words "Corbett House" at their conclusion. The Association remained in those quarters for the balance of the decade, usually subletting office space to other organizations.

Since its formation in 1935, the CAAE had been registered as an organization under the laws of Ontario. In the early sixties, while consideration was being given to the substantial revision of the constitution, it was decided to seek a federal charter instead. After the constitution was approved by the annual meeting in June 1963, application for the charter was made, and eventually approved in the fall of 1964 (CAAE Exec. Sept. 22, 1964). For a time thereafter, the Association inserted " (1964)" after its name on some of its publications, but this practice did not persist.

Finance

The Thomas years, like the earlier decades in the life of the CAAE, were a constant struggle in terms of financing the organization. The long campaign to secure a federal grant in support of the general expenses of the Association was successful in 1966, but both before and after that date, there were periodic crises when revenues were less than were needed to meet current expenditures, including the Director's salary.

The CAAE was extremely fortunate throughout this decade to have the loyal support and expert volunteer leadership of H.H. Edmison, an official of the Argus Corporation, as its Treasurer. He helped see the organization through its periodical financial crises, led a continuing effort to raise funds from corporations for the CAAE, and interested in the work of the Association several other prominent businessmen, most notably Mr. Ron Ritchie, who chaired the Executive for a time early in the decade, and Mr. Henry Sissons, who helped with fund raising and became President of the CAAE for two years beginning in 1969.

At the outset of the decade there were three main sources of funds, memberships (individual and organizational), donations from governments and businesses, and project funds. The Finance Commitee concentrated largely on securing donations. The Director raised most of the project money. The Finance Committee was very active in this period. Centered in Toronto, it concentrated most of its activity in the Toronto and Montreal areas, where many of the large corporations were located. There was something of a pause in fund raising in the interval just after Roby Kidd left in the spring of 1961 and, by late in the year, the situation was bleak. Early in 1962 a part-time fund raiser was employed for some months to assist the Finance Committee and the situation was improved somewhat (CAAE Exec. Dec. 12, 1961; Feb. 14, Mar. 21, May 16, 1962; AM 1962, 1963). Part of the problem had been the lapse in securing project funds. Thomas took over the directorship at a time when the organization's finances were at a low ebb. There were several other periods in the latter years of the decade when finances were at a crisis stage, in spite of the acquisition of the federal grant beginning in 1966. The minutes of the Board and Executive meetings throughout the late Sixties make frequent references to the organization's financial problems. The receipt of a $25,000 bequest in 1967 was helpful, some of it being used to cover expenses of moving into the new headquarters and the rest being invested (CAAE AM June 23, 1967; Bd. June 13-14, 1969). In 1967 too, much of the library of the Association was sold to the Ontario Institute for Studies in Education for approximately

$50,000, at least partly for financial reasons (CAAE Exec. May 25, Sept. 14, 1967). Several CAAE budgets in the late Sixties showed deficits and the organization was consistently living on borrowed funds. At the last Executive meeting before Thomas left the Association, in early 1970, the Treasurer described the financial situation as "particularly grim" (CAAE Exec. Feb. 13, 1970). The Association was not in a strong state to cope with the period of trial and indecision which followed after his departure (CAAE AM May 22-23; Exec. Sept. 9, 1970).

The most important event in terms of the long term financial picture was the securing of an annual supporting grant from the federal government. Efforts had been made since the very early years of the Association's life to get such a grant, but all these efforts had been unsuccessful. Early in 1965, Henry Sissons agreed to take charge of the process of seeking the grant once again and, after a pause occasioned by a fall election, consultations went forward. At the Board meeting in late January 1966, Dr. Bert Wales, the President, announced that word had been received of an agreement whereby the federal government would provide an annual grant of $30,000 or one third of the Association's annual expenditures, whichever was less, this arrangement to remain for an initial five-year period (CAAE Bd. Jan. 21-22, 1966). A few months later, Thomas referred in his annual report to (CAAE DR 1966):

> The grant from the federal government which has provided the first four months in succession since my assumption of office without constant worry over whether we could pay our staff.

As indicated above, this financial stability was not characteristic of the balance of the decade, although the federal grant was maintained. An attempt was made, in concert with the ICEA, in late 1969 to persuade the federal government to raise the level of their support, but this was not successful (CAAE Exec. Dec. 14, 1969; Jan. 21, and Bd. Jan. 30, 1970).

The financial relationships between the national office and the divisions has already been described. The divisions were not very successful in raising funds, but became increasingly insistent as the decade progressed that they be active participants in national decision-making. In the latter years of the decade, some divisions had considerable funds in their provincial accounts, while the national office had a severe shortage (CAAE Bd. Jan. 28-29, 1967; Exec. Nov. 5, 1969). The national Finance Committee moved in 1969 to get a full audited picture of divisional finances (CAAE Exec. Feb. 20, 1969). There were times in late 1969 and subsequently when the national organization could not meet its quarterly budget payments to the divisions (CAAE Bd. Oct. 6, 1969) and early the following year the national body asked for "loans" from the divisions, in cases where they had surplus in other accounts (CAAE Bd. Jan. 30, 1970). The financial relations with the divisions were a constant source of grief by the late Sixties and certainly contributed to the eventual breakdown of the system.

Membership

Membership in the CAAE increased steadily during the decade, doubling in the period from 676 individuals (1960-61) to 1,266 (1968-69) and 112 organizations (1960-61) to 273 (1968-69). There was a sharp jump in 1963-64, largely due to the efforts of the B.C. and Saskatchewan groups (CAAE Exec. Nov. 6, 1963). Six months later an item in the newsletter, *Interim*, pointed out that in B.C., Saskatchewan and Nova Scotia the existence of the provincial organizations appeared to explain the substantial increases in those provinces, whereas the numbers had remained "fairly stationary" in the other provinces (2,[3], 1964).

A position paper on membership was discussed by the Board early in 1968 and led to a decision to create a standing committee on the topic which was to involve active participation by the divisions and to undertake a membership campaign (CAAE Bd. Jan. 12-13, 1968). In the subsequent two years there are several references in the minutes to the development of this effort and in early 1969 it was reported that the recent campaign had increased membership by 65 per cent (CAAE Exec. Mar. 20, 1969). It is hard to see, from the annual figures, how this could have been so.

There were frequent discussions about the level of membership fees, pointing out from time to time that the current fee was not covering the costs of services rendered to members. The matter of inaugurating a "professional membership," at a higher rate, was discussed but never adopted (CAAE AM June 2, 1962; Bd. Jan. 12-14, 1968). Early in his time on the staff Thomas raised the matter of possible joint memberships with other organizations, such as of those in university extension work. Although the idea was referred to the committee studying the constitution, nothing further seems to have come of it (CAAE Exec. Nov. 20, 1961).

A review of the minutes and reports of the Association reveals that a great deal of time and energy went into discussing membership matters. Apparently concerted efforts were made from time to time to recruit additional members for the CAAE, but except for the substantial increase in the middle of the decade (most of it coming from the three provinces) all that was accomplished was a modest growth from year to year, even though this was a time of very rapid expansion of the field as a whole. A doubling of membership in the decade was an accomplishment, but it is clear that only a very small portion of practicing adult educators were interested in membership in the organization.

Staff

When Thomas joined the CAAE in September 1961, it was as Associate Director. Arthur Pigott had been appointed Director on May 1 of that year, on the departure of Roby Kidd, and remained in that position for a little over a year. Thomas took his place in September 1962. Pigott's chief interest in the field was in education for employment and he was active as a speaker and consultant in that area. His knowledge of the broader field of adult education was somewhat limited, however, whereas Thomas had completed doctoral studies in adult education and had varied experience as a practitioner. It was clear that the Association could not employ two such senior officers for long, and the relationship between the two was cordial, but somewhat uneasy. At a "closed session" of the Executive in June of 1962, it was decided to ask for Pigott's resignation and appoint Thomas as Director instead, as of September 1.

Several staff members left the Association in the closing months of Kidd's tenure. The veterans of the professional staff who carried over into the Thomas years were Isabel Wilson, the National Secretary of Citizens' Forum, and Diana Ironside, who was in charge of the library and information services. Eleanor Graham, the editor of *Food For Thought*, also carried over from the Kidd years but she resigned in 1962 and Thomas took over that role.

The size of the staff grew fairly steadily during the decade, rising from nine when Thomas took over to fifteen when he left. He recruited good people and in his report for 1966-67 he commented (CAAE DR 1966-67:9): "For the first time since my assumption of office as Director in 1962, I am able to come before the annual meeting representing a group of reasonably experienced staff." But he was quick to point out that the staff was greatly overworked.

The staff functions performed through most of this period included that of Director and journal editor, which Thomas combined; the Citizen's Forum and Public Affairs position, filled by Isabel Wilson; Program Officer, filled by Diana Ironside until 1964 and then John Cornish until 1966; the direction of the library and information services, performed by Diana Ironside (1962-63), Brenda Docent (1963-65), Lola Bratty (1465-68) and Anne Setchell after that time (there was an assistant librarian throughout the period); from early 1966, a Managing Editor of Continuous Learning, Donald MacNeil, who subsequently took on program functions as well, and eventually became the caretaker administrator of the CAAE's affairs after Thomas' departure in 1970; beginning in 1967, a part-time consultant on school board adult education, Milton Pummell; and with the beginning of the Commission on the Community College in 1968, three staff members on that project. In addition to the foregoing, there were usually four secretarial staff members, a bookkeeper and a membership secretary. When Thomas went on leave for the first four months of 1968, teaching and travelling in Africa, Mr. Gower Markle of the Steelworkers' Union and a long-time member of the CAAE Board and Executive served as Acting Director as necessary.

Thomas was greatly concerned about the welfare of the staff and gave a lot of time and energy to cultivating an *esprit de corps* among his colleagues. He worked actively with the personnel committee and encouraged periodic reviews of job classifications, salary scales and fringe benefits packages. A new pension plan was introduced in 1961, salaries were reviewed and scaled upwards significantly in the following year, a major review of personnel practices was prepared and implemented in 1963, sick leave provisions regularized in 1966, and new salary scales were adopted in 1968 and 1969.

Thomas was modest in his own salary demands and on at least two occasions, when he arrived in 1961 and again in 1968, opted for a lower salary than the top figure offered him. On more than one occasion, the shortage of funds in the Association's accounts led Thomas to defer the salary due him until the cash was available (personal communication Aug. 10, 1983).

When Thomas left the CAAE in late February 1970, there were 15 staff members, three of those on the community college project (and paid for out of the grant). Of the other 12, nine had resigned by the end of the year, a reflection of both the dwindling resources and the confusion of aims in the Association. These developments demonstrated dramatically how vital to an organization such as the CAAE is an able and energetic director who can inspire and lead its activities, raise project funds and generally make things go.

Relations with the ICEA

One of the goals Thomas pursued during his time as Director of the CAAE was to establish and maintain active, effective relations with the French Language counterpart organization of the CAAE, the Institut Canadien d'Education des Adultes (ICEA). Thomas attributes his deep concerns and aspirations in this matter to the fact that his mother was from Quebec and that he had spent some of his early years in that province and had a particular attraction to the French language (personal communication, Sept. 29, 1983). The Sixties were stressful times in Canadian Confederation, the years of the Quiet Revolution, and of mounting concerns about the gulf between English- and French-speaking Canada. In the world of adult education, although a French language organization had grown up as a committee of the CAAE originally, there had been a complete separation for some years. Kidd, Thomas' predecessor, although very successful in many aspects of his work, did not seem to have much success cultivating sustained working relations with the ICEA, which was founded in the early Fifties. When Thomas became Director, however, he was determined to establish satisfactory relations with the ICEA and he devoted a great deal of time and effort to bringing that about.

Relations with the ICEA took various forms. There was an attempt to hold a continuing series of joint committee meetings and, at times, joint Executive meetings, out of which came plans for several joint activities. Most basic of all, a firm relationship and understanding were created with respect to fund raising with the federal government. The principle of equality was established whereby the federal government would treat the two organizations equally. At first it might have been felt in the CAAE that because it represented the great majority of the nation, the English-speaking community, it should have received preferred treatment in any grants from Ottawa. In fact, however, it was to be only a few years later, in the time immediately after Thomas' departure, that the equal treatment understanding may have been what saved the Association. In a period when the CAAE's activities were at a very low ebb, it was the insistence upon equal treatment on the part of the ICEA which may have prevented the CAAE from losing the federal supporting grant.

In early December of 1961, Thomas and Diana Ironside met with representatives of the ICEA and reported to the CAAE Executive that "it was hoped that regular meetings between our two Executives could be held in future" (CAAE Exec. Dec. 12, 1961). The National Council endorsed the proposal at its next meeting, as well as the suggestion that the two organizations co-operate in fund seeking (CAAE NC Mar. 4, 1962). The first such joint executive meeting was held later in 1962 and out of this came the suggestion of a joint committee to be established which could plan for jointly sponsored activities (CAAE Exec. Sept. 22, 1962). This joint meeting did not take place until the fall of 1963, but in the meantime the CAAE held its annual meeting in Quebec City in June, which several ICEA members attended. There was discussion at the time of a possible further bilingual national conference in 1964, but this was apparently not pursued (CAAE Exec. Mar. 4, 1963).

Early in 1964, the ICEA was helpful to the CAAE in organizing a tour of Western Canada by a panel of speakers from Quebec, and during that year also the two organizations negotiated jointly with the ARDA administration for substantial consultations on training for community development workers, which were carried out the following year. The next major co-operative venture was a North American adult education conference, which was held in Montreal in the fall of 1967. It was in fact an inter-American conference, with some representation from Latin American countries as well, and although Thomas took much of the leadership in organizing the conference, he worked closely with representatives of the ICEA in the planning and execution of the meeting as well as with the continuing committee which arose from the conference.

A joint Executive meeting between the CAAE and the ICEA was held in December of 1968 in Montreal. Out of this came agreement on forming a joint Committee on Public Affairs, through which the two organizations could co-operate in bringing matters of national importance to the attention of the Canadian people (CAAE Exec. Jan. 16,1969). Other matters were discussed as well and were followed up in a more informal meeting the following spring. The annual report for the year described the relationship between the two organizations as "more mutually satisfactory than ever before" (CAAE AR 1968-69:A-28). In November 1969, not long before Thomas left the directorship, a further substantial joint meeting was held in Toronto. Discussed at that time were ambitious plans for further joint approaches to the federal government, the development of a national, bilingual declaration about adult education, and for a substantial project involving the holding of national consultations and the preparation of a publication on "adult education and public affairs" (CAAE Exec. Dec. 16, 1969). An anonymous article, likely written by Thomas, appeared in *Continuous Learning* at this time which reviewed current co-operative projects between the two organizations, those mentioned briefly above, and commented that there had recently been a "marked increase in co-operation" between the two bodies (ICEA, 969).

It was shortly after this that Thomas left his position with the CAAE and the organization fell into a period of inactivity and ineffectiveness. The CAAE was not in a position to carry out its business effectively and the relationship with the ICEA was not pursued, at least for several years, although there was continuing consultation with respect to the sustaining grant which the two organizations were receiving from Ottawa. It remained for Ian Morrison, when he took up the post of Director a few years later, to revive and further the co-operation between the two organizations.

Program Activities

Since the early years of the CAAE, it had been engaged in service to adult education practitioners and agencies, and also to members of the general public, the latter largely in the field of citizenship or public affairs education (Selman 1981, 1982). This continued to be the case in the Thomas years. As the field of adult education expanded, new specialties developed within the field, those practicing in related fields became increasingly interested in adult education, and new groups of learners, or clientele, each with special needs, became identified. At the same time, the rapid social and political change which was taking place during the Sixties threw up certain issues and dramatized the needs of certain groups. The program of the CAAE reflects clearly much of this.

The Association continued its practice, which had been instituted in the early Fifties, of holding a national conference approximately every second year. The decade began with a major event, the 1961 national conference, which was co-sponsored with the ICEA. The next was held in April of 1964, on "Learning to Live in the City." A special conference on the community college was held in Ottawa in June of 1965. In September of 1966, in Vancouver, a national conference was held on matters of professional concern, entitled "Adult Education: An Emerging Profession." Thereafter, beginning with the conference of 1968 and through into the beginning of the next decade, the meetings were preoccupied with the internal concerns of the organization.

The End of the Forums, the Joint Planning Commission and Study-Discussion

The Sixties brought the termination of several programs for which the organization—and Canadian adult education—had gained an enviable reputation internationally in the field of adult education. Three of the best known adult education programs in the world— National Farm Radio Forum, Citizens' Forum and the Joint Planning Commission, all CAAE activities—were discontinued during this decade. Similarly, the well known CAAE project involved in the promotion of study-discussion programs in the liberal arts was also brought to a close when the supporting grant funds ran out.

The first of these to be terminated was the study-discussion program. Having begun in 1956 under the name Commission for Continuous Learning (Selman 1982), the project was supported initially by the Fund for Adult Education (FAE), an American foundation, and promoted the use and development of study-discussion materials in Canada. It was subsequently renamed Living Library, acquired additional funding from Encyclopedia Britannica of Canada, but ran out of grant funds in 1961. At the first Executive meeting held after Thomas joined the staff, the chairman of the committee for the project made an appeal for $7,000 from the CAAE budget to continue the work. This was rejected on the grounds that the project had been a demonstration one and had done its work (CAAE Exec. Sept. 22, 1961). For a few years after this, arrangements were made with the Readers' Club of Canada (which was operated by a former CAAE staff member) to hold and distribute the study-discussion courses, but there was little activity and early in 1964, the project was terminated (Living Library, 1964).

The accomplishments and international reputation of National Farm Radio Forum, a joint project of the CAAE, the Canadian Federation of Agriculture and the Canadian Broadcasting Corporation, have been extensively documented (Corbett 1957; Ohliger 1967; Selman 1981, 1982; Sim 1954). The number of listening groups participating in the Farm Forum had been gradually declining since the early 1950s. Special efforts made in 1962 produced a slight increase in the number in the 1962-63 season but it declined again the following year, and in 1964-65 there were only 230 registered listening groups, involving approximately 2,000 persons. Early in 1965, the Board of Farm Forum decided to terminate the program at the end of that program year and to transfer its assets and liabilities to the Canadian Federation of Agriculture (Ohliger 1968). So ended the life of perhaps the most famous Canadian adult education program. There had been a suggestion within the CAAE as early as 1961 that it might withdraw its financial support of Farm Forum (CAAE Exec. Dec. 12, 1961), but it remained a full partner to the end, partly out of deference to Ned Corbett, the past Director, who had been the chief architect of the project and who represented the Association on the Farm Forum Board.

The CAAE had a more direct involvement in Citizens' Forum than Farm Forum. There was no third sponsoring organization in the case of the Citizens' Forum (just the CBC and the CAAE) and the offices of the project were at the CAAE headquarters. The program has been fully described elsewhere (Corbett 1957; Ohliger 1967; Selman 1981, 1982; Wilson 1980) and, as in the case of the Farm Forum, it was in a state of decline by the time Thomas joined the organization. In early 1961, the chairman of the committee responsible for Citizens' Forum reported to the National Council that the listening group aspect of the program was declining, receipts from the program were down 18 per cent from the previous year, and he raised the question as to "whether this investment is paying satisfactory dividends" (CAAE NC Jan. 20, 1961).

Throughout the next several years, efforts were maintained to sustain the program. Various experiments with the radio and television versions were tried. The television program was reaching a larger audience than radio had and the volume of mail from listeners increased. But the listening group aspect of the program had almost disappeared. In 1963-64, there were signs of lack of interest on the part of the CBC and the program lost even its longstanding name. The television program was changed to "The Sixties" and the radio version was converted to an open line show. Citizens' Forum had thus been changed out of all recognition and, for all practical purposes, had ceased to exist.

The CAAE did not give up easily on Citizens' Forum and the relationship with the CBC. In late 1963, "summit talks" between the two organizations were held and efforts made to bolster the interest in co-operative activity (CAAE Exec. Nov. 6, 1963). In the following year, Thomas reported that the relations with the CBC were "strained" and raised questions about the future of the project (CAAE Exec. Feb. 21, 1964). The CAAE journal continued to carry notices of "The Sixties" and the radio show, "Cross Canada Check-up," in the summer of 1965, but in the following year, it was decided formally to disband the Citizens' Forum Committee (CAAE Bd. Jan. 27-28, 1967). It would appear that one last effort was made to interest the CBC in co-operative activity. A comprehensive "Proposal to the Canadian Broadcasting Corporation" (undated, but likely 1966) appears in the files, which makes the case for "re-invigorating" the association between the two organizations. This was not to be, as the CBC applied more commercial standards to its public affairs programming (Peers 1979) and apparently had less interest in sustained association with organizations such as the CAAE.

The last of the longstanding major CAAE projects to be discontinued during the decade was the Joint Planning Commission. Founded in 1947, the J.P.C. was a consultative body serving more than a hundred agencies, public and private, interested in adult education and the social and cultural development of Canada (Clark 1954; Corbett 1957; Selman 1982). It was a successful model of such consultation and co-ordination and had been the object of study by visitors from many countries (Clark 1954).

The J.P.C. continued its pattern of three meetings a year well into the 1960s, although the number of organizations participating on a regular basis began to decline. A high point in 1964 was when Prime Minister Pearson addressed one of the meetings, on International Co-operation Year. Early the following year, the long-time chairman of the J.P.C. Walter Herbert, resigned and was replaced. With the decline in the number of those attending the meetings, it was decided to give up the pattern of three meetings a year and to have ad hoc sessions from time to time, as topics of interest suggested themselves. This new approach did little to revive the J.P.C.'s fortunes and in January 1968, the Board of the CAAE accepted a recommendation to terminate the work of the Commission (CAAE Bd. Jan. 12-14, 1968). It has also been suggested that a reason for the demise of the J.P.C. was that in order for such a body to function successfully at the national level in Canada as the Sixties progressed, it would have to be able to function in the two official languages, something the J.P.C. was not equipped to do (Alan Thomas, personal communication, Aug. 10, 1983).

Program Committee and the Public Agenda

In the summer of 1963, at the time of the restructuring of the Association and the creation of the Board of Directors, it was decided to set up what came to be known as the Special Programs Committee. Its role was to survey social and political developments and to suggest and organize special programs, apart from those likely to be taken on by other standing committees (CAAE Exec. July 25, 1963). The committee was chaired by Gordon Hawkins, a former member of the CAAE staff, and continued in existence for a little over a year. When Hawkins resigned in the fall of 1964, the committee was allowed to lapse, the Executive deciding that it could undertake the role (CAAE Oct. 23, 1964). During its brief existence, the Program Committee took responsibility for two significant ventures— a tour of Western centres by a panel of speakers from Quebec, and a speaking tour by a leading expert on the education of women. The CAAE's concern with both of these topics preceded the Program Committee, but the committee helped bring the projects to fruition.

As early as 1961, soon after he joined the staff of the CAAE, Thomas had made the suggestion that the Association organize a speaking tour in the West for a party of leading French Canadians, in an effort to promote understanding between the two regions (CAAE Exec. Dec. 12, 1961). The idea was implemented by the Program Committee in early 1964, with financial assistance from the Citizenship Branch, Ottawa. Two of the three speakers, Jeanne Sauve and Claude Ryan, were later to achieve very high profiles in Canadian life and the third, Guy Beaugrand-Champagne, was a leading adult educator from Quebec. The team visited five large centres in the West in February 1964, speaking to public meetings and appearing in the media. The Director's report to the Executive late in the month termed the project a success (although attendance was not all that was hoped) (CAAE Exec. Feb. 21, 1964) and, later in the year, two members of the touring panel wrote articles for *Continuous Learning* on their experience (Ryan 1964; Beaugrand-Champagne 1964).

Another important concern in the Sixties was the women's movement. The CAAE had become involved at least as early as 1962, when it published (edited by Eleanor Graham of the staff) the report of a CBC conference on "The Real World of Women" (Graham 1962). The Program Committee picked the matter up in 1964 and early the following year arranged a tour of Montreal, Toronto and Vancouver by Dr. Virginia Senders, an expert on the continuing education of women from the University of Minnesota (*Interim*, 2, [7], 1965; CAAE DR 1965). The CAAE continued its interest in this field in subsequent years, carrying items about outstanding programs and reviews of books and reports on the subject in its newsletters and journal.

The Program Committee also helped to develop the early stages of the "Health of a Nation" project (CAAE Exec. July 2, 1964), a significant program response to the Royal Commission on Health Services (the Hall Commission). This project was carried out in the spring of 1965 in co-operation with the CBC and the Canadian Institute on Public Affairs. The following report, taken from the CAAE document, "Proposal to the Canadian

Broadcasting Corporation" (1966) indicates the scope of the project:

> Four TV broadcasts and five radio programs were prepared on the basis of wide
> consultation. The CAAE assembled a kit of materials as a background for discussion
> and some 2, 300 of these were sold to adult education agencies across the country
> in support of activities in their regions and to individual members of the listening
> audience. The CAAE itself published a 16-page pamphlet outlining the major
> recommendations of the Hall Report. Quite apart from its inclusion in the kit,
> some 25,000 copies of this pamphlet have been sold.

The document also described a series of meetings and educational events which had
been held in seven different cities in Canada. This was clearly an example of the CAAE
calling upon its experience with the Forum projects and applying the techniques to this
new educational task.

During the balance of the decade, the Association carried out several other programs
which, like the three foregoing examples. involved responding in an educational manner
to matters which came to the fore in the public life of Canada. The volumes of the Royal
Commission on Bilingualism and Biculturalism report, as they appeared, were summarized
in the same way and were thereby made available to large numbers of Canadians. In 1968
when the federal government appointed a Task Force on Federal Government Information,
the CAAE persuaded the Task Force to hold "pilot conferences" for the purpose of testing
public perceptions and reactions in relation to its task and asked the B. C. and Nova Scotia
divisions to arrange such meetings.

Programs Related to Standing Committees

The Association maintained several standing committees during the decade on areas of
program which were of continuing interest and importance. Some of these, such as those
on school boards and residential education, had originated in the previous decade; others,
on poverty and on research and training, were established during the Thomas years. The
activities of five of these committees will be dealt with here.

Residential adult education was a matter of continuing interest in the field and had
been for some decades. The folk school movement had been active in Ontario, and to a
lesser extent in Manitoba, the leadership training and group development movements had
a particular interest in residential adult education, and the leadership of several residential
facilities had a particular interest as well. A standing committee on residential adult
education was maintained throughout the Sixties, having been established in 1956. It
appears to have been particularly active in the early years of the decade. A seminar on
residential adult education was organized in January of 1963 and another later in the same
year, co-sponsored with an Ontario-based group. In April of 1966, an issue of *Interim* was
devoted to residential adult education and an attempt was made to compile a directory of
adult education residential centres (*Interim* 3, [1], 1966). Plans for a conference on this
aspect of the field were indicated in February of 1969, but no account of this event is
available. *Continuous Learning* carried articles about residential education from time to
time (*CL* 1, [4], 1962; Sim 1969).

Perhaps the most active of the standing committees was that on communications.
This was an area in which Thomas had a professional interest, his doctoral dissertation
having dealt with an aspect of it. It was also an area of policy in which the CAAE had
taken a consistent interest since its earliest days (Faris 1975; Selman 1981, 1982).

Leadership was also provided during the Sixties by Arthur Knowles, who was chairman of the CAAE Executive for some years as well as chairman of the communications committee. Within the first year of joining the Association, Thomas expanded the functions of its standing committee on film to become the committee on communications and he and Knowles became a strong and influential leadership team which continued throughout Thomas' tenure. The minutes of the Executive, National Council and Board of Directors throughout the decade indicate that a great deal of attention was given by the CAAE to its own activities in this field and to helping shape public policy—several briefs to government were prepared on matters related to communications during the decade (see below), several day-long meetings of the committee and other interested persons were held, public conferences were organized on communications topics in 1965 and 1967, and a survey was conducted of TV stations in 1963 concerning their educational and cultural programs. The CAAE co-sponsored a TV series, "Exploring the Universe," with the CTV network in 1963, encouraging the formation of listening groups. It performed the same function with another series, "Metropolis—Creator or Destroyer," the following year, and for a time in 1964, the CAAE explored the possibility of becoming the distributor for Canada of TV programs produced by National Educational Television in the United States. The foregoing are only representative examples of committee activities. As well, the Association's journal carried a great deal of material on communications and communications policy during the decade. The Thomas-Knowles combination of energy, professional knowledge and active concern produced a great deal of useful activity.

A standing conrmittee on labor and education was maintained during the period. Its function was mainly one of keeping the lines of communication open between the CAAE and adult educators within the labor movement. Thomas, like his predecessor, had a great interest in labor education. From time to time he took part in courses designed to train instructors within the unions and, in 1966, the CAAE convened a meeting of specialists in adult instruction to advise the Canadian Labor Congress on its educational program. In 1964, an issue of *Interim* (2 [4], 1964) was devoted to education in the labor movement and the chairman of the standing committee reported from time to time to the Board of Directors.

Another very active committee, and program area, was that of school boards and adult education. The Sixties was a period of rapid expansion of school board sponsored adult education in Canada and the CAAE played a very active part in those developments, as it had in the previous decade (Selman 1982). Thomas worked closely in this matter with Dr. Bert Wales, who headed up the outstanding adult education program of the Vancouver School Board, chaired the standing committee for part of the decade and served as President of the CAAE from 1965 to 1967. Wales was perhaps the leading figure in school board adult education in the country and was a useful link with the Canadian Education Association, who frequently served as chief resource person at CAAE-sponsored meetings and conferences devoted to school board (and later, college) adult education. Dan Mewhort, Bert Curtis and Milton Pummell, the latter serving as a consultant in this area on the staff of the CAAE in the latter part of the decade, also made major contributions to this work. Several conferences on school board adult education were sponsored during the decade—one following the national conference in 1961; two for the Western Region (Regina and Edmonton) in 1964; and one for representatives of larger urban centres in the fall of 1966. Many items about school board adult education appeared in *Continuous Learning*. An issue of *Interim* in late 1966 was devoted to that area (3 [3], 1966) and, beginning early in 1967, a special newsletter for this sector, entitled *Accent*, was launched. This was edited by Milton Pummell and appeared several times a year until mid-1969 (last issue 3 [1] 1969).

In 1965, in response to the rapid increase in programming for the educationally disadvantaged, the Association created a standing committee on literacy (CAAE Bd. June 2, 1965). At the same time. concern for matters related to the extent of poverty in Canada was expressed and, after a few months, these two areas were brought together under a standing committee on poverty, chaired by Gower Markle, of which a group concerned specifically with literacy or adult basic education became a sub-committee. When John Cornish joined the staff in 1964, he was asked to assemble material about literacy education (CAAE Exec. Mar. 5, 1965) and the Association became increasingly active in the field, holding a national seminar on adult literacy in March of 1966 under a grant from the Training Branch of the Department of Citizenship and Immigration. This was held in co-operation with Frontier College. The CAAE held a further workshop on adult basic education jointly with the Elliott Lake Training Center at the Center in the fall of 1968. Considerable attention was given in CAAE publications to the field of basic education, two issues of *Interim* focussing on that area (4 [1], 1967; 5 [1] 1968) and several substantial articles appearing in *Continuous Learning* towards the end of the decade (Brooke 1969; Niemi and Anderson 1969; Webb 1970).

Several other standing conmittees were maintained by the Association in these years but appear to have sponsored little, if any, program activity. Committees on rural adult education and governments in adult education had functioned in the Fifties, but both appear to have lapsed in 1963 with the reorganization of the CAAE. The committee on governments held a substantial conference directly after the national conference of 1961. A committee on university non-credit activities was disbanded in 1962, when it became apparent that this function was being performed by CADESS, the university extension organization. A committee of professors of adult education was formed in 1966 and met on one occasion during that year, but apparently not again. Somewhat more active was a committee on training and research (later research and professional development) which was formed in 1963. An effort that year to secure a large foundation grant for training purposes was unsuccessful, and there seems to have been little activity subsequently.

Citizenship and Voluntary Action

Since its creation the CAAE had engaged in various forms of citizenship education, the Forum projects being the best known. In this connection, many activities were conducted co-operatively with the Citizenship Branch of the federal government, the Canadian Citizenship Council and other organizations in the field of education about public affairs.

Arising from meetings held soon after Thomas arrived (CAAE Exec. Sept. 22, 1961), a project funded by the Citizenship Branch was launched which resulted in the publication of four "program guides" for use by citizenship convenors and program chairpersons in voluntary organizations. The subjects were (1) Canadian Nationalism, (2) Public Responsibility, (3) Know Your Community, and (4) Leader's Guide to Citizenship Programs. Each publication contained suggestions about techniques and topics and lists of resources for those planning programs. Advertisements and descriptions of the materials were carried in successive issues of *Continuous Learning* during the summer and fall of 1962 and in the first issue of *Interim* in the fall of 1962, but no information has been located concerning the extent of use or sales of these booklets.

One of the most substantial program projects during these years was devoted to the subject of voluntary action. In 1962, in response to suggestions made by the Canadian Home and School and Parent-Teacher Federation, consideration was given to a project which would involve "study of the activities of voluntary organizations" and lead to developing "a program for training in leadership in voluntary organizations" (CAAE Exec. Apr. 25, 1962). In July of 1964, a substantial proposal for a three-year project to this end, which had been developed by a committee representative of several national voluntary organizations (National Council of Jewish Women, Y.W.C.A., Women's Institutes, Red Cross, Junior Leagues, etc.) was formally presented to the CAAE Executive, with a tentative budget of $12,000 over three years and the assurance that the Citizenship Branch, Ottawa, had indicated a willingness to finance at least some parts of the work (CAAE Exec. July 2, 1964). The project was approved and began operation in the fall, under the chairmanship of Mrs. Mozah Zemens of the National Council of Jewish Women.

In the subsequent three years, the broadly based committee met regularly, a monograph on "Voluntary Participation in Canada: A Comparative Analysis," was commissioned and completed, a special issue of *Interim* (3 [2], 1966) was devoted to the project, and in 1967, regional workshops were held in Regina and Vancouver and a national seminar in Toronto. The original funding for the project ran out in 1968 and further deliberations were required as to its future. The reaction of the CAAE Executive was somewhat testy. Apparently the committee requested an advance from CAAE funds (against an expected outside grant) and a further outright grant of $3,500 from CAAE funds. The latter was turned down and in the end, an advance of $1,000 agreed upon (CAAE Exec. Apr.17, 1968).

Further funds from the Citizenship Branch were forthcoming the following year and the committee entered into an ambitious program involving eight studies related to government/voluntary associations relations. Each topic was to be the subject of a background paper, a seminar and then the publication of a pamphlet which was to receive wide distribution. In the end only two of these topics were developed, "The Advisory Board or Council" and "Grants, Contracts and Subsidies." In the annual report for 1968-69, it was stated that the pamphlets on each were being distributed to approximately 15,000 persons in the English version and 5,000 in the French. Although it was recognized that the Voluntary Action Committee was doing important work, the Board and Executive came to feel that the outside grants were not fully covering the costs of the projects and they also were concerned that the relatively large requests for funds from government for this work might interfere with the main supporting grant being received annually. Thomas kept this matter under control, but within months of his departure there was an open clash between the CAAE governing bodies and the committee and thereafter there was considerable tension in the relationship (CAAE Bd. May 21; Exec. Sept. 9, 1970).

New Partners and Concerns

During the decade, the CAAE entered several new program areas as a result of changes and opportunities in the field. That the CAAE responded to these opportunities, many of which involved working with new groups of specialists who were not generally seen as part of the field of adult education, was a result largely of Thomas' leadership and his readiness to see the CAAE's concerns to relate to all who had an impact on adult learning, not just the traditional adult educators who had made up the membership of the organization.

The two groups which illustrate this point most clearly were those involved in human relations training and those in guidance and counselling. The human relations training project (HRT) was a classic case of Thomas' actions preceding his opportunity to consult with his Executive. Early in 1963, at a time when the CAAE was badly in need of project funds, Thomas secured a grant of $5,000 from the Citizenship Branch to organize a national "consultative conference" on HRT. When the matter was presented to the CAAE Executive in early 1963, Thomas ran into some serious questions as to whether this was an appropriate concern for the CAAE (CAAE Exec. Jan. 15, 1963). The event was held, however, in late April, and arising out of that came a request from the group that they be constituted as a standing group affiliated with the CAAE. In the end the CAAE decided to form a Commission for HRT, which would function as an affiliate (CAAE Exec. Jan. 24, 1964). In the subsequent period, the Commission had difficulty raising sufficient funds to carry out its activities, but did conduct a series of regional or provincial "labs" (CAAE AR 1966-67). The Commission was reactivated in the following year under the leadership of Michael Clague and a most successful national conference was held in April 1968 (CAAE Exec. April 17, 1968; AR 1967-68). The Board of the CAAE continued to have concerns as to whether the Commission was a drain on CAAE resources (CAAE Bd. June 5-6, 1968). By early 1969, questions were being raised as to when the Commission's affiliation would come to an end (CAAE Bd. Jan. 31-Feb. 2, 1969). After a planning meeting in Toronto in the fall of 1969 and a further national conference in February of 1970, just before Thomas' departure, the HRT group founded an autonomous organization and terminated its formal links with the CAAE (CAAE Exec. Feb. 13, April 8, 1970).

The involvement in a project on guidance and counselling, although briefer than that with the HRT specialists, was in some respects parallel to it. Once again, it appears that Thomas raised some funds from government, this time from the National Employment Service, which made possible a project which he had trouble selling to his Executive. There was some question at the outset, in mid-1963, as to whether the project would involve the CAAE in a professional area outside its proper concerns, but once again, Thomas carried the Executive with him (CAAE Exec. July 25, Nov. 6, 1963). Fortunately, grants totalling approximately $9,000 were secured to support the event, a most successful national conference was held in November, and a series of successful publications were prepared for practitioners. When, as in the case of the HRT group, the guidance and counselling committee expressed a wish to affiliate with the CAAE while it went through an organizational stage in creating an independent body, the affiliation was approved, but a further request for secretarial services was refused (CAAE Exec. Jan. 24, 1964). A further national conference under CAAE auspices held in the fall of 1965 led to the formation of an autonomous Canadian Guidance and Counselling Association and, after some disagreement over the disposition of the surplus from the meeting, an amicable parting of the ways was the outcome (CAAE Bd. Jan. 21-23, Exec. Mar. 3, 1966).

In both of these cases, two important features of the Thomas years were evident. One was the familiar problem of the Director having to find funding where he could and undertake activities which might not otherwise be high priority for the Association. The other was that Thomas' view of the centrality of adult learning, as distinct from adult education, led him to a wider view of the concerns of the Association than most leaders of the CAAE shared.

The CAAE sponsored activities on other specialized professional concerns as well. In 1962, with financial assistance from the Canadian Conference on Education and the Citizenship Branch, a seminar was organized on Teaching Machines and Programmed Instruction which was held in Toronto. The papers presented were published as the first special supplement carried by *Continuous Learning*, in the spring of 1962 (*CL* 1 [2]). Little information is available, but it appears that a seminar on Measurement and Evaluation was carried out in April of 1965.

A further major project involved the training of community development workers in association with ARDA, the Agricultural Reconstruction and Development Agency of the federal government. In December 1964, after some months of negotiations with ARDA and the ICEA, a contract was signed under which the two adult education bodies would provide consultation to ARDA on the training of community development personnel. The CAAE Board was enthusiastic about the project (CAAE Bd. Dec. 3-5, 1964) and it involved co-operation with the ICEA, which pleased Thomas. That the project was also well financed, with a good margin for overhead expenses, made it ideal (CAAE Exec. Oct. 23, 1964). It was managed by a joint committee on which all three organizations were represented. Two national seminars and a series of meetings of the management committee produced a printed report, which was submitted to the Minister at the end of April 1965 (CAAE Bd. June 2-3, 1965). It was hoped that further activities of this kind would be funded, and the matter was discussed further as late as March 1967, by the CAAE Executive. but no further project materialized (CAAE AR 1965-66; Exec. Mar. 7, 1967).

Commission for the Community College

The most substantial project undertaken by the CAAE during the Thomas years was the Commission for the Community College. Thomas and others had a particular interest in the community college as a source of opportunities for adult education and at least as early as March of 1963, Thomas raised with the Executive the matter of programming in that area (CAAE Exec. Mar. 4, 1963). A year later, he engaged in consultations with the Canadian Education Association about a possible seminar on college development in Canada, and after he reminded the CAAE Executive of the Kellogg Foundation's interest in the college movement, they authorized him to explore the possibilities (CAAE Exec. May 26, 1964). More and more items about community colleges appeared in *Continuous Learning* in 1965. In June of that year, a conference on Adult Education and the Community College was held in Ottawa in connection with the annual meeting. This meeting is seen by the college movement in Canada as the beginning of the process which led eventually to the creation of a national college association (Outline History of the ACCC n.d.). A printed conference report was published. In May 1966, a National Seminar on the Community College was organized by the CAAE and, this time, co-sponsored with several other national organizations interested in the college movement. The emerging college systems in B. C., Alberta, Ontario and Quebec were examined at this conference. Early in 1967, the CAAE assisted with a seminar on the subject held in Ontario for provincial purposes, and when reporting to the Board at the end of January, Thomas indicated that he was "pursuing the possibility of a National Commission for Community

Colleges in Canada, sponsored by the CAAE for three years" (CAAE Bd. Jan. 28-29, 1967). Soon thereafter negotiations with the Kellogg Foundation were begun in earnest (CAAE Exec. Mar. 7, 1967) and by the fall, the project was approved in principle (CAAE Exec. Oct. 26, 1967). In mid-December, Thomas informed the Executive that he had heard by telephone that Kellogg had approved a three-year grant of $202,800 for the project, which was to begin on April 1, 1968 (CAAE Exec. Dec. 13, 1967). Mr. Bert Curtis of Algonquin College, Ottawa, a longstanding member of the CAAE Board, was named chairman of the new Commission at the same meeting. Some consternation was expressed over the fact that the original request had been for $250,000 and that the reduction had largely been at the expense of amounts provided for overhead costs. The budget and constitution of the new body were carefully worked through in the ensuing months, there clearly being some concern that the new Commission might come to dominate the CAAE (CAAE Exec. Aug. 12, 1968). In the early fall of 1968, *Continuous Learning* formally announced the composition of the Board of the new Commission and that Robert Gwilliam had been named the Project Director. The Commission was described as follows:

> Over a three year period, it will cover statistical services and information exchange to the colleges, giving aid for special studies of curriculum, administration, faculty relations and professional programs. A major national conference will be convened each year. (Commission for the Community College 1968:203)

The Board of the Commission was representative of six provinces and made up largely of persons connected with the colleges rather than with the CAAE.

The National Commission for the Community College was a particularly successful venture but was not without its problems, as far as the CAAE was concerned. The project, as planned, carried out its work for three years, concluding at the end of 1970, almost a year after Thomas' departure. The Commission organized many activities intended to assist and influence the community college systems as they emerged and developed across the country. They included: annual major conferences; workshops and specialized conferences on such topics as transferability of credit, staff development, finance and Canadian studies; co-operation with the Dominion Bureau of Statistics; publication of a tabloid newsletter, "College Canada" (25,000 to 45,000 copies per issue); a series of "hearings" each year in various parts of the country to stir interest in college development and get local input; and information services of various kinds. The Commission amassed a list of 85 colleges by the end of its first year of operation, which grew to 105 by a year later. It was a goal of the Commission from the beginning to aim towards the creation of a permanent, autonomous organization of colleges after the Kellogg project concluded, and it was apparent from the beginning that there was support for such an outcome. As Curtis, the chairman of the Commission has put it:

> None of us envisioned the size, scope, and strength of the development of the community college movement....By the time the Commission had travelled the country and held meetings (say one and a half years into the three year project), it was obvious that the community college movement was bigger than the CAAE and that a separate association was wanted by the college people....By the time we came to the colleges' assembly in November, 1970, there were 153 voting delegates and there were 151 votes for the formation of an association. (personal communication, Jan. 6, 1984)

It was an idea whose time had come. At the assembly in November 1970, most colleges in Canada, Ministries of Education and other related associations were represented and the objectives and guidelines for the new organization were approved. The Commission was made possible by the largest grant the CAAE had received in its history and by any standard must be judged an outstanding success.

There were some problems along the way. The Director of the project (the staff was up to four at one point, but was usually three) was judged not to be performing satisfactorily and it was arranged that he resign, early in 1970. The CAAE Board and Executive felt at times that they were not being kept adequately informed about the project (CAAE Exec. Jan. 16, Mar. 20, 1969; Feb. 13, 1970), but it was sorted out to everyone's satisfaction in the end.

International Activities

International relationships had been a major theme in CAAE activities during the directorship of Thomas' predecessor. Thomas also had an active interest in such work and acted internationally as opportunities presented themselves.

The most ambitious project during the decade involved relationships with adult education organizations and leaders elsewhere in the Americas. With the Canadian centennial in mind, suggestions were made as early as 1963 that the two major American adult education associations, the Adult Education Association of the U.S.A. (AEA) and the National Association of Public School Adult Educators (NAPSAE), be invited to hold a joint conference in Canada in 1967, with the CAAE and the ICEA. The matter was discussed at the CAAE annual meeting in June of 1963 and such a plan was authorized (CAAE AM June 1, 1963). When it was discussed at an Executive meeting later in the month, Thomas reported that the American bodies had suggested the proposed conference be widened to include all of North America (CAAE Exec. June 27, 1963). It appears that the American leaders were anxious to involve Mexicans in a regional consultation but were aware that strong initiatives from the United States would not be well received by the Mexican organizations. The American bodies offered to pay the expenses of the two Canadian Directors to go to Mexico and try to arrange such a meeting (CAAE Exec. Jan. 24, 1964).

Arising out of these beginnings and subsequent meetings in the United States and Mexico, a North American Conference on Adult Education, attended by some 125 delegates, was held in Montreal, October 22-24, 1967. In the end, the two American organizations, AEA and NAPSAE, did not hold their conferences in Canada, but sent representatives to the international meeting. There was difficulty along the way arranging satisfactory Mexican representation, but in the end, several Mexican educators did attend. Atempts to secure funding for the meeting from the Ford Foundation were not successful, but grants were obtained from the Canadian Commission for UNESCO, the Quebec government and from the Citizenship Branch, Ottawa. There was also a plan that out of the conference would come a North American Bureau of Adult Education, a parallel organization to a European regional body already in existence (CAAE Bd. Jan. 28, 1967; Exec. Mar. 7, May 25, 1967).

The conference approved the establishment of an Inter-American Committee for Adult Education, with Thomas as its first chairman. There were to be four members of the committee from each of the three participating countries, with Canada divided equally between the CAAE and the ICEA. Subsequent meetings of the committee in Mexico City in June of 1968 and in Washington a year later extended the contacts, but difficulty in maintaining satisfactory Mexican representation continued. A further conference planned at one time for Mexico in 1971 was never held. When Thomas left the directorship in 1970, he continued to serve as a CAAE representative on the committee, but the necessary continuing support and co-operation were simply not there. The committee ceased to meet beyond that year (CAAE Exec. Oct. 27, 1967, Dec. 14, 1969; Bd. Jan. 30, 1970; AM June 6, 1968; *CL* 7, [3], 1968:131).

Late in the decade, an International Projects Committee was established. Although its functions were subsequently to become quite broadly defined, during Thomas' tenure the immediate task appears to have been to provide a means by which funds from the Canadian International Development Agency could be received and channelled to projects in India for which they had been raised by Roby Kidd, former Director and member of the committee (CAAE Bd. Oct. 6, 1969; Exec. Nov. 5, 1969, April 8, 1970).

Other Programs

Brief reference will be made to several other significant programs and projects carried out during the period.

Thomas had been active in educational travel activities while at Columbia University and had great interest in that field. The CAAE had a committee on educational travel for a few years in the latter half of the decade, assisted member institutions with planning for educational travel to other parts of Canada, experimented with audiotape aids for tours, and, in the fall of 1969, organized a major conference on education travel methods which was held in Ottawa.

One unusual program activity, held in 1967, involved the staff of the Association as consultants or process experts. The Steel Company of Canada hosted a three-day "Industrial Confrontation" in Hamilton, at which that firm and others made public statements about their activities. Members of the public and organizational representatives were given an opportunity to respond and critique the firms' positions. Alan Thomas and Milton Pummell represented the CAAE and managed the process of the meeting. Although Thomas reported to the Executive that the meeting had been very successful and that more would be held (CAAE Exec. Mar. 7, 1967), there is no evidence of further such meetings.

A committee on consumer education was active in 1968 and the following year, holding several meetings. Attempts to get funding for a major activity in this field which appeared hopeful in the fall of 1969 (CAAE Exec. Nov. 5, 1969) were not in fact realized and likely were left in abeyance after Thomas' departure a few months later.

In late 1967, the Association arranged a contract with the federal Department of Industry under which the CAAE prepared a course of study for industrial development officers in the department. The course was developed by staff employed for the purpose, field tested with a group in June of 1968, and submitted in completed form in July. It consisted of a 250-page typescript course of studies under ten major headings.

One noteworthy project during the period was a series of study tours across Canada for foreign service officers of the Department of External Affairs. These were designed to help acquaint newly hired officers with the various regions of Canada, before they went abroad to represent Canada elsewhere. The CAAE designed the tours, in co-operation with External Affairs, conducted some program events which were held in Ontario, and involved some of the divisions of CAAE in conducting events in other regions. There was a reasonable amount of overhead money available in the project and co-operating divisions did well financially as a result of taking part. There were four such tours arranged in the late Sixties.

The foregoing represent not all but perhaps the major program activities conducted by the Association during the Thomas years. Some other potentially major programs were discussed but were dropped when necessary outside funding could not be obtained. These included the development of a curriculum for adults on science, a computer-assisted information system on programs and materials for adult education, and a major five-year program for training and development in the field. The organization of program activities and solicitation for supporting funds was a constant preoccupation of the Director, as it had been throughout the Association's history. Within only a few weeks after Thomas' departure in early 1970 the lack of income for projects brought on, or deepened, the financial problems of the organization.

Services

The Association's Journals

Alan Thomas used the journal of the Association as one of the chief instruments at his disposal for achieving his ends. He was a man of ideas; he sought to change the course of national thinking with respect to the role and significance of learning in national life. Clearly one of the avenues open to him to influence others—national policy makers, educators, and of course the field of adult education itself—was the journal of the Association, which had been published continuously since 1936. When Thomas joined the staff of the CAAE, its journal was called *Food For Thought*, as it had been since 1940. He wanted the publication not just to be a source of articles about random aspects of the field but a leading intellectual force for the movement. He wanted the CAAE to support an ideology, and the journal was a means of stating the case he wanted to make (personal communication, Aug. 10, 1983).

Thomas thought that the title, *Food For Thought*, was rather innocuous, and did not convey the sense of purpose and direction he sought. In the very first month he was on the staff of the Association, he worked out a series of suggested changes in the journal and the editor, Eleanor Graham, brought them forward to the Executive meeting in late September 1961. The proposals included a change of name, a reduction from eight to six issues a year, and as Thomas is quoted in the minutes as saying, that the journal become "one of the liveliest magazines in the country" (CAAE Exec. Sept. 22, 1961). The changes proposed, which were approved by the Executive, were to come into effect with the new year, 1962. Volume 1, Number 1 of the new journal, *Continuous Learning*, was dated January-February 1962. It was slightly larger in format and generally more sprightly looking than its predecessor. A bit of style and tone was added with the use of such headings as "Intelligencer" as the title of the news section, "Parameter" as the title of an article length comment section, and the continuation of Roby Kidd's "Ensemble" column. Although Thomas clearly wished to use the journal to provide intellectual leadership and persuasive influence in the Canadian community, it is noteworthy that he chose to try to

do so in the name of the CAAE. The journal featured the symbol of the organization, a stylized tree of knowledge, and the name of the Association prominently on the cover of the journal consistently throughout the decade. *CL* was used as a house organ for the CAAE, carrying much information about the organization's activities and concerns.

Eleanor Graham remained as editor of *CL* for only the first three issues. From that point on, Thomas took over the task, with the help of an assistant editor. This arrangement was maintained until 1966, when Don MacNeill joined the staff as Managing Editor of the journal. There were several distinct changes in style or format during the decade. With the first issue in 1966, there was a new layout, more use of open space, bold black lines used between news items, and a generally more striking appearance. Two years later, perhaps as an economy measure, the paper stock became thinner and the print more compact, with less open space. In the meantime, with the first issue in 1967, soon after the official opening of "Corbett House"—the name given to the new offices—a line drawing of the headquarters was used on the cover of the journal, thus reinforcing its connection with the Association itself. The last issue edited by Thomas before he left the Association was the first number in 1970.

Nine more issues were produced before the journal ceased publication, in the rather chaotic and demoralized period of the early Seventies. At the special membership meeting in December of 1970 where basic decisions were made about the future of the Association, the former Director, Roby Kidd, offered to work vith a volunteer group for a period of time to keep the journal going. It was agreed that a group based at Kidd's institution, the Ontario Institute for Studies in Education, would take over the editorial duties for a two-year period, until the CAAE was ready to resume responsibility for it (CAAE Exec. Jan. 12, 1971). In the end, this arrangement was maintained for only one year, the last issue appearing as Vol. 10, No. 6, dated Nov.-Dec., 1971.

There is little information available as to the circulation of *CL*. In her report to the National Council in early 1961 on *Food For Thought*, Eleanor Graham has stated that the circulation of the journal had been approximately 1,800 copies a month and that this had been the case for the previous six or seven years (CAAE NC Jan. 20, 1961). The only other firm figures on circulation which are available are for *CL* during its first full year of publication, 1962. Circulation showed a steady increase during the year, moving from 1,896 to 2,071, with an average of 1,934. At the end of 1972, there were 498 subscribers to *CL*, in addition to the CAAE members, who received it as part of their membership services (CAAE NC Feb. 8, 1963). Although no other circulation figures have been located, it is known that the membership of the Association doubled over the decade, increasing by approximately 750, so it may well be that the monthly circulation increased by approximately that amount, at least.

There were a number of regular features in *CL* which helped to give it a distinctive flavor and some consistency. The most important influence was that of Thomas himself. He consciously used the journal as a means of advancing his ideas. He wrote the editorial for almost all issues, "Parameter" for most, and many other articles over the years (personal communication, Aug. 10, 1983). There were periods during which he wrote a substantial percentage of the content, anonymously or in his own name. The next most important person, in terms of the content of the journal, was Roby Kidd, the former Director of the Association. Having become by 1960 one of the most prominent adult educators in the world, Kidd had access to a wide range of information about the field, and he conveyed aspects of this to readers of *CL* during the decade through his regular column, "Ensemble." He also contributed several major articles. Kidd lived in several places and held several responsible positions during the decade—in Ottawa, India and Toronto—and his contributions to the journal represent a rich collection of fact and comment. A third consistent feature of the journal was its reporting on CAAE affairs. This was often covered in "Intelligencer," in articles and reports on CAAE meetings, including annual meetings and major conferences, occasional sections headed "CAAE News" or something similar, lists of office-holders in the Association, reprinting of submissions the CAAE had made to public bodies, and towards the end of the decade, sometimes the entire annual report of the Association. Although Thomas wished to use the journal to reach a wider audience than just the CAAE membership, its function as a vehicle for informing the membership about the work of the Association was very prominent.

The content of *Food For Thought* during the Fifties increasingly emphasized matters of professional concern in the field (Selman 1982) and this trend continued in the Sixties. Also prominent were Thomas' efforts to point out the relationship between the potential of learning and the public issues of the day. In his study of the evolution of the CAAE journals, Walter Stewart (1983) identified two main foci in *CL* during 1965, a year he examined in detail. One was the "clearing house" function—news about adult education people, programs, training opportunities, etc. The other was what he termed "articles on current adult education issues and on the relationship of adult education and current social issues" (Stewart 1983:44). He notes the number of articles on education for women and the number of what he terms professional articles. He sums up his observations by calling *CL* "a trade or craft magazine for adult education rather than a professional journal" (p.47). He characterizes the journals during the 1950s and 1960s as being directed at "an increasingly narrow audience," largely institution-based adult educators and a field which was "becoming increasingly professionalized and institutionalized." With respect to Thomas' ideas, as they were revealed in the 1965 issues, he sees a reflection of "the challenges confronting democracy" (pp.61, 66).

A closer examination of the contents of *CL* during this decade indicates some alternative and further observations. Certainly, compared to previous decades, there is much more material in the journal which is addressed to the professional interests of adult educators. These items include: several long directories of professional training programs at universities in Canada, the U.S. and abroad, sometimes taking up most of the issue; articles on research and research needs; articles on the development of the field in particular institutional settings, such as education in industry and in the emerging college systems; commentaries on the statistical work of the Domunion Bureau of Statistics concerning adult education; examinations of the characteristics of professionalism as they apply to adult education; theoretical pieces on such matters as the nature of skills; examinations of emerging fields of specialty, such as continuing professional education, adult basic education and education for women; and several pieces on the roles, functions and social relevance of adult education.

There were several special issues and supplements to the journal. It was annnounced at the time of the introduction of the new title and format that there would be such special issues from time to time, but there were in fact few. The first, which appeared in the second issue (*CL* 1 [2], 1962) was a supplement on Teaching Machines and Programmed Instruction. The largest supplement, which was published early in 1966, was on "Religion and Adult Education." Other topics receiving such treatment, sometimes declared to be special supplements and sometimes just a concentration of articles on a particular subject, included Canadian foreign aid, educational television and an innovative program in the Lakehead area, "Town Talk."

A review of the articles provides an indication of the emerging aspects of practice and of programming and of the social issues to which the field was responding. A sampling of these topics includes the changing role of women, pollution and other environmental concerns, Expo 1967, poverty, community development, international relations and foreign aid, French-English relations in Canada, aging and education for older people, education for prisoners, manpower training, retraining, and education for the disadvantaged. The journal also gave considerable space to printing submissions which the CAAE had made to Royal Commissions and other public bodies.

Thomas had his eye particularly on the policy makers and adult education leaders in editing the journal. There was criticism from time to time, especially from the provincial divisions presumably reflecting the views of the grass roots membership, that the journal was not of interest or use to them (CAAE Bd. June 22, 1967; June 5, 1968). Earlier in the decade. Thomas had acknowledged criticism of the journal when he commented in an editorial that there were readers "who quite legitimately urge us to be more practical in our approach" (Thomas 1963e:149). If one was looking to *CL* to be a practical manual of practice in the field, one was bound to be dissatisfied with it. Practical in that sense it was not, and was never intended to be. A review of the journal from this distance in time also reveals that there were times during the decade when the journal was somewhat thin and with little obvious sense of direction. These times were the exception, however. By and large, when reviewing the entire run of *CL* for the decade, one is struck by the dynamism and earnestness of effort which clearly informs all aspects of the journal. At these times, it seems truly a journal of ideas, an effort to stir the field of adult education and other educational decision makers to new thought about the role of adult learning in Canadian society.

Other Publications

The Sixties were an active period as far as the publications program of the CAAE was concerned. Some items represented a continuation of the sort of publications the Association had produced in the past: Farm and Citizen's Forum support material; occasional pamphlets on a variety of subjects; the Association's journal; and the publication of a further book of readings on the development of the field in Canada. But in addition, an impressive range of other publishing activities was undertaken. This included several specialized newsletters; precis and comments on significant public documents such as Royal Commission reports; and the White Paper on the role of adult learning in Canada, which was used as a vehicle for a major advocacy effort. Taken together, this publication program represents an impressive effort to serve the field, the members of the Association, and interested members of the public. It is a further manifestation of the ambition and "reach" which Thomas displayed in his efforts to influence both his colleagues in adult education and the broader society.

The Forum projects both came to an end during the decade, but while they continued, they involved major publication efforts. *Farm Forum Guide* continued much as it had in the previous decade (Selman 1982), involving news of Forum group activities and other materials as well as the background information on the broacast topics. The Citizens' Forum pamphlets remained much the same as before—restricted to information on broadcast topics. But as the program experimented with having several broadcasts deal with aspects of the same topic and leaving some topics open so that current topics could be inserted closer to broadcast time, the pattern of publication was altered. With the termination of these two major projects, the end of an important era for the Association was reached, and in the case of Citizens' Forum, staff time was released for other tasks.

Some impression of the scale of the publications effort of the Association can be gained from the periodic comprehensive listings published in *Continuous Learning* and the newsletters. The annual report for1967-68, for instance, listed eight publications for the year, over and above the journal. The report for the following year lists five different periodicals and five other publications, one of which had sales in the 20,000 range. In the summer of 1968, the journal carried a listing on the inside and outside back cover which listed 16 publications being distributed by the Association, 12 of which were published by the CAAE.

The Association had a commitment, under the terms of one of the grants obtained from the Fund for Adult Education in the late 1950s (Selman 1982), to publish a volume of readings on adult education in Canada, a successor volume to *Adult Education in Canada*, which was published in 1950. Like the earlier volume, this one was edited by Roby Kidd. It appeared in 1963 under the title, *Learning and Society,* consisting of 414 pages of text and including approximately 60 different authors, all the items except the editor's contributions having been published previously, many in the CAAE journals. This volume reflected clearly the advancing professionalism in the field, when contrasted vith the earlier volume (Selman 1982). There were 1,500 copies printed in the first run, at a cost of $6,000, one-third of which came from the FAE funds (CAAE Exec. May 14, June 27, 1963). Advertisements for the volume appeared in the journal for several issues in early-mid-1963 and when the book appeared later in the year, three book reviews were published in the same issue (*CL* 2 [6], 1963:272-83).

One of the most significant facets of the publications program in the Sixties might be summmed up under the heading "public affairs and advocacy." As part of its efforts in the field of education about public affairs, the Association launched into a new field under Thomas' leadership—the production of precis of public documents, most notably the reports of important royal commissions. This work was done largely by Isabel Wilson, the outstandingly skilled staff member who had for many years been the editor/author of the Citizens' Forum pamphlet series. Few Canadians, even those interested in the subject, were likely to acquire and read the full reports of royal commissions. The CAAE decided to publish a precis of some such reports and make them available at a very low cost (usually 10 cents per copy), for the benefit of interested persons and organizations.

The report of the Fowler Committee on Broadcasting was summarized in *Continuous Learning* (Broadcasting 1965). The first separate publication was prepared in connection with the Hall Commission on health services for Canadians, which was also the subject of a major programming effort, in 1965 (see above). By early the next year, approximately 25,000 copies of the pamphlet had been sold, a best seller by Canadian standards (CAAE Bd. Jan. 21-23, 1966). A pamphlet summarizing the report of the Royal Commission on Taxation was published in 1967. The most ambitious venture of this kind consisted of the publication of summaries of the successive volumes of the Royal Commission on

Bilingualism and Biculturalism, as they appeared in the latter years of the decade. The summary of the first volume was advertised late in 1967 and the original printing consisted of 15,000 copies in English and 5,000 in French. It was necessary to print an additional run of the English edition (CAAE AR 1968-69) and, in the spring of 1969, it was stated in *Continuous Learning* that "more than 25,000" had been distributed (*CL* 8 [2], 1969). The resumé of volumes 2 and 3 of the report were published by the time Thomas left the Association early in 1970 (*CL* 9 [1], 1970), and others followed in the ensuing months. Publications on national policy concerning adult education and on the manpower policy of the federal government were also published in quantity and will be dealt with below under advocacy activities.

A major publication effort in these years was the production of a series of newsletters for the field. These will be dealt with in the section under information and research, below. Their production was clearly a recognition of, and effort to serve, emerging new interest groups and specialized areas of practice in the field.

Reference has been made in the program section above to the several publications issued by the Association in the fields of citizenship education and the project on voluntary action in Canada. There were also several publications arising from the community colleges project.

A number of other publications were issued. They included: a booklet on how to learn French, which was subsidized by the Citizenship Branch and published by the University of Toronto; a substantial pamphlet on the history of extension work of The University of British Columbia; the separate publication of supplements which had been incorporated in the journal (the one on "Religion and Adult Education" was an especially big seller); and a series of modest, article and monograph length items, such as surveys of training needs for particular groups of practitioners. In 1967, the Association announced the beginning of a new series of "basic, informative, vital manuals on adult education" (*CL* 6 [5], 1967:226), referred to as the "How to..." series. The first and, as far as is known, only pamphlet published in the series was written by Milton Pummell of the staff on the topic *How to Start an Adult Education Program* (1967) aimed at school boards.

Information, Research and Library Services

In keeping with his ambitions for the CAAE, Thomas had high expectations for the Association's activities as a source of information and research data for the field. The level of activity maintained in these areas was impressive but, as in some other areas of the Association's work, was in the long run found to be beyond the CAAE's means. With the near collapse of the organization after his departure, almost all of these activities ceased.

After Thomas joined the staff in 1961, he supported strongly the work of Diana Ironside and the support staff in the library, and this policy continued throughout the decade. The report of the committee responsible for overseeing this work which was made to the National Council early in 1963 indicated that an active program of work was being maintained, including an active acquisitions, cataloguing and lending program, the preparation of bibliographies, issuance of news releases and the publication of a bi-monthly Association newsletter, *Interim*, launched late the previous year (CAAE NC Feb. 8, 1963). The library was regularly described in *Continuous Learning* and elsewhere as the "CAAE National Research Library in Adult Education." The information services of the Association were maintained at an active level throughout the decade, even after major portions of the library were sold in 1967. The Association devoted three pages of *Continuous Learning* in the last issue of 1967 to advertising the information services, emphasizing three in particular—"Information Service Sheets," "Trends" and directories (*CL* 6 [6], 1967:ff.286). The latter were to be directories of personnel and appear to have been restricted to the field of school board adult education. The information service sheets were lists of books, pamphlets, articles, films and tapes available from the CAAE, separate ones prepared for 14 different areas of specialty. By 1969, "over 1,000" persons were on the mailing list for this service (CAAE AR 1968-69). The service sheets were available flee of charge, but "Trends" cost $2.00 per quarterly issue or $6.00 for the year. This series began in 1968 and each issue contained an annotated list of current holdings and new materials of significance, each issue being devoted to a single area of practice. Only three issues appeared, however, and the series ceased in 1969.

The Association sold the bulk of its library holdings in 1967. For some years it had been a matter of discussion within the Association as to whether it could satisfactorily maintain and staff a sizeable library collection. Early in 1960, when the CAAE was facing the prospect of having to move its office, the chairman of the Executive pointed out that it was difficult to plan for the space required in view of the uncertainty concerning "the housing and future of the CAAE library" (CAAE Exec. Jan. 26, 1960). It is clear from the Executive minutes later in the year that discussions were entered into with the Toronto Public Library concerning their acquisition or management of the CAAE's collection (CAAE Exec. Feb. 23, 1960). The very serious financial situation of the Association in late 1966 and early 1967 apparently led to the revival of such a plan. By this time, the former Director of the Association, Roby Kidd, was chairman of the Adult Education Department of the Ontario Institute for Studies in Education (OISE) and negotiations were entered into with that organization for a possible purchase. The Board authorized the Executive in January to explore the conditions under which the library might be sold (CAAE Bd. Jan. 28-29, 1967) and Thomas' mid-year report to the same meeting made it clear that OISE was the prospective buyer. During the spring, a period during which the financial position of the Association was particularly grim (CAAE Exec. Mar. 7, May 25, 1967), discussions with OISE officials were carried forward. In June a formal letter was sent offering the transfer in return for a purchase price of $50,000 and later in the same month such an arrangement was formally approved by both the Board and annual meeting of the Association (CAAE Bd. June 22; AM June 23, 1967). What was sold to OISE was not the whole of the library collection but the bulk of it, the Association retaining those portions needed to support their information services.

Four newsletters were published by the Association for varying lengths of time. The longest running of these was *Interim*. It was a general newsletter for the field and was clearly part of Thomas' efforts to promote the professionalization of the field. It was to appear in the months between the bimonthly publication af the journal and was clearly aimed at adult education practitioners. Each issue was identified as being about a particular area or topic, or for those working in a particular sector of the field. A lead article and usually some other items were related to that field and then other miscellaneous news items followed, to fill out the issue. It was mailed free of charge to members and to others who requested to be on the mailing list. *Interim* began publication in late 1962 and was published fairly regularly until 1966. From 1967 to 1969, only one issue was published each year. The annual report for 1968-69 explained that this was due to "budgetary restrictions." Like so many other CAAE activities, *Interim* did not survive Thomas' departure.

A second newsletter was *Accent.* It was issued for those engaged in school board sponsored adult education programs and was managed in consultation with the standing committee on this aspect of the field. The first issue appeared in March of 1967 and the publication continued until 1969, during which time a total of eight issues were published. It was edited by Milton Pummell, the part-time staff member who worked in this area.

For a short period in 1968 and 1969, the CAAE published a newsletter entitled *Meeting Poverty.* This had been issued previously by the Special Planning Secretariat of the Privy Council Office, Ottawa, but was taken over by the CAEE, under contract, in the spring of 1968 (CAAE Exec. April 17, 1968). The newsletter was sent to approximately 4,000 persons, presumably to a mailing list which was also taken over from the government department. Three issues were published by mid-1969 and there is reference to a fourth being prepared (CAAE AR 1968-69), but such a further issue has not been discovered.

The fourth newsletter was *College Canada*, which was a publication of the Commission for the Community College and has been referred to above.

The Association co-operated with the ICEA and OISE in the publication of a directory, *Non-degree Research in Adult Education in Canada 1967-68* (1968). Edited by James Draper of OISE (English) and Paul Belanger of the ICEA (French), this was the first of a series of such directories which were compiled in subsequent years.

In view of the financial resources and staff time available, it was a tribute to Thomas and his colleagues that so many varied and useful publications and information services were made available during the decade. It may be seen as an integral part of the effort, inspired by Thomas, to have an influence on the thinking and development of the rapidly growing field. An indication of how crucial Thomas' leadership was to these accomplishments was the fact that almost all of them failed to survive his departure from the organization.

Advocacy Activities

Since the earliest days of the CAAE, the organization had acted as an advocate on behalf of adult education and in the interest of widening the learning opportunities for adults in Canadian society. Whereas in the very early years it had made pronouncements on broad matters of social policy, it had since the late 1940s tended to concentrate its attention more narrowly on matters directly related to adult learning (Faris 1975; Selman 1981, 1982). Thomas and the other leaders of the Association throughout the 1960s attached great importance to this function as well and a great deal of energy and resources were invested in such efforts.

The advocacy activities may be seen as falling into several categories, as indicated in the earlier section on Thomas' leadership.

Two cases of attempting to influence the methodology of public inquiries were particularly noteworthy. Thomas was of the view that how royal commissions and other such public bodies carried out their hearings and presented their reports could have a major impact on the educational value for Canadians of the whole process. The Commission on Agriculture and Rural Life in Saskatchewan in the early Fifties was seen by many as an exemplary model, one which maximized the educational impact of the public inquiry process. When in 1963 the federal government appointed the Royal Commission on Bilingualism and Biculturalism, the Commission convened a series of preliminary hearings designed to clarify its mandate and provide an opportunity to discuss its procedures. The CAAE communicated its views by correspondence to the co-chairmen of the commission in the late summer and presented a formal brief in early November (CAAE Exec. Sept. 19, 1963; Royal Comnission 1963). The brief stressed the importance of the potential educational impact of the commission's proceedings. It recommended regional hearings and forums in all parts of the country and also that the commission not leave it to various groups to come foward but actively go out and seek the views of certain significant groups at the local, provincial and national levels. In short, it recommended ways to facilitate what it termed "a prolonged two-way exchange between the commission and the citizens of Canada" (Royal Commission 1963:245).

A somewhat similar effort was made in connection with the federal government's Task Force on Government Information. When it was appointed in 1968, the Association approached the commissioners with the suggestion that if they would finance the meetings, the CAAE, through its partners, would convene regional meetings at which the views of a variety of organizations could be presented and discussed. Such events were held in Vancouver in December 1968 and in Halifax the following month. The ICEA held a meeting in Montreal (CAAE Bd. Sept. 20, 1968; Exec. Nov. 14, 1968; AR 1968-69). A similar proposal was made to the Senate Committee on Poverty in the fall of 1969, but the Committee decided to organize such meetings itself (CAAE Exec. Nov. 5, 1969).

The Association made presentations and presented briefs to a number of public inquiries during this period. In general it may be said that the main thrust or direction of these presentations was to recommend that Canadian society be so ordered that there would be maximum opportunities and encouragement for all Canadians to learn and to play an active, participating role in Canadian life. A list of the bodies to which submissions were made suggests something of the range and magnitude of these efforts:

1961 - Senate Committee on Manpower and Unemployment
1962 - National Centennial Council Committee on Manpower and Training (Ontario)
1963 - Royal Commission on Taxation
1964 - Senate Committee on Aging
     - Select Committee on Youth (Ontario)
1965 - Royal Commission on Bilingualism and Biculturalism
1967 - Parliamentary Committee on Broadcasting
1968 - Parliamentary Committee on Broadcasting—Supplementary Brief on Television
1969 - Royal Commission on the Status of Women
     - Task Force on Federal Government Information
1970 - Senate Committee on Poverty

One of the most ambitious attempts to influence public opinion and policy was the preparation and publication in 1967 of *A Report to the Canadian People on Manpower Development* (CAAE 1967b). The federal government had played an active role in stimulating and to some degree financing vocational and technical training since 1919 (Beck 1968). The Technical and Vocational Training Assistance Act of 1960 had significantly stepped up the pace of this work but still operated on the assumption that vocational training was a provincial prerogative, and this led to increased friction in federal-provincial relations (Wilson et al 1970). In 1967, the Pearson government passed the Adult Occupational Training Act. By its terms, the federal government entered directly into the field of adult vocational training and retraining on the grounds that it had the power to do so under its responsibility for general economic development, labour mobility and the general level of employment (Dupre et al 1973; Wilson et al 1970).

The CAAE had for some time been giving attention to this matter. In his report to the Board in January of 1966, Thomas had stated that he proposed to "undertake a study of the vocational training legislation" (CAAE Bd. Jan. 21-23, 1966). Early in 1967, the full text of the federal bill was printed in the journal and an editorial urged the government to engage in a wider public discussion of the matter (*CL* 6 [2], 1967). A full issue of the newsletter, *Accent*, was devoted to the matter in August. In October, Thomas indicated to the Executive that he was preparing a report on the legislation (CAAE Exec. Oct. 26, 1967). The Board approved the document in mid-January, 1968, and the "Report to the Canadian People" was issued, appearing both in *Continuous Learning* and as a separate pamphlet (CAAE 1967b). It was sharply critical of both the manner in which the new federal-provincial arrangements were negotiated, with no opportunity for public discussion, and also of some features of the plan itself. It was particularly critical of the eligibility for training regulations, under which the trainee must have been out of school for a full year and have previously been in the labor force for three years. These and other criticisms of the Act and of procedures established under it were currently forthcoming from several quarters (Wilson et al 1970). Two months later, while Thomas was on leave in Africa, the Acting Director, Gower Markle, reported to the Executive that the CAAE was receiving "most favorable comments" on the statement (CAAE Exec. Mar. 8, 1968).

This report was in certain respects a unique venture for the CAAE. Although it had frequently made submissions to public bodies which were soliciting opinion, the CAAE had not before spoken out in such an ambitious way on an issue about which a public response had not been invited. The statement may properly be seen as a manifestation of both Thomas' ambitions for the organization and as an illustration of how his concept of the learning society was applied in practice to an area of public policy. The preparation and publication of the statement was an example of the flair and ambition which Thomas displayed. It may also be seen as an extension of the same approach which the year before had led to the most ambitious of all attempts to influence educational policy, the *White Paper on the Education of Adults in Canada* (CAAE 1966b).

In the Association's Annual Report for 1965-66, the following statement appeared (p.16):

> The White Paper: This season marked the CAAE's largest adventure in policy determination in some years, if not in its history. It is more than 20 years since the Association has issued a formal manifesto, and five since it participated in the formulation of the statement issued by the World Conference. For all these reasons it was considered appropriate, if not urgent, for the Association to make a new public pronouncement. On April 5, in almost all provincial capitals, and at Ottawa, members of the Association participated in the release of this document. Of the 25,000 copies printed, roughly 20,000 have been distributed; about 15,000 free of charge and 5,000 sold. The price is set to cover mailing and promotion costs, but in no case has price been allowed to interfere with distribution to our colleagues. It was stressed at the time of release that the document was meant to open a discussion of national policy on these matters. It is hoped that it will be useful as a basis for

discussion for the next two years and that by that time a new version will be issued. There are some indications that closer co-operation with ICEA can be arranged in a revised edition. The response to the White Paper both as to its design and content has been most heartening. Any suggestions for the further use of the statement will be welcome. A one-minute promotional film spot for showing on the national TV network is being produced in co-operation with the CBC.

Thomas had taken the lead in urging that the organization prepare a new statement of its principles, one which would promote the concept of the learning society. The Board meeting held in December of 1964 marked the beginning of the process. Out of a general review of CAAE activities, in which concern for public policy was given high priority, came a proposal that "a statement of national policy from CAAE" be prepared and published, and a committee was established to give guidance to the process (CAAE Bd. Dec. 3-5, 1964). The subsequent preparation of the White Paper was largely Thomas' work, with first the committee and later the Board and Executive providing advice. The whole process took over a year. Thomas sought advice from public relations professionals concerning the release and publicity for the paper and worked through the provincial divisions, where he could, in arranging the local press conferences. The television spot announcement referred to above resulted from a $1,500 grant the Association made to the CBC for the purpose and, some months after the release of the paper, it was reported that the spot had been run "sporadically" across the country (CAAE Bd. Jan. 28-29, 1967).

The main ideas contained in the White Paper have been described in an earlier section. It was an attempt to spell out some of the implications of the concept of the learning society for the goals and operation of the educational system. It consisted of eight closely packed printed pages in an 8 by 11 inch format, with a wrap-around cover. The contents were presented under four headings: "Living is the Fifth Freedom," "Principles," "Proposals," and "Conclusion." What was impressive about the whole effort was not only the ambitious nature of its contents but also the extent of the effort to make the statement known. It was highy unusual for the CAAE or any of its divisions to "go public" in the way utilized in this case. The influence of any such attempt at advocacy is impossible to measure, but it can be said that the White Paper was the most ambitious attempt at public advocacy on behalf of adult education which had ever been undertaken by the CAAE up to that time in its history. It was inspired and written, and the promotional process largely devised, by Thomas himself.

A Decade of Leadership

Thomas announced in December of 1969 that he would resign from the directorship, effective the end of February 1970. He had been offered a position as Executive Assistant to Robert Stanbury, a Minister in the Trudeau government who was soon to take up the Communications portfolio. Thomas also felt that he had been Director of the CAAE long enough for the Association's good.

For several months in early 1968, Thomas was on leave in East Africa, lecturing at several universities. He returned in the spring of that year and found himself facing a particularly difficult situation. On the one hand, the funds from the sale of the Association's library, which might have been expected to shore up the organization's finances for a time, had largely been expended. During his absence there had been little, if any, effort to raise funds for projects. As a result, the Board of the Association went to the Annual

Meeting in June with a budget showing a sizeable deficit. And the annual meeting and conference which followed revealed some strongly felt dissatisfactions with how the Association was functioning. In commenting on the meeting in an editorial a few weeks later, Thomas referred to "anger, dismay and charges of irrational, irresponsible leadership" (Thomas 1968b:151). The divisional structure of the Association was proving too difficult for the small organization to manage, and as well, some divisions felt that the organization was out of touch with the needs of its members and that the national Board of Directors was tending to go its own way rather than take appropriate direction from the provincial bodies.

A further passage from Thomas' editorial perhaps indicates something of his feelings at the time (Thomas 1968b:149):

> Is the CAAE less valuable because it lives on the edge of the society, stumbles from bankruptcy to bankruptcy and faces a constant, never receding crossroad? Or is it that adult education, now institutionally powerful, on the verge of respectability, is less comfortable with a not-quite respectable, somewhat ramshackle, national organization? Can learning ever be respectable, ever be totally institutionalized into a permanent revolution?

There were other indications of some discouragement in ensuing months. In his annual report in 1968, Thomas suggested that the "sense of movement" in the CAAE was in need of strengthening (CAAE AR 1967-68: 12). At other times he expressed concern about the general tone of the discussions about the future of the Association (Thomas 1969e). As Thomas has put it, he found the CAAE in a discouraging state when he returned from his leave and he "just did not want to start again" (personal communication, Aug. 10, 1983). He had served as Director as long as he thought he should; he was offered an attractive position in Ottawa and he decided to make the move. He may have been reinforced in that view by his discomfort with the directions being taken by the Association by the time he left. There was emerging a model of future operations which he did not believe would work (personal communication, Aug. 10, 1983).

In his farewell editorial in *Continuous Learning*, Thomas wrote of his pleasure in having worked with the adult education community, referring to it as "the best company of any in the world," and characteristically, he returned to his old theme of learning and threw out a challenge (Thomas 1970:2, 4):

> My tenure as Executive Director has just spanned the Sixties. The curious thing is that in all the endless summations of that decade to which we have been treated in the past six weeks or so, none of those trained eyes and ears seemed to have noticed what we have....What we have seen individually and collectively has been and remains a renaissance, we have seen learning bursting free from the institutions of the society and confronting them one after another, in particular, confronting the institutions of education. Nor has this learning been confined to the young. It has emerged everywhere. It has not yet directly confronted the scattered and diffused institutions of adult education, but very soon it will, and I do not believe we are ready. We are not learning fast enough ourselves or perhaps understanding the real meaning of the tumultuous events in which others seem to have been engaged.

Alan Thomas was a person of very considerable intellectual powers and he aimed at a basic rethinking of the concept of adult education and its role in society, and sought to build a close relationship between social policy in Canada and the role of adult learning. In his words he sought for the CAAE and for Canada "to combine learning and action in a way no society [had] ever done before" (Selman 1983:17). He also aspired to move the CAAE into the forefront of national affairs; that is, to attach learning to all matters of public policy (personal communication, Mar. 10, 1982).

To these ambitious tasks, Thomas devoted tremendous energy. He made countless trips back and forth across the country with an impressive quantity of conferencing, public speaking and writing, and a quality of sustained personal communication which anyone involved in these events found truly impressive. During the 1960s, a time when the federal government was providing strong leadership in education and social policy generally, Thomas led the creation of an integrated adult education organization as well. In a period when it seemed worth striving for, Thomas spoke to Canada of a national policy for adult education and of a central place for adult learning in Canadian society. Such was the courage and range of the man. The wonder was not that his goals were not fully realizable, but that he dared to reach for them.

By the late Sixties, a national time of "agitation," as one of our cultural historians has termed it (Ostry 1978), the forces of populism and the shift in power in Canada from the national to the provincial level began to be felt in the CAAE, as they were in the broader society. Some of the key figures in the Association became disenchanted with the form of organization which had been built up and began to argue for a change. It was decided to disband the divisional structure and adopt instead a more grassroots, participatory model. It was the end of an era for the CAAE, as it soon proved to be for Canada too.

As the country entered the Seventies, a period of strong centrifugal forces in Canadian Confederation, Thomas' concept of a comprehensive national policy concerning adult education seemed a remote hope. It is probably fair to say that this element of his message was the one which had been least understood at the best of times by his colleagues and generally did not receive strong support from the provincial divisions.

However, his vision of the learning society and his emphasis on the power and primary importance of learning, as distinct from education, was to have lasting impact. For many adult educators in Canada, Thomas' ideas about learning provided a fresh and inspiring view of their task and its relationship to individual and social betterment. It prepared many to understand and enter into the discussion of lifelong education and related concepts which gained prominence in the early Seventies in Canada, and in the international community.

And Thomas' ideas had lasting impact on the CAAE as well. After a time of difficulty and general ineffectiveness for a few years in the early Seventies, the organization found its feet again by the middle of the decade. Beginning in the fall of 1974, Thomas served for four years as the President of the CAAE. By this time, he had returned from Ottawa to Toronto to become Chairman of the Adult Education Department of the Ontario Institute for Studies in Education. He and the new Director of the Association, Ian Morrison, were chiefly responsible for reviving the fortunes of the organization and for setting it back on the path of advocacy for the learning society and the adult learner, a thrust which the organization has maintained to the present day. So while the form of the organization adopted by the CAAE at the time of Thomas' departure in 1970 was other than what he had created during the decade of his leadership, the basic views he had conceived and promoted about adult learning were to stand the test of time, reinforced by educational leaders from many parts of the world in the years to follow, and provide the guiding ideas for the CAAE itself up to the present day.

References

(In the following list of sources, the Association's journals, *Food For Thought* and *Continuous Learning* are Abbreviated *FFT* and *CL*. Abbreviations used include: CAAE = Canadian Association for Adult Education; Bd = Board of Directors; Exec. = Executive Committee; DR = Director's Report; AM = Annual Meeting.)

Adamson, E. (1966), "Measuring the Need for Adult Basic Education," *CL*, 5: 115-26.

Andrew, G.C. (1963), "Reflections 3," *CL*, 2: 28-29.

———. (1967), "What's Past is Prologue," *CL*, 6: 5-15.

Armour, L. (1981), *The Idea of Canada*, Ottawa: Steel Rail Publishing.

Beaugrand-Champagne, G. (1964), "L'emotivite a la recherche d'accords possible." *CL*, 3: 229-232.

Beck, J.M. (1968), "Canadian Federalism in Ferment." In Leach (1968).

Bothwell, R., Drummond, I. and English, J. (1981). *Canada Since 1945: Power, Politics and Provincialism*, Toronto: University of Toronto.

Brebner, J.B. (1970), *Canada: a Modern History*, Ann Arbor: University of Michigan,

"Broadcasting in Brief," (1965). *CL*, 4: 285+.

Brooke, W.M. (1972), *Adult Basic Education*, Toronto: New Press.

CAAE. (1963), Submission to the Royal Commission on Taxation, *CL*, 6: 285-286.

———. (1966), *Adult Education: An Emerging Profession*, Toronto:CAAE.

———. (1966b), *A White Paper on the Education of Adults in Canada*, Toronto: CAAE.

———. (1967), *Brief to the Parliamentary Conrmittee on Broadcasting*, Toronto: CAAE.

———. (1967b), *A Report to the Canadian People on Manpower Development*, Toronto: CAAE.

———. (1968), "A Directory of Graduate Programs in Adult Education," *CL*, 7: 15-33.

———. (1969), *Report of the Committee on Philosophy, Structure and Operation of the CAAE*, Toronto: CAAE.

———. (1969b), "Brief to the Royal Commission on Status of Women in Canada," *CL*, 8: 27-30.

CAAE/ICEA. (1961), *National Conference on Adult Education*, Toronto: CAAE.

Clark, C. (1954), *Joint Planning Commission*, Toronto: CAAE.

Dennison, J.D. (1981), "The Community College in Canada: An Educational Innovation," In Wilson (1981).

Doerr, A.D. (1981), "Education and Constitutional Reform: An Overview," In Ivany and Manley-Casimir (1981).

Draper, J.A. (1971), *Citizen Participation: Canada*, Toronto New Press.

Dupre, J.S. et al (1973), *Federalism and Policy Development: The Case of Adult Occupational Training in Ontario*, Toronto: University of Toronto.

Edmonds, A. (1979), *The Years of Protest 1960/1970*, Toronto: McClelland & Stewart.

Faris, R. (1975), *The Passionate Educators*, Toronto: Peter Martin.

Faure, E. et al. (1972), *Learning to be*, Paris: UNESCO.

Graham, E. (Ed.). (1962), *The Real World of Women*, Toronto: CAAE.

Granatstein, J.L. et al. (1983), *Twentieth Century Canada*, Toronto: McGraw-Hill Ryerson.

Houle, C.O. (1984), *Patterns of Learning*, San Francisco: Jossey-Bass.

ICEA. (1969), *CL*, 8: 293-294.

Ivany, J.W.G. and Manley-Casimir, M.E. (Eds.) (1981). *Federal-Provincial Relations: Education Canada*, Toronto: O.I.S.E. Press.

Kallen, D. (1979), Recurrent Education and Lifelong Learning: Definitions and Distinctions. In Schuller, T. and Megarry, J. (Eds.). *Recurrent Education and Lifelong Learning*, London: Kogan Page.

Kettle, J. (1980), *The Big Generation*, Toronto: McClelland & Stewart.

Kidd, J.R. (Ed.) (1963), *Learning and Society*, Toronto: CAAE.

Leach, R.H. (Ed.) (1968), *Contemporary Canada*, Toronto: University of Toronto.

Legasse, J.H. (1971), "The First Years of Comnunity Development in Manitoba," In Draper (1971).

Lengrand, P. (1970), *An introduction to Lifelong Education*, Paris: UNESCO.

Lotz, J. (1977), *Understanding Canada*, Toronto: NC Press.

McClusky. H.Y. (1982), "The Legacy of the AEA/USA," *Lifelong Learning: The Adult Years*, (Sept.).

Martin, W.B.W. and Macdonell, A.J. (1978), *Canadian Education: a Sociological analysis*, Scarborough: Prentice-Hall.

Myers, D. (1973), *The Failure of Educational Reform in Canada*, Toronto: McClelland & Stewart.

Non-Degree Research in Adult Education in Canada 1967-68 (1968), Toronto and Montreal: CAAE; Department of Adult Education, OISE; and ICEA.

Ohliger, J. (1967), *Listening Groups: Mass Media in Adult Education*, Boston: CSLEA.

Ostry, B. (1978), *The Cultural Connection*, Toronto: McClelland & Stewart.

Outline History of the ACCC and Current Developments (n.d.), Toronto: Association of Community Colleges of Canada.

Peers, F.W. (1979), *The Public Eye*, Toronto: University of Toronto.

Pike, R. (1981), "Contemporary Directions and Issues in Education: A Sociologist's View of the Last Twenty Years," In Wilson (1981).

Pummell, M. (1967), *How to Start an Adult Education Program*, Toronto: CAAE.

Ryan, C. (1964), "L'ouest Canadien a l'ecoute du Quebec," *CL*, 3: 156-162.

Selman, G. (1969), *Towards Co-Operation: the Development of a Provincial Voice for Adult Education in British Columbia 1953 to 1962*, Occasional Papers in Continuing Education, UBC Extension Department. No. 3.

———. (1980), *The British Columbia Division of the CAAE: 1961-1971*, Occasional Paper, Pacific Association for Adult Education. No. 7.

———. (1981), *The CAAE in the Corbett Years: A Re-evaluation*. Occasional Papers in Continuing Education, UBC Centre for Continuing Education. No. 20.

———. (1482), *Roby Kidd and the CAAE 1951-1961*, Occasional Papers in Continuing Educetion. UBC Centre for Continuing Education. No. 22.

———. (1983), The CAAE 1935 - 1982. *Learning*, 3 (4): 14-19.

Sim, R.A. (1954), *Canada Farm Radio Forum*, Paris: UNESCO.

———. (1969), "Residential Adult Education," *CL*, 8: 149-157.

Sloan, E.P. (1972), "The Canada NewStart Program: An Overview," In Brooke (1972).

Stamp, R.M. (1970), "Government and Education in Post-war Canada," In Wilson (1970).

Stevenson, H.A. (1973), "Ten Years to Know-where," In Myers (1973).

———. (1981), "Educational Policy and the Future," In Wilson (1981).

Stewart, W. (1983), *A Comparison of a Historical Model of the American Literature in Support of Adult Education With the Literature in the Journals of the CAAE*, Unpublished Major Paper (M.Ed.), University of British Columbia.

Tewnion, J. and Robin, K. (1978), "Origins of the Alberta Association for Continuing Education," *Journal of the Alberta Association for Continuing Education*, 6 (1): 6-10.

Thomas, A.M. (1956), "New Horizons for Education." *FFT*. 17: 74-77.

———. (1957), "London—And After," *FFT*, 17: 230-233.

———. (1959), "Who are the Professionals?" *FFT*, 19: 362-369.

———. (1959b), "The Making of a Professional," *FFT*, 20: 4-11, 45.

———. (1961), "The Learning Society," In *CAAE/ICEA* (1961).

———. (1961b), "Something to Think About," *FFT*, 21: 180-182.

———. (1961c), "Parameter," *FFT*, 21: 217-219.

———. (1961d), "Parameter," *FFT*, 21: 262-264.

———. (1961e), "Parameter," *FFT*, 21: 314-316.

——. (1961f), "Parameter," *FFT*, 21: 357-362.

——. (1961g), "The Learning Society." In *Adult Education in British Columbia: The next Decade*, Report of Conference of B.C. Adult Education Council. May 11-12. Typescript multilith.

——. (1962), "Parameter," *CL*, 1: 16-20.

——. (1962b), "The Intelligencer," *CL*, 1: 49-51.

——. (1962c), "Parameter," *CL*, 1: 84-89.

——. (1962d), "Summary and Evaluation," *CL*, 1: 121-124.

——. (1962e), "Parameter," *CL*, 1: 188-191.

——. (1962f), "Opinion," *CL*, 1: 277-729.

——. (1963), "The Making of a Professional," In Kidd 1963.

——. (1963b), "Opinion," *CL*, 2: 4-5.

——. (1963c), "Editorial," *CL*, 2: 52-53.

——. (1963d), "Editorial," *CL*, 2: 100-101.

——. (1963e), "Editorial," *CL*, 2: 148-149.

——. (1963f), "Continuing Education and the Professors," *CL*, 2: 179-184.

——. (1963g), "Editorial," *CL*, 2: 196-197.

——. (1963h), "Pas comme les autres," *CL*, 2: 208-212.

——. (1963i), "Parameter," *CL*, 2: 269-271.

——. (1964), "Editorial," *CL*, 3: 5-8.

——. (1964b), "Parameter," *CL*, 3: 18-20.

——. (1964c), "Editorial," *CL*, 3: 52-53.

——. (1964d), "Parameter," *CL*, 3: 82-83.

——. (1964e), "Editorial," *CL*, 3: 101-04.

——. (1964f), "A New Flag: a New Country," *CL*, 3: 112-14.

——. (1964g), "Editorial," *CL*, 3: 148-149.

——. (1964h), "Parameter," *CL*, 3: 166-169.

——. (1964i), "Adult Education in Canada: Annual Review," *CL*, 3: 200-205.

——. (1964j), "Editorial," *CL*, 3: 242-244.

——. (1964k), "Parameter," *CL*, 3: 272-274.

——. (1965), "Editorial," *CL*, 4: 1-3.

——. (1965b), "Editorial," *CL*, 4: 49-51.

——. (1965c), "Editorial," *CL*, 4: 97-99.

——. (1965d), "Editorial," *CL* 4: 151-154.

———. (1965e), "Adult Education in Canada; Annual Review," *CL*, 4: 193-97.

———. (1965f), "Editorial," *CL*, 4: 241-242.

———. (1965g), "Parameter," *CL*, 4: 157-159.

———. (1966), "Editorial," *CL*, 5: 1-3.

———. (1966b), "Editorial," *CL*, 5: 49-51.

———. (1966c), "Editorial," *CL*, 5: 97-100.

———. (1966d), "Editorial," *CL*, 5: 145-146.

———. (1966e), "The Annual Review," *CL*, 5: 193-199.

———. (1966f), "Editorial," *CL*, 5: 241-244.

———. (1966g), "Why the CAAE?" In CAAE (1966).

———. (1967), "Editorial," *CL*, 6: 1-2.

———. (1967b), "Corbett and the Centennial," *CL*, 6: 25-27.

———. (1967c), "Editorial," *CL*, 6: 49-53.

———. (1967d), "Editorial," *CL*, 6: 97-99.

———. (1967e), "Editorial," *CL*, 6: 145-147.

———. (1967f), "Editorial," *CL*, 6: 195.

———. (1967g), "The Annual Review," *CL*, 6: 171-177.

———. (1968), "Editorial," *CL*, 7: 97-101.

———. (1968b), "Editorial," *CL*, 7: 147-151.

———. (1968c), "Editorial," *CL*, 7: 193-197.

———. (1969), "Editorial," *CL*, 8: 1-3.

———. (1969b), "Editorial," *CL*, 8: 97-99.

———. (1969c), "Editorial," *CL*, 8: 145-148.

———. (1969d), "Editorial," *CL*, 8: 193-194.

———. (1969e), "Notes on an Issue," *CL*, 8: 241.

———. (1970), "Editorial," *CL*, 9: 1-4.

———. (1970b), "Convergences." In Lowe. J. (Ed.), *Adult Education and Nation Building*, Edinburgh: University of Edinburgh.

———. (1980), "Learning and Power," J. Roby Kidd Lecture, Winnipeg: CAAE

———. (1981), "Other Voices, Other Rooms: The Emergence of New Educational Constituencies in the 1980s," In Ivany and Manley-Casimir (1981).

———. (1981b), "Education: Reformation and Renewal in the '80s?," In Wilson (1981).

———. (1983), *Learning in Society*, Occasional Paper. Canadian Commission for UNESCO. Ottawa. No. 41.

Wilson, I. (1980), *Citizens' Forum: Canada's National Platform*, Toronto: O.I.S.E.

Wilson, J.D. (Ed.) (1981), *Canadian Education in the 1980s* Calgary: Detselig.

Wilson, J.D. Stamp, R.M. and Auudet, GP. (Eds.) (1970), *Canadian Education: A History*, Scarborough: Prentice-Hall.

Originally Published in *Occasional Papers in Continuing Education*, University of B.C. Centre for Continuing Education, No. 24, 1985. Republished with permission.

Part 4

Adult Education in British Columbia: General History

*F*rom the very beginning of my studies of the history of adult education, I turned my attention to my native Province, British Columbia. My university thesis was devoted to the major role which The University of British Columbia had played in the field. My first major research undertaking after my thesis was an ambitious one, a study of the emergence of adult education in the years of colonial government and in the early years of Provincial status, up to 1914. British Columbia had not been a great innovator in this early period, but it had developed a broadly based service and in subsequent years it was to provide leadership of national stature in four areas: the provision of correspondence education; the Extension program of The University of British Columbia; the adult education offerings of the school boards; and the role in particular periods of the Provincial Department/Ministry of Education in providing leadership to the field.

In this first of three sections devoted to the history of adult education in British Columbia, I have included two monographs which are quite extensive in their coverage. The first was written as a general history of the field in B.C. and to the best of my knowledge is the only attempt at a Provincial history anywhere in Canada. Entitled *The Invisible Giant*, it was published in 1988 by the Centre for Continuing Education of The University of British Columbia. At the time I completed the study there did not seem to be a regular commercial publishing outlet for such a monograph-length account, so I was grateful that once again, Jindra Kulich of U.B.C. was willing to include it in his series of Occasional Papers. In writing the account, I drew on a lot of my previous work on aspects of the story, but also did a substantial amount of new research. One is of course painfully aware of the gaps in the story which still remain and other shortcomings of this pioneer effort, but I felt it was time to have a crack at presenting the overall story.

The other, shorter paper provides greater detail about an important aspect of the overall story, the leadership provided by government in two significant periods in the field's history in B.C. The first part of the paper draws on my research into public policy and governmental activity during the Depression of the 1930s. The second deals with the remarkable period from 1976 to 1983, when the Continuing Education Division of the Provincial Ministry of Education, under Dr. Ron Faris, was providing dynamic leadership for the field and significantly influencing the direction of its development. I had some involvement in the events of the latter period and had a very high regard for the achievements of Faris and his colleagues in the Ministry.

4.1

The Invisible Giant:
A History of Adult Education
in British Columbia

I. The Nature of the Enterprise

*W*hy have I chosen to refer to adult education as an "invisible giant"? Both words have significant implications. Few persons realize how "gigantic" the adult education enterprise is in our province. A recent Statistics Canada study has concluded that approximately 21 per cent of adults in British Columbia take part in some organized adult education activity each year. This represents some 405,300 people, more by far than the number of children and youth who attend all the schools in the province.

But this educational giant is invisible as far as most people are concerned, for several reasons. First, adult education is widely dispersed in our society. If the average person one might ask knows anything at all about what is meant by the term adult education, it is likely as a reference to "night school," the classes that are held at the local school in the evening hours. And indeed this is one major segment of adult education. But there are now at least three other sources of adult education programs in the province which account for a larger portion of this activity—employers, voluntary organizations, and the largest of all, the colleges and institutes. There are other significant sectors as well. The point is that adult education is so widely dispersed in our communities that it is not apparent— even to someone who is actively engaged in one segment of it—just how far-flung the whole field is.

Also, in most organizations which offer adult education, it is a secondary, relatively low priority or marginal activity for that organization. School authorities and universities, for instance, tend to see their adult education activities as secondary (if that) and are chiefly concerned with their full-time day students. Businesses or industries which may run substantial training programs in good times, tend to cut back drastically on such activity at the first sign of financial difficulty. Other major providers of adult education— unions, professional associations, the military, voluntary organizations, churches and synagogues, to name only a few—may see their efforts in adult education as of secondary importance, often as a means to achieve the primary goals of the organization rather than as ends in themselves.

It was very revealing that in 1971, when the Department of Education in Victoria asked Statistics Canada to prepare a special centenary report on the work of the Department during the 100 years since B.C entered Confederation, although B.C was by far the most active province in Canada in school board-sponsored adult education, not one word in a 160 page report was devoted to that subject. The point is not that the Department of Education deliberately set out to ignore the interest of adult education but that it probably didn't even think of it, when instructing the federal agency as to what it wished included.

The third main reason why adult education is 'invisible" is the fact that it tends to be a part-time or marginal activity in people's lives. One of the famous definitions of adult education is that it consists of "all activities with an educational purpose that are carried on by people engaged in the ordinary business of life." Because the adults' main preoccupations in life are understandably elsewhere, there is little consciousness of adult education as a separate entity. It was revealing that when in the mid-1980s there was such a battle over school board budget cuts, all the focus was on the impact of the reductions on children, when the adult education programs of the boards were probably the sectors which were hardest hit.

And the final reason why we know so little about adult education is that because it is so widely dispersed in society and is so frequently a low priority activity for the sponsoring body, information about it is difficult to gather. We can quickly determine from the reports of public educational institutions how many part-time students they had, but what of business, professional bodies, health associations, unions, churches and avocational interest groups? A group of doctoral students in the Adult Education program at U.B.C. set out in 1974 to gather complete statistics on participation in adult education in the province but in the end had to settle for very general estimates about some parts of the field. The student of adult education is in a situation that is perhaps similar to that of an archaeologist who finds a few groups of tiles from a mosaic in ancient Knossos, mounts them in a frame and then sketches in what the balance of the design might have looked like.

So it is with the "invisible giant" of adult education. The account which follows relies on information which is available about the nature and history of adult education in British Columbia, but the author is as aware as anyone that this account represents only some of the tiles of the larger mosaic.

It would be useful at the outset to take a closer look at what we mean by adult education. There is a liberal amount of chaos in the terminology of the field. There is not even agreement on what to call it. "Adult education" is a commonly used term, but in some institutions other phrases are used to refer to the same thing. Many school boards, colleges and institutes use the term "community" or "continuing" education. Other institutions use continuing studies or extension. Even "lifelong" education, which logically embraces all education, from birth to death, and "recurrent" education, which has particular reference to the alternation of work and education during the adult working years, are sometimes used as synonymous terms.

There is a sense in which adult education is used as an administrative category rather than a definition. When, for instance, a 40 year old woman returns to full-time study at a college or university to continue her education, the system counts her as a full-time "regular" student. If that same person decided to study part-time, but still in the daytime, she would likely be recorded as a regular part-time student. But if she studied on a part-time basis in the evening, she would commonly be included in the category of extension, or adult or continuing education student.

So it should be recognized that there is considerable lack of precision with respect to the boundary lines of adult education. Generally, what the author intends to include are those activities (apart from full-time attendance at institutional programs) which are purposefully planned to assist persons of adult years to learn the things which they need and wish to know. Typically, adult education programs are undertaken on a part-time basis, over and above "the ordinary business of life," or if the programs are full-time, they are usually of relatively short duration. Adult education is usually engaged in on a voluntary basis (though there are exceptions). The key phrase here is "purposefully planned," by an agency or by the learner him/herself. A great deal of learning on the part of adults takes place outside of educational programs, but no attempt will be made here to account for that broader phenomenon.

People decide to engage in adult education for a variety of reasons. One commonly used breakdown of the motivations consists of: vocational, social, recreational and self-development. The first of these is self-explanatory and is sometimes described as learning "to do a job better or to do a better job." For many Canadians in recent years, it has been to enable them to get a job, period. The social reasons for adult education may run the gamut from learning how to be a better parent, to be a member or a leader in organizational activities, or to work in the community for some social change. Recreational or avocational reasons for learning are of tremendous variety, from the proverbial basket weaving to any number of other interests—physical, mental or social. Self-development is usually meant to include such areas as enhancing the person's general capacities to think and to express ideas and also widening the person's horizons or powers of appreciation. These four areas are sometimes summed up in two phrases—to increase the person's "life chance" and "life space." Yet another typology is used as the basic framework for the description of the field in section III.

Not only is adult education offered by many organizations and engaged in for a variety of reasons, it also takes many different forms. The best known and most traditional of these is where there is a "class" and a "teacher." But we need to think as well of the discussion group or study club where the members may be taking turns providing leadership, or teaching each other, meeting without the presence of an "expert" in the normal sense. In recent years there has been rapid expansion of learning "at a distance" from the teacher or expert, where the learner is sitting in front of a computer terminal or a television screen, or is studying at home as a correspondence course student. Adult education takes many forms and may be designed by some institution or expert, or by the learners themselves.

In the account which follows, I have adopted an approach which involves some criss-crossing of the territory. In section II, there is a mainly chronological account. In III, the field is examined in terms of the functions performed by adult education in the lives of people. In the last section (VI), I have identified some of the most noteworthy achievements in the field in B.C. This seems to be a satisfactory approach in many ways, but does involve the need to refer to some programs and developments on more than one occasion. Efforts have been made to make this repetition painless and to stress different elements in different places.

A word about footnotes: there aren't any. I have decided that the nature of the paper is such that it required either endless footnotes, a lesser (and inadequate) number, or none at all. Where there are direct quotes, I have indicated the source in the text. For the rest,

I have tried to supply an appropriate statement about sources in general and a bibliography which makes quite clear where I have relied on the work of others.

II.   Historical Overview: Some of the Chief Actors

The division of the history of almost anything into periods of time is an artificial construct, but sometimes can be helpful in identifying trends and milestone events. For the purposes ot this study, three periods will be used: from the early years of European settlement to 1914; from 1914 to 1954; and from 1954 to the present.

Before 1914

European settlement in what is now British Columbia began in a small way in the 1820s with the establishment by the Hudson's Bay Company of Fort Langley on the Lower Fraser, and of Fort Victoria in the early 1840s on Vancouver Island, but got under way in earnest in the late fifties as a result of the gold rush in the Lower Fraser Valley. The earliest evidence we have of adult education activity in the province was recorded in Margaret Ormsby's centennial history of B.C. She states that in 1854, a group of settlers at Craigflower, outside Victoria, formed a study group and took turns presenting papers to each other on such subjects as "theology, natural history, geography or history." Such an example is an appropriate symbol for this earliest period because, although by the outbreak of World War I the foundations had been laid for the emergence ot many government-sponsored services, a great deal of what went on in the early decades was under private sponsorship—community and voluntary organizations, churches, unions and private businesses.

An important and impressive amount of adult education work in the early decades was provided by missionaries, clergy of various denominations and church organizations. There has probably never been a time when the churches have not been important providers of opportunities for adults to learn (the reference here is to non-proseletyzing type of activity), but in the early years, before other organizations and institutions entered the field, the work of the churches was particularly important, not just to their members, but to the community as a whole.

In a number of the communities which emerged in British Columbia in the latter decades of the century, the churches were the first organizations to provide opportunities for adults to pursue their learning in an organized way. The earliest example, perhaps, was the work of an Anglican missionary who founded the Fort Hope Reading Room and Library in 1959, which is thought to be the first library in the province. Three years later, the Yale Institute was established, again under Anglican auspices. Similar organizations were subsequently founded by churches in Nanaimo, Barkerville, Hedley and Trail, to name only a few. Typically, these church institutes maintained libraries and reading rooms, offered occasional lectures, and frequently sponsored choirs and other cultural activities. The newspapers of the period also provide ample evidence of the impressive role played by many of the clergy as lecturers on a variety of non-religious subjects for the benefit of the community as a whole, under both church and other auspices.

Of importance too was the educational work carried out by the churches for two particular groups, Native Indian people and Asian immigrants. One of the most colorful examples in this period was the work of William Duncan, an Anglican missionary, who conducted educational work among both young and adult Indian people on the North

Coast, beginning soon after his arrival in 1857, and five years later persuaded some 350 Indian people to move with him to found a new community in the forest, Metlakatla. The story of that community is significant from many points of view, but among them is the educational dimension, which was noted by various visitors at the time. The native people were trained to be farmers, blacksmiths, carpenters and merchants, and established a brass band. Also well known for their work among Indian people were Reverend Thomas Crosby and his wife (Methodists), who worked in Fort Simpson in the 1870s, initially, engaging the community in building a church and a school, learning arts and crafts and the manufacture of household goods, and studying English and other subjects at night school. Many other examples of such work could be listed, by several of the major denominations, and in various parts of the province.

When many thousands of Asian workers were brought to the province in the early decades of settlement, little thought was given to their cultural integration into the life of the area—indeed many interests were opposed to the idea—but several of the Churches responded to the need. In this case it was the Methodists who led the way. The work began in Victoria in 1868 and subsequently expanded to other centers, most notably Vancouver, where large numbers of Chinese adults were taught English. The Presbyterian and Anglican denominations took up the work as well (in some cases with Japanese immigrants too), and records have been found of such work in Vancouver, Victoria, New Westminster, Sapperton, Nanaimo, Union (Cumberland), Nelson, Kamloops, Kaslo and Steveston. It is clear that some tens of thousands of Asian immigrants were affected by this work.

A second major category of adult education carried out in this period was that offered by a variety of community or voluntary organizations. Five examples which will be mentioned here are the mechanics' institutes, the Y.M.C.A.s and Y.W.C.A.s, the Farmers' Institutes, the Women's Institutes, and various kinds of private schools.

The mechanics' institute was an organization founded in Britain early in the 19th century. It started as an attempt to provide scientific education for "mechanics" (workmen, especially the more highly skilled), but soon became general educational and cultural organizations. Many hundreds of these institutes were founded in Britain and elsewhere in North America by mid-century and B.C. got in on the movement in its waning stages. The most active and outstanding institute in B.C. was the one in Victoria, which was founded in the mid-sixties and continued for about twenty years. It sponsored a library, many interest groups, lectures and classes, debating societies, an orchestra and periodic exhibitions. Other communities which had mechanics institutes included New Westminster, North Vancouver and Vancouver, Nanaimo and Barkerville. The colonial and subsequently the provincial governments provided small annual grants to the institutes for a time.

The work of the Y.M. and the Y.W.C.A.s is relatively well known, but what may not be fully appreciated is that prior to the entry of the school boards into the field of adult education early in the present century, it was the Y.M.C.A., in both Victoria and Vancouver particularly, which provided the major evening class offerings, largely vocational and academic in emphasis. This was far from all that these organizations did, however. The earliest ones were founded in the 1880s, and although their existence at first was sporadic, the Ys provided many social, recreational and educational activities—the latter including reading rooms, interest and cultural groups, debating societies and mock parliaments, discussion groups and class activities.

The Farmers' and Women's Institutes had some characteristics in common. The former organization was founded in 1897 and the W. I.s in 1909. They provided a mixture of vocational education and social amenities for their members and generally were aimed at improving the quality of life in rural areas. Both organizations, though voluntary ones, received a large measure of government support in the form of modest grants, the services of experts to teach courses and address meetings, the support of regional field staff of the Department of Agriculture, literature, and other forms of assistance. There were approximately 80 Farmers' Institutes and 47 Women's Institutes in the province by 1914.

Quite another type of community organization was the private or proprietary school operated as a business. These have always existed in the province since the early years of settlement, and played an important role especially before the school boards began to provide comprehensive night school offerings. This sort of thing was a prominent feature in the newspapers in the early years, which carried many advertisements for individual tutoring services and specialized schools of various kinds, including of course the familiar business and secretarial schools. In Victoria, as early as 1859 and increasingly during the sixties, local private schools were advertising evening instruction in academic and commercial subjects. John Jessop, the man who subsequently became the first Superintendent of Schools for the province, was running a private school in Victoria in the sixties. In 1862 he established evening classes as well, in academic and commercial subjects (and a "singing school"), for which he received some public support from the Colonial government. Local commercial schools appeared in 1888 and these and other types of private schools became plentiful in Victoria, New Westminster, and as it gained prominence, especially in Vancouver.

In addition to these five detailed examples, many other kinds of community organizations were active in adult education—service clubs, unions, fraternal and ethnic societies, and cultural organizations of various kinds.

As time passed, especially after British Columbia joined Confederation in 1871, the two senior levels of government began to provide more and more educational services. In the case of the Dominion government, this took various forms. The most ambitious efforts in this period were in the field of agriculture. An experimental farm was established in Agassiz in 1889 and further developed in subsequent years. Promotion of improved dairy farming was carried out largely by means of local short courses. Early demonstrations of this technique were held in 1895 and they began on a regular basis in 1901. They were held in co-operation with the provincial department, and where possible, with the local Farmers' Institute, and usually lasted five days. Work in seed production and improvement was also carried out, and information conveyed by means of publications and lectures. Other departments of the Dominion government also carried out work in the province. The Geological Survey of Canada produced many useful publications. The Department of Marine and Fisheries organized Marine Schools offered annually in Victoria (beginning in 1903) and in Vancouver (beginning in 1907), as well as other ports across the country, the Vancouver school being considered the most successful in all of Canada.

Provincial government services expanded considerably during these early decades. In some respects agriculture led the way at this level as well. Provincial (and state) departments of agriculture throughout North America had developed a tradition of commitment to education as a means of promoting the efficiency of agricultural practice and the quality of rural life. The use of the Farmers' and Women's Institutes for this purpose has already been mentioned. The B.C. Department also supported a variety of other specialized organizations under the terms or the Agricultural Societies Incorporation Act, which was passed in 1873. By 1893, there were thirteen groups registered under the Act and by 1912 this number grew to 76. They ranged all the way from groups that sponsored annual exhibitions to ones like the fruit growers and cattle breeders, which carried out sustained information and educational work. The Department of Agriculture also sponsored schools, short courses and demonstrations on agricultural subjects, this activity expanding markedly after the re-organization of the Department in 1909. For instance, in the year 1914, 37 short courses in fruit packing alone were given by the Department. The Bureau of Mines was also active in educational work. In 1896, for instance, courses of lectures on the practical aspects or prospecting were offered in the three main population centers. And regulations governing the mining industry led to a variety of educational programs, in areas such as upgrading the knowledge of mine personnel (as it affected safety standards) and first aid to the injured. Government support of the mechanics' institute movement has been mentioned. There were also important developments with respect to libraries in the province. Although early legislation was not very generous or effective, some support was provided for community libraries. In addition, a scheme of "travelling libraries," boxes of 100 books which were sent from Victoria on three-month loan to small centers, was inaugurated in 1898. By 1914, there were 120 such libraries in circulation.

Of particular importance because ot the developments which were to flow from these beginnings, were actions taken by the Department of Education. Two lines of development are particularly relevant here: the launching of the Teachers' Institutes and the inauguration of school board adult education programs. John Jessop, the first Superintendent of Schools for the province, suggested in 1873 the organization or provincial teachers' conferences or institutes in order to promote the in-service development of members of the teaching profession. He organized the first of these the following year. They lasted three or four days, were held most years thereafter, and were usually attended by several hundred teachers. Beginning in 1885, local and regional institutes were organized as well. This pattern continued until the B.C. Teachers Federation was created in 1916.

Although John Jessop had suggested as early as 1877 that local school boards conduct evening classes for adults who wished to continue their education, by the time this development came about early in the next century, the initiative came from the local level and the Department had to be persuaded. The Vancouver School Board was the leading actor in these developments. An experimental set of classes was run successfully by a committee of teachers in Vancouver in the fall of 1907, but subsequent appeals to the Department by the Vancouver Board and by the B.C School Trustees' Association brought no results in terms of enabling legislation.

In 1909, the Vancouver board felt it was time for more decisive action and they authorized a more formally-cndorsed program, under the leadership of John Kyle, a teacher of technical subjects (and an outstanding artist). There were this time 966 registrations in ten different courses, held in six centers in the city, and once again the board enlisted the support of civic bodies and the Trustees' Association in trying to persuade the provincial govemment to act. They were successful this time, the government amended the Public Schools Act in 1910 to empower boards to conduct night classes and to provide financial support for this work from public funds. The response from other boards was not overwhelming in the immediate future. The first year under the grants (1910-11) six school boards applied for support. Of a total enrollment of 2,005, 1,628 were in Vancouver. By 1913-14, the total enrollment had risen slightly, to 2,311, drawn that year from only five centers, with Vancouver accounting for 1,749. The major expansion of night schools lay in the future, but a beginning had been made and supporting policies put in place.

In this period from the earliest days of European settlement to the outbreak of the first World War, the development of adult education was sporadic, and was carried out by many different agencies. The bulk of the work, for much of this period was undertaken by a wide range of private and voluntary organizations, but with the growth of population, particularly after 1890, government services of various kinds developed rapidly, especially in the Departments of Agriculture and Education.

1914-1954

These forty years were tumultuous ones in the life of the province—and of the whole world. Two World Wars and the Great Depression of the 1930s left their mark on our society, and also produced a need for learning on an enormous scale on the part of many of our citizens. The population and economy of the province continued to grow at a rapid rate and the "boom and bust" nature of the province's economy was amply demonstrated.

Both World Wars created conditions in which a large proportion of Canadians were thrown into unaccustomed roles, whether in the armed forces, in wartime industries, or in other aspects of their lives. As one of our historians has put it, "As soldiers, Canadians had everything to learn" (Morton p.41). Training within the forces, for military roles, will not be dealt with here, but it is clear that many thousands of British Columbians in the armed forces were learning at a rate they had never before experienced. In industry, at home, in many instances it was a case of expanding already established enterprises, be it logging, mining or fishing, but in the case of the shipyards, for instance, and in the Second World War aircraft production, expansion and innovation were on such a scale as to create entire new industries, with all the training of new personnel which was required. Although information is lacking, a tremendous amount of adult education clearly was carried out during the wars to train the "back home" population in such matters as first aid, homekeeping amidst wartime shortages, and during the Second World War, many skills related to air raids and other possible emergencies.

The University of British Columbia was established in 1915. Having been created in wartime, the institution turned its attention, among other things, to the rehabilitation of veterans. In the period 1917 to 1921, U.B.C. ran a series of concentrated courses for returning veterans in a range of vocational subjects, including assaying and other mining specialties, engine operation and maintenance, machine shop techniques, general electrical work, steam engineering, drafting, telegraphy, and specialties in forestry and agriculture. In all, some 1,300 men were helped in this way to equip themselves for civilian life. Following the Second World War, the University's efforts were largely devoted to providing degree credit programs for veterans who wished to advance their careers by university study.

During and immediately following both World Wars, a great deal of study and activity were devoted to "reconstruction." What had gone wrong with society? How could Canadians build a better, more peaceful world? The Protestant churches played a particularly active role in such work, as did some of the political parties. The activities of the Methodist Church during the First World War and of the United Church during the Depression years and the Second World War provided a "curriculum" for a broadly-based study group movement, very much in the social gospel tradition. Many thousands of Canadians were thus engaged in thoughtful study of the nature and goals of life in our society. As well, there were in British Columbia a number of very vigorous voluntary organizations concerned with the study of social and public affairs issues. These included the Councils of Women, the Women's School for Citizenship, the League of Nations Society (and later, the United Nations Association), the Parent-Teacher Federation and other groups.

One of the major elements in the provision of adult education during these decades was programs offered by the local school boards. The growth in enrollments in school board adult education was not particularly spectacular. They had reached approximately 4,000 by 1914-15, got as high as 7,600 in the prosperous twenties, slumped during the Depression and again during the War, and then rose sharply in the post-war period. Enrollments doubled between 1945 and 1950, from 8,000 to almost 17,000. The most spectacular story, as always, was that of the Vancouver Board's program. At the conclusion of the War (1945), enrollments in night school classes in Vancouver stood at 3,317. By 1954, this figure had reached 14,071, and was increasing at more than 10 per cent a year. The other aspect of the school board picture which should be noted is the large number of boards which became involved in adult education. Whereas in 1914, only five school boards claimed grant funds in support of night schools, by the end of the Twenties, this number had reached almost 70, many of these local programs being very small. Due to re-organization of school districts into fewer, larger districts, this number was reduced by half by the end of the Thirties (larger school districts had been formed), but this was still a substantial figure. When the rapid expansion of programs came about in the Sixties, it was no doubt important that so many of the boards had already had some experience with the provision of classes for adults.

In his study of the development of school board adult education, B.E. Wales rightly pays tribute to the important work of John Kyle. Kyle had been in charge of organizing the trail-blazing work by the Vancouver School Board in night schools beginning in 1909, and in 1913 the Department of Education employed him as Director of Technical Education, placing him in charge of night schools as well. His leadership of that enterprise was of outstanding quality and vigor over the subsequent 20 years. Kyle was successful in interesting a large number of the boards in this work, as the figures quoted above indicate. He also encouraged the boards to advertize their classes widely in the community so that potential students could learn of them. He insisted that the night school programs, which were largely vocational in emphasis at this stage, be developed in close liaison with the relevant industries. In his 1916 report, he stated, "behind the technical education movement in each district there should be found an advisory committee." This element of school board adult education, especially in the Vancouver area was fully developed and was clearly an important reason for its success over the years, and especially in the period of rapid expansion following the Second World War. Another significant development in the Department of Education at the time was the leadership being given to correspondence education (which had been initiated in 1919) by J.W. Gibson. He took over this work in 1929 and in subsequent years greatly expanded the curriculum and made it more relevant to adults in the province.

The story of adult education in B.C. during the Great Depression of the 1930s is a particularly interesting one, for at least two reasons. The first of these is simply to see how a service which prides itself on being responsive to the needs of the learners actually responded to the conditions of the times. The second arises from the fact that during this period, government for the first time, at least in any sustained way, used adult education as one of the means of implementing its policies. The reference here is to the Liberal government of Dufferin Patullo, which was elected in late 1933 on an "interventionist" platform reminiscent of the New Deal Roosevelt administration in the United States. Adult education was used by the new administration, under the Minister of Education, George Weir, who was a professional educator, as at least one means of providing both practical and morale-raising activities for many citizens of the province. This may be seen as a humanitarian and necessary response to the deep problems of a depression-ridden society, or it may be seen as an effort by the private enterprise establishment to provide constructive activities for the populace, in the hope that they would not listen to the blandishments of the communist and other revolutionary elements which were so vocal in those desperate times. At any rate, the latter half of the Thirties was a period during which government provided particularly strong leadership in the field of adult education, to an extent not paralleled until the late Seventies.

The Department of Education took a series of important initiatives during the latter half of the Thirties. It appointed an advisory committee, "Adult Education: British Columbia," to supervise the services to be provided to unemployed persons. These included night classes in practical subjects provided free of charge through the local school boards; the provision of organizers of educational programs in several of the larger camps for unemployed men in the province; an expansion and wider provision of correspondence courses in a variety of subjects; and financial and other assistance to the educational work of several voluntary organizations, most notably the Self-Help program of the Vancouver Council of Women, the housekeeper training program ot the Y.W.C.A. and the vocational courses being operated by the United Church organization, A.O.T.S. Other measures taken by the Department included the inauguration of a community drama service, which included the organization of several hundred drama reading groups, and the organization ot the Provincial Recreation Program (Pro-Rec), which involved some tens of thousands of adult British Columbians in recreational activities, including a great deal of leadership and coach training work as well. At no previous time had the government provided such vigorous leadership in adult education. Some further significant initiatives followed from a re-organization of the Department of Education in 1952, but this will be dealt with in the next section.

The government also took important steps in the field of vocational training, especially concerning apprenticeship. There had been unregulated forms of apprenticeship in some trades since the early years of the century, but no system of regulation. Beginning in 1926, the Building Trades Association in Vancouver created an Apprenticeship Council on the basis of the voluntary participation of some of its member companies. Saturday classes were run at Vancouver Technical School. There were 925 apprentices in that scheme by 1935, and in that year the government responded to appeals from the Council and elsewhere by securing the passage of the first act which regulated the apprenticeship scheme in the province. By 1939 there were 368 apprenticeship agreements registered under the Act. By the end of the period under review, 1954, there was a dominion-provincial apprenticeship agreement in force and in that year, 1,511 apprentices were taking instruction by evening classes or correspondence courses and 217 were attending daytime classes.

One of the most significant developments during these years was the emergence of the Extension Department of The University of British Columbia as a leading agency in the field. Mention has already been made of the vocational training activities the University conducted for First World War veterans. The major story during the 1920s was extension work carried out by the Faculty of Agriculture of the University, with the assistance of federal grants. Agriculture offered short courses in various parts of the province and courses of longer duration on the campus. The peak year in the early period was 1921-22, when eight off-campus short courses were offered, involving 732 registrants. Other work included visits and consultation by field workers, surveys of practice, soil testing, and the distribution of publications. In 1923 the federal grants were discontinued but the Faculty continued its extension work as best it could, until the early Thirties, when the government slashed the University's budget. The other form of extension conducted in these early years was a lecture service, which made faculty available to speak to community organizations, at their request.

By the early Thirties almost all of this activity had come to a halt, following the wholesale cuts in the University's budget by the Tolmie government. An opportunity for a new start presented itself in the mid-Thirties, when the University decided that $30,000 of a grant from the Carnegie Corporation of New York would be used to re-establish extension work. A major program of lectures throughout the province was conducted in the year 1935-36, and during the year it was decided to give permanent leadership to such work by means of creating a Department of University Extension. Gordon Shrum took over the direction of the Extension Department from Robert England, at the beginning of its second year of operation and in a very few years the Department was transformed from the newest and smallest in the country to one of the largest and most highly regarded. He was resourceful in finding funds from outside the University to make expansion of programs possible, he recruited able staff, and he provided vigorous, imaginative leadership.

In the succeeding two decades the U.B.C. Extension Department made outstanding achievements in several areas. In agriculture and rural life, the Department ran a series of Youth Training Schools in various parts of the province and an eight-week residential school at the University, in addition to a range of technical short courses and conferences in specialized subjects for producers. In the fine arts, a full-time drama specialist operated a range of services in that field, including play reading groups throughout the province (with a play lending library to service these groups), for a time a "theater of the air" on radio, short courses around the province, and beginning in 1938, a very successful annual Summer School of Theater. An instructor in the field of home economics was employed until the late Fifties, organizing and teaching courses and providing a great deal of service to the Women's Institutes of the province. A specialist in child development, family life education, and increasingly from the late Forties on, in human relations training and group development, provided leadership and publications which had a national reputation for excellence in those areas. The Department did outstanding work in the field of audio-visual services, operating a substantial provincial library of materials and giving leadership and services to the National Film Board film councils and circuits in the province. The Department also maintained a large program of co-operative education among the fishermen of the province, with at times up to three full-time professional staff. The Department served as the provincial headquarters for both National Farm Radio Forum and Citizens' Forum, the national projects of the Canadian Broadcasting Corporation and the Canadian Association for Adult Education, which involved weekly radio broadcasts and local discussion groups. These are but a few of the most noteworthy programs run by university extension in this period. By the early Fifties the U.B.C department was recognized as one of the top such units in the country. Registrations for its services well outnumbered those involved in all the school board programs combined.

The educational activities of the Parent-Teacher Federation of the province should also be mentioned. Formed in 1922, when it already had 60 local associations, this organization was particularly strong during this period and established a very active leadership development and human relations training program. Under its own auspices, or as was frequently the case, in co-operation with the U.B.C Extension Department, the P-T Federation through the 1950s and early 1960s organized regular series of training courses for its leaders and other interested members. With a membership of 30,000 by 1950 and 52,000 a decade later, this was a large and active organization which gave a great deal of attention to both parent education and leadership development.

Finally, reference should be made to library services. The general field of libraries as a resource for adult learning cannot be dealt with here, but it clearly was an important aspect of the field. Library work took a great step forward in 1919, when a new Library Act was passed and the Public Library Commission was created to carry out planning and provide leadership for the field. The pioneering demonstration project in regionally-based library services carried out in the Lower Fraser Valley beginning in 1928 under the leadership of Helen Stewart may perhaps be seen to fall in another area of professional service, but its impact on the future development of library service, both in B.C. and elsewhere—and therefore on the resources for adult learning—has been profound. As well, in the decades before the field of adult education became organized as a professional field, it was frequently librarians who spoke out most effectively on behalf of adult education.

One milestone for the field was the first directory of adult education services, which was published by the Vancouver Public Library in 1929, entitled "Why Stop Learning?" and containing a directory of programs offered by 38 agencies, listed under 74 subject matter headings. The most thorough survey of adult education in British Columbia ever conducted was carried out by the Public Library Commission in 1941, at the request of George Weir, then Provincial Secretary. It described the work of various public and private agencies in the field, providing enrollment statistics in some cases. The report included descriptions of approximalely 30 government departments and agencies and several hundred private and voluntary groups (the 186 Women's Institutes, for instance, were listed as just one of these). The report concluded with a series of strong recommendations calling for government leadership in the further development and co-ordination of adult education.

The year 1954 is taken as the dividing line between this period and the next because it was in this year that the first provincial organization of adult educators was formed. By this time, adult education had become a broadly based enterprise in the province and an increasing number of persons were coming to identify themselves with the field. Those employed professionally in this work were mainly in the school boards and the University

extension department, with a few elsewhere. As well, however, there were increasing numbers of leaders of voluntary organizations who saw the relevance of adult education and adult learning to the success of their work and who were ready to devote time to the advancement of the field of adult education.

Since 1954

The last 35 years, although the shortest of the three periods being considered, is perhaps the most eventful in terms ot the provision of and participation in adult education activities. The results of two Statistics Canada studies, one carried out in 1960 and the other in 1983, dramatically demonstrate the growth of the field in recent decades. According to these reports, in 1960, 5.3 per cent of adults in British Columbia had taken part in adult education courses of some kind in that year (the national average was 3.6 per cent). In 1983, the figure for B.C. had climbed to 21 per cent (and the national average to 19 per cent). These changes were the result of a number of factors, some having to do with forces in society such as technological change and social development, some to do with the increasing range of opportunities by which adults could continue their education, and perhaps some arising from a changing outlook on life on the part ot the individuals. For an increasing number of people, the concept of education, or perhaps more accurately, of learning, had been transformed. Education, instead of being seen as it had been traditionally, as "preparation for life," was being seen increasingly as an ongoing part of life. For some, this choice was made voluntarily; for others—largely for vocational reasons—it was forced upon them.

This was a period of continued growth in the population and economy of the province for the most part, and as the population grew, the provision of social services, including education, was expanded. Federal government policies provided stimulus and resources on an unprecedented scale. The school board segment of adult education flourished in B.C. for a time and the province created whole new systems ol education at the post-secondary level, the colleges and institutes, the Institute of Technology, two new universities, a television agency and the Open Learning Institute. As the scope and complexity of post-secondary and adult education increased, several organizations of adult education practitioners emerged and the provincial government commissioned several important public inquiries on aspects of the field. In the latter half of the Seventies, the Ministry of Education (the name was changed from Department to Ministry in 1976) created the largest, most highly respected government leadership team in Canada in the field of adult education, only to dismantle it completely in the wake of austerity budgets and the "privitization" philosophy of the present decade. In the 1970s and 1980s, for a variety of reasons, there has been a strong resurgence of the private sector in this field.

Although it was not a direct provider or organizer of adult education, the actions of the federal government and its agencies during this period were of basic importance. The manpower training legislation passed by Ottawa in 1960, 1967, 1982, and 1985 provided funds for the expansion and creation of vocational training facilities as well as a portion of operating expenses, on a shared cost basis. Following the decision in 1966 on the part of Ottawa that it would play a more direct role in the design and purchase of programs and the selection and maintenance of students, it became directly involved in a great deal of adult training or education. It also stimulated the growth and development of basic education and English as a second language provision in the province. Through various agreements, the federal authorities also made important contributions in such fields as health and rehabilitation education, second language (bilingualism) training, citizenship education, labor education, agricultural extension, community development, and a variety of local projects under such programs as the Company of Young Canadians, Opportunities for Youth and the New Horizons Program.

One of the major developments in the whole history of adult education in this province has been the contributions of the school boards to the field. The pioneering work of the Vancouver board and the broadly based nature of school board adult education as it developed in earlier decades have already been described. In 1952, the government created a new unit in the Department of Education, the Community Programs Branch, placing under it both recreation and adult education, and put in charge of this work one of the ablest persons in the civil service, L.J. (Laurie) Wallace. As a result of his leadership, which among other things included the first-ever conference of school board night school directors in the province, held in 1955, and because of the outstanding ability of many of the directors, this aspect of adult education in the province "took off" and for some 15 years at least, led all of Canada in this work. The number of school boards operating adult education programs grew from approximately 40 at the end of the War to approximately 70 by the mid-Sixties.

A national adult education publication stated in 1964 that of the full-time directors of adult education employed by boards in all of Canada, approximately 70 per cent were in B.C. Perhaps most significant of all, a Statistics Canada report published in 1963 indicated that school board adult education enrollments in the province were proportionately about twice as large as the national average, with no other region anywhere close to the B.C. figures. Total enrollment in school board adult education grew from 20,000 in 1953-54 to 70,000 in 1962-63, and 162,000 by 1969-70. During the 1960s, the number of full-time directors grew from 6 to 54. Another significant figure is that whereas at the beginning of the 1960s, approximately 75 per cent of the school board enrollments were in Vancouver and the balance in the rest of the province, by the end of the decade these proportions had reversed. A major shift in the content of these programs also took place. In the early Fifties, approximately half the enrollments were in vocational courses. Although such enrollments grew by 50 per cent in that decade, by the early Sixties, the proportion had fallen to 20 per cent, and it remained at that figure through the decade.

The almost explosive growth of school board programs came to an end in the early Seventies, when the Department let it be known that it would welcome school boards turning their adult education programs over to the emerging community colleges. Something approaching two-thirds of the boards took this step and school board enrollments fell off in the Seventies from the high of 180,000 in 1970-71. In 1983-84, the last year for which we have full statistics available, there were 145,000 registrants in the programs of 22 school districts.

The Vancouver board continued to provide important leadership in this sector of the field, not only in British Columbia, but nationally as well. Graham Bruce, who took over direction of this work during the War, and Bert Wales, his associate who succeeded him in 1959, were outstanding leaders in both school board and broader adult education circles. As in earlier periods, the Vancouver board continued its pioneering work. It led in the dramatic expansion of vocational adult education (the Vancouver Vocational Institute was opened in 1949), academic study for adults and other non-vocational areas. The early

Sixties were a particularly strategic period: the Vancouver program conducted the Vancouver Experiment in co-operation with both senior levels of government, which demonstrated the advantages of full-time adult academic study; it opened the King Edward Senior Matriculation and Continuing Education Center (1962), the first such full-time, day and evening adult studies center in Canada; and it was a key agency in the launching of the community college movement in the province, Vancouver City College being the first of these (1965) and Wales being named as its Director.   In addtion, in 1962, the Vancouver board was the first in Canada to approve and publish a formal policy declaration stating its responsibility for the education of the adults as well as the children in its district. Throughout the subsequent years, the Vancouver board has been the leading agency of its kind in the province and certainly one of the leading voices in the early Seventies which resisted the government's unsuccessful attempt to transfer responsibility for adult education mainly if not entirely to the colleges.

This period brought the creation of the system of community colleges and provincial institutes in the province, beginning in 1965. Various parties in the province had been calling for a college system, the School Trustees' organization and some member boards perhaps being the most insistent. It is generally agreed that a study issued in 1962 by the President of U.B.C., John B. Macdonald, was particularly influential. The government produced enabling legislation the following year and the first colleges opened their doors in 1965. The "community college," as distinct from the "junior college" model was adopted in B.C and from the beginning it was envisaged that the colleges would play an important part in the provision of adult education, evening and part-time studies, over a wide range of academic, vocational and general or community education areas. (Here the dividing line between what is adult education and what is called something else— post-secondary education?— becomes difficult to define.) In general it is true to say that the colleges began, in the sixties, with strong links to their communities and were able to respond to local situations and local needs, but that the general tendency, especially after the passage of the Colleges and Institutes Act of 1977, has been towards centralized control and decision-making. Following the opening of the initial colleges in 1965, it was some 10 years until the whole province was brought within the service areas of the 14 (now 15) community colleges. In addition, several "institutes' were created—college level institutes such as the College of Art and the Justice Institute of B.C., which have a province-wide mandate, but within a specialized subject area.

It was clearly the view of some of the Ministry officials that the colleges, perhaps because they already were dealing with an adult clientele, were in a better position than the school boards to provide adult education services in the communities they were serving. This led to the initiative in the early Seventies, already mentioned, to persuade the boards to vacate the field. The majority of boards, but generally those in the small centers, did this, but the province was left with a "mixed" system, and the government provided no leadership in differentiating the roles in the field of the two institutions. Indeed it can be said that policy in the Department of Education continued to favor the college-based adult education programs. Over time, the colleges played a larger and larger role in the field. From a total of approximately 5,000 adult education registrations in 1970-71 in college programs, the numbers increased rapidly during the decade (as did the number of colleges) to a figure of 155,000 by 1979-80 (approximately equal to that of the School boards at that time) and to 220,000 in 1983-84, the most recent figures available. The

Statistics Canada participation study published in 1984 shows the community colleges as the largest provider of adult education in the province, followed by voluntary organizations, employers and school boards (and others) in that order. Although some figures vary markedly from one institution to another, the general picture of the content areas covered by college and institute programs in 1983-84 is that community education and general interest programs accounted for 63 per cent of the registrations, vocational and professional courses for 25, and basic education and English as a second language for 11.5. The college and institute sector was likely the most rapidly growing part of this field during this period.

Another major sector of the field in this period was the continued development of university level extension work and that of the Institute of Technology. In the Sixties two new public universities, the University of Victoria and Simon Fraser University, were created. The Victoria institution had been active for more than a decade (in its previous existence as Victoria College) in this field and it greatly expanded its activities after being accorded university status, maintaining a program which combined non-credit and degree credit courses, with continuing professional education increasing in importance, especially in the last decade. Simon Fraser University, after a relatively inactive period of some years in this field following its creation, devoted much of its efforts to degree and diploma credit studies, and a number of other specialized projects. The B.C. Institute of Technology put great emphasis on the field of continuing education from the outset, providing access to its programs by part-time study, offering a large number and variety of programs for the benefit of those in business and industry, and technical fields generally, and doing important pioneering work in the field of distance education. The University of British Columbia, meanwhile, continued to expand its extension work, still largely in non-credit areas, and in this period, under the leadership of John Friesen, upgrading the general intellectual level of its program. Of particular note in the late Fifties and early Sixties were: the further development of work in the fine arts; a group discussion project in the liberal arts, Living Room Learning, which at its height was operating in 66 different B C. communities; and several special projects in the field of public and international affairs. In the mid-Sixties, the University severely reduced its financial support of adult education activities and Extension was forced to eliminate many programs, reduce staff and concentrate on programs which could maintain themselves from fees (continuing professional education), could be funded by external sources (leadership training for Native Indian leaders), or which the University was still willing to fund, such as degree credit offerings.

Satisfactory enrollment figures for this sector of the field are difficult to obtain. A Statistics Canada report for 1975-76 indicates a total of approximately 50,000 adult education registrations for the three universities, but by the mid-Eighties it would likely be approximately three times that number, with U.B.C. representing about half the total. In the case of B.C.I.T., selected figures are available. Opening in 1964, evening classes began the following year and Industry Services (which offered special courses for those in industry) in 1970. By 1980-81, Industry Services served 2,743 registrants and evening classes 27,006. By 1980-81, distance education enrollments stood at 1,400, and in addition, experimental work had been carried out leading to the formation of the public educational television channel, The Knowledge Network.

The Knowledge Network of the West (KNOW), now known generally by the first two words only, which was created in 1980, was a product of the innovative leadership in the Ministry of Education at the time. It is a telecommunications network which is designed to assist the educational institutions and other Ministries of the province with the development and delivery of courses and materials. Not only does it deliver courses and informational programming, but it is also capable of transmitting on a closed circuit basis for a variety of purposes. At the time of writing, KNOW is being amalgamated with the province's other specialized distance education institution, the Open Learning Institute. O.L.I. was created in 1978 to provide correspondence courses or distance education to the people of the province in three main subject matter areas—basic education, career technical training, and university level programs. By the fall of 1979, there were 750 students enrolled and four months later, 2,400. Growth continued at a rapid rate, the latest figures indicating that in the year 1986-87, O.L.I. had a total of 19,592 registrations, career/ technical being the largest of the three sectors. In the fall of 1984, an Open University Consortium of B.C. was created, which was aimed at making the combined use of distance education courses available from O.L.I. and the three universities, O.L.I. serving as the accrediting body for degree purposes in cases where that served the student's interest.

An area of major expansion in adult education during these decades was that of continuing professional education. It became increasingly obvious in the post-war period that new knowledge was being acquired at such a rapid rate that professional people, even more urgently than previously, had to continue to learn if they were to be able to carry out their roles in society in a satisfactory and responsible fashion. The same was obviously true for a range of "near professional" and higher level technical occupations. In response to such needs, continuing professional education took a great leap forward. The organizing agencies for this activity have varied from one field to another, but have in the main been the professional associations, the pre-service training institutions for the professions (university faculties, B.C.I.T., in some cases, colleges and institutes), and in many cases, the employing institutions as well (hospitals, business and industry, educational institutions, etc.). Comprehensive information about such activity is very difficult to gather and would require more space than is available here. Some aspects only will be touched upon.

In the early Sixties, an awareness of the heightened importance of continuing education for the professions became particularly evident to the professions themselves and to those responsible for pre-service professional education, which in those years was mainly The University of British Columbia. The Faculty of Medicine created a department to give leadership to this work and worked closely with those from other health care fields. University Extension worked closely with some other professional areas—engineering, law, education, commerce, agriculture, forestry, etc.—encouraging the expansion or inauguration of continuing education programs. Some of these were based at the University (or in other educational institutions) and some drew their energy and leadership (law and nursing, for instance) largely from the professional group itself.

By 1972-73, courses for the health care professions sponsored by U.B.C. attracted over 7,000 registrants. By 1985-86, the figure was 13,373. The nursing professional body, the RNABC, played a direct role in organizing many continuing education programs, but with the publication of an important series of reports in the early Seventies, changed its role largely to that of standard-setting and accreditation. Continuing Legal Education, which operates out of the professional association's office in Vancouver, involves approximately 7,000 course registrations a year. The teaching profession is served by all three universities, and does a great deal of continuing education through sections of the professional organization. Several of the professions have looked at the possibility of "mandatory continuing education" for their membership, but most have decided against such a policy. Continuing professional education has grown in the past three decades into a major sector of adult education, and many agencies are involved in this work.

Mention has been made of the fact that according to the most recent comprehensive Statistics Canada report, employers now represent the third largest source of courses taken by adults. Research on this sector of the field is skimpy, but it is clear that many employers, perhaps especially those whose work force require a high degree of technical knowledge, see this as a task they must assume, at least in part. A survey of the electronics industry in the province, conducted in 1985, revealed that a high percentage of such firms either provided training for technical staff or purchased such training from elsewhere. Probably the largest industrially based training program in the province is that operated by the B.C. Telephone Co. That work was begun in a small way soon after the company was founded, but the first full-time trainer was not appointed until 1956. For the next 20 years, training activities expanded considerably, located wthin the several operating units. First on an "experimental" basis in 1978 and then two years later as a permanent arrangement, these several units were brought together in a Department of Education and Training. This operation moved to new quarters in Burnaby in 1983, where there is a staff of 189 people in the department, 62 classrooms available, over 300 courses in the instructional catalogue and an annual operating budget of over eleven million dollars. In 1987, the Education Center offered 2,300 courses, which served 21,600 registrants. Programs operate under the guidance of advisory committees for each company "discipline", such as construction, engineering, computer communications, customer service and marketing. It is not surprising that industrially-based training is expanding at the present time, it being the declared policy of the federal manpower authorities to purchase proportionally more of their training places in the future from industry rather than from the educational institutions.

There has been an expansion in recent years of the role played by the private or proprietary training schools in the province. They have for many decades been a prominent source of training in certain fields, especially certain business skills and specialties. Their presence was perhaps less obvious during the bulk of this period, as the programs of the public educational institutions were growing so rapidly in almost every field. But since the federal government has adopted the policy referred to above and since the provincial government announced a similar intention (in their case, in an attempt to "downsize" the public sector in all fields) there has been new opportunity for the private sector in vocational training to expand and flourish. In 1985 there were well over 250 private career training schools operating in the province, providing 35,000 students with training. A Private Career Training Association has been in operation since 1977, devoted to advancing the interest of this work. It currently has something over 50 members and is concerned as well with the general improvement of standards and recognition of training in the private sector.

There are a number of important dimensions of adult education in this period which can be placed under the general heading of Community Education. Many of these activities are part of the public sector (community centers, community schools, etc.) and many are in the private and voluntary sector. In projects such as the Britannia Center, there is a mixture of public and private initiative. The following brief description can mention only a few aspects of this work. Community education is here used to refer to those aspects of adult education which are less "institutional" and more closely related to community concerns and interests than are some institutional offerings.

Like some other agencies which provide community education services, the community center movement, which emerged with dramatic speed in the late Forties, has offered a mixture of recreational and educational activities. In the City of Vancouver, 18 such centers were established in the 20 years beginning in 1948. In a single month in 1970, for instance, there were 160,000 participants in center programs in Vancouver alone, approximately half of whom were adults. Such work throughout the province typically drew financial support from the provincial government, the municipality, and of course from student fees. During the 1950s and the following decade there was very rapid growth in the number of Recreation Commissions operating these programs in the province, the number reaching 375 by 1965.

Another dimension of community education is represented by the activities of organizations providing educational and other services for recent immigrants. There was a substantial expansion of this work in the late 1950s, when civic Citizenship Councils were established in many cities in the province. The Immigrant Services Society and a wide range of other ethnic and inter-ethnic organizations continue to operate at the present time, offering cultural orientation, language instruction and a wide range of other educational and support services.

The community school movement has been another significant dimension of community education in recent decades. These are public schools (usually elementary schools) which are organized according to a scheme developed first in Flint, Michigan, and which involves establishing a close working relationship between the school and the neighborhood it serves, the resources of the community being called upon to enrich the activities in the school program and the school providing a range ot recreational and educational services of interest to the members of the community, sometimes including activities of a social change or community development nature. The first such school in B.C. was established in North Vancouver in 1971 and by 1980, there were forty such schools in the province. A few have fallen victim to the budget cuts which have affected the school boards in recent years, a situation which has not been helped by the Ministry of Education's consistent lack of interest in the community school movement.

A notable achievement of this period in the field of community education has been the Britannia Community Services Center, located in East Vancouver. This "village" or cluster of services, which emerged from various citizens' movements in the 1960s, but did not formally open its doors until 1976, contains a community school and various other elements and is devoted to serving and assisting with the social and cultural development of its area, a modest-income, heavily "ethnic" region of the city. Britannia has been outstandingly successful in involving the people of the area in the management and program of the agency and has provided a broad educational program as well as other services. The Britannia Center has gained a national, and even international reputation for its strongly community-related organization and program.

A feature particularly of the 1960s and 1970s in the province were a number of projects and programs which fell under the heading of community development. The relevance of community schools and the Britannia Center to such work has been mentioned. The National Film Board of Canada, through its Challenge for Change project and several of the social development projects typical of the late Sixties such as the Company of Young Canadians and other federally funded bodies, did significant community development work. In many cases, such projects were strongly supported by adult educators and their institutions. Most community development has been a casualty of recent shortages of funds, as well as of changes in dominant political and social philosophies.

Any such review of agencies in the field is clearly inadequate, particularly when it comes to trying to do justice to the vast array of private and voluntary organizations which make significant contributions to the field. A list of such groups would include ones in such areas of concern as health and safety, public affairs, social and cultural development, outdoor and environmental concerns, religious or spiritual development, and a wide range of avocational interests, to name only some. These represent a major portion of the invisible giant that is adult education in the province.

III. Historical Overview: To What End?

The previous section was in large part devoted to an examination of the organizations and institutions which provided adult education opportunities over the years. In some cases, we have considered briefly the nature of the programs or services they delivered. This enterprise, so varied, and growing at such a rapid rate over the decades, "prospered" because it was meeting people's needs. One of the most important characteristics of adult education is that by and large, people take part only if they wish to do so—only if they see some satisfactory outcome for themselves in return for the time, energy and funds expended. The nature of the benefits expected varies from person to person and from situation to situation. They may be vocational, social, recreational, spiritual, or related to some other aspect of self-development. Sir Josiah Stamp, an English industrialist and economist, put it well in the 19th century, when he said that the functions of adult education were to equip the individual "to earn a living, to live a life and to mould a world."

"...to earn a living..."

A major proportion of adult education as it has developed in B.C., as elsewhere, has been for the purpose of vocation, using that term in its broadest meaning. It is a natural human characteristic, perhaps, and this is something which is greatly emphasized in North American society—to want to "get ahead" and to perform one's daily work in a responsible and satisfactory fashion. Indeed many, if not most immigrants to Canada have come to this country because it held promise of reward for effort and opportunities for a better life in economic terms. Modern rates of technological change have also "forced" many Canadians to change their occupation, or change substantially the way they carry out their current one.

Seen from the point of view of society and public policy, vocational education has also received high priority indeed. For instance, governments have seen the basic importance of having an efficient system of food production in this country and both provincial and federal governments have heavily subsidized educational services for primary producers in order to bring this about, by means of district agriculturalists, demonstration farms, applied research activities, information systems, support of Farmers' and Women's Institutes, etc. Governments have also seen the vital importance in today's world of having a highly trained and resourceful work force. No part of adult education in Canada in recent decades has been as heavily subsidized as technical and vocational education. Government selects students for training, if necessary moves them to another part of the province (or country) where training is available, covers the cost of their training, and if needed, pays the students' living expenses while they are in training.

So from the point of view of both the individual and the society as a whole, vocational education is a matter of very high priority and it is no surprise, therefore, that education "to earn a living" has been such a large segment of the field.

When those early settlers in Craigflower, near Victoria, in 1854, gathered periodically to read papers to each other about agricultural practices (the earliest example of adult education in the province we know of), perhaps adult education for vocational purposes was launched in B.C. Newspapers in the early years of settlement abounded in advertisements for proprietary schools in vocational subjects. The first Superintendent of Schools in the province, John Jessop, was clearly ahead of his time, but as early as 1877, called in his annual report for the school boards of the province to become active in providing night schools, which he clearly saw as being mainly vocational in their efforts. The Department of Education took the initiative in 1874 to promote the in-service training of school teachers by means of organizing Teachers' Institutes, which subsequently became province-wide and functioned at both a provincial and regional level. The Provincial Department of Mines began offering instruction in its areas of concern as early as 1896. The B.C. Telephone Company began training programs for its employees in 1890 and the B C. Electric Company was doing so at least as early as 1906. The craft unions played an important role in the training of their members and journeyman members, the Typographical Union becoming active in this work in Vancouver as early as 1893. Among the professional groups, the medical doctors were organizing educational events for their members at least as early as 1902. The federal government Department of Marine and Fisheries began its marine schools in Vancouver in 1907.

Perhaps the largest scale educational effort in the vocational field before 1914, however, was that in the field of agriculture. Soon after British Columbia joined Confederation in 1871, the province began work in agricultural extension, even though agriculture did not become a Department on its own until the early Nineties. This activity was described briefly in the previous section. With the passage of the Agricultural Instruction Act in 1913 by the federal government, greatly increased funds became available to the province for this kind of work. The co-operative movement had got its start in B.C. in the 1890s and by 1914, the movement was active among producers (dairymen and fruitgrowers, particularly) and through co-operative stores.

Vocational education for the larger urban centers was provided by some of the means mentioned above, but also through other organizations. Over the turn ot the century, the most important provider of such courses, especially in Victoria and Vancouver, was the Y.M.C.A., which in the mid-Nineties began to offer classes in vocational subjects in both centers. In Victoria the program was even termed an "evening college" and in both centers there was a considerable range of vocational as well as other subjects offered. Although we are accustomed today to seeing school board programs which are extremely diversified in terms of the type ot course offered, in the early years, the offerings were overwhelmingly vocational. The advertisement for the Vancouver program in 1909 was headed, "Young Men and Women: Prepare For Promotion." The vocational emphasis of the program could not have been made more clear.

Both World Wars, the second of course on a much larger scale, caused a tremendous expansion in adult education in the vocational sector. Information about this activity in World War I is particularly elusive, but the vast expansion ot the shipbuilding, munitions, mining and lumbering industries in the province in the 1914-18 period clearly required the training of many thousands of workers, much of it presumably taking place on the job. It has already been pointed out that more than 1,300 veterans of the First World War attended vocational courses organized by the University, in at least 11 subject matter areas, plus several branches of agriculture. Much similar work was presumably carried out under other auspices.

The Twenties, especially the middle years of the decade, were prosperous times and a period of rapid development in some business and industrial sectors. Supported by funds made available by Ottawa under the Agricultural Instruction Act of 1913, agricultural work was expanded, under both government and university auspices. School board programs in several centers, with Vancouver leading the way, as always, expanded vocational offerings. Apprenticeship training was enhanced by the passage of provincial legislation in 1935 which regulated this activity. In 1919 the federal government passed the Technical Education Act, which provided matching funds to the provinces to finance facilities and programs, including in-school education. During the Twenties these funds helped to make possible modest progress in this field in B.C., including the building of technical schools in Vancouver, Victoria and New Westminster, the growth of vocational courses in night schools, and the beginning of vocational correspondence courses.

The depression years of the 1930s produced some important initiatives, many of them in order to produce activity for people rather than having them languishing in unemployment. A number of these programs which were described in the previous section, were vocational in character. Under federal legislation late in the decade (1937), the relatively new Extension Department at U.B.C. was able to get funds to enable it to launch a remarkable series of what were called Youth Training Schools. These were two week residential courses which provided mainly vocational training, for both men and women.

At the end of the decade, the Dominion government became more active in this work, and these measures were dramatically expanded with the beginning of the war and the urgent need lor trained people both within the armed forces and in the civilian war effort. An even larger effort, as far as B.C. was concerned, was the training of civilians for work in wartime industries, most notably shipbuilding and aircraft production. The year 1943 was the peak year for employment in this work, and training programs in both educational institutions and on the job were also at their peaks, some training being operated on a shift, 24-hour-day basis. Legislation in 1940 had the effect of shortening apprenticeship programs so journeymen could be turned out more quickly to meet the needs of wartime industry. In 1942, in Vancouver alone, the St. John's Ambulance Association trained 7,361 instructors in the fields of first aid and home nursing.

The immediate post-war years were a boom time in economic activity, as the Canadian economy converted to peacetime needs and developed rapidly in order to meet demands which had been deferred during the war, and the demands of the families established by the men and women as they returned to normal peacetime occupations and pursuits. Veterans returned to their education, many having come home with considerably altered goals from what they had held before the war, and with financial and educational benefits from the government which made it possible for them to pursue these ambitions. Veterans swelled the size of educational institutions, especially those which provided a means of completing their high school standing, university, vocational and professional training programs. The school boards and certain proprietary schools did important work in providing opportunities for high school completion. The University of British Columbia made remarkable efforts in responding to the needs of the veterans.

The Fifties saw the beginning on a whole new scale of the provision of vocational and technical education, with the provincial government establishing a series of vocational schools in the province and the Vancouver School Board, in the lead once again, creating the Vancouver Vocational Institute. Organized labor and industry stepped up their educational activities as well.

Conditions in the late 1950s conspired to bring about another major thrust in vocational adult education. It was a time of economic downturn and the number of unemployed workers in the country grew to unaccustomed heights. In 1957, the Western countries were shocked to hear of the successful launching of the first earth satellite, or Sputnik, by the U.S.S.R. The West's assumed leadership in technical training and research came under serious question and the Diefenbaker federal government, in common with other Western nations, gave serious attention to strengthening technical and vocational education, and to the retraining of many unemployed workers.

The result was the landmark federal legislation, the Technical and Vocational Training Assistance Act of 1960, which made previously undreamed of amounts of money available for this work—both facilities and programs. Funds were made available to the provinces on a matching funds formula. To this measure we owe the great expansion of the vocational school system, the creation of the B.C. Institute of Technology, the great expansion of vocational training in the school system, as well as support for some elements of the emerging community college system. One indication of the expansion of vocational education in this period was that enrollments in vocational classes sponsored by the school boards went from 9,000 to 34,000 during the decade. The rapid expansion of vocational training in many cases required the academic upgrading of potential students in order to make it possible for them to cope with the vocational courses.

Ever since the passage of the Agricultural Instruction Act of 1913, federal actions in the field of vocational and technical training had been based on the assumption that education was a provincial responsibility under the constitution. All Ottawa could do was to make federal funds for this purpose available, which it did on a matching funds formula, leaving the decision to the provinces as to whether they would get on with the work. During the early Sixties, under the Technical and Vocational Training Assistance Act, Ottawa received a great deal of criticism from the provinces, who complained that Ottawa's action in providing the funds was forcing the provincial government's hands (which was indeed the objective) and they complained also about federal "interference" in how the funds were being spent.

Tiring of this state of affairs, Ottawa took a different position beginning in 1966. It now asserted that the federal government, under its constitutional responsibilities with respect to the economic well being of the country, had the power to act on its own authority with respect to manpower training (which it carefully differentiated from education) and that under new legislation, the Occupational Training Act (1967), it would have the power to select candidates for training, purchase training for them from whatever source was appropriate, and when necessary, provide maintenance allowances for trainees during the period of training. These principles have governed the actions of the federal authorities under this and successive legislation. Such arrangements have provided vocational training in the province for many tens of thousands of adults. Training under these programs, which have changed in emphasis as conditions changed (further legislation in 1982 and 1985), was provided for 8,625 persons in 1967-68; 21,720 in 1969-70; 35,967 in 1978-79 and 32,036 in 1983-84. These figures include full and part-time trainees, but the vast majority were the former. Something less than 10 per cent of the figures represent those in full-time language or basic education training.

Another very important development in the last 20 years has been the rapid expansion in continuing professional education. Some information about this field was provided in the previous section. The basic point is that because the professions, by definition, are dealing with complex and advanced levels of knowledge, they have recognized, perhaps to an extent not matched by any other occupational groups, the necessity of their continuing to learn throughout their active years of practice.

As our society becomes more complex and new knowledge is generated at ever increasing rates, the way in which we carry out our vocational roles is tending to become technologically more sophisticated. Whole new industries requiring highly trained technical personnel are being created. Many existing jobs require new levels of skill and knowledge. And all too many Canadians lack the basic intellectual skills which are necessary if they are to be able to cope with these changes. Adult education which is relevant to the way British Columbians make a living has been prominent in the past and will perhaps be of even greater importance in the future.

"...to live a life..."

Activities related to living a life, apart from what will fall into the other two categories being utilized here, are of an enormous variety, and only a few selected examples can be mentioned. And here we are faced with the fact that the same course or program, such as academic upgrading, horticulture or the fine arts, may be used by one person for vocational purposes and by another for recreational or life-expanding purposes.

In the early years of settlement in the province, it is activities in this category which seemed to dominate the adult education scene. The record of the church institutes and mechanics' institutes which were formed in some cases almost as early as the communities themselves, indicate a concern for the amenities of life. These organizations typically provided a reading room containing books and newspapers; lectures, both occasional and in the larger centers, series as well (lectures on such subjects as "The Catacombs of Rome," "Rambles in the North West" or "An Evening with Longfellow" are frequently noted, and series on "The Psychology of Medicine," "The Elements of Geology" and many on literary subjects); debating societies in some of the larger organizations; study groups on literary or other subjects; dramatic clubs; and in the case of the largest of these organizations, the Victoria Mechanics' Institute, an institute orchestra. In the boomtown years of Barkerville, St. Saviour's Anglican Church was the sponsor ot the Cariboo Church Institute, which provided lectures, concerts, "lecture concerts," band concerts and "magic lantern shows." These were typical of such efforts in the early years of settlement.

A wide variety of independent study groups, literary, drama and music societies, debating and mock parliament groups were formed in the early years, some seeming to disappear after a short time and some, like the Collingwood or Bursill Institute of Vancouver and the Alexandra Club of Victoria having a longer life. Much of this sort of activity took place within the program of the Y.M.C.A. as well. Of particular interest were several organizations founded in the pre-war years which provided a fairly comprehensive program in the arts and sciences. In Victoria, a leading example was the Natural History Society of British Columbia, the program of which included regular lectures and discussions as well as a variety of field trips. Perhaps the most ambitious of these organizations was the Vancouver Art, Historical and Scientific Association, the work of which included many types of educational activities, exhibitions, musical events and which as well may be credited with the organization of what later became the public museum in Vancouver. In New Westminster, there was no organization of the range and stability of the two just mentioned, but the mechanics' institute, during its checkered career, performed many of the same functions. In the case of all of these organizations, they were actively supported by some of the leading citizens of the community. In his study of such organizations, Ian Hunt has termed these groups "mutual enlightenment" organizations and it is clear that they had significant social and perhaps political purposes, as well as cultural and educational.

The role of the churches has been referred to in connection with the church institutes. It should be pointed out as well that in at least three other respects the churches played an important part in adult education in this early period. The first is the recognition that an important aspect of adult education, then as now, has to do with people's religious growth and development, and the churches, of course, played an important and continuing role in this connection. Secondly, the churches sponsored a great deal of other educational activity themselves—lectures, study and interest groups, debating societies, and in the case ot the Methodist Church particularly, a great deal of English language instruction for Asian immigrants. The other main contribution of the churches was the activity of many outstanding ministers both as community leaders (in educational activities of various kinds) and in some cases as teachers and lecturers. The Rev. Henry Fiennes-Clinton of St. James Anglican Church in Vancouver was a leader in the organization of the Vancouver Reading Room, precursor of the public library, organizer of the Seamen's Institute, and frequent lecturer on church history and architecture. The Rev. John Gardiner of the Methodist Church worked in both Vancouver and Victoria giving leadership to language instruction for Asian immigrants and training teachers for that work. The Rev. H.H. Gowan of New Westminster and Victoria gave leadership to language instruction too, was an effective organizer and leader of a variety of educational and cultural organizations and was one of the most popular lectures in the area on literary subjects. The Rev. Percival Jenns ot St. John's Anglican Church in Victoria ran several educational programs in connection with the Church, and for some thirty years gave lectures on chemistry and other aspects of science.

The role of many of the churches in educational activities was particularly crucial in the early years of the development of the area, before other special purpose organizations and public institutions were created to take up the task. In subsequent years the churches concentrated more on education among their own adherents, and of course this work, although not well known beyond the church membership, has continued to be of very great importance in the lives of many people.

During the First World War, educational efforts were directed predominantly towards the goals of the war effort. The year 1916, however, marked the creation of one of B.C.'s remarkable cultural organizations, the Vancouver Institute. This organization has for most of its life been associated with The University of British Columbia, and rests on co-operation between "town and gown." It has an unbroken history of activity ever since its creation and conducts a series of Saturday night lectures given by outstanding experts, in recent years attracting many hundreds of people each week.

The Twenties were largely a period during which already existing services were continued in their development, the number of school boards offering programs increasing, with very modest development of non-vocational courses. A few specialized study group organizations such as the Burrard Field Naturalists Club (Vancouver) came into being. The Vancouver School of Decorative and Applied Arts (later the School of Art) was founded in 1925 and opened up opportunities for many interested in the fine arts. Radio broadcasting came into widespread use during the decade, an important source of cultural fare. In 1929, it became possible for the first time to complete the high school program by means of correspondence courses from the Department of Education. This was also a decade of fairly active development of library service—the Vancouver system, for instance, opening its first branch library in the city; the Public Library Commission carrying out a comprehensive study of library services in the province; and the ground work being laid for the important new development, the regional library service, which materialized in the next decade.

The decade of the 1930s and the depression conditions faced by so many British Columbians provides many examples of work of this kind. In fact it should be noted that in many of the reports of government services during the depression years, specific reference was made to the fact that the intent was to help raise the "morale of the people." To a degree unequalled at any other time in our history, government saw as one of its goals to help citizens of the province "live a life" that was rewarding, and to offset the desperation and discouragement which were being faced by so many. A public policy with respect to adult education which embraced a view of the whole person, rather than seeing the adult learner in just a particular role as worker, student, or one seeking hobbies or recreation, was a remarkable feature of the period and has not been seen since. The role of the government in supporting the work of the Vancouver Council of Women among the mothers of families on relief (Self-Help) was in keeping with this philosophy, and the government also ran programs on its own. The latter included the large-scale Provincial Recreation program (Pro-Rec), which enrolled tens of thousands of citizens in recreational activity and included a great deal of training work, and also a community drama program, which sponsored the formation of hundreds of play-reading groups and provided assistance to them.

Much of the work of the Extension Department of the University, created in 1936, was in this category. The chief initiatives in the program of the Department in the Thirties were mainly in the liberal arts and the humanities. A lecture service for the community was continued, evening classes in a wide variety of mainly non-vocational areas was built up, an audio-visual service of film slides, 16 mm films and recordings was established, study courses on various social science, educational and family life subjects were developed, a summer school of the arts was launched, a quite remarkable series of services in the field of drama were established. The role of the new department, as summarized by its long-time Director, Gordon Shrum, was that of assisting with the cultural development of the province.

Another area of expanding activity during this period was education about health and safety. The Red Cross and St. John's Ambulance Associations strengthened their work during this time and as it turned out, developed a strong base on which to build wartime services. Much of their work was conducted under the sponsorship of other groups. The Greater Vancouver Health League, created during the decade, symbolized new efforts to promote health education on a broad community front.

The post-Second World War period brought a number of important developments. Many persons who had been involved in urgent war work, at home and abroad, were relishing the opportunity following the war to pursue their own interests and hobbies and there was a great expansion of adult education related to these areas. A great deal of that was based in the emerging community center and neighborhood house organizations. This post-war period has been caricatured as the "basket weaving" period in the development of adult education in Canada and like all good caricatures, it contains much truth, even if it is an oversimplification. Clearly related to this development came the dramatic expansion of school board adult education beginning in the Fifties. From 1955 to 1957, for instance, night school enrollments increased by 50 per cent, and as B.E. Wales, the historian of this work has pointed out, a great deal of the expansion during this period was in the fields of general interest and recreation-related subjects.

The Community Arts Council of Vancouver began its remarkable life in the promotion of the arts and education about them in the post-war decade. In 1954, it received a national award from the Canadian Association for Adult Education for its programs.

The Extension Department was presented in the late 1950s with an opportunity to develop an ambitious new program based on what was called the study-discussion method. This involved the organization of small groups of people who read certain material each week and then met to discuss the ideas involved, under the leadership of persons who had received some training in leading group discussion but who were not subject matter experts. Financed by the Fund for Adult Education, an American subsidiary of the Ford Foundation, this project was called Living Room Learning. It began in a small way in 1957-58 with 29 groups in three different communities, and by the early Sixties was for several years operating more than 125 groups, in as many as 66 different communities in the province, utilizing at one point as many as 24 different courses, and involving approximately 1,600 persons per year. This program was a casualty of budget cuts in the Extension program in 1964.

Beginning slightly earlier than Living Room Learning and based on very similar methods, the Vancouver Public Library launched the local version of the Great Books program. This involved the study and discussion of some of the seminal books of the Western tradition and was developed (by the sponsoring American foundation) into a multi-year program, with a parallel program for children and teenagers as well. Launched locally in the mid-Fifties, this program was maintained for more than twenty years.

The yeasty, populist years of the 1960s were a period of continued interest in private pursuits of many kinds and the non-vocational elements in the programs of school boards, the University and the community centers grew rapidly. Important new participants on the adult education scene appeared in this decade with two additional public universities being created and the system of community colleges beginning in mid-decade. Many voluntary organizations—the churches, the Y.M. and Y.W.C.A.s, a variety of special interest groups and proprietary schools expanded their offerings as well.

The emergence of the Women's Movement dates from the 1960s as well and, in educational terms, this led to the creation of many programs which were aimed at assisting women to make decisions about their lives, assess their interests and capacities, and further personal development. A major step in this period was the foundation of the Women's Resources Center under U.B.C. extension auspices, but located in the downtown area. Earmarked funding from the Ministry made it possible for interested colleges to establish women's access centers in the late Seventies.

The Sixties, especially the latter part or the decade, brought the beginnings of great expansion in the fields of adult basic education (ABE) and the teaching of English as a second language (ESL) to adults. Although both fields had received some attention earlier, the dramatic expansion of vocational and technical education programs in the early Sixties under the TVTA Act had brought fresh revelation of how many potential students in such programs did not have sufficient knowledge of the language or enough basic education to allow them to take advantage of the vocational training which was increasingly becoming available. The federal authorities began to develop curricula and to purchase full-time ABE and ESL programs for their trainees, and this in turn led to the expansion of interest in these fields and in the number of experienced teachers available. In the case of ESL, a strong provincial professional organization emerged in the late Sixties and The University of B.C. began teacher training courses especially tor this group. Strong leadership in both fields was provided by Vancouver Community College, their programs being among the leading ones in Canada. When the provincial government greatly expanded its role in adult education in the late Seventies, the provision of ABE and ESL was a top priority for the Continuing Education Division and by various means it assisted in the further expansion of this work. In the four year period 1978-79 to 1981-82, for instance, the number of ESL students in the province increased from 9,600 to 22,820 (and the number of contact hours of teaching from 553,500 to 1,462,000); and the number of ABE students from 4,157 to 18,661 (and contact hours from 16,462 to 72,777). A further significant development lying behind these figures is that in addition to the many students in both fields who were sponsored by the federal manpower programs, a larger and more rapidly growing segment of both fields was made up of part-time students who were developing themselves through such study as their circumstances permitted. Especially in the field of ESL, a great deal of instruction was also being provided by voluntary and other organizations (including the universities) whose work is not reflected in the statistics for the school boards and the colleges presented above.

Another feature of the field which emerged in the Sixties and took on increasing significance with each passing year since was the provision of education appropriate to the needs of older people. Early efforts in the field took the form of workshops and conferences for those working professionally in the field and as well, programs with and for older people aimed at identifying the educational needs and interests of that age group. Since those early years, this work has been taken up by many organizations, including those of older people themselves, and many educational institutions also have lowered or waived registration rates in their regular programs for older people. Through the federal government's New Horizons program, financial assistance has been available for a number of special educational projects organized by groups of older people for themselves.

These are a few of the noteworthy accomplishments in adult education in the province which have particular relevance to the non-vocational elements of life. The lively adult education scene in B.C. has produced many outstanding programs in these areas, a number of them having gained widespread recognition in Canada and beyond for excellence of concept and performance.

"...to mould a world..."

The traditional concept of a liberal education is that it would help make the person capable of being a free and independent person, able to express ideas, sort the valid from the spurious or propagandistic arguments, and make well considered decisions as a free and independent citizen. The intention here is to focus more narrowly than that, on types of education which deal with matters clearly related to one's functioning as a citizen. It is clear, of course, that certain types of basic education—a satisfactory level of literacy and the ability to use the working language of the society—are necessary for citizenship, but these and other aspects of general education have been considered in the section above.

It has been said that many of the early leaders of the English working class gained confidence and competence in expressing themselves and in organizational affairs from their participation in Methodist bible classes, study circles and church government. This is undoubtedly also the case for many British Columbians. Hidden in the fabric of our social and political development are many influences which have equipped and disposed men and women to play an active part in the organizational and political life of our communities. We could look to the churches, the unions, the Y.M. and Y.W.C.A.s, the Farmers' and Women's Institutes and the like as the training ground for many a citizen and leader.

There is much evidence that in the early decades of our development, many citizens were anxious to develop their capacities for action as members of their communities. In the 1890s there was a strong trend in the development of debating societies and mock parliaments. In Vancouver, in 1911, a "league" of debating societies from various organizations was formed and competitions among the groups were held on a regular basis. Also of importance in this connection were such groups as the Men's Canadian Club, which was established in 1906 and the women's counterpart organization which was formed three years later, the aim of which was to help their members become informed about community and national affairs. However, several organizations went beyond providing information for members and played an active part in advocacy and political action. Examples of such organizations include the Council of Women, established in both Victoria and Vancouver in 1894, and the Farmers' and Women's Institutes. Whereas the Council of Women was established primarily for the purpose of social action, the Institutes had a variety of functions, of which such activity was one.

The political parties themselves were a source of stimulation for learning about public affairs. It is difficult, if not impossible to differentiate their propagandistic efforts from what might properly be termed educational, but both have been of value in drawing people to consideration of and participation in public affairs. Although little is known of their work in this connection, it appears that the early socialist parties in B.C. were very active in providing educational opportunities for their adherents, just as the C.C.F. party was when it emerged in the early 1930s. The churches too, arising out of their social gospel concerns for the nature of society, took an active part in such work. On a number of occasions over recent decades the churches, Protestant and Catholic, have made public pronouncements on matters of policy and have engaged large numbers of their members in a study of social questions. Examples of church-sponsored statements which were widely studied in the early years include the Methodist Manifesto on Peace and War, published in 1914, the "Message from the Chaplains" issued at the end of the war, the radical and controversial Manifesto of the Methodist General Conference of 1918, and the United Church's major statement entitled "Christianity and the Social Order," which was published in 1934.

Prior to and during the First World War, many women's organizations, already existing ones and new, special purpose ones, did a great deal of work, some of it educational, to promote the cause of women's suffrage, a goal which was successfully realized when women received the vote in 1917.

The U.B.C. Extension Department had a strong interest in public affairs. The Department became the provincial center at the beginning of the Second World War for the film distribution network being established by the National Film Board. Under the dynamic and controversial leadership of John Grierson, the NFB, in co-operation with the Wartime Information Board, took up the task of helping to unify the nation behind the war effort, and subsequently, to move on to its broader mandate of citizenship education. A distribution system for NFB films was based in the Extension Department and much work was done by way of forming and supporting local film councils and film circuits and training people in the use and appreciation of film. The Extension Department also became the provincial office of the two CBC-CAAE public affairs programs, National Farm Radio Forum and Citizens' Forum. Listening groups for both programs were organized throughout the province and the provincial secretary for both programs were staff members of the Department and were responsible for collating feedback from the groups and broadcasting it back to the groups on a weekly basis. Also of importance in this connection was the program of education about co-operatives for the fishermen of the province which the Department began in 1939, with financial assistance from the Dominion government. At the time, according to the historian of the co-operative movement, Ian MacPherson, the fisheries co-operatives were the liveliest and most dynamic part of the co-op movement in the province, and the work of the Extension Department in assisting with the organization of co-operatives and credit unions was central to this work.

The period of reconstruction thinking during the latter part of the Second World War was a lively time for education about public affairs. The role of Farm Radio Forum and Citizens' Forum and the National Film Board have already been referred to. Typical of the period was a conference held in Vancouver in mid-May of 1944 involving some 144 organizations of which organized labor groups were the most prominent and sponsored by the Industrial Reconstruction and Social Development Council. The theme of the conference was "Post-War Rehabilitation and Reconstruction" and a number of recommendations on social policy were approved and publicized, including some on adult education.

The immediate post-war period stimulated the activities of several organizations interested in international affairs as well, the League of Nations Society being active in the inter-war years and giving way to the United Nations Association after the Second World War. The Canadian Institute of International Affairs also had strong branches in the main centers.

Particular reference should also be made to the emergence in the late Forties and Fifties of what might be termed the group development, leadership training or human relations training movement. The U.B.C. Extension Department provided a great deal of the leadership in this field, a major portion of it in co-operation with the parent-teacher movement. The Department provided staff specialists who led work in this kind of training, organized training events led by outside experts, and developed study guides and other teaching materials for use by those interested in this area.   Many of the methods and techniques which were developed in this human relations training field found their way into various branches of education, practices in organizational life, and training in government and business and industry.   It also helped to develop skills which in many cases were used in community affairs.   A grant from the Fund for Adult Education made it possible for the Extension Department in the early Sixties to enter into three-year projects with both the Council of Women and the B.C. School Trustees Association to strengthen their educational work among their members.   Programs about public affairs within the regular evening class program were also expanded at this time.   These grants, plus a subsidy provided by the Board of Governors of the University, made it possible to expand short course activity in public and international affairs.

Another significant product of this period was the work of the Citizenship Branch of the federal government in promoting efforts among established and "New Canadians" as well towards what later was termed multi-culturalism. The immediate post-war decades were ones of very extensive immigration to Canada. The federal government took a lead in working with ethnic groups and other organizations and individuals interested in the reception and welfare of immigrants, and in citizenship policy generally. They sponsored the creation of what were usually called Citizenship Councils, provided assistance to them and made possible communication among the councils, including periodic regional conferences of councils, the first or which in B.C. was held in 1957.   There were approximately 10 councils in B.C. and they conducted a wide range of educational activities, as well as rendering practical assistance of various kinds to newcomers to the country.

The 1960s was a decade of widespread social and political agitation in Canada, as elsewhere.   It was a period of populist movements, the growth of single-issue advocacy groups (women's issues, environmental concerns, disarmament, Vietnam, Native Rights, etc.) and it was also a period of strong leadership from the federal government. Canada's "War on Poverty" measures, including Manpower policies, work under the Agricultural Reconstruction and Development Act (ARDA) and several programs to subsidize local initiatives by young people, all contributed to a range of educational and social development programs in B.C. This was a period during which liberal social and educational philosophy was strongly challenged and a number of programs were created which were aimed at a basic examination of community life and economic and social relationships.

Community development in various forms became a prominent feature of the educational scene. In this connection, the National Film Board, perhaps reviving something of the spirit of its first director, John Grierson, moved into an active role in the animation of social change through its project, Challenge for Change. The program had two main thrusts; one, a series of films aimed at encouraging citizens to take an active part in community affairs and, the second, a pioneering venture in placing film-making (and later videotape) equipment and training in the hands of those engaged in community development projects. Both aspects of Challenge for Change were utilized in B.C.; the best known example of the second being a long-term community development project in Bridgeview, a district in Surrey.

Reference has already been made to two other projects which were concerned with community development, in the broad sense, the Community School movement and the Britannia Center. Community education, that is, efforts to link educational provision to the concerns of the community and to the quality of life in the local area, have a long and important history in Canada. A belief that the neighborhood elementary school could play a key role in the development of its region, dealing with the adult community as well as the children in its charge, goes back in Canada to at least the 1920s.

The period of NDP government in the province, 1972 to 1975, was one which generally supported educational change and community development approaches. The Community Resource Boards which were created were a natural form for promoting social development. The efforts of the government directed towards the further development of the college system in the province laid the foundation of a system which could be more responsive to educational needs at the community level. And as long as that government remained in power, the colleges were left relatively free to be responsive to local situations, although few of them were outstanding in this regard. The new college legislation of 1977 reinforced trends towards system-wide governance and discouragement of responsiveness to unique local needs.

As a final example of adult education which is related to the learner's role as citizen, reference should be made to the longstanding efforts of organized labor in the training of its leaders and interested members for their responsibilities within the union organizations. Local, provincial and national labour bodies have been active in such education since 1945, the longstanding "weekend institutes" dating from the latter years of that decade. Human rights educational activities began in Vancouver in 1951 and were pursued vigorously during that decade. When the Canadian Labour Congress was formed in 1956, the pace of educational activity picked up, more extensive training programs were organized in the region, co-operative relationships were developed with Simon Fraser University and a number of B.C. union leaders attended the annual eight week residential Labour College of Canada, which began in 1963. In 1975, union-sponsored education took a substantial step forward when the federal government began a program of financial support for the educational programs of the main labour bodies, annual grants which still continue.

Participation in adult education is under almost all circumstances a voluntary act. The fact that there has been such rapid and continuous growth in adult education in the province is a clear indication that for one reason or another, be it vocational, social, recreational, or in order to expand personal interests or skills, adults in this province in steadily increasing numbers have turned to education as a key to their prosperity, development and enjoyment of life.

IV. Public Policy and Advocacy

One of the most important determining factors affecting the extent and nature of adult education in the province has been the policy of government, and of public agencies of all kinds towards this field. The following account deals with some of the highlights in the development of public policy over the years, some aspects of which have already been mentioned in the preceding sections.

Public Policy

The earliest use of public funds in support of adult education in what is now B.C. actually predates the province. In 1865, the government of the Mainland Colony of B.C. provided a supporting grant for the British Columbia Institute of New Westminster, the forerunner ot the mechanics' institute of that city. In 1866, after the union of the colonies, the government of the United Colony made grants to the New Westminster and Barkerville institutes, but these ceased after two years. One of the earliest pieces of legislation of the newly created provincial government in 1871 was An Act Respecting Literary Societies and Mechanics' Institutes, under which grants for such bodies were made until the year 1878.

In the late 1880s, the Provincial Library and Museum were created and in 1891, province-wide library activity was fostered by the passage of the Free Libraries Act. Also in the early Nineties, the Department of Agriculture expanded its educational activities, and launched its regular information bulletin series. The late 1890s was a creative period for publicly sponsored aspects ot the field—the Provincial Bureau of Mines giving courses in the three main centers, the Farmers' Institute Act (1896) laying the foundation for the expansion of that activity, and the provincial travelling library service being launched.

Public school adult education emerged after the turn of the century. In 1909, the Vancouver board launched an ambitious evening program and during the ensuing months, with the help of the school trustees' organization, persuaded the government to amend the Public Schools Act (1910) in order to provide official recognition and financial support for night school work. In 1913, John Kyle, who had organized the Vancouver program, was hired by the Department of Education and put in charge of both technical education and night schools.

Agricultural extension, which was considerably expanded by the government in 1909, developed dramatically beginning in 1913 with the help of funds made available by the federal legislation, the Agricultural Instruction Act. So although the adult education movement in the province before the First World War was largely provided by the voluntary sector, government was beginning to play a role, especially in agriculture, public libraries and at the end of the period, in the public school system.

The period of the Great Depression of the 1930s represents an important stage in policy development because as the effects of the Depression years created widespread social and economic distress, the government responded to people's needs in an unprecedented fashion. The most important single feature of the 1930s, as far as adult education was concerned, was the broadening of both the purpose and the extent of public provision in this field. This came about under the Patullo government, (which came to power in late 1933), and much of it as a result of the leadership provided by the Minister of Education, Dr. George Weir. The public library service of the province took a great leap forward with the development of the regional library system model, which was tested in the Lower Fraser Valley region in the early Thirties and subsequently ulilized elsewhere. Correspondence education, which had begun in 1919 under government auspices, was greatly expanded in the 1930s and B.C. was well ahead of other provinces in this work by 1935.

Local night school enrollments fell off badly during the decade, but had reached new highs by the late Thirties. The government underwrote some kinds of vocational night school courses, making it possible for the local boards to offer them free. The apprenticeship system in the province was regularized and expanded under the Apprenticeship Act of 1935. Technical and vocational education generally operated at a modest level, the supporting federal legislation having expired in 1929. The province maintained a minimal program, however, concentrating largely on classes for the unemployed inside and outside the relief camps. This work expanded greatly after 1937, however, when the federal government provided funds and leadership under the Unemployment and Agricultural Assistance Act, which in turn merged into the Second World War programs. The government also encouraged the university to expand its adult education activities and this work moved forward rapidly in the latter half of the decade.

A number of important programs were undertaken by the government in response to the distress and despair which many citizens experienced as a result of the depression. Government reports frequently referred to the need to bolster the "morale" of the people. The Minister of Education appointed a Provincial Advisory Committee on Adult Education to advise on activities to be provided for the desperate and unemployed. Under this committee, vocational classes were made available for the unemployed; a large-scale and much admired recreational program, Pro-Rec, was developed; a social and cultural development small-group program for women in the Vancouver area was co-sponsored and funded by the government, in association with the founding organization of the project, the Council of Women; and a large-scale community drama program was organized by the Department of Education.

In the mid and late Thirties, the variety of government-sponsored educational activities for adults had increased greatly and perhaps equally significant, government's perception of the purpose of its efforts had taken on philosophical overtones which had not been experienced previously—and have not since.

The period 1955 to 1970 was one of vigorous expansion in public provision. School board-sponsored adult education programs grew enormously during this period, with boards in B.C. leading all the rest of Canada in this respect. Strong leadership came from L.J. Wallace of the Department of Education during the Fifties and the Vancouver board's program continued to lead the way. In the Sixties, enrollment in school board programs in the province quadrupled, as did the number of classes, and by the end of the decade, 69 boards offered programs, with 54 employing full-time directors. The Vancouver board created the first full-time adult education institution in 1962, the King Edward Senior Matriculation and Continuing Education Centre, which operated until it merged into Vancouver City College (now Vancouver Community College) when the latter was founded in 1965. U.B.C.'s extension program grew rapidly during the Fifties, becoming one of the most outstanding programs in the country, suffered a setback in the mid-Sixties due to budget cuts, but reached its highest ever levels of activity by the end of the decade.

The new colleges, institutes and universities were just beginning to develop their adult education work by 1970, but the pace of growth was picking up.

Federal initiatives, in the form of the Technical and Vocational Training Assistance Act of 1960 and the Adult Occupational Training Act of 1967, transformed adult education in the vocational and technical areas. By the end of the Sixties, the impact on the field of the vocational schools, the first colleges and the B.C. Institute of Technology (which had been financed largely out of the federal funds) was impressive. Apprenticeship in the province had developed steadily, except for the recession in the late Fifties and early Sixties.

By the end of the Sixties, the adult education scene in the public sector was becoming increasingly complex. Organizations of adult educators representative of the various aspects of the field had emerged. Each of these organizations was involved to some extent in trying to influence public policy. In 1971, the Department of Education convened a conference, the first of its kind under public auspices, to examine problems of coordination in the public system.

Although the Ministry (formerly the Department) of Education had appointed a part-time director of night schools as early as 1913, it was not until 1962 that a full-time person was appointed and even then, the leadership exercised by the Ministry was sporadic, and necessarily limited. The outstanding exception to this was the mid to late Thirties, as described above. With the appointment in 1976 of Dr. Ron Faris to head this work (an experienced bureaucrat and doctoral graduate in the field of adult education) a new era began. Dr. Faris and the team of colleagues he was able to build up around him in subsequent years had a very different view ot the Ministry's role than had his predecessors. Whereas earlier directors had administered government grants and generally did what they could to encourage public institutions to expand their programs, Dr. Faris saw it as government's role to give leadership to the development of the field and to encourage qualitative improvements, in terms of both the professional leadership and the outreach of programs to meet the needs of all segments of the population. He persuaded his Ministry to appoint a Committee representative of the public educational institutions (which he chaired), which issued a discussion paper, held hearings throughout the province and produced a report in 1976, which served as a blueprint for many subsequent actions. Developments included the appointment of a standing Ministry Advisory Committee on Adult Education; stimulation by means of research studies, conferences and special programming grants of activity in underdeveloped but high priority areas (adult basic education, English as a second language, services to handicapped persons, services to women, the elderly and single parent families); research studies, publications and practice manuals designed to assist the practitioners in the field; special subsidies for innovative programs and services; the improvement of data collection for the field; and the sponsorship of a series of conferences about adult and lifelong education for policy makers.

In addition to this expanded role on the part of the Ministry itself, this period brought the rapid expansion of adult education programs offered by public institutions. The need for continuing of lifelong learning on the part of the adult citizen was widely accepted. and for a variety of reasons—vocational, citizenship, self-development, academic upgrading—increasing numbers of persons took part in adult education. Many school boards in the province turned their adult education programs over to the new colleges in the early Seventies, but the remaining ones stayed in the field. The colleges, B.C.I.T., the other institutes and the universities all expanded their programs enormously in the last few years.

Particular mention should be made of the major initiatives of the provincial government in the area of distance education. The Open Learning Institute was created in 1978 specifically for the purpose of delivering educational programs by distance education to all parts of the province, program areas to include post-secondary, technical and vocational and adult basic education. In 1980, the Knowledge Network of the West was established, to assist other institutions in the system to convey programs to their students and the general public by means of a telecommunications network. These two agencies were combined to form the Open Learning Agency, effective in 1988.

Arising out of a conference which the Ministry co-sponsored with several provincial educational organizations and which was held in Vancouver in late 1979, the Ministry initiated a process designed to develop a series of Ministry policy statements on adult education. Drafts were prepared by the Ministry Advisory Committee, circulated to the field for comment, and then rewritten in the Ministry and issued as policy papers. The first of these statements, an overall or general policy, was issued by the Ministry in March of 1980. A second, on Community and General Interest Education, followed in May. An Adult Special Education policy was released in March, 1982 and was followed by one on Adult Basic Education (including ESL), released in April of that year.

The first sign of trouble concerning this process came in 1981, when a new Minister of Education called a halt to it and indicated his unwillingness to accept some of the work already completed. The Ministry has since dismantled the Continuing Education Division, has terminated virtually all of the work which had begun in the late Seventies and publicly announced its intention to discontinue providing leadership in this field.

Co-ordination of adult education services within the public sector is an element of public policy which deserves special mention. In 1971, the senior continuing education official in the Department of Education, A. L. Cartier, pointed out that the articulation of adult education services among adult education agencies would be one of the main difficulties in the future. This was the same year in which the Department encouraged the school boards to turn their programs over to the colleges, which would certainly have simplified the picture had it been fully acted upon. Approximately a third of the boards stayed in the field, however, and little if anything was done to deal with the considerable overlap in roles between those two sets of institutions. When the Faris Committee carried out its work in 1976, this issue was an emotionally "loaded" one. In its report, the Committee made an effort to define institutional roles but what was done still contained much overlap and grounds for confusion.

An effort was made in 1981 to examine the question. With financial assistance from the Ministry, the Directors of Adult Education of the eight school districts in the Douglas College region and the Dean of Continuing Education of the college jointly undertook a study of the relative roles of the several agencies and of the basis on which an articulation of services might be arrived at. A key conclusion was that as long as the Ministry based financial support of institutions on the number of enrollees and at the same time had no satisfactory way of acknowledging for financial purposes co-operative arrangements between and among them, the result was likely to be competition rather than co-operation. Faris reported in that same year that when he was assembling information from government departments and crown corporations to be included in the directory of adult education services which was to be published, he encountered a great deal of suspicion and reluctance to provide information, the departments fearing this was a prelude to someone attempting to take over their programs. When, in 1983, Faris was demoted and instructed to cease providing leadership in the field of adult education, he was told that one area in which he could continue his efforts was that of promoting co-ordination and "efficiency" in the system. But no policy initiatives were forthcoming to facilitate such work.

The matter of co-ordination remains where it has always been. Those responsible for the direction of institutional programs are left to exercise their judgment in the matter. This has worked reasonably well, but especially in the areas of overlap between the school boards and the colleges and institutes, there have been problems in some geographic areas, and at some times. It would appear that governments which see virtue in competition or "free enterprise" in other areas are just as committed to that principle for the field of adult education as well.

Advocacy

Some of the features of public policy towards adult education have been described. A related part of the story consists of the efforts which have been made over the years to shape or influence government's attitude toward such activity. What role should government play in the provision of opportunities for adult education, and what services should it and the public educational system provide? These questions have been the subject of many representations to government over the years. There has also at times been a persistent effort by those in government to persuade the public educational institutions to behave in certain ways.

The colony of British Columbia joined Canadian confederation in 1871 and we have evidence that in that very first year of the province's existence, efforts by members of the mechanics' institute in the provincial capital led to the passage of An Act Respecting Literary Societies and Mechanics Institutes. From those early years until the formation of provincial organizations devoted to adult education in the 1950s, advocacy on behalf of the field had to come from interested citizens, other educators or from allied professions. There was not a great deal of this, but some examples can be given. When the provincial organization of school trustees and the Vancouver School Board were attempting to persuade the government in the early years of the century to amend the Public Schools Act in order to empower local boards to operate night schools, not only did the School Trustees Association and the Vancouver Board make representations to the government, but so did the Vancouver City Council and The Central Ratepayers organization in that city.

The librarians of the province were drawing the importance of adult education to the attention of the government as early as 1922, and when the Public Library Commisson was asked by the Provincial Secretary to carry out a survey of the field in 1941, the Commission included in its impressive report strong recommendations as to the government's role in the field. They asserted:

> The next forward step in the march of educational progress in British Columbia ought to be the creation of means whereby men and women of mature age may have at their command facilities for knowledge such as have for generations been given the child.

They called for the creation of a strong agency within the Department of Education which for the field of adult education would be a "Directing, Controlling, Co-ordinating, Unifying, Centralized Authority." Their recommendations, in summary, were described by the authors as:

> [T]o the purpose and end that there may thus be organized and established, as speedily as possible, a province-wide system of adult education comparable in scope and organization with that of the public school.

No organization of professional educators, as they evolved in subsequent decades, could have put the case more strongly. Indeed the Public Library Commission's recommendations went beyond what most adult educators would subsequently seek.

The predominant phenomenon of recent decades has been the efforts on the part of professional or career adult educators, and their associations (to be described in the next section), to persuade government to accord higher priority to adult education. Research has shown that something of the order of 250 submissions by adult education organizations have been made to government since 1973 about policies in the field. These have included requests for greater visibility within government structures, stronger leadership from government, declarations of government policy, increased resources of various kinds for the field, and increased attention to the needs of particular groups. But as the field became increasingly professionalized, and as some of the institutions in the system developed large programs, there developed a degree of ambivalence with respect to how strong the leadership coming from the Ministry of Education should be.

In the buoyant period of the late Fifties to the early Seventies, those who were in charge of institutional programs tended increasingly to take the view, "Give us the tools and we will do the job." They argued for increased resources to be made available by government, but were no longer always arguing for strong and co-ordinated leadership from that quarter.

Two factors were especially significant in this connection. When the college system began to develop in the mid-Sixties, and especially after the government attempted to shift responsibility for adult education from the school boards to the colleges, a substantial portion of the professional manpower in the field began to take a jaundiced view of the leadership coming from government. By the time of the public inquiry into government policy towards adult education which was carried out in 1976 (the "Faris Committee,") opinion in the field was very divided. Submissions coming from many community organizations and from some institutions continued to call for strong leadership from government. Others, most notably those in the school board sector, but also some voices from the community and other professional sectors, were arguing for more funding, but less "control" from government. This arose in some cases from a distaste for government's apparent favoring of the colleges as deliverers of programs and in other cases from those who felt that government should route more of its adult education funds to the private sector.

As previously described, the school board-based adult education enterprise in the province, which had flourished for almost two decades—the mid-Fifties to the early Seventies—was the outstanding one of its kind in Canada and had built up a considerable head of steam and confidence in its own ability. The Directors of these programs were on the whole successful "educational entrepreneurs," who felt they knew the needs of their communities and who were accustomed to being left alone to do their iobs, within budgetary limits.

When the NDP government came to power in 1972, fresh winds began to blow. When first the report of the government appointed College Task Force of 1974 seemed to favor the colleges over the school boards, and then Dr. Ron Faris (who was known to have the same views) became Executive Director of the new Continuing Education Division in 1977, these forces had to be taken seriously. Although Faris's social democrat views were not by any means representative of those of the Social Credit government under which he was operating, he was accorded considerable freedom by his Minister and Deputy. Faris was generally critical of the adult education programs in the province, largely for what they were not doing rather than what they were doing. He felt the institutions were not trying hard enough to meet the needs of disadvantaged persons in their communities. By various means he and his colleagues set out to shift the priorities of adult education in the school board and college systems. In a significant number of cases, this "interference" with local adult education programs was resented. So that by the late Seventies, there were mixed signals incorporated into advocacy efforts.

The case was consistently made over the years for government to affirm and give increased prominence to its responsibilities in the field of adult education. The most frequently mentioned recommendation was that government should develop and state its policies for the field. It was also recommended by various parties that the government's commitment to adult education be placed "in statute." In other words, there was concern that what has since in fact happened to government's commitments to adult education, namely their drastic reduction, might happen; and it was felt that if government's commitment to the field was stated in law, there would be less likelihood of it subsequently being brushed aside.

One of the most interesting features of the story, especially in the period 1976 to 1982, was the role of officials within the public service in creating opportunities for advocacy to government and senior officials. The Continuing Education Division was painfully conscious at all times of the "marginality" of government's concern about adult education. Faris and his colleagues were therefore constantly looking for ways in which persons and agencies in the community could be encouraged to press their case for an increased or more effective government role in the field.

The most significant characteristic of the field of adult education in British Columbia has been its failure to establish a political constituency for the field. In the last two decades particularly, there has been a great deal of advocacy activity within the system, but it has by and large consisted of the professional or career adult educators engaging in dialogue with the ministries of government. In the decades before the organizations of adult educators came into being, whatever efforts were made had to come from elsewhere. When the first provincial organization devoted to adult education was formed in 1954, and for about a decade thereafter, the leaders of a number of voluntary associations—the Y.M. and Y.W.C.A., the Council of Women, the Women's Institutes, the Parent-Teacher Federation, etc—were prominent in the affairs of the organization. But with increased professionalization and a change in the nature of the provincial adult education organization in the early Sixties, it is clear that adult educators neglected their links with the voluntary sector and tended to narrow their interests and to draw in upon themselves and their institutions. This had the unfortunate effect of narrowing the circle of those who felt themselves to be involved in the welfare of adult education.

Interestingly, it was in the Continuing Education Division of the Ministry that there appeared to be the clearest realization of what was happening. One can see many of the initiatives of the Division after 1976 directed towards the goal of involving elements of the community in shaping the field. The most obvious attempt to include such other parties was the strategy employed in organizing the three Lifelong Learning Conferences of 1979-82. Organized directly by one of the provincial professional organizations, but according to strategies developed by Faris and his Division, this venture involved several other groups, such as the school trustees, college council members and college teachers. It is significant that these initiatives have not been followed up since the Ministry has ceased to provide leadership in the venture, but it was its early success that appeared to lead to the Ministry's decision to launch the policy development process undertaken in the early Eighties. The situation in this province contrasts sharply with that of Alberta and Saskatchewan, where by pursuing different strategies, adult educators have been more successful in recent decades in building a political base of support for the field. The result of the B.C. situation has been that when in recent decades adult education has been greatly downgraded in terms of public priority, the field has not been able to summon an effective base of support from citizen groups of various kinds.

It would appear that organized adult education has been largely ineffective in its advocacy activities. It would be difficult to identify any single issue on which advocacy from the field has made an important difference. Calls for strong, co-ordinated leadership by government which were made in the Forties brought no discernible response. During the period of rapid growth and development from the mid-Fifties to the early Seventies— a time of increasing professionalization and institutionalization—much of the advocacy originated with the growing number of professional bodies in the field, and with the possible exception of some adjustment in the provision for high school completion programs for adults, appeals for change were largely ignored. Submissons from the field, some of them very substantial and carefully reasoned, were often barely acknowledged and requests for meetings with Ministers or senior officials were more often than not rebuffed.

With the coming to power of the NDP administration in 1972 and through the years of the Social Credit governments which have succeeded it (at least up to 1982) there were at the helm ministers or other officials with agendas of their own for the field of adult education. The field was catapulted from a period in which there was little sense of direction for government's role in the field to one in which government had a clear sense of where it wanted to go and did not wish to be diverted or distracted. In the NDP years, there was readiness to change but a singleminded concentration on the further development of the college and institute system. After 1976, under the leadership of Faris and other senior officials, there were lines of development firmly held to by these leaders. They overwhelmed the system with initiative, orchestrating expressions of opinion from the community as it suited their purposes.

But events since 1982 have made it clear that advocacy on behalf of adult education has next to no impact in the political arena. In the last five years, the government has publicly announced that it no longer intended to play a leadership role in this field. It has totally dismantled the Continuing Education Division of the Ministry. The volume of advocacy activity on behalf of adult education has slowed to a trickle in this period, it generally being felt that "no one was listening." To their credit, several of the associations of adult educators have sent out exploratory probes from time to time to see whether the wind had changed, and when, as in the case of literacy education, there have been grounds for encouragement, efforts have been renewed. Generally, however, the improvements which appeared to have been made during the Seventies in government's acceptance of responsibility for leaderhip and support for adult education have proven to be illusory, or at best, short term. Efforts mounted by the field of adult education to dissuade government from its retreat from leadership in this field have been unsuccessful.

V. Movement and Profession

It is commonly observed by students of the field of adult education that it has over time been transformed from a social movement to a profession. Or to put it another way, that adult education is becoming professionalized. Adult education was seen by many of its exponents in the early decades of its development as a means ot improving society. This was, of course, to be achieved through the education of individuals, but the effects would be a better world in which to live. It is no accident that many of the early leaders of adult education in our country, as in many others, came out of the churches, the Y.M.C.A. and various reform organizations. Adult education was seen by many of its pioneers as a means of enabling the democratic system to function more effectively or to bring about a fairer distribution of the benefits of our society by giving many adults a "second chance," in cases where they had missed out on opportunities in their youth to further their education. The latter was very much the case made by Jessop, Kyle and others in promoting the progress of night schools. And here are the words of a report by the B.C. Public Library Commission in 1922:

> It is not the education of children that will save the world from destruction; it is the education of adults. It is the adult who must be released from his prejudices, his narrow customs. His habits, his nature, his outlook must be broadened and enabled until they attain to civilized citizenship.

It is not without significance that when the first of the semi-annual conferences on adult education was held in December of 1954, the main topic of the day's discussion was "Education for Citizenship."

The 1950s brought several developments which were signs of an emerging professional spirit in adult education. Recent research has indicated that this was true for the country as a whole, but nowhere was the trend more obvious than in British Columbia. In 1954, the three leading adult education agencies, the Department of Education, the Vancouver School Board and the Extension Department of the University, took the lead in steps which led to the formation of the first adult education organization in the province, the B.C. Adult Education Council. It sponsored a series of semi-annual conferences about adult education and led in turn to the formation of two successor organizations, the B.C. Division of the Canadian Association for Adult Education (which existed for roughly the decade of the Sixties) and the Pacific Association for Continuing Education (PACE), which is active at the present time. In 1955, L.J. Wallace of the Department of Education organized the first-ever conference of school board night school directors. This was clearly an important event in relation to the dramatic expansion of school board programs which began at that time, and it also contributed to building a sense of cohesion among the growing number of full-time adult educators in the province. In the following year, 1956, Dr. Roby Kidd, the Director of the Canadian Association for Adult Education, came at the invitation of the University and taught the first degree credit course in adult education which had been offered in the province. The University followed up on this event by inaugurating in the following year what was the first degree program in adult education in Canada. By the end of the Fifties, therefore, there were a considerable number of full-time adult educators working in B.C., an organization had been formed which provided a means of consultation among them, and professional training was available in the form of a masters degree (and beginning in 1966, a diploma and a doctorate) at The University of British Columbia.

In the subsequent decades, a number of more specialized organizations of adult educators have been formed in the province, in keeping with the expansion and specialization in the field. The school board adult educators decided in 1963 to form an association, what for most of its existence has been called the B.C. Association of Continuing Education Administrators, and when it was officially constituted two years later, it welcomed into membership the college and institute-based adult educators as well. The Sixties saw the beginning of the rapid expansion of technical and vocational education for adults and a provincial chapter of the Canadian Vocational Association was formed in 1964. (It went out of existence when PACE was formed in 1972.) The specialists in English as a second language formed a provincial association, TEAL, in 1967. Approximately half of its members were teachers of adults and the other half worked in the school system.

The Seventies brought further organizations. Two of these related particularly to training in and for business and industry, the Training and Development Society of B.C. (formed in 1974) and the Private Career Training Association of B.C. (established in 1977). In 1976, educators from the Community School movement and others interested particularly in education as a key to social change formed the Association for Community Education in B.C. Those involved in the delivery of adult basic education formed a provincial association in 1979. Two other groups, the Society of Vocational Instructors of B.C. and the Adult Special Education Association (later renamed "Network"), were formed subsequently.

This means that there are at the time of writing at least nine different provincial organizations representing elements of the field of adult education. One organization, PACE, sees itself as concerned with the whole field of adult education. Others are specialized in terms of representing either institutons (public or private) or specialized content areas. The "umbrella" organization, PACE, tries to provide a common meeting ground by enabling each of the other organizations to name a representalive to sit on the PACE board. The presidents of all organizations are invited to come together periodically to discuss matters or mutual interest.

The various associations have quite different interests, however. PACE (partly because of its strong links with the national organization, the Canadian Association for Adult Education), the Association for Community Education, the Adult Basic Education Association, and the Adult Special Education Network, tend to represent the "movement" dimension of adult education. They put stress on the interconnection between the further education of adults and improvement in social justice and the social order. The other associations named tend to be more predominantly concerned with professional or institutional dimensions of the field. These differences in emphasis or priorities make it difficult for the organizations to act collaboratively, or even to maintain effective communication. Specialization in the field is accompanied by the risk of balkanization. Earnest efforts are continuing on the part of several of the leaders of these organizations to maintain contacts across the field, but it is a difficult struggle. Just as adult education itself is extremely varied and dispersed in our society, so it is proving difficult to achieve anything approaching a community of interest among the many working professionally in the field. The question clearly is whether it will be reasonable in the future to see adult education as one, or several fields.

Professional training and research are an important part of the story of the field. As in the case of the field as a whole, it is no simple matter to define the limits of the subject. A number of the most senior positions in adult education in the province are held by persons with no formal training in the field of adult education. This may continue to be the situation over the long run, but certainly at the present time is an indication that the field is in only a partial stage of professionalization.

It has already been mentioned that The University of British Columbia launched a masters degree in adult education (within the Faculty of Education) in 1957 and that this was the first such program in Canada. This development came about largely due to the initiative of John Friesen, the Director of the Extension Department, and Alan Thomas, who held a joint appointment in the Faculty of Education and the Extension Department. The first degree was awarded in 1960. Thomas headed up the program until 1961, when he left the University, and Coolie Verner then became the Head and first full-time appointment in the academic program. The degree was available only by part-time study for the first several years, but as other staff were added (there are currently eight faculty), full-time study became possible. A doctoral degree was added to the offerings in 1966, with the first such degree being awarded two years later. A Diploma Program was also inaugurated in 1966 and was at first made up of a selection of the graduate courses. In 1980, a special series of undergraduate courses were introduced and formed the Diploma curriculum. Non-credit continuing professional education courses for adult educators were offered regularly, beginning in 1960 administered by the Extension Department. These involved several hundred adult educators each year and during the Seventies and early Eighties included as well a cluster of varied training programs each spring under the title, "Chautauqua by the Pacific."

Training which has relevance for the field of adult education does not by any means all emanate from the adult education program at U.B.C. Individual courses in adult education have been offered for more than ten years at the University of Victoria, and it is possible to earn masters or doctoral degrees at both Victoria and Simon Fraser in other fields, but with some degree of emphasis on adult education. In addition, there is a degree of overlap between aspects of adult education and other fields such as social work, recreation, and of course other specializations within the field of education. A number of Community School co-ordinators, for instance, have been trained in other fields.

Another dimension of training in the field has been represented by the Instructors Diploma Program. When the government began its province-wide system of vocational schools (and subsequently melded most of them with the colleges), they employed as instructors large numbers of qualified journeymen who knew their trades, but had not had training as instructors. The Department of Education provided what was at first called the

Vocational Instructors Program for this group, a series of four courses offered by face-to-face instruction. The Department turned the administration of this program over to the Extension Department of U.B.C. beginning in 1968-69. The name was changed to the Instructors Diploma in 1972, and it remained at the University until 1986, when it was transferred to the Vancouver Vocational Institute. Non-formal training in the field of adult education aimed particularly at those working in business and industry has been provided for some years by both the B.C. Institute of Technology and Vancouver Community College. In addition, Finning Tractor, the B.C. Telephone Co. , the Workers' Compensation Board and other agencies have done a great deal of training for their own personnel and others, in such areas as program development and the instruction of adults.

The graduate program at The University of B.C. has been the major center for research in the province, though much significant work has been done by individuals elsewhere, most notably in the other universities. It is in the nature of graduate programs to generate a major thrust in research. Faculty are expected to maintain a substantial research program and students are required to produce research both within individual courses and as degree requirements in the form of graduating essays, theses and dissertations.

Adult education has clearly become much more professionalized in recent decades than was the case earlier. Some of the significant earmarks of a profession—the complex subject matter, the body of theory and accumulated knowledge, professional training being available—have been developed. A great deal of the thinking about adult education as a field of practice is currently contained within the idea of the delivery of expert services. Many adult educators see it as their task to be proficient in the specialized services they are paid to deliver, be it the design of courses and curricula, the teaching of certain content, the evaluation of programs, or the administration of a service.

There are those who are concerned lest the delivery of expert services of this type become the total pre-occupation of adult educators. Some of these are in what has been termed the "social reformist" tradition of adult education and wish to see the field retain something of the sense of being a movement. To what end? Reverend Moses Coady, the major figure in the internationally famous adult education program based in Antigonish, Nova Scotia, termed it "the high objective of social progress" and he described adult education as "a mass movement of reform." Other, perhaps most, adult educators today see no such social program as inherent in the work that they do and tend to separate the expert services which they render from the ultimate use to which the learner—and society as a whole—put the results of learning. Small wonder, then, that adult education is such a dispersed and disparate enterprise in our society.

VI. The Past as Prologue

It is a familiar maxim that the most dependable way of making a judgment about the capacity of a person or an organization to perform well in the future is to rely not on their promises of marvels they will perform in the years to come, but rather on their past actions. What have they been able to do in meeting challenges and responding to opportunities in the past? It is perhaps appropriate to apply something like the same standard as we now come to contemplate the future of adult education in British Columbia.

There are grounds for expecting great things of adult educators and adult education, relying on past performance as a guide. As we look back over the history of the field in British Columbia, it is clear that there is a record of major achievement in some parts of the field. It is appropriate to identify some of these. All have been mentioned in the previous sections, but are singled out for special mention again here in this final chapter.

First, it should be pointed out that the field as a whole has a remarkable record of vigorous and responsive action. In every national study that has been undertaken, British Columbia has over the years consistently come out at or near the top in terms of participation rates in adult education. In certain sectors of the field such as school board adult education, non-degree aspects of university extension, and English as a second language instruction, there have been periods of time when the work in this province has been the most outstanding in Canada. The field of adult education in British Columbia has attracted a considerable number of creative, energetic and resourceful people who have a long and outstanding record of achievement.

The earliest accomplishment in the field which will be singled out is what was achieved by the Department of Education in the province under the leadershjp of J.W. Gibson and his colleagues in the development of correspondence education. Gibson took charge of this work in 1929 and within a few years, especially after the Liberal government came to power in 1933 and he could count on the support of the Minister of Education, George Weir, Gibson expanded the correspondence course service of the Department considerably, provided a complete high school program, and in other ways as well, made the correspondence courses more relevant and accessible to adults as well as the children of the province, including men in the relief camps. It was in recognition of the outstanding achievement of this work that Gibson was asked to prepare a special appendix to the national survey of adult education which was conducted by the Canadian Association for Adult Education in 1935, and also that the then newly-established international congress on correspondence education held its second world conference in Victoria in the Thirties.

The Fraser Valley Regional Library service was launched in that region in the summer of 1930 under the leadership of Helen Stewart. The project had been conceived by the Public Library Commission of the province, which had also raised funds from the Carnegie Corporation of New York to underwrite the first three years of operation. The important innovation in library service which was involved in the project was that instead of every town in a region developing its own small library collection and service, these things would be done on a regional basis and holdings anywhere in the system were accessible, on call, if necessary, to everywhere else. Such arrangements have long since become a common basis of library development, throughout B.C. and elsewhere in the world, but the demonstration project in the Lower Fraser Valley was an important pioneering venture and Helen Stewart was kept busy travelling to many parts of the world explaining how the new system worked. Locally, the test came in 1934 when the outside funding ran out and the 22 communities involved, in the depth of the depression, had to make a decision at the polls as to whether the regional library system would be assumed as a local tax expense. In 20 of the 22 communities, the answer was yes.

The Community Self-Help program of the Depression and early war years was an example of initiative on the part of a voluntary organization which was supported as well by government resources. It is included here both because of its importance in its own right and also as an example of the admirable readiness of the Department of Education under the leadership of Weir as Minister and Kyle as the official in charge of adult education to respond to the conditions of the times. And the times were terrible, of course. The Great Depression had hit B.C. and Vancouver harder than any other part of Canada. In the year 1933-34, the Vancouver Council of Women began a project of providing material and psychological support to the mothers ot families on relief in the city, forming groups of eight or so mothers who met weekly in homes and there received a combination of practical instruction in such areas as the remaking of clothes, the recovering of furniture and low budget meal planning, etc., and as well had an opportunity for regular social contact with others. To these very practical subjects were added others: instruction in arts and crafts, music and drama groups, and a variety of other activities. The program was described at the time as being aimed at "the prevention of spiritual tragedies" and it was clearly aimed at both practical and morale-boosting goals. By the spring of 1934 there were 257 women participating in the groups. In the following year the Department of Education joined in the effort by providing a back-up administrator for the project, arranging the availability of required space in schools and elsewhere for special events, and paying for a variety of materials which were needed in the work— cloth, printing services, seeds for home gardens, etc. Registration in the program climbed to 1,691 women in the peak year (1937-38) and continued until 1941-42, when there were 1,130 participants. In the final year's report, it was stated that women from 8,000 homes had been involved in the work.

The recently-created Extension Department of The University of British Columbia established a remarkable record of achievement in the latter years of the Thirties. Dr. Gordon Shrum took over the direction of the Department in its second year of operation and in a remarkable burst of leadership, recruited staff and found resources from various sources which made possible the development of adult education services. Dorothy Somerset, who was a drama specialist, developed a multi-faceted service in that field in a remarkably short period, including a play lending library, some hundreds of local play reading groups around the province, a "theater of the air" through which plays were produced on the radio and listening groups (up to 127 at its peak) organized to listen and discuss them, and beginning in 1938, a Summer School of Theater. In addition, she guided the development of work in several other areas of the fine arts. Making use of funds available from the federal government, the Extension Department organized teams of teachers who traveled around the province, spending two weeks in each of the towns which requested their services and conducting Youth Training Schools for unemployed young adults of the area. In the last two years of the decade, some 39 of these short courses were run, with an average attendance of 53, and as well, an annual eight week residential course was established on the campus. Federal funds from another source made possible the launching of an educational program among the fishermen of the province which was devoted to promoting the development of co-operatives in the fishing industry. A number of the larger co-ops in the province owe their origins to this work. A remarkable beginning was made in the field of audio-visual services as well. With support from the National Film Board of Canada and other sources, the major film library in the province was established in the Extension Department and the Department became the organizing center tor the far-flung series of film councils and film circuits which were established under the sponsorship of the Film Board. These are but a few of the services established in a very short period of time in the pre-war years by university extension under Gordon Shrum's leadership. Other accomplishments of national reputation were to follow.

The adult education program of the Vancouver School Board, as the previous pages of this study reveal, could be recognized for a number of important contributions to the field. The emphasis here will be placed on several vital contributions which were made in the span of a very few years in the late Fifties and early Sixties. They have mainly to do with the development of programs which made it possible for adults to complete further academic study, to the grade ten or grade twelve levels especially. Prior to that time, there was a growing consciousness of the need for such educational opportunities, but the path to gaining such qualifications on the part of adults was discouragingly slow, both because the programs available could be taken only on a part-time basis and because adults were still required to complete some course work which might have been relevant to youth still in school but was of little or no relevance to adult students. As a result of continuing negotiations with the Department of Education and the successful demonstration projects such as the Vancouver Experiment and the King Edward Center, which have already been described, the adult education personnel of the Vancouver Board, headed by B.E. Wales, brought about academic programs designed especially for adults and demonstrated the impressive response there was from the community if opportunities for full-time, reasonably rapid progress towards such academic qualifications were available to adults. In the same period also, the Vancouver Board approved and issued its "Guiding Principles" on adult education, the first such declaration from a school board in Canada that it recognized it had a responsibility for the education of adults as well as the children of its district.

One of the most remarkable projects in the field of adult education in the province was the Living Room Learning program run by the Extension Department of The University of B.C. beginning in 1957. Funds secured by the Department from an American foundation, the Fund for Adult Education, made it possible at that time for Extension to employ someone to attempt to establish in the province a network of study-discussion groups for the study of liberal arts subjects. Study-discussion as a methodology relied on groups being formed which would meet regularly to discuss whatever the topic under study was to be. The subject matter of the study course was provided not by expert speakers but by selected readings, which group members read and analyzed before coming to the meeting and then discussed under the guidance of group leaders who were not expert in the subject matter, but who had been given some training in the art of discussion leadership. (The Great Books program was another example of a study-discussion program and began slightly earlier than Living Room Learning, under the auspices of the public library.) It was by no means a foregone conclusion that such a program could be made to work. It required the organization of groups to take part, a formidable problem of recruitment in itself; the finding and training of volunteer discussion leaders (there were no funds to pay them); the recruitment of co-ordinators in various towns of the province (there being an intention from the beginning to make this a province-wide program); the selection of appropriate study courses, including the creation of a series of Canadian programs, much of the other material available originating in the United States and having too American a slant; and the establishment of a province-wide network to sustain the whole operation. Knute Buttedahl, who had been working in the field of human rights education, was recruited by the Department to head up the project and he achieved remarkable results. In the first year of operation the program involved 29 groups in three communities, with 346 participants. By the time Buttedahl left the project in 1961, it was operating in 66 different communities in the province, 126 groups were involved, with 1488 members. The American foundation officer responsible for the project, for which they had given parallel grants to several other institutions in North America, said on several occasions that the foundation achieved more for dollars invested in the program at U.B.C. than they had anywhere else. The program continued under other leadership at U.B.C. until 1964, when it was a victim of the severe budget cuts the University administration imposed on the Extension Department. A brief revival later in the Sixties was of limited success, in its way demonstrating just how essential the special leadership qualities of Knute Buttedahl had been.

Recognition should be accorded to Vancouver Community College for several aspects of its activities on behalf of adult students, but particular reference will be made to its work in the field of English as a second language (ESL), especially in the formative years of the late Sixties and early Seventies. The Vancouver School Board had a long history in the field of ESL, going back to the 1930s. The field began to pick up speed in the Sixties as the federal manpower training authorities began to provide ESL training for some of those who were selected for vocational training. Mel Henderson was in charge of this work for the board, beginning in 1964. He was also a key figure in the establishment of teacher training courses in ESL, which began at U.B.C. in 1966. Pat Wakefield took over the leadership of this work for the board in 1970 but soon thereafter she, and responsibility for ESL, were transferred from the school board to Vancouver Community College. The explosive growth in this work really began in 1972, when it fell into two main divisions—the full-time courses for the federal Manpower students and the half-time and other part-time programs, both on the campus of the college and elsewhere through night classes and through the Neighbourhood English Classes, which were held in many locations throughout the community. In the span of just five years, 1971 to 1975, enrollments in the College's ESL classes increased from just a few hundred to over 3,000—320 of whom were studying English full-time and 1,410 were studying for three hours per day. Night school students had represented the bulk of enrollments until 1972 and stood at 606 by 1974-75. The neighbourhood classes had begun in 1971 and by 1975 enrolled 525 persons in the year. This ESL program was by far the largest in the province, and perhaps in all of Canada. It was meeting the needs of the federal manpower program, which paid all the costs of their students, but also through other financial arrangements and innovative programming on the part of the adult educators involved, it was as well providing a broadly-based community outreach service.

Reference has already been made in an earlier chapter to the outstanding record of service of the Britannia Community Services Center. The achievements of this project should clearly be recognized in this list of outstanding programs in the field, but it is not necessary to repeat some of the information. It should perhaps be said, however, that although in the fields of adult education and social work, there is a great deal of emphasis placed on the need to establish and run programs with, rather than just for the people to be served, Britannia has been more successful in this regard than almost any other project. This is a tribute to careful and skilled planning, and also to the leadership, both lay and professional, which have been demonstrated in the Britannia project since its inception. Michael Clague, the Director of the project for its initial years, has been widely recognized as one of the key factors, if not the key reason, why this was achieved. Britannia provides a number of community services, draws budget from several public sources, and is recognized as a creative and responsive provider of social and educational services to its region.

The Women's Resources Centre, which comes administratively under the Centre for Continuing Education (previously called the Extension Department) of U.B.C. and grew out of its Daytime Program in the mid-Seventies, is located downtown in the City of Vancouver and provides counselling and educational services for women who are considering the course of their lives and preparing themselves for their future activities. There is only one key paid professional staff person employed by the Center and much of the service provided by the program is carried out by trained volunteers. Counselling services of various kinds are provided through the Centre and a large range of group and class programs as well. By the mid-Eighties, the Center was serving approximately 1,400 women per month with their various services. The report for 1985-86 indicated that in that year, the volunteers had provided some 7,000 hours of service to the Center. The Women's Resources Centre has been singled out in international publications as one of the outstanding agencies of its kind in the world and each year it receives visitors from various countries who are wishing to see its work at first hand. Pat Thom, its founder, and Anne Ironside and Ruth Sigal, its directors, have received wide recognition for their contributions to this field.

The final project to be described is very different from the others in that it is a device of government policy, rather than a project which delivers services directly to adult students. It may be seen as representative of the many creative measures adopted by the Continuing Education Division of the provincial Ministry of Education in the period 1977 to 1982, during which it provided such strong leadership in the development of adult education services in the public educational system. It was the conviction of Ron Faris, the head of the Division, that although the public institutions, the school boards and the colleges, were doing much useful work in the provision of adult education in their communities. they were not pursuing as vigorously as they might the provision of service to some of those most in need of them, the educationally disadvantaged. He had in mind particularly the provision of adult basic education, English as a second language for immigrants, and education for the handicapped. The Continuing Education Division was not in a position to tell the institutions "what to do." But they did have some control over the purse strings. So when additional financial resources became available in the system in 1977, rather than put all the funds into the regular grant systems through which adult education in the institutions normally received support, Faris established a "Special Projects Fund." The funds were allotted by college district and could be claimed by either school boards or colleges, but the requests coming from each district had to be co-ordinated at the district level. A small amount of money, some $117,000, was made available in this way in the first, experimental year, but the annual allotment subsequently reached $500,000. These funds could be applied for by institutions and it was made known that they would be made available only if the projects in question were considered to have merit in terms of pioneering new, more effective service to the priority groups referred to above. Advisory panels from the field were recruited to jury the submissions and advise the Continuing Education Division about the grants to be awarded. This administrative device was clearly successful from several points of view. It allowed the Division to have an impact on the directions of innovation in the system, it was successful in stimulating the establishment of new programs and techniques for serving the priority groups, and it brought about the accelerated growth of such work. In the years in which the policy was maintained, programs which were designed to provide educational services to the priority target groups grew at a faster rate than did the field as a whole.

The ten projects just described are of course just ten among many which could have been selected. They seem to this writer to demonstrate some of the characteristics that are required if the field of adult education is to continue to rise to the challenges which lie ahead.

In the record of achievement which is represented by these projects—and many others which have been mentioned in the pages of this study—a number of essential qualities have been demonstrated. First it is clear that adult education in British Columbia has attracted a large number of remarkably able persons to this field of activity. In some cases it would appear that the nature of the field itself, the pleasure of working with adult persons who were seeking to improve their knowledge and skills or to widen the horizons of their lives, was the attraction. For others, what mattered may have been other goals, the attainment of which involved adult education as an instrument. Those other goals have included such things as improving the quality of democratic life in our society, improving the lot of certain groups—women, immigrants, the poor, working men and women, the educationally disadvantaged, or the handicapped—or it may have involved the promotion of certain causes, such as the co-operative movement, cultural development, respect for human rights, environmental concerns, or certain social or philosophical views. It appears that the "great deeds" that have been accomplished in adult education in the province have in every case been accomplished by, and under the direction of, persons of great ability who clearly cared deeply about what they were doing and about the benefits which could flow if they did their work well.

In some, but not all cases, it seemed to be important that the project was based in an agency which was recognized by the community and highly regarded by many. This was not necessarily a public institution, but perhaps we tend to know more about projects in the public sector.

It is worth stressing that the programs and projects which seem to be of importance are in no instances "90 day wonders." They are achievements which have been the result of sustained effort over a period of some years. Here again, the fact that most of the examples chosen were ones based in a organization or institution which had a continuing existence beyond this adult education project being described may be significant. The stability and resources of the sponsoring body may be an important element in making a particular program or project possible. The quality being identified here is that of persistence over a long enough haul to make considerable achievement possible.

Another quality which jumps out from the story of all these projects is competence. In many, but not all cases, one might properly term it professional competence. But in all, the competence was clearly there. If passion were all that were required, this would indeed by a very different list. What has been seen in project after project here was passion coupled with the competence to see the job through.

There is another quality, one perhaps based in part on competence but which goes beyond it. Perhaps the term creativity comes as close as any. The creativity involved in this case, however, is not that of the dreamer; it is rather a kind of applied inventiveness, a response to real life situations. The Britannia Community Services Centre was an original, creative response to a set of circumstances which existed at a certain time and place. What was attempted there was firmly rooted in a knowledge of what was needed and what might be possible. It—and many other projects described in these pages—were examples of what Coady was referring to when he urged his fellow Nova Scotians to "use what they have to secure what they have not."

Singular achievements such as those described in this study were made possible by the efforts of people who cared deeply about what they were engaged in, had the competence to carry it out and the persistence to see it through. Great things do not happen just because some institution or organization decides that something should take place. They happen only when there is a person or a group who will take charge and see the job through.

There are many fine achievements in the record of adult education in this province. There are signs in contemporary society that adult learning, and therefore adult education, are going to be at least as necessary—if not more so—in the future than they have been in the past. How as a society we respond to those needs will depend in large measure on both the quality and commitment of adult educators. In Mao's China, the expression was, "both expert and red." In present day British Columbia, the "red" may not be such a good idea, but the basic notion is the same—both commitment and competence.

Not many of us aspire to great, trail-blazing achievement. We are quiet people, going about our chosen tasks and wishing to perform them in a responsible, competent and in many cases, caring way. But we are ready to salute great achievement when we see it—in the record of the past or when it emerges around us in our own day. The history of any field is largely one of everyday achievement. In the case of adult education in British Columbia, there has been an admirable record of such everyday achievement, and there have been some great deeds done.

All of this promises well for the future. But the events of the Eighties suggest that changes may be on the way which will profoundly affect the field of adult education. There have been—and are—in effect, two "economies" of adult education. There is a sector, in many respects the most visible and best known, which operates largely on the basis of a fee for service economy. As long as institutions retain a policy of adult education having to pay its way financially and as long as decisions as to what services will be delivered and what courses may be held rest on a cost recovery principle, then we are operating within that "break even" economy. Thanks to the resourcefulness of so many adult education "entrepreneurs," very considerable achievements have been realized by such means. The "Robin Hood Principle" whereby profits are made in one part of a program to subsidize something else, is a familiar part of the adult education scene, here as elsewhere.

There is a second economy or sector of adult education, one where much of the cost of providing courses and other services must come from sources other than fees. This is mainly because the persons being served—the poor, the educationally disadvantaged, the unemployed, the handicapped—simply do not have the disposable income which enables them to pay fees which cover costs. In addition, much work with these groups cannot be organized on the basis of mailing a brochure or placing an advertisement in the paper. There is staff time involved for social animation and working intensively with the clientele groups, necessary in order to secure the success of the program, but not recoverable out of student fees. The reader is invited to review the list of significant achievements which are described earlier in this section. Not one of them was, or could have been financed only out of learner fees.

What has been experienced in the depression years of the early 1980s is that the first of the two economies of adult education, although it felt the pinch like everything else, survived. Fees were raised, small classes were cancelled, corners were cut, but programs went on. In the other economy, with subsidies removed or reduced, staff cut back and funds "unearmarked," whole programs for potential learners disappeared, waiting lists to get into many classes became hopelessly long and special provisions for groups requiring special services in many cases totally disappeared. In many instances what is happening is that the private and voluntary sectors are responding as best they can to the needs and we are witnessing a fundamental change in the field of adult education.

We have long been accustomed to the fact that in the world community, in spite of all the efforts to the contrary, the gap between the richer nations and the poorer nations is widening. Within our own society, there is growing recognition that the same thing is happening, and that we will increasingly see a deeply divided society. The "haves" will be able to come to terms with and make their way in the post-industrial, high tech world, and will reap economic rewards. Many other persons and groups either will not have that choice open to them or will reject it, and will suffer certain consequences, poverty and alienation among them.

Adult education as an organized movement has tended to serve those who already have the most formal education. Every participation study ever conducted confirms this fact. It presumably will continue to serve the needs of the "haves" in Canadian society, and also hopefully continue to provide a "second chance" for those who wish to move in that direction.

But a "new" element is emerging in adult education now. The term is put in quotation marks because what now may be seen as new in Canadian adult education is as old as the movement itself, has strong roots in Canada, but may not have been as visible in recent decades as it now is. It has to some extent gone underground while the professionalization and the institutionalization of adult education has taken place. In many parts of the world this sector of adult education is known as "popular education." It leaves institutionalized adult education to do its job, but has little to do with it. It has much in common with the original adult education movement: it seeks a better world, a more just and co-operative society, with adult education being used as one of the instruments to that end. It is based in many organizations and is allied with or part of many citizen groups and movements. It is assuming the name of popular education here too.

Many elements of the story of adult education as presented in these pages fit comfortably within a popular education movement. But the author is very much aware that the projects from the past about which information is available tend rather to be those which are related to the public sector and the large institutions. Much of the giant is indeed invisible.

The events of the Eighties, to some extent building on the Sixties and the years between, appear to indicate that in North America, the mainstream of adult education has lost its capacity to respond to the full range of human concerns. An increasingly professionalized field has developed a capacity to respond relatively effectively to the dominant social and economic elements of our society. It is important that this be done, and done well. The last several decades have witnessed great progress of this kind. But mainstream adult education in Canada appears less able than it once was to serve the needs of all the people. Perhaps it is romanticizing to think that it ever did, though we have some outstanding examples.

There seems strong indication at the present time of an emerging popular education movement in Canada and British Columbia. A history of adult education in our province written some years hence will be able to provide greater perspective on this phenomenon. The history of this field, however, is increasingly becoming two histories, that of institutionalized, professionalized adult education as it emerged in the province over the past thirty years particularly, and a popular education movement which is of the people and is an instrument of spiritual, cultural, social and political change.

Sources and References

A Note About Sources

This monograph is based on sources which have been examined over a period of the last 30 years, but mainly in the latter half of that time. A number of the published works are listed in the bibliography which follows. A note about some other sources which have been used:

Organizational Correspondence/Files: At various times a detailed search has been carried out of the files of certain organizations. Some examples are:

- B.C. Adult Education Council 1954 - 1961
- B.C. Division of C.A.A.E. 1961 - 1972
- U.B.C. President's Office and Faculty of Agriculture re extension work 1915 - 1936
- U.B.C. Extension Department 1936 - 1970
- B.C. Association of Continuing Education Administrators 1965 - 1985

Journals/Newsletters: A large number of journals and newsletters published by organizations of adult educators in BC., the Canadian Association for Adult Education, and both federal and provincial departments of government have been consulted. For the most part, such sources are not listed separately in the bibliography which follows.

Newspapers: Some years ago, I carried out a careful study of newspapers for the pre-1914 period in Victoria, Vancouver, New Westminster, Nanaimo, North and West Vancouver, and Barkerville. Much of this research was reflected in G. Selman (1971a), below. Newspapers have been consulted for specific dates, events, projects, since that time.

Government Department Annual Reports: Many such reports have been consulted over the years. At the federal level, this has included particularly Agriculture, Labor, Secretary of State, Manpower and Immigration, and Canada Employment and Immigration Commission. At the provincial level the emphasis has been on Agriculture, Labor, Education and the Provincial Secretary.

Statistics Canada/Dominion Bureau of Statistics: There is reference in the bibliography below to two particularly significant statistical reports on participation in adult education in Canada, but many others have been consulted, most of them reports on particular sectors of the field. Statistics Canada and its predecessor have not been consistent in their coverage of the field and parallel statistics over even five year periods are not available.

Interviews/Personal Contacts: Having been actively engaged in adult education and in organizations of adult educators, provincial and national, since the early 1950s, and being interested in the history and development of the field from the beginning, I have made notes on events and interviewed key figures from time to time. Information gathered in these ways has inevitably found its way into this study.

Student Research: As a faculty member in the Adult Education program of the Faculty of Education, U.B.C. since 1974, I have had the opportunity of supervising the research of many students who have done historical and related work on the field. A great deal has been learned and recorded as a result of student research, and a number of these studies are listed in the bibliography. Some students have done excellent research for term papers within courses, but though I have profited from some of these, I have not attempted to list them.

Allen, A.T. (1981?), *Forty Years Journey*, Vancouver: Privately printed. n.d.

Allen, R. (1973), *The Social Passion*, Toronto: University of Toronto.

Baehr, M.L. (1983), *Agricultural Extension in B.C.*, Unpublished M.Ed Paper, University of B.C

Bigsby, K.M.(1977), *Continuing Education at Capilano, Douglas and Vancouver Community Colleges*, Unpublished M.Ed. Paper, U.B.C.

B.C. Committee on Continuing and Community Education (1976), *Report*, Victoria: B.C. Ministry of Education.

B.C. Department of Education (1955), *Report of the Provincial Conference of Night School Directors*, Victoria: Department of Education.

B.C. Parent-Teacher Federation (1965?), *History of the Parent-Teacher Movement in B.C.*, Vancouver: B.C.P.T.F., multilith.

B.C. Ministry of Education (1977), *Directory of Provincial Government Adult Education Programs and Services*, Victoria: Ministry of Education.

———. (1981), *Adult Education in British Columbia: A Handbook*, Victoria: Ministry of Education.

B.C. Public Library Commission (1942), *Preliminary Study of Adult Education in B.C.*, Victoria: B.C.P.L.C.

B.C. Royal Commission on Education (1960), *Report*, Victoria: Province of B.C.

B.C. Task Force on the Community College (1974), *Report: Towards the Learning Community*, Victoria: Department of Education.

Brooke, W.M. (1972), *Adult Basic Education*, Toronto: New Press.

Buttedahl, K. (1973), *Living Room Learning in B.C.*, Vancouver: University of B.C. Centre for Continuing Education.

Canada Secretary of State (1984), *One in Every Five*: Ottawa: Secretary of State & Statistics Canada.

Canada, Statistics Canada (1964), *Participants in Further Education in Canada, 1960*, Ottawa: Statistics Canada.

Canadian Association for Adult Education (1982), *From The Adult's Point of View*, Toronto: C.A.A.E.

Carle, J.J. (1982), *Analysis of Member Education: A Study of the CCF Party in B.C.*, Unpublished M.A. Thesis, U.B.C.

Carlisle, M.M. (1986), *Early Agricultural Education in British Columbia: The Pioneering Role of the Farmers' Institutes.* Unpublished M.A. Thesis, U.B.C.

Cassidy, F. (Ed.) (1984), "Creating Citizens," *PACE Papers* 1, Vancouver: Pacific Association for Continuing Education.

Cassidy, F. and Faris, R. (Eds.) (1987), *Choosing Our Future*, Toronto: Ontario Institute for Studies in Education.

Clague, M. et al. (1984), *Reforming Human Services*, Vancouver: University of B.C. Press.

Coady, M.M. (1939), *Masters of Their Own Destiny*, New York: Harper and Bros.

Dampier, L.P. (1977), *Towards a Public Policy for Adult Education in B.C.: A Review,* Unpublished M.Ed. Paper, U.B.C.

———. (1986), *Courage and Conviction: The YMCA in Vancouver 1886 - 1986*, Vancouver: YMCA.

Davison, C.V. (1969), *Survey of Adult Basic Education Instructors*, Unpublished M.A. Thesis, U.B.C.

Dennison, C.J. (1987), "Housekeepers of the Community: The B.C. Women's Institutes 1909 - 1946," in Welton.

Dennison, J.D. and Gallagher, P. (1986), *Canada's Community Colleges*, Vancouver: U.B.C. Press.

Dickinson, G. (1978), *The Undereducated of B.C.*, Vancouver: University of B.C. Department of Adult Education.

Douglas, J. (Ed.) (1959), *Modern Pioneers 1909 - 1959*, Vancouver: B.C. Women's Institutes.

Draper, J.A. (Ed.) (1971), *Citizen Participation: Canada*, Toronto: New Press.

Dupre. J.S. et al. (1973), *Federalism and Policy Development: The Case of Adult Occupational Training in Ontario*, Toronto: University of Toronto.

England, R. (1980), *Living, Learning, Remembering*, Vancouver: U.B.C. Centre for Continuing Education.

Fennema, L.J. (1982), *The History and Development of the Continuing Education Division of Vancouver Community College 1974 - 1981.* Unpublished M.Ed. Paper, U.B.C.

Faris, R. (1975), *The Passionate Educators*, Toronto: Peter Martin.

Fidler, J. (1984), *Program Development Management Systems* (B.C. Telephone Co.)., Unpublished M.Ed. Paper, U.B.C.

Foster, J.K. (1970), *Education and Work in a Changing Society: B.C. 1870 - 1930*, Unpublished M.A. Thesis, U.B.C.

Fournier, R.M.E. (1981). *Educational Brokering and the U.B.C. Women's Resources Center*, Unpublished M.A. Thesis, U.B.C.

———. (1983), *The Third Alternative: Co-ordinating Adult Education in Surrey and Whiterock*, Surrey: Surrey School Board and Kwantlen College.

Gilroy, M. and Rothstein, S. (Eds), *As We Remember It*, Vancouver: University of B.C. Press.

Gibson, B.C. (1961), *Teacher-Builder: The Life and Work of J. W. Gibson*, Victoria: Privately Printed.

Gray, C.W. (1973), *Movies for the People*, Montreal: National Film Board.

Hacker, G.C. (1933), *The Methodist Church in B.C. 1859 - 1900*, Unpublished B.A. Thesis, U.B.C.

Harrison, M.J. (1975), *The Social Influence of the United Church of Canada in B.C. 1930 - 1948*, Unpublished M.A. Thesis, U.B.C.

Harrison, N. (1981), *Continuing Education Relationship between the College and School Districts of the Douglas Region*, Victoria: Ministry of Education.

Harshaw, J.P. (1966), *When Women Work Together* (YWCA), Toronto: Ryerson.

Hellaby, H.A. (1925), *Oriental Missions in B.C.*, London: Society for the Propagation of the Gospel in Foreign Parts.

Hill, A.V. (1967), *Tides of Change*, Vancouver: Prince Rupert Fishermen's Co-op. Association.

Hodgson, P. (1987), *Project Literacy B.C.*, Unpublished M.Ed. Paper, U.B.C.

Holmes, M. (1959), *Library Services in B.C.*, Victoria: Public Library Commission.

Hunt, A.l. (1987), *Mutual Enlightenment in Early Vancouver*, Unpublished Ed. D. Dissertation, U.B.C.

Innis, M.Q. (1949), *Unfold the Years: A History of the YWCA in Canada*, Toronto: McLelland and Stewart.

Ivany, J.W.G. and Manley-Casimir, M.E. (Eds.) (1981), *Federal-Provincial Relations: Education Canada*, Toronto: Ontario Institute for Studies in Education.

James, A. (1975), *The Women's Resources Center - 1974*, Unpublished M.A. Thesis, U.B.C.

Johnson, F.H. (1964), *A History of Public Education in B.C.*, Vancouver: U.B.C. Press.

———. (1981), *John Jessop: Goldseeker and Educator*, Vancouver: Mitchell Press.

Jothen, K. (1985), *Employer-Sponsored Training: Analysis of the B.C. Electronics Industry*, Unpublished M.A. Thesis, U.B.C.

Kalef, R.H. (1984), *Betsy MacDonald: Adult Educator*, Unpublished M.Ed. Paper, U.B.C.

Kidd, J. R. (Ed.) (1950), *Adult Education in Canada*, Toronto: CAAE.

Kidd, J. R. (Ed.) (1963), *Learning and Society*, Toronto: CAAE.

——. and Selman, G. (Eds.) (1978), *Coming of Age*, Toronto: CAAE.

Kidd, N.L. (1985), *Curriculum Development in Adult Basic Education in B C.*, Unpublished M.Ed. Paper, U.B.C.

Knox, D. (1982), *The Distance Education Services of the B.C Institute of Technology 1973 - 1981*, Unpublished M.Ed. Paper, U.B.C.

Kulich, J. (1971), "Training for Adult Educators and Research in Adult Education at the University of British Columbia, Canada," in *Yearbook of Adult Education 1971*, Heidelberg: Quelle & Meyer, 33-54.

——. (Ed.) (1976), *Former U.B.C. Extension Directors Reminisce 1936 - 1976*, Vancouver: University of B.C. Center for Continuing Education.

——. (Ed.) (1986), *Adult Educators and Their Associations*, Vancouver: Pacific Association for Continuing Education (PACE Papers 2).

MacPherson, I. (1979), *Each for All*, Toronto: MacMillan of Canada.

McBride, B.E. (1982), *An Analysis of the Factors Affecting the Re-Entry Process of Mature Women*, Unpublished M.Ed. Paper, U.B.C.

Macdonald, J.B. (1962), *Higher Education in B.C. and a Plan for the Future*, Vancouver: University of B.C.

McGechaen, A. (1971), *Role of the National Film Board in Adult Education in B.C. 1942 - 1970*, Unpublished M.A. Thesis, U.B.C.

Mugridge, I. and Kaufman, D. (Eds.) (1986), *Distance Education in Canada*, London: Croom Helm.

Nitkin, B. (1982), *The Open Learning Institute: Origins and Development*, Unpublished M.Ed. Paper, U.B.C.

Ormsby, M. (1964), *British Columbia: A History*, Toronto: MacMillan of Canada.

Peake, F.A. (1959), *The Anglican Church in B.C.*, Vancouver: Mitchell Press.

Powell, M.P. (1967), *Response to the Depression: Three Representative Women's Groups in B.C.*, Unpublished M.A. Thesis, U.B.C.

Ouinn, M.F. (1988), *A History of the Pacific Association for Continuing Education 1972 - 1987*, Unpublished M.Ed. Paper, U.B.C.

Roberts, P. (1981), *Inter-Agency Co-ordination of Adult Education in North Vancouver*, Unpublished M.Ed. Paper, U.B.C.

Robinson, D.J. (1986), *Continuing Education in a Professional Nursing Association*, Unpublished M.A. Thesis, U.B.C.

Rouillard, H. (1952), *Pioneers in Adult Education in Canada*, Toronto: Thomas Nelson & Sons.

Sandiford, P. (Ed.) (1935), *Adult Education in Canada: A Survey*, Toronto: University of Toronto.

Selman, G. (1963), *A History of the Extension and Adult Education Services of the University of B.C. 1915 to 1955*, Unpublished M.A. Thesis, U.B.C.

———. (1966), *A History of Forty Years of Extension Service by the University of B.C. 1915 - 1965*, Toronto: CAAE.

———. (1969), *Toward Co-operation: The Development of a Provincial Voice for Adult Education in B.C. 1953 - 1962*, Vancouver: University of B.C. Centre for Continuing Education.

———. (1971a), *Some Aspects of the History of Adult Education in B.C. before 1914*, Unpublished manuscript, University of B.C. Centre for Continuing Education.

———. (1971b), "Adult Education in Barkerville 1863 to 1875," *BC Studies*, 9: 33-54.

———. (1971c), "Mechanics' Institutes in B.C", *Continuous Learning*, 10 (3): 126-131.

———. (1971d), "Origins of Public Locally Sponsored Evening Classes in B.C.," *Continuous Learning*, 10 (4): 199-207.

———. (1975a), *Adult Education in Vancouver before 1914*, Vancouver: University of B.C. Center for Continuing Education.

———. (1975b), *A Decade of Transition: The Extension Department of U.B.C. 1960 to 1970*, Vancouver: U.B.C. Center for Continuing Education.

———. (1976), *Adult Education in B.C. During the Depression*, Vancouver: University of B.C. Centre for Continuing Education.

———. (1977), *A Chronology of Adult Education in B.C.*, Vancouver: University of B.C Centre for Continuing Education.

———. (1980), *The B.C. Division of the Canadian Association for Adult Education 1961 - 1971*, Vancouver, PACE Occasional Paper No. 7.

———. (1984), "Government's Role in Adult Education 1933-39 and 1976-83." In Cassidy (1984), 4-34.

———. (1987a), "Adult Education and Citizenship." In Cassidy and Faris (1987), 36-49.

———. (1987b), "The Fifties: Pivotal Decade in Canadian Adult Education," *Canadian Journal for the Study of Adult Education*, 1 (1): 5-24.

Sparkes, R.G. (1977), *Adult Education, Community Development and the Challenge for Change Program*, Unpublished M. Ed. Paper, U.B.C.

Shaw, R.L. (1957), *Proud Heritage*, Toronto: Ryerson.

Skolrod, A.H. (1967), *The B. C. Teachers' Federation*, Unpublished Ed.D. Thesis, University of Oregon.

Thomas, Audrey, (1976), *Adult Basic Education and Literacy Activities in Canada 1975-76*, Toronto: World Literacy of Canada.

———. (1983), *Adult Literacy in Canada*, Ottawa: Canadian Commission for UNESCO.

Thornton, J. (1971), "Adult Education in B.C.," *Journal of Education*, No 18 (special issue) University of B.C.

U.B.C. Adult Education Research Center (1973), *Pioneering a Profession*, Vancouver: University of B.C. AERC.

Verner, C. (Ed.) (1964), "Adult Education in B.C.", *Journal of Education*, No.10 (special issue).

Verner, C. and Dickinson, G. (1974), *Union Education in Canada*, Ottawa: Labour Canada.

Wales, B.E. (1958), *The Development of Adult Education in B.C.*, Unpublished Ed.D. Thesis, Oregon State University

Welton, M. (Ed.) (1987), *Knowledge for the People*, Toronto: Ontario Institute for Studies in Education.

Wilson, J.D., Stamp, R.M. and Audet. L-P.(Eds) (1970), *Canadian Education: A History*, Scarborough: Prentice-Hall.

Witter, S.R. (1979), *Historical Study of Adult Education in the Women's Institutes of Canada and the YWCA of Canada 1870 - 1978*, Unpublished M.Ed. Paper, U.B.C.

Vainstein, R. (1966), *Public Libraries in B.C.*, Victoria: Public Libraries Research Study.

Young, W.D. (1969), *The Anatomy of a Party: The National CCF 1932 - 1961*, Toronto: University of Toronto.

Originally published by University of British Columbia Center for Continuing Education, No. 25 (1988), *Occasional Papers in Continuing Education*. Reprinted with permission.

Government's Role in Adult Education: Two Periods of Active Leadership in British Columbia, 1933 - 1939 and 1976 - 1983

A review of the history of adult education in the province of British Columbia makes it clear that there have been two periods during which the government, through the Department (now the Ministry) of Education, has played a particulatly vigorous and prominent part in the evolution of the field. The first of these occurred during the latter portion of the 1930s, when measures were taken to help British Columbians cope with the devastating effects of the Depression. The second commenced in the late 1970s and continued up to the fall of 1983. As a result of vigorous policy and professional leadership from the Ministry during these periods, the quality and outreach of adult education in the province was materially advanced.

This article describes the role of government leadership, the methods employed and something of the impact which government had on the field in these two periods. The intention is not to provide a detailed history of adult education in these years. Rather, it is to assess the relationships between the government and the field. Even so, little reference is made to the impact of government departments, other than Education, in areas such as vocational training.

The adult education scene in British Columbia was very different in these two periods. In the mid-Thirties, participation in publicly-sponsored adult education activities was still at a very modest level. A number of school boards in the province (66 in 1929, for instance), ran small "night school" programs, as they were called then. The Department of Education had established a program of correspondence courses which was attracting increasing numbers of adults. There was, as yet, no system of community colleges, however, and the province's only university, prior to an influx of foundation funds in the middle of the decade, maintained only a modest extension service. There were few, if any full-time adult educators. In Canada, at least, the education of adults had yet to become the object of research and professional training. For the officer responsible for night schools in the Department of Education, this was only a part-time commitment.

By the mid-Seventies, the picture was very different. The publicly-sponsored adult education system in the province was a major enterprise. School board sponsored programs, of which B.C. had more during the Sixties than any other province, had been reduced somewhat as some boards turned their responsibilities in this area over to the community colleges. They were still a major part of the system, however. The colleges, which had begun to develop in 1965, were, by a decade later, serving almost every region of the province and maintaining substantial adult education programs. There were three public universities, all of which were actively engaged in adult education. There were, as well, a growing number of special purpose post-secondary institutions, the largest being the British Columbia Institute of Technology. The Ministry of Education was soon to create a Division of Continuing Education with a senior official at its head. The field of adult education was becoming professionalized and there were several associations of adult educators in the province. Professional training for the field was available at the undergraduate and graduate levels at the University of British Columbia.

In the 1930s, adult education, both here in British Columbia and in North America as a whole, was in its infancy as a professional field and as an aspect of government-sponsored services. Forty years later, the field had come of age in many respects and the public educational system was providing services used annually by hundreds of thousands of adults.

The two periods discussed in this article have not been the only ones during which effective leadership has been provided by government in the field of adult education. This is far from the case. As early as 1913, the Department of Education appointed a person of outstanding ability, John Kyle, as Director of Technical and Adult Education. Kyle had earlier been the leader of the pioneering school board adult education program in Vancouver. He was effective, over the time during which he was in charge of this work, in encouraging other boards to program for adults.

A further substantial step forward was taken by the government in the early 1950's, under the vigorous leadership of Mr. Laurie Wallace (later to go on to high posts in the civil service of the province). At this time, adult education work was combined with the recreation service. Both advanced rapidly. It was not until 1962, however, that an officer of the department was able to devote full time to the supervision and promotion of adult education. Although useful work was done, he and his successor were relatively minor officials and had very limited resources available. The late Fifties and Sixties were, nevertheless, a period of major growth in school board adult education (Cartier, 1971).

Special circumstances during the two periods being described in this study made possible major steps forward in publicly-sponsored adult education. In both cases, there were Ministers of Education who were genuinely interested in the work, albeit for different reasons. In addition, the climate was right for an expansion and basic change in adult education services. Greatly increased resources were made available, particularly in the second period.

The Morale of the People: 1933-1939

The 1930s are synonymous with the Great Depression. The Twenties had been prosperous times for British Columbia on the whole, especially following the sharp, but brief, recession of the first two years of the decade. The Depression, when it came full force, hit British Columbia particularly hard. In common with the rest of Western Canada, the nature of the province's economy, with its heavy reliance on primary resources and exports, was such that it was especially vulnerable to the forces at work. The policies which were adopted by the federal government to combat the depression were such that the burden fell especially heavily on the West, and, in particular, on the agricultural and the export industries of B.C. By the time the census was taken in 1931, 25.06 per cent of wage earners in B.C. were unemployed, a higher figure than in any other province. This figure almost doubled by 1933, at the depth of the Depression.

It has been suggested that the development of adult education in Canada, and elsewhere, has taken place in distinct phases and that important new programs and periods of growth have come about as responses to national crises (Thomas 1961). Just as the individual adult seems to experience certain "teachable moments" at times of challenge or change in life, so nations rise to the challenges they face, in part by means of new government programs designed to assist men and women to cope with the needs of the times. It can be amply demonstrated that during the Depression, surely one of the most traumatic events in Canadian experience, there was such a response. Both senior levels of government and a range of local agencies initiated educational programs in an effort to help people cope with distress and demoralization. The provincial government, especially after the Liberals came to power in late 1933, responded by strengthening vocational and academic educational opportunities for adults, launching the Provincial Recreation Program, which was the first of its kind in Canada, and supporting the related efforts of a variety of voluntary associations.

The most important feature of the 1930s, with respect to the development of adult education, was the broadening of both the extent and purpose of public provision. The extent of government's role, and that of government supported public educational institutions, increased greatly. In the field of vocational education, for example, provision by both senior levels of government became the dominant factor. Especially during these years, it was government which had the funds. There also was increasing support for the idea that government had the major responsibility for ameliorating the harmful effects of the Depression.

The purposes as well as the extent of public provision were expanded in this period. Prior to this time government had seen its role in adult education to be largely in the field of remedial education and occupational training. Now there developed an increased willingness, in response to the distress and dislocation caused by the Depression, to relate adult education to the general welfare or "morale" of the population. Previously such considerations tended to be the concern of voluntary and private service organizations. Now government demonstrated a readiness to cater to the needs of the whole person, to be concerned with how the individual felt about self and society.

Presumably such a change in orientation did not result from pure and wholly altruistic concerns for the citizen's welfare. In part, at least, it was a response to the frightening realities of depression conditions. It was clear that if steps were not taken to ameliorate the situations in which so many people found themselves, there might be an inclination for them to adopt radical approaches aimed at changing existing social and economic arrangements drastically. While there was, of course, genuine concern about human suffering and misfortune, there was also political concern about the stability and perpetuation of existing systems. Accordingly, the public services went beyond social or citizenship concerns. Public participation and funding were extended into education for personal self-development and the cultivation of the liberal arts. By the end of the decade public adult education services had not only greatly increased in volume but also were extended over a much wider range of concerns.

The Conservative Tolmie government, which was in office from mid-1928 to late 1933, took few, if any, significant steps in the field of adult education. The government headed by T.D. Patullo, which held office throughout the balance of the decade, introduced a number of important new programs. The key figure in this connection was Dr. George M. Weir, the Provincial Secretary and Minister of Education. Weir, known as a progressive in his approach to educational matters, had been principal of the Normal School in Saskatoon before joining The University of British Columbia as professor of education in 1924. In his history of education in British Columbia, F. Henry Johnson (1964) describes Weir as a "dynamic crusader" and quotes Bruce Hutchison's description of him as having "the zeal of a real reformer."

Weir's interest in adult education had been clearly demonstrated before he entered the government. As early as 1930, in his speeches about the future of education in the province, he stressed the importance of adult education (Vancouver *Sun* April 3, 1980; March 9, 1932). Johnson refers to Weir as "the great champion of adult education in British Columbia." During his time as Minister of Education, several significant measures in this field were enacted or implemented by the government. These included a major expansion of correspondence courses into areas of particular interest to adults; the development of a number of programs designed to serve the unemployed; the introduction of the Provincial Recreation program; the appointment of a provincial advisory committee on adult education to guide the development of services to the unemployed; the creation of the Department's community drama program and the co-sponsorship, with the private sector, of several programs, most notably "Self-Help."

Weir gave strong support to John Kyle's promotion of local school board night schools (Wales 1958). Weir also had a strong influence on the decision by the University during the middle years of the decade first to experiment with an expanded program of university extension and then to create a department to give continuing direction to this work (Selman 1963). He was also a close associate of Dr. E.A. Corbett, the director of the newly-established national association for adult education, and played an active part in the development of that body (Faris 1975a).

Although the initiatives of the provincial ministry took various forms, only a few examples will be described here, each revealing a different aspect of the willingness to respond to the urgent needs of people facing the economic and social crisis. This account will not deal with such significant matters as efforts to increase the availability of vocational education, the expansion of provincial library services and the influence of night school programs.

1. Education in the relief camps

A distinctive, some would say notorious, feature of the Depression years was the role of the relief camps throughout Canada. Single and transient men were housed and engaged in public works projects in return for room and board, clothing and a minimal per diem allowance. Most of the camps in B.C., as elsewhere, were located in remote areas. There was much discontent in the camps. Strikes, acts of violence and other forms of protest were common.

The federal officials who were responsible for the installations encouraged the provinces to send teachers into them. The response in British Columbia was significant, but hardly in keeping with the need. The two main educational efforts consisted of the operation of "schools" in four of the larger camps and the provision of correspondence courses free of charge wherever there was interest in them. The schools were supervised by a single teacher in each centre. In 1934 there were 146 students in the four schools. J.W. Gibson (1935), the Director of high school correspondence work, described activities in the camps in the spring of 1935 in this way:

> In two of the larger camps resident instructors were employed whose business it was to supervise the studies of the men in connection with their correspondence courses, and to look after books and other educational equipment supplied. In each of the two camps referred to a separate building for study purposes was erected and a third one is nearing completion. The Department of Education supplied all camp students with free books and equipment loaned out to them through the camp foreman.

Correspondence instruction in the camps began as a voluntary effort on the part of instructors at Vancouver Technical School. These instructors offered, in December, 1933, to prepare and mark correspondence courses to be organized through the Department of Education for men in the camps. Things moved quickly. By mid-January, nearly 350 men had registered. In the end, a total of 1,347 men took correspondence courses under this scheme, a combination of volunteer effort and Departmental support and organization.

2. Educational relief measures outside the camps

In addition to the special provisions which the provincial government made for men in the relief camps, it undertook several kinds of special educational programs for those on relief who were not in camps. Such activity did not begin until the Liberal government came to power in late 1933. Soon after entering office, George Weir appointed a committee known as the "Adult Education, British Columbia" committee to oversee and co-ordinate activities for the unemployed undertaken by the Department. John Kyle was a member of the committee and directed the activities which were conducted under its auspices.

The first mention of specific measures involving education for the unemployed appeared in the Department's report for 1933-34. There it was reported that classes for the unemployed, organized in co-operation with local school boards, had been held in three centres and attended by 360 persons. The Department also co-operated with the Department of Mines, in response to the great interest in gold mining at the time, in offering courses of 20 lectures in 22 centres (again, through local night school programs) to a total of 2,136 students. This program was continued in three subsequent years with registrations of 1,174; 1,454 and 893 respectively.

In the year 1934-35, Kyle's report on the work conducted under the Adult Education Committee described classes on vocational subjects which were conducted, for the most part, in school buildings. Centres were located in Vancouver (5), North Vancouver (2), West Vancouver, New Westminster and Victoria (1 each). Courses in English (for New Canadians) and Spanish were the only non-vocational subjects. Other subjects included auto mechanics, cabinet making, clothing, home economics, etc. There had also been a series of radio lectures sponsored by the committee on "The Social Problems of British Columbia" and a night class course on economics, given in Vancouver. Similar programs were offered in subsequent years, the volume diminishing as emergency wartime programs came into effect.

Reference should also be made to a series of training courses for household helpers which were co-sponsored by the Young Women's Christian Association (Y.W.C.A.) of Vancouver and the Department of Education. The program was initiated in early 1934 by the Y.W.C.A., at first as a one-day-a-week program for five weeks and, subsequently, for twelve weeks . By the time the third series began the following year, the Department had joined as a sponsor, paying the salary of the teacher. Participants in the program were referred by welfare agencies at the outset. As time went on, the Y.W.C.A., which was heavily engaged in other projects involving contacts with unemployed women, tended to recruit more of the students on its own. The program carried on until 1936 at least. It was a further significant example of government working in combination with voluntary organizations.

3. Self-Help

One of the most interesting and important adult education programs in the Thirties was the Self-Help movement, which operated in the Vancouver area. It was directed to women and families in distress as a result of the depression. It involved a beneficial and perhaps unique partnership between voluntary organizations, individuals and government, the latter paying much of the bill. Self-Help was predominantly non-vocational in its emphasis. It was directed at both increasing the morale of those enrolled, through association with others and through instruction in arts and crafts, drama and other fields, and at teaching skills for the homemaker which would enable her to carry out her duties more effectively and economically.

Self-Help had its origins in the work of the Vancouver Council for Women. During the year 1933-34, the Council organized a new program for mothers of families on relief. Those who joined were formed into groups of eight and given instruction in sewing, knitting and/or quilting, the materials being provided by the Council. As noted in the Council's minutes, the objective of the works was "the prevention of spiritual tragedies through fear and suffering" (Powell 1967). A great deal of emphasis was placed on social as well as instructional aspects of group activities.

By the spring of 1934, there were 257 women participating in the program. The work had started out under the direct sponsorship of the Council of Women but in May of 1935 a separate organization, the Community Self-Help Association, was formed. This step appears to have been taken to facilitate relations with the provincial government, which by this time had adopted the project, bringing it under the auspices of the Adult Education Committee. Several references are made over the years in the departmental reports to the aims of the program. The most expansive of these appeared in 1938-39:

> Under the stress of present social and economic forces families feel isolated, lonely and discouraged, and tend to become apathetic or actively anti-social. Through membership in the ninety groups of our organization they acquire various skills, broaden their outlook, make new friends, and find an outlet for energies of mind and heart.

Instructional activities were carried out through Self-Help Centres, with space being made available, free of charge, in schools, and through Self-Help groups which met in people's homes. They were concerned, for the most part, with the teaching of skills in several domestic arts as well as related arts and crafts. The groups generally met weekly.

They were kept small, each led by a volunteer. Monthly "rallies" were usually held at a nearby school and involved all the small groups in the region. Speakers on educational and cultural subjects were heard, handicrafts exhibited, and on occasion, choral and dramatic works performed by member groups.

Total registration began at 430 in 1934-35, climbed to 1,691 in the peak year (1937-38) and gradually declined to 1,130 in the final year of operation (1941-42). Main school centres numbered three in the first year and were up to 16 or 17 for most years thereafter. The number of small groups was stated to be 65 in 1936-37, the only year for which a figure was given.

4. Provincial Recreation Program

One of the best known programs inaugurated in B.C. during the decade was the Provincial Recreation Program or "Pro-Rec" movement. Weir announced the commencement of the new service in November of 1934. In the words of the Department's annual report (1934-35):

> The aims and objects of the new work were to protect the youths of British Columbia from degenerating effects caused by enforced idleness and to build up the morale and character which rest on a good physical basis.

Classes were held in school buildings and other appropriate facilities which could be made available, such as church and community halls, as well as swimming pools. In its peak year, 1938-39, the program operated in 114 centres and served 21,493 people, 9,141 of whom were unemployed. The program included a wide range of physical activity for both sexes, mainly team sports (volleyball, basketball, soccer, etc.) as well as gymnasium and pool exercise activities (calisthenics, dancing, apparatus work, boxing, etc.). In addition, an increasing amount of summer outdoor activity was added each year. Although much of the work was purely recreational, a great deal of emphasis was placed on instruction in the various areas. There was also considerable in-service training for the staff.

In some respects, the most interesting aspect of the Pro-Rec movement was that it represented both a type of activity and a reason for undertaking it which extended the services of government in the field of education into new areas. The stated purpose for this new program was frankly described as an effort to boost the morale of the population. This was both a sign of the times and an important extension of government's reasons for involvement in adult education activity.

5. Community Drama

In 1937 the Department of Education created a School and Community Drama Branch. It was intended to stimulate interest in drama, particularly in rural communities, and beyond that "to teach discrimination between worthy and unworthy use of leisure and to provide for the enjoyment of leisure" (Johnson 1964). The Department divided the province into 15 "drama districts" and each had its own annual drama festival. There were 177 adult community drama groups and 86 high school clubs active in the peak year of this work (Vancouver *Sun*, October 20, 1939). When the drama activity under the sponsorship of the Department is added to the somewhat parallel work sponsored in this period by The University of B.C.'s Extension Department, it represents a remarkable flowering of interest and participation in this field at the close of the decade.

Although information about adult education development in the Thirties is fragmentary, there were two general surveys carried out—in 1935 and at the end of the period—which provide something of an overview. In 1934, meetings were held in Toronto aimed at creating a national organization to serve and promote the interests of adult education in Canada (Corbett 1957; Faris 1975; Selman 1981). It was decided, in order to determine the extent of adult education in the country, to carry out a national survey, under the general direction of Dr. Peter Sandiford. In his comments in the report, Sandiford took the general position that adult education was to be "the next general forward step in government service to the people" and that government should play a leadership and co ordinating role. He saw one of the chief purposes of adult education as "the solution of the great problem—how to restore, maintain and enhance the morale of the people" (Sandiford, 1935).

Just after the end of the decade, the British Columbia Public Library Commission carried out a survey of adult education at the request of the Minister of Education and published its findings and recommendations in *A Preliminary Study of Adult Education in British Columbia: 1941*. This was the most thorough survey ever undertaken of adult education in the province. What is perhaps most impressive about this report, apart from the vast amount of activity it reflects, is the belief expressed that adult education should in the future become organized at the provincial level on a scale comparable with in-school education and that such a system should seek to support all aspects of adult development.

The Library Commission, like Peter Sandiford, was in favor of strong leadership and co-ordination from the government. Its recommendations called for legislation to create a Division of Adult Education in the Department, the appointment of a Director who was professionally qualified in adult education, and the creation of a Council of Adult Education which would determine policies and on which a variety of community organizations, public and private, would be represented. Perhaps because the country was plunged into the war by the time the report was published, the recommendations were not acted upon, and indeed more than 40 years later are still in many respects ahead of their time. Nevertheless, changes brought about in the second of the periods to be studied in this article have brought adult education as close to the vision outlined those many decades ago as we have ever been.

Moulding the System: 1976-1983

The social and economic scene in British Columbia in this recent period has been, for the most part, different from that of the depression years. British Columbia's heavily resource-based economy performed well during the latter half of the Seventies but was especially vulnerable, as it had been in the 1930s, to the economic downturn in the 1980s. Unemployment (in common with the rest of Canada), took a sharp upward turn in the mid-Seventies (Deaton 1983). As the effects of the recent sharp depression were felt this situation became even more extreme. Unemployment rates were much worse than the national average and substantially greater than in the other "have" provinces. Because of the beneficial effects of welfare legislation, federal and provincial, which had been put in place in intervening years, there was not, however, the same degree of desperate poverty and suffering in this recent Depression as there was in the 1930s.

Summing up economic developments during 1983, Peter Newman pointed out that "two separate societies" were evolving in Canada (1984). One is involved in new, "high tech" development and has benefitted from the economic recovery of 1983. The other has experienced little or no recovery, continues to have high levels of unemployment, and has limited prospects for long-term improvement. This has been the case for many British Columbia communities.

The same dichotomy persists in the field of adult education. Those who already have a relatively advanced level of education know how to take advantage of the educational services available. They have the income to enable them to take advantage of the "enrollment economy" sectors of the field, that is, those programs which pay for themselves largely out of student fees. Those who do not know how to "work the system" are not as efficient and motivated in seeking out educational opportunities. The more heavily subsidized services in the field, adult basic education and English as a second language, are most relevant to many in this group. It is these services which have been drastically reduced as a result of budgetary restraint and the relatively low priority accorded them by government and educational institutions. There are, indeed, two societies in adult education.

When compared with the 1930s, adult education in British Columbia has been strikingly different in this recent period. This has been especially true of the public sector. In the Thirties there were few if any full-time workers in the field and few who identified themselves as adult educators. By the mid-Seventies, there were many hundreds who did so. A major expansion in adult education offerings by school boards took place in the latter half of the 1950s. Throughout the Sixties, British Columbia led the nation in this aspect of the work.

With the creation of the college system in the province, beginning in 1965, some boards turned the work over to the new institutions, but the combined total of registrations in the college and school board programs increased steadily. By the program year 1975-76, college development in the province was virtually complete. In that year, 31 school boards offering programs attracted approximately 141,000 registrations and the 14 colleges, approximately 98,500. The B.C. Institute of Technology and the three public universities also had large and growing adult education programs by this time, The University of British Columbia having by far the largest.

Increasing numbers of persons in the province were working part or full-time in adult education and many of these consciously associated themselves with the field. An adult education association had begun as a co-ordinating council of agencies in 1954. It became a personal membership association in 1962, being known as the B.C. Division of the Canadian Association of Adult Education (CAAE). Beginning in 1955, those responsible for school board adult education met periodically. In 1965 they formed an organization concerned largely with administrative matters. As the college system developed, college-based adult educators joined with their school board colleagues in the membership of this organization, which was called the B.C. Association of Continuing Education Administrators (BCA-CEA).

With the dramatic expansion of technical and vocational education following the federal legislation in this field in 1960 and 1967, the number of professionals engaged in that sector of adult education grew rapidly. A national organization, the Canadian Vocational Association, was formed in 1963. In the following year a B.C. provincial chapter was organized. Discussions took place in the early 1970s aimed at an amalgamation of this body, the BCA-CEA and the B.C. Division of the CAAE. The result was the formation of the Pacific Association for Continuing Education. In the end, BCA-CEA decided to become affiliated with the new organization while maintaining a separate existence as well. Other, more specialized organizations, interested areas such as industrial training and English as a second language, also were formed. A further contributing factor to the professionalization of the field was the inauguration, in 1957, of a graduate degree program by The University of British Columbia. This was the first such program in Canada.

In 1972 the government of Premier W.A.C. Bennett was defeated at the polls by the New Democratic Party (NDP) under the leadership of David Barrett. During the approximately three years the NDP government remained in office, few if any major initiatives were taken in the field of adult education. Several measures in related areas had an impact on the field, however. The government appointed a Task Force on the Community College in late 1973. Submitted the following year, the Task Force's report charted the further expansion of the college system and placed great emphasis on the adult education mission of the colleges (Report, Task Force on the Community College, 1974).

The number of colleges in the province was increased from nine to fourteen by the NDP. All parts of the province were brought within the service area of a college. This development provided a basis for an expanded service to adults. The number of college adult education registrations almost doubled in the three years. With respect to the universities, the government announced that it had a particular interest in any proposals which would increase the outreach activities of these institutions. In pursuing this goal, the government provided designated funding for a number of projects, most of which were in the field of adult education.

The Barrett government also appointed a Commissioner of Education, John Bremer, whose task it was to stimulate change in the educational system. Although little if any of his work was directed specifically at adult education, the atmosphere created by the activity of such a "change agent" encouraged and stimulated all parties interested in change in the educational system. Not many months before Bremer was summarily dismissed by the government, he brought Dr. Ron Faris in as his assistant. A British Columbian, Faris had provided leadership in the development of community colleges and educational media in Saskatchewan. He "survived" both the Bremer firing and the change of government in 1975 and was to become a key figure in the subsequent development of adult education in the province.

Finally, with respect to the impact of the NDP administration on the development of adult education, it should be mentioned that a month before the defeat of the government, Eileen Dailly, the Minister of Education, made a major policy speech in which she stated it was the intention of the Ministry to "implement a policy of recurrent education for the Province of British Columbia" (Dailly, 1975).

The activities of the Commissioner of Education and the apparent openness of the NDP government to suggestions for change encouraged provincial adult education organizations to make major recommendations for improvements in the system. In October 1973 the twenty professional staff members of the University of B.C. Centre for Continuing Education submitted a 35 page brief, containing 28 recommendations, to the Commissioner of Education. The major recommendations endorsed lifelong learning as the major planning concept. They also called upon the government to give increased priority to continuing education and to create an "advisory council or board to assist with the development of this sector" (U.B.C. Centre for Continuing Education, 1973).

The BCA-CEA was also active in advocacy activity in this period, making several submissions. The first, submitted in April, 1973 was on finance and administration. The next was in February 1974 on the structure of the Department of Education in relation to adult education. In December of that year a further submission suggested that a commission be established to study the field as well as make recommendations for future development and policies. More detailed suggestions about the proposed commission, offered at the request of the Minister, were submitted in May, 1975 (Submissions 1973, 1974; Letter, G.A. Thom, President of BCA-CEA, to Hon. E. Dailly May 6, 1975).

The most comprehensive submission in this period came from the Association for Continuing Education, soon renamed the Pacific Association for Continuing Education (PACE). This brief was submitted in January 1974. Entitled *Organizing for Lifelong Learning*, the statement made sixteen major recommendations, among them the restructuring of the Department of Education in order to provide leadership in the field. Co-ordination for a "system" of adult education for the province was also recommended as was the publication of a policy statement by the Department "which places continuing education as a full partner with other forms of publicly supported education" (Association for Continuing Education, 1974).

It appears from the correspondence of the period that Dailly was considering the appointment of a commission or task force to undertake a study of adult or continuing education. No such action was taken by the NDP government before its defeat at the polls in late 1975. Shortly before the defeat of the government, Dr. Faris was sent on a fact finding mission to the United Kingdom and Western Europe. He subsequently submitted a report on recurrent education (including paid educational leave) and the British Open University (Faris, 1975b) to the Minister. The Minister announced, some weeks later, the adoption of recurrent education as government policy. Major initiatives in the field of distance education awaited the new administration.

When the new Social Credit government took office, Dr. Pat McGeer, a professor in the Faculty of Medicine at the University of B.C., became the Minister of Education. He recruited Dr. Walter Hardwick, also from the faculty of U.B.C., as his Deputy Minister. Shortly before this appointment, Hardwick had also served as U.B.C.'s Director of Continuing Education. He had also been an alderman of the City of Vancouver and was active in many aspects of public affairs. McGeer and Hardwick were both persons of energy and imagination. They were determined to improve the efficiency and effectiveness of the educational system. They also sought to make use of the most recent developments in educational technology as a means of making especially post-secondary and adult education more available to British Columbians in all parts of the ptovince.

Faris remained in the Department of Education after the Social Credit victory. For a brief period he retained his position as Superintendent of Communications. Having earned his doctorate in the field of adult education at the Ontario Institute for Studies in Education in Toronto, Faris had been one of the chief architects of the progressive community college and educational media policies in Saskatchewan before he came to British Columbia. With that background, and having recently been overseas to study emerging educational policies, including distance education, he possessed knowledge and experience which were valued by the new Minister and his Deputy.

McGeer and Hardwick actively sought out avenues for improvement and innovation, especially in the post-secondary field. Before the new government was many months in office, they launched three major inquiries into aspects of the field. One was on the delivery of university programs to non-metropolitan areas of the province. The others were on technical/vocational education and adult/community education. The intention at the outset, according to Deputy Minister Hardwick, was to establish a comprehensive Post-Secondary and Training Act, which would govern the whole system with separate, subsidiary sections including one on Adult Education (Cassidy 1984). The recommendations from these three studies were to provide input into the draft legislation. This comprehensive plan was never fully implemented. Nevertheless, the study of adult education did incorporate a number of recommendations which were to be implemented subsequently.

Given his academic qualifications in the field of adult education and the considerable bureaucratic experience in the field he had gained in Saskatchewan, Faris was the logical choice as chairman of the committee to study that area. Following the completion of the committee's work, he was appointed Executive Director of a newly created Continuing Education Division within the Ministry. As a result, adult education was accorded more visibility and a higher level of representation within the Ministry than it had ever had before.

In the years after his appointment as Executive Director in 1976, Faris gave strong leadership to this division. He utilized the authority inherent in his appointment, the resources available to him, the influence and powers of persuasion he could bring to bear and his ideas and professional skills. Faris and the team of colleagues he was able to build up had a major impact on the adult education services provided by the public sector. It is not possible, in the space available, to attempt a complete description of the activities undertaken by the division, but the following is an attempt to explore some highlights.

1. Policy Development

Although the public educational system in British Columbia had been active in the field of adult education for many years, there was little in the way of clearly articulated policy in the area. In an effort to correct the situation, the Ministry appointed the Committee on Continuing and Community Education in early summer 1976. As noted above, Ron Faris was selected as its chairman. The Committee, commonly referred to as the Faris Committee, was made up of 23 persons, all but one of whom were employed in the public education system.

Cassidy (1984) has provided a detailed description of the committee, its procedures and recommendations, which it is not necessary to repeat here. Certain features should be stressed, however. Faris strongly believed in the importance of approaching the task in a way which encouraged a high degree of participation on the part of interested citizens and organizations. It was decided to begin by preparing and circulating a preliminary statement which described the task, defined key terms, and identified the issues. Interested parties were invited to prepare submissions and, if they chose, to attend one of the public hearings held by the committee in all parts of the province.

In all, 199 submissions were presented to the committee, ranging from letters from individuals to fairly comprehensive, formal briefs. In addition, brief questionnaires distributed at the public meetings were completed by approximately 280 persons. The committee completed its work within the six month time limit stipulated by the Minister, submitting its report in December, 1976. The report contained 110 recommendations and in many respects served as a blueprint for the subsequent activities of the Continuing Education Division. A few of the leading recommendations were as follows:

1. lifelong learning be adopted as basic to the planning of the total public education system;

2. the government develop and place in legislation a statement of purposes and goals with respect to the development of adult education in the province;

3. an administrative mechanism be established within the Ministry of Education to provide more rigorous provincial leadership and coordination for adult education;

4. the provincial government create public advisory and intra-governmental coordinating mechanisms for adult education at the provincial level;

5. the institutional role of varying public adult education programming agencies be clearly defined and related to one another in a systematic and co-ordinated manner.

As Cassidy (1984) has subsequently pointed out, not all of the committee's recommendations have been implemented by the Ministry. Many have, however, and a great many more provided direction for the activities of the Division's staff.

After the Division of Continuing Education was officially created and Faris was named its Executive Director, a process was begun which aimed at influencing the policy of the Ministry, and that of educational institutions in the public system, in selected areas of practice. In each case, in keeping with a desire to secure maximum participation from the field, Faris designated an area for study, appointed a study or advisory committee representative of the practitioners and institutions in the field, and employed an expert person to prepare a report and recommendations, on the advice of the group. In this way a series of what were titled "discussion papers" were prepared and published in the period 1979 to 1981.

The discussion papers dealt with the following subjects: adult basic education, non-traditional learning programs for women, English as a second language, and family learning activities. These papers, although published by the Ministry, were not statements of Ministry policy. However, in some cases they clearly led to action by the Ministry. In all cases they had the effect of raising consciousness in the field. Although "discussion papers" were not used, somewhat the same approach was followed in other areas of interest, including the special needs of seniors and single parent families.

The Committee on Continuing and Community Education called for statutory provision for a policy-making body on adult education within the Ministry. No action was taken on this matter. When the Colleges and Provincial Institutes Act was passed in 1977, it did not provide for a council on adult education, parallel to those established on institutional management, academic education and occupational training. An Advisory Committee on Adult and Continuing Education was created instead. It met for the first time in June of 1978. Appointed by the Deputy Minister and related to his office, this committee was initially made up of educators from various organizations in the public system—the school boards, colleges, provincial institutes and universities. Due attention was also given to representation from rural and urban settings. In 1981, for the first time, school trustees and college council members were added to the membership.

The Advisory Committee's terms of reference were broadly defined, providing for initiatives from the members, the Continuing Education Division and the Deputy Minister's office. The financing and co-ordination of adult education in the public system received much of the Committee's attention. Perhaps the most substantial task undertaken by the committee was its work in the policy development process, described below. The committee met several times a year and maintained approximately the same level of activity until 1983, when as part of the Ministry's restraint measures, both its size and its operating budget were substantially reduced.

The policy development process, referred to above, may be seen as an outgrowth of the Faris Committee report and, perhaps, the earlier representations of concerned adult educators. In any case, it was the immediate result of the decisions announced at a conference held in November, 1979. The Continuing Education Division of the Ministry took the initiative in organizing the conference, on "The Changing Face of Education in the 1980s." Additional co-sponsors were the School Trustees and the B.C. Association of Colleges. The B.C. Association of Continuing Education Administrators was responsible for the organization of the event. The hope was to engage a substantial number of elected school trustees and college board members in consideration of policy related to adult education and lifelong learning. It turned out that quite a number of such persons agreed to take part in the conference. When Jim Carter and Andy Soles, assistant deputy ministers in the Ministry of Education, rose to speak, they announced that the Ministry intended to launch a policy development process concerning adult education. First with reference to the field as a whole and subsequently on each major section of it, the Ministry would prepare a draft policy statement, send it out to the field for comment, redraft it in the Ministry, as required, and then issue it as an official Ministry policy. So began a policy development process which continued until early 1982.

It has been mentioned that the Ministry Advisory Committee on Adult and Continuing Education played a part in the process. The Committee prepared draft policy statements, after being vetted by the Ministry, were sent out for comment. Once the responses were received, Ministry staff made whatever changes they felt were necessary and then issued the policy statements, over the Deputy Minister's signature.

This procedure was followed, apparently without hitch, for the first three policy statements. The first of these was on "The Provision of Continuing Education in the Public Educational System of British Columbia." It was issued in March, 1980. This document was followed by statements on "Community Education and General Interest Programs" and "Adult Basic Education Programs, Including English as a Second Language Training." The latter was distributed in August, 1980, shortly before Dr. Hardwick left his position as Deputy Minister. It was understood in the field that these three statements represented government or ministerial policy.

When the new Minister of Education, Mr. Brian Smith, undertook a series of fact-finding meetings around the province in fall, 1980, he was asked about the policy on adult basic education (ABE). His response was that this statement was not Ministry policy in the full sense, but only a statement issued by Ministry officials. When the matter was pursued with the Deputy Minister, Mr. Jim Carter (Hardwick's successor), the Minister's comments were confirmed. It was stated that the first two policy papers which had been issued raised no problems and could be confirmed as accepted policy. But because of its financial implications, the statement on ABE could not be taken as policy and would have to be processed by a policy development procedure in the Ministry (Minutes, Ministry Advisory Committee, Dec. 9, 1980).

In the end, it was more than a year later that the ABE statement, considerably altered, was issued by the Deputy Minister. It was accompanied by another policy statement which had been developed in the interim on Adult Special Education. As the Deputy's covering letter indicated, by that time, the government had adopted a policy of fiscal restraint and the policies being issued were to be seen as "guidelines for efficient and effective use of limited resources" (Covering letter, March 25, 1982). It became clear that this aspect of the policy development process, which had begun in November, 1979, had come to an end early in 1982. A further draft policy statement, on part-time vocational programs, although prepared by the Ministry Advisory Committee, was never sent out for comment.

2.   Developing the C.E. Division's Capacity for Leadership

One of the striking features of the period under consideration is the fact that during these years the Ministry was able to exercise more vigorous and effective leadership in the field of continuing education than ever before. This was due to the personnel and resources made available to the Continuing Education Division and the working procedures adopted by Faris and his colleagues. Prior to Faris' appointment as Executive Director in 1976, the role of Ministry administrator of continuing education, which had only been part-time until 1962, had been seen essentially as one of maintenance. Ministry personnel had, with varying degrees of effectiveness, done what they could to encourage school boards (who had been the only providers for much of the time) to mount comprehensive programs. With limited time at their disposal, the Ministry personnel recognized that leadership in program development would have to come largely from the institutional level. Much of the energy in the Ministry was devoted to managing rather than leading the system, therefore.

Faris had a very different concept of the role of the Ministry. Far from wishing to leave the leadership in the public system at the institutional level, he believed that government had an important leaderhip role too. He believed that the state had a responsibility to ensure that the public system provided adequately and equitably for all those in need of its services. In the words of John Lowe (1975), to whose writings on these matters Faris referred frequently:

> Only the state is in the position to take the overall view, to determine norms of provision, to locate gaps and see that they are filled, to encourage research and development and to execise regulatory supervision. (p. 160)

Faris' advanced training in adult education and prior experience in public sector management gave him the intellectual and organizational skills required to work effectively towards these goals.

At the crucial stages of developing his Division, Faris received strong support from his Minister and Deputy Minister. Within two years of being appointed, he was able to assemble a core staff of four administrators and arranged to have several other specialists attached to his group on secondment from institutions in the system. In this way, it was possible for Faris and his colleagues to spend considerable time in the field, exercising influence and providing leadership.

Faris' methods of operation also extended the leadership capacity of the Division. He and his colleagues developed a network of personal relationships in the field which was used effectively to influence professional and institutional behavior. In addition, they were skillful in calling on the services of other institutions and organizations. By making relatively modest grants available to other bodies, they elicited very considerable assistance with projects directed at the improvement of the field. While some institutions came to be somewhat wary of these arrangements, the "burden" was astutely distributed around the system and much good work resulted which otherwise would have been beyond the means of the Continuing Education Division.

3.   The Continuing Education Projects Fund

At the time Faris was appointed to head the Continuing Education Division in early 1976, the Ministry was in a period of retrenchment. Prior to his appointment the Ministry had cut the per instructional hour grant to school boards for continuing education from $10 to $5. As additional funding became available in 1977-78, instructional grants were raised to $7. Another portion, $117,000, was put into a fund to be used for innovative projects. The thinking behind this move was the same as that which led the Faris Committee to recommend an innovative project development fund. It was clear that if all the funds were simply used to restore the per instructional hour grants to their previous level, then the system would, by and large, operate along the same lines as it had before. By contrast, if some of the money was put in a special fund and made accessible only for services or programs judged to be innovative, pilot or demonstration work which would improve the system in some significant way could be encouraged. As a result, the funds might have a more useful impact locally, and in the system as a whole.

The plan for the distribution of the special funds was set up on the basis of college regions. A portion of the funds was set aside for each region. The school boards with continuing education programs and the college in a region were required to co-ordinate and assign priorities to their applications for special funds before submitting them to the Ministry. Initially there were two main categories of projects, adult basic education and community or general education. Subsequently, adult "special education" projects were added as well. Field based "juries" were set up each year to assess the applications and advise the Division on their relative merits. The insistence that each region set priorities forced some of the decision-making back to the local applicants. Perhaps it also had benefits in at least some regions by promoting the idea of co-ordination at that level. The decisions made at the local level were not always adhered to by the Ministry, however. When it was seen, for instance, that a project which had been accorded low priority in one region had potential benefits for the whole system, it was moved up the list by the provincial jury.

It is clear that the special projects fund, formally referred to beginning in 1981 as the Continuing Education Project Fund, had great potential for the Division and for the field as a whole. As far as the Division was concerned, it represented a major means of bringing about change in directions it perceived as desirable. This was, for instance, a time of major growth and development in the field of adult basic education. Courses and services in this area were badly needed, especially as the federal funding for such work was sharply reduced. ABE was not a part of the field which could be expected to support itself on the basis of student fees. By designating ABE as a high priority area for special project funding, the Ministry encouraged initiatives in this area and also made experimental, pilot and demonstration efforts possible.

The hope and expectation was that at least some of the courses and services developed as a result of the project system would subsequently, after an initial subsidization for a year or two, be incorporated into the regular services of the sponsoring institution. This happened to a considerable degree in the early years of the system, while budgetary resources were generally on the increase. As budget restraint became a feature of institutional life, this was less the case.

The Continuing Education Division put considerable effort into evaluating the C.E. Project system, commissioning and printing an evaluation of the first year of operations (Report, Committee on the Assessment of the C.E. Project System, 1978). It also commissioned directories of projects approximately every two years, starting in 1980. These were distributed to all public continuing education institutions as well as interested persons, with the hope that the information included would reinforce the impact of the various projects assisted by the fund.

The Division also held meetings most years on "creative use of the system." These were attended by representatives of the applying institutions. Considerable stress was also placed on—and sometimes special funding provided for—the circulation of reports on projects which were judged to be of particular interest or relevance to others in the field. For instance, a report containing a proposal for innovative measures of co-ordination of adult education services between Kwantlen College and the Surrey School Board was seen as having possible application in other areas of the province and was widely distributed.

As confidence in the benefits of the special project system was gained, the size of the fund increased. From an initial investment of slightly over $100,000 in 1978-79, the fund grew to approximately $500,000 in 1981-82, only to be slashed by 80% as a result of budget restraint in the following year.

In the years during which it was funded at a reasonable level, the Division's Continuing Education Project System produced many beneficial results for the publicly-sponsored adult education system in the province. It also gained considerable recognition in the educational community across Canada for both its basic concept and the innovations it made possible.

4. Promoting Services in Priority Areas

A basic priority during the Faris years was the extension of adult education services in the public system to people who were educationally disadvantaged. Such people had not been well served prior to that point. The public education institutions in the province— the school boards, colleges and institutes, and the universities—had built up large programs. Because of the funding arrangements, however, these programs were based largely on a "market economy," the costs having to be recovered largely from student fees. In the school board programs especially, organizing and programming staffs were of necessity small, leaving little time for planning and carrying out innovative programs. These factors combined to produce a system, even though it had grown considerably, which did not respond easily to the needs of disadvantaged groups.

Given a commitment on the part of Faris and his colleagues, and to some extent the Minister and Deputy Minister as well, to filling the gaps in the service, the problem became one of influencing the behavior of the system, without at the same time becoming overbearing or diminishing initiative at the local and institutional level. Faris' strategy ranged over several fronts. First of all, the activities of the Faris Committee in 1976 were conducted in such a way as to elicit responses by, and on behalf of, a wide range of those most in need of better provision. The final report of the committee (1976) identified many of these needs and thereby provided something of an agenda for future activity.

Many of the Division's research and in-service professional development activities (see below) were also aimed at documenting unmet needs and bringing them to the attention of practitioners. The discussion papers described earlier were intended in part to show both Ministry officials and field-based practitioners the nature and scope of the educational needs in the several areas studied. The methods employed in carrying out these studies focussed on substantial input from committees drawn from the field. This process not only assisted in the provision of useful information but also served to strengthen the special needs groups and those working on their behalf.

The Continuing Education Project system was directed particularly at encouraging innovative projects in relation to the needs of disadvantaged groups. Other funds were used for the organization of workshops and conferences relevant to areas of special need. And perhaps most important of all, Faris added staff to his team who could spend much of their time providing services to practitioners in these areas, organizing workshops, conducting in-service development, developing new curricula, publishing newsletters, and undertaking other support work.

By all of these means, the Continuing Education Division sought to influence institutional provision and community demand for effective service in areas of special need. The top priority areas for much of this activity were adult basic education (literacy and life skills training as well as high school completion), English as a second language, and adult special education (services for handicapped persons). In each of these areas, the full range of strategies described above was brought to bear. Some other areas which received special attention included education for women, older persons, rural and isolated persons, single parent and poverty level families, as well as citizenship education and community development.

5.   Data Collection and Research

As a foundation for policy development, a means of gaining recognition for the field and a way of documenting educational need, Faris and his colleagues put considerable stress on data collection and research activity. Data collection and publication about the field of practice were transformed in this period. In co-operation with the Statistical Services section of the Ministry, annual "Continuing Education Data" publications were produced. Annual directories of the adult education activities of provincial ministries and crown corporations were also published. Directories of institutions and key adult education personnel in the public system were issued or commissioned from time to time, as were lists of Ministry and institutional publications of interest to the field. Much of the latter information was also provided by means of various newsletters.

The Division also carried out research on topics of special interest, usually with the assistance of researchers on contract. Many of these studies were carried out as part of the strategy of promoting increased attention to priority areas. The Discussion Paper series described above was an example of this approach. Other commissioned reports on such topics as social indicators, the single parent family and teaching resources were also published.

6. In-Service Professional Development for Practitioners

A great deal of initiative and resources went into efforts by the Division to influence and improve the practice of the personnel who were in charge of adult education programs within the public system. One aspect of this thrust consisted of a regular series of annual conferences on lifelong learning for continuing education administrators. For some purposes, rural and urban centre administrators met separately. Conferences were also held for administrators on specialized subjects such as adult basic education, areas of special need and the use of social indicators. In addition, there were many workshops for teachers in such areas as adult basic education, adult special education and English as a second language.

Another aspect of in-service development consisted of a series of manuals for practitioners which were financed by the Ministry and prepared under contract by other persons and agencies. Examples of this included: a manual entitled *Introduction to Teaching Adults*, which consisted of both text and audiotapes; the *C.E. Programmers Manual*, a comprehensive guide to program planning; and *Getting; to Know Your Community*, a guide to community-based needs analysis.

Within the priority areas, such as adult basic education, adult special education and English as a second language, to which the Division gave special leadership, a large number of publications were commissioned. These included curricula for instruction, guides to resource materials, and publications and videotapes on particular aspects of program planning and teaching.

The Division worked closely with the professional associations in the field as a whole and also in the specialized branches of activity such as ABE and ESL. Where such organizations did not already exist, as in the case of adult special education, it sponsored periodic meetings until those in the field were ready to form an association. The annual conferences on lifelong learning, the first of which gave rise to the adult education policy development process, were co-sponsored with other organizations. The Division also commissioned a survey in 1981 of training needs in the field of adult education.

The several newsletters published by the Division were another form of assistance to practitioners. Separate newsletters for ABE and ESL were initiated in 1979 and a general publication was begun in 1981, incorporating the other two. This in turn ceased publication in the fall of 1983, a victim of fiscal restraint.

In-service development activity absorbed a great deal of the energy and resources of the Division and was one of its major commitments. The brief description presented here is but a sampling of the overall effort.

7.   Reponse to the Economic Depression

As the economic depression hit the province in the early Eighties, the Continuing Education Division was affected in two main ways. First, the fiscal restraint policy of the government resulted in a drastic reduction of the resources of the Division. Staff were cut, many services discontinued and supporting grants to the colleges and school board adult education programs were severely reduced. The elimination of the C.E. Project system has already been mentioned. In addition, the Division was specifically instructed not to promote new demands on the services of the Ministry, but to concentrate, rather, on efforts to increase efficiency and co-ordination in the field.

In keeping with the changing mandate, resources were made available to several studies of co-ordination of services among adult education agencies. Noteworthy in this respect was the Kwantlen College-Surrey School Board project, already mentioned, and the earlier (1981) study of relationships between Douglas College and the school district continuing education programs in its service area. The Ministry Advisory Committee also formulated a proposal on local learning centres as a relatively low cost way to co-ordinate and deliver services for adults at local and neighborhood levels.

The major exception to the directive barring new initiatives in the field was the Division's sponsorship, beginning in mid-1982, of the "Adult Education Consortium on Economic Dislocation." Colleges and school districts serving areas where the unemployment level was particularly high were invited to confer on mutual concerns and formally constituted the consortium. The consortium continues to operate. The C.E. Division has assisted in some of its activities, making possible the part-time assistance of a skilled community worker and financing several publications, including the Consortium's newsletter, *Tough Times News*, which first appeared in December, 1982. A resource kit for adult educators (Clague 1983), containing ideas for projects which might be used in the local community, was also produced with the assistance of the Division. The consortium came about as a result of leadership from the C.E. Division. It has been studied by several other provinces and has received wide recognition in the field for being an innovative and appropriate response to the present "tough times."

In addition to the activities described above, all of which related to the Continuing Education Division, reference should be made to public policy initiatives in this period which were carried out by other sections of the Ministry of Education.

Major activities were launched in the field of distance education. The study conducted in 1976 on the delivery of university programs in non-metropolitan areas resulted in a recommendation that the existing universities, under the leadership of Simon Fraser University, deliver programs in the Interior, by a variety of means (Report, Commission of University Programs, 1976). The universities were asked to begin planning such a service. While this was happening, a Distance Education Planning Group was commissioned by the Ministry to study the potential for and means of using distance education methods (Report, Distance Education Planning Group, 1977).

Drs. McGeer and Hardwick also became interested in the model of the British Open University. Concluding that the universities were so busy competing with each other that they were not likely to produce a satisfactory joint project (Shore 1984), the Ministry initiated the Open Learning Institute in 1978, a correspondence instruction institution. Two years later, they created the Knowledge Network of the West (KNOW), a television network utilizing satellite communication and carrying both open and closed educational television services throughout the province. By means of these steps, the provincial authorities greatly expanded the educational services available to adults in the province.

Despite its limited resources the Continuing Education Division experimented with the use of the Knowledge Network to reach a variety of target audiences. Several programs were aimed at improving the instructional skills of some 18,000 part-time instructors in the system. One series, developed in co-operation with the Ministry of Human Resources and the Foster Parents' Association, was developed to strengthen foster parenting skills. Another, in co-operation with the Ministry of Labour, focussed on how individuals and communities could more effectively cope in tough economic times.

Some other projects deserving of particular mention had a close link to the work of the Continuing Education Division. Reference has been made earlier to the work of the Division with respect to promoting more effective provision to meet the educational needs of women, handicapped persons and the under-educated. In each of those areas, the Ministry took steps designed to augment its other activities. In the case of services to women and handicapped persons, the Ministry provided earmarked funds to each of the colleges for some years to enable them to staff special services. In the field of adult basic education, the Ministry established a special bursary program for potential ABE students who needed financial assistance in order to begin or continue their studies.

Two Periods of Dynamic Leadership

In the two periods examined, government officials provided particularly effective and vigorous leadership in the development of adult education services in the public system. The reasons and conditions were different, but the evidence is clear.

The basic posture or political philosophy of government in these two periods was strikingly different. In 1933, when the Liberal Patullo government came to power, it had been elected on a "New Deal" platform. It was clearly committed to an interventionist role in helping people to cope with the devastating effects of the economic depression. It is not surprising, therefore, that the administration took bold initiatives in this field, as in others. The fact that the Minister of Education, George Weir, was a professional educator who had considerable interest in adult education before he entered office predisposed him, no doubt, to utilize adult education as one of the avenues for social intervention.

The Social Credit Government of William Bennett, when it came to power in late 1975, had a very different orientation. It was a conservative party. Having been elected on a platform emphatically opposed to that of the social democratic, interventionist policies of its predecessor, the new government was an unlikely sponsor of significant initiatives in adult education, especially of the type subsequently developed by the Continuing Education Division. The explanation of its leadership role lies in three areas.

First of all, Dr. McGeer, the Minister in charge of Education in the formative period following the election, was a professional educator and an advocate of bold initiatives in his field. He had a particular intetest in the application of new technology as it related to the task at hand. He recruited as his Deputy-Minister, Walter Hardwick, a man of ideas and energy, who had an active interest in adult education. Hardwick had been involved in the development of the college system and had a commitment to widening access to educational opportunity for the people throughout the province. It was a strong leadership team which was committed to imaginative initiatives and open to new ideas.

The second factor in the situation was Dr. Ron Faris. As has been described, he had strong views about the leadership role of government and adult education's role. These views were not, on the whole, shared by the government for which he worked, but the senior figures in his Ministry, at least in the formative years of the Faris era, were willing, to a point, to give him his way, within the limits of the resources available. Faris' advanced professional training in adult education and his earlier experience in government contributed to a sophisticated style of operation on his part. He used the potential influence of his position effectively and maximized the impact of the resources he and his colleagues had available.

The third reason contributing to the extent of the Division's influence on adult education activities of the public institutions of British Columbia was the nature of the system itself. The adult education programs in these institutions had, for some decades before the Faris years, been outstanding in their extent and variety. Participation rates in adult education had consistently been higher in B.C. than in any other province in Canada (Selman 1980). The program sponsored by school boards had led all Canada in that sector of the field since at least the early 1950s. The University of British Columbia's extension program was one of the most outstanding in the country. The community college system was virtually complete by the time Faris took up his post. It was based on an institutional model, that of the comprehensive community college, which accorded considerable importance to the adult education function. The programs of the two newer universities and the provincial institutes, including the B.C. Institute of Technology, were also growing rapidly.

So, in this period the adult education enterprise in the public sector was a large and rapidly expanding one, especially until the onset of sharp budgetary restraint in the early Eighties. College and Institute enrollments in adult education grew from 98,458 in 1975-76 to 193,904 in 1980-81 (Ministry of Education, 1981-82 Continuing Education Data). Enrollments in school board programs grew from 140,952 to 156,118 in the same period, even though the number of boards offering programs decreased from 31 to 27 during that time. The leadership and influence which were exercised, therefore, was exercised in relation to a vital and expanding field of activity. There was a significant—and growing—number of able and energetic leaders in the public adult education system at this time, many of whom welcomed the leadership being exercised and were ready to take advantage of the opportunities it provided.

One question which should be raised about the policy of the Pattullo government concerning adult education is whether its active and innovative role arose mainly from the conviction of the importance of such activity in the development of the people of the province, or whether it was more a series of expedient measures designed to prevent civil unrest and despair. Certainly considerable stress was given in public statements to the role of the new programs in raising the morale of the people. It is obvious that this was a major reason why such programs found favor with the government. On the other hand, it appears that Dr. Weir himself supported adult education, not just as a way of coping with the emergency but as part of his overall educational philosophy and view of desirable human development.

How influential Dr. Weir's views were in the minds of his colleagues in the Pattullo government is not known. The distress and demoralization caused by the conditions of the Depression called for measures aimed at providing constructive activities for adults. No sooner were those conditions alleviated than the country was involved in the Second World War, with all its unusual demands on the Canadian people. It is therefore not possible to determine what the government's policies in this field would have been in more normal times.

In the case of the Bennett government of the Seventies and Eighties, there appeared to be no commitment to a social philosophy which would explain its vigorous leadership role in adult education. The explanation lies rather in the three factors described above. So long as the McGeer-Hardwick team remained at the head of the Ministry of Education, and times were relatively good and fiscal resources available, Faris and his colleagues had a reasonable level of support from above as well as the funds with which to act.

In the early Eighties, fiscal restraint resulted in a perhaps more focussed approach to priorities. Less supportive leadership took over in the Ministry. The Division's freedom of action was greatly reduced. Not only were resources diminished, but the Division was clearly instructed to concentrate its efforts on maintenance and cost reduction in the system, avoiding initiatives which would result in new or additional demands on the Ministry. It appears that these most recent developments are a result partly of fiscal restraint, but also of the dominant philosophical position of the Social Credit government being brought to bear on the Continuing Education Division to an extent which it had not before.

In these two periods, almost fifty years apart, the Department/Ministry of Education provided strong and imaginative leadership in the field of adult education, to an extent beyond that of any other time in the Province's history. The conditions of the two periods, both in society as a whole and within the field of adult education, could hardly have been more different. The scale of the initiatives in the later period were vastly greater than in the Thirties. The sophistication of the measures taken in the Seventies and Eighties, in terms of the methodologies and other professional aspects of adult education practice, was immeasurably greater. The essential elements of dynamic leadership, imagination and ability, as well as a conviction that the public authority should respond to the needs of the people, especially those in greatest need, were present on both occasions.

References

Association for Continuing Education (B.C.), *Organizing for Life-Long Learning*, Occasional Paper No. 2, A.C.E., 1974.

British Columbia Public School Reports for years indicated.

Cartier, A. (1970), "The Growth of Public School Adult Education," *The Journal of Education*, No. 18 (Winter 1970): 75-81.

Cassidy, F. (1984), "Fostering the Learning Society: Continuing Education Policy in British Columbia 1976-1980," *PACE Papers* I.

Clague, M. (1983), *Tough Economic Times*, Vancouver: Typescript.

Corbett, E.A. (1957), *We Have With Us Tonight*, Toronto: Ryerson.

Dailly, E. (1975), "Address to the Association of Canadian Community Colleges," Nov. 12.

Dampier, L.P. (1978), *Towards a Public Policy for Adult Education in British Columbia*, Occasional Paper No. 6, Pacific Association for Continuing Education.

Deaton, R. (1983),"Unemployment: Canada's Malignant Social Pathology," *Perception*, 6 (5): 15-19.

Discussion Paper: Adult Basic Education, Victoria: Ministry of Education, 1979.

Discussion Paper: English as a Second Language for Adults, Victoria: Ministry of Education, 1979.

Discussion Paper: Family Learning Activities, Victoria: Ministry of Education, 1981.

Discussion Paper: Non-Traditional Learning Programs for Women, Victoria: Ministry of Education, 1979.

Discussion Paper: Women's Access Centres, Victoria: Ministry of Education, 1979.

Faris, R., (1975a), *The Passionate Educators*, Toronto: Peter Martin.

———. (1975b), *Report on: A) Recurrent Education B) The British Open University* October 3, 1974, Available from author.

Gibson, J.W. (1935), "Adult Education in British Columbia," appendix to Sandiford, P. (Ed.) (1935), *Adult Education in Canada: A Survey*, Toronto: University of Toronto.

Johnson, F.H. (1964), *A History of Public Education in British Columbia*, Vancouver: University of British Columbia.

Lowe, J. (1975), *The Education of Adults: A World Perspective*, Paris: UNESCO.

Newman, P. (1984), "Brave hopes, fearful times," *Maclean's*, Jan. 2, 1984, 22-24.

Powell, M.P. (1967), *Response to the Depression*, Unpublished M.A. Thesis, University of British Columbia.

Public Library Commission (1942), *A Preliminary Study of Adult Education in British Columbia: 1941,* Victoria: Public Library Commission.

"Report, Committee on the Assessment of the Continuing Education Project System," 1978, typescript.

"Report Committee on Continuing and Community Education in British Columbia," 1976.

"Report, Distance Education Planning Group," Victoria, Ministry of Education," 1977.

"Report, Task Force on the Community College in British Columbia," Victoria: Department of Education, 1974.

Sandiford, P. (Ed.) (1935), *Adult Education in Canada: A Survey,* Toronto: University of Toronto. Typescript mimeo.

Selman, G.R. (1963), *A History of the Extension and Adult Education Services of The University of British Columbia 1915 to 1955,* Unpublished M.A. Thesis, University of British Columbia.

——. (1976), "Adult Education in British Columbia during the Depression," *Occasional Papers in Continuing Education,* University of B.C. Centre for Continuing Education, No. 12 (1976).

——. (1977), "A Chonology of Adult Education in British Columbia," *Occasional Papers in Continuing Education,* University of B.C. Centre for Continuing Education, No. 14 (1977).

——. (1980), The British Columbia Division of the Canadian Association for Adult Education 1961 - 1971, *Occasional Paper No. 7* (1980), Pacific Association for Continuing Education.

——. (1981), "The Canadian Association for Adult Education in the Corbett Years: A Re-evaluation," *Occasional Papers in Continuing Education,* University of B.C. Centre for Continuing Education, No. 20 (1981).

——. (1983), "Public policy concerning adult education in British Columbia," *PACE Newsletter,* 13 (1): 15-21.

Shore, V. (1984), "KNOW—An Electronic Classroom for B.C.," *University Affairs,* Jan., 1984, 3-4.

The Third Alternative: Co-ordinating Adult Education in Surrey and White Rock, Kwantlen College and Surrey School Board, 1983, Rose Marie Fournier, Project Co-ordinator.

Thomas, A.M. (1961), "The Learning Society," *in National Conference of Adult Education,* Toronto/Montreal: CAAE/ICEA.

Thomas, Audrey (1983), Adult Illiteracy in Canada: A Challenge, *Occasional Paper, No. 42,* Ottawa: Canadian Commission for UNESCO.

University of British Columbia, Centre for Continuing Education (1973), "A Statement about Continuing Education in British Columbia and Recommendations Concerning Future Developments."

Wales, B.E. (1958), *The Development of Adult Education in British Columbia,* Unpublished Ed.D. Thesis, Oregon State University.

Originally published in Cassidy, F. (Ed.) (1984), *PACE Papers 1,* Vancouver: Pacific Association for Continuing Education, pp. 3-34. Reprinted with permission.

Part 5

Adult Education in British Columbia: The Early Years

*O*ne of my most substantial and most memorable research undertakings was the study of the emergence of adult education in the colonial period of what is now the Province of British Columbia and up to the outbreak of World War I. I was attracted to the subject at least in part by the fact that the topic had not been researched on a thorough basis by anyone else. F. Henry Johnson had a chapter on adult education in his history of public education in the province, but it concentrated mostly on the role of the school boards and the Department of Education. Dr. Bert Wales of the Vancouver School Board had written his doctoral dissertation on the development of adult education services in the Province, but he paid little attention to the pre-war period and focussed his study mainly on the work of the school boards in the field. Basing my research on a much broader definition of adult education than these other two men had, I cast the research net much more widely than they had attempted to do. Rather than rely mainly on the reports of government departments and of the school boards, I based my work to a large extent on the newspapers of some of the major towns. The indexes to the newspapers were prepared in almost total ignorance of the field of adult education, so rather than rely on them, I was forced simply to go through entire files of newspapers, which were available in microfilm in the University Library. Days, weeks and months were devoted to that task, as the time could be found. This was in the period before I became a Faculty member and research time had to be found somehow out of my life as a programmer and administrator. I am not sure when it all happened, as I look back over the years in question, but by the year 1971 I was able to pull together a manuscript (which was not intended for publication) which incorporated the results of my research.

Using this manuscript as the main source of information, I subsequently wrote several articles and monographs about the field in the early years. The one which was the most colorful in some respects was about adult education during the heyday of the town of Barkerville. Barkerville, which was the centre of a gold mining boom in the 1860s and early 1870s, and was said for a brief period to have been the largest centre west of Chicago and north of San Francisco, was famous for the number of saloons in town, but was also an active centre of adult education activity. One of the earliest settlers in the area had started a newspaper and, as a result, we have a remarkable day-to-day account of the development of the community. The editor was clearly enormously interested in the educational and cultural life of the community and the pages of his newspaper provide a remarkable record of such matters. I was able to put together a coherent account of adult education in the community (subsequently to become perhaps the best known ghost town in the Province) and was pleased when the editors of *BC Studies* agreed to publish it in 1971.

Several years later I prepared a somewhat more ambitious study of adult education in Vancouver prior to 1914. The basic facts came once again from my original research document, but in this case, the picture was much more complex than the Barkerville story and the period to be covered was a more extended one. This study was published as a monograph in 1975 by the Centre for Continuing Education of The University of British Columbia.

In much the same way, I used the original research when I came to write my general history of adult education in the Province, *The Invisible Giant*, which was included in the previous section. Much of the material on the pre-1914 period which appeared in that document was based on my earlier study.

I also tackled other sorts of subjects, ones not based on a focus on a particular community. One of the most interesting revelations arising out of my earlier research was the number of "mechanics' institutes" and somewhat similar "church institutes" which I found had existed in the early years. These organizations were modelled on ones which had existed in Great Britain at the time and were clearly "transplants" from the former home communities of the immigrants in the area. The institutes were important centres of educational, cultural and social activity for some communities in the early years of settlement and for a time the larger institutes received financial support from public funds. Information about these organizations having emerged from my research on several towns in the area, I put together a comprehensive account of their rise and decline, which was published in 1971 in the journal of the Canadian Associsation for Adult Education, *Continuous Learning*. Later in the same year I wrote a somewhat parallel description of the emergence of publicly sponsored evening classes at the local level in the Province in the pre-1914 period. The article was carried in the same journal. This was a period of only small beginnings in such work, but the local school boards in B.C. were subsequently to provide national leadership in this type of work.

5.1

Adult Eduction in Barkerville 1863 - 1875

*N*o attempt has previously been made to present an account of the adult education and related cultural activities which existed in Barkerville and the nearby communities on Williams Creek during their heyday, from the early 1860s to 1875. The story is a unique one, just as Barkerville's story is unique. Barkerville sprang into existence during the gold rush of the 1860s and soon became the largest community in the northwest. Within a decade it rapidly dwindled in size, and became one of the ghost towns of the Province. Yet during its brief period of prominence, it was large enough to sustain a number of educational and cultural organizations offering an interesting range of activities. Many towns in this province and elsewhere have flourished and faded away, but none reached the size or contained the rich social diversity characteristic of Barkerville at its height.

The story of the Cariboo Gold Rush and the development of Barkerville, Cameronton, Richfield and the other nearby communities has been presented in detail by various authors and is well known (Elliott 1958; Ludditt 1969; Ormsby 1958). Prospectors pushing on from the earlier discoveries on the Lower Fraser found gold on Williams Creek in February of 1861. By August the search brought them to the site of Richfield, the earliest settlement in the Barkerville area. Some 80 men stayed in Richfield through that winter and the first sizeable influx of population appeared in the spring of 1862. By March, 20 business establishments had been established at Richfield. In August, Billy Barker and John Cameron struck it rich a mile or so down the creek. Within a month the first cabins began to go up near these claims, at what were to be the communities of Barkerville and Cameronton, although most of those who stayed in the area through the following winter lived at Richfield. Before the middle of the following May (1863), more than 2,000 people arrived at Richfield. Businesses were soon established at the other two communities as well. F.W. Ludditt gives us a picture of the incredible pace of development during the season:

> Countless cabins now were erected on the hillsides of the creek. By the end of the year over three thousand claims had been located. At the height of the mining season the population had risen to four thousand miners and businessmen. (Ludditt 1969:37)

1863 was in many respects the big year for discovery in the area, but gold production figures continued to grow for the next several years. After the first wave of discoveries had been made by individual miners or small groups, the methods of operation began to change. As Dr. Ormsby has pointed out, "the days of the rocker and the sluice were past" (Ormsby 1958:212); the solitary prospector or the small group with little capital could not hope to make their way in that area any longer. Mining conditions were such that only the larger companies could afford to provide the equipment and construct the large scale machinery, water wheels and shafts required to develop the claims. By 1867, the number of men actually working on the diggings had considerably decreased from the earlier peak.

The communities in the area were, in the meantime, developing at an exciting pace:

> The growth and development of Richfield, Cameronton and Barkerville was steady after 1863. They gradually became mining towns rather than mining camps and soon contained the businesses, societies, schools and churches that related to a growing society. (Ludditt 1969:73)

Ormsby has stated that it is impossible to estimate the population of the Cariboo mining communities in this period. Some figures went as high as 16,000, "but officials doubted whether the total population of British Columbia was much in excess of the Vancouver Island figure of 7,500" (Ormsby 1958:209). Bruce Ramsay, in his guidebook to Barkerville, indicates that the Chinese population alone was estimated to be 8,000 at one point (Ramsay 1961).

Barkerville, at the time of its rapid growth in 1864, was colorful, but not particularly attractive:

> The following year the merchants came, and wooden buildings, generally of whipsawed lumber, were erected in an irregular fashion on an irregular street. Because the creek was subject to freshets and flash floods, most of the houses were on log posts, hardly two of the houses the same height. Consequently, the sidewalks in front were at varied elevations and made walking unsafe. Overhead the signs of various businesses protruded over the muddy, filth-strewn, hole-pitted, eighteen-foot wide street. (Elliott 1958:27)

The early educational opportunities for adults were centred in Cameronton. The key figure in these developments was John Bowron. Bowron arrived on the creek in the spring of 1863. He had beeen born in Quebec, received his early education there, and studied law for a time in Cleveland, Ohio. He came West with the "Overlanders" in 1862, arrived in Quesnel in September of that year and, like many of that party, proceeded to the coast for the winter months. After returning to Williams Creek, he travelled all over the mining area.

> It was during those early weeks, and later, when he did some prospecting on his own, that he conceived the idea of forming a society where men could meet and talk and once again feel themselves to be part of the world of music, books and the arts that had been left behind on entering the goldfields. (Ludditt 1969:125)

Within the first few weeks of arriving in the area, Bowron interested a few others in the idea and founded the Cariboo Literary Society. The first meetings were held in his small cabin in Cameronton. A further step was taken the following year, when this group decided to create a library for the community. In the name of the Cariboo Literary Institute, they raised $1,000 by public subscription and then appealed to the Colonial government to supply a building in Cameronton to house the library. One was in due course provided and the library opened its doors to the public on June 7, 1864.

There is some disagreement on two points related to the early days of the library. The first has to do with whether the government or Bowron himself supplied the library building. Ludditt, in his history of Barkerville, states that the government supplied the building (Ludditt 1969). Wolfenden (1947), in her pioneer work on the libraries of the Province, states that the building was constructed at Bowron's expense. On a more significant point, there is disagreement as to who was the first librarian of the Institute. Holmes (1959), in her historical account of library service in the Province, states that "Florence Wilson of Victoria" was the librarian for the first year, after which Bowron assumed the post. Other historians, including Ludditt (1969), Wolfenden (1947) and Elliott (1958), state that Bowron was the librarian from the outset. Bowron certainly held that position (and was Secretary of the Institute) by the summer of 1865 and remained the dominant figure for a decade.

The sole purpose of the Cariboo Literary Institute soon became the maintenance of the library. Wolfenden states in her article that "lectures, debates, musical and dramatic entertainments were sponsored" (Wolfenden 1947:180), but the record does not bear this out. The local newspaper, the *Cariboo Sentinel*, which first appeared in June of 1865, gave detailed attention to the activities of the Institute and other educational and cultural events, and with the exception of a lecture for the benefit of the Institute given in September of 1865 *(Cariboo Sentinel* (hereafter *C.S.*) Sept. 2, 1865), there is no mention of such events actually being sponsored by the Institute itself.

The Institute and the library remained in existence for a decade, the last known reference to the latter appearing in the *Cariboo Sentinel* in November of 1974 (Nov. 7). Maintaining the library was clearly a struggle throughout the period. But maintained it was, thanks to the devoted efforts of a small group of supporters, most notably John Bowron himself.

Ludditt (1969) states that when the library opened it contained 300 volumes. The first issue of the *Sentinel*, on June 6, 1865, carried an advertisement as follows:

Reading Room and Circulating Library

The terms of subscription have been reduced to two dollars per month; above 100 volumes of New Works have been only lately added to the Circulating Library. Parties are solicited to subscribe. John Bowron, Librarian *(C.S.* June 16, 1865)

The Institute advertised the library and reading room in the *Sentinel* frequently over the next few years. Sometimes the item was similar to the item presented above. Beginning in July of 1866, a second, longer form of advertisement appeared, as it did frequently thereafter. This item listed the officers of the Institute, quoted the subscription rates ($2.00 per month and $5.00 per quarter), listed some of the significant books in the collection (stating that there were "about 500 volumes" in stock), and indicating that the hours of service were 10 a.m. to 10 p.m. (*C.S.* July 19, 1866). These ads state that the President of the Institute was Mr. J.S. Thompson. Thompson was a lawyer and one of the best known and respected citizens of the whole area. He, like Bowron, was active in the local dramatic society. He served for a time as editor of the *Cariboo Sentinel* and was the first representative of the area in Parliament after the Colony joined Confederation in 1871, having been elected on the first occasion by acclamation. No doubt the support of such a prominent and influential person as Thompson was extremely important to the Institute over the years.

In 1866, Bowron was appointed Postmaster for the area and the post office and library were combined in the same building. In the meantime, Barkerville had come to the fore as the largest, most influential centre in the area and it was decided to move both of these facilities there from Cameronton. The *Sentinel* reported that the post office and library "were removed from Cameronton to the old Parlor Saloon, Barkerville, where they shall remain until the new buildings are ready for their reception" (*C.S.* April 15, 1867). Bowron had purchased the residence of a Mr. Winnard and housed both services there. The library opened in its new quarters on May 11, the newspaper referring to it as a large room housing "the News Room and Library" *(C.S.* May 13, 1867).

The library was growing in size and diversity and receiving some support in the community. But it seems that there were not enough people in that rugged frontier town who would support the library over the long haul. The *Sentinel* reported in July of 1868 that the "public reading room" would close if more subscribers could not be obtained. A few days later it reported that the room had closed *(C.S.* July 19, 1868). But some way of carrying on must have been devised for in mid-September the Institute ran another advertisment which indicated that it was still open and providing service (*C.S.* Sept. 16, 1868). Two days later, on September 18, Barkerville burned to the ground in an hour and twenty minutes. Only one building in the community was saved. In the list of properties destroyed was the entry "John Bowron, library and post office—$4,000" *(C.S.* Sept 22, 1868). The town was rebuilt with impressive speed and on October 27, the newspaper reported that the library had been "re-opened and replenished with a good stock of books...," 200 of which had been supplied by Mr. Chartres Brew, the Gold Commissioner. Judging by the reports in the *Sentinel*, the library struggled on for several years after that, although the most prosperous time for Barkerville had passed. There were indications in May of 1869 that more members were urgently needed if the service was to continue, subscription having fallen to sixty, far below the required 100 *(C.S.* May 22, 1869). Reports in August referred to the serious debts of the organization *(C.S.* Aug. 14, 1869). There was a further flurry in April of 1870, when Bowron was dismissed as Postmaster (see *C.S.* April 2, 1870). The future of the Institute was in jeopardy and was the subject of a meeting in late May (*C.S.* May 28, 1870). The Institute survived that crisis. An advertisement appeared in the paper in mid-September announcing reduced fees for the library ($1.00 per month), signed by Bowron, still in the capacity of librarian *(C.S,* Sept. 10, 1870).

Things seem to have gone from bad to worse thereafter. The regular advertisements in the *Sentinel* no longer appeared. In January of 1872, J.S. Thompson, the President of the Institute, left the community to take up his seat in the House of Commons. In May of 1873, a meeting was held of interested persons "for the purpose of taking steps for the re-organization of the Cariboo Public Library." A collection was taken up and a committee appointed to carry the matter forward. Bowron acted as the secretary of the meeting, but when the work of the committee was reported a week later, it was stated that a Mr. Jonathan Nutt had been appointed librarian (*C.S.* May 10 & 17, 1873). Bowron had in the meantime been appointed Mining Recorder at Richfield (subsequently being appointed as Government Agent (1875) and Gold Commissioner (1883) until his retirement and death in 1906).

In early June the Sentinel reported that the library was once again open to the public and made an appeal for the return of missing books (*C.S.* June 7, 1873). (This had been a recurring problem, such appeals having been made as early as 1867.) The final reference to the library was a rather plaintive notice which appeared in the paper in late 1874. It reminded readers of the existence of the library and expressed the hope that more use would be made of it now that "the long winter evenings have set in" (*C.S.* Nov. 7, 1874).

One very striking aspect of the history of the Institute and the library is the degree of support that was provided by certain elements in society. The surprising thing is not that the organization had such serious problems, but that it survived as long as it did and continued to provide the level of service that it did. The contribution of John Bowron, of course, was crucial, as was the support of prominent citizens such as J.S. Thompson, the Institute's President. The Institute was also afforded remarkably strong and constant support from the *Cariboo Sentinel*. The newspaper seemed to take advantage of any excuse to mention the library. On occasion, the acquisition of a noteworthy single book, or the receipt of a box of books from a donor would be the subject of an item in the new columns (see for instance *C.S.* Sept. 3, 1866). The newspaper repeatedly encouraged citizens to become subscribing members, stressing its value particularly to those who lived in the area all year round. At the time of the move to Barkerville it stated that the institution "well deserves the support of the community" (*C.S.* May 13, 1867). When in the summer of 1868 it appeared that the library would close because of lack of revenue, the Sentinel urged, "Let the friends of literature rally at once and see what can be done" (*C.S.* July 16, 1868). In an article on the institutions which had been lost in the fire, the paper commented, "The oldest and perhaps the most useful was the library and reading room" (*C.S.* Oct. 2, 1868). The *Sentinel* gave space generously to announcing and reporting on any fund-raising events which were fior the benefit of the Institute. Throughout the whole period, under its various owners and editors, the *Sentinel* gave outstanding support to the Literary Institute and the library.

Help was forthcoming from elsewhere as well, both inside and outside the community. When Governor Frederick Seymour visited the area in the spring of 1866, he went to see the library, gave encouragement to those connected with it and promised to send additional books for the collection. Three boxes of them arrived in late June (*C.S.* June 28, 1866). A year later an additional box was received from "the government" (*C.S.* July 1, 1867). Governor Seymour visited the area again in August of 1867 and once again he visited the reading room (*C.S.* Aug. 12, 1867). But the most significant help, of course, came from within the community. A number of persons made contributions to the funds of the Institute over and above paying their regular subscription, but no details are known. Mention has already been made of the lecture given in September of 1865 in the reading room in Cameronton by the Reverend A.C. Garrett as a fund-raising event. Later in the same month the Cariboo Glee Club and others staged "a grand musical entertainment" for the benefit of the reading room and the event was later described as "the most successful in every sense that has ever been held here" (*C.S.* Sept. 30, 1865). Two years later, a visitor in the community, Mr. Legh Harnett, gave two lectures in Barkerville, the second of which was offered for the benefit of the Institute (*C.S.* Sept. 5 & 9, 1867). In August of 1869, the Reverend Thomas Derrick of the local Methodist church gave a lecture at the Royal Theatre, for the Institute. It was announced that "the proceeds will be devoted to the liquidation of a debt contracted by the Directors of the Cariboo Literary Institute". It was a most successful affair (*C.S.* Aug. 14 & 21, 1869). It can be seen that in these ways, many persons in the community who were in a position to be of assistance to the Institute and its library did what they could.

Only fragmentary information is available about the size of the library, its circulation, and the number of persons served. It has already been mentioned that there were approximately 300 volumes in the collection when the library was opened. In July of 1866 the Sentinel referred to the library as having "upwards of 500 volumes of standard works (*C.S.* July 2, 1866), and later in the year the columns of the same paper report that as of October 1, there were 104 subscribers to the library and 437 books (*C.S.* Oct. 22, 1866). As has been mentioned, the library closed in the middle of 1868 because there were so few subscribers, 100 being stated as the required minimum. It is not known whether any books were saved in the fire later that year, but as has been mentioned, the Institute received a gift of 200 books from Chartres Brew, the Gold Commissioner, as the nucleus of the new collection. A press report of May, 1869 stated that there were only 60 subscribers and once again indicated that a minimum of 100 was required (*C.S.* May 22, 1869). No further figures in relation to either the holdings or the membership are available for the declining years of the library service.

The library sponsored by the Cariboo Literary Institute was not the only one in the area, but little is known of the others. The Reverend John Sheepshanks is said to have brought 250 books with him when he was based briefly at Antler in the early 1860s. Elliott, in his history states that "private libraries also existed on the creek: the Occidental Cigar Store had novels, while the Roman Catholic and Anglican Churches had books of a more serious nature" (Elliott 1958:30). The Cambrian Hall, which was built in 1866 as a result of the efforts of Welsh citizens (and rebuilt after the fire) was described as to be used as a "Meeting House and News and Lecture Room" (*C.S.* June 4 1866). The library of the Catholic Church came to public notice briefly in 1868. Just five days after the fire, "the St. Patrick's Lending Library" based in the church at Richfield was written up in the *Sentinel* and an advertisement appeared listing the rates as $3.00 per quarter and $5.00 per year. The paper commented that "the library is well stocked with useful and interesting books and the terms are very liberal" *(C.S.* Sept. 16, 1838). A further ad was run for the library on October 2, shortly after the fire (and the destruction of the Institute's library), but no further notices appeared. There is a record of one other reading room in the area. The third issue of the *Sentinel,* in June 1865, carried an ad for the Parlor Saloon which contained in it a notice of, "A First Class Reading Room! All the latest English, American, Canadian and Colonial papers taken in" *(C.S.* June 24, 1865). This establishment ran advertisements in the *Sentinel* regularly thereafter and these never failed to mention the reading room until May of 1866, when that part of the ad was deleted.

Frequent mention has already been made of the *Cariboo Sentinel.* It was, in its way, an educational influence in the community. It was started by George Wallace, who arrived in Barkerville in May of 1865. He had had some newspaper experience in Victoria prior to that. The paper was first published on June 6 of that year, at first a weekly and then bi-weekly, sometimes suspending operations for a few weeks during the winter. Within a year, Wallace sold the paper to Allan Lambert, who had also come from Victoria, where he had worked on the *Colonist.* After a short period Lambert sold out to Robert Holloway, who carried on for the balance of the life of the paper—until the fall of 1875. The *Sentinel* gave strong support to all educational and cultural activities in the community and also carried from time to time a considerable amount of locally produced poetry (especially that of John Anderson) in its columns.

Two protestant denominations in the area were active in educational activities. The most prominent in this respect was the Anglican church, especially during the tenure of Reverend James Reynard from 1865 to his departure in August of 1871. When he first arrived, Mr. Reynard and his congregation acquired an old building and converted it into a church, only to have it destroyed in the great fire of 1868. They then began to raise funds in order to have a new church built. The fruit of this effort was a new St. Saviour's Church, which was opened on September 18, 1870, and became perhaps the best known building in Barkerville. Mr. Reynard's church had an active educational program long before that building was available, however. He organized a Church Institute along the lines of those existing in Great Britain (see Kelly 1962). There were other church institutes in British Columbia in the early years of the colony, but as far as can be determined, none was more active than Barkerville's. The *Sentinel* carried the following news item on December 19, 1868:

> *Cariboo Church Institute*—On Monday evening next, December 21, the elementary and other classes, as under, will assemble. The Bible classes on Wednesday and Friday evening are open to the public. On alternate Thursday evenings there will be an entertainment of singing and reading, or lectures on popular science, or history, or music. The fee for the course of elementary classes will be ten dollars. The proceeds will be devoted to church purposes.

F.A. Peake, the author of *The Anglican Church in British Columbia,* quotes a letter Mr. Reynard wrote at approximatelly the same time in which he indicated his plans to organize an institute and the proposed schedule of activities (Peake 1959:43-45).

The *Sentinel* carried notices of public meetings which occurred in the course of the Church Institute's activities. The first of these was a lecture by Mr. Reynard on "John Bunyan and Pilgrim's Progress," which was given to a "large and attentive audience" in the following month *(C.S.* Jan. 16, 1869). Reports followed of a band concert, two evenings of song and readings, and two lecture-concerts on "English Ballads," Mr. Reynard both lecturing and singing. In a financial statement published in the *Sentinel* as part of his campaign to raise funds for the new building, Mr. Reynard showed an income item of $235.25 as "Net proceeds of lectures, etc." *(C.S.* June 23, 1869). The most outstanding occasion perhaps was a concert on September 20, 1869, to raise funds for the Church Institute at which the Welsh Glee Club performed as well as church members, which was attended by Governor Seymour *(C.S.* Sept. 22, 1869).

In the following year the Church Institute was, if anything, even more active. In February and March of 1870, advertisements ran in the *Sentinel* which once again set out the schedule for the week and which put more stress on the availability of a reading room and study materials than had previously been the case. An indication of the popularity of the Church Institute's events is provided by the fact that although the new church building became available for use in the early fall of 1870, many of the meetings, both before and after that time, were held in the Theatre Royal building rather than in the church. Public events that season included a music concert given by Mr. Reynard, two performances of general musical entertainment and a band concert. This last meeting, which was reported as being "very well attended," included as well a "magic lantern show," a recent innovation in the community *(C.S.* April 29, 1871). Nothing else is known of the work of the Church Institute, but even these activities represent an impressive achievement on the part of Mr. Reynard and his church.

There is some indication that the Weslyan Methodist Church was also active in educational affairs. It has already been mentioned that the minister, Reverend Thomas Derrick, gave a lecture for the benefit of the Literary Institute in August of 1869. Earlier that year, he had given two public lectures in his own church. In early January he spoke on "Enthusiasm," admission fee, one dollar. The proceeds were to be used to help retire the church debt. A long report on the lecture appeared in the *Sentinel* and described the church as being "well filled" (*C.S.* Jan. 9, 1869). The following month he lectured on "Stumbling Blocks and How to Remove Them" and once again the newspaper carried a long summary (*C.S.* Feb. 13, 1869). At various times during this period there were references to Mr. Derrick's lecturing at the nearby community of Van Winkle.

The most active cultural organization in Barkerville was certainly the Cariboo Amateur Dramatic Association, the members of which were often referred to simply as "the Amateurs." A number of prominent local citizens were active in the group, including Bowron, J.S. Thompson and the poet, John Anderson, who also wrote plays and poetry for the group and usually appeared in a singing part. Over the years the group staged a large number of performances, often as frequently as one a month. The evidence seems to indicate that their first performance was given in June of 1865. An advertisement in the *Sentinel* of June 24 for the Parlor Saloon stated that "A Theatrical Entertainment will be given once a week by the Cariboo Amateur Dramatic Association." The next edition carried an enthusiastic review of the performance and expressed the hope that more would be forthcoming (*C.S.* July 1, 1865). It is not clear whether the group performed regularly thereafter, as suggested in the ad.

The society felt that it needed a more adequate and perhaps more appropriate hall for its presentations and during 1866 and the following year a number of interested people began to raise funds for the building of a theatre (Ludditt 1969). The campaign was successful and culminated in the construction of the Theatre Royal, which was officially opened with a performance on May 11, 1868. This building was an important asset to the community and was used for a wide variety of educational, cultural and social events. Ludditt relates that when the building, as rebuilt after the fire, was eventually torn down a few years previous to his account, it was revealed that five different floors had been laid on top of the original one.

The opening night was a gala occasion. The *Sentinel* carried advance advertising of the event and through the news columns repeatedly reminded its readers to attend. The account of the evening included a highly enthusiastic review of the Amateurs' performance and indicated that 250 people had attended, with others having been turned away (*C.S.* May 14, 1868). Four further performances of different works were presented in the following two months, each followed by long and laudatory reviews in the newspaper. Other touring theatre and music groups appeared in the theatre from time to time.

In September, the building was destroyed in the fire. The circumstances surrounding the rebuilding of the theatre are not known, but the "grand re-opening performance" was held on January 16, 1869, and presented to a "crowded house" (*C.S.* Jan. 23, 1869). There were frequent performances through the 1869 and 1870 seasons, with special occasions arranged over the Christmas and New Year holidays. It may well be that the rebuilding of the theatre and its upkeep were proving to be a serious burden on the community. In September of 1870 there was mention in the paper that the theatre was in debt and the Amateurs were selling "shares" in the building in an attempt to raise money

(*C.S.* Sept. 24, 1970). In the meantime, performances continued over the next few years, always followed by a long and appreciative account in the *Sentinel*. On a number of occasions, the performances were advertised as being a benefit for some individual in the community, usually a woman who had lost her husband.

The fact that the Amateurs continued to function successfully into the 1870s, when the community generally was on the decline, is a tribute to the energy and, possibly, talent of the performers and an indication of the strong support they had earned in the community. The group offered several performances in the spring of 1872, most to good houses but at least one, "somewhat thinly attended" (*C.S.* Sept. 28, 1872). In November of that year, three key members left the community (*C.S.* Nov. 16, 1872). Only one performance was offered the following year, a benefit in early March. The next notice was for a presentation held a year and a half later, in October of 1875. In a somewhat wistful notice, the newspaper commented that the excitement surrounding the occasion was like "days gone by" (*C.S.* Oct. 16, 1875). There was a long review of the event in the paper and some indication that there would be a further performance in November, but with that same issue the *Sentinel* ceased publication and it is not known whether any further productions were actually offered (*C.S.* Oct. 30, 1875).

There was also considerable musical activity in Barkerville in these years. Reference has already been made to the amateur activities in the churches and in association with the Dramatic Society, and as well to the fact that touring professional groups often appeared. There was musical activity associated with several of the saloons in the area and the *Sentinel* would occasionally refer to a particular performance, or even, on occasion, to the fact that a particular musician in one of the establishments had received a new piece of music which he or she would perform. Special mention was made of one couple who arrived in 1867 and set up "The Concert Hall, Richfield", where the wife, Mrs. Lange, who was described as being an accomplished artist, played sophisticated music on the piano while the customer consumed appropriate alcoholic beverages—presumably Mr. Lange's department (*C.S.* June 27 & July 22, 1867).

A number of Welsh citizens in the area had an active glee club whose activities were centred on the Cambrian Hall. But as has been pointed out, they played a part in the musical activities of the broader community as well. The group occasionally gave a public concert on their own (see *C.S.* May 22, 1869). Among these various groups, the Dramatic Society, the churches and the glee club, there were quite a number of amateur vocalists and on at least one occasion there was a concert in the Theatre Royal by "the amateur vocalists" and the *Sentinel* encouraged everyone inteested to attend in order to encourage these persons in their development as musicians (C.S. May 22, 1869). The only evidence of instruction in instrumental music is the reference by Elliott in his book to Mr. J.B. Melanion. He was said to be "an excellent violinist who played with the Paris opera. A carpenter by trade, he taught music to some of the Barkerville boys" (Elliott 1958:29).

There were several organizations in the community which offered educational activities for their members. The Welsh group has already been mentioned. Their building, the Cambrain Hall was described as being devoted to "literary, moral and religious meetings" (*C.S.* Jan. 15, 1867). There were Masonic organizations in the city, among both the white population and the Chinese. In the summer of 1867 it was announced that a local Caledonian Society was being organized and in September the *Sentinel* reported that "in order to increase the information of its members," a brief lecture was to be given at each meeting of the group prior to the handling of regular business (*C.S.* Sept. 12, 1867).

Apart from the church institute, there were two examples in Barkerville at this time of what we would refer to today as "evening classes for adults." The first was connected with the name of "Mons. B. Deffis." The earliest reference to him appears in an item in the *Sentinel* on October 7, 1867, where it was stated that he was staying in Barkerville through the winter and would give "lessons in French, Spanish [and] English grammer" [sic]. The writer commented that , "this is a good opportunity afforded miners to employ profitably the long winter months" (*C.S.* Oct. 7, 1867). During the following May, notices were run three times of new classes beginning at that time. That fall, similar notices were carried, arithmetic having been added to the list of subjects and $12.00 per month being stated as the fee (*C.S.* Oct 16, 1868 and later dates). The following fall, a news item was carried in four successive issues (beginning October 29, 1869) once again announcing the classes, this time including English composition and "private lessons in the dead languages if desired." There is no indication of what enrolments there were in these courses.

The other occasion on which evening classes were offered came considerably later. In early October, 1871, the *Sentinel* carried an advertisement for a Night School which was to be supervised by Mr. John Mundell (the teacher in the local public school, which had been opened the previous year). There were to be five classes weekly, in subjects which were unspecified but were presumably the regular school subjects. The fee was announced as $5.00 per month (*C.S.* Oct. 7, 1871). A news item a week later indicates that the school house, which had been announced as the location for the classes, had proven to be inconvenient and that the program was to be moved to the Cambrian Hall instead (*C.S.* Oct. 14, 1871). There is no indication as to registration in these classes, but it is known that Mr. Mundell left the community in March of the following year (Ludditt 1969).

One other educational organization should be mentioned. In late August of 1869, a notice appeared in the paper of a meeting of "the Barkerville Pickwick Club." It is referred to as a philosophical discussion group and the impression is conveyed that it was not a new organization in the community. The topic of the next meeting was described as being "a departure from the ordinary class of topics selected by the club for their literatry and discursive exercises" and because the topic did not involve "profound or abstract doctrines," members of the public were invited to attend (*C.S.* Aug. 21, 1869). On three more occasions over the following six weeks reference was made in the *Sentinel* to the activities of the club and then it too dropped out of sight, never to reappear.

During this decade there was at times a surprising amount and variety of educational activity for adults in the Barkerville area. It was an extremely difficult community in which to establish and maintain such work because of the percentage of the population that was transient, and also the considerable portion of even the "permanent" population which left the area during the winter. As we have seen, some provision for educational activities on the creek was made as early as 1863 and by 1868 and 1869, a wide range of activities were under way. Leadership was given to these enterprises by a relatively small number of devoted and able men and women. And it seems to have been the case that there was at least a small corps of people in the community, apparently drawn from several of the ethnic groups, who had some education and were persuaded of the importance of educational and cultural activities to their own lives and that of the community as a whole.

It should not be forgotten that the Barkerville of those days was no ordinary town. It had all the characteristics of the frontier community and was swept from time to time with rumours—some well based and some not—of exciting new discoveries in the area. While we may observe that there was considerable educational and cultural activity in Barkerville by 1869, it should be remembered that by the middle of that year there were eighteen saloons in that community and nearby Richfield combined. The local newspaper reveals a constant procession of businesses being sold and going bankrupt, partnerships being dissolved, and property being auctioned. It was in many respects a rapidly changing and unstable community. And yet much was attempted—and achieved—in the direction of social and individual betterment.

But the Barkerville of those boom days was short-lived. In many respects, the community began to go downhill by the latter part of 1869. The decline became a skid by the early 1870s and by 1873 many of the longest-established businesses had been sold at auction or simply closed (Ramsay 1961). The *Cariboo Sentinel* ceased publication in the fall of 1875 and, by the early 1880s, the total population on the creek had fallen to two or three hundred (Ludditt 1969). The end of an era had come for Barkerville and with it the end of a stimulating story of people attempting to build a better life for themselves and their community in the rough and ready surroundings of a frontier mining town.

References

Cariboo Sentinel newspaper, various dates.

Elliott, G.R. (1958), *Quesnel: Commercial Centre of the Cariboo Gold Rush*, Quesnel: Cariboo Historical Society.

Holmes, M.C. (1959), *Library Service in British Columbia*, Victoria: Public Library Commission of B.C.

Kelly, T. (1962), *A History of Adult Education in Great Britain*, Liverpool: Liverpool University Press.

Ludditt, F.W. (1969), *Barkerville Days*, Vancouver: Mitchell Press.

Ormsby, M.A. (1958), *British Columbia: A History*, Toronto: MacMillan of Canada.

Peake, F.A. (1959), *The Anglican Church in British Columbia*, Vancouver: Mitchell Press.

Ramsay, B. (1961), *Barkerville*, Vancouver: Mitchell Press.

Wolfenden, M. (1947), "Books and Libraries in Fur-Trading and Colonial Days," *British Columbia Historical Quarterly*, 11, (3). (July 1947).

Appeared originally in *B.C. Studies*, No. 9 (1971), pp. 38-54. Reprinted with permission.

5.2

Adult Education in
Vancouver before 1914

*I*t has been necessary, in connection with this study, to arrive at a satisfactory definition of adult education for present purposes. Because the research being carried out was the first attempt to review many of the primary sources available, it seemed wise to be as inclusive as possible. I therefore turned to the language of the well known *1919 Report* on adult education in the United Kingdom which defined it as:

> All the deliberate efforts by which men and women attempt to satisfy their thirst for knowledge, to equip themselves for their responsibilities as citizens and members of society or to find opportunities for self-expression. (Cited in Waller 1956:59)

This formulation made it appropriate to include a variety of activities which might have been excluded by a narrower, more technical definition which we might find appropriate today.

It should also be pointed out that in the account which follows, the references in the text have been kept to a minimum. Because much of the material included has been gathered from newspaper sources, there are places in the text when almost every sentence could be followed by a citation, in most cases to the Vancouver *News Advertiser*. Instead, references have been kept to a minimum, usually in the case of direct quotes.

Vancouver—indeed the whole of British Columbia—was late to be settled compared to many other parts of North America. But once established, it grew very rapidly, passing through a physical and social evolution in a few decades which was experienced by many older communities over a much longer period of time. This may help to explain the erratic development and short duration of some of the organizations and forms of adult education which appeared in the city in this early period. For its size, and considering its youth, Vancouver had by 1914 developed a relatively wide range of adult education activities.

* * *

The story of the development of Vancouver from its beginnings in the 1860s until the outbreak of the World War in 1914 is an amazing one. The period of early settlement through to the early 1880s was one of feverish industrial activity around the two main mills on Burrard Inlet, at Moodyville on the north shore and Hastings Mill on the south—but the number of people involved was small. Burrard Inlet was still seen by many as a recreational area for New Westminster. Although the timber industry developed at a constantly quickening pace, with at times as many as forty ships in the harbour either loading or waiting their turn, and while the Inlet was rising to a position as one of the greatest timber ports in the world, still the growth of permanent settlement was small. Vancouver's historian, Alan Morley, has referred to this period as "a quiet, placid and on the whole idyllic time:"

> The population...continued to increase in the measure necessary to conduct the business of a flourishing port, but only to that extent. The inlet settlements had little attraction for the speculators and minor capitalists who, since 1871, had been arriving in considerable numbers in B.C. in anticipation of the coming of the railroad. (Morley 1961:62)

But the next few years changed all that. By 1882, it became clear that Burrard Inlet would be the terminus of the railway, although at first it was assumed that it would be at the eastern end of the Inlet, at Port Moody. As soon as it was decided that Coal Harbour, at the village of Granville, would be the actual terminus, the rush was on. From an estimated population of 400 in 1881, the town increased to 2,000 in 1886. There were 100 buildings in the town in February of 1886 and 800 by June. Lots which sold for $300 in March were sold again for $1,000 in June. Granville was incorporated as the City of Vancouver in April. The great fire which wiped out the city in June of 1886 caused but a pause in the wave of expansion.

From 1886 to 1892 was a great boom period for the city. With the extension of the railway from Port Moody in 1887, and the inauguration of the trans-Pacific shipping routes, the transportation and communication links which were to be the vital factors in the growth of Vancouver, were solidly established (Roy 1960). From this point, there was no question that it was in due course to become the dominant centre in the province. By 1888 there were 8,000 persons in the city and by 1892, 15,000. There was big money in the community, including most obviously the investment being made by the Canadian Pacific Railway (C.P.R.). Capital was coming in from all parts of the world, especially Central Canada, the United States and Great Britain, and although there was as yet a very modest industrial base (mostly lumbering and fish canning) Vancouver was becoming the supply centre and regional financial centre for the whole Province. In this boom period, cultural and educational activities took a pronounced step forward and it is particularly obvious from the evidence that the early years of the 1890s were a definite peak as far as this work was concerned.

In the mid-1890s, Vancouver was a victim of the severe world-wide Depression. By 1893 it was hit hard. At its early stage of development the city was very vulnerable to a shortage of credit and capital. Contracts were cancelled, wages fell, the land boom was temporarily over and unemployment was high. Things began to move again by late 1897 and the Klondike gold rush, although its main financial benefits fell to Victoria and Seattle, provided a spark that set affairs moving again. The boom which followed was of unprecedented proportions and had profound effects on Vancouver. The population rose from 20,000 in 1898, to 26,000 in 1901, 45,000 in 1905 and 120,800 within expanded boundaries in 1911. The population of Vancouver was approximately fifteen per cent of that of the whole Province in 1901. By 1911, the figure had increased to over thirty per cent. This period was referred to by Alan Morley as "The Golden Years" in the development of the city and certainly they were times of remarkable growth and development. They were also times of elegance among a broad upper social class, which was demonstrated in a variety of ways such as dress, architecture and social activities. There was a fantastic real estate boom and the newpapers were full of grandiose schemes for expansion, most of which materialized!

There was a brief recession in 1907-1908, but this represented just a pause in the surge of development as far as Vancouver was concerned. This period too marked the high point of antagonism on the part of some citizens towards the large numbers of Asian immigrants in the city, whose numbers exceeded 20,000 by that time. In September of 1907, an unruly mob of 15,000 men actually invaded the "Chinatown" area, plundered, broke windows, and attacked many persons. This incident was a manifestation of an anti-Asian sentiment which was widely shared in the community and endorsed by many public figures. A further depression set in by 1912 and remained with the city until the outbreak of the war.

In these pre-war years, Vancouver was a city of grand schemes and ambitions. By 1898, when the population stood at approximately 20,000, the popular slogans of the day were predicting 100,000 residents by 1910. By 1908, when the population stood at something over 60,000, the city boasted a "Progress Club" and a "Half Million Club" which were energetic boosters of the future of the place. In the summer of 1914, as war clouds were gathering and the city was in a severe depression, a "Pageant of Vancouver" was "a success beyond the dreams of the promoters," with "crowded streets and cheering multitudes" (Vancouver *News Advertiser* (hereafter *N.A.*) June 13, 1914). Vancouver looked to the future with boundless optimism.

Mechanics' Institute

By the late 1860s, there was intense rivalry between Moodyville, the company town adjacent to Sue Moody's mill on the north shore of the inlet, and Stamp's Mill (soon renamed Hastings Mill) on the south shore. Morley suggests that it was in response to Moody's creation of a masonic lodge at Moodyville, that J.A. Raymur, the manager of Hastings Mill, set up the New London Mechanics' Institute on the south shore in January of 1869. It seems more likely, however, that to the extent that rivalry was involved at all, Raymur was responding to Moody's launching a mechanics' institute the previous fall. The Institute soon changed its name to the Hastings Mill Mechanics' Institute and it apparently collected a small library, which was located in a company boarding house near the mill. Little information is available about the activities of the institute. Morley states that it was officially opened by Rev. Arthur Browning. A New Westminster newspaper reported in May of 1871 that Reverend Thomas Derrick had spoken at the institute the previous week on "Enthusiasm." It is probably safe to say that little in the way of educational activities was undertaken by the organization except for the maintenance of a library and reading room. The only other references to the institute were in connection with two benefit performances for the institution held in the early 1880s.

There is no clear evidence as to why the institute ceased to function. It appears that it was maintained until the community outside the mill area became attractive enough that the men at the mill chose to live there rather than in the company boarding house. Then the company closed down the boarding house, and the reading room with it (Walker 1966).

Vancouver Reading Room and Public Library

About a year later, three prominent citizens, under the leadership of Rev. H.G. Fiennes-Clinton, the Rector of St. James Anglican Church, gathered up as many of the institute's books as they could find, raised some money, and called a public meeting at which the Vancouver Reading Room was formally organized. Established at first on a subscription fee basis, the library was supported by a modest grant from the city by 1888 and was put on a free service basis. Negotiations with the city in 1890 resulted in significant improvement in the grants from that source and in the creation of a Library Board on which the city had formal representation. The increase in funds made it possible to add to the collection, expand the library and reading room and employ a paid librarian. The next decade brought considerable expansion in the size of both the collection and circulation figures, but these did not keep pace with the remarkable growth of the city.

In 1898, a special meeting of the Library Board was held to consider the necessity for a new and larger building. This set in motion a series of events which, after many delays, led to the eventual construction of a new building and a vast improvement in the city's library services. The new library building came about as a result of a gift from Andrew Carnegie, and the amount he provided, $50,000, was made available on the customary terms—that the municipality was required to provide the site for the building and to guarantee that it would subsequently provide annually for the operation of the service an amount equal to at least ten per cent of the capital grant. After much detailed discussion over many months as to whether to accept the gift, the selection of a site and the approval of architect's plans, a contractor was finally selected in October of 1901. Construction was under way by the beginning of 1902 and was completed the following year.

The new building provided greatly expanded and improved facilities for the library, of course, and also made it a much more impressive and attractive place to visit. It provided space in which the specialized library services and collections could be more fully developed. In 1901 there were 6,878 volumes in the city lending library (actually down from a few years previous) and 210 in the reference collection. By 1905, there were 11,013 volumes in the library and by 1913 there were 34,000. The increase in circulation was even more spectacular. It rose from 44,000 in 1903 to 79,504 in 1910, 178,098 in 1911 and 330,000 in 1913 (figures from newpaper accounts). In the two years 1912 and 1913, six branch libaries were opened in different sections of the city. A children's department was opened in 1909 and the reference section was greatly strengthened beginning in 1910.

By 1911, the building was taxed to capacity. The *News Advertiser* ran a full page illustrated article on the institution in February of 1912 and stressed the difficulties under which the service was operating, referring to it as "a public utility grossly overworked and miserably underpaid" *(N.A.* Feb. 4, 1912). The chairman of the Board, Mr. Edward Odlum, made vigorous representations to the City Council on two occasions in early 1913 in which he stressed the urgent need for more space, money, books and staff. He pointed out that the very large circulation which had been experienced the previous year (265,000 volumes) had worn out many of the books and that in order to maintain that pace and to serve a city the size of Vancouver, 100,000 volumes were required, a far cry from the current 34,000. The librarian subsequently made the statement that no library had ever maintained such a circulation on so few volumes. By this time, however, the city was facing the serious depression of the immediate pre-war years and no substantial steps were taken to improve the situation. The library had come a long way since the days of the subscription service launched in 1887, but it faced serious problems which remained unresolved at the end of the period under review.

Commercial Libraries and Reading Rooms

There were a considerable number of these institutions in the city during this period. The first of these was one operated by Diplock's Book Store beginning in January of 1891. In order to make use of the 3,000 volume collection, subscribers were required to pay $2.00 per quarter, which entitled them to borrow three books at a time. By the early years of the new century, there were several such commercially operated libraries in the city.

Several reading rooms were operated during these years. The Vancouver Hotel announced in November of 1893 that it had opened a new reading room on its premises. When the Collingwood Institute (see below) was opened in 1911, it maintained a library and reading room. In the fall of 1912, a ratepayers' meeting in the suburb of Kerrisdale decided to set aside a room in their municipal hall to be run as a reading room and quiet games room. And in the same month, the All Saints Church announced that it was going to remedy the lack of such service in the East end of the city by opening a free reading room on their property at Victoria Drive and Pandora Street.

Young Men's Christian Association

In the early fall of 1886, a letter appeared in the Vancouver *News* lamenting the absence of a free reading room in the community and expressing the hope that a Y.M.C.A. would be formed to meet this need. When, by the end of September, no action was forthcoming, the *News* urged the mayor to call a public meeting to set things in motion (Vancouver *News* Sept. 14, 18 & 30, 1886). A meeting was held in late October and a further one early in November at which a Y.M.C.A. was formally organized and plans laid for a building and program. The report of the first meeting indicated that it was intended "to open a reading room and gymnasium and institute a lecture course." The subsequent session arranged for monthly meetings of the members, at which it was intended to have programs of "a literary character, selections of prose, poetry, songs and debates to form part of the order of exercises." Progress was rapid in the coming weeks and in late December, work was begun on the construction of a two-storey building for the Association.

The year 1887 was largely given over to the completion of the building, soliciting memberships and funds and the inauguration of group activities. The building was opened in October. The first group activities were religious in character; Bible classes and Sunday afternoon gospel meetings. In addition, the Association maintained a reading room and a social room, which were open from 9:00 a.m. to 10:00 p.m. This reading room was therefore opened just a few weeks before the Vancouver Reading Room became available, the latter at first on a subscription basis.

1888 to 1898

For most of the next decade, the Y.M.C.A. remained active and conducted a variety of educational activities. Much of this came under the general heading of lectures. Musical evenings were held from time to time as well. The reading room was maintained throughout the period but little is known about it. In 1893, shortly following the opening of the Association's new building, the Y.M.C.A. entered the field of educational classes for the first time. In mid-October it was announced that courses in writing, arithmetic, bookkeeping, French and shorthand were to be given. The instructors included some well known and outstanding persons. This program was expanded the following year to include other subjects such as architectural drawing, music and "elocution." It was announced that classes in any of those subjects would be started as soon as ten students had signed up for a course. There do not appear to have been further classes until after the turn of the century. One other educational program, the debating and discussion group called the "Current Topics Club" functioned for a few years in this period. It was announced in September of 1894 that such a group was to be formed and this was accomplished in late October. It soon had 25 members and was meeting regularly, discussing topics of current interest. The group continued to meet in the two following years, but did not start up again in the fall of 1897, when the Association closed its doors for a period. However, in the following months, when the rooms were being operated as a Young Men's Home, a "Young Men's Debating Society" was meeting.

1898 to 1914

The Association was reorganized in 1898 and a paid general secretary was appointed. By the fall of 1899, the organization was operational once again and continued to be active throughout the remainder of the period, especially after a move into new premises in 1905. In this 15 year period, a very active program was built up. The Association was heavily involved in evening class activity before the public school authorities took up that task. Early in 1906, the following announcement appeared in the newspaper:

> The educational agencies in connection with the Y.M.C.A. now include evening classes for men who are working during the day and desire to use part of their leisure time in preparing for promotion. Mr. Edgar Murphy, principal of the Admiral Seymour School, is engaged as teacher of arithmetic and business English while Mr. J.R. Cunningham of the Vancouver Business College is the instructor in the penmanship and bookkeeping classes. (*N.A.* Jan. 20, 1906)

In the fall of that year, classes were started again, the year being divided into two ten-week terms. It was announced that classes would be arranged on any subject for which there were 12 students. By November of 1907, 125 students were taking the courses being offered. The following year, 160 students were registered in 13 subjects. In 1909, 191 students took courses. Subjects mentioned at the time were arithmetic, business English, penmanship, architectural drawing, freehand drawing, plan reading and estimating, gasoline engines and first aid (*N.A.* Dec. 15, 1909). When the Vancouver School Board started its night school on a large scale in 1910, the Y.M.C.A. ceased offering most of its classes, although work in public speaking and salesmanship were begun as late as 1913 and 1914, respectively.

The Association also maintained its active program of regular public lectures. In addition, a number of specilaized educational organizations were operating under Y.M.C.A. auspices. In the fall of 1902, an active Literary Society was formed which continued to meet until at least 1907. At that time it was amalgamated with the Debating Society. The latter had been founded in October of 1903 and was very active. It gave important leadership to the Vancouver Debating League in future years (see below) and was also active in its own right as late as the fall of 1913, at least. Reference has been found in early 1912 to a "Tuesday Club", which arranged lectures and discussions on both religious and secular subjects. In the fall of the year, an "Efficiency Club" was formed. It was made up of men in business, but its program ranged over a wide variety of subjects, some of them related to business but others of general interest. This group was still active in the program year 1913-14.

The Association also maintained its reading room. It was described in early 1901 as "supplied with standard magazines and papers." The annual report given in January of 1903 indicated that the room was kept open from 8:00 a.m. to 10:00 p.m. six days a week and 2:00 to 5:30 on Sunday, and that 45 papers and magazines were kept in stock. When the new building was opened in late 1905, expanded facilties became available. A description of the new facilites mentioned not only a "members' reading room" which contained magazines and reference books, but also a "newspaper room."

Young Women's Christian Association

The Vancouver Y.W.C.A. was founded as a result of a series of meetings which began in the fall of 1897 and culminated in May of the following year. The Y.W. put chief emphasis on maintaining a residential facility for girls and young women and providing other services of benefit to these groups, such as the Travellers Aid and an employment bureau. In 1910, for instance, their employment bureau received 3,000 requests from employers for personnel.

No details are available on the educational work of the Association until well after the turn of the century. In the program year 1906-1907, classes in Bible study, physical training and embroidery were operating, involving a total of 70 women. Press reports in February of 1908 indicated that during the previous year, classes in English literature, Bible study, French, shorthand, dressmaking, embroidery, physical training and choral music had been held, with a total enrollment of 150. Millinery, first aid, domestic science and "elementary subjects" were added the next year. Unlike the Y.M.C.A., the Y.W. maintained its modest program of classes after the Vancouver School Board began its night classes. In the fall of 1912, it even held a "class rally" in late September to launch the program for the fall. It included the same sort of subjects as had been given previously and at the annual meeting later in the year it was reported that 317 women and girls had taken part in the "classes and clubs" during the year. This increased to 400 the next year (Y.W.C.A. Annual Report 1913). Additional subjects in the program during these last two years of the period included "expression and voice culture," home nursing and Shakespeare.

Church-Sponsored Lectures, Literary and Debating Societies

As in other centres in the Province during this period, the churches were very active in providing lectures for both their members and the general public. Many different congregations became involved in this work. The most active were the Methodists, Presbyterians and Congregationalists, with the Anglicans, Unitarians and some others also conducting programs. These events ranged all the way from single lectures to ambitious series and included a wide range of subject matter.

Some of the churches organized literary societies and debating organizations. Five or six congregations organized mock parliaments. When the Vancouver Debating League was founded in 1911, at least six churches had teams taking part in the first or succeeding years, the Kitsilano Presbyterian team winning the competition in the year 1911-1912.

Ad Hoc Lecture Activity

There was a great deal of lecture activity in Vancouver, as elsewhere, which was either offered on an isolated, ad hoc basis, or was offered under the auspices of organizations which were not primarily educational in character. For instance, a number of lectures were arranged on matters related to the British connection. In the spring of 1889, the noted British political figure and exponent of Imperial Federation, G.R. Parkin, spoke on Imperial Federation to a large meeting chaired and arranged by the mayor. In the spring of 1907, the Imperial Order of Daughters of the Empire offered a public lecture series on "imperial subjects," the first of which was given in mid-March on "Track of Empire" by Sir Charles Tupper. In the fall of 1909, Mayor C.S. Douglas chaired a public meeting at which a Reverend gentleman from Ireland spoke on "Ireland's Relations to the British Empire." A year later, the United Services Club organized a large public meeting at which G.H. Cowan spoke on the "naval Question." Literary topics, travel and international affairs were the most frequent subjects as far as other lectures were concerned.

Two special series deserve separate mention. The Rev. H.H. Gowen, who had formerly lived in New Westminster and was now a Congregational minister in Seattle, had given lecture series in Victoria in 1903 and 1905. In 1906 and again the following year, he did so in Vancouver. On the first occasion, the lectures were given for the benefit of the Victorian Order of Nurses and consisted of two series of weekly lectures, one in the afternoon and one in the evening of the same day. The fee was $2.50 for the series, with half price for public and private school students and for professional nurses. The topics were all about literature and were different for the two series. They included: "Poets of Today," "Novels and Novelists," "Sonnets and Sonnet Writers," "The Poets of the Renaissance," and "The American Pantheon of Poetry." Both of these ambitious series were reasonably well attended. In the fall of 1907, a similar double series was again announced, this time the lectures dealing more with individual writers such as Swinburne, Blake, Stevenson and Omar Kayam. Less detail is available on the lecture activities of Mr. A.N. St. John Mildmay, but they were considerable. During the fall and winter of 1909-1910, he gave a series of weekly lectures on literary subjects which were held in a private home but were open to the public at fifty cents per lecture. In the spring of 1913, he gave a series of seven weekly lectures in a public hall on classical and more recent authors which was described as intended to stimulate interest in the Arts section of the new University of British Columbia, which was being planned at the time.

Other Literary and Debating Societies

A. Vancouver Institute

During the winter season, 1890-1891, while Vancouver was still a very small community, two local leaders, Rev. E.D. McLaren and Mr. W.H. Gallagher, proposed that if a meeting room in the city-owned Market Hall was made available to them free of charge for three evenings a week, they would arrange a series of free entertainments consisting of "popular science, music, literature and debates" (*N.A.* Nov. 11, 1890). The City Council provided the room and there followed a remarkably successful series of events, the hall frequently being filled to capacity. When the time came in March to conclude the series, the hall was reported as "never before so crowded" for the final concert and in response to popular demand, the season was extended by a few weeks. This was not attempted again the following year.

B. Burrard Literary Society

The story of this organization from its founding in 1889 until its dissolution in 1908 is one of the most interesting chapters in the story of adult education in the pre-war years. In a period when such organizations typically lasted a relatively short period of time, this one maintained an active program consistently for almost 20 years. It appears to have been a "closed" group in the sense that one had to be formally admitted to membership before one could take part in its activities. It is unusual, however, for such a group to receive as much press coverage as this one did. There were some prominent citizens such as Mr. Jonathan Rogers in the group. One of the pioneer members noted that there were also a number of prominent socialists in the organization (Vancouver City Archives docket on the B.L.S.). It is not known precisely when the group was organized, but evidence indicates that this was likely in the fall of 1889. For much of its life the organization seems to have specialized in the standard forms of debating, although from time to time there were indications that some meetings consisted of a lecture followed by a general discussion of the topic. Although it met normally on its own, there were occasional meetings with other groups. The Society appears to have been well organized. The normal pattern, apparently, was to set out the topics for the term at the first meeting in the fall and again in the spring; or in some years, to divide the program year up into three periods. Topics discussed were numerous and varied, most of them related to significant political questions of the day. Little information is available about the dissolution of the organization. The group started again as usual in the fall of 1907, setting a schedule of topics in early October and again in mid-November. The last press report of a meeting which has been located appeared on January 23, 1908. As far as can be determined, this marked the end of this remarkable organization which had a long and useful life and more than ten years previously had already been described as "one of the oldest and most useful institutions in the city" (*N.A.* Oct. 4, 1896).

C. Vancouver Mock Parliament

This organization was in operation for several years in the early 1890s, although information about its activities is fragmentary. In November of 1890, the press reported that 28 persons had come together and formed the "Vancouver Mock Parliament, Literary and Debating Society." Eighty persons took part in the first debate, held a week later, and 100 in the one a few days later. Several meetings were reported in early 1891 and again in 1893. Meetings were noted in March and April of 1894, but nothing further after that. In late 1897 an attempt was made to reform a mock parliament, but nothing seems to have come of that effort.

D. Mount Pleasant Literary Society

This organization was active during 1901, but it is not known how long it was in operation. The first reference to it which has been found mentioned that the Burrard Club had arranged to debate against the Mount Pleasant Literary Society in mid-February of 1901. There was also some reference to the fact that this group held mock trials as well. In November of the same year, the newspaper carried a list of topics for the Society's meetings through into January of the following year. There was also further indication that mock trials were staged regularly. There were no further indications of the activities of the group.

E. Vancouver Debating League

Beginning in 1911, a number of organizations in the city which had debating clubs or were interested in such activity came together in the Vancouver Debating League. The organization was formed in November of that year, as a result of initiative taken by the Debating Club of the Y.M.C.A. Such organizations had apparently proven successful in some other centres. Two meetings held during that month resulted in the formation of the League, which had as its stated purposes to improve the public speaking skills of the participants and to keep matters of public interest before the membership of the societies taking part. There were ten organizations taking part in the League the first year. The first debates were held in December and the balance in the early months of the following year. In March of 1912, the League sponsored an oratorical contest which was held at the First Presbyterian Church and attended by more than 600 persons. The League functioned in each of the next three years—through to the end of the period under review. The number of participating groups increased to 20 by 1913, and in the words of the League's historian, were "representative of practically all the political, educational, religious and literary organizations in Vancouver and New Westminster" (Ginn 1913:7). By early 1914, in addition to the churches represented, there were teams from the Collingwood Institute, Law Students, South Vancouver Liberals, Y.M.C.A., West End Club and Knights of Columbus. One further group, the Round Table Debating Club, was mentioned later in that year.

F. Collingwood Institute (Bursill Institute)

In late 1911 or early 1912, John F. Bursill, a well-known newspaper man and literary figure, founded the Collingwood Institute and Free Library in the South Vancouver area. The Institute, often referred to as the Bursill Institute, became a focal point for a variety of literary, musical and social activities. In spite of the fact that the organization was consistently hampered by debts, many of its activities were outstandingly successful. An "entertainment" held in February of 1912 attracted an audience of approximately 300 and a sketch written by Bursill himself was the main item on the program. "Several hundred people" attended a similar event the following month (N.A. Feb. 16, Mar. 20, 1912). Mr. Charles Hill-Tout lectured at the Institute in the fall of 1913 and in February of 1914 a gala musical and literary evening featuring the works of Charles Dickens was held. Bursill was well known in the area as the leading expert on Dickens and he lectured frequently on topics connected with the life and writing of the great Victorian novelist. The Institute also maintained a library from its very early stages, although little is known about it. The Vancouver *Daily World* stated in January of 1915 that there were 2,500 books in the collection. There was a reference at one point to a Collingwood Mock Parliament, which may have been connected with the Institute.

G. Shakespeare, Dickens and Burns Clubs

The newspaper carried an announcement in October of 1904 that an organizational meeting was to be held that month for a local Shakespeare Club. Little is known of this group, but it was still operative in 1913. In January of that year, in an article about F.W. Dyke, a prominent local musician, the following passage appeared:

> For five or six years he has been an enthusiastic member of the local Shakespearean Society of which Mr. E.C. Kilby is the moving spirit, and which meets together regularly to read and discuss the plays of the master dramatist. (*N.A.* Jan. 5, 1913)

There was also a Dickens Club in the city. It was a small, exclusive group for some years, but the membership was widened somewhat in 1911 on the occasion of the centennial of Dickens' birth. The only references to a local Burns Club which have been found were carried in the press in early 1912, in which two successive "regular meetings" were mentioned.

The Vancouver Art Association, the Historical and Scientific Association and City Museum

In 1889, the Vancouver Art Association, the first organization of its kind in the city, was founded by a small group of interested citizens. It was expanded five years later to include historical and scientific fields of interest and thereafter became, along with the Y.M.C.A., one of the two most outstanding voluntary associations in the city in terms of their adult education activities. On January 18, 1889, the *News Advertiser* carried a letter to the editor signed by "Art" which stressed the growing interest in art in the city and announcing a meeting to be held that evening to discuss plans "to promote art in every desirable way." What happened at the meeting was summarized in the press account of the meeting:

> The meeting held at Mrs. Webster's Art Bazaar...was numerously attended and it was unanimously resolved that the aims and objects of the association be for the mutual assistance of its members in the prosecution of art studies and by every means to cultivate a taste for and to further the interest of art in the City of Vancouver....Hopes were expressed that an art association here would soon be started, and that this city...might before long boast an art gallery.... (*N.A.* Jan. 20, 1889)

There two leading figures in these developments were Captain and Mrs. H.A. Mellon. Captain Mellon was an industrialist in the city and both he and his wife gave active support and leadership to this organization and its successor for many years (although both stoutly refused to become president at any time).

The Vancouver Art Association, which has been described as the city's first permanent cultural group, must have been formally established within a few days of that first meeting. The press announced a meeting of the organization (not necessarily the first) for early February and within two months, "nearly forty" persons had joined (*N.A.* April 10, 1889). The first major event sponsored by the new group took place in late June in the form of a loan exhibition. It was opened on June 28 by Rev. H.P. Hobson, the President of the

Association, who paid tribute to "Mrs. Webster, Mr. Ferris, Captain Mellon and others" for their efforts in launching the organization. In mid-November, the Association opened its own rooms with "a most successful 'at home'." It was announced at that time that art classes were to be inaugurated under the sponsorship of the Association and according to Wylie Thom's study (Thom 1969), Mr. Will Ferris was the first teacher. The Association also began creating "a collection of objects of art and of historic interest" (*AHSA Journal* 1917:3). At the beginning of 1890, the new organization was described as being "in a flourishing condition" and plans were being laid for the most ambitious event yet, an art exhibition. This was held during October and included 350 pictures, half of them painted by the pupils and members and the rest loaned by members and friends. The exhibition was open for five days and each evening some dramatic or musical performance was presented for those in attendance.

There was a falling off of activity on the part of the Association for several years from this point on. There was a newspaper notice of an "art reading and social gathering" held in March of the following year, and some indication that these were weekly affairs, and there is indication that painting classes were held in the following summer. Attempts were made in both 1892 and 1893 to widen the scope of the organization to include historical and scientific (especially archeological) interests but neither of these produced immediate results. Mrs. Mellon is generally seen to be the key figure in the formation of the Art, Historical and Scientific Association. It had been her intention ever since 1887 to form a group which would take an interest in the history of British Columbia and the Vancouver area. She turned her hand first to the Art Association, but continued her interest in the other idea and worked for the extension of the Art Association to include the other function as well. At a public meeting held on April 17, 1894, called "for the purpose of considering if an effort should be made to revive the interest formerly taken in Art, History and Science," it was agreed to form the Art, Historical and Scientific Association of Vancouver (A.H.S.A.)(*AHSA Journal* 1917:3). Rev. Norman Tucker, Rector of Christ Church, was named the first President, a position he held for the next three years. Mrs. Mellon became Vice President and Mr. H.J. De Forest, Secretary. In the following month, the Vancouver Art Association was formally dissolved and its exhibits and funds turned over to the new organization. Thus was founded the organization which for many years thereafter was to play such an important part in the cultural and educational life of the city.

The activities of the A.H.S.A. in the succeeding twenty years were impressive in terms of their variety, quality and benefit to present and future citizens of the city. The organization was fortunate in being able to attract strong leadership which was well connected socially and financially in the city. The A.H.S.A. did not ever have a particularly large membership. It reached something over 50 by 1901 but had fallen to approximately 40 the following year. By 1908, it had come up to only 65 and by 1912, to 130. The financial fortunes of the Association were remarkably stable for an organization of its type, another reflection of the fact that the Association was ably led and well connected. Memberships brought in a modest but steady income. The city made a grant to the Association beginning in 1903 of $100 per year. The amount remained the same until 1905, when the museum was opened in the Carnegie Library and the city began to pay a salary to the curator. In 1907 the city's grant was $850 and by 1912 this had risen to

$2,500. Other funds were raised by means of entertainments, excursions, balls and voluntary contributions.

The two activities to which the A.H.S.A. most consistently gave its attention were lectures for the general public and the development of what later became the city museum.

A. Lectures

A general lecture series for the public, usually free of charge, was given almost every year, but varied widely in number. Five were given in 1895, the first full year of operation, and this represented the average for the next several years, after which it increased slightly. The subject matter was extremely varied, ranging over the many fields of interest encompassed by the scope of the organization. The lectures appear to have been on serious subjects and tended to be scholarly rather than "popular" in character. The lecturers included the outstanding authorities in the area, with occasional visiting speakers. It would appear that the lectures were of a uniformly high standard. The full text or long excerpts were sometimes subsequently printed by the local newspapers. On several occasions, what might be described as courses of lectures on the same or related topics were offered. Topics included English literature, geology, mining, religions and the history of the province. In a press report on a meeting of the Board of Directors of the Association which was carried in late January of 1912, it was announced that plans were being made to provide some lectures each year for members only, in addition to the regular series for the general public. By that time there were over 100 members and it was decided it would encourage other people to join, and be a useful service to members to arrange such a series. There were six such lectures arranged the first year and three in each of the next two years. The lectures offered on this basis did not seem to differ in any noticeable way from the other series

B. Vancouver Museum

It has already been pointed out that the predecessor of the A.H.S.A., the Art Association, had begun a collection of items of artistic and historic interest. Whatever materials that organization collected were turned over to the A.H.S.A. in the spring of 1894. According to the Journal of the A.H.S.A., once the organization was founded, "energetic steps were taken to develop the small art collection into the nucleus of a museum" (*AHSA Journal* 1917:4). A public exhibition was organized in November of 1894 which contained pictures and curios and the growth of the collection was steady from that point on. At the first annual meeting in January of 1895, the President reported that the Association had begun to collect treasures of art and remains of Indian life and stamps and specimens of various kinds. The Association moved into new rooms in February of 1896 and the city directory referred to its quarters as "museum and lecture rooms."

During 1898, significant new steps were taken. Representations were made to the City Council pointing out that the museum collection was an important asset to the city and asking for financial support for that aspect of the Association's work. Reference has already been made to the success of that application and the level of grants accorded in the following years. The year 1898 was also (presumably a result of the grant) the first occasion on which purchases were made for the collection. In the fall of 1899, having been successful in securing a grant, the management committee of the Association decided to approach the City Council again, this time asking for space in the public library which could be used to house the museum. These representations did not produce the desired results at the time, but they foreshadowed what was to come about a few years later. Thereafter, increasingly frequent notices appeared in the papers concerning donations of significant items to the museum collection. At the annual meeting early in 1901, it was made clear that the Association still wished to transfer the museum and the Association's property to the city. Negotiations to that end apparently progressed slowly for the next two years. The A.H.S.A. decided in 1903 to make further formal representations to the city and this time they were successful. As a result of these discussions, the city entered into an agreement with the Association which established the basis on which a public museum could be created. The city would supply suitable premises for the new museum— which turned out to be on the third floor of the new library building at Main and Hastings— and once the collection was moved in, it would become the Vancouver Public Museum, to be maintained by the city and managed by the Association. Under the arrangement, the mayor and two aldermen were to become members of the board of directors of the Association.

After a further delay of some two years, the Vancouver Museum was formally opened in the Carnegie Library building on April 19, 1905 "amidst great festivities." A lengthy newspaper account of the occasion described the displays as "a handsome and extensive collection of Indian relics, curiosities, valuable stones and other specimens" (*N.A.* April 20, 1905). The museum grew and prospered in its new location. Attendance increased tremendously in succeeding years. The large numbers of people who visited the museum and the growth in the collection itself caused acute space shortages by the beginning of the World War. It was a creditable achievement on the part of the A.H.S.A. to build up a museum collection under very difficult circumstances and to keep it going until the time when the City Council could be convinced that it was a valuable civic asset which should be housed and supevised as a public institution. Even after that decision was made, the Association continued its connection with the institution and continued to give valuable leadership to its improvement and expansion.

C. Other Activities

Reference has already been made to the fact that in the first year of its existence, the A.H.S.A. organized a large public exhibition of art work and curios. It was held in November of 1894 and was officially opened by the Governor General, the Earl of Aberdeen, who was visiting the area at the time. No further shows of this kind were sponsored by the Association. The A.H.S.A. staged a number of fund-raising ventures over the years. Musical evenings were held quite frequently from 1894 to 1899. Litrary evenings held under the title of "conversaziones" were held from time to time in 1896, 1899 and 1902. Three outstandingly successful balls were organized in 1906 and 1907.

By virtue of a combination of hard work, good management and attracting able leadership with useful political and social connections, the A.H.S.A. was able to accomplish a great deal. Their lecture activities were of an outstanding number, regularity and quality and their efforts in connection with the museum left Vancouver in their debt.

Groups Related to the Arts

A. Instrumental Music

After one false start in 1886, the Vancouver Philharmonic Society was formed in 1889, performing both instrumental and vocal music. The Philharmonic and Orchestral Society was formed in 1893 and continued to perform over the next decade. The Vancouver Choral and Orchestral Society was launched in 1904, followed in 1911 by the Vancouver Musical Society. It was not until 1911 that a strictly instrumental group on a large scale was formed, its first concert—and the first orchestral concert given in the city—being offered in March of the following year. A chamber music group gave a series of concerts during 1911 and a Scottish Philharmonic Society was active beginning in 1912. Mention should also be made of the City Band, a brass band formed in 1886 which remained active through until 1914, took part in many ceremonial occasions in the city, and during the summer season regularly gave outdoor concerts. At least two other brass bands were active for shorter periods during these years.

Mention should be made as well of the Vancouver Women's Musical Club. Like its counterpart in Victoria, this organization was formed not for the purpose of performing music, but to provide opportunities to listen to it. It is not known exactly when the group was organized, but it was certainly in operation as early as the fall of 1906. In that year it was arranging bi-monthly morning concerts of instrumental and/or vocal music for its members. Such activities were held each year thereafter. This organization was significant not only because it made it possible for its members to hear performances of good music on a regular basis but also because it provided an opportunity for a large number of local artists to perform.

B. Vocal Music

Mention has been made above of several groups which performed both instrumental and vocal music. In addition to this, there were a large number of organizations, all of them apparently short-lived, which concentrated on vocal music only. The earliest of these was the Vancouver Glee and Madrigal Society, which was organized in 1887. The Vancouver Operatic and Dramatic Society, which was active from 1893 to 1897, lasted longer than any other group in the period. Isolated references have been found to a variety of other groups, especially in the period after 1910, but little is known about their work.

C. Drama

Several references to drama groups have been found, but only the Garrick Dramatic Club, which was organized in 1888 and was active until at least 1913, continued in existence for any appreciable length of time.

D. Painting, Drawing and Related Arts

Organized activities in these fields was relatively late in developing. As described above, the Vancouver Art Association was founded in 1889, to be replaced in 1894 by the Art, Historical and Scientific Association. Both organizations arranged exhibitions which included the work of local artists and the former had an active program of painting classes.

The Vancouver Arts and Crafts Association was formed in 1900. It included representation from several different areas of artistic endeavour, held public exhibitions and conducted lectures and classes during 1900 and the following year, but became less active after that, dissolving when several key leaders left the city. In 1904, a longer-lasting organization, The Studio Club, was organized. It remained active until 1913, organizing art classes, maintaining its own studio space, and holding annual exhibitions of members' and other art work. It has been criticized as having degenerated into a social club, but it did make a contribution over the years by stimulating participation and interest in the arts (Thom 1969). The Studio Club was intended for the amateur. In 1908, several of the professional artists in the city came together to form the British Columbia Society of the Fine Arts and the main focus of the Vancouver art world shifted to this new and active organization. Its annual exhibitions, which continued until the beginning of the War, became the art event of the year, received a great deal of attention from the press and were the subject of serious art criticism. Towards the end of the period an organization devoted to handicrafts was formed in the city. The Vancouver Branch of the Canadian Handicrafts Guild was established in September of 1912 for "the preservation and promotion of handicrafts...and actively working for the benefit of their fellow men and women." The organization attracted a number of prominent citizens to its board. In the summer of 1913, it opened a shop in downtown Vancouver (with the help of a $500 grant from the provincial government) where craft work from across Canada was sold, the proceeds going to support handicapped and native Indian artists, as well as other worthy purposes. The Guild also sponsored public lectures and other fund raising events.

E. Instruction in the Arts

In addition to the organizations already mentioned, there were many and varied opportunities in all of the foregoing fields, as well as in other arts and crafts and the dance, for the interested individual to receive instruction. In the very early years, many individuals advertised their services as teachers. This was especially common in instrumental music, dance, and painting and drawing. In subsequent years, commercial companies entered the field. These included the Academy of Music (1889), the Vancouver Conservatory of Music (1896), The Columbia Commercial College (1896), the Vancouver Art School (1905), several dancing academies and a number of others.

Public Educational Authorities

The participation of public educational authorities in the provision of adult education opportunities for the city of Vancouver began in a small way in the year 1900 and culminated in the fall of 1909 with the permanent establishment of a night school program. As early as 1900, the annual report of the public schools of the province indicated that there were both part-time and full-time students taking first and second year university level work at Vancouver College. Vancouver College was the name adopted by Vancouver High School under an agreement by which it had become affiliated with McGill University in 1899. In December of the following year, the same institution sponsored a public lecture given at O'Brien's Hall by Mr. Oliver Bainbridge. This was perhaps the first extension or adult education activity offered by any public school authority in the city, apart from making the regular curriculum available to part-time students.

In 1906, McGill University College was created in Vancouver and it took over the university level work which had previously been provided by the local school board through Vancouver College. In the spring of 1907, this institution offered its first extension activity in the form of a lecture by the Superintendent of Education for the province, Mr. Alexander Robinson, on "Captain Vancouver—His Explorations." The Literary Society of the College, which normally involved only students in its activities, arranged this public lecture. Judging by the account of the proceedings in the press, this was seen to be a significant step by the institution. There was considerable formality involved in the meeting and in the introduction of the speaker, and the meeting hall was filled to the doors.

Night school classes under the auspices of the school board began in early 1907. An announcement in the newspaper on January 12 under the heading "Night Classes," read as follows:

> A meeting of persons interested in the formation of night classes for instruction in Mathematics, Engineering Mechanics, Descriptive Geometry, Geometrical and Mechanical Drawing and other subjects will be held in the Principal's room, Central High School, on Monday, January 14th at 8:00 p.m. (*N.A.* Jan. 12, 1907)

Arising out of the discussions at that meeting, in which the experience of the city of London, England with such classes was referred to frequently, a committee was appointed to carry the matter forward. Among others, it included Mr. John Kyle, who was to play a particularly significant role in the future of this work. Events moved rapidly after that. The committee met the next day to discuss plans for the program. They were of the opinion that it was largely elementary subjects which were needed and decided to place newspaper advertisements in order to test the demand. The model provided by the system in the United Kingdom was apparently very much in their minds. It was decided that each course would consist of 14 lessons and that the courses would be handled in such a way that the student would be in a satisfactory position to write examinations in the various subjects which were set by the British authorities. There was, however, to be no formal affiliation with a British agency.

On January 18 and for the next four days the *News Advertiser* carried an advertisement headed "Night Classes" which listed a number of subjects in which the board was prepared to offer instruction in the term January to June. Students of both sexes were encouraged to indicate their interest in the program by contacting the Secretary of the School Board. It was stated that the fees per course had not been set but would not be more than $3.50. The subjects listed included six courses on different applications of drawing (Mechanical, etc.) elementary mathematics and chemistry, experimental physics, building construction, "Steam—first stage," theoretical and applied mechanics, music, domestic science and manual training. On the first day the advertisement was run, the newspaper carried two news items in its columns drawing readers' attention to the new program.

There was apparently a reasonably promising response to the advertisements, because the following notice was carried by the *News Advertiser* on January 29 and 30:

> Meetings for the formation of classes will be held as follows:
> January 30 at 8:00
> Mathematics—Principal's Room, Central School
> Experimental Physics, Mechanics and Steam—City Superintendent's Office
> Drawing—School Board Office

January 31 at 8:00
Building Construction—Principal's Room, Central School
Manual Training, Woodwork and Domestic Science—School Board Office
Music—City Superintendent's Office
Course in each subject will include 14 lessons
Fee for the first stage in any subject $2.50.
Fee for advanced stage in any subject $5.00.
All desiring to join the classes must be present on the above dates.

In a press report of a school board meeting held in early March, the Superintendent, Mr. Argue, "reported that that the night classes in the high school in Experimental Science and Geometrical and Freehand Drawing were well attended considering their recent establishment, and their success for the future was assured" (*N.A.* Mar. 30, 1907). These then were the first night classes offered by the Vancouver school authorities (starting approximately six months later than the ones in Victoria).

In the fall of 1907, the school board night classes were not offered, but McGill University College ran courses in several subjects. A first meeting to organize the classes was held in early October, when it was made clear that this work could be taken for credit towards college certificates. No details are available concerning enrollments in the various courses offered, but a press report of a school board meeting early in 1908 contained the following statement:

> In October night classes were opened in the University College. Instruction in English Literature, Latin, French, Mathematics, Mechanical Drawing was offered; and while these classes have not been as well attended as they should be, a fair beginning has been made. (*N.A.* Jan. 7, 1908)

With this development, the province had its first example of university level extension work. As far as is known, the College did not repeat this experiment.

The school board did not offer night classes in the fall of 1908, but it continued its interest in the matter and took steps towards the eventual establishment of a continuing program. The board decided at a meeting in October that at the provincial convention of school trustees which was to be held in Revelstoke a few weeks later, it would support a resolution in favour of offering such classes. Two weeks later, the Vancouver City Council passed a resolution unanimously which endorsed these proposals. At the subsequent trustees' convention, the following resolutions were passed unanimously:

> That the Board of School Trustees be given power to conduct night classes for all pupils who are not included under the clauses of the Public Schools Act. That government assistance by way of a grant be given Boards conducting night classes. (B.C.S.T.A. 1908:10)

Although no action had been taken by the government in this matter by the fall of 1909, the Vancouver School Board decided to go ahead that year with the inauguration of an ambitious night school program. In early October of 1909, a story about the opening of night schools appeared in the press under the following headline, "Night Schools Begin Shortly: New Departure under Auspices of Vancouver School Board Should Prove Very Popular." The story indicated that "final arrangements" had been made to inaugurate the program. A list of courses to be offered was included, along with details about the four schools to be used for classes. The instructional staff was described as "made up of practical men" and those who were expected to be interested in the opportunity were referred to as "young men and women." On the same day, the newspaper carried an advertisement placed by the school board which was headed, "Young Men and Women! Prepare for Promotion!". The vocational emphasis of the program could not have been made more clear. The ad listed the courses being offered and indicated that the fee would be $3.00 per course (*N.A.* Oct. 5, 1909).

The response was most gratifying. In that first full year of operation, 601 persons took courses, some more than one, making a total of 966 registrations (Wales 1958). Ten different courses were given, held in six different centres. The enrollments by subject were as follows:

Arithmetic	276	Drawing	36
English	288	Modelling	9
Bookkeeping	209	Quantity Surveying	15
Engineering	39	Building Construction	22
Mathematics	21	Architecture	51

The four main schools used and the numbers attending classes at each were: Central (159), Fairview (108), Mount Pleasant (168) and Seymour (166).

The unexpectedly heavy response to the new program caused problems. The size of the enrollments and the consequent demands on the school board in terms of providing instructors, space and supplies was more than had been anticipated. The response of the board to this situation was summed up in a press report on the board meeting held in mid-October, which was headed, "Popularity of Night Schools So Great that Board Will Have to Apply for Provincial Government Aid." The article indicated that the board anticipated a deficit of $3,000 on the operation, one-third of which it could find out of its own budgeted funds and the balance of which it would seek from the province, via the Vancouver City Council. It is not known what the outcome of these financial negotions was, but with the amendments to the Public School Act which were introduced by the government and passed by the legislature early in 1910, the financial burden in connection with night classes was reduced, if not removed entirely, by virtue of the grants which the province thereafter provided towards the remuneration paid to the teachers of approved night school courses.

In subsequent years, the night schools in Vancouver operated at a consistently high level. In 1910-11, the second year of operation, enrollments increased to 1,628. One innovation that year, which was to be repeated for several years thereafter, was the holding of a large rally to mark the opening of the fall term, at which the mayor presented prizes to the top students in the previous year. Some non-vocational subjects such as citizenship and music were added to the list of courses. When the classes were re-opened in January, courses in shipbuilding, mechanics, first aid, embroidery and millinery were added. In February, another innovation was made, when the music classes themselves sponsored a public lecture and performed musical selections.

In the year 1911-1912, enrollments increased once more, to 2,011. New subjects included French, German, navigation, physical culture, wood carving, copper work and "Cooking for Men." The music program was futher expanded with beginners' work being conducted on Monday evening, the choral society on Tuesday and an orchestra on Thursdays. A debating club was started among the students. Further embellishments appeared in March of 1912, when the bookkeeping and shorthand classes held "a second social evening for this season," including music, recitations and refreshments. The program that year was held in eleven different centres and involved 49 instructors.

In the year 1912-1913, enrollments were sown to 1,420, but in the following year, the last before the war, they were up again to 1,749. Some interesting detail on an aspect of the program was provided in the fall of 1914 by an article by G.A. Laing, the Director of Technical Education for the Board, which was submitted at the Editor's invitation to *The B.C. Federationist,* the labour newspaper, and printed in their first issue in October. It described the program in general and stressed the courses in elementary subjects, the building trades and engineering. In reference to the building trades courses, the author stressed that the classes were suitable not just for apprentices, but also for "men who already have a practical acquaintance with some branch of the trade." The two elementary courses mentioned were workshop arithmetic and workshop drawing. There was a three-year course in carpentry and technical courses in sheetmetal work, building construction, quantity surveying, architectural drawing and architecture. In the engineering program, there were courses in preliminary mathematics; two years in both mechanical and steam engineering; two years in machine construction and drawing; and a two-year course in electrical engineering. The article mentioned courses in some other fields such as the arts, commercial subjects and domestic science and put heavy stress on the practical nature of all the programs (*B.C. Federationist* Oct. 3, 1914).

McGill University College did not offer extension credit courses again after its initial effort, but in the academic year 1908-1909 and again the following year, it sponsored brief series of lectures for the public. The only two lecturers whose names are known were John G. Davidson and Lemuel Robertson, both of the college staff and both of whom were to play significant roles in university extension work in later years as faculty members of the University of British Columbia, which was created in 1915.

Reference should be made to the role of the South Vancouver School Board and its brief participation in the field of adult education. In January of 1910, the press carried an account of the first meeting of the Board in the new year at which Mr. Spencer Robinson was re-elected as Chairman. In his remarks to the meeting, he said:

> The establishment of night schools in our Municipality, where boys and girls could receive special training for some trade or business, would be practical help [sic]. Your Board are unanimously agreed on this point, and it only remains for the Government to make the necessary grant for the carrying on of this valuable branch of educational work. (*N.A.* Jan 22, 1910)

At the time, of course, the Vancouver School Board already had its program under way. Within a few weeks, the Public Schools Act was amended so as to provide support for this work. True to its word, the South Vancouver Board launched a night class program the following fall. It was prepared to offer instruction in English, commercial arithmetic, bookkeeping, shorthand, building construction, dressmaking and sewing. The arrangement was that if 20 or more students enrolled in any class, no fees would be charged. It is not known how many courses were actually held, nor what the enrollments were. Figures for the South Vancouver district did not appear in the Department of Education statistics for the year. By early November, teachers were appointed and classes confirmed, Mr. Kyle of the Vancouver district having given useful advice in this connection. Some of the classes were apparently quite small at the outset, but continued to grow during November. A shorthand class had over 30 students. On the other hand, English and arithmetic classes held at Cedar Cottage were so small they had to be combined. A dressmaking class at Central Park was so large it had to be split into two. In the second term, the dressmaking and building construction classes were reported as being well filled, but pupils were "wanted in most other classes" (*N.A.* Jan. 19, 1911). In subsequent years, the South Vancouver Board apparently left it to the larger program run by the Vancouver district to serve the needs of students in both areas.

Private Tutoring and Other Academic Evening Instruction

The public institutions did not provide the only instruction in academic subjects. A variety of other sources were available including private tutors, commercial schools which offered some academic subjects and private educational institutions.

There were a number of private tutors who advertised in the newspaper from time to time. The first noted was a Professor Heinrich Pottmeyer, who advertised instruction in French and German, each three nights per week, in the fall of 1888. By September of 1911, six private tutors were advertising at the same time.

There were a number of private institutions which specialized in academic tutoring. These included a School of Elocution run by a Professor Wenyon (1896); the Vancouver Conservatory of Music which for a time offered languages as well (1896); the Columbia Commercial College, which at one point has an academic department (1897); the Vancouver Night School, which offered predominantly academic subjects and to a lesser extent commercial ones (1903-1905); the Sprott-Shaw Business Institute, which offered foreign languages for a time (1906); and the Vancouver School of Expression (1911).

Something of the general demand for instruction was revealed by an article which appeared in the Vancouver *Province* in the fall of 1909. The paper was running a series of articles on "The Symptoms of an Educational Crisis" in support of the need for a university in the province. One of the articles dealt in part with the extent of private tutoring which was going on:

> There is a steady demand for mathematical, linguistic and even for classical private tuition. Vancouver has had the advantage of several good business colleges and does a surprising amount of business with American correspondence colleges.... One experienced teacher reports that he often spends forty to fifty hours per week tutoring single pupils mostly attending or preparing for Canadian university courses.

It added that some tutors in Vancouver, who only a short time ago had a precarious income, "are now besieged" (*Province* Oct 9, 1909).

In addition, there were several private academic institutions which offered regular instruction to young people during the day on a full-time basis and also gave courses at night. The first of these was Weltham College, which was active in this field from 1891 to 1893. These included lecture series on astronomy and electricity and a series of four chamber music concerts. The college closed in 1893. Buckland College also conducted work of this kind. The advertisements for the college which ran in the fall of 1896 indicated that it offered preparation for matriculation, law and public school teachers' examinations and that it offered both day and evening classes. Evening classes in French were given in 1898. In 1907, Columbian College, the Methodist institution in New Westminster, announced a series of what it called "University Extension Lectures to be held in Vancouver." The Principal, Rev. Mr. Sipprell, was to lead off with a lecture on

"The Theory of Sight-Sensations and Our Ideas of Space." There were to be four lectures in the series, given in fortnightly intervals and free to the public. The series had the "double object of interesting the public in University work, and of giving them the results of the study of specialists in departments of high interest" (*N.A.* Feb. 27, 1907).

Evening Instruction in Commercial and Technical Subjects— Private Schools

This was a large field of activity in Vancouver during these years when the city was developing so rapidly and the business and industry of the area, especially in the boom periods, were increasingly large users of trained men and woman. It is difficult, if not impossible to present an orderly and fully accurate account of the various business schools in the area because with notable exceptions there was a procession of short-lived operations, with personnel shifting from one to the other. Schools came and went, some going bankrupt and some being taken over by other institutions. One of the most successful, for instance, the Sprott-Shaw School, absorbed six competing schools at various times.

The earliest entries into the field were individuals offering instruction in commercial subjects. These appeared as early as 1888, but by the middle of the next decade, incorporated companies began to take over this field of activity. The first of these was Pacific Shorthand and Business College, which appeared in 1894 and like many of its successors, offered instruction in business subjects both day and evening. Some of the most prominent firms which appeared in the field in subsequent years included Columbia Commercial College (founded in 1895), H.B.A. Vogel Commercial College (1898), Pitman's Business College Ltd, (1898), Vancouver Business College (1903), 20th Century Shorthand (1904), Vancouver Night School (1904), Sprott-Shaw Business University (later College—1904), and Central Business College (1910). Some of these organizations taught academic and technical subjects from time to time as well.

Other Technical and Vocational Education

J.K. Foster, in his study of the development of vocational education in the province, has pointed out that the general background factor to the development of training of this kind was the decline in the relative significance of the "frontier" occupations, especially between 1870 and 1890, and the increasing need for a more highly skilled and knowledgeable work force (Foster 1975).

A. Public Policy and Organized Labour

Some of the labour unions, especially the craft unions, took an active interest in the development of both in-school and out-of-school technical training. Some of the unions were actively involved in educational programs for their members and co-operated closely with the local school boards when they entered the field, supporting their night classes in technical and vocational subjects. Some also sought a role in determining the nature of the programs. When the sheetmetal workers approached the Vancouver Board in 1913 asking it to take over the admninistration of their educational classes, the union suggested that an advisory committee to the program be established on which they would have representation. This was arranged. The following year, G.A. Laing, Director of Night

Schools for Vancouver (John Kyle having joined the staff of the Department of Education that year) invited the Trades and Labour Council to appoint delegates from the building trades unions to sit on a newly formed technical advisory committee. The committee was to assist the school board on questions of technical education.

B. Organized Labour's Participation in Educational Programs

The craft unions were the labour groups which were most actively involved in the education of their members and which also secured some degree of control over the apprenticeship system as it related to their fields. The Vancouver Typographical Union was founded in 1888. In the early 1890s members of this group were faced with a problem when linotype machines were introduced by the two local newspapers, the *World* and the *News Advertiser*. In June of 1893, in order to get around this problem, the union negotiated with the two newspapers an arrangement whereby journeymen could go on a lower salary scale ("machine scale") for brief periods while they learned to operate the linotype machines. The local Typographical Union had at its disposal the well developed apprenticeship system worked out by its parent international union. It established clear guidelines concerning the educational requirements of those entering the field, established policies on the range and duration of the duties to be performed by apprentices, and kept careful records of the progress and experiences of the apprectices. In 1908, the International Union inaugurated a correspondence course for apprentices, providing a systematic review of the main subject matter to be mastered. These were adopted in Vancouver and, in 1910 and 1911, the Vancouver local purchased technical books to be used by apprectices who were following the correspondence course. In the following year the union organized a series of lectures by journeyman union members for the apprentices. This was subsequently expanded in association with the school board night school program. Also in 1912, the local entered into an agreement with the employers to the effect that when any person was accepted by the employer for a trial period of employment, the apprentice candidate had to write a union examination in spelling, grammar and English usage. It was also arranged in that year that there were opportunities for an exchange of apprectices between shops so the workman could get a wider range of experience than would be available to him in a single establishment. Finally, in 1914 the union created a club for apprentices, the "Caxton Apprenticeship Club of Vancouver," where certain educational and other activities could be carried out.

The sheetmetal workers were also active in education. In 1909, the union organized a class on different aspects of the trade for apprentices and ran it successfully. They then approached the Vancouver School Board and asked them to organize such classes in the future on behalf of their members. Regular sheetmetal classes were begun in 1913.

C. Training in Industry

Although increasingly during this period, the government regulations concerning the qualifications of certain categories of workers made it necessary to provide training of some kind, it was still true that before the World War, "management became involved in training only under exceptional circumstances" (Foster 1975: V,2).

Apart from the examples already mentioned, the earliest instance of training programs in industry was that of the British Columbia Telephone Company. They began the training of telephone operators in their Vancouver exchange in 1890 and continued that practice until 1907, when the training was transferred to the Seymour exchange at 555 Seymour, where it continued until 1912. In 1913, a training school for operators was established in a new building adjoining the Fairmont office at Tenth and Prince Edward. Mary Dickson was the head of the school and 36 pupils advanced from one class to another. They attended classes for eight hours per day for three weeks and in addition to their technical training, all student operators were given a course in voice culture. On the other hand, all construction, installation, maintenance and repair personnel were trained right on the job.

The British Columbia Electric Company was also active in training for its personnel. In January of 1906, the city Medical Health Officer gave a series of lectures on first aid to employees of the company. This was apparently part of a larger program. In the same year the company introduced a three-year course of training for employees working as electrical technicians. The program was opearated by "the B.C. Electric Technical School" and the costs were met partly by student fees. The company provided instructional space and equipment. The program, which was continued until 1920, covered advanced theoretical concepts and principles in the field of electricity and electrical engineering. This program led to the establishment in 1912 of a company commercial training course as well. In 1909, the city passed a by-law which made the training of conductors and drivers on trams compulsory. There had been an informal system of oral exams begun by the company the previous year, but this was replaced beginning in February of 1909 with a regular course of lectures, followed by examinations. This program eventually became an integral part of the company routine, with its own specially equipped lecture room. By 1910, an additional educational activity was in operation within the company in the form of the B.C. Electric Co. section of the National Electric Light Association. Papers on technical subjects were presented to regular meetings of this group, usually by group members but occasionally by visiting speakers.

By 1911, the Canadian Pacific Railway was heavily involved in first aid instruction. In February of that year it was reported in the press that eleven "mechanical employees" had passed examinations after taking the St. John's Ambulance course. In October plans were announced for an ambitious national competition in proficiency in first aid, with competitions in each area, region and in the end, at the national level. The company was described as "the foremost railway in North America in teaching its employees first aid" (*N.A.* Oct. 11, 1911).

D. Mining

Considerable educational activity was carried on in this field in the 1890s, a decade of rapid expansion in the mining industry of the province. Early in 1896, the Provincial Department of Mines offered in Vancouver a series of six lectures on different aspects of mining. This series, which was presented in Victoria and New Westminster as well, was given by the leading experts in the province and was well attended. The Art, Historical and Scientific Association sponsored a series of lectures on mining given by G.F. Monckton in 1895. There were six lectures in the series, followed by a seventh on the geology of Burrad Inlet. At least some of the lectures included chemistry tests of minerals and other demonstrations. Mr. Monckton and a partner opened the Vancouver School of Mines early in 1896. Its program was devoted to the training of assayers and mining engineers.

Some weeks later it was announced that the proprietors had found it necessary to enlarge the school. No further mention has been located of the Vancouver School of Mines, but in the fall of 1896, the British Columbia School of Mines was advertising for students, perhaps a successor to the other organization. Early in 1898, a School of Placer Mining was offering instruction. The press described the program as "practical classes" and stated that men who were intending to go to the Klondike were taking them. In the fall of that year, an organization called the Institute Columbia was advertising, offering classes in geology, mineralogy and chemistry, both day and evening.

In 1912, the Vancouver Mining Club, the forerunner of the Vancouver Chamber of Mines, was formed. By October of that year, the organization had collected an interesting display of mineral samples which was available for viewing by the general public. Late that year or early in 1913, the name was changed to the Chamber of Mines and in late January a lecture was organized for the members on "Modern Surface Equipment of Coal Mines." In the fall, the *News Advertiser* ran a long illustrated article on the Chamber which indicated that it maintained a reading room, a "bureau of mining information" and "the best museum of provincial minerals extant" (*N.A.* Oct. 5, 1913). Further lectures for the members were offered quite frequently in the following months, most of them on mining topics.

E. Marine Schools

In the fall of 1907, a Marine School organized by the Federal government was started in Vancouver and became the most successful of its kind in all Canada. In the next seven years, a total of 198 lectures were given as part of this program, with average attendance in Vancouver ranging from a high of 29 for the 1908-1909 series to 12 in 1912-1913. Instruction in this vocational area was also offered through the local Seamen's Institute.

Business Clubs and Trade Groups

Brief comment should be made about several other educational programs conducted by business or trade groups. The Vancouver Board of Trade organized public lectures from time to time on subjects related to the economy of the province. Two examples which might be mentioned are an address on "Trade Between Great Britian and the Colonies" given by a British Member of Parliament in September of 1891 and a lecture on forest conservation presented in the spring of 1910 by the Federal Inspector of Forest Reserves.

In 1894, the local sugar refinery established a Reading and Social Club for interested employees. In 1902, there was mention once again of the "Sugar Refinery Literary Club," which may or may not have been the same organization. In 1912, the B.C. Electric Railway Co. opened new club rooms for its office staff and announced that the organization which was to have the use of the premises was intended to provide opportunities for "social intercourse and the moral and intellectual edification of its members" (*N.A.* Nov. 2, 1912). Early in 1914, reports indicated that there was a particularly active photography section of the club, which arranged lectures for the membership.

At least three organizations devoted to the study of business were formed in the latter years of the period. In the fall of 1910, the press reported that a Businessmen's Club had been formed, "to take up the study of the science of business building" [sic]. What sounds like a similar group, the Business Science Club of Vancouver, was founded early in 1911.

It was apparently a branch of an organization which had originated in Chicago and provided an opportunity for the members to gain greater understanding and knowledge of business practices. In the fall of the following year, mention was made in the press of the Pickwick Club of Vancouver. Its objects were described as "the improving of the knowledge of its members in subjects relating to finance, law, business and politics" and its membership was limited to twenty. Nothing further is known about the activities of these groups.

Brief reference might also be made of the local branch of the Life Insurance Salesmen and of the Canadian Bankers Association, both of which arranged lectures for their members on matters related to their work. The same can be said of the Provincial Funeral Directors and Embalmers Association, which held its first annual convention in Vancouver in the fall of 1012, the program of which contained a number items aimed at in-service development for persons in that business.

In-Service Development of Teachers

A. School Teachers

In these years, the teachers in the Vancouver area were organized at three levels, each of which conducted professional in-service development activities. The Provincial Teachers' Institutes began in 1874 and met most years thereafter. Considerable numbers of Vancouver and district teachers took part in these meetings. The regional organization in which the Vancouver teachers played a part was the Mainland Teachers' Institute. It was formed in 1885 and met regularly thereafter, the name being changed in 1905 to the Coast Teachers' Institute. The regional body met for two days during the Christmas school break, normally in the early days of January. The meetings alternated between Vancouver and New Westminster. They appear to have been devoted mainly to professional in-service development activities.

The Vancouver teachers organized at the local level early in 1889, forming the Vancouver Teachers' Institute "for the purpose of mutual improvement and to further the cause of education in the Province." Judging from the accounts of their first few monthly meetings, the sessions were given over almost exclusively to the discussion of professional topics, usually on the basis of the delivery of a paper on some aspect of teaching, followed by a discussion. Such topics as "Canadian History," "School Discipline," "Teaching Composition" and "Teaching Literature" were typical. There is little information available about the affairs of the local Institute over the years, but it is known that by the turn of the century it had almost 200 members.

B. Sunday School Teachers

There developed during this period a very active in-service training program for those involved in Sunday School activities in several Protestant denominations—at both the local and provincial levels. As in the case of the school teachers, attention was given in these programs to both content and methodology.

C. Kindergarten Teachers

For a brief period in the late 1890s, there was an active Kindergarten Club in Vancouver. At a meeting held in late March, 1898, the club was officially formed, its stated aim being "to promote the study of kindergarten methods of teaching." The group met on a monthly basis throughout that year and became so large and active by the fall of 1899 that it was divided into two branches. However, by the spring of 1900, the organization seems to have disappeared.

In-Service Development in Other Professions

It is not known when the local Nurses' Association was formed, but a press account in the fall of 1906 indicates that it was holding meetings on a monthly basis at that time and that the programs consisted of lectures on topics of professional interest. There was further indication of such work in the fall of 1913. Early in 1914, the press indicated that the Public Health Nurses' Association was operating in-service development activities. In announcing a lecture by the school dentist to a meeting soon to be held, the report stated:

> This is one of a course of lectures planned by the Public Health Nurses' Association, and all nurses and others interested in public health matters are cordially invited. (*N.A.* Feb. 18, 1914)

No information has been located about educational activities for the legal profession, but on several occasions the press mentioned lectures which were arranged by and for the Law Students' Society. The earliest of these which was noted was given on November 10, 1908, by C.M. Woodworth on law relating to marriage and divorce. Other topics about the law included "The Mechanics' Lien Act" and "Summons Procedure." Other, non-technical subjects such as "The Hudson's Bay Route" were covered on occasion. "Mock Chambers" and mock parliaments were also held.

Several branches of the engineering profession organized educational activities. The earliest specific reference noted was to a meeting of the local branch of the Canadian Society of Civil Engineers in December of 1910 at which papers on "Testing of Concrete Pipes" and "Railway Organization and Cost Keeping" were delivered and discussed. Other reports indicate that this group was actively engaged in this kind of activity for the next few years. For instance, the announcement of their first meeting in the fall of 1913 contained a list of topics to be covered at meetings during the coming year, including such as dredging, town planning and dock construction. In December of 1913, a two-day meeting of the British Columbia section (other notices had been for the Vancouver Branch) was announced at which a number of technical papers were to be delivered. Approximately 150 engineers attended that meeting. Only one meeting was noted of the Corporation of B.C. Land Surveyors, it being held in January of 1912. A local section of the American Institute of Electrical Engineers was formed in the fall of 1911, but nothing is known of its activities. Finally, a British Columbia Association of Gas Engineers was formed in early 1914. It had a total of 84 members, 60 of whom belonged to the Vancouver local.

The architects were active at two levels. The provincial body held meetings from time to time, hearing lectures on such topics as "Some Phases of Fireproof Construction" and "Specifications." The Vancouver chapter also arranged lectures for its members. Two topics which were noted were "The Modern Landscape Architect" and "City Planning and What it Involves."

The Chartered Accountants Student Society of British Columbia was active in educational work by the fall of 1912. A press announcement at that time indicated that the group had recently heard a lecture on "Business Investigations" and that a series of lectures had been arranged for the ensuing year.

Press reports indicated that the Home Economics Association was involved in such work by the fall of 1913. The teaching of home economics, ceramics, and the evolution of the home were among the topics discussed at the regular monthly meetings which were held during that year at least.

National and Ethnic Organizations

A. The Canadian Clubs

The Men's Canadian Club, designed "to foster the spirit of national patriotism" and other related values, was formed in Vancouver in the latter part of 1906. The club seems to have been a success from the beginning and attracted as speakers outstanding persons from all parts of Canada and abroad. A year after its formation, the president reported that the club had outgrown almost every available hall in the city. The club's main activity was to arrange lectures for its members. The first indication that the Women's Canadian Club of the city had been formed appeared in November of 1909 and it is assumed that it, like its counterpart in Victoria, was formed earlier that year. The women's group conducted a program along similar lines to that of the men's club. In addition, however, it undertook in the program year 1912-1913 a special series of lectures on British Columbia history, which was arranged by the president, Mrs. Jonathan Rogers.

B. Ethnic and Regional Organizations

There was the usual range of ethnic and regional organizations in Vancouver during these years, but for the most part their activities were more social than educational, and as such do not come within the terms of this study. The Sons of England were perhaps as active as any in terms of educational activities for the general public. A lecture on Shakespeare and Dickens held at the First Congregational Church in March of 1907 and one on naval matters ("Through Shot and Shell") held in February of the following year were typical of their events. The Society of Londoners, which was formed in the fall of 1910, also organized an active program of music, literary evenings and discussions to which all were invited.

There were also in these years active organizations devoted to the understanding and propagation of the French language and culture. As early as the spring of 1888, L'Institut Canadien Francais de Vancouver was formed. It established club rooms and maintained a supply of French language newspapers and literature there. Within a month, it was reported that the group was meeting "with great success" and that its membership was alrteady "very large." In the spring of 1904, a local branch of the Alliance Française was formed. (It was at first referred to as the "French Alliance" in the press.) Little is known of their activities, but by 1907, at least some members were meeting on a weekly basis studying works of French literature.

Women's Organizations Related to Education and Public Affairs

A. Council of Women

The leading women's organization in many respects, and certainly the most comprehensive in terms of its membership was the local Council of Women. Like similar councils elsewhere in the country, the organization was interested in the education of its members (and that of the affiliated organizations) especially to the end that they could undetake informed and effective social action in the interests of improving their communities and the nation, with particular emphasis to areas which affected the welfare of women and children. As part of this process, considerable educational work was organized for the purpose of informing its own membership, and on occasion, events were organized for the benefit of the general public. The Vancouver Council was organized in 1894 and was soon conducting a very active program which clearly involved considerable study of many social questions of public concern. Some of the many topics to which they gave study were labour conditions, the situation of East Indian women, housing, recreation, industrial and technical education, laws affecting women and children, public health, child wefare and city beautification. The Council was also active in seeking the franchise for women at both the local level and at senior levels of government.

B. Educational Clubs

The Educational Club of Vancouver, which was formed in 1908, intended to "study the problems of politics and society which form the background of educational work; and to develop enthusiasm for ideas in general." Early meetings brought together many of the leading figures in educational circles in the city. A year or so later, a women's section of the organization was formed, the earliest meeting of which that has been noted being held in January of 1911. There is a possibility of confusing this group with another, the Women's Educational Club of Columbian College. The College was a Methodist institution located in New Westminster which had been in operation since 1892. By 1913, there was an affiliated Women's Education Club in both Vancouver and Victoria. The former conducted an active educational program for its members. Little is known about the activities of the University Women's Club of Vancouver. A press report stated that it was holding meetings in the spring of 1910. At that time it was indicated that the club had arranged two dramatic readings for interested members of the general public, but no other information is available about their activities.

C. Women's Suffrage Organizations

Beginning in 1912, just after women received the vote at the municipal level, and increasingly as the campaign for women's suffrage at other levels gained momentum, there was organizational activity aimed at expanding the franchise or educating women for informed use of the vote. These organizations included the "Women's Forum," the B.C. Equal Franchise Association and the Pioneer Political Equality League.

Sailors' Organizations

It is clear that a certain amount of educational work for sailors was carried on during this period by organizations set up for the welfare of sailors in the port of Vancouver, but the information about this work is far from complete. In the summer of 1892, the Sailor's

Rest was founded in the city. It provided recreation and entertainment, and when possible, lectures. A reading room containing newspapers, periodicals and books was available by the following year and the press carried notices from time to time of concerts staged for the benefit of the work. This organization seems to have disbanded by 1895. In the fall of 1897 or early the following year, a fresh start was made. At that time, Rev. H.G. Fiennes-Clinton of St. James' Church gave leadership to the establishment of a Seamen's Institute which was at first housed in a building adjoining the church. The *Vancouver Directory* for 1897-1898 lists the organization as providing "reading and recreational rooms" which were "open every evening." This organization continued in existence throughout the balance of the period under review, and beginning in 1907, it worked in close association with the Missions to Seamen organization, which was also sponsored by the Anglican Church. Some indication of the activities of the Institute is provided by the reports to the annual meeting in the fall of 1909, for instance, which indicated that during the year there had been 11,858 visits by seamen to the Institute, 4,023 had been present at the entertainments, "several men" had been interested in the first aid course, and 49 men had been prepared in what was called the Institute "Nautical Academy" to write the examinations in navigation and all had passed. This particular program had been the "fullest and most brilliant success." In the fall of 1907, a Vancouver Branch of the British and Foreign Sailors' Society was established. This organization appears to have sponsored what was called the Stathcona Institute, which provided services to sailors. Captain Eddy, who also lectured at the Marine School operated by the Dominion government, conducted classes in navigation for the Strathcona Institute two nights a week which were reportedly "well attended."

Education for Asian Immigrants

As in the case of Victoria and other centres in the Province, the churches were active in missionary work among oriental immigrants.

A. Chinese

When the railroad was completed to the West Coast in 1886, a large number of Chinese who had been engaged in that project were thrown out of work and many of them joined the small Chinatown which already existed in Vancouver (Willmott 1970). The history of the growth of that community does not form part of this study, but it should be pointed out that for at least three decades after the turn of the century there was serious hostility to the Asians in the community, producing the levying and periodic increases in the head tax against them; the serious riots and attacks on the Chinese and Japanese districts in 1907; and the activities of the Asiatic Exclusion League and others which aimed at reducing their numbers and limiting their role in society. The work which was carried out by the churches on behalf of these groups was done in the face of a widespread body of public opinion against them.

Missionary work among the Chinese people in Vancouver began as early as 1888. The Methodist and Presbyterian Churches began active educational work in the early 1890s among the Chinese. Rev. John E. Gardiner, who had previously done significant work of a similar kind in Victoria for some years on behalf of the Methodists, conducted language classes and missionary work in Vancouver from 1894 to 1896. Work among the women included teaching "English, sewing, knitting and other household arts" (Osterhout 1929:184). An item in the *Methodist Reader* in October, 1899, stated that "Our night schools have reopened after a short holiday. At Vancouver we have enrolled nearly fifty pupils." Disappointingly little is known about the work of the Presbyterian Church among the Chinese in this period. By 1894, the Presbyterians had four Chinese schools operating in Vancouver which opened five nights a week for classes for adults (Kennedy 1938:36).

Little is known about the development of this work in the early years of the new century. Reports delivered to the quadrennial General Conferences of the Methodist Church give some indication of that denomination's efforts. In 1906, it was reported that the work among the Chinese in the city included night schools, Bible classes and street preaching and that there were five missionaries and four teachers engaged in the work. Only the missionary work was referred to in the reports for 1910, but in 1914 it was stated that at that time there were 125 Chinese students in their night schools in Vancouver. The Presbyterian women's society continued its activities on behalf of Chinese women. In 1913 they reported they were conducting English classes in homes in Chinatown for women and girls. In addition, instruction was given in knitting, crocheting and making of children's shoes. The following year it was reported that there were 70 people in the evening classes for Chinese and that there had been such an eager response to this work that the classes were maintained throughout the summer months, when attendance "had scarcely gone below seventy." Instruction was given in spelling, reading and composition four nights a week from 8:00 to 10:00.

The Anglican Church was also active in this work. In the early 1890s a night school for Chinese was opened at Christ Church and a Chinese Mission Aid Association was formed to support work among these immigrants in the diocese. F.A. Peake states: "A room on Pender Street was obtained for the school which had the support of the clergy of Christ Church and St. Paul's as well as of a number of enthusiastic women." In 1893 the school was moved to larger premises on Pender, "where it would be possible to have a reading room and sitting room, chapel, kitchen and rooms for a dozen or so men to live." Ten years later the work was moved to a building on Homer Street. The school was open five evenings a week, "with an average attendance of thirty-five Chinese pupils and four volunteer teachers" (Peake 1959).

The Society for the Propagation of the Gospel also played a role in such work, beginning in 1905. A book about their activities stated in 1925 that "over 20,000 Chinese have passed through the night school of the Vancouver mission during the last twenty years." It further states, however, that the bulk of that activity had taken place in the eight years prior to 1925. So how much of it was carried out before 1914, and what the character of that was, is not clear. It did state that two missions with their own buildings were operating in Vancouver before 1925 (Hellaby 1925:45 & 90). Finally, in an article about private tutoring activity in the city of Vancouver which appeared in the press in the fall of 1909, refeence was made to the fact that private tutors in the city had been getting work "instructing Asiatic students in the English they assiduously demand" (*Province* Oct. 9, 1909).

B. Japanese

The number of Japanese in the Province was much smaller than that of the Chinese, but significant work was done in the field of adult education. Missionary work began in the late 1880s, but it appears that the first English language classes were not offered until a Methodist layman, Mr. Shinkichi Tamura, made his house available for this work in 1891. Classes were held five days a week and were staffed mainly by volunteers from the Methodist Church. Some 30 to 40 students attended these classes. The historian of this church activity among the Japanese has commented that the teaching of English "later became one of the most important services which the Japanese Christian Church rendered to the Japanese Canadian community and through which the church became the most powerful institution to help Japanese assimilate into Canadian Communities" (Mitsui 1964:11). It is an indication of the energy and resourcefulness of this group that by 1896, the night school activity for their people was run and financed by the Japanese themselves. The following year, there were over 30 students in the night school language classes. In addition, women missionaries formed groups of women and girls which met in homes and where, according to Rev. T. Komiyama, who has written about this work, instruction was given in "the Canadian way of cooking, etiquette and customs, and so on, and of course the language" (Komiyama undated:5). By 1907, there were 80 night school students in the program run by the Methodist Church, and in 1914, there were 95.

The Methodist Church was the dominant force in Christian missionary and educational work among the Japanese in the city. The Anglicans carried on some work, however. In 1904 they opened a school for Japanese, primarily a day school for the children. In 1909, in an upstairs room over their mission building on 2nd Avenue, they expanded the work with an upgraded day school for the children and sewing and reading classes for the women.

C. East Indians

Only one reference has been located to educational activities among the East Indian immigrants. In his work on the activities of the Anglican Church in the Province, F.A. Peake states that efforts on behalf of the East Indians began in 1913, when English classes were organized for these immigrants for the first time (Peake 1959).

Organizations Devoted to the Study of Science

Although little is known about their activities, there is evidence during this period of several organizations which were devoted to the study of specialized branches of science. The earliest of these which has been noted was the B.C. Entomological Society. The press reported that it was formed in January of 1902 and that at its first meeting members brought specimens for examination and discussion. The first annual meeting was held a year later in Victoria and was attended by six persons. The next word of this group came in December of 1911, when the press reported a one-day annual meeting in Vancouver. At that time, in addition to normal business, a scientific paper was delivered and reports were heard "from the four districts represented in the Provincial Society."

The Vancouver Naturalist Field Club was formed in late 1905 or early the following year. The first activity of which evidence has been found was a field trip taken in late August of that year. At the first annual meeing, held in October, William Burns, the Principal of the Normal School, became President of the group. Meetings resumed in January of 1907 and the following month a very active program for the ensuing spring and summer was printed in the local press. Notice was carried of the next annual meeting in the fall of the year (erroneously referred to again as the first annual meeting) but no further word of the organization has been discovered.

In 1909, the British Columbia Academy of Science was formed in Vancouver. The stated purposes were to foster research and to bring together people from various branches of science who had hitherto been working separately. In December of that year, the *News Advertiser* carried a long account of a lecture by Dr. J.F. Clarke to this group on "The Forest Resources of British Columbia," one of the few instances which has been noted of scientific interest in that important aspect of the Province's resources. In the fall of 1910, the group held its meetings in the rooms of McGill College, one lecture being delivered on "Four Dimensional Space" and another on "The Calendar."

In the fall of 1911, the Vancouver Archeological Society was holding meetings. Professor Charles Knapp of Columbia University addressed a meeting of this organization on "The Roman Theatre" in late November. As usual with this group, the public was invited to attend as well, free of charge. Further lectures were given in January and February of 1912. The press reported in the fall of that year the proceedings of the annual meeting of the "Vancouver Branch of the Archeological Institue of America," and this may have been the formal name of the Vancouver group. This account revealed that a number of prominent citizens were members of the group, Judge F.W. Howay being the President at the time. Accounts of further meetings appeared from time to time, the audience for a lecture about Rome by a visiting professor from Stanford University having "crowded the hall of the King Edward High School" in March of 1913. In January of the following year, the press carried an account of the group's recent annual meeting and a list of several lectures which were scheduled for the coming months.

A Vancouver Branch of the Royal Sanitary Institute of London, England, was founded in 1912. Dr. J.G. Davidson of McGill College spoke during October to what must have been one of its first meetings on "Light and Heat." The press report described the group as "lately formed." In the following February the group met in the city testing laboratory and heard a lecture on "Sanitary Ideals in Chemical Engineering." In the fall of that year, the organization arranged a series of weekly lectures on "Water" which was described as being of use to those preparing to be sanitary inspectors or "lady health visitors." This series carried on into the following year, the press reporting early in January the thirteenth lecture in "the Sanitary Science Series." The group was organized at the provincial level as well and this body held in late October the "first public health congress" held in the city, at which prominent persons gave scientific and technical papers on a wide range of topics.

Agricultural Organizations and Exhibitions

Vancouver was not, of course, primarily an agricultural community. There were very few agricultural organizations based in the city, although some of the provincial bodies held their annual meetings in the city from time to time. The Vancouver newspapers took considerable interest in agricultural matters and carried advertisements and notices for the various agricultural fairs in the general area, most prominently the annual exhibition held in New Westminster in the early fall. While it lasted, the exhibition of the Delta Agricultural Society held each fall at Ladner's Landing also was given coverage. This was also true of the Richmond Fair at Eburne.

The first association which was actually based in Vancouver was the Vancouver Poultry Association, which was holding meetings and preparing for a show by the fall of 1894. It later became the Vancouver Poultry and Pet Stock Association. A struggling Vancouver Horticultural Society was meeting by January of 1905, with only ten persons attending its annual meeting at that time. It apparently went out of existence subsequently, because during the fall of 1913, as a result of several meetings, a Vancouver Horticultural Association was formed, "to have lectures and papers at intervals during the winter months on subjects interesting to lovers of horticulture." Vancouver's first horse show, arranged by the "Hunt Club and Livestock Association" was held in mid-March of 1908 and a second one a year later.

Although the matter had been under discussion as early as 1902, and an Exhibition Association had been active since 1907, Vancouver did not hold its own comprehensive exhibition until the late summer of 1911, the first of what was to be an annual event held at Hastings Park.

The Newspapers

Finally, some reference should be made to local newspapers as an educational influence. It might be useful to comment on the development of one leading local newspaper by way of illustration of the educational efforts that were made. The example chosen is the *News Advertiser,* the newspaper which was followed most closely for the purposes of this study. In the fall of 1898, in addition to its regular content of news, editorials and advertisements, the *News Advertiser* began to carry a "Literary Notes" column approximately weekly. It contained information about new books, the people in them, information out of biographical works and other related material. The apparent intention was to encourage subscribers to read some of these other works. For some time this material appeared under the heading, "Books and Writers." In 1901, material began to be printed frequently about art, music and various aspects of literature. The whole front page of a second section which was published in the Sunday edition began to be devoted to such material. In December of that year, "The Poet's Corner" began to appear periodically, containing poetry from various sources. The reader had the feeling in this case that this material, which appeared sporadically, was mainly designed as a filler. By 1906, a great deal more special interest material was being carried, again, especially in the weekend paper—under such headings as poetry, photography, books, music. These sections contained not only criticism, but also general information about these fields. In 1910, the paper expanded greatly in volume and this tendency to print specialized informative material was accentuated, appearing under such headings as the home, cultural subjects, historical and scientific topics, economics, regions of the province and special articles on individual cities and natural resources. Of particular interest to the historian, for example, was a series of biographical articles about prominent citizens which was run weekly beginning in 1913 under the heading, "The Story of My Life." By 1914, the special feature material carried on the weekends was even further expanded, including long articles on such subjects as "Garden, Field and Farm," cooking and other household arts, automobiles, etc., in addition to the kinds of topics mentioned above. From the turn of the century, and especially after 1910, those who wished to do so could get a great deal of useful information about a wide variety of subjects from the pages of their daily newspaper.

References

AHSA Journal (1917), *Journal of the Art, Historical and Scientific Association of Vancouver*, Vancouver: Trythal and Son.

BCSTA (1908), *Report of the Fifth Annual Convention of the British Columbia School Trustees Association*, Vancouver: A.H. Timms.

Foster, J.K. (1975), "Vocational Education in British Columbia 1970-1930," (Draft of M.A. Thesis, University of British Columbia.

Ginn, R.W. (1913), "Oratory and War: Vancouver Debating Leagues's Development," *Westminster Hall Magazine and Farthest West Review*, 4, (5).

Hellaby, H.A. (1925), *Oriental Missions in British Columbia*: London: Society for the Propagation of the Gospel in Foreign Parts.

Kennedy, M.E. (1938), *The History of Presbyterianism in B.C. 1861-1935*, Unpublished M.A. Thesis, Union College of British Columbia.

Komiyama, Rev. T. (undated), "Missionary Work among the Japanese in Canada," Unpublished manuscript in Archives of Union College of B.C.

Mitsui, T. (1964), *The Ministry of the United Church of Canada Amongst Japanese Canadians in B.C. 1892-1949*, Unpublished M.S.T. Thesis, Union College of B.C.

Morley, A. (1961), *Vancouver From Milltown to Metropolis*, Vancouver: Mitchell Press.

Osterhout, S.S. (1929), *Orientals in Canada*, Toronto: United Church of Canada.

Peake, F.A. (1959), *The Anglican Church in British Columbia*, Vancouver: Mitchell Press.

Roy, P. (1960), *The Rise of Vancouver as a Metropolitan Centre 1886-1929*, Unpublished B.A. Thesis, University of B.C.

Thom, W.W. (1969), *The Fine Arts in Vancouver 1886-1930: An Historical Survey*, Unpublished M.A. Thesis, University of B.C.

Wales, B. (1958), *The Development of Adult Education in British Columbia*, Unpublished Ed.D. Thesis, Oregon State College.

Walker, E. (1966), "Vancouver Public Library—Before Carnegie," *B.C. Library Quarterly*, 20, (2).

Waller, R.D. (1956), *A Design for Democracy*, London: Max Parish.

Willmott, W.E. (1970), "Approaches to the Study of Chinese in British Columbia," *B.C. Studies*, No. 4.

YWCA (Young Women's Christian Association of Vancouver) *Annual Reports*, various years.

Originally published in *Occasional Papers in Continuing Education*, No. 9 (1975), Vancouver, University of British Columbia Centre for Continuing Education. Reprinted with permission.

5.3

Mechanics' Institutes in British Columbia

*I*n the past twelve years, we have celebrated three centennials in British Columbia—the anniversaries of the founding of the Mainland Colony (1958); the union of the two colonies, Vancouver Island and the Mainland (1866); and B.C.'s joining Confederation. The present year is also the centennial of a significant step in the development of adult education in the early years of our history—the date on which the Provincial government first provided public financial support for the mechanics' institutes and literary societies. These grants were maintained for less than a decade, so it is perhaps understandable if our commemoration of the event is somewhat restrained. There were, however, a number of mechanics' institutes and similar organizations in British Columbia in the latter part of the nineteenth century, and the story of their work forms a significant chapter in the history of adult education in this area.

Mechanics' institutes originated in the United Kingdom in the early years of the nineteenth century. At the outset, they were intended primarily to serve skilled tradesmen, providing instruction in various branches of science which were related to the "mechanics'" work. It is common knowledge that the movement, which expanded at an extraordinary rate, did not for long reach the intended audience. Nevertheless, as Thomas Kelly has pointed out, a great deal of important work was carried on, both in the field of science and in general basic education (Kelly 1962). In subsequent years, there came to be two main types of institutes. Those in Northern England and Scotland concentrated particularly on technical education, whereas in the South, many institutes were dominated by middle class elements and became "general literary and scientific societies, with the emphasis on the library, general lectures and social activities rather than on classes" (Kelly 1962:198).

In his study of the mechanics' institute movement in Ontario, Foster Vernon has made it clear that both of these tendencies were reflected in that area. Many of the institutes (there were 311 by 1985) concentrated on library, social and general education activities, but in the case of others, considerable classroom instruction was conducted, in both basic education and technical courses. The Department of Education in Ontario for a period even saw the institutes as the chief agency through which "the upgrading of workers in the technical arts could be achieved" (Vernon 1969:481).

There were few mechanics' institutes in British Columbia and generally speaking they, like their counterparts in southern England, were dominated by the middle class rather than by workingmen and put their chief emphasis on the development of libraries, plus some lecture activity. The exceptions to this were the institute in Victoria, which maintained a large and varied program for much of its life, and the one in New Westminster, which conducted regular classes for a brief period in the early 1890s. The institutes in B.C. were varied in their activities and development, and in view of their general character, it is appropriate to describe along with them several "church institutes" which were active in similar work for brief periods, and certain literary societies which aimed at a broad public service along the same lines.

Government Policy

The institues in B.C. were autonomous bodies which were organized on a voluntary basis to meet local needs. The sole exception, if it can be so judged, was in the case of New Westminster, the capital of the Mainland Colony of B.C. There, in 1865, the Governor, Frederick Seymour, provided the leadership which led to the formation of the British Columbia Institute. He made available an unused government building to house the library and arranged for an initial government grant of $300 in support of the organization. This was the first grant from the public purse in support of the institutes. In the following year, when the two colonies, British Columbia and Vancouver Island, were united, the new colonial administration provided support for both the New Westminster and Cariboo (Barkerville) institutes. This policy was shortlived, however. When Nanaimo applied for similar assistance in late 1867, it was turned down (Victoria *British Colonist* Dec. 6, 1867). The grants to the other two were terminated the following year, likely a result of the economic depression then facing the colony.

Soon after the colony joined Confederation and B.C. became the sixth Province of Canada, the provincial administration revived the grants. Henry Johnson, the historian of the educational system in B.C., has stated that it was pressure from the Victoria institute which brought about this step (Johnson 1964). He may well be right because, in the first budget brought in by the government following the passage of "An Act Respecting Literary Societies and Mechanics' Institutes" (1871), there appeared an item of $500 for support of these organizations. When the government spokeman was asked in the legislature how the money was to be used, he said it was to be a grant to the Victoria institute; whereupon members representing Nanaimo, New Westminster and the Cariboo rose in turn to point out that flourishing organizations of the same kind were active in their constituencies and were no less worthy of support. The government hurriedly gave assurances that further funds would be provided in supplementary estimates (Victoria *British Colonist* Mar. 29, 1872). The following year, Burrard Inlet (Moodyville) was added to the list and by 1876, there were eight centres, those already mentioned plus Hastings (Vancouver), Comox and Cowichan. The grants ranged from $500 for Victoria to $75 for Comox, with five institutions receiving $250. Only three of these centres received funds in 1878 and by 1879 grants were discontinued entirely, for reasons which are not clear (B.C. Public Accounts, several years).

Mechanics' Institutes and Literary Societies

Little is known about the work of the earliest organization of this type which was formed in B.C., the Nanaimo Literary Institute. It was founded in 1863, the successor of a church institute organized by the local Anglican minister the previous year. The group maintained a modest library and arranged occasional lectures. In the season 1874-75, and perhaps other years as well, it sponsored regular series of lectures and in the fall of 1880 formed a Debating and Elocution Club. Its meeting rooms were used for a variety of community functions from 1865 on and although no activities of the institute itself have been identified beyond 1880, the meeting rooms continued to be in use for at least another decade.

The Cariboo Literary Institute was established in Cameronton in 1864 and was soon after moved to the boom town of Barkerville, which was not only the largest centre on gold-laden Williams Creek, but soon became the largest city west of Chicago and north of San Francisco. This institute remained in existence for a decade under the guiding hand of a remarkable man, John Bowron, and concentrated entirely on the difficult task of maintaining a library in the rough and ready, boom and bust atmosphere of that area. The latest reference which has been found to the organization was in 1874, after Barkerville was well into its decline towards the ghost town it became for many years.

The story of the Victoria Mechanics' Institute, which was active from 1864 to 1886, is one of the most interesting aspects of adult education in B.C. in this early period. It arose out of an attempt to form an organization to provide lectures during the winter months and a number of speakers at the organizational meetings made reference to how the institutes had been managed in the United Kingdom (Victoria *British Colonist* Nov. 26, 1864). At least three future Premiers of B.C. took part in the affairs of the Victoria institute over the years and many prominent citizens were connected with it at times. It built up a modest library, employed a paid librarian, and in the end its collection became the nucleus of the city library. The institute maintained a program of lectures and courses over the years, the latter including series on such subjects as "spectrum analysis" and "electricity." Debating and elocution classes, exhibitions of arts and manufactures, and essay and poetry contests were also conducted. The institute even had its own orchestra for several years and staged a great many "entertainments," mainly as money-raising affairs. By the mid-1880s, however, support for the institute waned, its debts grew to an alarming level and the organization disbanded, the library being turned over to the city.

In New Westminster, the institute had a chequered career. The British Columbia Institute was founded in 1865 and made a start on a library collection and a museum, but disbanded three years later. It was succeeded by a "Mechanics' Literary Institute," which sponsored lectures sporadically over the next decade, had several spurts of activity, but by the mid-1880s was in trouble, being disbanded and reorganized on at least two occasions in the next few years. In 1890, the city government separated the management of the library from the mechanics' institute, the latter being entrusted with the task of organizing evening classes in "the mechanical and manufacturing arts" (New Westminster *British Columbian* Nov. 6, 1891). Over the next two years, classes were offered in such subjects as commercial specialties, elocution, drawing, mathematics and arithmetic, theoretical and applied mechanics, and experimental physics. There was a satisfactory response to these offerings for two years, but for reasons unknown, the classes ceased and the organization disappeared in the summer of 1893.

The story of the institutes in the small sawmill communities on Burrard Inlet, Moodyville (later incorporated into North Vancouver) and Hastings Mill (later part of Vancouver), can be quickly told. There was intense rivalry between the two towns in the early years, and it is felt that the founding of a mechanics' institute at Moodyville in late

1868 was the chief reason for the mill manager at Hastings Mill on the south shore of the inlet doing likewise. Neither institute was particularly active. The Hastings Mill organization, which maintained a small library in the company boarding house, petered out about 1886, its books subsequently forming the nucleus of the Vancouver Reading Room (later the public library). The Moodyville Institute remained in existence until 1900, its modest library being its chief activity.

Church Institutes

Brief mention should be made of several of these organizations, which were usually founded by clergymen in connection with their local churches and provided a library and reading room and sometimes a program of lectures and other activities. Reference has already been made to St. Paul's Literary Institute in Nanaimo, founded in 1862. A similar organization had been established in 1859 at Fort Hope (now Hope) by the Anglican clergyman there. It is not certain whether a local church was responsible for the founding of an institute at Yale in late 1862, but the Anglican minister was certainly the key figure in its revival twenty years later. The most active of all was the Cariboo Church Institute organized by Rev. James Reynard of St. Saviour's Anglican Church in Barkerville, which operated from 1868 to 1871, providing lectures and concerts, elementary academic courses and bible and music study. Somewhat later, in 1896, an Anglican clergyman founded a "free libary and sitting room" in connection with his church in Rossland. In Hedley, another mining town, the Methodist church established a library and literary society in 1903. There may have been other organizations of this type as well, but the foregoing are all that have been identified at this time.

As indicated by the foregoing, it is clear that the mechanics' institutes in British Columbia showed little resemblance to the original institutions in the United Kingdom. By the time such organizations were founded in B.C., mechanics' institutes and literary societies were a common and widespread movement in Great Britain and Eastern Canada. The names were adapted for local use, presumably because they were widely understood in general terms among the educated middle class, but the activities varied greatly from one community to another, depending on local needs, interests and resources, and on the wishes and capacities of local leaders. It is not known whether any "mechanics" were served by these organizations, but it is clear from what little is known of their work that they provided a wide variety of educational opportunities, intellectual stimulation and wholesome entertainment during the formative years of many of the province's main population centres.

References

B.C. Public Accounts, *Sessional Papers*, several years.

Johnson, F.H. (1964), *A History of Public Education in British Columbia*, Vancouver: University of British Columbia.

Kelly, T. (1962), *A History of Adult Education in Great Britain*, Liverpool: Liverpool University Press.

Vernon, F. (1969), *The Development of Adult Education in Ontario, 1790-1900*, Unpublished Ed. D. Thesis, Ontario Institute for Studies in Education.

Victoria *British Colonist* newspaper.

Originally published in *Continuous Learning*, 10 (3), 1971: 126-130. Reprinted with permission.

5.4

Origins of Local Publicly Sponsored Evening Classes in British Columbia

*T*he school boards and universities in British Columbia have developed large adult education programs as part of their service to the people of their communities. They have been joined in the task in recent years by the community colleges and the Institute of Technology, additional partners in the public sector of education. It was only a few decades ago that there was no publicly-sponsored activity of this kind anywhere in B.C. Little is known of the early stages of this work, but recent research makes it possible to begin to see the broad outlines. This article represents the results of some of this exploratory research.

The title of this article has been worded in such a way as to exclude a number of adult education activities which were publicly sponsored, in that they were made available by the Provincial or Federal governments, but which were not primarily a result of local initiative. This account does not, therefore, include the Marine Schools organized by the Dominion Department of Marine and Fisheries or the dairy schools and other activities arranged by the Dominion Department of Agriculture. At the provincial level, it does not include the many and varied educational activities of the Department of Agriculture (short courses, Farmers' and Women's Institutes, etc.); courses given by the Bureau of Mines; support for mechanics; institutes and local libraries; or the services provided by the provincial library, archives or museum. The focus here is on locally arranged evening classes sponsored by public educational institutions

In this, as in so many other areas of social service, local initiative was ahead of official public policy. Private schools, individuals and voluntary organizations (most notably the Y.M.C.A.) pioneered in the provision of opportunities for evening study in academic, commercial, technical and general interest subjects. It was not until 1906 that a local school board ran an evening class program; 1909 that such a program was successfully launched on a large scale; and 1910 that the provincial government provided grants in support of such work. In years prior to that, a series of local efforts—privately and publicly sponsored—had tested the need and experimented with different forms of service.

Forerunners

A study of the newspapers in several leading centres in the province reveals that before public schools and school boards began offering night school classes, others had pioneered in this work. In Victoria as early as 1859 (when the town still had fewer than 5,000 inhabitants), and increasingly during the 1860s, local private schools—and individual teachers from the schools—were advertising evening instruction in academic and commercial subjects (See *Victoria British Colonist* Dec. 13, 1859). In 1861, the man who subsequently became the first Superintendent of Schools for the Province, John Jessop, opened a private boys' school inVictoria. In the fall of the following year, he conducted evening classes as well, offering a range of academic and commercial subjects, and a "singing school." The work holds special interest because, in 1865, Jessop's school became publicly supported our of funds granted by the colonial government (the Colony ofVancouver Island). In a sense, the evening classes which he continued for the subsequent two or three years thus became the earliest example of publicly-sponsored night school work in B.C. (Victoria *British Colonist* Aug. 16, 1867). Other individuals advertised classes from time to time, including local artists who taught mechanical and "scientific" drawing. Local commercial schools appeared by 1888.

The public school teacher in the gold boom town of Barkerville advertised night classes in the fall of 1871, but it is not known whether they materialized (Barkerville *Cariboo Sentinel* Oct 7 & 14, 1871). In New Westminster, the Roman Catholic boys' school ran an "evening school" for "young men" in academic and commercial subjects as early as 1886 (New Westminster *Guardian* Oct. 5, Nov 17, 1886). In that same year the principal of the public school in Nanaimo, E.B. Paul, along with another member of his staff, taught night classes in acdemic subjects in a room provided by the local Anglican church (Nanaimo *Free Press* Aug. 11, Oct. 16, 1886). In Vancouver, private schools were conducting evening classes as early as 1891 and frequently thereafter (Vancouver *News Advertiser* Mar. 13, 17 & 20, 1891).

Special mention should be made of the role of the Y.M.C.A. in this work. In both Victoria and Vancouver, this organization maintained large evening class programs in academic and other subjects long before the school boards entered the picture. In Victoria, the Y. program began in a small way in the fall of 1889, commercial and other vocational subjects predominating. Classes were offered again the following year, and then there was a gap until 1895, when this work was revived for a three-year period (at one point being described as the Y.M.C.A. "Evening College"). The organization fell on evil days for some years after that and when it was reconstituted in 1903, the class program was revived. It grew into a major community service in subsequent years, with 170 students enrolled in a wide variety of subjects at its height in the fall of 1912 (Victoria *Colonist* Oct. 26, 1912). Whereas in several of the large centres the school board began evening classes in 1910 (when government grants became available), in Victoria the board did not get into this work until the fall of 1913, perhaps because the Y.M.C.A. was already providing such a comprehensive service. In Vancouver, the Y. conducted classes in 1893 and the following year, but nothing further until 1903. The work was revived at that time and by the fall of 1908, 160 students were registered in thirteen subjects. During 1909, there was a total registration of 191. The school board launched its night school in 1909 in Vancouver and the Y. offered few classes thereafter. In the case of both these centres, the Y.M.C.A.

had shown the way and accomplished a great deal on slender resources (Vancouver *News Advertiser* Oct. 18, 1908).

Public Policy

The Superintendent of Schools, John Jessop, was publicly suggesting government support for evening classes as early as 1877. In his annual report at that time he pointed out that such work was being conducted in San Francisco and other places and should perhaps be experimented with in the larger B.C. centres. There was no apparent response to this intitiative. In Victoria, a few classes were conducted in 1906. The Vancouver School Board launched an experimental night school program in the fall of 1907. The following year it gave no classes, but worked successfully through its delegates to the annual meeting of the B.C. School Trustees' Association to secure passage of resolutions by that body calling for monetary and other support from the Department of Education for night schools (BCSTA 1908). In 1909, Vancouver began its comprehensive night school program and called upon the government once more for assistance.

Government response came early in 1910 in the form of amendments to the Public Schools Act. These formally authorized school boards to conduct night schools. The regulations stipulated that night class students must be fourteen years of age or older and that twenty would be the minimum class size. Teachers were required to have an acceptable teaching ceretificate. The Department would pay from two-fifths to four-fifths of the teachers' remuneration, with rural districts receiving the higher amount. Subject matter was to consist of the regular academic school subjects. The night schools were to be supervised for administrative purposes by the Technical Branch of the Department of Education and inspected for academic purposes by the regular school inspectors in the districts. (The regulations were to apply, of course, only to those classes for which grants were to be sought.)

The response from the school districts was not exactly overwhelming. In the first year under the grants (1910-11) six centres applied for support. Of the total enrollment of 2,005, 1,628 were in Vancouver. By 1913-14, the total enrollment had risen slightly to 2,311, drawn that year from only five centres, with Vancouver accounting for 1,749 (Public Schools Annual Reports). The major expansion of night schools in the province lay in the future.

Victoria

Although Victoria was slower than some centres to launch school board night classes under the provisions of the 1910 amendments, there had been a long history of involvement by the public schools and school personnel in this kind of work. In 1896 and again two years later, the South Park School offered lecture series for the public, the proceeds of which were to be used to strengthen the school library. In 1898 the city high school presented a single lecture. In 1901, the Spring Ridge school formed a "Mothers' Club" which met regularly on a monthly basis every year until 1912, the meetings consisting usually of lectures on the school program, child care or related topics. This was perhaps a forerunner of the parent-teacher organization. In 1904 and again the following year, the "Principal and Faculty of Victoria College and High School" presented a series of lectures for the public. On the first occasion, proceeds were to be used to buy equipment for the science department of the school, but for the second series only a nominal fee was charged and the newspaper stated that "the primary object is education" (Victoria *Colonist* Oct. 4, 1905). Another important step was taken in 1905, when manual training classes, which had been offered in the daytime since 1901, were made available in the evening as well. A slightly wider range of offerings became available the following year, when as a result of initiatives taken by "the gentlemen teachers of the city schools," English, arithmetic and bookkeeping were added (Victoria *Colonist* Sept. 20, 1906). There were no further evening classes offered by the schools until 1913, but in January of 1908, A.J. Pineo, a faculty member at the College (and a key figure in the Y.M.C.A. program as well) conducted an evening course in chemistry for interested medical and pharmacy students.

When the school board entered the field in the fall of 1913, a wide range of courses was offered including academic subjects, design, manual training, gasoline engines, sheet metalwork, dressmaking, cooking and a special course for those preparing for the civil service exam. Classes were offered in three different schools on five nights a week and the fees were three dollars per term "and upward." There were 384 enrollments in the first year.

Vancouver

As will be described below, Vancouver College and McGill College conducted night classes as early as 1900. The school board entered the field early in 1907. In mid-January the local newspaper carried a list of subjects which might be offered by the board in the evenings and invited all who were interested to attend a meeting. (The organizing committee included John Kyle, Supervisor of Drawing and Art in the Vancouver system, who was to direct the much larger program which was to be launched two years later and was subsequently to give vigorous leadership to night class work throughout the Province after he joined the staff of the Department of Education.) It is not known how many persons enrolled for the courses but, at a subsequent school board meeting, classes in Experimental Science and Geometrical and Freehand Drawing were described as being "well attended considering their recent establishment" (Vancouver *News Advertiser* Mar. 10, 1907). Classes were not offered the following year but, as mentioned above, the school board was active in seeking support for this work from the Province.

Although no action had been taken by the government in this matter by the fall of 1909, the Vancouver board decided to go ahead that year with the inauguration of an ambitious night school program, under the direction of John Kyle. In early October, the program was announced publicly and a long list of proposed courses was carried in the newpaper. It was clear from the announcements that the program was wholly vocational in emphasis, the advertisements for the courses being headed, "Young Men And Women! Prepare for Promotion!" Fees were $3.00 per course (*N.A.* Oct. 5, 1909). The response was gratifying—601 persons took part in the program, with a total of 966 registrations. Arithmetic, English and bookkeeping each enrolled over 200; engineering, drawing and architecture were the largest of the remaining classes. These numbers exceeded expectations and imposed some financial burdens on the Board which it sought to relieve by renewed requests to the Province for financial support.

By the following year, provincial grants in support of night schools hads been made available. For the next four years—until the outbreak of the war—enrollments in Vancouver remained at a consistently high level. They rose to 1,628 in 1910-11, to 2,011 in 1911-12, fell off somewhat the following year and came back up to 1,749 in 1913-14. A variety of academic and general interest courses were added after the first year and the number of vocational subjects, still the core of the program, was greatly increased. Close links were established with organized labour, especially the craft unions, and three-year programs were organized in a number of specialized vocational areas. By 1914, the Vancouver night school program was solidly established and already developed to a fairly advanced stage.

Other Centres

The other centres in the province had smaller populations and less is known about evening class activities there. In New Westminster, some pressure was brought to bear on the school board as early as January 1909 by the local Trades and Labour Council, which was interested in a night school. The board explained that it was not as yet empowered to undertake such work (New Westminster *British Columbian* Jan. 16, 1909), but when the legislation was amended in 1910, the board was quick to respond to the opportunity and conducted a program for each of the four remaining years prior to the war. Three other communities launched night school programs in the first year supporting grants were available—Nanaimo, Extension and South Vancouver. In the case of the latter, its enrollments did not appear on the official lists in the report of the Department of Education, but it is known from newspaper sources that it did conduct classes. The South Vancouver School Board (which was subsequently incorporated into Vancouver) went on record in January of 1910 as being in favour of providing night school classes for young people in its district. It took the position, however, that it was not as yet empowered under the Act to undertake this work. When the Act was amended a few weeks later, they set the wheels in motion and established several classes the following fall. Enrollment statistics are not available, but it appears from press accounts that classes in shorthand, dressmaking and building construction were certainly held. Groups taking English and arithmetic were so small they had to be combined (*N.A.* Nov, 25, Dec. 9, 1910). In subsequent years South Vancouver apparently left the task to the much larger Vancouver program to serve their district as well.

In 1911-12, the districts of Coal Creek, Cumberland and Ladysmith, all coal mining areas, launched night schools. The following year, Duncan and Hosmer were added to the list; and in 1913-14, Victoria and Thrums began their programs. It is entirely likely that during this period some other centres, like South Vancouver, held classes which for some reason did not qualify for grants and did not appear in the Department's reports (suggested in Wales 1958 and confirmed by other evidence). Details about such programs await further research.

Post-Secondary Institutions

There were several instances during this early period of post-secondary institutions conducting adult education activities. Weltham College, a private institution in Vancouver, began such work in 1891. In the next two years brief lecture series on astronomy and electricity were given in the evening for the general public and were well attended. A series of four chamber concerts were given during May of 1893. Later in the same decade, Buckland College, also in Vancouver, offered some of its regular courses at night, but it is not certain that this work was at the post-secondary level. In the meantime, the Methodist Church had founded Columbian College in New Westminster, which had a provincial charter to grant theological degrees and was affiliated with the University of Toronto. In the fall of 1893, the College sponsored a series of debates, lectures and entertainments which were open to the public. It was announced in the fall of 1899 that some of its regular courses would be given in the evening for part-time students, but it is not known whether these materialized. During the next decade, some evening classes were certainly given but, as far as can be determined, not in the post-secondary aspects of the College's curriculum. Occasionally lectures and recitals were held. These included two lecture-recitals on the development of classical music (1903), three lectures on classical literature (1914) and five on religious pedagogy (1914).

In the public sector, the first in the field appears to have been Vancouver College. (This was the name adopted by Vancouver High School under an agreement by which it became affiliated with McGill University in 1899.) As early as 1900, the annual report on the public schools of the province indicated that there were both part-time and full-time students taking first and second year university-level work at the college (B.C. Public Schools Annual Report 1900). In December of 1900, a lecture sponsored by the college was given in a public hall in the city. It has already been mentioned that in the fall of 1904 and again the following year, the staff of Victoria College and High School offered a series of lectures for the public in that city.

In 1906, McGill University College was created in Vancouver, and it took over the university-level work which had previously been conducted through Vancouver College. In the spring of 1907, with considerable fanfare, the new institution offered its first extension activity in the form of a lecture on "Captain Vancouver—His Explorations" by the Provincial Superintendent of Education, Alexander Robinson (*N.A.* Mar. 16, 1907). In the fall of the same year, McGill College offered courses in the evening which could be taken for credit towards college certificates. These included English literature, Latin, French, mathematics and mechanical drawing. As far as can be determined, such courses were not offered again in subsequent years, but in 1908-09 and again the following year, brief series of non-credit lectures were presented. The only two lecturers whose names are known were John G. Davidson and Lemuel Robertson, both of the college staff and both of whom were to play significant roles in university extension work in later years as faculty members of The University of British Columbia (*N.A.* Nov. 14, 1909; Selman 1963). So although The University of British Columbia did not open its doors until the fall of 1915, some adult education activities at the post-secondary level had been conducted by public institutions over the previous fifteen year period.

There are several aspects of the development of this work in British Columbia which deserve comment. It is significant, first of all, that organized labour played a part in the initiation and subsequent development of night schools in several centres. In most other aspects of adult education during these early years, it was middle class elements which provided stimulus, leadership and participants. In this case, the craft unions especially played a leading part; some of them having conducted educational activities on their own before public authorities took up the task. There has not been space here to develop this aspect of the story, but it should be noted that training programs in some vocational areas were stimulated by ever-widening government regulations concerning the qualifications of those performing certain tasks. It is no coincidence, for instance, that several coal mining communities were among the first to conduct classes. Following several serious accidents in coal mines in the province, regulations required new levels of training for certain categories of workmen. Finally, it should be noted how small most of these communities were when classes were begun. This can perhaps be explained by the fact that because B.C. was developed so late compared to other parts of the continent and because many immigrants brought with them experience with such activity in other parts of the world, this work was perhaps begun here sooner than would otherwise have been the case. But although publicly-sponsored night school programs were relatively late in starting in British Columbia compared to some other centres in North America, they were to develop rapidly in subsequent years and in due course to provide significant national leadership in this field.

References

British Columbia, *Annual Report of Public Schools*, various years.

BCSTA, British Columbia School Trustees Association. *Report of Fifth Annual Convention*, 1908.

Cariboo Sentinel, Barkerville newspaper.

News Advertiser, Vancouver, newspaper.

Nanaimo *Free Press* newspaper.

New Westminster *British Columbian* newspaper.

Selman, G. (1963), *A History of the Extension Services of the University of British Columbia 1915 - 1955*, Unpublished M.A. Thesis, University of British Columbia.

Victoria *British Colonist* and *Colonist* newspapers.

Wales, B. (1958), *The Development of Adult Education in British Columbia*, Unpublished Ed.D Thesis, Oregon State University.

Originally published in *Continuous Learning*, 10 (4), 1971: 199-207. Reprinted with permission.

Part 6

Adult Education in British Columbia: The Great Depression

*S*oon after changing my position in early 1975 from being Director of the Centre for Continuing Education to joining the teaching faculty in the Adult Education Program of the Faculty of Education, I was faced with the unaccustomed luxury of deciding how to use my summer non-teaching time for research work. For reasons I don't fully recall, I decided to investigate what had happened to the field of adult education in the province during the Great Depression of the 1930s. As I recall the subject appealed to me because of the relatively short time frame involved (thus making it hopefully doable in the three months or so I had available) and because it would fill in another piece in my long-term goal of writing a comprehensive history of the field in the province. I had also picked up intriguing bits of information about the period from several other sources. Peter Sandiford's 1935 survey of adult education in Canada (written as part of the organizational stages of founding the Canadian Association for Adult Education), Henry Johnson's history of public education in the province, and Bert Wales' doctoral dissertation on the development of adult education in the public system all contained some significant information about those years. I had also heard about a few of the chief actors in the story from my aunt, Mrs. Rex Eaton, who had worked at senior levels of the Provincial civil service in the pre-war period So while I am not very clear as to why I turned to this subject for my research, the foregoing factors may have had something to do with it. Whatever the reasons, the subject turned out to be a deeply interesting one.

The immediate product of the summer's research was a monograph on *Adult Education in British Columbia during the Depression*, which was published in 1976 and which is reprinted in this section. In subsequent years I made use of the material in other work, most notably in my general history of adult education in the province, *The Invisible Giant*.

What came to have particular meaning for me, arising out of this research and writing, was that as I deepened my knowledge of the Depression period, I came to two important conclusions. One was that in those years, adult education was seen to a degree not equalled before or since in our province's history as one of the instruments government could utilize in pursuing its major goals. One of these was frequently referred to in the documents of the period as helping to improve "the morale of the people." I felt that it was extremely significant that adult education, which has frequently been a strictly marginal activity in our society, appears at that time to have loomed large in the government's thinking. The other important fact was that whereas in most instances we tend to see adult education as significant in enabling adults to play this role or that in society (as worker, citizen, parent, organizational member, etc.) during the Depression period it was seen as an important factor in a more comprehensive view of our citizens—how they felt about themselves and their role in their society. This struck me as quite the most profound notion about the role of adult education that we have ever seen emanating from government.

In the late Eighties I was invited by the continuing education people at the University of Syracuse, who had a large grant from the Kellogg Corporation in support of various forms of historical work in the field, to an invitational seminar on documentation in adult education. Out of that meeting, or the project of which it formed one stage, came a proposal for a volume of writing about adult education between the two World Wars, with some emphasis on workers' movements. I had not paid special attention to workers' education, but indicated that I could make a contribution based on the earlier research I had done on the Depression years. In the chapter which I subsequently wrote for inclusion in this book, which I entitled "The Morale of the People: Reflections on Adult Education in British Columbia in the Great Depression," and which is included in this section, I took the opportunity to develop the foregoing points at some length. This volume was published in 1990, some 15 years after my original research on the subject. My deepening understanding of the Depression period and of the role of adult education during those years has been one of my most abiding research interests.

6.1

Adult Education in British Columbia during the Depression

*T*he 1930s are synonymous with the Great Depression. The Twenties had been prosperous times for British Columbia on the whole, especially following the sharp but brief recession of the first two years of the decade. In 1929 the per capita income in B.C. was the highest of any province in the Dominion (Ormsby 1964; Robin 1972). Because of the nature of the province's economy, however, the short-run and seasonal picture could vary greatly from the overall trends. Vancouver, the chief population centre, had a long history of unemployment problems. It had established relief camps for unemployed single men in the early Twenties. In 1925, at the height of the business boom, Vancouver had 1,800 men on the relief dole during the winter months. In his remarkable biography of his mother, Rolf Knight indicates that when she moved from Toronto to Vancouver in 1928, their experience indicated that "the depression was already on" (Knight 1974:103). Reports in the Vancouver *Sun* in September of 1929, before the stock market crash, revealed that the number of families on city relief at that time was already up sharply over the previous year (*Sun* Sept. 17, 1929).

The Depression, when it came full force, hit British Columbia and Vancouver particularly hard. In common with the rest of Western Canada, the B.C. economy, with its heavy reliance on primary resources and exports, was especially vulnerable to the forces at work. As was clearly demonstrated in the report of the Federal Rowell-Sirois Royal Commission, the policies which were adopted by the Federal government to combat the Depression were such that the burden fell especially heavily on the West—on Agriculture and the export industries of B.C. (Smiley 1963). By the time the census was taken in 1931, 25.06 per cent of wage earners in B.C. were unemployed, a higher figure than in any other province at the time. This figure almost doubled by 1933, at the depth of the Depression. In September, 1931, over 35,000 people in B.C. had registered for unemployment relief. Six months later the figure had doubled. By the beginning of 1933, it had reached 85,750 and three months later, 118,538 (Lane 1966). By 1933, the per capita income in the province had fallen 47 per cent from the 1929 level.

British Columbia was affected not only by the blow to its own people and economy, but also by the fact that many people came from other parts of Canada, especially from the Prairies, in the hope of finding it easier to get along on the coast than in their home areas. Much of the burden of caring for, or at least coping with the influx of transient people, fell on Vancouver itself. Its charter made the city responsible for making "suitable provision for its indigent and destitute." The burden of relief expenditures soon overwhelmed the city and was subsequently shared with the provincial and federal authorities, but this remained a matter of dipute among the three levels of government throughout the Depression. In 1933, $2,391,000 was spent on relief in Vancouver, of which the city's share was $1,100,000.

In terms of social unrest, the city felt the effects of the Depression from the very beginning. Within weeks of the crash in late October, 1929, there were disturbances in Vancouver—the unemployed demonstrated, raided the city relief office and clashed with police. Demonstrations became commonplace. The "occupation" of Victory Square and the reading of the Riot Act by the Mayor in 1935, the launching of the trek to Ottawa later in the year, and the occupation of the post office and other buildings in 1938, were but the most dramatic incidents of a troubled decade for Vancouver. The city made unofficial efforts throughout the period to discourage the transients—the "untouchables" as Rev. Andrew Roddan termed them—from settling in Vancouver, but many stayed, in spite of efforts to "keep them moving" (Roddan 1932).

It has been suggested that the development of adult education in Canada, and elsewhere, has taken place in distinct phases and that important new programs and periods of growth have come about as responses to social crises (Grattan 1955; Thomas 1961). Just as the individual adult seems to experience certain "teachable moments" at times of challenge or change in his or her life, so the nation rises to the challenges it faces, in part by means of new programs designed to assist men and women to cope with the needs of the times. It can be amply demonstrated that during the Depression, surely one of the most traumatic events in the Canadian experience, there was such a response. Both senior levels of government and a range of local agencies initiated educational programs in an effort to help people cope with the distress and demoralization resulting from the impact of the Depression. At the Federal level, provision for vocational and technical education was greatly strengthened and significant assistance for other forms of education such as work among those who were in the relief camps, the fishermen, and certain categories of rural youth. The Provincial government, especially after the Liberals came to power in late 1933, responded by strengthening vocational and academic educational opportunities for adults, launching the Provincial Recreation Program, which was the first of its kind in Canada, and supporting the efforts of a variety of voluntary associations through the "Self-Help" activities and in other ways. Publicly supported agencies such as The University of British Columbia and local school boards provided new services as did a variety of voluntary, service and religious organizations.

There also appears to have been considerable effort put into study of what had gone wrong with Canada's economic and social system, and into mobilizing for bringing about changes. The formation of a new political party, the Co-operative Commonwealth Federation, was the most obvious outcome of this activity and represented, among other things, the search for new avenues to social justice which was going on so actively during the decade. There also seems to have been an educational by-product of the tendency toward co-operative and group approaches to coping with the difficulties of the Thirties. By the end of the period there had been a remarkable development of study group activity, drama clubs and a variety of small group approaches to learning and self-development. There were also the beginnings of interest in leadership training for those involved in this type of activity.

Other significant developments in adult education during the period were perhaps less related to the circumstances of the Depression years. The Fraser Valley Regional

Library project had been started in the late Twenties but demonstrated its success in the Thirties and influenced the development of library service elsewhere in the Depression decade and later. Much of the activity of the newly-established Extension Department at U.B.C., although directed at the concerns of the day, represented the application in British Columbia of ideas concerning the university's proper relationship to the community, ideas which had been developed earlier, in other places.

The most important feature of the 1930s, with respect to the development of adult education, was the broadening of both the extent and the purpose of public provision in this field. The extent of government's role, and that of government supported public institutions, increased greatly. In the field of vocational education, provision by both senior levels of government became the dominant factor. Especially during these years, it was the government which had the funds and there was increasing support for the idea that government had the major responsibility for ameliorating the harmful effects of the Depression.

Not only the extent of public provision but also the purposes to be served were expanded. Whereas prior to this time government had seen its role in adult education to be largely in the field of remedial education and occupational training, there developed an increased willingness, in response to the stress and dislocation caused by the Depression, to be concerned with the general welfare or "morale" of the population. Prior to this time such considerations tended to be the concern of voluntary and private service organizations. Now government demonstrated a willingness to cater to the needs of the whole person, to be concerned with how the individual felt about himself/herself and his/her society. Such a change in orientation did not come about presumably out of pure and wholly altruistic concern for the citizen's welfare, but at least partly was a response to the frightening realities of Depression conditions. It was clear that if steps were not taken to ameliorate the situation in which so many people found themselves, there might be an inclination to adopt radical approaches aimed at changing drastically the existing social and economic arrangements. There was, of course, genuine concern about human suffering and misfortune. There was also, obviously, political concern about the stability and perpetuation of existing systems. Public services went beyond just social or citizenship concerns. Public participation and funding were extended into education for personal self-development and the cultivation of the liberal arts. By the end of the decade, public adult education services were not only greatly increased in volume, but were also extended over a much wider range of concerns.

The Conservative Tolmie ministry, which was in office from mid-1928 to late 1933, took few if any significant steps in the field of adult education. The government headed by T.D. Patullo, which held office throughout the balance of the decade, introduced a number of important new programs. The key figure in this connection was Dr. George M. Weir, the Provincial Secretary and Minister of Education. He had been principal of the Normal School in Saskatoon before joining The University of British Columbia as professor of education in 1924. He was known as a progressive in his approach to educational matters, a fact amply demonstrated by the terms of the important Putnam-Weir Commission report on the future of education in the province which he had helped to prepare in 1924-25 . In his history of education in British Columbia, F. Henry Johnson describes Dr. Weir as a "dynamic crusader" and quotes with approval Bruce Hutchison's description of him as having "the zeal of a real reformer" (Johnson 1964:113).

Dr. Weir's interest in adult education had been clearly demonstrated before he entered the government. Although the Putnam-Weir report did not deal with adult education, it did put great stress on the need for the curriculum to be closely related to real life situations and also on the need for a satisfactory program of physical education (Johnson 1964). As early as 1930, in his speeches about the future of education in the province, Weir was stressing the importance of adult education (*Sun* April 3, 1930 & Mar. 9, 1932). Johnson refers to Weir as "the great champion of adult education in British Columbia" (Johnson 1964:230) and during his time as Minister of Education several significant measures in this field were enacted or implemented by the government. These included a major expansion of the correspondence courses into areas of particular interest to adults, a number of programs design to serve the unemployed, the introduction of the Provincial Recreation program, the appointment of a Provincial Advisory Committee on adult education to guide the development of services to the unemployed, the creation of the Department's community drama program, and the launching of several programs of adult education—most notably the "Self-Help program—which involved a partnership between government and voluntary agencies. In addition, Weir gave strong support to John Kyle of the Department in his active promotion of local school board night schools (Wales 1958). Weir was also a strong influence in the decision by the University during the middle years of the decade first to experiment with an expanded program of university extension and then to create a department to give continuing direction to the work (Selman 1963). He was also a close associate of E.A. Corbett, the Director of the newly-established national association for adult education, and played an active part in the development of that body (Faris 1975).

One question which should be raised about the policy of the Patullo government concerning adult education is whether their active and innovative role in that field arose mainly from the conviction of the importance of such activity in the development of the people of the province or whether it was seen more as a series of expedient measures designed to prevent civil unrest and despair. Certainly considerable stress was given in public statements about some of the new programs concerning their usefulness in raising the "morale" of the people. It seems obvious that this was a major reason why such programs would find favour with the government. On the other hand, it appears from his public statements, some made well before he was in office, that Weir himself supported adult education not just in order to cope with the emergency but as part of his overall educational philosophy and view of desirable human development. How influential his views were in the minds of his colleagues in the government is not known. The distress and demoralization caused by the conditions of the Depression called for measures providing constructive activities for adults in the province. No sooner were these actions taken than the country was plunged into the Second World War, with all its unusual demands on the Canadian people. It is therefore not possible to determine what the government's policies in this field would have been in more normal times.

One means of assessing the adult education provisions at the beginning of the decade under review is to examine the directory of adult education offerings which was published by the Vancouver Public Library in late 1929. Entitled "Why Stop Learning?," it was the first such directory to be published in Vancouver, and probably in the province (Copy in V.P.L. & see *Sun* Jan. 6, 1930). The publication was organized under 74 subject matter headings from Aeroplane Construction to Zoology and included others such as Art,

Bookkeeping and Accounting, Dancing, Literature, Matriculation, Plumbing and Nursing. A total of 38 different agencies were listed as sponsors of instruction.

What was most obvious from examining the directory was the prominence in the listing of the Vancouver School Board night school on the one hand and the considerable number of proprietary technical, commercial and art schools on the other. (As far as can be determined, 22 of the agencies listed were of this latter type.) Because the directory was intended for use in Vancouver, it did not, of course, reflect the availability of services elsewhere. It did not, for instance, refer to the academic correspondence courses which were available from the Department of Education (but which were up to this time not taken by many adults). With respect to night schools, it reflected the services of the Vancouver system only. This was, however, by far the largest such program in the province, its registrations in these years representing more than the total of all the other school boards combined. Many other school boards offered classes (66 in 1929, up from 49 the year before) but most offered just one or two and, like the Vancouver program, they were overwhelmingly vocationally oriented. The work of several voluntary organizations was represented as well. These included the Y.M.C.A., Y.W.C.A., Council of Jewish Women, several other religious organizations, and several devoted to the study of scientific subjects.

What was not included, which represented then, as it does now, a very substantial segment of adult education activities, was work carried on by organizations for their own members. This would have included religious, service and fraternal organizations, professional and trade groups, unions, business and industry, educational, debating and study groups and a number of organizations interested in literature and the arts. The impression that one forms about adult education at the time is that, apart from the night schools and the proprietary schools, provision was minimal. The Y.M. and Y.W.C.A. had been active over the years and still gave a few classes each year, but largely a repetition of a very few tried and true practical subjects. Taken as a whole, what was available was overwhelmingly vocational in emphasis. It was left to the next decade to bring great changes in this.

Although information about adult education developments in the province in the Thirties, especially in the private sector, is fragmentary, there were two general surveys carried out—in 1935 and at the end of the decade—which provide something of an overview. In 1934, meetings were held in Toronto aimed at creating a national organization to serve and promote the interests of adult education in Canada (Kidd 1950; Corbett 1957; Faris 1975). It was decided, in order to determine the extent of adult education in the country, to carry out a national survey under the general direction of Dr. Peter Sandiford of the Univeristy of Toronto. The survey in British Columbia, interestingly enough, was carried out by E.A. Corbett, then of the University of Alberta Extension Department. Adult education activity in B.C. is reflected in the various chapters of the report and some reference to the details will be made below. In an appendix to the document, there is a summary by J.W. Gibson of the B.C. Department of Education which purports, apparently, to be a general description of the field in the province but which is in fact only an account of the activities carried out by the Department itself. Taking the survey report as a whole, however, what is perhaps most obvious is the greatly increased role of government and other public agencies in the field and the fact that a much greater effort than at the beginning of the decade was being devoted to other than vocational programs. Sandiford's general position was that adult education was to be "the next general forward step in government service to the people" and that government should play a leadership and co-ordinating role. He saw one of the chief purposes of adult education as "the solution of the great problem—how to restore, maintain and enhance the morale of the people" (Sandiford 1935: XX, 7). This was clearly a reflection of the Depression times in which the survey was conducted. With respect to adult education in B.C., Sandiford summed up as follows:

> The Government of British Columbia...plays the chief part in Adult Education. The work on the whole is fairly well co-ordinated and financed, but here again we see the need of bringing the various activities within the general "set-up" of provincial education. (Sandiford 1935: XX, 7)

Another comment of a general kind on developments in the province is provided by a report in a Vancouver newspaper in late 1938 in which Dr. Gordon Shrum, the Director of the Extension Department at U.B.C., on his return from national meetings, sums up his conclusions. He said that B.C. was leading all other provinces in the variety of its adult education programs and in the response to them. He added:

> No other Province is doing the school and community drama work which is being carried out under the provincial Department of Education in B.C. And there is no other program of recreational education that compares with that being conducted by Ian Eisenhardt [Provincial "Pro-Rec" program] The most significant thing being done in Canada is the work being accomplished by the Dominion-Provincial Youth Training Plan. (Vancouver *Province* Nov. 25, 1938)

Just after the end of the decade, the Public Library Commission of the province carried out a survey of adult education at the request of the Minister of Education and published its findings and recommendations in *A Preliminary Study of Adult Education in British Columbia: 1941* (B.C.P.L.C. 1942). This was the most thorough survey which had yet been undertaken. It described the work of the various public and private agencies in the field, providing enrollment statistics in some cases. The report included descriptions of approximately 30 public departments and agencies and several hundred private and voluntary groups (all of the 186 Women's Institutes, for instance, were just mentioned as a group). Agencies described ranged from the Departments of Education and Agriculture to the Vancouver Folk Society and the Alpine Club. What is perhaps most impressive about this report, apart from the vast amount of activity it reports, is the belief expressed that adult education should in the future become organized at the provincial level on a scale comparable with in-school education and that such a system should seek to support all aspects of adult development. The chief emphasis was on the all-round development of the citizen. The committee was chaired by E.S. Robinson, Head Librarian of the Vancouver Public Library, and included two other profesional librarians and a lawyer with considerable experience in library affairs. The committee, like Peter Sandiford, editor of the national survey of 1935, was in favour of strong leadership and co-ordiantion from the government. Their recommendations called for legislation to create a Division of Adult Education in the Department, the appointment of a Director who was professionally qualified in adult education, and the creation of a Council of Adult Education which would determine policy and on which a variety of community organizations, public and private, would be represented. Perhaps at least partly because the country was plunged into the problems of the War by the time their report was published, the recommendations were not acted upon, and indeed more than 35 years later are still in many respects ahead of their time.

In the account which follows, emphasis is given to those programs or projects which broke new ground in terms of adult education in the province, which related in a significant way to the conditions of the Depression period, or were so outstanding in terms of scale or national leadership that they merit separate treatment. Over and above these programs, however, a vast and varied array of adult education activity took place during the period. Many departments of government, Federal and Provincial, carried out large programs. Two examples would be the educational and informational activities of the Department of Agriculture, through its field personnel, demonstration projects, courses and publications program and through its support of the Farmers' and Women's Institutes; and the contribution of the Provincial Department of Health, by means of its public health personnel and clinics, its courses and publications. Private and voluntary associations of various kinds contributed mightily to the educational opportunities available to adults. A partial list of such organizations would include business and industry, trade associations, union and professional groups, religious and service organizations, cultural groups, organizations interested in health and safety matters, fields of science and other special interests, and a range of groups concerned with aspects of citizenship such as the Canadian Clubs and the Councils of Women. A significant contribution was also made by the proprietary schools which offered instruction in a wide range of content areas, from business skills to arts and crafts. Particular mention should be made as well of the two national mass media agencies which were created in the period, the Canadian Broadcasting Corporation, which was established in 1936, and the National Film Board, which was formed in 1939.

Technical-Vocational Education

A large segment of adult education, perhaps larger proportionally at the beginning of the decade than at the end, consisted of technical and vocational education. At the beginning of the decade, such work was being funded under the terms of the federal Technical Education Act of 1919, which had been extended for a further five-year period when it expired in 1929. This act provided matching funds to the provinces to finance facilties and programs, including in-school education. During the Twenties, these funds had made possible modest progress in this field in B.C., including the building of technical schools in Vancouver, Victoria and New Westminster, the growth in vocational courses in night schools, and the beginning of vocational correspondence courses. In the 1930s, as the Depression conditions worsened, to the more longstanding realization that a more highly trained work force was needed, was added the further stimulus of the necessity to provide people with meaningful activities in order to bolster their morale. The federal Vocational Education Act of 1931 having failed to be proclaimed, the province was forced to proceed on its own already strained finances to provide modest numbers of programs, concentrating largely until late in the decade on courses for the unemployed, both inside and outside the relief camps.

The Federal government came to the aid of the provinces in 1937. The Unemployment and Agricultural Assistance Act was passed providing a sum of one million dollars for the training of young men and women between the ages of 18 and 30 (See Dupre 1973). In order to qualify for assistance under this Act, the person had to be unemployed, registered with the Unemployment Service, and in needy circumstances. Each province made separate agreements with Ottawa under the Act. British Columbia organized its cost-sharing agreement under the following six schedules:

A. Forestry Training
B. Mining Training
C. Urban Occupational Training
D. Recreational and Physical Training
E. Rural Occupational Training
F. Student Aid

This "Youth Training Program" as it came to be called, provided funds in support of vocational training for the balance of the decade. By 1939-40, additional schedules had been added to the agreement with Ottawa to cover "Industrial Training for War Work" and an "Aircraft Mechanics School" and work in these areas was beginning.

The apprenticeship system in B.C. made great strides during the Thirties. Such arrangements had existed in various trades since the early years of the century at least, but there was no satisfactory system of regulation; this led sometimes to the exploitation of the apprentice. Beginning in 1926, the Building Trades Association in Vancouver created an Apprenticeship Council on the basis of the voluntary participation of some of its member companies and did much useful work in the succeeding years arranging and regulating apprenticeships and staffing evening and Saturday classes in several trades at the Vancouver Technical Scool. The number of apprentices increased significantly by the early Thirties, reaching a high of 925 by 1935 (B.C. Public School Reports, various years). In the meantime, the Council continued to press for government regulation of this activity, supported by press editorials (*Vancouver Sun* Dec. 13, 1929) and in 1935 the Liberal administration secured the passage of an Act Respecting the Training of Apprentices. This established a regulated system, including terms of service, training provisions, the responsibilities of the parties concerned and minimum levels of remuneration at the different stages. Within a very few years, trades coming under the Act included carpentry and joinery, painting and decorating, sheet-metal working, plumbing and steamfitting, electrical work, auto maintenance, sign painting, ship and boat building, repairs of electrical appliances and jewelry manufacture and repair. Classes were subsequently made available for most of these areas and correspondence instruction in some. Statistics on numbers in the apprenticeship programs under the Act were rather inconsistently presented in the reports of the Apprenticeship Branch in these early years, but it is known that there were 261 in registered programs in 1936, 180 in 1938, and 368 in 1939.

Night Schools

Night schools under the sponsorship of the local school boards, with grant aid from the Department of Education, had been operating in B.C. since 1909 (Selman 1971; Wales 1958). The number of school boards which participated had gradually increased over the years but had fluctuated widely from year to year. Vancouver, the first into the field on a large scale, had by far the largest program, its enrollments consistently representing half or more of the total for the whole province. From the beginning the night schools had been overwhelming vocational in emphasis. Courses in academic subjects and in domestic science had been added in the mid-Twenties. Total enrollments had reached a peak of almost 7,400 in the province in 1924 but had dropped off in subsequent years, increasing again by 1930-31. Enrollments during the Thirties began the decade at 7,179 in 1930-31, dropped to 4,600 in 1932-33 and rose again to 8,069 by 1939-40 (B.C. Annual Reports on Public Schools). The decline in the early and mid-Thirties was a reflection of depression conditions. Many potential students found even the minimal fees which were charged to be more than they could afford. The Vancouver *Province* commented on the decline of enrollments in 1934, stating that there was a falling off in attendance "by reason of young people losing interest in their self-improvement when continuously unable to find employment (*Province* Sept. 5, 1934). In 1931, the Department of Education reduced by almost half the supporting grants which it paid the school boards for approved courses.

The range of courses offered underwent significant change during the period. In addition to vocational and academic subjects, school boards began to expand the number of avocational and liberal arts subjects. New courses which appeared during the decade included drawing, pottery, weaving, folk dancing, play production, current events, economics, short story writing and the history of art. The provincial Director of Night Classes, John Kyle, actively promoted such work in his contacts with the school boards and in his annual reports put increasing emphasis on their relevance to the better use of leisure time. In 1934, W.K. Beach, the director of night classes for Vancouver, described the kinds of people who benefitted from night schools during the Depression:

> ...unemployed persons improving skills, unemployed persons for help in getting jobs, hobbyists, those lacking basic general education, new Canadians, homemakers and, those taking courses for leisure time purposes or for the satisfaction gained from attending. (Quoted in Wales 1958:166)

By the end of the decade, night school enrollments were rising again and the grants from the Department of Education had been increased, amounting to 75 per cent of the approved level of night school teachers' remuneration in rural school districts and 25 per cent in the larger urban centres.

Relief Camps

A distinctive, some would say notorious, feature of the Depression years was the role of the relief camps throughout Canada, where single and transient men were housed and engaged in public works projects, in return for room and board, clothing and a minimum per diem allowance (Lane 1966; Tanner 1965). The Provincial Tolmie administration had established a large number of work camps beginning in 1931, but a dispute arose with Ottawa over the shared cost arrangements. The Federal government took over the program in the summer of 1933 and operated camps for three years thereafter, under the Department of National Defence. Most of the camps in B.C., as elsewhere, were located in remote areas of the province. There was much discontent in the camps, where strikes and other forms of protest were common.

Efforts were made to provide comforts and constructive recreation for the men in the camps, but they were minimal. The Federal officials encouraged the provinces to send teachers into the camps. They also asked Frontier College, the national voluntary organization which for several decades had been sending labourer-teachers into remote frontier "communities," to provide as many men as possible for service in the camps. It is not known how many Frontier College field workers were assigned to the 83 major relief camps in B.C. The Federal authorities also encouraged churches and other voluntary organizations to provide books, magazines and other "comforts" for the men. A number of organizations responded, including the Vancouver *Sun* newspaper, which collected books through its carrier depots (*Sun* Feb. 2, 1934, etc.). Most if not all camps had some sort of library.

The response by provincial authorities to the invitation to provide educational activities in the camps was significant, but hardly in keeping with the need. The two main educational efforts consisted of the operation of "schools" in four of the larger camps and the provision of correspondence courses free of charge wherever there was interest in them. The four camps in which school were established by the Department of Education were University Hill (Vancouver), Otter Point (Sooke), Deroche (Harrison Mills) and Wilson's Landing (Kelowna). The schools were supervised by a single teacher in each centre. In 1934 there were 146 students in the four schools and thus it is clear that there would have been few enrollments in any one subject. A special course for camp cooks was given at the University Hill Camp, attended by 25 men. J.W. Gibson, the Director of high school correspondence work, described activities in the camps in the spring of 1935:

> In two of the larger camps resident instructors were employed whose business it was to supervise the studies of the men in connection with their correspondence courses, and to look after books and other educational equipment supplied. In each of the two camps referred to a separate building for study purposes was erected and a third one is nearing completion. The Department of Education supplied all camp students with free books and equipment loaned out to them through the camp foreman. (In Sandiford 1935: append. pp.4-5)

Correspondence instruction in the camps began as a voluntary effort on the part of instructors at Vancouver Technical School. Under the leadership of Col. F.T. Fairey, the Vice Principal of the school (later to become Deputy-Minister of Education), teachers there offered in December 1933 to prepare and mark correspondence courses for men in the camps, which were organized through the Department of Education. Things moved quickly; by mid-January there were 350 registrants in the six subjects offered, and by mid-February, 800 (*Sun* Jan. 11, Feb. 10, 1934). The annual report of the Department indicated a total of 871. The following year the report stated that in 1934-35 there had been 458 students in the courses run by Vancouver Technical School (11 teachers were involved in the work) and 590 other men in the camps had taken other correspondence courses from the Department. In his article written in the spring of 1935, Gibson stated that in addition to those who had taken the technical courses, 280 men took elementary school subjects during the year (in six subjects) and 681 took high school courses (in 22 subjects), making up a total of 1,347 men in the camps who had studied by correspondence.

Educational Relief Measures Outside the Camps

In addition to the special provisions which the Provincial authorities made for men in the relief camps, it undertook several kinds of special educational programs for those on relief who were not in the camps. Such activity did not begin until the Liberal government came to power in late 1933. Soon after entering office, Dr. Weir appointed a committee known as the "Adult Education, British Columbia" committee to oversee and co-ordinate activities undertaken by the Department for the unemployed. John Kyle was a member of the committee and directed the activities which were conducted under its auspices. The committee was made up of four civil servants plus Mrs. Paul Smith, M.L.A., who was a leader in women's voluntary organizations, and Mr. Harry Charlesworth, the Secretary of the Teachers' Federation. The first mention of specific measures involving education for the unemployed appeared in the Department's report for 1933-34. There it was reported that classes for the unemployed, organized in co-operation with the local school boards, had been held in North Vancouver (151 students), West Vancouver (183) and Victoria (26). There was also a report that the Department had co-operated with the Department of Mines, in view of "the great demand in the country for gold", in offering courses of 20 lectures in 22 centres (through the local night school program) to a total of 2,136 students. This program was continued in the three subsequent years with registrations of 1,174, 1,454 and 893, respectively.

In the year 1934-35, Kyle's report on the work conducted under the Adult Education Committee is more detailed. Reference has already been made to the work in the relief camps. The other activities consisted of vocational classes, the Self-Help activities (see below) and recreational classes for the unemployed (see Pro-Rec, below). The vocational classes were for the most part conducted in disused school buildings, the centres being located in Vancouver (5 schools), North Vancouver (2 schools), West Vancouver, New Westminster and Victoria (1 each). Courses in English for New Canadians and in Spanish were the only non-vocational subjects. Other subjects included auto mechanics, cabinet making, clothing, home economics, etc. Reference was also made to a series of radio lectures sponsored by the committee on "The Social Problems of British Columbia" and a night class course on economics given in Vancouver by a U.B.C. professor.

In 1935-36, vocational classes for unemployed not in relief camps were conducted in eleven schools. In the following year, the report lists for the first time the number of students in each vocational course. Total enrollment was 916 for classes in 19 schools in five centres. In 1937-38, some of the work which had been under the committee was absorbed into the provisions under the new Dominion-Provincial Training Plan. Classes not supported by the Fedral grants were held in four centres, with a total enrollment of 329. There were 1,186 enrollments under Youth Training (under the Dominion-Provincial arrangement) in Vancouver, Victoria, Nanaimo and Abbotsford. By the following year, Youth Training had risen to 1,855, and the courses not supported by the Federal funds had shrunk to 99 persons, all enrolled in English for New Canadians classes in Vancouver. The same pattern obtained in 1939-40, with 1,772 enrollments in Youth Training and 90 enrolled in English classes. The picture became somewhat blurred in the last year of the decade as Youth Training began to be used not only for training of the unemployed but also to meet certain wartime workforce needs.

Reference should also be made to a series of training courses for household helpers which were co-sponsored by the Young Women's Christian Association of Vancouver and the Department of Education. The course was initiated in early 1934 by the Y.W. on its own, at first as a five-week program (one day a week) and subsequently lenghened to twelve weeks. By the time the third series began the following year, the Department had joined in as a sponsor and paid the salary of the teacher. Participants in the program were referred by welfare agencies at the outset, but as time went on the Y.W., which was heavily engaged in other projects involving contacts with unemployed women, tended to recruit more of the students on its own. The program carried on until at least 1936.

Self-Help

One of the most interesting and important adult education programs of the Thirties was the Self-Help movement, which operated in the Vancouver area. It was directed to women and families in distress as a result of the Depression and involved a beneficial and perhaps unique partnership between government, which paid much of the bill, and voluntary organizations and individuals. It was predominantly non-vocational in its emphasis and was directed at both increasing the morale of those enrolled, through association with others and through instruction in arts and crafts, drama and other fields, and also at teaching skills for the homemaker which would enable her to carry out her duties more effectively and economically.

Self-Help had its origins in the work of the Vancouver Council of Women. During the year 1933-34, the Vancouver Council organized a new program for mothers of families on relief. Those who joined were formed into groups of eight and given instruction in sewing, knitting and/or quilting, the materials being provided by the Council. In the words of the Council's minutes, the objective of the work was "the prevention of spiritual tragedies through fear and suffering" (Quoted in Powell 1967:73) and it is clear that a great deal of emphasis was placed on the social as well as the instructional aspects of the group activities. By the spring of 1934, there were 275 women participating in the program. The work had started out under the direct sponsorship of the local Council of Women, but in May of 1935 a separate organization, the Community Self-Help Association, was formed. This step may have been taken in order to facilitate relations with the Provincial government, which by this time had adopted the project, bringing it under the auspices of the Adult Education Committee. Several references are made over the years in the Departmental reports to the aims of the program. The most expansive statement along these lines appeared in the report for 1938-39:

> Under the stress of present social and economic forces familes feel isolated, lonely and discouraged, and tend to become apathetic or activley anti-social. Through membership in the ninety groups of our organization they acquire various skills, broaden their outlook, make new friends, and find an outlet for energies of mind and heart. (B.C. Public Schools annual report 1938-39)

There was persistent emphasis in the annual reports on the provision of services to the poor, those on relief or receiving pensions, and "borderline families" which were next thing to it. In the second year of operation, Mrs. G.G. Ross, the Director, presented the enrollment statistics in terms of 255 (46 per cent) participants being on relief, 41 (7 per cent) on pensions and 254 (46 per cent) "borderline or other," a total of 550. By the following year, the proportion of those on relief or pensions had increased slightly, but by 1941-42, the last year of the program, only 17 per cent were on relief.

The instructional activities of the Community Self-Help Association, carried out through Self-Help centres (space made available free of charge in schools) and through Self-Help groups (which met in people's homes), were conducted for the most part with the teaching skills in several domestic arts and crafts. In the second year under government sponsorship, for instance, the subjects taught were listed as quilt, rug and dressmaking, knitting, spinning, weaving, dyeing, carding, toymaking, embroidery and fancy work, dramatics, folk dancing, discussions, and the circulation of books and magazines. This was a fairly typical list of activities over the years, with budgeting, choral work, physical recreation (through the Pro-Rec program) also being included in most years. Home nursing, vegetable gardening and canning and even "Air Raid Precaution Training" were added in the early War years. The program operated on the basis of main regional centres located in city schools. The interest groups, which generally met weekly, were kept small, each led by a volunteer. They met in people's homes for the most part and in each region there was a monthly "rally" at the centre, to which members in all the sub-groups in that district were invited. At the rallies, speakers on educational and cultural subjects were heard, handicrafts exhibited and on occasion, choral and dramatic works produced by the member groups were performed.

Statistics on the program were not uniformly presented in the annual reports and it is therefore difficult to trace the development of the work in any systematic way. Total registration began at 430 in 1934-35, climbed to 1,691 in the peak year (1937-38) and gradually declined to 1,130 in the final year of operation (1941-42). The number of main school centres began at 3 the first year and was up to 16 and 17 for most years thereafter. The number of small groups was stated to be 65 in 1936-37, the only year for which a figure was given. The number of drama groups and weavers' groups both reached 10 at their highest point. An additional 2,594 persons were registered in physical fitness activities in 1938-39, the high point of such activity. In her report for 1941-42, the last full year of the program, Mrs. Ross stated that Self-Help had provided service over the past years to "over 8,000 families."

For two years only, 1934-35 and the following year, reports on the Self-Help work contained as well an account of classes run by the O.A.T.S. (As One That Serveth) organization, an interdenominational Christian men's organization which was active in the field of vocational education (See Harrison 1975; *Sun* Oct. 7, 1929). For these two years the A.O.T.S. organized in downtown Vancouver a "polytechnic school" for unemployed men. There were five classes held the first year and at least eight the second, on various business and technical subjects (drafting, commercial art, commercial arithmetic, etc.) and an "English for New Canadians" course each year. M.J. Harrison's account of the work states that a total of "over 1,000" people attended these classes in the two-year period (Harrison 1975:61). After 1934-35 there is no further reference in the reports to this work and it is likely that it was absorbed into the regular program for unemployed persons which was being run by the Department.

Correspondence Instruction

Correspondence instruction had been begun by the Department of Education in 1918 and through the Twenties it had consisted largely of elementary school subjects and several courses in aspects of mining. In 1929, the new Conservative administation made provision for the advancement of this work, enlarging the offerings into high school subjects. J.W. Gibson was placed in charge of this work and under his vigorous leadership, rapid strides were made in subsequent years, not only in academic high school subjects, but also in a wide range of technical and vocational areas as well. When he became Minister of Education, Dr. Weir also gave strong support to this work, announcing its further expansion to cover senior matriculation subjects (*Province* June 5, 1934). The Sandiford survey of adult education in Canada which was issued in 1935 indicated that B.C. was well ahead of other provinces in this work (Sandiford 1935: Ch. XIII). By 1937, 88 high school and technical vcourses were available by correspondence.

There are few figures available on the number of adults taking correspondence courses prior to 1940, when the annual reports began to include these figures separately. Kyle reported in his summary of the year 1930-31 that 45 per cent of those taking vocational correspondence courses were adults (over 18 years). Writing in 1935, Gibson stated that since 1929, "approximately 2,800 students had enrolled in high school subjects and about a third of them were over 18 years of age at the time of enrollment" (not including those in the relief camps). At the time Gibson was writing, there were 967 students registered in high school and vocational subjects, "almost 40 per cent" of whom were 18 or older. It is noteworthy that fees for taking correspondence courses were then graduated according to age; those under 18 (and also dependents of returned soldiers, families on relief and those in sanitoria and hospitals) paid no fee. Students who were 18 or 19 paid $2.00 per course; 20 or 21 paid $3.00; and over 21 paid $5.00. In the year 1939-40, 872 adults were registered for correspondence courses.

Provincial Recreation Program

One of the best known programs inaugurated in B.C. during the decade was the Provincial Recreation or Pro-Rec movement (Arnold 1973). On November 9, 1934, Dr. Weir announced the inauguration of the new service. In the words of the Department's annual report:

> [T]he aims and objects of the new work were to protect the youths of British Columbia from degenerating effects caused by enforced idleness, and to build up the morale and character which rest on a good physical basis. (B.C. Public Schools Report 1934-35; also *Sun* Nov. 9, 1934)

Mr. Ian Eisenhardt, who had been working for the Vancouver Parks Board, was appointed to head up the new program. Under his leadership, and with the resources made possible by government support, the program expanded very rapidly in the first and subsequent years. It was the first program of its kind in North America and was widely recognized as an important pioneering effort (Arnold 1973). Within a few weeks of the announcement of the program, it became necessary to clarify who was eligible to take part. In early January, 1935, Eisenhardt stated that the programs were "primarily designed for the benefit of unemployed young men and women, but anyone over 16 is eligible to take part" (*Sun* Jan. 16, 1935).

Classes were held in school buildings and other appropriate facilities which could be made available, such as church and community halls and swimming pools. In the first few months, 19 centres were established in six communities (eight of them in Vancouver). By the end of the season (March 31), 3,000 people had joined the centres and 2,689 came regularly to classes. From these figures in 1934-35, the program rose by its peak year, 1938-39, to 114 centres and 21,493 registrations (9,141 of whom were unemployed), and there were 165 full- and part-time paid staff. The program included a wide range of physical activities for both sexes, mainly team sports (volleyball, basketball, soccer, etc.) and gymnasium and pool exercise activities (calisthenics, dancing, apparatus work, boxing, etc.). In addition, an increasing amount of summer outdoor activity was added. There was also considerable in-service training for the staff during the summer.

In some respects, the most interesting aspect of the Pro-Rec movement is the fact that it represents both a type of activity and a reason for undertaking it which extended the services of government in the field of education into new areas. The stated purpose for which this new program was launched was frankly described as an effort to boost the morale of the population. This was both a sign of the times and an important extension of government's reasons for involvement in adult education activity.

University Extension

The University of British Columbia was founded in 1915 and from its very early days was engaged in extension work, including agricultural extension, vocational courses for veterans and widespread lecture activity (Selman 1963). Almost all extension work was brought to a halt in the early Thirties when the Tolmie government reduced their support of the University by two-thirds over a two-year period. A fresh start was made in 1935 when $30,000 of a grant made available by the Carnegie Corporation was used by the University to survey the needs of the province for extension work and to conduct a remarkable program of almost 900 lectures by faculty members throughout the province during the 1935-36 academic year. As that year was drawing to a close, Dr. L.S. Klinck, the President of the University, who was a strong supporter of adult education and who was encouraged by Dr. Weir in this regard, urged the Board of Governors to provide continuing direction to such work by creating a Department of University Extension and appointing a full-time Director. This action was taken by the Board in April, 1936, and Mr. Robert England was named Director. He reamined in the position for only one year and was then replaced by Dr. Gordon Shrum, who retained it for 16 years.

The direction of the development of U.B.C.'s extension service was the reflection of a decision made by Dr. Shrum and others to reject the more traditional pattern of extension credit and other lecture courses prevalent in most Canadian universities and instead, in his words, to have the University "align itself with the new trend in adult education which advocated a more general and vocational training for the average adult" (*Extension Department Annual Report 1943-44*). Shrum set about, with very slender resources, to build up the work and staff of the Department. The project which most knowledgeable observers feel was the most outstanding one developed under his leadership was the Dominion-Provincial Youth Training Schools. Securing the use of funds under the Federal legislation (via the Provincial authorities) he organized a series of two-week residential short courses for young unemployed men and women in various communities in the province. The schools provided training in some vocational subjects, along with a variety of cultural and social activities. After a few trial shorter courses in March of 1938, the program was fully operational for the remaining two years of the decade and at that time, 39 courses were run, with an average attendance of 53. A travelling instructional team of five persons was employed to staff the courses, with an additional group of five employed for a few months in the second year. Courses were put on at the request of the communities and local committees were responsible for all local arrangements and recruiting. The Department could not keep up with the demand for the courses. The first of what was to be a long series of eight-week courses was held at the University in early 1940.

Beginning in 1939, the Extension Department conducted an educational program for fishermen in the co-operative marketing and harvesting of the fishery. Modelled somewhat on the well-known program of St. Francis Xavier University in Nova Scotia, this work was barely launched before the outbreak of the War, but even in its first year carried out impressive work by means of public meetings, study clubs, consultation with directors of co-operative organizations and other educational activities. Five study courses were developed and in 1938-39, there were 179 study groups. The total continued to grow for some years thereafter.

Under the leadership of Miss Dorothy Somerset, the Department's activities in the fine arts, especially in the field of drama, rapidly developed into the most outstanding of its kind in Canada. By the fall of 1939, a comprehensive drama program was being offered including a Summer School of Theatre (begun in 1938), a "drama school of the air" involving C.B.C. broadcasts and local study groups (122 in 1938), a play lending library and annotated list of plays for the use of drama groups, a study course for local groups on the history of the theatre, and short courses in theatre skills, which were offered at the request of local groups.

A short-lived involvement in broadcasting directly from the campus lasted for two years in the late Thirties. In 1937-38, 206 broadcasts originated at U.B.C., but continuing technical difficulties appear to have forced an end to this work by 1939. The foundation of what was to become substantial activity in the field of audio-visual services and the promotion of the use of film was laid in early 1939 when the Dominion Government Motion Picture Bureau (later the National Film Board) decided to make U.B.C. Extension Department a "regional repository" for its materials. By the end of the decade, the U.B.C. Extension Department was already one of the major adult education agencies in Canada.

Community Drama

In 1937, the Department of Education created a School and Community Drama Branch and appointed L. Bullock-Webster as provincial organizer. It was intended to stimulate interest in drama, particularly in rural communities, and beyond that, in the words of a Department bulletin, "to teach discrimination between the worthy and unworthy use of leisure and to provide for the enjoyment of leisure" (Quoted in Johnson 1964:231). The Department divided the province up into 15 "drama districts" and each had its own annual drama festival. There were 127 adult community drama groups and 86 high school clubs active at the time (*News Herald* Sept. 1, 1939; Sun Oct. 20, 1939). When the drama activity under the sponsorship of the Department is addded to the work sponsored by the Universty Extension Department, it represents a remarkable flowering of interest and participation in this field at the close of the decade.

Library Services

Public libraries had progressed well in the Twenties, with the assistance of the Public Library Commission that had been created in 1919. The most important developments in this field in the 1930s were undoubtedly the successful carrying out of the experiement with the Fraser Valley Regional Library system, the subsequent decision by the municipalities concerned to continue the service at their own expense, and the extension of regional or union libraries to other regions of the province (Ley 1971; Gilroy and Rothstein 1970).

The Public Library Commission, following a survey of library needs in the province conducted in 1927, decided to experiment with rural library services based on regions. They successfully sought funds in 1928 from the Carnegie Corporation to finance the project, the first of its kind in North America. It involved small communities banding together, financially and administratively, to provide public library service to the combined geographic area, using a common pool of books which could be moved anywhere in the region. Carnegie provided $100,000 and the service began in August, 1930, under the leadership of Miss Helen Stewart, formerly of the Victoria Public Library. The demonstration project was judged to be remarkably successful and in 1934, when the special funding ran out, 20 of the 22 municipalities involved voted in favour of continuing the service at their own expense. In the meantime, legislation had been passed by the Provincial government to faciltiate such regional arrangements and later in the decade similar schemes were established in the Okanagan, the Kootenays and on Vancouver Island.

Public libraries in the province, like other public services, were on difficult days during the Depression. The budget of the Public Library Commission was sharply reduced early in the decade and the Vancouver Public Library, for instance, had its grant from the city reduced by almost half in 1933. The staff was reduced to half its former size and the library was closed for the two summer months. The Vancouver library entered the field of adult education programming for the first time during this decade, sponsoring an annual course of lectures beginning in 1934, and each year thereafter for eight years.

The provincial travelling libraries, boxed sets of books which were sent out to remote areas where no other service was available, continued to operate in the period and rendered particularly valuable service to the relief camps. The "Open Shelf" library service, a mail delivery service operated by the Public Library Commission, expanded rapidly in the late Twenties (Province May 31, 1931), but in 1933 fell on evil days when as a result of budget cuts the staff member in charge of it had to be dismissed. Three years later, however, the service was re-organized and the collection was greatly expanded, with the assistance of the Provincial Library (Holmes 1959).

Public Affairs

This was a time of trouble for Canadian society and there was widespread concern about public affairs questions and the political and economic system generally. British Columbia was a strong centre of interest in and support for socialist ideas. By the late 1920s, socialist support in the province was rallied mainly behind two parties, the Canadian Labour Party and the Socialist Party of Canada. In his study of dissenting groups in the Canadian West, Walter Young states that in the case of the latter party, "much time was spent in the discussion and analysis of the writings of Marx and Engels" and that at one point, "membership in the party was...restricted to those who could demonstrate a sound knowledge of Marxist doctrine" (Young 1969:11). Dorothy Steeves states in her book about the events of this period that in 1932 the B.C. Socialist Party ran classes on "Marxian economics and the materialist conception of history" at its headquarters in downtown Vancouver (Steeves 1960:77). There were also a series of "C.C.F. Clubs" formed in the province during the organizational period of the new national party, the Co-operative Commonwealth Federation, and they conducted study group activity as well. In his study of the C.C.F. party, Young has stressed its commitment as a movement to education through study clubs, reading lists, correspondence courses, study guides and summer schools. Study groups and lecture series were conducted regularly by the C.C.F. in succeeding years. Other political parties conducted educational activities as well, but not on anything like the same scale.

A large number of other organizations conducted meetings and in some cases study groups on political and social questions. A review of newspaper announcements during the period indicates the activities of the League of Nations Society, the Men's and Women's Canadian Clubs, the Council of Women, the University Women's Club, the Women's International League for Peace and Freedom, and public affairs groups in the Y.M. and Y.W.C.A.

Various groups associated with the United Church were active in the study of social issues (Harrison 1975). A major statement entitled "Christianity and the Social Order," which was published in 1934, was the subject of widespread study in B.C. before and after its publication. Both the "Evangelism and Social Service Committee" of the church and an allied organization, the "Fellowship for a Christian Social Order" were also active in promoting study of social and economic policy. Mention should also be made of Rev. Andrew Roddan and the First United Church of Vancouver. Mr. Roddan was a dynamic leader of his congregation, which carried out substantial programs of relief and emergency assistance for the unemployed in the city, especially those in the "hobo jungles" and others in the area of his downtown church. Of importance in the context of this description of public affairs education at the time was Mr. Roddan's preaching ministry, especially the remarkable Sunday evening meetings at his church. On these occasions, he spoke on current moral and social issues, attacking wrongdoers with great vigour and eloquence. He attracted large crowds, many of them from among the ranks of the unemployed, and the meetings, which involved considerable discussion, often were very rowdy and colourful. Roddan (or his occasional guest speakers) often clashed vigourously with radical views expressed by his listeners and the Sunday night meetings came to be regarded by many as "the best show in town." Communists were often out in force and sections of the audience more than once broke out into "The Red Flag" song. The meetings were also seen by many to be a significant educational force, involving as they did a lively discussion of many public issues of the day in which a wide variety of points of view were vigourously represented (Roddan 1945).

This section on public affairs or social education is an appropriate one with which to close this survey. It emphasizes the point that during the decade under review, not only the amount, but also the range of adult education activity in the province increased very considerably. The widespread concern which surfaced in the Depression about the nature of Canadian society and which was accompanied by a flowering of small group approaches to study and discussion of such issues, carried on into the wartime period and was adapted to a consideration of the problems of reconstruction. It added strength to what has been termed the "social reform" tradition of adult education, a characteristic of the field which became less prominent in the postwar period (Faris 1975; Cotton 1951).

References

Arnold, T.C. (1973), *The Status and Influence of Sport and Physical Recreation Activities in British Columbia during the Depression and World War II*, Unpublished M.P.E. Thesis, University of British Columbia.

B.C.P.L.C. (B.C. Public Libary Commission) (1942), *A Preliminary Study of Adult Education in British Columbia: 1941*, Victoria: Typescript multilith.

Corbett, E.A. (1957), *We Have with Us Tonight*, Toronto: Ryerson.

Cotton, W.E. (1951), *On Behalf of Adult Education*, Boston: Centre for the Study of Liberal Education for Adults.

Dupre, J.S. et al. (1973), *Federalism and Policy Development*, Toronto: University of Toronto.

Faris, R. (1975), *The Passionate Educators*, Toronto: Peter Martin.

Gilroy, M. and Rothstein, S. (1970), *As We Remember It*, Vancouver: U.B.C. School of Librarianship.

Grattan, H. (1955), *In Quest of Knowledge*, New York: Association Press.

Harrison, M.J. (1975), *The Social Influence of the United Church of Canada in British Columbia 1930-1948*, Unpublished M.A. Thesis, University of British Columbia.

Holmes, M.C. (1959), *Library Service in British Columbia*, Victoria: B.C. Public Library Commission.

Johnson, F.H. (1964), *A History of Public Education in British Columbia*, Vancouver: University of British Columbia.

Kidd, J.R. (1950), *Adult Education in Canada*, Toronto: Canadian Association for Adult Education.

Knight, R. (1974), *A Very Ordinary Life*, Vancouver: New Star Books.

Lane, M.E. (1966), *Unemployment During the Depression*, Unpublished Graduating Essay (History), University of British Columbia.

Ley, R. (1971), *A Brief History of the Fraser Valley Regional Library*, Abbotsford: Fraser Valley Regional Library.

Ormsby, M. (1964), *British Columbia: A History*, Vancouver: MacMillan.

Province, Vancouver *Province* newspaper.

Powell, M.P. (1967), *Response to the Depression*, Unpublished M.A. Thesis, University of British Columbia.

Robin, M. (1972), *Rush For Spoils*, Toronto: McClelland & Stewart.

Roddan, A. (1932), *Canada's Untouchables*, Vancouver: privately printed.

Roddan, A. (1945?), *The Church in the Modern City*, Vancouver: privately printed.

Sandiford, P. (1935), *Adult Education in Canada: A Survey*, Toronto: University of Toronto.

Selman, G. (1963), *A History of the Extension and Adult Education Services of the University of British Columbia 1915 to 1955*, Unpublished M.A. Thesis, University of British Columbia.

Smiley, D. (1963), *The Rowell-Sirois Report: An Abridgement of Book I*, Toronto: McClelland and Stewart.

Sun, Vancouver *Sun* newspaper.

Tanner, T.W. (1965), *Microcosms of Misfortune*, Unpublished M.A. Thesis, University of Western Ontario.

Thomas, A.M. (1961), "The Learning Society," in Canadian Association for Adult Education, *National Comnference on Adult Education*, Toronto: Canadian Association for Adult Education.

Wales, B. (1958), *The Development of Adult Education in British Columbia*, Unpublished Ed.D. Thesis, Oregon State University.

Young, W.D. (1969), *Democracy and Discontent*, Toronto: McGraw-Hill Ryerson.

Originally published in 1976 as No. 12, *Occasional Papers in Continuing Education*, by the Centre for Continuing Education, The University of British Columbia. Reprinted with permission.

6.2

The Morale of the People: Reflections on Adult Education in British Columbia in the Great Depression

*T*he Province of British Columbia, whose economy was based in large part on primary industries—forestry, mining and fishing—was especially hard hit by the Great Depression of the 1930s (Thompson & Seager 1985). Federal government policies adopted to combat the Depression exacerbated the economic difficulties of the Canadian West, which relied heavily on agriculture and the export of raw materials (Smiley 1963). By 1931, relatively early in the Depression, British Columbia had the highest unemployment rate in Canada. The four Western provinces had the sharpest declines in the country in per capita personal income. In addition, because the coastal area of B. C. has a more moderate climate than does the rest of the country, many unemployed transient persons from elsewhere in Canada "headed West." Many stayed for some years, in spite of concerted efforts to "keep them moving" (Ormsby 1964; Robin 1972). Many persons—and families—in the province found themselves in a desperate situation.

Provincial elections in late 1933 brought to power a Liberal Party government which promised a "new deal" and which represented a distinct shift to the left in provincial politics. The Premier described his position as "socialized capitalism" and spoke in terms of a "war on poverty" (Thompson Seager 1985:242). The government may properly be described as having a small "l" liberal point of view, and as combining "the philosophy of 19th century liberalism with its respect for individual rights and the point of view of the 20th century that planning must go into the new social order" (Ormsby 1964:460). (The new Premier of B. C., T.D. Pattullo, told his friends that Franklin Roosevelt, in preparing his inaugural address, must have been studying Liberal campaign literature in B. C.!)

Like most governments which place a great deal of emphasis on social planning, the Liberal Pattullo administration attached importance to the utilization of experts from outside government in developing the "new social order" which it had promised (Ormsby 1964; Thompson & Seager 1985). In selecting his Minister of Education (who was also appointed Provincial Secretary), he was able to choose someone who was himself an expert (not a common occurrence in the parliamentary system). This was Dr. George Weir, the former co-chair of a landmark government commission of inquiry which studied the B. C. school system in 1924-25 and produced a report which had substantial impact for at least 30 years (Johnson 1964). Weir had been appointed professor of education at The University of British Columbia in 1924 and had subsequently become head of a newly-created Department of Education, a position from which he took leave of absence in order to run for political office. Weir was also an enthusiastic supporter of adult education, having frequently made speeches about the field before he entered political life ("Adult Education Stressed" 1930; "Dr. George Weir Speaks" 1932, for instance). He was a high profile minister in the government and had the strong support of the Premier (Mann 1978). Perhaps this fact, coupled with his recognized expertise in the field of education, allowed him to move with assurance into innovative areas and to acquire the financial resources to support his projects, even in those lean times.

With respect to the field of adult education, Weir already had in place in his Department two outstanding individuals. The first was John Kyle, who had been in charge of technical education and night schools since 1913, having previously given leadership to the pioneering work of the Vancouver School Board's adult education program. The other was J.W. Gibson, the director of correspondence education, who was in the process of transforming the Department's work in that field into one of the most outstanding programs of its kind in the world (Selman 1988). Weir further strengthened the team by hiring, again from the Vancouver Board, Mr. Ian Eisenhardt, who was to lead in the creation of what became an internationally-renowned provincial recreation program, "Pro-Rec" (Arnold 1973).

Aims and Achievements

In those Depression years, to a degree which has not been achieved since, adult education became an important instrument of government policy. This is not to say that enormous sums of money were spent on it by today's standards, or that anything approaching today's variety of institutional programs was available. Rather it is intended to point out that there was a clear connection between the political platform of the government and its actions in adult education, between the rhetoric of its overall policies and that used to descibe the new measures which it undertook in adult education. In many respects, other measures enacted in the early months of the new government's tenure—an increase in the "relief" payments; a Work and Wages Act which included a raise in the minimum wage; financial assistance to key industries which were in trouble; a start on economic planning and a study of an unemployment insurance scheme; negotiations with Ottawa concerning altered tax arrangements; and the launching of major public works projects—were clearly more spectacular steps towards "a new deal" than actions taken in adult education (Ormsby 1964; Sutherland 1960). But many measures were initiated in the field of adult education which were clearly aspects of an overall strategy on the part of the government intended to promote the desired "new social order": free courses of instruction in vocational subjects; courses in household arts (and free material to work with) for mothers of families on relief; and a vast new recreational program intended to build up the "morale" of the people. An indication of the consciousness of the special quality of some of these measures was that in the reports of the Department of Education at this time, the new, special programs were dealt with in a separate section (called "adult education") and reported on separately from the traditional "Night School" and "Correspondence" work. As well, the Minister appointed an advisory committee containing community representatives, whose responsibility related only to the new programs being undertaken.

A second noteworthy and unprecedented feature of the adult education projects created by the new government was its general goal. The phrase most frequently used in the various government reports of the period spoke in terms of addressing "the morale of the people." Reports on the innovative recreation program organized by the province spoke of aiming "to build up the morale and character" of participants, and on another occasion of "maintaining morale" (*British Columbia Public Schools Report* (hereafter *BCPSR*), 1934-35:75; 1938-39:79). An overall report on adult education for 1934-35 referred to "the preservation of their skill, self-respect and morale" (p. 68). And a report on the Self-Help project, which will be described later, stated that it was aimed at "preserving the morale of the people" (*BCPSR*, 1936-37:78).

There are at least two points to be emphasized in this connection. The chief of these, for present purposes, is that the goal of this work was conceived at the time as being related to the whole person. The goal was not described, as is generally the case in adult education, as having to do with one or more of the social roles of the adult—as worker, parent, citizen, or homemaker—but with the person as a total entity—how adult citizens felt about themselves and their society. This tends not to be the way we think of the functions of adult education, and is certainly not the feature of it which we use to "sell" the importance of the field. In the case of British Columbia, at any rate, it is not the sort of idea or rhetoric which has appeared in similar government documents at any time since the 1930s.

The other point to be considered is that such language being used in reference to the goals of adult education is very much a reflection of the liberal point of view so typical of the Western democracies in this period (and since). The matter is seen very much in individualistic terms. Also, there was lurking behind such terminology the ever-present connotation that it was vital to help people be in better spirits, better "morale," in the then-current times of trouble, rather than have them succumb to the blandishments of those advocating the overthrow of the system. Depending on one's inclination, one can see these programs, therefore, as arising from altruistic concern about the citizens' welfare, or from the fear that unless something was done to cheer people up, they might turn to the voices of the far left—or the far right—alternatives which were very lively specters during the thirties (Lower 1953; Mann 1978; Thompson & Seager 1985) . Most observers see a combination of altruism and political realism in the approach.

Although the worst years of the Depression brought a falling off in the more traditional adult education activities such as school board night schools (Wales 1958), the new Liberal administration started a number of new ventures and began to provide financial support for a number of what it judged to be particularly worthwhile projects in the private sector. Foremost among the activities under direct sponsorship were a range of vocationally-oriented training programs which were offered free of charge (mainly through school board night school programs) to persons who were on relief or social assistance of some kind. The list of vocational subjects offered is a long one and concentrates largely on occupations related to the industries of the province. Among these, incidentally, was a considerable surge of interest in small scale and low tech gold mining procedures—a mark of the times, and the region. Secondly, the Minister gave strong support to J.W. Gibson, his able officer in charge of correspondence education, providing increased resources and enabling his unit, which served both children and adults, greatly to shift the emphasis to the latter. During this period, the Correspondence Branch of the Department enhanced its already considerable reputation in this work. An entirely new field of activity for the Department was the sponsorship and servicing of local play-reading groups throughout the province. By 1939, 177 adult groups were operating (in addition to an even larger parallel service being run at the time by the University Extension Department) (Selman 1976). A major new venture of the period for the Department was a "Provincial Recreation" program, known as "Pro-Rec." This was announced in late 1934, was based on a Scandinavian model, and was the first program of its kind in North America (Arnold 1973). Classes and other activities were held in schools, churches, and other community space available, and the program involved a great deal of instructional, as well as recreational, activity. By 1938-39 the program was operating in 114 centers and approximately 21,000 persons (9,141 of whom were unemployed) took part. The language used in government reports on the project concerning its aims were much along the lines described already—"to build up morale and character" (*BCPSR* 1934-35:75). And finally, in this list of directly-sponsored activities, reference should be made to the fact that the Department provided a number of teachers and a great deal of teaching material for educational work conducted within the "Relief Camps" for unemployed men which were being operated throughout Canada during this period by the Canadian government (Swettenham 1968; Thompson & Seager 1985).

The fourth noteworthy characteristic of the new measures taken in adult education at this time was the willingness demonstrated by the Department of Education to enter into various kinds of arrangements with the voluntary sector in the delivery of new types of service. There had been a tendency in Canada, as in the United States, to use public money in the field of education by means of public institutions. This was perhaps a legacy of the fact that many immigrants in North America were fleeing societies which were elitist in social and cultural terms, often based on domination by church and other private interests. There was a widespread determination that North American society should be more open to individual merit and initiative, and there was a general reliance on public educational systems as part of the social arrangements which would make this possible. It was, therefore, a significant departure from usual practice which was adopted in the emergency and a further dimension of the "new deal" approach. Such co-operative ventures with the private and voluntary sector generally did not continue in the post-Depression period, and certainly not in the post-WW II period.

There were a number of such partnerships created; four will be mentioned as examples. The Vancouver Council of Women, a coordinating and joint action vehicle for women's organizations in Canada, had created a project in early 1933 which involved forming small groups of mothers of families on relief for the combined purpose of providing social contacts and teaching the women how to stretch their resources by means of clothing remodeling, furniture repair and recovering, knitting, weaving, preparing nutritious meals on low budgets, and other household arts. Donations of materials from commercial companies arranged by the Council of Women made it possible to maintain the program at very low cost—and without charge to the members of the groups. This program was known as "Self-Help," and in addition to the regular weekly working meetings of the small groups which have been described, other clubs and activity groups formed— pottery making, choirs, play reading, and acting groups. Generally, the program had the effect not only of teaching practical skills, but also of providing a basis for new friendships and associations and a time away from household routines. By the end of the first year of operation, some 257 women were involved in the program. The Department of Education, seeing the practical and psychological value of such work and realizing that the project simply could not function without the volunteer leadership of Council of Women members, proposed that government funds be donated both to pay for the consumable supplies which were required for the classes (on an increasingly large scale) and to provide an office and co-ordinator for the work. This blend of voluntary effort and government support proved entirely satisfactory and continued until the early years of the War. At its peak (1937-38) the program involved 1,691 women, and when it was terminated in 1942, over 8,000 women had been involved (*BCPSR* for years mentioned).

Other projects will be more briefly described. The Vancouver YWCA began a series of three-month programs to train unemployed women who wished to get jobs as maids or housekeepers. The government approached the organization and arranged to cover some of the costs of the training, while leaving the operation of the program in the YWCA's hands. An interdenominational men's Christian organization, the AOTS (As One That Serveth) was financed by the Department so it could operate a "polytechnic school" for unemployed men in downtown Vancouver. This program ran for at least two years, enrolled some 1,000 men, and taught vocational subjects, along with a few classes in English as a second language. The final program to be mentioned involved a group of teachers at the Vancouver Technical School who wrote and tutored a series of correspondence courses in technical subjects to be taken, at no cost, by interested men in the federal relief camps in the province. The Department of Education agreed to assume all the costs of the program, and as many as 871 men were enrolled in the courses in the peak year, 1934-35 (*BCPSR*, 1934-35).

The other dimension of liaison with the voluntary sector took a different form. It was the decision on the part of the Minister to appoint an advisory committee to give the Department advice on the development of its adult education activities. This was the first time such a committee had been established, and it appears to have been concerned not with the longer-established work (night schools, correspondence courses), but only with the special measures being taken to respond to the Depression emergency. The committee was made up of a mixture of Department officials and representatives of community organizations. It remained in existence for only three years—during the depth of the Depression. (Such a committee was not appointed again by the Department until 1978.)

In these four respects—adult education as a significant instrument of government policy; the philosophical thrust behind its measures; the creation of new adult education services; and new kinds of partnerships with the private and voluntary sector—the approach of the Liberal administration and the responsible minister, George Weir, were innovative, and may appropriately be seen as a clear response to the traumatic Depression conditions. Certainly they stand out in sharp contrast to the activities of the preceding Conservative government. A few dimensions of this work, such as the Self-Help program and the recreation program, carried on into the World War II period, but by the end of the War no trace remained of either of these special programs or the philosophical and policy stance which had been adopted by the Liberal government. (Pattullo and Weir left office in 1941.) Of course, the wartime conditions of full employment removed the need for many of these measures.

How are we to see this phenomenon which took place during the Depression years, and which presumably was duplicated in at least some of its aspects in other jurisdictions? As has been suggested earlier, there are at least two views which can be taken. On the one hand, the measures adopted by the Liberal government and the Department of Education may be seen as a case of government responding to the desperate needs of many persons and families who were at risk in the bleak conditions of the Depression years. Others have preferred to stress the view that such "new deal" approaches were based primarily on fears, on the part of Western governments, that if things were not done to alleviate the desperate conditions in which many citizens found themselves, they would espouse radical ideas and seek the overthrow of the present system. As one student of education in the province in these years has put it, this was a case of the state looking to its own "protection and perpetuation" (Mann 1978:105). These two views concerning the motivation of governments in this period are not mutually exclusive.

Both the projects undertaken and the language used to describe and justify them, appear to fall in the classic liberal philosophical tradition. The approach was in terms of promoting individual welfare and was not directed at the social system as a whole. The concept was one of providing "relief" and boosting the morale of individuals, not addressing the nature of the society which had produced the crisis. (Other elements in society were of course taking this other approach.) The emphasis was on getting people through the crisis, not on transforming the society in any significant way. The goal was the stability of the state, not changing it (Macpherson 1965).

This having been said, however, one of the most intriguing elements of the story of these Depression years is the fact that, to a degree perhaps unequalled at any other time in the modern adult education movement, leaders in government and public service had a purpose for their efforts in adult education which involved the whole person. Whether it was rhythmic gymnastics, English as a second language, vocational training, or skill courses for homemakers, the reasons stated for delivering the services were consistent: to improve the morale of the people. The intention here is not to engage in polemic about the appropriateness or justifiabilify of such an aim, but rather to point out its unusual character. To a degree unequalled in any other period since the emergence of the modern adult education movement, the purpose of the public authorities in the field were stated in terms of the total sensibilities of adult persons and how they felt about themselves and their society.

Reflections from the 1980s

The B. C. Context

The passage of some 50 years since these events makes possible considerable perspective on the nature and uniqueness of the actions of the Liberal administration in that earlier period. We see their initiatives now out of our experience with a vastly expanded, considerably professionalized and institutionalized field of adult education. Also, we now have the context of a society with a welfare "safety net," which was not in place during the desperate Thirties.

It is reasonable to ask whether the significant actions taken during the Thirties were built upon in subsequent decades or in any way can be seen to have influenced subsequent actions by government. Such questions do not lend themselves to precise or definitive answers. But it is likely reasonable to state that there has been little, if any, influence that has carried over. The reasons are not hard to find; conditions have altered greatly. The Depression was followed by the crisis of World War II, and in many respects, the wartime experience obliterated the conditions which had been brought on by the Depression. In the post-war period the economy was booming and employment was at a high level, at least until the late Fifties. By that time a conservative government was in power in the province (Social Credit Party) and, except for a brief interlude in the early 1970s, has remained in power ever since. Economic conditions have varied over the years, but we have not experienced a depression of the depth and duration of that of the Thirties (though the one of the early 1980s was severe), and when such times have come, most people have been protected to some degree by the welfare measures in place. So conditions have been different, and the social philosophy of the governments in power have been different.

A further point which should be made is that there has been little in the way of permanent or declared official policy in the field of adult education in the province. Several pieces of legislation authorize or allow public institutions to be engaged in adult education, but little is said beyond that. There has been lots of administrative action in support of adult education activity but very little stated policy. A concerted effort to correct this situation was launched by government in 1979, but was in the end overtaken by the economic recession of the early Eighties and government's determination to downsize the scope of government action (Cassidy 1984; Selman 1984).

The first characteristic of government action in the 1930s, which was identified above, was that government utilized adult education as a significant instrument of government policy. This has at no time been the case in the subsequent period. Adult education has been a thriving enterprise in British Columbia over the decades, but this has largely been as a result of energetic and imaginative leadership from individuals—within the public service and outside it—and with the assistance of unexceptional levels of government support. Adult education has generally remained in a marginal and minor position in policy terms, and the leadership coming from within government has been minimal. The important exception to this took place in the latter half of the 1970s and into the early 1980s, when a progressive and innovative Minister of Education (who, interestingly enough, had crossed the floor from the Liberal to the Social Credit Party) appointed an able senior official in charge of adult education in the Ministry and gave him enough staff and funds to enable him to exert real leadership in the field. A change of leadership in the Ministry and the financial crisis of the early Eighties combined to bring this initiative to an abrupt end.

The proclivity of government in the Thirties to see the role of adult education as supporting the overall outlook of the citizen has not re-occurred. The conditions have not ever been the same as in the Thirties, and governments in the province have been business-oriented and conservative in their views. Certain national cultural institutions such as the Canadian Broadcasting Corporation and the National Film Board have seen themselves in such a role, but government at the provincial level has not. The closest we have come to it, perhaps, has been in the approach adopted by continuing education leaders in the Ministry of Education in the late Seventies in their efforts on behalf of certain disadvantaged groups—the undereducated, those in need of English as a second language, older people, and single-parent families below the poverty line (Cassidy 1984). What was true of the continuing education unit in the Ministry was not true of the government as a whole, however.

In the category of innovation in the types of adult education services provided by government, certainly there have been significant developments in the subsequent decades, and very great expansion, but except for the measures just mentioned, this has not been an outstanding feature of the field. The school boards, colleges and institutes, and universities have been enabled to expand their offerings over the years, and participation rates in adult education in B. C. are among the highest in Canada, but government's role in bringing this about has not been particularly outstanding. There has been concern in government at certain times about the outreach of services to the rural and small town areas, and the Open Learning Agency, created in the late Seventies, has an unusually ambitious mandate in this regard.

The fourth remarkable feature of the Thirties was the variety of alliances which were created between the public and private sectors. There has been comparatively little of this since that time. During the progress of a comprehensive study of adult education in the province which was conducted by a government-appointed committee in 1976 (B. C. Ministry of Education 1976), some committee members wished to submit recommendations in this area, but were steered off this course of action by Ministry officials, who said it was out of the question and would get in the way of implementing other proposals. The matter was shunted to a category "requiring further investigation" (which it has not received). When a Ministry Advisory Committee on Adult Education was created in 1978, its membership was made up entirely of professional educators from the public educational institutions.

The Broader Context

Looking back on the 1930s from the present period, one is struck by a link between the grounds for policy which were expressed in British Columbia in the Thirties and the case which has been developed by the proponents of lifelong learning and lifelong education over the last two decades. Of course, lifelong education is promoted on various grounds, but there is a particular "stream" in the literature of that concept which is closely related to the rhetoric of the 1930s. In what follows, this will be pursued by reference to the work of J. Roby Kidd and Alan Thomas in Canada during the Sixties; Lengrand and the *Learning to Be* report early in the Seventies; and certain international work in Europe since that time, especially that of the Council of Europe and the UNESCO Institute at Hamburg.

It should be mentioned by way of introduction to this discussion that there has been a thread running through the literature of liberal adult education for some decades which comes close to reflecting the philosophical position being identified here. The same can be said of some elements of the human potential movement. What we are focusing on here, however, are attempts to develop or propose a *public* policy which is grounded in a view of the whole person rather than the person in his/her various (usually compartmentalized) social roles.

In the early 1960s Alan Thomas, who was Director of the Canadian Association for Adult Education (CAAE) for most of the decade, burst onto the Canadian adult education scene as a thinker of dynamic and original ideas. He drew on the ideas of John Dewey, Marshall McLuhan, and Roby Kidd. If his message were to be summed up in a phrase, it would be the one he used as the title for his address to the landmark National Conference on Adult Education in Ottawa in the fall of 1961, "The Learning Society" (Thomas 1961).

Thomas called on adult educators to focus their attention on learning rather than education and throughout the Sixties he developed the idea of a learning society and its implications for both public policy and the practice of adult education. Representative of the further development of his thinking are two publications, *A White Paper on the Education of Adults in Canada* (CAAE 1966), which explored some of the implications of his ideas for public policy, and a paper prepared in 1985 under the title "Learning in Society" (Thomas 1985), which further elaborated the analysis.

Thomas' views, which may be described as liberal in philosophical terms, were based on the transforming power of learning in the lives of individuals and on the "saving" potential of learning if it is harnessed to public and social purposes. At a time approximately a decade prior to the more internationally visible final report of the UNESCO Faure Commission, *Learning to Be* (UNESCO 1972), Thomas was exploring many of the same ideas. A few brief quotations from some of his writings will convey the direction of his thinking:

- The only human, dignified way to respond to change is by learning (1961).
- Learning, the true currency of post-industrial society (1961).
- Learning together always breeds effective relationships among men (1964).
- ... A whole new moral code, of which learning and competence are cornerstones (1965).
- Morality lies in the learning, in the activity itself, and not in the effect of the subject matter (1966).
- In every act of learning there is both an act of surrender and a great release of energy (1970) (quoted in Selman 1985:11-12).

The point being made here is that in the work of Thomas, an approach to public policy and adult learning was being developed which shared some elements—in terms of the relevance to "the whole person"—with the position adopted back in the 1930s. Some of the same ideas are found in the work of Roby Kidd in the Sixties as well, especially in his text for the field, first published in 1959, and in his remarkable lectures delivered in Saskatchewan in 1966 (Kidd 1959; 1966). In the case of both Kidd and Thomas, we see a shift in focus from education to learning, from pedagogy to mathetics. And in the work of both there is an emphasis on the impact of the act of learning on the total human personality.

By the end of the Sixties, there was emerging in the work of the Council of Europe and UNESCO a very similar point of view. The Council of Europe's development of the concept of *education permanente* put particular emphasis on the cultural and personal impact of lifelong learning (Kallen 1979; Simpson 1972). Although UNESCO's sustained work on lifelong education had relevance to many schools of thought about adult life and educational policies, they have come to be strongly identified with a liberal-humanistic view (Knapper & Cropley 1985).

Paul Lengrand was the chief architect of UNESCOs early work on the concepts of lifelong education and lifelong learning. Rereading his first published statement on the subject, *An Introduction to Lifelong Education* (1970), one is reminded of the "sense of crisis" to which he was clearly responding. Although the nature of that crisis at the end of the 1960s was very different from that of the 1930s, there was somewhat the same sense of rallying people to the nature of the urgent situation and of the need for maintaining morale in the face of the forces at work. Lengrand expressed concern about the human condition and the many challenges facing society. People must go on learning "if they do not want to find themselves on the losing side" (p. 9). In words very reminiscent of the Depression, Lengrand speaks of the need "to help humans to become more fully themselves" and of the dangers of boredom; "boredom is to the soul as perilous, as fatal an evil as is a virus to the organism" (pp. 21-22). He emphasized the role which learning can play in man "resuming control of himself" and in putting the emphasis on "being rather than on having" (pp. 40-41). It would be possible to push too far with the attempt to see connections between the mentality of the Depression and that of the emergence in recent decades of the current concept of lifelong learning, but there is certainly a similar sense of response to crisis and a clear thread of liberal or liberal-humanist views present in both cases. Further insight into the sense of crisis prevailing at the time is provided by works such as P.H. Coombs' *The World Education Crisis: A Systems Analysis*, which had been published in 1968.

In 1972 the report of UNESCO's International Commission on the Development of Education, entitled *Learning to Be* in the English version, burst upon the world of educational planning. As in the case of Lengrand's earlier work, the seven commissioners were obviously deeply impressed by the dangers facing contemporary society and, as well, by the varied critiques of existing educational systems which had appeared on the world scene in both the developing and the more industrialized countries. In terms which spoke clearly to the experience of the 1930s, the report pointed out that education had been "the select instrument by means of which existing values and balances of power have been maintained" (UNESCO 1972:55) and that no political system could "forego securing its foundations through its educational systems and other means" (p.150). The report developed the notions of lifelong learning/education and that of "the learning society," professing a belief in "scientific humanism" as a basis for action. It emphasized as well the need to shift from a pedagogical perspective to one of mathetics. Among the basic assumptions stated at the outset of their report was that "only an over-all lifelong education" could enable the individual to cope in the modern world and that the aim of the person must be "to build up a continually developing body of knowledge, all through life—learn to be" (p.vi). Although the various roles which the adult plays in life were fully acknowledged in the report, the focus kept coming back to the individual man and woman, their view of themselves and of their society.

Following the publication *of Learning to Be*, UNESCO asked its Institute for Education in Hamburg to devote a major effort to the development of the concept of lifelong education. The first major publication to result from that work was *Foundations of Lifelong Education*, edited by R.H. Dave (1976). Once again, we find language reminiscent of that of the 1930s. In his chapter on philosophical foundations, B. Suchodolski gives emphasis to "the problem of overcoming alienation" and to "boredom, hopelessness and disintegration," certainly common themes of the earlier crisis, and he stresses that education, which he interprets as "the intensification of human development," is the most essential response to such conditions (pp 71-72). Elsewhere in the volume, P.N. Kirpal deals with many of the same themes, his commitment to "a new humanism," or "evolutionary humanism," being drawn upon in support of the idea of lifelong learning (p. 107).

Only two other studies which have emerged from UNESCO's exploration of the concept of lifelong education will be referred to. In a volume edited by A.J. Cropley, *Towards a System of Lifelong Education* (1980), a number of themes dealt with are relevant to the experience of the 1930s. One is the elaboration of the "lifewide" as well as the lifelong dimension of such a system and the redefinition that is required of public and private elements of the field. The reaching out for new relationships with the voluntary sector, which we saw in British Columbia during the Depression years, takes on significant implications in this context. In a later volume by Knapper and Cropley (1985), there is an elaboration of the idea of the whole person, which was a striking feature of policy in the Thirties. The authors point out that although in their view the idea of lifelong education need not necessarily serve liberal-democratic values, its development in the literature of the field since 1970 has been based on the assumption that it does, and lifelong education is usually defined as "education for 'liberation', 'self-realization', and 'self-fulfillment'". These are regarded as inevitable results of "forms of education that seek to develop 'whole' beings" (Knapper & Cropley 1985:19).

It may be pointed out, in conclusion, that while in recent years such humanistic views have influenced or infused much of the literature of lifelong education/learning, we have at the same time been hearing a somewhat complementary view from the analytical philosophy school of writers about adult education. In an early statement of the analytic school, *Values, Education and the Adult* by R.W.K. Paterson (1979), the author states the case: "Education . . . directly touches our personal being, tending our identity at its roots, and ministering directly to our condition as conscious selves...." (p. 15). Another prominent proponent of the analytical approach, Kenneth Lawson (1982), comments that "education implies a concern for moral and evaluative issues consistent with a humanistic approach" (p. 97).

It is clear that in many ways over the last 30 years, the literature concerning lifelong learning and the learning society has devoted considerable attention to themes which were prominent in the "new deal," Depression years of the Liberal government in British Columbia. It is of course not the intention to claim any causal relationship between the two phenomena, but rather to note some common themes—most notably the emphasis on learning's impact on the whole person and the new kind of relationship between the public and private sectors of providers which is required in "the learning society."

References

"Adult Education Stressed" (1930, April 30), *Vancouver Sun*, p. 7.

Arnold, T.C. (1973), *The Status and Influence of Sport and Physical Recreation Activities in British Columbia During the Depression and World War II.* Unpublished Master's Thesis, University of British Columbia, Vancouver.

B. C. Ministry of Education, (1976), *Report of the Committee on Continuing Education in British Columbia,* Victoria: Ministry of Education.

B. C. Public School Reports, 1930-41, (BCPSR) Victoria: King's Printer.

Canadian Association for Adult Education. (1966), *A White Paper on the Education of Adults in Canada* Toronto: CAAE.

Cassidy, F. (Ed.) (1984), *Creating Citizens*, Vancouver: Pacific Association for Continuing Education.

Coombs, P.H. (1968), *The World Educational Crisis: A Systems Analysis,* Oxford: Oxford University.

Cropley, A. J. (Ed.) (1980), *Towards a System of Lifelong Education,* Oxford: Pergamon.

Dave, R.H. (Ed.) (1976), *Foundations of Lifelong Education,* Oxford: Pergamon.

"Dr. George Weir" speaks to rotary (1932, March 9), *Vancouver Sun*, p. 10.

Johnson, F.H. (1964), *A History of Public Education in British Columbia,* Vancouver: University of British Columbia.

Kallen, D. (1979), "Recurrent Education and Lifelong Learning: Definitions and Distinctions." In T. Schuller and J. Megarry (Eds.), *Recurrent Education and Lifelong Learning* (pp. 45-54), London: Kogan Page.

Kidd, J.R. (1959), *How Adults Learn*, New York: Association Press.

Kidd, J.R. (1966), *The Implications of Continuous Learning.* Toronto: Gage

Knapper, C.K., and Cropley, A.J. (1985), *Lifelong Learning and Higher Education,* London: Croom Helm.

Lawson, K. (1982), Lifelong Education: Concept or Policy, *International Journal of Lifelong Education*, 1 (2), 97-108.

Lengrand, P. (1970), *An Introduction to Lifelong Education,* Paris: UNESCO.

Lower, A.R.M. (1953), *Colony to Nation,* Toronto: Longmans Green.

Macpherson, C. B. (1965), *The Real World of Democracy,* Toronto: CBC Enterprises.

Mann, J.S. (1978), *Progressive Education and the Depression in British Columbia.* Unpublished Master's Thesis, University of British Columbia, Vancouver.

Ormsby, M.A. (1964), *British Columbia: A History,* Toronto: Macmillan.

Paterson, R.W.K. (1979), *Values, Education and the Adult*, London: Routledge and Kegan Paul.

Robin, M. (1972), *The Rush for Spoils*, Toronto: McClelland & Stewart.

Selman, G. (1976), *Adult Education in British Columbia During the Depression*, Vancouver: University of B. C. Center for Continuing Education.

Selman, G. (1984), Government's role in Adult Education: Two Periods of Active Leadership in British Columbia. In F. Cassidy (Ed.), *Creating Citizens* (pp.3-34), Vancouver: Pacific Association for Continuing Education.

Selman, G (1985), *Alan Thomas and the Canadian Association for Adult Education 1961-1970*, Vancouver University of B. C. Center for Continuing Education.

Selman, G. (1988), *Invisible Giant: A History of Adult Education in British Columbia*, Vancouver: University of B. C. Center for Continuing Education.

Simpson, J.A. (1972), *Today and Tomorrow in European Adult Education*, Strasbourg: Council of Europe.

Smiley, D.V. (1963), *The Rowell/Sirois Report: Book I*, Toronto: McClelland & Stewart.

Sutherland, J.N. (1960), *T.D. Pattullo as Party Leader*, Unpublished Master's Thesis, University of British Columbia, Vancouver.

Swettenham, J. (1968), *McNaughton* (Vol. 1), Toronto: Ryerson Press.

Thomas, A. (1961), "The Learning Society." In *National Conference on Adult Education in Canada*, Toronto: Canadian Association for Adult Education.

Thomas, A. (1985), Learning in Society, in Canadian Commission for UNESCO, *Learning in Society: Toward a New Paradigm*, Ottawa: Canadian Commission for UNESCO, 15-34.

Thompson, J.H. and Seager, A. (1 985), *Canada 1922-1939*, Toronto: McClelland & Stewart.

UNESCO (1972), *Learning to Be*, Paris: UNESCO.

Wales, B.E. (1958), *The Development of Adult Education in British Columbia*. Unpublished doctoral thesis, Oregon State University, Corvallis.

Originally appeared in Rohfeld, R.W. (Ed.) (1990). *Breaking New Ground: The Development of Adult and Workers' Education in North America.* Syracuse: University of Syracuse Kellogg Project. pp. 273-292. Reprinted with permission, Syracuse University Resources in Adult Education, Adult Education Program.